SPERM DONATION, SINGLE WOMEN AND FILIATION

SPERM DONATION, SINGLE WOMEN AND FILIATION

Elena Ignovska

intersentia
Cambridge – Antwerp – Portland

Intersentia Ltd
Sheraton House | Castle Park
Cambridge | CB3 0AX | United Kingdom
Tel.: +44 1223 370 170 | Email: mail@intersentia.co.uk

Distribution for the UK:
NBN International
Airport Business Centre, 10 Thornbury Road
Plymouth, PL6 7PP
United Kingdom
Tel: +44 1752 202 301 | Fax: +44 1752 202 331
Email: orders@nbninternational.com

Distribution for the USA and Canada:
International Specialized Book Services
920 NE 58th Ave Suite 300
Portland, OR 97213
USA
Tel.: +1 800 944 6190 (toll free)
Email: info@isbs.com

Distribution for Austria:
Neuer Wissenschaftlicher Verlag
Argentinierstraße 42/6
1040 Wien
Austria
Tel.: +43 1 535 61 03 24
Email: office@nwv.at

Distribution for other countries:
Intersentia Publishing nv
Groenstraat 31
2640 Mortsel
Belgium
Tel.: +32 3 680 15 50
Email: mail@intersentia.be

Sperm Donation, Single Women and Filiation
Elena Ignovska

Note: This book is the product of a PhD project under the supervision of Professor Gerd Verschelden, University of Ghent, Faculty of Law, to whom the author is very grateful.

ISBN 978-1-78068-336-2
D/2015/7849/95
NUR 822

British Library Cataloguing in Publication Data. A catalogue record for this book is available from the British Library.

To my family,
our history, presence and future

FOREWORD

On 10 September 2014, Ghent University Law School (Belgium) awarded Elena Ignovska the degree of Doctor of Law. It was my privilege to supervise her three year research project resulting in this doctorate, which was funded by the Basileus Erasmus Mundus Action 2 Programme of the European Commission. The present volume is the commercial edition of her dissertation, which was entitled "Affiliation of Children Conceived by Sperm Donation to Single Women: The (Im)possibility to Establish Fatherhood from an International Perspective with a Focus on the Republic of Macedonia".

This book holds a methodologically well thought-out analysis of the complex and captivating issues connected with deliberate solitary motherhood both in international law and in the national law of ten European countries. It is a legal dissertation based on empirical, sociological and ethical literature. This multifaceted approach helps to develop the author's argument. Discussing the topic from interdisciplinary, national and international viewpoints and in a historical context offers a clear perspective for finding universal solutions. This opens the until now mostly nationally perceived field of family law up to international observation, and thus enhances the discussion on affiliation in the Macedonian family law context.

From a fitting abstract position, the author offers in Part II an original analysis using three different perspectives: the standpoint of the single mother with the desire to have children, the viewpoint of the sperm donor, and thirdly the perspective of the children, born of single mothers who were fertilised with donor sperm. One of the key issues is whether the right to have access to assisted reproductive technology of the deliberately solitary mother combined with the protection of the donor's anonymity isn't inevitably in conflict with the child's fundamental human rights, including the right to know one's genetic identity, the right to family life (and to have a relationship with one's parents) and the right to due process. The author makes a comparative assessment throughout the whole thesis, by collating the position of children born of single mothers fertilised with sperm from an anonymous donor and the position of children of heterosexual couples or (of secondary importance) of children born to single mothers whose fathers are known.

As a conclusion, Ms Ignovska expresses a well founded, balanced and nuanced preference to give priority to the fundamental rights of the child over the desires of single mothers and donors.

The bibliographical unit encompasses not only legal documents, court judgments and literature, but also medical websites, newspaper articles and public and governmental opinions.

The author has dealt with the subject in a thorough and creative way, resulting in refreshing insights. The sense of nuance as well as an understanding for the position of all actors, are clearly the strengths of this PhD thesis. The combination of the legal, ethical and sociological positions of the participants of the reproductive project of single women conceiving children with the assistance of sperm donors is enriching. The author clearly shows her ability to keep up with an evolving research topic, to find the rationale behind the policy, and accordingly to anticipate future action in terms of turning policy into law and its consequences.

Elena Ignovska already proved to be a researcher with a particularly broad view on the law when she was working at the University Ss. Cyril and Methodius in Skopje (FYR of Macedonia). Even before she came to Ghent, she had acquired expertise in the fields of family law, the law of succession, and sociology of the family, all subjects which proved to be extremely relevant for this research project. Her constant drive to gain more in-depth knowledge and to further improve her research skills is witnessed by her additional degree in Bioethics. During her time spent in Ghent, Ms Ignovska was always eager to present and discuss her work in progress, in order to get extra feedback, looking for new perspectives. During our discussions, I was impressed by her very extensive knowledge of the literature and her exhaustive and creative thinking about the subject, always proceeding in a very cautious way with all appropriate differentiations and nuances, understanding the position of the three main actors: the single woman, the sperm donor and the child.

This book offers innovative perspectives, not only for Macedonian citizens, but for all legal scholars. It reminds us that, in the words of Karl Marx, the philosopher's task is not so much to describe the world, but to change it. The author's hope has been to cast light on the problems of children conceived by sperm donation to single women in Macedonia, and to advance their perspectives. May this aspiration come true in a practical sense. I have no doubt that this thesis will prove to be of value for the development of Macedonian Family Law in the next years or decades.

Prof. Dr Gerd Verschelden
Director of the Institute for Family Law
Ghent University, Belgium

CONTENTS

LIST OF ABBREVIATIONS

ART	assisted reproductive technologies
Brussels II	Council Regulation (EC) No 2201/2003 of 27 November 2003
bis Regulation	concerning Jurisdiction and the Recognition and Enforcement of Judgments in Matrimonial Matters and the Matters of Parental Responsibility
CCC	Convention on Contact concerning Children
CEDAW	Convention on the Elimination of All Forms of Discrimination Against Women
CRC	Convention on the Rights of the Child
Draft Recommendation	Draft Recommendation on the Rights and Legal Status of Children and Parental Responsibilities
ECECR	European Convention on the Exercise of Children's Rights
ECHR	European Convention on Human Rights
ECLSCBOW	European Convention on the Legal Status of Children Born Out of Wedlock
ECtHR	European Court of Human Rights
HEFA	Human Fertilisation and Embryology Authority
ICCPR	International Covenant on Civil and Political Rights
ICESCR	International Covenant on Economic, Social and Cultural Rights
IVF	in vitro fertilisation
UDBHR	Universal Declaration on Bioethics and Human Rights
UDHGHR	Universal Declaration on the Human Genome and Human Rights
UDHR	Universal Declaration on Human Rights
"White Paper"	Report on Principles Concerning the Establishment and Legal Consequences of Parentage

INTRODUCTION

> "Science enhances the moral value of life, because it furthers a love of truth and reverence – love of truth displaying itself in the constant endeavour to arrive at a more exact knowledge of the world of mind and matter around us, and reverence, because every advance in knowledge brings us face to face with the mystery of our own being".
>
> Max Planck, *Where is Science Going?*
> Translated by James Murphy (1932)

The enormous progress of science is eagerly welcomed with regard to the growing prosperity of humankind. On the road of unstoppable scientific progress, some intrinsic human values have been endangered, thus confronting humanity with manifold moral and legal dilemmas. The possibilities, such as the assisted reproductive technologies, teeter at the very edge of ethical sensitivity regarding life and the application of science.

At the very essence of the circle of existence is reproduction, as a process of continuing the human species and thus striving for eternity. What was once considered a natural process following coitus is now more than ever a planned and conscious transformation of human life when people are ready and willing to undertake the parental role.

The first test tube baby – Louise Brown, born in Great Britain in 1978 – was probably the most famous baby in the world. Louise Brown was not only a product of conception by her parents, but also of a new and revolutionary concept in reproductive medicine, thus starting a revolution in modern families all over the world. Until Louise was born, the ethical and legal aspects regarding the process of giving birth and founding a family were focused around debates on contraception, abortion, sterilisation and, inevitably, women's bodily integrity. In vitro fertilisation (IVF) breached the exclusivity of a woman's body in which, until then, conception always took place. A woman's body, specifically her womb, no longer has primacy in the process of conception. IVF also breached the exclusivity and even outdated the modus of conceiving a child: coitus between a man and a woman. From here on, IVF has created opportunities for modelling and indeed manipulating the act of human conception, arising from the new scientific developments in bio-reproductive medicine. These new opportunities became the only possibility for some parents to have genetically related offspring.

The conception of a child by a single woman with a donation of genetic material but not of a father, and posthumous reproduction are now an integral part of contemporary natal policy. An increasing number of mono-parental families and children who will grow up with the absence of one parent has emerged as a trend. This in turn dilutes the quality of parental relationships, depriving children from having two parents as a desired and preferred context for its development, and as such, one protected in articles 7 and 8 of the United Nations Convention on the Rights of the Child (CRC).

Following drastic scientific, sociological and legal changes in the recent years, there is no universal model of family and family relationships anymore. On the contrary, the definitions of marriage, kinship, parenthood and family differ in various state legislation and, what is more, each family becomes model of its own. Changes in the family laws are encouraged by the prerogatives of each individual as a holder of the right to reproduce and, consequently, to found a family.[1] Given that *family* is a union composed of parent(s) and child(ren), the research more closely focuses on reconciling the human rights of the progenitors with the human rights of the child conceived with medical assistance.[2] Even though the recent family law debates are predominantly paedo-centric,[3] one cannot avoid questioning why in the discussions of alternative family formations the focus is always on the welfare of the child when the emphasis on the acceptability of techniques for medically assisted reproduction is usually on the parents.[4]

A common feature of national family legislation in Europe is that the donor should not be considered a father as a principal rule. Consequently, provisions for establishing fatherhood do not apply in cases in which the conception occurred through assisted fertilisation. Regulations of that kind compromise articles 12, 2 and 18 of the CRC.

The reasons why the scope of the research is limited to single women solely (excluding partner families that face the same issues) are twofold. Firstly, single women families illustrate how assisted reproductive technologies are changing family laws in contemporary societies by making it possible to conceive a child by realising one's individual reproductive right without a partner. This leads to a responsibility of the legal system to manifest greater flexibility in adjusting family provisions to the new circumstances created by introducing ART. Secondly, the issues are treated differently due to the different contexts surrounding both families – absence or presence of a father in the child's life. Two parents will raise the child conceived in the second context, even though the father will be a social

1 In the legal framework of article 12, and to a lesser extent article 8 of the European Convention on Human Rights (ECHR).

2 Through article 8 (ECHR) protecting the right to respect for private and family life and its derivate – right to identity.

3 Almeida S., "The Right to Respect for (Private and) Family Life in the Case-Law of the ECtHR; the Protection of New Forms of Family", *Academia.edu*, p. 25, available online: https://www.academia.edu/2269426/The_right_to_respect_for_private_and_family_life_in_the_case-law_of_the_European_Court_of_Human_rights_the_protection_of_new_forms_of_family.

4 Pennings G., Mertes H., "Ethical Issues in Infertility Treatment", *Best Practice & Research Clinical Obstetrics & Gynecology*, Vol. 26, No. 6, 2012, p. 855.

and legal but not biological/genetic parent. The child conceived in the first context is destined to be fatherless intentionally and from birth. A confrontation between both contexts (single mothers by choice and couple families) for conceiving a child with assisted reproduction is a subject of analysis for the purposes of re-examining the accuracy of the biological criterion as suitable for satisfying the legal needs of the newly created realities. Nevertheless, inevitably, the suggestions proposed in this book should apply to both contexts.

1. RESEARCH QUESTIONS AND TOPICS OF INTEREST

The reproductive right and consequences of its realisation are introduced through the perspective of universal human rights, the application of these principles in ten different European positive national family law jurisdictions (with a later focus on the Republic of Macedonia), and their evaluation through the practice of the European Court of Human Rights (ECtHR). This introduction draws attention to the diagnosed discrepancies with the aim of searching for the answers to several questions of common interest. The subsidiary questions of the research are: (1) is assisted reproduction a function of realising the reproductive right of prospective parents or a function of protecting the best interests of the prospective children; (2) how are the overlapping interests between children and the other participants (the parents and donors) resolved in terms of protecting children's right to their genetic identity; and (3) how does assisted reproduction affect the affiliation within the family? The answers to these questions bring the content closer to the more central questions: is the legal family primarily a social or biological construct and therefore is parenthood a twofold concept: (a) *social* when it comes to executing (carrying out) the parental role, rights and responsibilities in the relationship with the child, and (b) *biological/genetic* when it comes to the genetic relatedness; further, what is the relation between them, and how does one evaluate the proportionality of their coexistence? The answers to these questions bring light to the main hypothesis: there is an inconsistency between treatments of children conceived "naturally" and "artificially" since the latter are often restricted in their access to judicial proceedings for establishing parenthood. From here on, the text will navigate towards the core questions with a focus on the national legislation of the Republic of Macedonia: (1) is the current impossibility of launching proceedings for establishing parenthood in relation to children conceived by ART to single women harmonised with the internationally ratified documents and the practice of the ECtHR, and consequently, (2) is there a need to introduce legal changes?

It remains clear that by changing the ways of conceiving children, the definitions and concepts of families are radically altered. Although more than 30 years have passed since the birth of Louise Brown, the participants in assisted reproduction – "the parents to be", the donors, third parties and children are still a part of an uncertain sociological experiment, scrutinising, changing and creating laws through new litigation, and national and international regulations. In these terms, the concept of parenthood (once having an exclusive meaning) is undergoing fragmentation into biological/genetic, legal and social parenthood, depending mostly on the intention and role that the parent will have or already has in the child's life. Therefore the overall goal of the research is to analyse the impact of the application of the assisted reproductive technologies in the changing family law, in particular, the provisions on affiliation in the Republic of Macedonia from a human rights perspective and in the context of the European legal family.

2. METHODOLOGY

The topic focuses on a concrete problem and envisages considerations of how the law is trying to solve it. The positions of the participants in the reproductive project are represented separately in different chapters. This is for the purposes of understanding the behaviour behind the social phenomena on the path of mediating between their contrasting interests, and possibly suggesting new solutions, therefore also taking a political approach.[5]

The work uses predominantly qualitative legal methodology.[6] Bearing in mind some of the advantages of the quantitative research, some statistical materials and information, and official records and surveys originally obtained for other purposes and by other researchers are used restrictively only as a secondary source of data.

The approach is mostly doctrinal, normative and therefore theoretical.[7] Accordingly, the research is conducted via selecting and weighing materials, taking into account the hierarchy, authority, and understanding of the social context and interpretation. Nevertheless, non-doctrinal methodological research

---

5 Hong Chui W., "Quantitative Legal Research", in McConville M., Hong Chui W. (eds.), *Research Methods for Law*, Edinburgh University Press, 2007, p. 48. See also Henn M., Weinstein M., Foard N., *A Short Introduction to Social Research*, Sage, 2006, and Dobinson I., Johns F., "Qualitative Legal Research", in McConville M., Hong Chui W. (eds.), *Research Methods for Law*, Edinburgh University Press, 2007, p. 20.

6 The simplest definition of qualitative legal research is that it is non-numerical and as such, is in contrast with quantitative (numerical) research. Nevertheless, both (qualitative and quantitative methodologies of research) are empirical since they are based on observations of the world. See Dobinson I., Johns F., "Qualitative Legal Research", in McConville M., Hong Chui W. (eds.), *Research Methods for Law*, Edinburgh University Press, 2007, pp. 17 and 18. See also Epstein L., King G., "Empirical Research and the Goals of Legal Scholarship: The Rules of Inference", *University of Chicago Law Review*, Vol. 1, No. 69, 2002, p. 3.

7 See the definitions and descriptions of these categories in Dobinson I., Johns F., "Qualitative Legal Research", in McConville M., Hong Chui W. (eds.), *Research Methods for Law*, Edinburgh University Press, 2007, pp. 17 and 18.

categories are also used, such as social considerations of the problems currently affecting the law (taken from newspaper articles or web-portals), analysis of the policy underpinning the existing law and possible proposition of changes or law reform.[8] Additionally, the current regulation regarding paternity of children conceived by sperm donation to single women is described, and the problem is located and defined with a common purpose of matching social realities with prescribed norms towards their better consistency.

The materials used during the research can be divided in two major categories: (1) primary sources (international conventions and other international documents,[9] the national legislation of the Republic of Macedonia,[10] and the case law of ECtHR), and (2) secondary sources (written commentaries on the legislation and the case law, books, monographs, journal articles, reviews, surveys, etc.). Both deductive and inductive reasoning is used in interpretations of the primary and secondary sources. The research is qualitative in an attempt to deal with the issue itself and not with different national systems and institutions. Concepts are based on legal norms and sets of statements that focus on interpretations and meanings. The purpose of this approach is to develop a better understanding of the researched phenomena. Inevitably, interpretations of meanings are a matter of subjective perceptions. In these terms, qualitative research is more "slippery" than quantitative statistics.[11] To exclude subjectivity as much as possible, the research also expands the scope to the circumstances surrounding the creation of the legislation, the other relevant laws and parallel factual situations. To avoid the threat of the predisposition to research as an advocate and not as an academic,[12] the structure is organised in a way to confront biased perspectives and contrasting opinions.

The research topic itself tackles different disciplines. The legal discipline is at the core of the research and provides the problem definition. Futhermore, due to

---

8 As defined categories of non-doctrinal qualitative legal research. See more Dobinson I., Johns F., "Qualitative Legal Research", in McConville M., Hong Chui W. (eds.), *Research Methods for Law*, Edinburgh University Press, 2007, p. 20.

9 The core sources are (1) the Universal Convention of Human Rights, (2) the European Convention of Human Rights, (3) the Convention on the Elimination of All Forms of Discrimination against Women, (4) the Convention on the Rights of the Child, the Oviedo Convention, the Universal Declaration on the Human Genome and Human Rights, the Universal Convention on Bioethics and Human Rights, the European Convention on the Exercise of Children's Rights, and the Convention on Contact concerning Children. Additionally, other documents also play a significant role in the analyses: the White Paper, the Principles of European Family Law regarding parental responsibilities, and the "Draft Recommendation".

10 The core sources are (1) the Family Law of the Republic of Macedonia, and (2) the Law on Bio-medically Assisted Fertilisation of the Republic of Macedonia.

11 Dobinson I., Johns F., "Qualitative Legal Research", in McConville M., Hong Chui W. (eds.), *Research Methods for Law*, Edinburgh University Press, 2007, p. 21. See also Ezzy D., *Qualitative Analysis: Practice and Innovation*, Allen & Unwin, 2002, p. 5.

12 Manderson D., Mohr R., "From Oxymoron to Intersection: An Epidemiology of Legal Research", *Law/Text/Culture*, Vol. 6, 2002, p. 159.

the nature of the problem, two very different legal disciplines necessarily overlap – civil law (i.e. national positive law of each state) and international law (i.e. universal human rights and freedoms). The sensitivity of the ethical aspects in the legal discussion over the issues of conception, reproduction, and individual rights and freedoms inevitably imposes even more interdisciplinary methodology. Therefore bioethical concepts and deliberations are used to evaluate and re-evaluate legal questions. There are at least three reasons why the use of ethics can be productive to conduct legal research. Firstly, both disciplines have the same subject and treat morality in a hermeneutic, normative, argumentative and interdisciplinary way since their purpose is to interpret social institutions and to guide human actions. They both use the argument as a central tool. Secondly, they overlap in content due to their intention to guide and regulate behaviour in order to make society and our lives better. Therefore they have many of the same central concepts such as human rights, freedoms, justice and democracy. Thirdly, ethics is beneficial to law since the legal system is a normatively open practice inevitably making references to moral ideas and exercises in ethics.[13]

The research also expands from its strict legal framework because it treats normative questions making suggestions regarding what the law ought to be, and therefore penetrates the political sphere. Since law and society coexist, sociology also contributes to the research. The other disciplines are used heuristically as a source of argument and inspiration that is incorporated into the legal argumentation.[14] The aim of this kind of approach is to enhance the strict legal norms with better understanding of the sensitive domain of family and private life respectively. Interdisciplinary research is more prone to innovation than mono-disciplinary research into law if the other discipline is used as heuristic device for generating new insights from which the target domain – the legal science – may profit. An integrative approach offers the best opportunity for exchanging knowledge, therefore liberating science from artificial and arbitrary disciplinary boundaries.[15] Acknowledging that natural sciences are prone to more exact results and conclusions, the question of measuring the truth in the humanities is rather difficult. In the search for more objective truth out of family law, as a complex set of objective and subjective private life conducts and human behaviour, *the correspondence theories of truths* will play an instrumental role. According to them, a statement is true if it correctly reflects the facts of the world; therefore the truth is determined by checking whether it fits the facts.[16] This concept will be instrumental in observing the credibility of the biological criterion

13 Van der Burg W., "Law and Ethics. The Twin Disciplines", in Klink B., Taekema S. (eds.), *Law and Method, Interdisciplinary Research Into Law*, Mohr Siebeck, 2011, p. 175.

14 Regarding the methodology for interdisciplinary research, see more in Klink B., Taekema S. "On the Border. Limits and Possibilities of Interdisciplinary Research", in Klink B., Taekema S. (eds.), *Law and Method, Interdisciplinary Research Into Law*, Mohr Siebeck, 2011, p. 10.

15 *Ibid.* p. 30.

16 *Ibid.* pp. 15 and 16 discussing the modern theories of truth dividing them into two categories: correspondence and coherence theories of truth.

as a determinant in the proceedings for establishing paternity in correlation with the reality of the existent family forms. In this sense, the research will move from elaborating facts and how things are (*de lege lata*) towards elaborating on values and how things should be (*de lege ferenda*). The knowledge of facts presumes knowledge of values and *vice versa*.[17] Even though facts and values are interconnected, there is no sharp distinction between them, especially not in the humanities. The statements about what the law is have both factual and evaluative dimensions.[18] Therefore the interpretation of the facts, social institutions and human behaviour will be crucial for evaluation of the relevancy of the hypothesis.

Since the purpose of the ECtHR is to assure appreciation of the fundamental rights through interpretation and appliance of the core human rights and freedoms on national levels, binding the concerned countries to adjust their legislation and administrative practice, the research will also inevitably parallel other European national regulations.

The Macedonian legal context is interesting for several reasons. Firstly, the Republic of Macedonia as a Member State of the Council of Europe is under scrutiny for its interpretations of the international conventions of the *ECtHR*. Notwithstanding the wide margin of appreciation in family law matters, it is important for the national legal system to harmonise within the European legal context. Secondly, on the one hand, Macedonian family legislation is relatively traditional,[19] while on the other hand, the context of the application of ART is relatively liberal[20] in comparison to some other European legislation. There is inconsistency even on the internal national level, since the Family Law and the Law on Bio-medically Assisted Fertilisation have contrasting evolutionary paths, even though they both tackle families in one way or another. Thirdly, the consequences of the relatively new regulation on the application of ART (dating from 2008) and its impact on the parent–child relationship are evident and appealing in practice a couple of years later, at the present time and in the future. This means that the conflicting cases in practice and before the courts are yet to come. Therefore it is necessary to examine why family law is reluctant to change, even when changes are already present in society, enabled among other factors by open access to bio-reproductive technologies. Introducing sperm donor inseminations for single women has already created fecund grounds for violating children's rights in

---

17 *Ibid.* p. 18. See also Putnam H., *Pragmatism: An Open Question*, Blackwell, 1996.

18 Dworkin R., *Law's Empire*, Harvard University Press, 1986, pp. 230–231.

19 In terms of not recognising official homosexual partnerships. This is important for the research topic, since a significant number of "single women" who decide to be inseminated by sperm donors around the world are lesbians who consider sperm donor insemination a joint parental project with their homosexual partner. See, for instance, Kelly F., "Equal Parents, Equal Children: Reforming Canada's Parentage Laws to Recognize the Completeness of Women-led Families", *University of New Brunswick Law Journal*, Vol. 64, 2013, p. 254.

20 In terms of the liberal possibilities allowed in the Law on Bio-medically Assisted Fertilisation as a general comparison with other European legislation. For more, see the explanation on the choice of the European national regulations encompassed in Part I: 3.1.3. Legal proceedings for establishing the paternity of ART conceived children.

the domain of their private and family life in a context of official secrecy over reproductive matters.

Beyond the national context, the filiation of children conceived by sperm donation is controversial, not only in Europe, but also worldwide. On this level, the accuracy of the issue and the necessity for investigating the possibilities is of broader and common importance.

PART I

MAPPING THE TERRAIN FROM AN INTERDISCIPLINARY AND INTERNATIONAL PERSPECTIVE

CHAPTER 1
TERMINOLOGY

For the purposes of discussing the law and ethics of reproduction in the era of medically assisted technologies, it is important to differentiate between the use and interpretation of the terminology in the literature depending on the historical and professional context. It is important for interdisciplinary research to induct harmonised terminology, which will be used in a consistent manner at least for the purposes of the work itself. The ethical and legal debates related to sensitive issues such as life, personal identity, reproduction and family are too abstract for the needs of exact scientific conclusion. Bearing in mind that they cannot be calculated with mathematical formulas, it is useful from the beginning to elaborate some of the different interpretations of the ambiguous terms depending on their context of interpretation. Along these lines, it is important to make a distinction between (1) *reproduction, procreation, insemination, fertilisation and conception*; (2) *wish, desire and need to have a child*; (3) *rearing, bearing and begetting a child;* (4) *progenitors/begetters, donors and parents (genetic, biological, social and legal);* (5) *kinship and family;* and (6) *"artificial insemination" and sperm donation as Assisted Reproductive Technologies (ART).*

The introduction and interpretation of the terminology will be a basic tool for the further discussion. The legal context will be mapped from an international perspective, narrowing it down to the European context and the interpretation of international documents such as the European Convention on Human Rights by the European Court of Human Rights. For purposes of comparative overview, the lenses of observation will also look at the national regulations in ten European countries regarding three topics: (1) the right of single women to use ART; (2) the right of the child to know the identity of the donor; and (3) the legal proceedings for establishing fatherhood in relation to children conceived with ART.

1.1. REPRODUCTION, PROCREATION, INSEMINATION, FERTILISATION AND CONCEPTION

An important change that announced the new era of human cooperation with medical science in the field of what before was considered the exclusivity of nature was introduced when the term "procreation" was replaced with the manufacturing word "reproduction". The differentiation between both terms – "reproduction" as referring to making children as a product in the laboratory, and "procreation" as referring to the natural conception following coitus – announced the beginning of the penetration of *in vitro* into humans' daily lives.[21] According to this logic, assisted reproductive technologies do not *procreate* children, but only *reproduce*. Therefore the focus of the term "reproduction" is on the adult agents' rights to "re-produce themselves" and not on the creation of progeny.

There is also a very thin line between the terms *insemination*, *fertilisation* and *conception* as they are very often used not only in medical surroundings – in the laboratory, but also in the religious, philosophical and ethical debates around the issue – in relation to "when does human life begin". From a technical point of view, sperm *insemination* is a medical technique for achieving *fertilisation* in a woman's body. Since it is done by unnatural methods (inserting sperm inside the genitals of a woman), it is also called *artificial insemination* or *intrauterine insemination*. Some gender studies criticise this terminology as offensive towards women's bodies and their decision-making capacity, as it emphasises women's passivity in procreation: women being considered as mere objects on which insemination is performed (something is done to them).[22]

Fertilisation, on the other hand, is the process of fusing into union two gametes of different sex resulting with a new cell called a *zygote*, potentially a new future individual person. The fertilisation can happen *in vivo* (i.e. in the women's body), but can also take place *in vitro* (i.e. outside the human body).[23] *Conception* is a term mostly used in *pro-life* and *pro-choice* ethical settings regarding the beginning of life. The meaning though is very close to that of *fertilisation*, differing mostly in the interpretation of the eternal question – is human life conceived after the fusion of gametes or at a later stage? Sometimes, it is used to describe more accurately the moment when the connection is made with the wall of the womb by the zygote, therefore representing the later stage of *fertilisation*.

Chadwick re-examines the consistency of the terms observing that: "there seems to be something odd saying that persons have a natural right to reproduce by artificial means".[24] The term *artificial insemination*, having the initial intention of distinguishing between *natural procreation* from *assisted reproduction*, does not correspond with the way the process tends to be treated, and is replaced with the terms *assisted insemination* and *bio-medically assisted reproduction*, therefore losing the artificiality and keeping the reproduction in the domain of intrinsic human nature.

---

21 Ramsey P., "Shall we 'Reproduce'? II Rejoinders and Future Forecast", *Journal of the American Medical Association*, Vol. 220, No. 11, 1972, pp. 1480–1485.

22 Zerjav T., "The Politicization of Singlehood", *CEU eTD Collection*, 2012.

23 VS Pages Comparing Difference between Things. Insemination vs. Fertilization: http://vspages.com/insemination-vs-fertilization-25363/.

24 Chadwick R.F., "Having Children: Introduction", in Chadwick R.F. (ed.), *Ethics, Reproduction and Genetic Control*, Routledge, 1990.

1.2. WISH, DESIRE AND NEED TO HAVE A CHILD

The lust for a child is differentiated and elaborated by Denier[25] using Frankfurt's *principle of precedence* scheme.[26] The gradation between the *wish, desire* and *need* for a child depicts their different importance and urgency for fulfilling, promoting, and elevating the realisation of the *child need* to be recognised as a human right. Applying Harry Frankfurt's scheme, the lust for a child actually belongs to the category of *constrained volitional needs* due to the reason that is generated by a very strong and urgent desire that remains present until it is not satisfied. Consequently, the non-fulfilment of a *constrained volitional need* causes distress, and in the case of involuntary childlessness, one suffers harm.[27]

The distinction of the content and meaning of the *wishes, desires* and *needs* is important to examine the legitimacy of the right to reproduce with the application of reproductive technology. The gradual evolution of their importance using the *principle of precedence* is in compliance with the notion that the ethical evaluation of certain rights should not be brought up by subjective sensations and feelings such as *wishes* and *desires*.[28] Hare argues that it is not necessary for all desires to claim their realisation and that a sentiment should not be a starting point of moral arguments.[29] Denier on the other hand elevated the *constrained volitional needs* to a level of rights, thus arguing that they should not be treated as personal sentiments.

According to Harry Frankfurt's hierarchy and the impact that a strong *child need* has on human life, the reproductive right should belong in the category of basic human rights. This is in concordance with some other authors who argue that a claim becomes a positive right when society recognises that claim as a basic need (not merely as a wish) for the well-being of a person.[30]

1.3. REARING, BEARING AND BEGETTING A CHILD

The distinction between *rearing, bearing* and *begetting* a child corresponds to the fragmentation of parental roles caused by assisted reproductive technologies.

---

25 Denier Y., "Need or Desire? A Conception and Moral Phenomenology of the Child Wish", *International Journal of Applied Philosophy*, Vol. 20, No. 1, 2006, pp. 81–95.

26 Frankfurt G.H., "Necessity and Desire", *Philosophy and Phenomenological Research*, Vol. 45, No. 1, 1984, pp. 1–13; Frankfurt G.H., *The Importance of What We Care About*, Cambridge University Press, 1988.

27 Denier Y., "Need or Desire? A Conception and Moral Phenomenology of the Child Wish", *International Journal of Applied Philosophy*, Vol. 20, No. 1, 2006, pp. 81–95.

28 Hare R.M., "In Vitro Fertilization and the Warnock Report", in Chadwick R.F. (ed.), *Ethics, Reproduction and Genetic Control*, Routledge, 1990.

29 *Ibid.*

30 Boivin J., Pennings G., "Parenthood Should be Regarded as a Right", *Archives of Disease in Childhood*, Vol. 90, No. 8, 2005.

Rearing refers to being a factual parent and executing the parental responsibilities and does not necessarily include a biological link with the child. *Rearing* is related to the role of the *social* or *legal parents*, related to "doing parenthood", and as such is an issue of custody disputes. *Bearing* a child on the other hand refers to caring for the child in pregnancy which could lead to giving birth. Therefore *bearing* a child is related to the gestational role of the mother which is essentially a biological role, and not to be confused with the role of the person contributing genetic material. This is especially important to emphasise since the leading presumption in the continental filiation laws was, and in most of the national legislation still is, that the mother of the child is the woman who *bears* and therefore gives birth to the child.[31] In contrast, the purpose and the intention of surrogacy agreements are to attribute the roles of *bearing* and *rearing* (usually also *begetting*) the child to different women: the surrogate woman, and the commissioning mother, respectively. *Begetting* a child refers to being genetically related to the child, and therefore to "being a parent". Since the roles of *begetting* and *bearing* do not have to coincide with the same person anymore, it is important for a discussion on the affiliation to clearly distinguish between the different roles of the possible fragmentation. *Begetting* as passing on one's genes to the child is the foundation of affiliation. Genes are rather passed completely by cloning rather than with assistance in reproduction when only half are passed. However, cloning for reproductive purposes is forbidden and, as it is a different topic, will not be tackled in the discussion. Nevertheless, the analogy with cloning can shed light on the over-estimated role of genes in the present legislation on affiliation. By analysing the differences of the multiple participating roles in the process of human reproduction, Chadwick points out that not all aspects of reproduction are related to the *need to have a child*.[32] In other words, some aspects of the *need to have a child* are more justified than others to claim that the application of assisted reproduction is necessary, and that is to claim that there is no other means to accomplish the same goal. In contrast to the *principle of precedence* that elevated the personal importance of satisfying the need, Chadwick associates the relevance of the claim to being the beneficiary of reproductive technology with the existence or non-existence of alternative solutions for accomplishing the specific role of parenting. In these terms, the specific *need to bear a child* is connected with the social role of being a parent, encompassing the need to care for the upbringing and development of the child. Therefore it is not questionable

---

31 This is also accepted in the White Paper as a first principle. Therefore, surrogacies are ruled in a manner of subsequent modification of the legal parentage, for instance later adoption by the commissioning parents that does not affect the legal maternal affiliation at the time of birth. See more in the *Report on Principles Concerning the Establishment and Legal Consequences of Parentage – The White Paper*, Committee of Experts on Family Law, 2006, p. 8.

32 See more Chadwick R.F. (ed.), *Ethics, Reproduction and Genetic Control*, Routledge, 1992, pp. 11–12. Chadwick uses the term *desire* not *need*. For the purposes of consistency with the above accepted Frankfurt's use of the term *need*, the use of the term *desire* (as used with the same meaning) is replaced with the term *need*.

that the *need to bear* a child can be very strong. Nevertheless, this fact cannot be an argument for access to ART if there are other alternative means at disposal, such as adoption. In these terms, *begetting* a child should be treated differently from *rearing* and *bearing* a child because there is no other substitute (such as adoption) for transferring the genes apart from the application of ART. In the case of embryo donation the transfer of the genes remains unaccomplished, while the ground for the priority of ART *vis-à-vis* adoption is weaker.

1.4. PROGENITORS/BEGETTERS, DONORS AND PARENTS (GENETIC, BIOLOGICAL, SOCIAL AND LEGAL)

The difference between *progenitors/begetters* and *parents* (mother and father) relates to the persons which *beget* ("are parents"), *bear* (*gestate*) or *rear* ("do the parenthood") the child, and therefore persons which are genetically related to the child, biologically and physically give birth to the child or execute the parental responsibilities. In legal terms, fulfilling the role of parenthood is the responsibility only of legally recognised parents,[33] accompanied by custody, financial support and inheritance rights, making parental responsibilities inherent to the notion of parenthood.[34] Accordingly, parental responsibilities are a collection of

[33] Recommendation No. R (84) 4 on Parental Responsibilities of the Council of Europe, 28.02.1984, in its Principle 1, paragraph 2 defines the use of the terms "father", "mother" and "parents", as referring to persons having a legal filiation link with the child. The White Paper refers only to "legal parents" (persons whose parentage has been established in a manner prescribed by law). The Draft Recommendation (see footnote 51) in its article 2 defines parents as "persons who are considered to be the parents of the child according to national law". Thus, the article makes it clear that the recommendation only refers to questions concerning legal parentage and not to the establishment of biological or gestational parenthood (which is a medical matter), nor to social or psychological parenthood. Despite this, still, the provisions on legal parentage (articles 6–18) are intended to provide a balance between "the biological truth" and "the social or psychological parenthood" reflecting the fact of mutual habitat with the child and who is responsible for the role of taking care of the child. See p. 31 of the Draft Recommendation.

[34] *Ibid.* Recommendation No. R (84) 4, in its Principle 1, paragraph 1 defines parental responsibilities as a collection of duties and powers which aim at ensuring the moral and material welfare of the child, in particular by taking care of the person of the child, by maintaining personal relationships with him, and by providing for his education, maintenance, legal representation, and administration of property. Brussels II bis (see footnote 138) in its article 2(7) uses the term "parental responsibility", meaning the entirety of rights and duties relating to the person or the property of a child which are given to a natural or legal person by judgment, by operation of law or by agreement having legal effect, including rights of custody and rights of access. Comparatively, the concept of "parental responsibility" comes under different names or sometimes even contents. "Parental rights and responsibilities" is used in Bulgaria, "custody" in Finland, "custody and guardianship" in Ireland and Sweden, "parental care" in Germany, "parental authority" in Denmark, France, Italy, Lithuania, the Netherlands, Poland, Spain and Switzerland, "parental care and guardianship" in Greece, "parental supervision" in Hungary, "parental power" in Portugal and "parental rights" in Russia and in the Republic of Macedonia. The term "parental responsibility" in singular has been used

duties and powers, which aim at ensuring the moral and material welfare of children, in particular: (1) health and development,[35] (2) care and protection, (3) maintenance and personal relationships, (4) education, (5) legal representation, (6) determination of residence, and (7) administration of property.[36] *Parenting by doing* recognises the reality of looking after children, while *parenting by being* acknowledges the genetic identification between the parent and the child on a level of fact.[37] In England and France there is a terminological difference between the term "father" (*père*) – the person fulfilling the parental role – and the term "genitor" (*géniteur*), reserved for the biological parent. In the Netherlands, the Dutch Civil Code (Book 1, title 11) introduced the legal concepts of "biological father", "begetter", and "donor", while the legal literature and case law have developed the concepts of "legal", "social", and "physiological" parentage.[38] *Legal parentage* is associated with the legally relevant facts for establishing parenthood, while *social parentage* is associated with a family tie based on the education and upbringing of a child by adults who are not its biological parents.[39] Begetters are different from biological parents in the sense that the first (in its specialist meaning under the Dutch law) presupposes that a child is conceived in a natural way, while the second only presupposes a genetic link between the parent and the child irrespective of the modus of conception.[40] Thus, the begetter (*verwekker*) is the biological father of the child as a result of sexual intercourse with the mother, whereas the donor is the biological father but not the *verwekker*.[41]

While the anthropology differentiated between *pater* as the man socially recognised as the father and *genetrix* as the man believed to be the physiological parent, Barnes even makes a further distinction between *genitor* and *genetrix* associating them with the supposed biological parent and the actual genetic

---

in the Hague Conference on Private International Law, and the European Commission. The term "parental responsibilities" in plural has been used by the Council of Europe and in the White Paperand the Draft Recommendation. This term is becoming increasingly established in Europe. For this reason, it will be a term used in this work too. See more in Boele-Woelki K. *et al.*, *Principles of European Family Law Regarding Parental Responsibilities*, Intersentia, 2007, pp. 27 and 31.

35 The Draft Recommendation, article 20.

36 White Paper, Principle 18, p. 23. The definition of "parental responsibilities" in the White Paper was taken from the Recommendation No. R (84) 4 (Principle 1) of the Committee of Ministers to Member States on Parental Responsibilities. Several paragraphs were added, in particular the expression "care and protection" including health, nourishment and welfare of the child, as well as the "determination of the residence of the child" as in concordance with the Convention on Contact Concerning Children of the Council of Europe.

37 Masson J., "Parenting by Being. Parenting by Doing – in Search of Principles for Founding Families", in Spencer J.R., Bois-Pedain A. (eds.), *Freedom and Responsibility in Reproductive Choice*, Hart Publishing, 2006.

38 Antokolskaia M., Boele-Woelki K., "Dutch Family Law in the 21st Century: Trend-Setting and Straggling Behind at the Same Time", *Nederlandse Vereniging Voor Rechtsvergelijking (Netherlands Comparative Law Association)*, Vol. 6, No. 4, 2002.

39 *Ibid.*

40 *Ibid.*

41 Explanatory Memorandum, Kamerstukken II, 1995–96, 24649, No. 3, p. 8.

parent. This author tries to make a connection between physical and social kinship, arguing that discrepancies may happen due to humans' culturally developed ideas about how biology works.[42] The old Roman law presumptions that the mother is always certain while the father is not are not obsolete nowadays and even more so when single women conceive a child with an unknown sperm donor.

The official criteria accepted as core principles on establishing parenthood confront the genetic, biological, social and legal criteria for becoming a parent.

The initial legal concept of parenthood fused the genetic, biological, legal and social relationships together. Under these terms, the Roman law presumption that *mater semper certa est* applied (the mother of the child is always certain, i.e. the woman who gives birth to the child will be considered as the legal mother). For the father, applying the Roman law presumption – *pater is est quem nuptiae demonstrant* – the father is the mother's married husband, with a possibility of rebutting his fatherhood if his biological relatedness with the child is contested, because he is always uncertain – *pater semper incertus est*. The conception of a child happens solely through sexual intercourse. Extra-marital children were discriminated against in comparison to children born within marriage mostly due to the desire to protect the institution of marriage. The biological relatedness between parents and children was a principal rule, with an exception of establishment of parenthood through adoption.

Today, with the application of the assisted reproductive technologies, family law is changing the definitions of family and parenthood. The introduction of the regulation of the new forms of conception of human life has not happened at the same latitude and time everywhere in the world. Some countries have disputed the ethical, religious and social justification of the process of assisting in the act of conception; others, despite heated debates, became pioneers in the harmonisation of their family law with the newly emerged ways of becoming a parent.[43] Despite the differences, the concepts of establishing parental roles and the corresponding family models have drastically changed almost everywhere in the world. In addition, family models arising from the application of the assisted technologies are still subject to constant change.

Machteld Vonk distinguishes four different types of mothers: (1) *biological and genetic mother* (the woman who supplies the ovum and gives birth to the child); (2) *genetic mother* (the woman who supplies the ovum, but does not give birth to the child); (3) *gestational mother* (the woman who gives birth, but does not supply the ovum); and (4) *non-biological mother* (the woman who raises the child but is not genetically related, nor has given birth to the child). In her qualification, there are only two kinds of fathers, thus creating a dichotomy between: (1) the

---

[42] Barnes J.A., "Physical and Social Kinship", *Philosophy of Science*, Vol. 28, No. 3, 1961, pp. 296–299.

[43] See *Comparative Analysis of Medically Assisted Reproduction in the EU: Regulation and Technologies*, Final Report (SANCO/2008/C6/051).

bio-father (the man who supplies the sperm); and (2) the *non-bio father* (the man who raises the child but is not genetically related to the child).[44]

Furthermore, Vonk illustrates three legal dimensions of the parent–child relationship: (1) *biological/genetic parenthood*; (2) *legal parenthood*; and (3) *parental responsibility*.[45] According to this author, there can only be two *biological* or *genetic parents*, which does not mean that they will be the *legal parents* or will exercise the parental responsibilities (e.g. when they are sperm/egg/embryo donors). *Legal parenthood* can also be granted only to two parents which may lead to full parental status if the holder also has parental responsibilities. They, however, can be granted to more than two persons (in England and in the Netherlands), but if they are obtained without *legal parenthood* the parental status is not full (e.g. when under certain circumstances the *social parent* – i.e. the stepparent – acquires parental responsibilities by court order).[46] Furthermore, Vonk supports the possibility for the legislator to abandon the concept that a child may only have two *legal parents*, since they are not necessarily *biological parents*, or at least the possibility for a jurisdiction that recognises the tripartite *legal parenthood* in relation to a child from a foreign jurisdiction.[47]

In the book *Bio-reproductive Ethics and Law*, the criteria for establishing *legal parental responsibilities* in the Republic of Macedonia are elaborated. These criteria can be summarised into three categories: (1) *biological/genetic criterion* (by the fact of biological/genetic relationship with the child);[48] (2) *legal criterion* (by the fact of additional legal action for becoming a parent); and (3) *social criterion* (by the fact of mutual family life with the child). Even though the *biological criterion* is taken as a core prerogative in the proceedings for establishing and rebutting the parental role, legal interventions in terms of intention-based consent accompanied with other administrative mechanisms in the cases of adoption and assisted fertilisation have stronger legal power to claim paternity.[49]

Different women/men can participate in different roles in the reproduction: (1) the woman/man who donates the ovum/sperm (genetic parents); (2) the woman/man for which the ovum/sperm is donated. The second category can be named

44 Vonk M., *Children and their Parents, A Comparative Study of the Legal Position of Children with Regard to their Intentional and Biological Parents in English and Dutch Law*, Intersentia, 2007, pp. 26–27.

45 *Ibid.* p. 7.

46 From a comparative survey, in many national legal systems, in practice the stepparents living with the child and his or her parent participate anyhow in the decision-making on daily matters concerning the child with the consent of the parent. See Boele-Woelki K. *et al.*, *Principles of European Family Law Regarding Parental Responsibilities*, Intersentia, 2007, p. 117.

47 *Ibid.*

48 The biological and genetic criteria are merged into one criterion because under thepositive legislation when the cited book was written as well as the book in front of you, surrogacy arrangements were forbidden in the Republic of Macedonia. Nevertheless, surrogacies were introuduced by amending the Law on Bio-medically Assisted Fertilisation on 9 October 2014 (Official Gazette of the Republic of Macedonia, No. 149).

49 Ignovska, E., *Bio- reproduktivna etika i pravo. Novite reproduktivni tehnologii i roditelskoto pravo*, Biggos, 2010.

differently according to different criteria: (a) *non-genetic parent(s)* – according to the genetic participation; (b) *intended parent(s)* – according to the purpose of the donation; (c) *social parent(s)* – according to the factual situation (i.e. mutual family life with the child); or (d) *legal parent(s)* – according to the legal attribution of parental responsibility. In the case of assisted reproduction, the beneficiaries of the donation will legally be the parents of the child, while the genetic men/women will only be *donors*, but not *legally recognised parents*. Donations in European Union countries are altruistic contributions for therapeutic purposes. In these terms, the role of the *donor* is usually accomplished and exhausted by the act of donation, and he ceases to exist in the child's life. The introduction of *non-anonymous donors* also introduced the possibility of further interaction between the donor and the child, and therefore started to change the perceptions of the concept of the *limited liability* of donors.

For the purposes of this book and as a present reality, the terms *donor* and *parent* do not coincide on at least three levels: their intention; legal attribution of paternity; and in most cases, family life realities. The principles of the "White Paper" set out by the Committee of Experts on Family Law restrict the terminological usage of parentage only to the legal one as parentage established in a manner prescribed by law, since the establishment of biological parentage is mainly a medical matter.[50] On the grounds of these premises, upgraded Appendix IV of the Draft Recommendations on the Rights and Legal Status of Children and Parental Responsibilities[51] makes it clear that it deals only with legal parentage. Nevertheless, the constitution of parentage as legal should "balance between 'the biological truth' reflecting biological and genetic parentage, and 'social or psychological parenthood' reflecting the fact with whom the child is living and who is or would be taking care of him or her".[52]

1.5. KINSHIP AND FAMILY

The continental legal systems follow the Roman law system of *consanguinity* for regulating affinity. This means that the blood relation is the foremost relevant factor for attributing kinship. Similar blood participation shows that the person is descended from the same ancestor as another person and is therefore affiliated. The *patrilineal system* of *consanguinity* can be *linear* as a direct, vertical line of affiliates descending from one another: son, father, grandfather, etc.; and *collateral* as an indirect, horizontal line of affiliates descending from the same ancestor but not from one another: brother and sister, cousins, etc. who could have the same father (*consanquinei*) or the same mother (*uterini*). The affiliation system

50 White Paper, 2006.
51 Appendix IV, Draft Recommendations on the Rights and Legal Status of Children and Parental Responsibilities, Explanatory Memorandum, CJ-FA (2011) RAP 5 prov. (Article 2).
52 *Ibid.*

of *consanguinity* is important for family law, providing that individuals can marry among each other up to the fourth degree collateral line of *consanguinity*. Marriage is almost universally prohibited up to and including first cousins mostly for medical reasons, i.e. preventing genetic disorders and inbreeding caused by incest. It is scientifically proven that the offspring of an incestuous relationship are at great risk of genetic disorders caused by autosomal recessive gene mutation which is doubled in closely blood-related relatives who carry two copies of the same gene, making the probability 1 in 16. It is highly probable that the offspring will have severe abnormalities, mental retardation or die early in childhood. Only around half of the children of incestuous relationships avoid such abnormalities. The risk of transferring the genetic disorder weakens (but is still present) as blood-related relatives become more distant.[53] Anonymous sperm donations pose a risk of incestuous relationships among siblings originating from the same donor. This risk was higher at the beginning of the application of sperm donations due to the lack of regulation or restrictive norms regarding the possible number of children conceived by one sperm donor. Even nowadays, some experts are calling attention to the accidental incest between half-sisters and half-brothers who often live close to one another.[54] They have warned that siblings that have been separated and have not been living together are exposed to the probability of developing incredible mutual affection for one another once they meet.[55] This is explained by the *Westermarck psychological effect* that refers to reverse sexual imprinting, i.e. people who live in close domestic proximity during the first (usually 6) years of their lives become desensitised to later sexual attraction. Lack of this kind of imprinting infers the opposite – siblings or half-siblings raised apart miss out on this, so if they meet each other as adults they experience incredible mutual attraction.[56]

The affiliation system of *consanguinity* is also important in inheritance law, thus, not only for the succession of human genes *inter vivos*, but also for the succession of property *mortis causa*, providing the heirs through two systems of (1) *ius accrescendi* (only the closest alive descendants become heirs, thus,

---

53 See more in Kingston H.M., *ABC of Clinical Genetics* (3rd edition), BMJ Books, 2002, p. 7.

54 Sperm Donation and Possible Inbreeding – Oops! "One Sperm Donor, 150 Offspring", *Human Biological Diversity*, 09/07/2011, available online: http://hbdchick.wordpress.com/2011/09/07/sperm-donation-and-possible-inbreeding-oops/; Krista A., "Genetic Sexual Attraction", *The Guardian*, 17 May 2003, available online: www.theguardian.com/theguardian/2003/may/17/weekend7.weekend2. See also Bouchard T.J., "Genetic Influence on Human Psychological Traits. A Survey". *Current Directions in Psychological Science*, Vol. 13, No. 4, 2004, pp. 148–151.

55 *Ibid.*

56 *Ibid.* The Westermarck effect was first developed by the Finish anthropologist Edward Westermarck in 1891. Westermarck E.A., *The History of Human Marriage* (5th edition), Macmillan, 1921. It has been criticised on grounds that childhood proximity cannot in itself produce sexual avoidance without the existence of social pressures and norms. See more in Eran S., Dalit S., "Incest Avoidance, the Incest Taboo, and Social Cohesion: Revisiting Westermarck and the Case of the Israeli Kibbutzim", *American Journal of Sociology*, Vol. 114, No. 6, 2009, pp. 1803–1842.

excluding the representation of more distant relatives); and its corrective (2) *ius representationis* (the descendants become heirs in the place of the previously died or are declared unworthy of inheriting heir). In the affiliation system of *consanguinity*, the next of kin is the closest person by blood.

The choice of factors we take as relevant when attributing kinship is important for family formation. Adoption of children not biologically linked and the "legitimation"[57] of children who are biologically linked (meaning that some biological children will be illegitimate) were the Roman law legally accepted exceptions of the system of *consanguinity*. Nowadays, ART application creates many more exceptions. The discussions on biology as an ontological essence *versus* sociology as a relationship factor in determining kinship were and still are very fierce among different groups of sociologists and anthropologists. On one side is the first group claiming biological determinism to be essential in affiliation relations. On the other side are representatives claiming the relevancy of sociological relations as crucial for building an affiliation relationship, arguing that the biological facts are just one of the conditions to which kinship systems must adapt.

A number of early studies in sociology tried to define the natural desire inherent to humans as individuals to create human families.[58] A number of early studies in anthropology also promoted blood-relatedness as ontologically prime, and only in the absence of relatedness was the fact of living together secondary in determining kinship. Many authors afterwards criticised the lust for "naturalness" as being an instrumental policy of constructing social roles of males as providers and females as responsible for the domestic realm, thus building the nuclear family in which the father should be "more certain".[59] Morgan as one of the most prominent American ethnologists, anthropologists and sociologists, who developed *the theory of social evolution* and set the ground for contemporary anthropology, argued that the first human domestic institution was not the patriarchal family but the maternal clan. The central role of the mother in determining the kinship and therefore the early social networks known as a *matriarchy* or a *gynocentric society* excluded the necessity of knowing the biological relatedness with the father, since the clan was related from the mother's side only. He addressed the later social evolution in the family forms that led to the dominance of the patriarchal family in the technological progress that not only changed property relations, but on a wider social scale also changed the systems of governance. Although there is no clear evidence of the true existence

---

57 As a difference between "legitimate" children born in marriage, and "illegitimate" children born outside wedlock.

58 Westermark E., *The History of Human Marriage*, Macmillan, 1891.

59 See more in Fortes M., "Introduction", in Goody J. (ed.) *The Developmental Cycle in Domestic Groups*, published for the Department of Archaeology and Anthropology by the Cambridge University Press, 1959; and later on in Yanagisako J., Junko S., Collier J.F., "Towards a Unified Analysis, Gender and Kinship", in Collier J.F., Yanagisako J. (eds.), *Gender and Kinship: Essays Toward a Unified Analysis*, Stanford University Press, 1987.

of the *matriarchy* as an early stage of development of human unity,[60] the influence of the Morgan's theory was enormous in later intellectual thought.

Morgan also claimed that human reproduction and the biological link between parents and children represent *real kinship*, while adoption is legal fiction, thus representing *fictive kinship*.[61] He showed flexibility in accepting the social reality when blood relatedness is absent. Malinowski also claimed that kinship is primarily psychobiological in nature and constituted by blood ties, which however can be substituted by culturally developed relationships, as for instance in the case of adoption.[62]

The controversial *inclusive fitness* and *kin recognition theories* propose the high importance of genes as an individual unique identification code, as a tool to possibly recognise the close genetic relatives of one another and who therefore engage in mutual social relations. These theories have many critics nowadays.[63] Holland argues that if observed carefully, both biological and social theories of kinship do not treat each criterion exclusively. Thus, he tries to harmonise both patterns for conceptualising kinship by contextualising them.

In the 1960s and 1970s anthropologists recognised that the biologically claimed concepts about kinship are suspect, especially bearing in mind the cultural context in which they were placed. The fiercest battle between the old biological concepts and the upcoming relational concept for determining kinship culminated with the work of Schneider who marked the turning point in anthropological studies.[64] He argued that what is given by birth *via* blood is a static state of *being* (a parent), while what is created and maintained by an interactive process of performance and care giving is an active state of *doing*, and therefore is the real parent–child relationship. He does not avoid the genetic reality as if it was non-existent, but he questions its necessity in the actual doing of parenthood.[65] Therefore for him, kinship is about relations and interactions for which the blood ties are irrelevant. The blood ties are relevant just as far as they are socially recognised and constituted. Apart from that, the function of performing particular relationships is a ground for defining the relationship as kinship. Many

60 See more in Lowie R.H., *Primitive Society*, Bony and Liveright, 1920. He concludes that there is no proof about the hypothetical existence of matriarchy. This is a dominantly present understanding nowadays too.

61 Morgan L.H., "Systems of Consanguity and Affinity of the Human Family", *Smithsonian Contributions to Knowledge*, Vol. 17, Washington Smithsonian Institution, 1870, available online: http://ia700407.us.archive.org/17/items/systemsofconsang00morgrich/systemsofconsang00morgrich.pdf.

62 Malinowski B., "Parenthood – the Basis of Social Structure", in Calverton V., Schmalhausen S.D. (eds.), *The New Generation*, Macaulay, 1930.

63 Holland M.P., *Social Bonding and Nurture Kinship: Compatibility Between Cultural and Biological Approaches*, 2004, available online: http://ssrn.com/abstract=1791365 or http://dx.doi.org/10.2139/ssrn.1791365.

64 See more in Schneider D., *A Critique of the Study of Kinship*, University of Michigan Press, 1984, p. 165.

65 *Ibid.* pp. 124–125.

authors draw a distinction between genetic relatedness as defined by science, and the culturally developed kinship systems, thus considering parenthood as a rather political and not natural concept, being negotiated on a case-by-case basis, just like adoption and fosterage.[66] Assisted reproductive technologies introduced "families of choice"[67] where the ties between family members have shifted from being conventionally defined as "ties of blood" to social obligations attached to individual judgments, and thus are more of a subject of negotiation than accepted as given.[68] This decentralised family relations from their core – sexual intercourse[69] – and brought about a notion of "defamiliarising" of what were once considered traditional kinship ties.[70] This was also criticised on the same grounds. Accepting that contemporary families are to a large extent negotiated (in terms of the statuses attributed to the parents), while not accepting negotiations over donors' roles in the children's lives (when mothers' set of fixed behaviour attached to a known donor does not allow any contacts with the child) is paradoxical.[71]

Contemporary anthropologists appreciate the biological links but relate kinship to concepts outside nature – in the culture and relations based upon emotions, affections and attachments, shared habitat, shared food, care, shelter, and even sleeping arrangements. Carsten conceptualises kinship as founded on actual relations of shared bodily and spiritual substance, which does not have to be related to tracking down genetic relatedness.[72] *Attachment theorists* claim that genetic relatedness *per se* is not a factor for developing attachments. On the contrary, other factors such as proximity, care, nurture and responsiveness to the infant's needs are relevant for building relationships between the child and the father, mother or any other caregiver. Weiss enumerates three aspects of manifestation of attachment – physical contact comfort, particular warmth, and security from danger – as especially important for building the relationship between child and parent.[73] The attachments and social bonds built in childhood

66 See more in Barnes J.A., "African Models in the New Guinea Highlands", *Man*, Vol. 62, 1962, pp. 5–9; Schrauwers A., "Negotiating Parentage: the Political Economy of 'Kinship' in Central Sulawesi, Indonesia", *American Ethnologist*, Vol. 26, No. 2, 1999, pp. 310–323 (p. 311).

67 As a term used in the context of international lesbian and gay communities. See more in Weston K., "Parenting in the Era of AIDS", in Stein A. (ed.), *Sisters, Sexperts and Queers Beyond the Lesbian Nation*, Plume, 1993; Weeks J., Heaphy B., Donovan C., *Same Sex Intimacies: Families of Choice and Other Life Experiments*, Routledge, 2001.

68 Dempsey D., "Donor, Father or Parent? Conceiving Paternity in the Australian Family Court", *International Journal of Law, Policy and Family*, No. 18, 2004, pp. 76–102, p. 78.

69 Strathern M., *Reproducing the Future: Anthropology, Kinship and the New Reproductive Technologies*, Routledge, 1992.

70 Franklin S., *Embodied Progress: A Cultural Account of Assisted Conception*, Routledge, 1997.

71 Dempsey D., "Donor, Father or Parent? Conceiving Paternity in the Australian Family Court", *International Journal of Law, Policy and Family*, No. 18, 2004, p. 95.

72 Carsten J., "The Substance of Kinship and the Heat of the Hearth: Feeding, Personhood, and Relatedness among Malays in Pulau Langkawi", *American Ethnologist*, Vol. 22, No. 2, 1995, p. 236.

73 Weiss R.S., "The Attachment Bond in Childhood and Adulthood", in Paros M.C., Stevenson-Hinde J., Marris P. (eds.), *The Attachment Across the Lifecycle*, Routledge, 1991.

are very strong and continue into adulthood too.[74] For Bowlby, the developments of the behaviour that operate in childhood create the essence of parenthood. For some other attachment theorists, sharing meals together not only just as an imitation of the first nutrition that happens in the women's womb, but also as a way of developing behavioural attitudes is a key to creating family kinship.[75] Richards even defines the family in terms of "the regularity of eating meals together".[76] The state of "being born and bred" as a social aspect also adds personal characteristics alongside or even more so than biological possessions.[77] A number of studies, researching the family patterns of indigenous people from different parts of the world found, other than biology, important elements of becoming kin – the social bond established by sharing common household and living arrangements.[78] Many cultural anthropologists since Levi-Strauss have argued that the reproduction of human beings is also the reproduction of social relationships.[79] All the ethnographies that emphasise the importance

---

74 Bowlby J., *The Making and Breaking of Affectional Bonds*, Tavistock, 1979, p. 129. He suggested that the attachment behaviour "characterize[s] human beings from the cradle to the grave".

75 Richards A.I., *Hunger and Work in a Savage Tribe: A Functional Study of Nutrition Among the Southern Bantu*, G. Routledge and Sons, 1932, p. 28.

76 *Ibid.*

77 Edwards J., *Born and Bred. Idioms of Kinship and New Reproductive Technologies in England*, Oxford Studies in Social and Cultural Anthropology, Oxford University Press, 2000.

78 Weismantel M., *Food, Gender and Poverty in the Ecuadorian Andes*, University of Pennsylvania Press, 1988, p. 169. Weismantel conducts a study of Zumbaqua Society. In Zumbaqua the parent–child relationship is defined by common life where the heart defines the home, and conjugal living and not blood relations are the key elements of determining parenthood; Carsten J., Hugh-Jones S., "Introduction", in Carsten J., Hugh-Jones S. (eds.), *About the House: Levi-Strauss and Beyond*, Cambridge University Press, 1995; Carsten J.,"Substantivism, Antisubstantivism, and Anti-antisubstantivism", in Franklin S., McKinnon S. (eds.), *Relative Values: Reconfiguring Kinship Studies*, Duke University Press, 2001, p. 227. They argue that the consumption of various foods, accommodation and so on develops the child's social identity as mutable and open to influences rather than given; Stafford C.L., "Chinese Patriliny and the Cycles of *Yang* and *Laiwang*", in Carsten J. (ed.), *Cultures of Relatedness: New Approaches to the Study of Kinship*, Cambridge University Press, 2000; Stafford C.L., *Separation and Reunion in Modern China*, Cambridge University Press, 2000. From research conducted in North Eastern China and in Angang, Taiwan, Stafford observes the family patterns – the care given to children creates enduring respect that manifests in caring for their old parents later on in life; Storrie R., "Equivalence, Personhood and Relationality: Processes of Relatedness Among the Hoti of Venezuelan Guiana", *Journal of the Royal Anthropological Institute*, Vol. 9, No. 3, 2003, pp. 407–428. Storrie observed that raising a child may produce a kinship even in the absence of natural ties, led by the common sentiment among southern Chinese that "the far away relatives are no better than close neighbours". By examining the life of the Hoti of Serrania de Maiqualida, Venezuelan Guiana, Storrie found that the morality of sharing transforms the unrelated to related. Because of this, co-residence is important and "those close *consanquini* who are not living together are forgotten, as their substance changes from shared to different" (pp. 420–422). Vilaca A., "Making Kin out of Others in Amazonia", *Journal of the Royal Anthropological Institute*, Vol. 8, No. 2, 2002, pp. 347–365. By examining the family patterns of Wari people living in Western Amazonia, Brazil, Vilaca observes that "the proximity and living together are so decisive in determining kinship that the genealogical kin who lives far away may be excluded from the kin circle".

79 See, for instance, Smart C., Neale B., *Family Fragments?*, Polity Press, 1999; Spaas L. (ed.), *Paternity and Fatherhood: Myths and Realities*, Macmillan, 1998, Strathern M., *Reproducing the Future: Anthropology, Kinship and the New Reproductive Technologies*, Routledge, 1992.

of environmental influences as important to create kinship relationships run against the genealogical assumptions, which they consider fixed and given, and therefore untouchable by environmental influences. They demonstrate that social and emotional bonds are relevant and determining and not genetic participation *per se* for creating kinship. Thus, the use of biology may be considered "strategic" to naturalise assisted kinship,[80] even though it is considered important only once it is questioned. If not questioned, parents will usually consider the emotional connections developed with their children through the process of nurturing and upbringing as a key pillar in constructing and constituting kinship.[81]

Applying the attachment theory to the right of the child to establish contact with the donor after reaching the age of 18 may be irrelevant, since the attachment bonds based on raising the child are already established.

Some recent studies promote the combination of both biological and cultural approaches in understanding not only what kinship is, but also what kinship does as an effect.[82]

Foucault has claimed that all historic periods developed certain conditions of truth based on what was at the time acceptable. He has argued that contemporary understandings of sexual dimorphism and reproductive physiology are recent phenomena and follow the development of modern biology and science.[83] In this light, kinship is a social and cultural dimension of constructing families, finding legitimation in blood ties through history depending on the preferred political set of values. The distinction between genetic (*genitor* or *genetrix*) and social parent has always existed in cases of step-parenting, adoption or non-paternity. It is only now that the new reproductive technologies have highlighted the ways in which biogenetic kinship is socially constructed, reaffirming that parenthood in relation to children conceived by genetic material donation is grounded in the legal concept of intent rather than in genetics.[84]

Family in Plato's view was fundamentally natural in character. He developed a sharp distinction between the private life in a family as led by the natural phenomena of affection and reproduction, and the common life in a state as led mainly by reason. For his student, Aristotle, however, both family and the state

80 Thompson C., "Strategic Naturalizing. Kinship in an Infertility Clinic", in Franklin S., McKinnon (eds.), *Relative Values. Reconfiguring Kinship Studies*, Duke University Press, 2001, p. 175.

81 Hirsch E., "Negotiated Limits. Interviews in South-East England", Edwards J. *et al.* (eds.), *Technologies of Procreation. Kinship in the Age of Assisted Conception*, Manchester University Press, 1993, p. 69.

82 Holland M.P., *Social Bonding and Nurture Kinship: Compatibility Between Cultural and Biological Approaches*, 2004, available online: http://ssrn.com/abstract=1791365 or http://dx.doi.org/10.2139/ssrn.1791365; Schweitzer P.P., *Dividends of Kinship: Meanings and Uses of Social Relatedness*, Routledge, 2000.

83 Foucault M., *The Order of Things. An Archaeology of the Human Science*, Vintage Books, 1994.

84 Shaw A., "The Contingency of the Genetic Link in Constructions of Kinship and Inheritance - An Anthropological Perspective", in Spencer J.R., Bois-Pedain A. (eds.), *Freedom and Responsibility in Reproductive Choices*, Hart Publishing, 2006, p. 75.

were natural and social constructions. For him the family sprouted out of the love and true friendship between the husband and wife as the leading pillars of the familial community. In *Politics*, he defined family (*οἶκος*) as a smaller cell of the political community (*πόλεις*) that is itself a special entity as a community or association (*κοινωνία*) that integrates its members in a mutual life.[85] As being a natural part of the bigger mosaic that constitutes the political system, the family transitions from animal existence to rational life that is possible only in an organised state. Attributing the natural component to the family due to the biological links between its members is an argument for naturalising the political system and the state too, and as such to bring the state closer to the individual who should be able to identify the organic relationship familiar to his own household. By making such identification, he also emphasises the social component of the family, stressing the mutual life between its rational members, which by definition has to be organised as well as the state itself.

Marriage as a formal institution of mutual life was a solid framework to reassure that sexual intercourse had happened between the married partners, and that the family was a continuation of one's own kind. For these purposes, kinship transitions from the time of primitive promiscuity, matriarchy and undetermined paternity, to the structured framework of monogamous marriage, leading to nuclear families.[86] Malinowski differentiated social and physical kinship, overlapping in the mother, while not necessarily in the father whose role is essentially social and may or may not be physical.[87] For him the family was composed of the woman and the children she takes care of, alone or together with the man with whom she is in a stable relationship. In these terms, the relationship between the man and the child was determined by the relationship between the man and the woman who bore the child. The man was eligible to be classified as the father depending on his social and real relationship and contribution to the mother, and therefore the child too. Kinship connections between the biological father and the child are even nowadays usually mediated legally by an existing intimate relationship between the biological mother and the child.[88] Feminists support single women's reproductive right to be exercised alone as a means of providing women with more choice and with the possibility of having children without marriage. Mary O'Brien argues that there have been two crucial moments

85 Provencal L.V., "The Family in Aristotle", *Animus*, Vol. 6, 2001, available online: www.mun.ca/animus/2001vol6/provencal6.htm#1.

86 See more in Morgan L.H., "Systems of Consanguity and Affinity of the Human Family", *Smithsonian Contributions to Knowledge*, Vol. 17, Washington Smithsonian Institution, 1870, available online: http://ia700407.us.archive.org/17/items/systemsofconsang00morgrich/systemsofconsang00morgrich.pdf; Morgan L.H. *Ancient Society*, Macmillan, 1877; Engels, F., *The Origin of the Family, Private Property and the State*, 1884, Introduction by Brewer P., Resistance, 2004, available online: http://readingfromtheleft.com/PDF/EngelsOrigin.pdf.

87 Malinowski, B., *The Family Among the Australian Aborigines: a Sociological Study*, University of London Press, 1913.

88 Dempsey D., "Donor, Father or Parent? Conceiving Paternity in the Australian Family Court", *International Journal of Law, Policy and Family*, No. 18, 2004, p. 97.

in the history of reproduction. The first one was the differentiation of the roles between the male as provider and the female as housewife, restricting women to the home so that the uncertainty regarding "who the father of the mutual children was" becomes, to some extent, reduced. This division downgraded the private sphere (reproduction, child rearing, maintaining the household) and celebrated the public sphere (production). The second crucial moment was the discovery of contraception that gave women control over their fertility.[89]

The presumption that a married husband is the father of the child born during marriage is still a valid legal argument in paternity disputes, unless proved otherwise. Adulterous women were considered criminals of the highest rank, among other reasons such as the dominant male's position in the family, and also due to the fact of disturbing and manipulating the genetic family tree.

Nowadays, the term *family* is even vaguer and therefore suitable for extended interpretations. If once the debate was over nuclear *versus* extended family, characterised by biology or the fact of mutual life and over whether the family depends on marriage or not,[90] nowadays the term *family* is the symbiosis of a diversity of forms. It has already been argued that if there is a caring relationship and commitment between an adult and child, then the absence of a biological link is not fatal to the engagement of article 8 of the ECHR.[91] Family (if we exclude partner-only families without children) can be formed by members who are or are not biologically related (e.g. adoption, heterologous donor insemination); who live or do not live together and share or do not share a common household (e.g. re-constructed families); by two members (woman/man with a deceased/divorced/ separated husband/wife/partner and a child or deliberately single woman and a child); two parents and one child/more children (hetero- or homosexual),[92] more than two parents holding parental responsibilities and a child/children (e.g. three parents in the UK,[93] and only recently, up to four parents in British Columbia in Canada);[94] parents and their parents and children and their children (as extended

89 O'Brien M., *The Politics of Reproduction*, Routledge & Kegan Paul, 1981.

90 See more in Mount F., *The Subversive Family: an Alternative History of Love and Marriage*, Counterpoint, 1983.

91 Lowe N., *A Study into the Rights and Legal Status of Children being Brought Up in Various Forms of Marital or Non-Marital Partnerships and Cohabitation*, A Report for the Attention of the Committee of Experts on Family Law, September, 2009, p. 8.

92 Two-parent families are still the dominating concept worldwide, even though several jurisdictions are considering a proposal to lift the restriction on more parents. See more in Antokolskaia M., "Legal Embedding Planned Lesbian Parentage. Pouring New Wine into Old Wineskins", *Familie & Recht*, February 2014, p. 2.

93 Also see the suggestions for family law reform in recognising the parenthood of more than two persons in Brennan S., "How Many Parents Can a Child Have? Philosophical Reflections on the Three Parent Case", *Western University*, 2013, available online: http://papers.ssrn.com/sol3/papers.cfm?abstract_id=1451926, referring to a case before the Ontario highest court which recognised the necessity for a change in the law in terms of introducing more persons in a child's life in concordance with the child's best interests (*AA v. BB*, 2007 ONCA 2, 83 OR (3d) 561).

94 See footnotes 942 and 943.

families) and so on. The new emerging trend of "modern families" are "families by choice of co-parenting partners" which refers to mothers and fathers that have relationships based on legal agreements for purposes of having and raising a mutual child rather than mutual relationship of affection, romance and sex.[95] This is a step further in the trend from single mothers by choice to co-parenting by choice, as one of the interviewed persons for the purpose of sharing their experience said: "why would you choose to be a single parent when you could co-parent?",[96] or "why only have a child when you could also provide a father".[97]

Some authors appreciate the nuclear family as it was, and consider that any divergence from its realm is potentially dangerous for developing a relationship and commitment necessary for the proper bringing up of children.[98] They blame the application of ART for the disturbance of the nuclear family ideal as a basic social unit, thus creating childless families, donor intruded families and parentless children.

John Harris criticises marriage as a moral and biological foundation, giving the family an institutional character. For him, the institutional family foundations depend on the political ideology to grant central focus to one of the following three dimensions: (1) society (family is a fundamental unit of society; thus society has an interest to ensure that there will be a next generation), (2) adults (the right to found a family as part of the human rights and freedoms of the individual), or (3) the child (securing the interests of the future generations).[99]

In the European context, at the present time, it is widely accepted that parenthood is more a social than a natural construct, even though many implications resulting from the application of ART are still under discussion.[100] Acknowledging not only the social but also the normative role that the family

95 See more in Carpenter L., "Meet the Co-parents", *The Guardian*, 15.12.2013, available online: www.theguardian.com/lifeandstyle/2013/dec/15/meet-the-co-parents-modern-families; Daily Mail Reporter, "Meet the 40-something Childless Singles Turning to "Co-parent partnerships where Raising a Family Doesn't Include Romance", *MailOnline*, 11.02.2013, available online: www.dailymail.co.uk/femail/article-2277027/Meet-40-childless-singles-turning-parent-partnerships--raising-family-doesnt-include-romance.html; Ellin A., "Making a Child Without the Couple", *The New York Times*, 08.02.2013, available online: www.nytimes.com/2013/02/10/fashion/seeking-to-reproduce-without-a-romantic-partnership.html?pagewanted=all&_r=0; Al Jazeera English, "Family on Your Own Terms", *The Stream*, 24.02.2014, available online: http://stream.aljazeera.com/story/201402242305-0023501.

96 *Ibid.* Carpenter L., "Meet the Co-parents", *The Guardian*, 15.12.2013.

97 Al Jazeera English, "Family on Your Own Terms", *The Stream*, 24.02.2014, available online: http://stream.aljazeera.com/story/201402242305-0023501 (5–6 min).

98 Singer P., Wells D., *The Reproduction Revolution. New Ways of Making Babies*, Oxford University Press, 1984, p. 53; Chadwick R.F. (ed.), *Ethics, Reproduction and Genetic Control*, Routledge, 1990; Mary Warnock in the Warnock Report.

99 Harris J., "The Right to Found a Family", in Scarre G. (ed.), *Children, Parents and Politics*, Cambridge University Press, 1989.

100 European Parliament, Directorate General for Internal Policies, Policy Department C: Citizens' Rights and Constitutional Affairs, Legal Affairs, *Recognition of Parental Responsibility: Biological Parenthood v. Legal Parenthood, i.e. Mutual Recognition of Surrogacy Agreements: What is the Current Situation in the MS? Need for EU Action?*, 2010, pp. 7 and 12.

plays and therefore accepting the necessity for making political decisions to shape family forms, we lean towards the flexible definition of family provided in *Bromley's Family Law*[101] with small modifications based on accepting the dichotomy between the fact of mutual life or the sole existence of the biological link. Along these lines, *the family* will be treated as a social unit whose relationships may fall under two categories: (1) common life: two persons living in a marital/ extra-marital relationship, or living together in a manner similar to spouses, or one parent living with one or more children; and (2) the sole existence of a biological link: two or more persons related by blood or marriage (for instance brothers and sisters).

The CRC offers a broad definition of family, reflecting the wide variety of kinship and community arrangements within which children are brought up around the world.[102] The Preamble emphasises the importance that family has as a fundamental group of society and as a natural environment for the growth and well-being of its members, particularly children. Article 5 recognises and appreciates the extended family, especially in its meaning for children and their evolving capacities. The Human Rights Committee also emphasised a flexible definition in two General Comments favouring a broad definition to include "all persons composing it in the society of the State Party concerned",[103] being aware of the discrepancies from State to State and even from region to region within a State.[104] It furthermore showed sensitivity towards appreciating nuclear and extended families, as well as various other forms of families such as unmarried couples and their children or single parents and their children if they exist in a particular society.[105]

The ECtHR and the European Commission on Human Rights have included several aspects in the concept of "family life": married parents and their legitimate minor child, cohabiting parents and their minor child, the mother and her minor child within and outside marriage, the man and the minor child which has been recognised, the biological father and the minor child in specific circumstances, close relatives such as grandparents and the minor child, foster parents and the minor child, and the non-biological parent and the minor child.[106]

---

101 Lowe N.V., Douglas G. (eds.), *Bromley's Family Law* (10th edition), Oxford University Press, 2007, p. 2.

102 Hodgkin R., Newell P., *Implementation Handbook for the Convention on the Rights of the Child*, UNICEF, United Children's Fund, 2007, p. 105, referring to CRC/C/2/Rev.8, p. 76.

103 *Ibid.* p. 77, referring to Human Rights Committee, General Comment No. 17, 1989, HRI/GEN/1/Rev.8, para. 6, p. 184.

104 *Ibid.* referring to General Comment No. 19 of the Human Rights Committee.

105 *Ibid.* referring to Human Rights Committee, General Comment No. 19, 1990, HRI/GEN/1/Rev.8, para. 2, p. 188.

106 Boele-Woelki K. *et al.*, *Principles of European Family Law Regarding Parental Responsibilities*, Intersentia, 2007, p. 16.

1.6. "ARTIFICIAL INSEMINATION" AND SPERM DONATION AS ASSISTED REPRODUCTIVE TECHNOLOGIES

The history of assisted reproductive technologies (ART) can be traced back to long before the first officially announced birth in the United Kingdom in 1978.[107] The term "artificial insemination" refers to the historical first form of assistance in the reproductive process – homologous (autologic) sperm insemination when the husband was not able to achieve intercourse with his wife. It was defined as "introduction of sperm into a woman's genital tract by any means other than sexual intercourse".[108] The term "artificial" was commonly used to symbolise that the conception did not occur through natural coitus. It was only afterwards that a new dimension of the term was accepted, acknowledging that there was nothing artificial about the conception or the children born as a result. On the contrary, it was just the process of conceiving that was assisted for the parents; therefore the later term "assisted insemination" replaced the previous.

The first human case is attributed to John Hunter in 1790 involving a woman's insemination with sperm from her husband. Sperm donations by third parties were not acceptable.[109] According to Bartholomew records and unofficial archives, heterologous (allogeneic) insemination came a century later. For some other authors, donor insemination was first used in clinical practice in the late 1930s.[110] In the United Kingdom, women conceiving through sperm donation were treated as if they had had intercourse with a third person, registering the birth in the husband's name, without revealing the origin to the children. In 1948, a Commission of experts considered the practice fundamentally wrong, especially in the case of sperm donor insemination, for several reasons: breach of marriage by introducing another party in the process of reproduction, thus introducing a situation similar to adultery into marriage;[111] and harmful effects towards the child exposed to conspiracy about his/her origin, equivalent to

---

107 Bartholomew G.W., "The Development and Use of Artificial Insemination", *Eugenics Review*, Vol. 49, No. 4, 1958, pp. 187–195.

108 *Report on Human Artificial Protection, Principles Set Out in the Report of the Ad Hoc Committee of Experts on Progress in the Biomedical Sciences (CAHBI)*, 1989, Scopes and definitions.

109 *Report of the Departmental Committee on Human Artificial Insemination*, Cmnd. 1105, Her Majesty's Stationery Office, July 1960.

110 Nachtigall R.D., "Secrecy. An Unresolved Issue in the Practice of Donor Insemination", *American Journal of Obstetrics and Gynecology*, Vol. 168, No. 6, 1993, Part 1, pp. 1846–1851.

111 See, for instance, similar cases regarding the treatment of donor insemination as adultery or not as described in Kaplan J.L., Tong R., *Controlling Our Reproductive Destiny. A Technological and Philosophical Perspective*, MIT Press, 1994, pp. 237, 238. The authors refer to the case *Oxford v. Oxford* (though the donor insemination was without the husband's consent) ruled on by the Supreme Court of Ontario, Canada in 1921. In this case, according to the Court's decision, adultery was considered a voluntary surrender of one's reproductive (not sexual) powers or facilities to another. The opposite decision, considering that for adultery to be committed there must be two persons physically engaged in a sexual act was handed down in the case *MacLennon v. MacLennon* by a Scottish Court in 1958.

fraud on personal identity, kinship and inheritance.[112] The same and even graver convictions were addressed to sperm donations in a later report that condemned the practice as dangerous to all the parties concerned as well as to society at large by underestimating the institution of marriage and deceiving children.[113] The worst conviction was that of an attempt of single women to procreate as being totally ignorant to the child's needs.

The first official birth through ART was in 1978, announcing that regulation had to follow. Therefore the British government formed the Warnock Committee (chaired by the philosopher Mary Warnock) to reflect on the possible effects of opening the doors of reproductive technologies on human lives. The Committee was medical in its approach, addressing primarily "infertility and its alleviation". This meant that unmarried women were not allowed to use ART, stressing the possible consequences of legally fatherless children. The Report acknowledged the fact that the register of births would no longer portray the true genetic record, since there would result a fiction that the husband of a woman who conceived by sperm donation will not be the genetic father of the child.[114] The Warnock Report led to medically regulated practice with the Human Fertilisation and Embryology Act in 1990. The aim of the Act was to normalise ART families to the existent model of a nuclear family.[115] The Act did not allow women to utilise treatment services unless "account has been taken of the welfare of any child who may be born as a result of the treatment (including the need of that child for a father)".[116] Nowadays, the compromise is achieved on a level where single women are allowed to be inseminated by sperm donation but in order not to neglect the right of the child to know the origin, the concept of anonymous sperm donors was removed prospectively for gametes donated after 1 April 2005.[117] Nevertheless, sperm donations to single women continue to neglect the need of the child for a father.

Sperm/intrauterine inseminations were historically the first medical form of technological assistance to achieve pregnancy. They are considered to be the least expensive of the various reproductive technologies with the highest success rate.[118] Nevertheless, assisted reproductive technologies encompass a wide range of possibilities to assist wanted reproduction such as: in vitro fertilisation,[119]

112 *Artificial Human Insemination: The Report of a Commission Appointed by His Grace the Archbishop of Canterbury*, London, SPCK, 1948.
113 *Report of the Interdepartmental Committee on Human Artificial Insemination, Feversham Committee*, 1958.
114 *Report of the Committee of Inquiry into Human Fertilisation and Embryology*, Department of Health & Social Security (Warnock Report), Her Majesty's Stationery Office, July 1984.
115 Sheldon S., "Fragmenting Fatherhood: The Regulation of Reproductive Technologies", *Modern Law Review*, Vol. 68, No. 4, 2005(b), pp. 523–553.
116 Human Fertilisation and Embryology Act (HFE Act), section 13(5), 1990.
117 Human Fertilisation and Embryology Authority (HEFA), Disclosure of Donor Information, Regulations 2004.
118 Balen A.H., Jacobs H.S., *Infertility in Practice* (2nd edition), Informa Healthcare, 2003, p. 369.
119 IVF is carried out outside the woman's body, in a laboratory. This is where the eggs are fertilised and then the resulting embryos are transferred to the woman's uterus.

zygote intra-fallopian transfer (ZIFT) or tubal embryo transfer, gamete intra-fallopian transfer (GIFT), intra-cytoplasmic sperm injection, or other activities that facilitate wanted pregnancy such as cryopreservation, or pre-implantation genetic diagnosis.

CHAPTER 2
INTERNATIONAL REGULATIONS

The degrading human treatment that left black marks on human history after the World War II increased international recognition of human rights, followed by human rights treaties as core prerogatives for building common ground for the future. Setting the key principles that represent minimum moral standards was an attempt to reconcile the damage not between States, but primarily between a particular state and the individual. Shifting to the human person as the most important agent worthy of protection, the focus of international attention resulted in the Universal Declaration on Human Rights (UDHR).[120] The Declaration was followed by (among others) the International Covenant on Civil and Political Rights (ICCPR)[121] and the International Covenant on Economic, Social and Cultural Rights (ICESCR).[122] These international documents also set the minimum standards for the protection of individuals and human dignity in the field of private and family life alone or in conjunction with the obligation of society to enable the conditions necessary to ensure the individual's physical and mental health through access to medical services for everyone. The more specific international regulation regarding particular groups worthy of particular protection (and out of interest for this work) was achieved by the Convention on the Elimination of All Forms of Discrimination Against Women (CEDAW)[123]

120 Adopted by the United Nations General Assembly on 10 December, 1948.

121 Adopted by the United Nations General Assembly on 16 December 1966 and in force as of 23 March 1976.

122 Adopted by the United Nations General Assembly on 16 December 1966 and in force as of 3 January 1976. Both Covenants were ratified by the Socialist Federal Republic of Yugoslavia (Republic of Macedonia as a successor country also succeeded the ratified international regulations) on 30 January 1971 with the laws on ratification: *Закон за ратификација на меѓународниот пакт за граѓанските и политичките права and Закон за ратификација на меѓународниот пакт за економските, социјалните и културните права.*

123 Adopted by the United Nations General Assembly in 1979. The former Yugoslavia signed and ratified the Convention on 17 July 1980 and 26 February 1982, respectively. The Convention was ratified additionally by the Republic of Macedonia on 18 January, 1994 (see more online: http://treaties.un.org/Pages/ViewDetails.aspx?src=TREATY&mtdsg_no=IV8&chapter=4&lang=en). The Optional Protocol to the Convention was ratified by the Republic of Macedonia into law from 24 June 2003 – *Закон за ратификација на факултативниот протокол кон Конвенцијата за елиминација на сите форми на дискриминација врз жената.*

and the Convention on the Rights of the Child (CRC).[124] The new scientific developments in the field of life-creation, and therefore in the fields of human dignity, planned parenthood, and private and family life, pointed to the need for a universal principle and regulation that was achieved in the Universal Declaration on the Human Genome and Human Rights (UDHGHR)[125] and the Universal Declaration on Bioethics and Human Rights (UDBHR).[126]

After establishing the principles, the need for an effective safeguard for their implementation was more than necessary.

The regional mechanism for ensuring protection on already established principles in Europe had already been established and implemented through the Council of Europe. The European Convention on Human Rights (ECHR)[127] that followed accepted in its preamble the responsibility to confirm, implement and ensure the rights set down in the UDHR. For these purposes, the European Court of Human Rights (ECtHR) as a supranational court was established in 1959 and in concordance with Article 19 of the ECHR. The main purpose of the Court is to ensure the enforcement and implementation of the ECHR in the Member States of the Council of Europe. The judgments of the Court are binding on the concerned Member States.[128] The national laws of each Member State are to incorporate the ECHR into their national legal system, and most of them have already done so.[129] Even though the Court does not have jurisdiction to annul national laws, the Committee of Ministers monitors the State's execution of judgments and whether additional measures are undertaken to address the violations. In these terms, the case law of the ECtHR unites the Member States under the umbrella of

---

124 Adopted by the United Nations General Assembly on 20 November 1989, and in force as of 2 September 1990. Former Yugoslavia signed the CRC on 26 January 1990, and ratified it on 3 January 1991. The reservation was made in article 9, paragraph 1 of the CRC, stating that "the competent authority of the SFRY may under article 9, paragraph 1 make a decision to deprive parents of their right to raise their children and give them an upbringing without prior judicial determination in accordance with the internal legislation of the Socialist Federal Republic of Yugoslavia". Subsequent to dissolution, the Government of the Republic of Macedonia deposited notification of succession with the Secretary-General, with effect from 17 September 1991, the date on which it assumed responsibility for its international relations. The official ratification of the CRC was 2 December 1993 (see: http://treaties.un.org).

125 Adopted at the UNESCO's 29th General Conference on 11 November 1997. The following year the United Nations General Assembly endorsed the Declaration. It was ratified by the Republic of Macedonia on 27 April as the law on ratification – *Закон за ратификација на Конвенцијата за заштита на човековите права и достоинството на човековото суштество во однос на примената на биологијата и медицината со дополнителниот протокол за забрана на клонирање на човечки суштества и дополнителниот протокол за трансплантација на органи и ткива од човечко потекло.*

126 Adopted at the UNESCO's General Conference, 19 October 2005.

127 Ratified by SFRY on 27 February 1997 as law on ratification – *Закон за ратификација на Конвенцијата за заштита на правата на човекот и основните слободи и на Првиот протокол, Протоколот број 4, Протоколот број 6, Протоколот број 7 и Протоколот број 11 кон Конвенцијата.*

128 Smith R.K.M., *The Essentials of Human Rights*, Oxford University Press, 2005, p. 117.

129 Keller H., Sweet A.S., *The Impact of the ECHR on National Legal Systems*, Oxford University Press, 2008.

the ECHR, interprets, acknowledges violations through binding judgments, and thus, modifies, amends and creates national laws.

In the realm of private and family life, though, the interpretation of human rights by the ECtHR is to a great degree dependent on the State's proclaimed values. The introduction of assisted reproductive technologies has made these interpretations even more sensitive to the particular State's ethical and legal tradition. Nevertheless, assisted reproduction has also increased the responsibility of the national regulations to reconcile with the benefits of science and the desirable practices, but without compromising the paradigms of human rights and freedoms, human dignity, the right to form a family, the freedom to decide the number and dynamics of childbirths, as well as the child's rights.

The reproductive rights and freedoms are in correlation with the obligations of the state, as being an essential factor for ensuring their implementation. The margins within which science and technology are allowed to enter national family law are still to a great degree dependent on the particular state policies regarding its interpretation of fundamental values to be protected. Therefore on the grounds of particular historical, political, social or even religious perceptions, the state itself orchestrates the level on which reproductive rights are enjoyed as exclusive prerogatives of human beings. The European Council recognised the specific nature of the family regulation as "heavily influenced by the culture and tradition" and consequently, dependent on the nationally proclaimed values and principles as a reason for difficulties in the context of harmonisation.[130] A very thin line could be drawn between the sphere of application of the assisted reproductive technologies and their impact on the gradual changing of the basic human functions such as reproduction, parenting and individual self-realisation. Therefore some boundaries regarding the implementation of the universal human rights principles on national levels are extensively interpreted, and yet some questions remain outside the universal human rights umbrella. For the reason of appreciating conceptual differences, the ECtHR developed the concept of *margin of appreciation* when considering whether a Member State has breached the ECHR. This doctrine allows the Court to take into consideration the fact that the Convention will be interpreted differently in different Member States according to their cultural, historical and philosophical differences. On the other hand, in the family law domain, there are authors who promote harmonisation of family law in Europe, questioning whether family law still remains so culturally specific.[131] Some fierce opponents of the "cultural constraints argument"[132]

130 Council Report on the Need to Approximate Member States' Legislation in Civil Matters of 16 November 2011, 13017/01 justciv 129, p. 114.

131 See Boele-Woelki K. (ed.), *Perspectives for the Unification and Harmonisation of Family Law in Europe*, Intersentia, 2003; Antokolskaia M., *Harmonisation of Family Law in Europe: A Historical Perspective, A Tale of Two Millennia*, Intersentia, 2006.

132 The "cultural constrains argument" is considered the main objection to family law harmonisation; see Antokolskaia M., *Harmonisation of Family Law in Europe: A Historical Perspective, A Tale of Two Millennia*, Intersentia, 2006.

consider that culturally imbedded rules are constructions that do not coincide with the modern notion of human rights.[133] In these terms, tradition is not "holy" and should not be protected at any rate. On the contrary, family laws are not an end in themselves but a means for promoting human rights besides the fact that they are imbedded in our culture.[134] Moreover, family is a social construct made by humans but not necessarily intrinsic to human nature. In these terms, it should be underlined that there is a distinction between unification and harmonisation of the law. While the first refers to application of identical rules in all national systems, which are bound by international or regional instruments, the second refers to the laws of the legal systems in a specific field, which are in harmony with each other, thus reducing differences to a minimum.[135] In these terms, the process of harmonisation of family laws in Europe as influenced by human rights and the interpretations of the ECtHR is not only feasible, but also desirable. For the Member States of the European Union, the necessity of bringing family laws together is even greater taking into account the prohibition of discrimination on grounds of nationality together with the right to move and reside freely within the Member States.[136] Measures have already been taken in other property-related family law fields,[137] and also in the sphere of divorce and parental responsibility.[138] In the past 50 years, the Court has been called upon and ruled on many issues of society, including families and affiliation, such as: abortion-related questions, the right not to be prevented from tracing one's origins by the right of mothers to give birth anonymously, adoption by homosexuals and others.[139] As such, the Court's interpretation of the Conventions in the light of present-day conditions[140] allows the notion of family life to adapt to changing societies, therefore having an indispensable role in evolving laws in Europe.[141]

---

133 De Groot G.R., "Op Weg naar een Europees Personen – en familie recht?", *Ars Acqui*, No. 44, 1995, p. 29.

134 Pintens W., Vanwinckelen K., *Casebook European Family Law*, Leuven University Press, 2001, p. 15.

135 Boele-Woelki K., "European Challenges in Contemporary Family Law: Some Final Observation", in Boele-Woelki K., Sverdrup T. (eds.), *European Challenges in Contemporary Family Law*, Intersentia, 2008, p. 413.

136 Articles 12 and 18(1) of the Treaty Establishing the European Community of 25 March 1975.

137 Such as maintenance obligations, property law between married and unmarried couples, and the law of succession of wills. See Boele-Woelki K. *et al.*, *Principles of European Family Law Regarding Parental Responsibilities*, Intersentia, 2007, p. 2.

138 Brussels II bis Regulation (EC) No 2201/2003, available online: http://eur-lex.europa.eu/LexUriServ/LexUriServ.do?uri=CELEX:32003R2201:EN:HTML.

139 *European Court of Human Rights: The ECHR in 50 Questions*, July 2012, available online: www.echr.coe.int/Documents/50Questions_ENG.pdf, p. 11.

140 See ECtHR cases *Marckx v. Belgium*, No. 6833/74, judgment of 13.06.1979 (paragraph 41 of the judgment states as follows: "the Court recallsthat this Convention must be interpreted in the light of present-dayconditions"), and *Burghartz v. Switzerland*, No. 16213/90, judgment of 22.02.1994 (paragraph 28 of the judgment states as follows: "[i]n any event, the Convention must be interpreted in the light of present-day conditions, especially the importance of the principle of non-discrimination").

141 Brussels II bis Regulation (EC) No 2201/2003, p. 3.

2.1. THE UNIVERSAL DECLARATION OF HUMAN RIGHTS, THE INTERNATIONAL COVENANT ON CIVIL AND POLITICAL RIGHTS AND THE INTERNATIONAL COVENANT ON ECONOMIC, SOCIAL AND CULTURAL RIGHTS

The UDHR sets out the fundamental human rights as a ground for harmonisation of all the other universal and regional documents. The Declaration safeguards discrimination by attaching the rights and freedoms to everyone without prejudice, among other grounds, based on birth or other status (article 2), and equality before the law in order to protect against discrimination (article 7). The same rights are confirmed in the ICCPR (article 2) and in the ICESCR (article 2(2)).

The Declaration entitles everyone on equal grounds to a right to access an independent court for a fair and public hearing (article 10), as well as to a right for an effective remedy for acts violating the fundamental rights (article 8). These rights are also provided for in the ICCPR (articles 14 and 26).

Family enjoys special protection by society and the State as a "natural and fundamental group unit of society" (article 16(3)). The right to marry and to establish a family is attributed to men and women of full age (article 16), while the other forms of establishing families are not addressed. Children though, are entitled to the same social protection irrespective of whether they are born in or out of wedlock (article 25(2)). Both motherhood and childhood enjoy special protection. The same rights are afforded by the ICCPR (articles 23 and 24), also affirming the right of each child to be registered immediately after birth, and in the ICESCR (article 10) complemented by the safeguard that children should not be discriminated against for reasons of parentage (article 10(3)).

Article 12 of the Declaration safeguards against arbitrary interference with an individual's privacy, family, home and correspondence in concordance with article 29 that safeguards respect for the rights and freedoms of others in a democratic society. Both the ICCPR and ICESCR, in their first articles, recognise the right to self-determination as a right to freely determine the political status and freely pursue individual economic, social and cultural development. The ICESCR also recognises the right to "enjoyment of the highest attainable standard of physical and mental health" as enabled by creating conditions which should ensure medical services for everyone (article 12 and article 12(d)).

2.2. THE CONVENTION ON THE ELIMINATION OF ALL FORMS OF DISCRIMINATION AGAINST WOMEN

In concordance with the principles of non-discrimination (articles 2 of UDHR, ICCPR and ICESCR), the equal rights of men and women in the enjoyment of all civil, political and economic, social and cultural rights (articles 3 of ICCPR and ICESCR), and the special protection afforded to women and children (article 10 ICESCR), the CEDAW specially deals with the definition and operation of the protection against discrimination against women. The Convention defines discrimination against women as "any distinction, exclusion or restriction made on the basis of sex which has the effect or purpose of impairing or nullifying the recognition, enjoyment or exercise by women, irrespective of their marital status, on the basis of the equality of men and women, of human rights and fundamental freedoms in the political, economic, social, cultural, civil or any other field" (article 1). Along these lines, states should undertake measures to ensure that the stereotyped concepts of the roles of men and women are eliminated (article 10(c)). Family issues and the right to start a family with a partner or at the level of individual access to health care clinics are dealt with in articles 12, 14(b) and 16. Women are guaranteed protection of their right to have a family and to "freely and responsibly decide on the number and spacing of their children", as well as to "access the information … and means to enable them to exercise these rights" (article 16(e)). Women should also enjoy "the same rights and responsibilities with regard to guardianship, ward-ship, trusteeship and adoption of children, or similar institutions where these concepts exist in national legislation" while protecting primarily the best interests of the child (article 16(f)). In the framework of establishing a family with the assistance of a health care institution, all women are entitled to family planning and access to health care services (articles 12(1) and 14(b)).

2.3. THE CONVENTION ON THE RIGHTS OF THE CHILD

The necessity and universal scope of the CRC are manifested by the fact that it is the most widely and rapidly accepted international legally binding document.[142] The Convention specifies the human rights of the special category of children who are vulnerable due to their immaturity as regards the age of majority, while

[142] Frith L., "Gamete Donation and Anonymity. The Ethical and Legal Debate", *Human Reproduction*, Vol. 16, No. 5, 2001, pp. 818–824, p. 820. See also Freeman M. (ed.), *Children's Rights. A Comparative Perspective*, Dartmouth Publishing, 1996.

capable as agents themselves of being entitled to certain civil, political, economic, social, health and cultural rights.

In concordance with the UDHR, article 2 of the Convention ensures respect for the rights of the child without discrimination of any kind, among other grounds, based on birth or other status. At the core of the Convention is the privileged position that children should enjoy when their rights are questioned especially in relation to the rights of other adult agents, among others their parents. In this light, article 3 boosts the best interests of the child as a paramount principle in all actions concerning children, "whether undertaken by public or social welfare institutions, courts of law, administrative authorities or legislative bodies". The question "what are the best interests of the child?" has often been re-interpreted and re-evaluated due to its vagueness and dependency on the particular circumstances. Therefore the question should be brought up and profoundly examined on an individual case-by-case basis by the authorities when making decisions according to the actual circumstances. This has been elevated as a state obligation, and omissions to fulfil the obligation have been punished as violations or no violations (if the state has considered the best interests of the child *vis-à-vis* the parents or other concerned parties) of the ECHR by the ECtHR in a number of cases.[143]

One of the most fundamental principles in respect for the personality of the child is the protection of their interests to be registered after birth, to be allowed to know his/her origin and to be taken care of by their parents (article 7). In this respect, states undertake to "respect the right of the child to preserve his or her identity, including nationality, name and family relations as recognised by law without unlawful interference" and, in the case of illegally deprived identity, to "provide assistance and protection to speedily re-establish the child's identity". Article 9 provides that the child should not be separated from his or her parents

---

[143] See, for instance, the ECtHR cases: *Pini and Others v. Romania*, No. 78028/01 and 78030/01, judgment of 22.06.2004 in which the Court found no violation of article 8 ECHR as interpreted in light of the CRC due to the fact that the Romanian courts upheld the priority of the best interests of the child, rejecting the applicants' claim to a right to create ties with the adopted children; *Morfis v. France*, No. 10978/04, judgment of 12.04.2007 in which the Court found no violation of article 8 ECHR as interpreted in light of the CRC, due to the fact that the French authorities viewed the child's best interests as a primary consideration; *Maumousseau and Washington v. France*, No. 39388/05, judgment of 06.12.2007 in which the Court found no violation of article 8 ECHR as interpreted in light of the CRC, due to the fact that the French authorities viewed the best interests of the child as a primary consideration; *Harroudj v. France*, No. 43631/09, judgment of 04.10.2012 in which the Court found no violation of article 8 ECHR as interpreted in light of the *CRC* which explicitly refers to the Islamic *kafala* as "alternative care" in comparison to adoption; *Maire v. Portugal*, No. 48206/99, judgment of 26.06.2003 in which the Court found violation of article 8 as interpreted in light of the CRC as a parent's right to be reunited with his or her child; *Monory v. Romania and Hungary*, No. 71099/01, judgment of 05.04.2005, in which the Court found violation of articles 6(1) and 8, as interpreted in light of the CRC and followed the precedence of the protection of the best interests of the child; *Emonet and Others v. Switzerland*, No. 39051/03, judgment of 13.12.2007 in which the Court found violation of article 8 ECHR as interpreted in light of the CRC.

against the child's will. As a supplement to this protection, article 18 sets forth the preference for the upbringing and development of the child to be the common responsibility of both parents. Article 12 ensures certain civil rights of the child to express views in matters that affect him or her, as well as to be heard in any judicial or administrative proceedings that affect these rights.

All these articles have been challenged by the case law and literature, especially in the field of private and family life and the affiliation of the child in relation to the parents and with regard to the new ways of establishing families, i.e. with the assistance of bio-medical technology.

Family affiliation in the Convention is expressed in terms of rights: the right of the child to know and be cared for by its parents, "as far as possible";[144] and the right of the child to preserve his or her identity, including family relations as recognised by law without unlawful interference. Blauwhoff proclaims the year of the introduction of the CRC as a year of progressive international and national recognition of individuals' interest in knowing the truth as a particular fundamental right,[145] which is based on the right to "private life" and the "personality right", respectively.[146] There has been a progressive recognition of this right under the case law of the ECtHR with articles 8 and 14 of the ECHR, even though many contradictions and ambiguities are still present.

Most countries in Europe have either made reservations[147] or firmly hold on to the "as far as possible" part of article 7. In this regard, there have already been objections to laws which do not allow adopted children to find out who their biological parents are.[148] There are many critics of the use of the word "*parent*" in article 7 as being vague in meaning, allowing different interpretations, and

---

144 The connotation "as far as possible" was incorporated in the Convention as insisted on by the delegations of the United States and Germany in response to the original draft submitted by a few countries (Algeria, Egypt, Iraq, Jordan, Kuwait, Libyan, Arab Jamahiriya, Morocco, Oman, Pakistan and Tunisia). For a commentary on the CRC, see Detrick S., *A Commentary on the United Nations Convention on the Rights of the Child*, Kluwer Law International, 1999.

145 Blauwhoff, J.R., "Tracing down the Historical Development of the Legal Concept of the Right to Know One's Origins. Has 'To Know or Not To Know' Ever been the Legal Question?", *Utrecht Law Review*, Vol. 4, No. 2, 2008, pp. 99 -116.

146 *Ibid.* Blauwhoff states that the "personality right" is protected in the German Federal Constitution or Basic Law under article 1 I in conjunction with article 2 I. The grounds of the right to know one's origin are derived from the "right to informational self-determination" as an aspect of this right. "A personality right" is also considered a basis of the right to know one's origin in the Netherlands (in the Dutch Constitution and in the *Valkenhorst II case* of the Dutch Cassation Court, 15 April 1994, NCJM-Bulletin No. 6, p. 652), and in Portugal from which "a right to one's personal history" is derived).

147 To prevent the controversies that article 7 may cause regarding anonymous donors or in the cases of adoption, several countries – the Czech Republic, Poland and Luxembourg – have entered reservations. See Detrick S., *A Commentary on the United Nations Convention on the Rights of the Child*, Kluwer Law International, 1999, p. 154.

148 See Ziemele I., *A Commentary on the United Nations Convention on the Rights of the Child. Article 7 – The Right to Birth Registration, Name and Nationality, and the right to Know and Be Cared for by Parents*, Martinus Nijhoff Publishers, 2007, p. 27 citing the CRC Committee, *Concluding Observations: Kazakhstan (Un Doc. CRC/C/15Add.213, 2003), Estonia (UN Doc. CRC/C/15Add.196*, 2003).

therefore incorporating all possible parents (biological, genetic, social and legal).[149] The limitation "as far as possible" presupposes that there could be circumstances that might limit the child's right to know, but an absolute prohibition on the right to know the biological parents is in contradiction with the purpose of the CRC.[150] Some authors have re-formulated that part into "the right to know as much as possible",[151] arguing that "truth is always better than deception".[152] For other authors the words "as far as possible" should only refer to cases in which the parents are dead, have repudiated the child or when state authorities have judged that parental care is not in the child's best interests because the parents are abusive or neglectful.[153] These authors suggest that the burden of proving that the child is better off without the parents (opposite to the general principle that a child is better off with both parents) should be assigned to the state.

There are also critics on the vagueness of how paternity and affiliation in article 8 of the CRC are addressed. The consideration is that there is an omission, bearing in mind that the original proposal of the article as submitted by Argentina aimed at protection of the child's genuine personal, legal and familial identity, and consequently, the biological relationship of the natural parent and the child.[154]

Article 2 of the CRC protects children from discrimination of any kind, irrespective of their or their parents' birth or other status, among other grounds. If we accept definitions of discrimination,[155] it remains questionable if "children of the new era" conceived with the assistance of biomedical technology do hold the same rights as children conceived *via* sexual intercourse under legislation that protects the donor's anonymity. These children are incapable of challenging their parenthood in civil proceedings and their life unfolds in ignorance of their genetic origin and therefore their personal identity.

The right of the child to know his/her genetic origin and the ascending right to be cared for by the parents as originating from the right to respect private and family life will be the main pillars of the discussion.

---

149 *Ibid.* from the communication between the CRC Committee and the States, as well as from the CRC's aims.

150 *Ibid.*

151 McGee G., Brakman S.V., Gurmankin A.D., "Gamete Donation and Anonymity. Disclosure to Children with Donor Gametes should not be Optional", *Human Reproduction*, Vol. 16, No. 10, 2001, pp. 2033–2036.

152 Trieseliotis J., "Identity and Genealopgy", in Bruce N., Mitchell A., Priestley K. (eds.), *Truth and the Child. A Contribution to the Debate on the Warnock Report*, Family Care, 1988.

153 Hodgkin R., Newell P., *Implementation Handbook for the Convention on the Rights of the Child*, UNICEF, 2007, p. 109.

154 Hodgson D., "The International Legal Protection of the Child's Right to a Legal Identity and the Problem of Statelessness", *International Journal of Law, Policy and the Family*, Vol. 7, No. 2, 1993.

155 Discrimination as a distinction, exclusion, restriction or preference, based on the accepted grounds, where the aim is to nullify or impair the recognition, enjoyment or exercise, on an equal footing, of rights and freedoms. See Detrick S., *A Commentary on the United Nations Conventions on the Rights of the Child*, Martinus Nijhoff Publishers, 1999, p. 73.

2.4. THE OVIEDO CONVENTION, THE UNIVERSAL DECLARATION ON THE HUMAN GENOME AND HUMAN RIGHTS AND THE UNIVERSAL DECLARATION ON BIOETHICS AND HUMAN RIGHTS

The Convention for the Protection of Human Rights and Dignity of the Human Being with regard to the Application of Biology and Medicine, also known as the Convention on Human Rights and Biomedicine or Oviedo Convention, was drafted by the Council of Europe.[156] This was the first legally binding international instrument setting the principles in the field of bioethics and applying the new developments of medical science to human beings.[157] In these terms, the Convention confirmed the principles set forth in both the UDHR and the ECHR. The Convention found its reasoning in the principles of bioethics: autonomy, confidentiality, beneficence/non-maleficence and justice.[158] The origin of the principles can be traced back to the Belmont Report and the activities of the National (American) Commission for the Protection of Human Subjects of Biomedical and Behavioral Sciences between 1974 and 1978. The Belmont Report established three principles used as a common language in bioethics from the beginning:[159] respect for persons (to make informed decisions and actions, as safeguarded by the possibility of informed consent), beneficence (to protect from harm and to secure well-being, as safeguarded by the assessment of risks and benefits), and justice (in terms of "equals ought to be treated equally" safeguarded by the division of subjects on two levels: individual and social).[160] The aims of the Oviedo Convention as defined in its article 1 are to protect the dignity and identity of all human beings, while guaranteeing everyone, without discrimination, respect for their integrity and other rights and fundamental freedoms with regard to the application of biology and medicine.

The Oviedo Convention was meant to be built by means of additional protocols dealing with the particular field of biomedical activities. The second protocol from 2002 deals with transplantation of organs and tissues of human

156 Signed in Oviedo, Spain in 1997, entered into force on 1 December 1999.

157 A more specialised and pioneering instrument regarding the application of ART was the *Report on Human Artificial Protection, Principles Set Out in the Report of the Ad Hoc Committee of Experts on Progress in the Biomedical Sciences (CAHBI)*, 1989. Principle 4 regulates informed consent and Principle 13 regulates anonymity, also allowing flexibility of the national legislation to provide the child with access to information regarding the manner of conception or even the identity of the donor.

158 For more on the Principles of Biomedical Ethics, see: Beauchamp T.L., Childress F.J., *Principles of Biomedical Ethics* (5th edition), Oxford University Press, 2001.

159 Jonsen A.R., *The Birth of Bioethics. An Historical Memoir of the Origins and Evolution of Bioethics in the United States, 1947–1987*, Oxford University Press, 1998.

160 See Gracia D., "History of Medical Ethics", in ten Have H.A.M.J., Gordijn B. (eds.), *Bioethics in a European Perspective*, Kluwer Academic Publishers, 2001, pp. 17–50.

origin, explicitly excluding organs and tissues for reproductive purposes and embryonic or foetal organs and tissues.[161]

The Convention sets two kinds of standards: for establishing individual rights which can be directly addressed to the courts, and for states' obligation to adopt the necessary legislation and thus to harmonise national laws. The principles set out in the Convention had an influence in the drafting of other international documents with universal scope, such as the Universal Declaration on the Human Genome and Human Rights (UDHGHR)[162] and UNESCO's Universal Declaration on Bioethics and Human Rights (UDBHR).[163] The commonly agreed principles on which they rest are: non-discrimination and non-stigmatisation based on genetic characteristics and individual genetic heritage;[164] equality, justice and equity, sharing of benefits, access to scientific and technical knowledge, and equitable access to health care in accordance with the person's medical needs, especially for women and children;[165] informed consent, autonomy to decide and individual responsibility;[166] privacy and confidentiality[167] as opposed to the private life, and the right to information about personal and familial origins.[168] Informed consent encompasses "prior free and informed consent of the person undertaking therapeutic medical intervention with a possibility to be withdrawn by the concerned person at any time and for any reason without disadvantage or prejudice".[169] When informed consent is given under circumstances of anonymity, the confidentiality of the personal information should be respected with the utmost protection as stated in article 9 UDBHR: "The privacy of the persons concerned and the confidentiality of their personal information should be respected to the greatest extent possible, such information should not be used or disclosed for purposes other than those for which it was collected or consented to".

Article 10 of the Oviedo Convention reaffirmed its consistency with article 8 ECHR as respect for private and family life, thus allowing restrictions to the respect for privacy for instance in cases where the judicial authority orders a

---

161 Article 2(3), Additional Protocol to the Convention on Human Rights and Biomedicine concerning Transplantation of Organs and Tissues of Human Origin, Council of Europe, 2002.

162 Adopted by acclamation at UNESCO's 29th General Conference, 11 November 1997. The following year, the United Nations General Assembly endorsed the Declaration.

163 Adopted at UNESCO's General Conference, 19 October, 2005.

164 Article 6 UDHGHR, article 11 UDBHR, article 11 Oviedo Convention.

165 Articles 10, 14(2)(a), and 15 UDBHR, article 3 Oviedo Convention.

166 Articles 5 and 6 UDBHR and article 5 Oviedo Convention.

167 Article 9 UDBHR and article 7 UDHGHR.

168 Article 10 Oviedo Convention. This concept was used in the *Report on Human Artificial Protection, Principles Set Out in the Report of the Ad Hoc Committee of Experts on Progress in the Biomedical Sciences (CAHBI)*, 1989. Principle 4 regulates informed consent and Principle 13 regulates anonymity, also allowing flexibility of the national legislation to provide the child with access to information regarding the manner of conception or even the identity of the donor.

169 Article 6 UDBHR.

test to identify and/or determine the affiliation link as an exception based on the principle of protection of the rights of others.[170] Even though the Convention deals with the possibility of carrying out tests which are predictive of genetic diseases and performed exclusively for health purposes, it also emphasised in its preliminary work that the intention is not to ban tests ordered by a court in the course of criminal proceedings or paternity tests.[171]

2.5. EUROPEAN FRAMEWORK

In the European framework (among Member States of the Council of Europe) and within the bounds of the right to found a family, private and family life, establishment of legal parenthood, parental responsibilities and children's rights, several legal sources are considered fundamental. Thus, the following text will introduce the research context from the prism of the application of the European Court of Human Rights of the above-mentioned international conventions and the European Convention on Human Rights, as being important on both a normative and applicative level. Extraction will be made of the case law in the following domains: (1) reproductive rights – the right to found a family for (a) a couple (right to access to ART and right to sperm and ova donation), and (b) an individual (competing interests between the individual of a couple regarding the reproductive choice in the use of ART and the right of a single person to found a family by adoption); (2) parental rights – establishing and rebutting of legal parenthood grounded in the marital presumption, out of wedlock and for the sperm donor; and (3) children's rights – the right to information about genetic origin and the right to be taken care of by both parents. Furthermore, an extraction of the relevant provisions will be made from the European Convention on the Exercise of Children's Rights and the Convention on Contact Concerning Children.

The Brussels II bis Regulation that affects family law and almost all civil matters related to attribution, exercise, delegation, restriction and termination of parental responsibility will be excluded from the text since its article 3(1) explicitly restricts the scope of its application in matters of establishing or rebutting of a parent–child relationship.[172]

The 1975 European Convention on the Legal Status of Children Born Out of Wedlock (ECLSCBOW), Recommendation No. R (84)4 on Parental

---

170 Article 10(63) and (64) UDBHR.

171 *Report on Principles Concerning the Establishment and Legal Consequences of Parentage – White Paper*, Committee of Experts on Family Law, 2006, p. 20, available online: www.coe.int/t/dghl/standardsetting/family/CJFA_2006_4e%20Revised%20White%20Paper.pdf.

172 Council Regulation (EC) No. 2201/2003 of 27 November 2003 concerning Jurisdiction and the Recognition and Enforcement of Judgments in Matrimonial Matters and the Matters of Parental Responsibility, repealing Regulation (EC) No. 1347/2000.

Responsibilities, the "White Paper" on Principles Concerning the Establishment and Legal Consequences of Parentage, the Principles of the European Family Law Regarding Parental Responsibilities and the Draft Recommendation will not be discussed in this part, but left in the part regarding legal proceedings for establishing parenthood.[173] The reasons for this structure are twofold. Firstly, it has been long recognised that the ECLSCBOW needs consolidation with Recommendation No. R (84)4, as well as updating in order to follow the changes in the new family formations.[174] Thus, in 1997 the CJ-FA gave Working Party No. 2 on the legal status of children the task of drawing up a report with principles relating to the establishment and legal consequences of parentage. Consequently, the Working Party presented the White Paper on Principles Concerning the Establishment and Legal Consequences of Parentage at the XXVIIth Colloquy on European Law on Legal Problems Relating to Parentage (Malta, 1997) which was adopted by the CJ-FA in 2001. The principles are recommended set of guidance when it comes to regulations regarding establishment of legal parentage (Part A), legal consequences of parentage (Part B), and possible legal consequences where the parentage has not been established (Part C) but not mandatory for the Member States. As such, the legal constellation in the field of parentage is still under construction. Secondly, the development of such regulation is partially the subject of this work, and the discussion will unfold later on, after examining the legal positions of the participants of the reproductive project of single women conceiving with assistance of sperm donor (the mother, the donor and the child).

2.6. THE CONSIDERATION OF THE INTERNATIONAL CONVENTIONS BY THE EUROPEAN COURT OF HUMAN RIGHTS

The ECtHR recognised the necessity that the rules originating from the ECHR "cannot be interpreted and applied in a vacuum". On the contrary, they must be

---

[173] See *infra* section 1. Establishing fatherhood through the prism of the "White Paper", the Principles of European Family Law regarding parental responsibilities, and the "Draft Recommendation".

[174] Lowe N., "An Evaluation of the Council of Europe's Legal Instruments in the Field of Family Law, A Report for the Attention of the Committee of Experts of Family Law (CJ-FA)", *Cardiff Law School Research Papers, No. 2*, Presented to the 36th Plenary Meeting of the CF-FA, Strasbourg, 15–17 November 2006, p. 10. See also the Draft Recommendation on the Rights and Legal Status of Children and Parental Responsibilities, Committee of Experts on Family Law (CJ-FA), Explanatory Memorandum, Revised version proposed by Nigel Lowe after the 4th Meeting held in Strasbourg, 16–18 March 2011; Preamble of the Draft Recommendation on the Rights and Legal Status of Children and Parental Responsibilities, Committee of Experts on Family Law Tasked to Draft One or More Legal Instruments on the Rights and Legal Status of Children and Parental Responsibilities (CJ-FA), Strasbourg, 13 July 2011; Appendix IV, Draft Recommendation on the Rights and Legal Status of Children and Parental Responsibilities, Explanatory Memorandum, CJ-FA, 2011 RAP 5 prov.

interpreted in the light of the integration and harmonisation of the international conventions, especially bearing in mind the special character of the Convention as a human rights treaty.[175]

In the sphere of application of article 8 ECHR, and the private and family life among parents and children, the Court mostly takes reference from the Convention on the Rights of the Child, as well as from the Hague Convention on the Civil Aspects of International Child Abduction[176] and the Hague Convention on Protection of Children and Co-operation in Respect of Intercountry Adoption.[177]

With regard to the CRC and its supplemental interpretation of article 8 of the ECHR, the Court judged in a number of cases.

In *Pini and Others v. Romania*,[178] even though the Court reiterated that the relationship between the adoptive parents (as applicants) and the adopted children should be considered the same as the relationship within a family, and as such be protected under article 8 of the ECHR, it still found no violation when interpreted in light of the CRC. The Court's rationale was grounded in the fact that the Romanian courts gave priority to the best interests of the child over the applicants' claim to a right to create family ties with the adopted children. The Romanian authorities took the children's opinions into account when they rejected the adoption and weighted children's interests higher than the applicants' right to found a family. In the Court's opinion, the right to private and family life for the applicants from the ECHR was legally weakened by the application of the children's best interests standard from the CRC.

In the cases of *Morfis (Greece) v. France*[179] and *Maumousseau and Washington v. France*,[180] the Court found no violation of article 8 ECHR together with articles 3 and 13 of the Hague Convention on the Civil Aspects of International Child Abduction as interpreted in light of article 3 of the CRC. The ECtHR restricted

---

175 *Loizidov v. Turkey*, European Court of Human Rights, No. 15318/89, judgment of 18.09.1996.

176 See, for instance, the cases: *Ignaccolo-Zemide v. Romania*, European Court of Human Rights, No. 31679/96, judgment of 25.01.2000; *Maumousseau and Washington v. France*, European Court of Human Rights, No. 39388/05, judgment of 06.12.2007; *Maire v. Portugal*, European Court of Human Rights, No. 48206/99, judgment of 26.06.2003; *Neulinger and Shuruk v. Switzerland*, European Court of Human Rights, No. 41615/07, judgment of 06.07.2010; *Monory v. Romania and Hungary*, European Court of Human Rights, No. 71099/01, judgment of 05.04.2005; *Karadzic v. Croatia*, European Court of Human Rights, No. 71099/01, judgment of 05.04.2005; *X v. Latvia*, European Court of Human Rights, No. 27853/09, judgment of 13.12.2011; *Bianchi v. Switzerland*, European Court of Human Rights, No. 7548/04, judgment of 22.06.2006; *Morfis v. France*, European Court of Human Rights, No. 10978/04, judgment of 12.04.2007.

177 See, for instance, the case *Pini and Others v. Romania*, European Court of Human Rights, No. 78028/01 and 78030/01, judgment of 22.06.2004.

178 *Pini and Others v. Romania*, European Court of Human Rights, No. 78028/01 and 78030/01, judgment of 22.06.2004.

179 *Morfis v. France*, European Court of Human Rights, No. 10978/04, judgment of 12.04.2007.

180 *Maumousseau and Washington v. France*, European Court of Human Rights, No. 39388/05, judgment of 06.12.2007.

the other parent's custodial right to be united with the child due to the fact that the national French authorities (where the child was taken) took the child's best interests as a primary consideration. In the first case, the Court acknowledged that the French authorities by considering the time spent with both parents and the young age of the child when making their decisions, thus constantly took into account the best interests of the child. The Court also took into consideration Recommendation 874 (1979) of the Parliamentary Assembly of the Council of Europe and the European Charter of Rights of the Child promoting as a general principle that "children should not be considered the property of their parents, but to be recognized as individuals with their own rights and needs". In the second case, the best interests of the child were interpreted in light of the principle that the child should not be separated from the mother and her family to which the child has already established familial ties, in comparison to, "out of concern for effective restoration of the father's role".

In the case of *Harroudj v. France*,[181] the Court found no violation of article 8 ECHR as interpreted in the light of the CRC, which explicitly addresses the Islamic *kafala* as "alternative care" in comparison to adoption. The Court found no family ties between the woman and the child in *kafala* foster care, and confirmed the decision of the French authorities, which refused permission for a French national guardian to adopt the Algerian baby under guardianship. Therefore the already existing social care lookalike family ties were not accepted as a ground to protect the alleged private and family life of the applicant. In contrast, the form of *kafala* was considered as decisive when it comes to founding family life. The Court also acknowledged that the French authorities did not allow the adoption due to the provision in the French Civil Code that allowed adoptions only if consistent with the national law of the country of origin of the child, which was not the case in Algeria. The Court considered that the French authorities made a fair balance between the public interest in safeguarding cultural pluralism, and the respect of private and family life. The balance was achieved by allowing children from different nationalities to retain ties with the laws of their country of origin, while also encouraging their rapid access to French nationality, which would eventually allow the adoption.

In contrast, the Court found a violation when interpreting article 8 in light of the CRC in a number of other cases.

In the case of *Maire v. Portugal*, the Court found a violation by the Portuguese authorities that failed to protect a parent's right to reunite with the child, thus failing to enforce a court decision to award custody of the child.[182] Relying on article 8 of the Convention, the French applicant complained of the Portuguese authorities' inactivity and negligence in failing to enforce the judicial decisions awarding him custody of his child abducted by his mother. The Court, like in

181 *Harroudj v. France*, European Court of Human Rights, No. 43631/09, judgment of 04.10.2012.

182 *Maire v. Portugal*, European Court of Human Rights, No. 48206/99, judgment of 26.06.2003.

the previous cases, reaffirmed that with regard to the reuniting of the child with his or her parent, the case should be observed through the prism of the CRC and the Hague Convention on the Civil Aspects of International Child Abduction. Nevertheless, the Court's decision was rather different from the previous cases by asserting that the Portuguese authorities did not take all the reasonably expected steps to enforce the French courts' decisions of affording custody to the father. Such negligence was considered inappropriate, especially in custody proceedings that need urgency in their conclusion, which consequently caused distant relations between the child and the parent from whom the child was separated. The ECtHR unanimously held that there had been a violation of article 8 of the ECHR due to the long period of dealing with the proceedings by the Portuguese authorities that eventually jeopardised the best interests of the child and caused circumstances that made it even more difficult for the applicant to reunite with his child.

A similar case is the case of *Monory v. Romania and Hungary*,[183] in which the Court found a violation of articles 6(1) and 8 of the ECHR. Since the case concerned an inter-country custodial dispute, the Court observed it through the prism of the CRC, claiming that the best interests of the child were not considered by the Romanian Courts, and the Hague Convention on the Civil Aspects of International Child Abduction, claiming that appropriate measures to ensure the parent–child reunification were not undertaken. Once again, the Court reiterated that custodial cases require urgent handling, as allowing a big gap in time could have irreversible consequences for the parent–child relationship, bearing in mind the age of the child. Therefore the Court established failure on the part of the Romanian authorities to handle the case with due diligence as regards the urgency of the case and the best interests of the child that go along with it. Consequently, the applicant's private and family life right to reunite with his child was also violated.

In the case of *Emonet and Others v. Switzerland*,[184] the Court found a violation of article 8 of the ECHR as interpreted in the light of the CRC. The case concerned an attempt of the mother's partner to adopt the daughter while they were living together for six years and the father of the child was deceased. Even though the applicants were claiming familial ties with the child, the adoption was conditional on the mother's termination of the parental legal ties with her child. According to the cantonal authority and article 267 of the Swiss Civil Code, the existing parental ties were severed on adoption by a partner of the mother, and not by a spouse of the adoptive parent. The ECtHR considered that a regulation of that kind interfered with the applicants' right to respect for their private and family life. It also held that the marital request in order to avoid the loss of the parental tie was not in concordance with the essence and meaning of article 8, which afforded

[183] *Monory v. Romania and Hungary*, European Court of Human Rights, No. 71099, 01, judgment of 05.04.2005.

[184] *Emonet and Others v. Switzerland*, European Court of Human Rights, No. 39051/03, judgment of 13.12.2007.

family ties irrespective of the marital or extra-marital nature of the relationship. Therefore the Court examined whether the present interference pursued a legitimate aim and was necessary in a democratic society. Even though the Court recognised the uniqueness of the situation, it also acknowledged the failure of the Swiss authorities to accept both existing biological and social realities, which did not benefit anybody. In contrast, they only infringed the private and family life of the applicants, which tried to make the social reality a legal fact.

2.7. EUROPEAN CONVENTION ON HUMAN RIGHTS AND THE MARGIN OF APPRECIATION IN THE FIELD OF FAMILY LIFE

The concept of "margin of appreciation" of the ECtHR is the flexible framework of the space for manoeuvre in which the national authorities are to apply their obligations under the ECHR.[185] The concept aims to balance the sovereignty of the Member States with their undertaken obligations from the Convention while maintaining the Court's role as an arbitrator between the states and their citizens.[186] The principles under which the concept operates are (1) effective protection (the priority is to effectively protect human rights and not to enforce mutual obligations between Member States)[187] and (2) subsidiarity and review (the state should decide for itself the appropriateness of the national regulation,[188] while the ECtHR only subsidiarily reviews and ensures that the state has remained within the limits, thereby safeguarding human rights).[189] Some authors have criticised the overwhelming role of the principle of subsidiarity, claiming that the ECtHR should interpret on grounds of rational and strict scrutiny in the European context, because its decisions set a European hierarchy of values, which cannot vary from state to state.[190] In this way, the Court should remain for the members of the Council of Europe a guide, and not allow overuse of the margin of appreciation in the field of conflicts between fundamental rights.[191] Even though,

185 Greer S., *The Margin of Appreciation: Interpretation and Discretion under the European Convention on Human Rights*, Council of Europe, 2000, p. 5.

186 Fenwick H., *Civil Liberties and Human Rights*, Cavendish Publishing Limited, 2005, pp. 34–37.

187 Van Dijk P., Van Hoof F., *Theory and Practice of the European Convention on Human Rights*, Kluwer, 1998, p. 74.

188 Clayton R., Tomlinson H., *The Law of Human Rights*, Oxford, 2000, p. 285.

189 Schokkenbroek J., "The Basis, Nature and Application of the Margin of Appreciation Doctrine in the Case-Law of the European Court of Human Rights", *Human Rights Law Journal*, Vol. 19, No. 30–31, 1998.

190 Marauhn T., Ruppel N., "Balancing Conflicting Human Rights: Konrad Hesse's Notion of 'Praktische Konkordanz' and the German Federal Constitutional Court", in Brems E. (ed.), *Conflicts Between Fundamental Rights*, Intersentia, 2008, pp. 246 and 247. See also Lester L., Herne H. Q.C., "Universality *v.* Subsidiarity: A Reply", *European Human Rights Law Journal*. Vol. 3, No. 1, 1998, pp. 73–81.

191 Marauhn T., Ruppel N., "Balancing Conflicting Human Rights: Konrad Hesse's Notion of 'Praktische Konkordanz' and the German Federal Constitutional Court", in Brems E. (ed.), *Conflicts Between Fundamental Rights*, Intersentia, 2008, p. 246.

very often, sensitive national matters are involved, making appreciation of certain rights also a political decision, the subsidiarity principle must be a result of rational examination, rather than a legal loophole.[192]

The possible interferences with the rights guaranteed under the umbrella of the Convention are always judged on an individual case basis, recognising the diversity of circumstances that add value to particular cases. Therefore the margin of appreciation can possibly pose limits only within specific cases.[193] The state's national regulations have to satisfy several requirements to qualify as permitted infringements of the Convention.[194]

The first requirement is existence of *prescribed law* in the national legal system, so that the consequences are foreseen and clear, while the information is accessible for people to guide their actions, thus, avoiding arbitrary decisions. Along this line, article 12 of the Convention allows infringements on the right to marry and to start a family if it is in concordance with the nationally prescribed law, stipulating: "men and women of marriageable age have the right to marry and to start a family, *according to the national laws governing the exercise of this right.*"

The second requirement is that the infringing norms should have *legitimate aims and purposes*, strengthened by the requirement of their *necessity in a democratic society*. Along this line, article 8 of the Convention allows infringements on the right to respect private and family life, stipulating that while "everyone has the right to respect for his private and family life" without interference by a public authority, the exception is allowed if "it is *in accordance with the law and is necessary in a democratic society*, in the interests of national security, public safety or the economic well-being of the country, for the prevention of disorder of crime, for the protection of health or morals, or the protection of the rights and freedoms of others". This formulation explicitly depicts the tension between balancing individual *versus* collective rights[195] and opens the space for the manoeuvre of the margin of appreciation even more, claiming the right to respect for private and family life to be far from being an absolute right.

The third principle requires that the infringing norms are *proportionate* (have reasonable proportionality between the objectives meant to be achieved by interfering with the Convention and the means used to achieve it.[196] This means that no restrictions in the law should be automatically justified if they are not related

---

192 *Ibid.* p. 247.

193 Lavender N., "The Problem of the Margin of the Appreciation", *European Human Rights Law Review*, No. 4, 1997, p. 382.

194 See *The Margin of Appreciation*, Council of Europe, available online: www.coe.int/t/dghl/cooperation/lisbonnetwork/themis/echr/paper2_en.asp.

195 Ostrovski A.A., "How the Margin of Appreciation Doctrine Preserves Core Human Rights within Cultural Diversity and Legitimizes International Human Rights Tribunals", *Hanse Law Review*, Vol. 1, No. 1, 2005, p. 50.

196 See Clayton R., Tomlinson H., *The Law of Human Rights*, Oxford University Press, 2000, p. 278.

to the achievement of normative goals.[197] In this line, article 6 of the Convention imposes a positive obligation on the states to ensure *the right to access to the courts* in civil and criminal matters. Still, the Court has acknowledged that the right is also not absolute, especially if its restrictions are in concordance with a legitimate aim, establishing a *proportional relationship* between the means that are used and the goals that are to be achieved. Moreover, the restrictions of the right to access the Court and therefore greater flexibility of the margin of appreciation is allowed in civil law cases when the authority of the national sovereignty is greater in comparison to criminal law cases.[198] Even article 14 (as a general prohibition of discrimination, among other grounds, also on grounds of birth or other status), alone or in combination with article 6(1) (as a right to a fair trial) could be infringed in cases of establishment of fatherhood in relation to children born with assisted insemination, if the accepted national moral standard promotes anonymity of the donor while protecting the social fatherhood of the presumed father. A relevant factor for interpreting whether an act is discriminatory is to compare whether the same act is considered discriminatory in other democratic societies too.[199] The non-discrimination prerogative has also the challenge of balancing individual rights and rights of the community. The case law of the Court distinguishes between two categories – *difference* and *discrimination* – arguing that if there is a reasonable and objective basis for the different treatment, it does not imply that the treatment is discriminatory *per se*.[200]

Human rights in the realm of private and family life have always been considered on the one hand significant, so to be characterised as fundamental, while on the other hand also subjective, allowing nation states to rule what family life encompasses based on their own morals and traditions. Extending the limits of the margin of appreciation to allow such morally, traditionally and culturally driven national family law regulations is in the intersection of the individual human rights and the nationally protected values. The individual rights in the field of family law are protected in article 8 – as rights to the respect for private and family life; article 12 – as a right to marry and establish a family; article 14 – as a general principle for non-discrimination; and article 6(1) – as a right to access civil law courts for solving family matter, among others, also

197 Storrow R., "The Pluralism Problem in Cross-Border Reproductive Care", *Human Reproduction*, Vol. 25, No. 12, 2010, pp. 2939–2943.

198 See: *Golder v. the United Kingdom*, European Court of Human Rights, No. 4451/70, judgment of 21.02.1975; *Bellet v. France*, European Court of Human Rights, No. 23805/94, judgment of 04.12.1995; *Z and Others v. the United Kingdom*, European Court of Human Rights, No. 29392/95, judgment of 10.05.2001.

199 See also *Runke and White v. the United Kingdom*, European Court of Human Rights, No. 42949/98, judgment of 10·05.2007; *Rasmussen v. Denmark*, European Court of Human Rights, No. 8777/79, judgment of 28.11.1984. The Court here also applied the European consensus standard, by referring to the way that the matter was regulated in the other Member States as being a relevant factor for interpreting discrimination.

200 *Relating to Certain Aspects of the Laws on the Use of Languages in Education in Belgium v. Belgium*, European Court of Human Rights, No. 2126/64, judgment of 23.06.1968.

to proceedings for establishing parenthood. Nevertheless, each state has its own system of regulating family life, right to marry, the criteria for discrimination, and even the criteria for establishing parenthood, thus promoting its own morals. Appreciating differences between the Member States sometimes collides with the protected human rights. The *European consensus standard* sets the limits of the margin of appreciation even further if, comparatively, particular breach is present in the national legal systems of more Member States. The space for calling upon this standard could be especially manifested, and even manipulated in the field of family life.[201] The *European consensus standard* has been criticised for not possessing enough grounds on which the human rights protected by the Convention could be infringed.[202] On the other hand, the standard has also been favoured as a tool that allows evolutive interpretation of the ECHR, thus striking a balance between development and stability.[203]

The margin of appreciation is the flexible system of "checks and balances", not in a Montesquieuian manner among the different authorities within a state, but on a wider European level of the individual, the state and the ECtHR. Three factors are guiding principles when the possible infringements of the Convention are allowed: (1) the *European consensus* standard, as a comparison among the regulations of the other Member States; (2) the nature of the right (absolute or relative character); and (3) the aim to be achieved by the contested measure enacted by the state.[204] In these directions, the problem of the impossibility of the child conceived by sperm donation to single women to establish fatherhood will be tackled from (1) a comparative overview of some Member States in the field of private and family life, reproduction and children's rights; (2) the nature of each right separately (the right to reproduce, to know the origin, and to private and family life) in a relational context; and (3) the rationale behind the aim to be achieved by accepting the current regulations, while examining if there is a space for its re-evaluation.

In fields of contested moralities, such as in the intersection between medically assisted reproduction and family life, the margin of appreciation is especially flexible.[205]

---

201 The *Marckx* case concerned an illegitimate daughter possessing minor legal status in Belgium. The Court remarked that the distinction between "legitimate" and "illegitimate" children was regarded as permissive and normal in many European countries, while recognising the developmental path towards their full recognition as equal.

202 Helfer L.R., "Coherence and the European Convention on Human Rights", *Cornell International Law Journal*, Vol. 26, No. 133, 1993, pp. 133–165.

203 Dzehtsiarou K., "European Consensus and the Evolutive Interpretation of the European Convention of Human Rights", *German Law Journal*, Vol. 12, No. 10, 2011, pp. 1730–1745.

204 *The Margin of Appreciation*, Council of Europe, available online: www.coe.int/t/dghl/cooperation/lisbonnetwork/themis/echr/paper2_en.asp.

205 Van Hoof W., Pennings G., "Extraterritorial Laws for Cross-Border Reproductive Care. The Issue of Legal Diversity", *European Journal of Health Law*, Vol. 19, No. 2, 2012, pp. 1–14.

2.8. THE CASE LAW OF THE EUROPEAN COURT OF HUMAN RIGHTS

2.8.1. THE CASE LAW IN THE FIELD OF REPRODUCTIVE RIGHTS AND THE RIGHT TO FOUND A FAMILY

2.8.1.1. The reproductive right of a couple

2.8.1.1.1. Right to access to assisted reproductive technology for a couple (competing public and private interests)

In the case of *Dickson v. United Kingdom*[206] the right to access assisted reproductive technology for a prisoner and his married wife was affirmed as protected under article 8 and article 12 of the ECHR. Kirk Dickson as a prisoner convicted of a murder with a 15-year sentence to imprisonment was not allowed access to ART facilities by the state authorities of the United Kingdom under three justifications: (1) the imprisonment itself excludes the possibility of begetting a child; (2) the public trust in the systems will be circumvented if prisoners are allowed to conceive a child; and (3) the consequences of conceiving a child with an absent parent are against the interests of the child itself. The ECtHR rejected the first two justifications, claiming that the inability to beget a child should not necessarily be a consequence of imprisonment and that the rehabilitative aims of imprisonment should be supported, while also maintaining public confidence in the penal system. Thus, the violation of the right to respect for private and family life, as well as to found a family, in the case could not be justified by claiming appropriate measures *necessary in a democratic society* to protect public order. The ECtHR agreed that the best interests of the child could be better protected if the child is raised by both parents. Nevertheless, the ECtHR recognised that the proportionality assessment between the competing individual and public interests was not balanced properly, therefore finding a violation of article 8, and initiating revisions of the public policy that forbids prisoners' access to ART.

2.8.1.1.2. Right to sperm and ova donation of a couple and in general

In the case of *S.H. and Others v. Austria*[207] the ECtHR confirmed the wide margin of appreciation when it comes to the complex ethical questions and keeping pace with the development of the new reproductive technologies. The Court acknowledged the supremacy of the Member State to decide the level on which a third party *via* sperm and ovum donation may interfere with conception.

---

206 *Dickson v. United Kingdom*, European Court of Human Rights, No. 44362/04, judgment of 04.12.2007.

207 *S.H. and Others v. Austria*, European Court of Human Rights, No. 57813/00, judgment of 03.11.2011.

Thus, a total ban on gamete donation (Lithuania, Italy and Turkey) and wide permissiveness are considered to fit in within the margins of appreciation of the Court. Two couples could not conceive naturally, for which they needed sperm and ovum donation respectively. Under the Austrian law, they could not benefit from the assistance of reproductive technology as it is allowed only for the purposes of homologous insemination, or exceptionally sperm donation on the condition that the insemination takes place in the woman's body. The rationale behind this regulation was to afford protection from fragmentation of the roles of the parents that would lead to a complex set of parental arrangements, as well as protection from the possibilities of misusing economically disadvantaged women to donate ova, which they would otherwise not do. The applicants complained that gamete donation under the Austrian law contradicted article 8 in conjunction with article 14 of the ECHR since the assisted reproductive procedure was allowed only for homologous insemination. While the ECtHR agreed that an interruption to using ART was against the right to private and family life in article 8, it also afforded supremacy to the state's national authorities to implement the application of ART in family life as regulated and prescribed by the national laws. Therefore the violation of the Convention was not detected, but the Court emphasised the need to keep legal pace with scientific development, supported by the comparative context of the already accepted European consensus of allowing gamete donations. The Court also called upon Directive 2004/23/EC on Setting Standards of Quality and Safety for the Donation, Procurement, Testing, Processing, Preservation, Storage and Distribution of Human Tissues and Cells of 31 March 2004, which explicitly states that the ethical considerations remain the responsibility of the Member States, and thus also the decision whether gamete donations are going to be an allowed practice or not. It furthermore confirmed that the ethical considerations did not come under the scope of the Directive and would be left to the discretion of the Member States.[208] This means that the Court took the stand of regarding the right to reproduce as relative and dependent on individual national regulations.

As an ethical issue for which there was no consensus in the Austrian legal context, and since the Austrian legislation never banned the possibility for seeking such a treatment abroad, the Court concluded that gamete donation did not exceed the margin of appreciation of the ECHR as stipulated in article 8, while not considering the need to consider it jointly with article 14 any further.

Some authors have criticised the wide interpretation of the Court of the margin of appreciation in the case, claiming that it focuses on the means–end rationality (proportionality argument) without interfering with the choice of

208 *S.H. and Others v. Austria*, European Court of Human Rights, No. 57813/00, judgment of 03.11.2011, § 53, calling upon § 12 of Directive 2004/23/ECon Setting Standards of Quality and Safety for the Donation, Procurement, Testing, Processing, Preservation, Storage and Distribution of Human Tissues and Cells of 31 March 2004.

ends.[209] As such, it does not pay attention to the European consensus standard that already exists in other European countries. Furthermore, it does not shed light on the interpretation of article 8 of the ECHR when it comes to gamete donations. The gap created may be a tool for restrictive regulations in relation to the right to procreate and the use of ART. The alternative solution of providing treatment elsewhere is not legally satisfactory because it has no connection with the recognition of reproductive rights in the country concerned. Moreover, it should not be taken as a justification for allowing restrictive laws in a country.[210] Therefore there is a concern that the decision may have harmful consequences by sending a message that in the field of contested morality, like in the case of gamete donation, any case can fit the margins of appreciation irrespective of its irrationality or inconsistency.[211]

2.8.1.2. The reproductive right of an individual

2.8.1.2.1. Competing interests between two individuals comprising a couple regarding the reproductive choice in the use of assisted reproduction

Even though both partners of a couple should equally possess the right to reproduce, the reproductive project can be carried out only by the couple together and not on the level of an individual right. In these terms, neither individual in a couple can procreate naturally or reproduce with the assistance of biomedical technology without contribution or the consent of the other party. Therefore the existence of the individual right to procreate in a couple is absurd. The *Evans v. the United Kingdom* case before the ECtHR proved this precisely.[212] Natallie Evans underwent *in vitro* fertilisation with her partner, resulting in six embryos, which were placed in storage prior to removing her ovaries due to ovarian cancer. Soon afterwards, the couple divorced and Natallie's partner withdrew consent for the further step of insemination of the embryos and therefore refused any parental role for the future. The national law seeks dual consent at any stage prior to insemination, thus restricting Natallie's chance to become a mother. While the case was ongoing, Professor John Harris reflected on it. He clarified that the eventual success of the woman to realise the reproductive project without the consent of her former partner would overrule the foundations upon which the entire Human Fertilisation and Embryology Authority is grounded. According

---

209 Van Hoof W., Pennings G., "The Consequences of S.H. and Others v. Austria for Legislation on Gamete Donation in Europe. An Ethical Analysis of the European Court of Human Rights Judgments", *Reproductive BioMedicine Online*, Vol. 25, No. 7, 2012, pp. 665–669.

210 Storrow R., "The Pluralism Problem in Cross-Border Reproductive Care", *Human Reproduction*, Vol. 25, No. 12, 2010, pp. 2939–2943.

211 *Ibid.* referring to the dissenting opinion of the judges Tulkens, Hirvela, Lazarova Trajkova and Tsotsoria in the case.

212 *Evans v. United Kingdom*, European Court of Human Rights, No. 6339/05, judgment of 10.04.2007.

to him, this was a threat to men, minimising and thus underestimating their role, which will end after the fertilisation of the egg.[213] Even though the case was overwhelmed by sympathising solidarity with the woman, the ECtHR ruled against her petition, thus finding that there were no violations of article 2 (right to life of the stored embryos), article 8 (right to respect for family life of the woman) and article 14 (prohibition of discrimination against realising the reproductive right) of the ECHR.

Informed consent as an accepted principle of bioethics and in the UDBHR encompasses "prior free and informed consent of the person undertaking therapeutic medical intervention with a possibility for withdrawal by the concerned person at any time and for any reason without disadvantage or prejudice".[214] In the case of in vitro insemination, the interpretation is that the withdrawal is possible at any time before insemination in the woman's body.

2.8.1.2.2. Right of a single person to found a family by adoption

The ECHR interpretation that the right to found a family does not include mono-parental families was upheld also in the cases of *X. v. Belgium and the Netherlands*[215] and *Di Lazzaro v. Italy*[216] in which the Commission reiterated that the Convention does not guarantee the right to adopt for a single person. This reasoning follows the outdated content of article 12 of the ECHR, according to which the right to found a family is guaranteed solely for men and women of marriageable age and not to single persons. Nevertheless, once mono-parental families are founded, they enjoy protection under the scope of article 8, as confirmed in the case of *Marckx v. Belgium*.[217]

The case of *Fretté v. France*[218] regards a refusal to found a family through adoption based on the ground of an unfit parent not being able to provide proper child rearing due to, as the authorities[219] claimed, the applicant's "choice of lifestyle", and, as the applicant appealed, "his sexual orientation". After rejection of Fretté's appeal, he complained that the refusal of authorisation for him to adopt infringed article 8, thus his right to private and family life, in connection with article 14 of the Convention, in view of the fact that the discrimination was made on grounds of his sexual orientation. The ECtHR noted that neither was there a sufficient number of studies that had tackled the possible consequences for

213 John Harris interview for BBC, 11 September 2002: http://news.bbc.co.uk/2/hi/health/2249442.stm.
214 Article 6 UDBHR.
215 *X v. Belgium and the Netherlands*, European Commission of Human Rights, No. 6482/74, judgment of 10.07.1975.
216 *Di Lazzaro v. Italy*, European Commission of Human Rights, No. 31924/96, judgment of 10.07.1997.
217 *Marckx v. Belgium*, European Court of Human Rights, No. 6833/74, judgment of 13.06.1979.
218 *Fretté v. France*, European Court of Human Rights, No. 36515/97, judgment of 26.02.2002.
219 Paris Social Services, Youth and Health Department.

children brought up by one or more homosexual parents, nor was there factual European consensus regarding the issue. On the contrary, the Court noted that the applicant's rejection under article 343-1 of the French Civil Code was primarily intended to protect children's interests and not to discriminate on sexual grounds. Therefore the Court found no violation of article 14 in conjunction with article 8, concluding that the Convention did not guarantee the right to found a family by adoption. The adoption cases are very different from the cases where the right to found a family with assisted reproduction is concerned. Nevertheless, the Court interpreted article 8 in light of not being able to offer a guarantee or protection of the right to start and found a family. On the contrary, according to the Court, the article only protects the already existing or presupposed private and family life. By analogy, this interpretation could also apply in similar cases (for instance in cases where single women claim to found a family in a country in which the practice of that kind is forbidden, or in cases where single women are simply denied the possibility to conceive a child by sperm donation).

The case of *Wagner and J.M.W.L. v. Luxembourg*[220] concerned a similar adoption restriction, this time for a single woman. Due to the restrictions, the adoption was executed in another country than the native country (adoption took place in Peru and the decision was not recognised in Luxembourg). In contrast with the previous case, the Court recognised the already created family life and therefore protected the family link between the mother and the child. The Court held unanimously a violation of article 6(1) and of article 8 in conjunction with article 14 due to the discriminating status of the child and the mother not being legally recognised in society, and thus failure of the Luxembourg courts to recognise already existent family ties. Along these lines, the Court protects already established family life and not a right to found a family and start family life under article 8 of the ECHR.

2.8.2. THE CASE LAW IN THE FIELD OF PARENTAL RIGHTS

2.8.2.1. Establishing and rebutting the parental legal affiliation grounded in the marital presumption

The case of *Kroon and Others v. the Netherlands*[221] concerned the marital presumption that the father of the child was the husband of the mother if the child was born during the marriage or 300 days after the dissolution of the marriage. A woman separated but not divorced from her missing husband, living

220 *Wagner and J.M.W.L. v. Luxembourg*, European Court of Human Rights, No. 76240/01, judgment of 28.06.2007.

221 *Kroon and Others v. the Netherlands*, European Court of Human Rights, No. 18535/91, judgment of 27.10.1994.

with another partner with whom she gave birth to a child, was barred from rebutting the marital presumption and from establishing family life due to the authorities' refusal to establish the fatherhood of her partner in the register of births. The ECtHR found a violation of article 8, pointing out that marriage is not the only place where family ties can be established,[222] reiterating that the crucial goal of the article is to protect the individual against arbitrary action by the public authorities. The Court also noted that the state must act in a manner to enable legal safeguards from the moment of birth or as soon as possible to integrate the child into his family. The Court also qualified the relationship between the partners as "family life", thus emphasising the obligation of the state's authorities to provide mechanisms for establishing family ties as expeditiously as possible, while legally solving the burdens. The Court acknowledged that the "respect of family life" would be accomplished if the biological and social realities prevail over the legal presumption, which in the case was only a legal burden despite the intention of the parties.

A similar situation of the impossibility to rebut the father's affiliation due to a marital presumption with a husband with whom the mother has ceased to live was highlighted in the case of *Chavdarov v. Bulgaria*.[223] The applicant (as a new partner of the woman, while the marriage was still not dissolved) was living with the mother during which period three children were born and registered as children of her husband due to the marriage presumption. After a while, the woman also left Mr Chavdarov to start a mutual life with another man, during which period the applicant was living with his three children. In an attempt to establish his fatherhood in relation to the children he was living with, his lawyer consulted him about the legal impossibility to rebut the paternity of the married husband. Mr Chavdarov complained before the ECtHR about his inability to establish fatherhood in relation to children of which he claimed to be both the genetic and social parent under article 8 of the Convention. The Court found that family life was indisputably existent since he was living with the children together with their mother and after their separation; therefore developing an emotional link was reliable under the notion of "family life". The Court's decision in this case was dramatically different in comparison to the previous, unanimously finding no violation of article 8, claiming that the legal impossibility of having biological paternity established was due to the applicant's passivity in using the national legal possibilities to become a legal father. Namely, after examining the national legal context, the Court found that there were other possibilities for him to establish his fatherhood such as adopting the children, or asking for their custody, as they were abandoned underage children. Since he had not undertaken such actions,

222 Similar opinion regarding not only the marital community but also extra-marital relationships as legal cradles for establishing fatherhood was also recognised in the case *Keegan v. Ireland*, European Court of Human Rights, No. 16969/90, judgment from 26.05.1994.

223 *Chavdarov v. Bulgaria*, European Court of Human Rights, No. 3465/03, judgment of 21.11. 2010.

the Court stated that it was his own passivity and not the irresponsiveness of the Bulgarian legal system to the obligations undertaken under the Convention, even though the impossibility of rebutting the presumption of the married husband remained. Nevertheless, the Court held that the current impossibility of establishing his fatherhood was not contrary to the "respect of his family life" but it was due to his inaction to use the possibilities available in the national legal system to establish his own paternal link in other alternative ways (not necessarily by rebutting the fatherhood of the husband). The Court noted that the margin of appreciation in cases of establishing parental links is wide, while also recognising the lack of European consensus on the issue of whether domestic legislation should enable the biological father to rebut the marital presumption of the husband's paternity.

A similar conclusion was drawn in the case of *Schneider v. Germany*.[224] The case, though, differed in two important ways: (1) there was no pretention of rebutting the legal fatherhood, and (2) it did not involve the factual family life of the child with the biological father (due to the marital presumption and the shared life of the mother with the husband after the birth of the child). The German courts refused the applicant access to information and contact with the boy of whom he claimed to be the biological father from an extra-marital relationship with a married woman. The Court declared the inadmissibility of his claim due to the fact that there was no social relationship between them resulting in any actual responsibility for the child, which was a condition for allowing any sort of protection of the relationship under the German Basic Law. Instead, it emphasised that the possibility for rebutting parenthood was an available legal option, even though not claimed by the applicant. In contrast, the ECtHR found a violation of article 8, concluding that depriving a person of having information and contact with his own affiliates is an infringement of their private life. The absence of actual family life in the case was considered not to be Mr Schneider's fault. The Court also concluded that the German courts should have also examined the best interests of the child when deciding the access of the biological father to already established family life with the presumed (thus legal) father. The Court also objected to the alleged possibility of rebutting legal fatherhood due to the fact that under the German Civil Code it would have been predetermined to fail. Furthermore, the justification of that kind was unacceptable because the goal of such proceedings is different from the applicant's petition aiming to access information and to establish contact with the child. Along these lines, the ECtHR concluded that the German courts protect the marital presumption mechanically, without examining either the child's best interests or the applicant's interests, and thus fail to balance between the competing rights. The ECtHR recommended that on a case-by-case basis, it should be examined which are the child's interests and

224 *Schneider v. Germany*, European Court of Human Rights, No. 17080/07, judgment of 15.09.2011.

how they can be balanced in the particular circumstances and in relation to the other interested parties.

The case of *Mizzi v. Malta*[225] also concerns the impossibility of rebutting the marital presumption, but this time from the husband himself. Following separation with his wife, a child was born and was automatically registered as the applicant's child. After DNA tests, the applicant confirmed that he was not biologically related to the child which led him to the decision to launch proceedings for rebutting his fatherhood. He was denied the possibility of civil litigation due to the fact that under the national law he was only entitled to do so if he also petitioned the adulterous behaviour of his wife and that the birth had been concealed from him. The ECtHR found a violation of article 6(1) as regards his inability to commence civil litigation to rebut his paternity which also violated article 8 as creating vagueness and uncertainty of his family relationships despite the genetic evidence. The Court also found a violation of article 14 in conjunction with article 6(1) and article 8 due to the restricted time limits[226] imposed on him to initiate the procedure for rebutting his fatherhood, which in turn did not apply to the other "interested parties".

A specific case regarding the value given to DNA tests when the marital presumption conflicts with the genetic reality of an adulterous relationship is *M.B. v. the United Kingdom*[227] before the European Commission of Human Rights. The case concerned a sexual relationship of a married woman outside her marriage. The woman was not able to conceive a child during 15 years of attempts with her husband. Nevertheless, she got pregnant whilst at the same time having an extra-marital relationship. She decided to keep the child and the marriage, refusing a parental responsibility agreement with the applicant. Nevertheless, her lover did not wish to give up his future relationship with the child who he thought was his. Thus, he applied to the Court for an order of parental responsibilities and contact with the child. The woman opposed any DNA tests that might disturb the presumption of legitimacy that her husband enjoyed. The Court protected the already created family life between the married couple, and refused further DNA tests. The Court considered that the child may have interests in knowing the biological truth, but in the particular case the child's best interests were related to preservation of the continuity of the existing family life. The applicant complained of deprivation of a fair trial contrary to article 6 of the Convention. He also invoked article 8 of the Convention arguing that family and blood relationships are part of his right to family and private life. In addition, he also stated that his child was

225 *Mizzi v. Malta*, European Court of Human Rights, No. 26111/02, judgment of 12.01.2006.

226 The restricted time limits for initiating civil proceedings for rebutting parenthood have a rationale of protecting children after establishing factual family life with the father. The exceptions are allowed after consent from the Constitutional Court. The same issue with this kind of regulation regarding the restricted time limits, the Court also noted in the case of *Roman v. Finland*, European Court of Human Rights, No. 13072/05, judgment of 29.03.2013.

227 *M.B. v. the United Kingdom*, European Commission on Human Rights, No. 22920/93, judgment of 06.04.1994.

deprived of the possibility to inherit from him, from substantial information to enable her to avoid marrying with prohibited degrees of relationship and from the correct knowledge of her genetic origins, which might be relevant to her health. He also claimed that he had been subject to discrimination contrary to article 14 of the Convention by not being allowed on equal grounds as that of the mother to recognise and register his parenthood. The Commission rejected his claim for a fair trial, since his petition was inadmissible in the first instance. It also rejected his claim that his child's rights would be violated if DNA tests were not performed, claiming that he was not the child's guardian or legal representative. The Commission also considered that there was no violation of article 8 since his family life was never established (no cohabitation nor demonstrable interest and commitment by the natural father to the child both before and after the birth, as well as rejection by the mother). Therefore the Commission found that "there are sound reasons of legal certainty and security of family relationships for States to apply a general presumption according to which a married man is regarded as the father of his wife's children and to require a good cause before allowing the presumption to be disturbed".[228] Therefore the best interests of the child were interpreted in the light of maintaining the security of the already existent family and not in the light of obtaining verification of the biological fact of the applicant. The Commission also dismissed the claim of discrimination, stating that the fact that women rarely find themselves in a position to prove their biological connection with the child is due to the natural difference between the genders and not to the discriminatory treatment of the Court.

The case of *Anayo v. Germany*[229] also included conflict between the marital presumption for establishing the fatherhood of the husband and the biological relationship of the extra-marital partner of the mother with the children (twins in the case). Following the extra-marital relationship parallel to the existing marriage, the mother of the child decided to continue marital life with her husband, whom by the legal marital presumption was already considered the father of the children. The marital partners and the Karlsruhe Court of Appeal denied Mr Anayo any contact with the twins because he did not hold any parental responsibilities for them, while he also did not have any factual social and family life. The German Basic Law protects the biological link between parents and children only under a condition of already existent family life, not including here the wish of establishing family life in the future. The ECtHR found a violation of article 8, hence the private and family life of the applicant, holding that the non-existent family life in the case was a result of the refusal of the mother and the legal parent against the efforts of Mr Anayo to establish contact with his children. Along these lines, the Court recognised that not only the existent family life, but also the desire to establish one, falls under the scope of article 8, when the reason

---

[228] See No. 18535/91, Comm. Rep. 7.4.93.

[229] *Anayo v. Germany*, European Court of Human Rights, No. 20578/07, judgment of 21.12.2010.

for its non-existence is not attributable to the applicant. In the case, the applicant showed a proactive attitude to establishing family life, even though he was barred both by the legal parents and institutionally. Furthermore, the Court found that the German courts did not examine profoundly if it was in the children's best interests to meet their biological father, while already having a legal father, despite the fact that the father demonstrated constant active behaviour. Therefore the Court again asked for a better balance in the relational context of all parties concerned when it comes to parental proceedings.

2.8.2.2. Establishing parental legal affiliation out of wedlock

Both cases of *Ahrens v. Germany*[230] and *Kautzor v Germany*[231] called upon article 8 (alone and in conjunction with article 14) regarding the refusal of the German courts to rebut paternity of an already established legal fatherhood *via* recognition of the child born outside a marital relationship. Mr Ahrens assumed that he was the biological father of a child whose mother had a common household relationship with another man who recognised the child as his. Both legal parents shared parental responsibilities over bringing up the child together. After asserting through medical tests that Mr Ahrens was the genetic father of the child, the Court of Appeal decided that the fact of already established family life between the child and the legal father was stronger than merely the biological connection and thus refused to permit Mr Ahrens to challenge the paternity of the legal father.

Mr Kautzor also assumed that he was the biological father of his former wife's daughter who was recognised by the mother's new partner with whom the mother shared a common household and family life. Mr Kautzor was precluded from civil proceedings for rebutting legal paternity on the same grounds – already established social, legal and family life with the legal father. Moreover, in his case, he was also precluded from the possibility of undergoing medical tests to prove his genetic connection with the child, since according to the Federal Constitutional Court he did not have the right to establish biological paternity without also establishing legal paternity. In his case, the ECtHR noted that there was a European consensus that existed in all 26 Member States that a procedure for the sole purpose of establishing biological fatherhood without formally challenging legal fatherhood was not recognised.

In both cases, the ECtHR found that even though the impossibility of establishing legal affiliation with their children interfered with the applicants' private and family life as protected under article 8, it did not violate the purpose of the article itself, since apart from the biological reality, social and family life was never established. On the contrary, the ECtHR considered that a violation of

[230] *Ahrens v. Germany*, European Court of Human Rights, No. 450071/09, judgment of 22.03.2012.
[231] *Kautzor v. Germany*, European Court of Human Rights, No. 23338/09, judgment of 22.03.2012.

the private and family life of the already established families would arise if their rights were reaffirmed. The Court furthermore emphasised that since there was no European consensus regarding the possibility of biological fathers establishing parenthood in relation to their children,[232] the margin of appreciation of the national regulations was wide in deciding their acceptable legal solution. The Court also rejected the claim under article 8 in conjunction with article 14, claiming that the different treatment between the applicants, the mother, the legal fathers and the child was not discriminatory, but intended to protect already established family life from external disturbances.

The case of *Marckx v. Belgium*[233] was a cornerstone case in establishing affiliation links outside marriage, therefore tackling the discrimination between "legitimate" as born in marriage and "illegitimate" children as born out of wedlock. The applicant claimed that as a single mother she was barred from establishing motherhood in relation to her baby daughter from her birth. Namely, the Roman law principle – *mater semper certa est* – did not apply under the former Belgian law. Therefore Mrs Marckx had to take additional legal action – firstly, to recognise her daughter, and secondly, to adopt her if she wanted to qualify for a wider range of rights and responsibilities in relation to inheritance (that go along automatically if parenthood is established in a marital relationship). The applicant claimed that the manner of establishing the parental link, the extension of the family ties towards the other relatives (e.g. grandparents), and the scope of rights and obligations granted to illegitimate children was discriminatory in comparison to children and families founded in marriage. Therefore she questioned if private and family life as protected in article 8 also encompassed the biological tie she had with her daughter, and if the legal consequences of such family life extend to the property and inheritance between them and other family members. The ECtHR found a violation of article 8 in conjunction with article 14 as the respect for private and family life should not discriminate between "legitimate" and "illegitimate" children. The different ways to establish motherhood based on grounds of the marital status of the mother were considered discriminatory towards the mother and children. The Court qualified an act as discriminatory if it "had no objective", did not pursue a "legitimate aim", and lacked a "reasonable relationship of proportionality between the means employed and the aim sought to be realized". Additionally, the Court acknowledged that "the Committee of Ministers of the Council of Europe regards the single woman and

232 The Court affirmed that even though comparatively, the majority of the Council of Europe Member States allowed the possibility for civil litigation in which the presumed biological father could challenge legal fatherhood established by acknowledgment, even when there was already established family life among them, there was also a significant minority of nine Member States in which the presumed biological father did not have the right to rebut the paternity of the legal father.

233 *Marckx v. Belgium*, European Court of Human Rights, No. 6833/74, judgment of 13.06.1979.

her child as one form of family, no less than others";[234] therefore family life exists irrespective of the partnership or single parent status. The Belgian legislation had a restrictive interpretation of family and relatives since the established affiliation of illegitimate children created legal bonds only with the mother and not with the mother's family as well. In the Court's opinion family life also included at least the family ties between near relatives (such as grandparents and grandchildren) since they constitute a substantive part of the family. The right to inheritance though, according to the Belgian authorities, gradually developed from recognition of adoption of an illegitimate child. In these terms, it could have never been equal with the right to inherit of legitimate children, since even at its utmost it excluded the other relatives of the mother. Namely, under the Belgian law, at the time of the case, while a "legitimate" child could have been fully integrated into his parents' families from the time of birth, an "illegitimate" child (even when adopted), could have never been integrated. Governments' reasoning for the adoption not to cover the inheritance rights between the other relatives was associated with the possibility of the relatives disapproving of it. The Court did not go on to discuss discrimination under these grounds, finding that the mere fact that the mother has to adopt her child was already discriminatory. Consequently, the Court did not find a violation of the patrimonial rights of the mother and daughter, reasoning that the violation already found on the other grounds was a prerequisite for the later discrimination.

A similar case that discriminated between "legitimate" and "illegitimate" children in the field of their inheritance was the later case of *Inez v. Austria*.[235] The ECtHR in this case found violation of article 14 in conjunction with article 1 of Protocol No. 1 (right to peaceful enjoyment of possessions). The applicant claimed that under Austrian law he was not legally entitled to inherit his mother's property in the same way as her other legitimate child because he was born out of wedlock. Even later on, the ECtHR dealt with similar cases. In *Mazurek v. France*[236] and *Merger and Cros v. France*,[237] the Court concluded that the French authorities treated children born in marriage and out of wedlock differently in the sphere of their inheritance rights. The Court found that an evident evolution of harmonising the national laws in the field of abandoning the terminological difference between "legitimate" and "illegitimate" children, and consequently, discrimination is already a European standard.[238] Therefore the Court found a

234 Referring to Resolution (70) on the Social Protection of Unmarried Mothers and Their Children, 15 May 1970.

235 *Inze v. Austria*, European Court of Human Rights, No. 8695/79, judgment of 28.10.1987.

236 *Mazurek v. France*, European Court of Human Rights, No. 34406/97, judgment of 01.02.2000.

237 *Merger and Cros v. France*, European Court of Human Rights, No. 68864/01, judgment of 22.12.2004.

238 Inheritance of children born in and out of wedlock, though, is not a European standard yet. There are still countries that hold reservations regarding article 9 of the European Convention of the Legal Status of Children Born Out of Wedlock which shows that the issue is still

violation of article 1 of Protocol No. 1 in conjunction with article 14, after which the national authorities took measures to change the national legislation.

In the case of *Camp and Bourimi v. the Netherlands*,[239] once again the *ECtHR* found a violation of article 14 in conjunction with article 8, due to discrimination against a child born out of wedlock to inherit from the father who died before the child's birth. In this case, neither was the child recognised (only proclaimed legitimate two years after the death of the father) nor was the marital presumption for establishing parenthood applied. Nevertheless, the Court found that the fact that the father died before the child was born was not a valid reason to take a different approach towards the child born out of wedlock as compared with a child born in marriage, or a child that had an opportunity to be recognised by a living father after being born. Therefore the Court found discrimination between persons in similar situations based on birth. Even though it acknowledged that the states enjoy a margin of discretion to qualify if the different treatment should be categorised as discrimination, the Court also underlined that in concordance with the case law, there have to be very weighty reasons to justify different treatment on the ground of birth out of wedlock to be considered in line with the Convention.

The case of *Mikulic v. Croatia*[240] concerned the impossibility of establishing fatherhood in relation to a child born out of wedlock. The child together with the mother filed a paternity suit with the Croatian courts, as being the only mechanism for establishing the parental link with the father who refused to recognise the child as his. The national law, however, did not provide the possibility of a court order for DNA tests of the presumed biological father as the only way to confirm the biological link, and thus his legal paternity. Therefore the applicants claimed before the ECtHR under article 8 that the domestic courts failed to decide the child's paternity claim while leaving her uncertain in regard to the personal identity encompassed under private and family life. She also complained under article 6(1) about the long paternity proceedings outside the reasonable time requirement, and under article 13 about the lack of any effective remedy to speed up the process since Croatian law does not oblige defendants in paternity suits to undergo DNA tests.

The ECtHR found a violation of articles 6(1), 8 and 13, emphasising that the Croatian courts failed to consider the best interests of the child in the paternity dispute. The Court supported the decision by acknowledging that the paternity procedure under the Croatian law did not strike a fair balance between the right of the applicant to certainty when it comes to the child's personal identity and the supposed father's refusal to undergo DNA tests as a prerequisite for establishing

controversial. For this reason, the White Paper has not set a principle on the matter. See more in the White Paper, p. 31.

239 *Camp and Bourimi v. the Netherlands*, European Court of Human Rights, No. 28369/95, judgment of 03.10.2000.

240 *Mikulic v. Croatia*, European Court of Human Rights, No. 53176/99, judgment of 07.02.2002.

the link with the child. The case represents an important step in the ECtHR's recognition of the child's right to know the genetic origin as part of personal identity and therefore private life, even though there was no existent family life between the child and the presumed father.

In the case of *Yousef v. the Netherlands*[241] the applicant claimed that he could not establish legal fatherhood in relation to his biological child born out of wedlock. The applicant did not recognise the child as his after her birth, while he was also not sharing the same household with the mother and the child. They only started living together later on and for no longer than a year. Afterwards, the applicant went to his home country of Egypt, retaining little or no contact with his child. Returning to the Netherlands after two and a half years, he tried to establish regular contact with his child. He repeatedly asked the mother of the child for permission to recognise the child as his while being constantly refused. After the death of the mother, her brother was appointed as a guardian of the child following the mother's will. The applicant initiated proceedings for establishing fatherhood in relation to his child, while being refused by the Netherlands' courts on grounds of protecting the best interests of the child. The suspicion was that the applicant wanted to misuse the proceedings for establishing parenthood just to be able to obtain a residence permit and security benefits in the Netherlands.

The applicant later on married and had another son. Nevertheless, he complained under article 8 that he was restricted from recognising his own biological child as his own. The ECtHR found no violation of article 8, claiming that the Netherlands' courts fairly balanced the interests by claiming that the child's best interests should prevail, while considering these in contrast with the claim of the applicant to establish fatherhood. The Court considered that the decision in favour of the applicant could have distanced the child from the family with whom she was already living and being taken care of.

2.8.2.3. Establishing parental legal affiliation for the sperm donor

The case of *J.R.M. v the Netherlands*[242] is at the heart of the problem when it comes to the impossibility of a sperm donor establishing fatherhood in parental proceedings. It has been confirmed many times before and afterwards that sperm donors do not qualify for the proceedings that will eventually make them a legal parent. On the contrary, there is widespread consensus among the international documents as well as among Member States that sperm donors should not be considered fathers of children. The importance of the case is precisely that the Dutch courts allowed paternal proceedings for sperm donors, despite the fact

---

[241] *Yousef v. the Netherlands*, European Court of Human Rights, No. 33711/96, judgment of 05.11.2002.

[242] *J.R.M. v. the Netherlands*, European Commission of Human Rights, No. 16944/90, Decision of 08.02.1993.

that they rejected his claim afterwards (while the rationale of the rejection is also relevant).

In the case, the applicant agreed to donate his sperm in order to enable a lesbian couple to become parents. The couple preferred a known donor so that they could afford to the child a right to know the biological father's identity, as according to them this seemed to be an important element for satisfying the child's best interest. The applicant paid regular visits to the couple and the child during the pregnancy and after the birth of the child. After a while, he expressed his wish to establish certain visiting arrangements, which was unacceptable for the couple. Consequently, he requested the Dutch Juvenile Court to determine an arrangement concerning his access to the child.

The application was admissible due to the fact of the combination of a biological connection and weekly contact with the child. Nevertheless, the Court refused the applicant's request for contact and access to the child considering it to be against the best interests of the child in the particular circumstances of disagreement by the legal parents. The judge considered that the fact of sperm donation in itself is not a sufficient basis for creation of family life within the meaning of article 8 of the ECHR and that agreements on rights and duties concerning the child are null and void.

This judgment may also mean that if the circumstances had been different in terms of the existing agreement of the parents regarding regular contact of the donor with the child, the donor might have been allowed particular visiting arrangements. This could mean that the possibility of attributing parental responsibilities to the donor is not excluded if several factors are in favour of it, one of which (lacking in the case) is intention and consent of all the concerned parties. If the circumstances were such, the Court might have ruled in favour of granting him access/regular contact with the child that may even lead to eventually gaining parental responsibilities. Nevertheless, it is important that the Court allowed the application to be admissible giving it due weight of investigation of the particular circumstances of the case.

After appealing to the next instances (the Court of Appeal and the Supreme Court),[243] the applicant also challenged articles 8 and 13 in conjunction with 6(1) and 14 of the ECHR. The Commission reaffirmed that it had been previously held that family life under article 8 implies personal ties in addition to biological parenthood that depend on many factors among which are cohabitation, as well as the circumstances of each particular case. Furthermore, it considered that the written consent of the donor to donate for purposes of satisfying the child-

[243] It is interesting to mention that the Supreme Court rejected the applicant's argument under the rationale that "family life" requires, apart from biological fatherhood, also the existence of additional circumstances, which in the case were considered of summary and not substantial character. Nevertheless, the Court confirmed that there is always "family life" between a biological father, including a donor and the child. Yet this was not enough to constitute legal consequences of "family life". See more in the facts of the case, *ibid.*

need of another couple, explicitly excluded him from any legal parental scenario. Regarding the complaints about the alleged violation of his right to access proceedings, the Court also considered them non-grounded since he used all the legal means at his disposal in the Juvenile Court, the Court of Appeal and the Supreme Court respectively. Therefore he was granted a right to access the Court, his case was administered and, after rejection of his claim, he used the right to legal remedy. This, though, could not be dealt with in the same way in most of the Member States which explicitly forbid legal proceedings for establishing fatherhood in relation to a child conceived by assisted insemination (including the Republic of Macedonia). Regarding the claim of discrimination against him by declaring his request for access and contact with the child inadmissible (whereas in a similar case a father of a legitimate child who procreated naturally[244] would not have received such a rejection), the Court also ruled in favour of the Dutch courts. The Commission noted that a comparison between him and a father who procreated naturally is not appropriate since they are not analogous, and therefore they do not raise a question of discrimination. This case should not be confused with sperm donations to lesbian couples under agreements between the parties but not in licensed clinics.[245]

In this sense, the recent Draft Recommendation[246] proposes that the establishment of parental affiliation in cases of medically assisted procreation should not differ, or at least should be grounded on the same rules as natural procreation. This would mean that the proposed presumptions for establishing paternity of the father in marriage as well as in registered or not registered cohabitant partnership would already solve the paternity issue from the time of birth. Additionally, this would exclude the possibility for legal paternal identification of the donor as a principle rule. Exceptionally, if the other criteria are fulfilled and if it is in the child's best interests, it would be possible for third parties to be attributed certain parental responsibilities.[247] Nevertheless, this presumption could only apply in cases in which couples are concerned and not in

---

244 Here the term "father of a legitimate child" is used wrongly. Since the distinction of legitimate and illegitimate children was initially drawn to distinguish among children born within or outside marriage, and afterwards considered to be a wrong nomenclature, the term has been later on replaced with a "father who procreated naturally". See also the case of *Marckx v. Belgium*, European Court of Human Rights, No. 6833/74, judgment of 13.06.1979.

245 The practice has shown up in several similar cases worldwide. The most recent one is before the Kansas court in which it was ruled that the man who donated sperm to a lesbian couple in response to a private advertisement and insemination that took place at home was the legal father of the child. The court held the contract for waiving all parental rights and responsibilities that they concluded to be void, because an authorised physician was not included in the process which is a condition stipulated for assisted reproductions in the Kansas Parentage Act, 1994. See more in Hyder H., *Craigslist Sperm Donor is Legal Father, US Court Rules*, bionews.org.uk, 27.01.2014, available online: www.bionews.org.uk/page_390812.asp.

246 Appendix IV, Draft Recommendation on the Rights and Legal Status of Children and Parental Responsibilities, Explanatory Memorandum, CJ-FA (2011) RAP 5 prov.

247 *Ibid.* p. 46.

single women cases, when the possibility to establish the fatherhood of the second parent is excluded.

2.8.3. THE CASE LAW IN THE FIELD OF CHILDREN'S RIGHTS

2.8.3.1. Right to information about genetic origin or personal history

The case of *Odièvre v. France*[248] concerned an adopted child's right to seek information regarding her genetic origin when born under rules governing confidentiality at birth. After obtaining non-identifying information regarding her genetic family, the applicant's request to also receive identifying information about her three brothers was rejected. The rules in France clearly rejected an application for disclosure of identifying details if confidentiality was agreed at birth. The applicant claimed under article 8 that the French authorities were infringing her right to obtain identifying information about her genetic roots which she considered to be an essential part of her identity, and private and family life. Furthermore, she claimed discrimination under article 14 on the ground of birth as not being treated equally regarding her rights towards the natural mother enjoyed by children who were not adopted. The ECtHR did not find a violation either of article 8 or of article 14 of the Convention. While the non-existence of family life was not disputed, the private life of the applicant was observed from the perspective of her right to obtain identifying information regarding her personal history. The Court confirmed that birth as well as the circumstances in which the child was born constituted an important part of personal private life, and was therefore protected under article 8. Nevertheless, the Court considered that in the case, several conflicting interests had to be balanced in a relationship context regarding the child's interests to know, the woman's interests to remain anonymous (in order to protect her health by giving birth in appropriate medical conditions), as well as the interests of the adoptive parents, the father and other members of the natural family. In this respect, the Court also acknowledged that the identifying information could possibly infringe substantial rights of the mother herself, the adoptive family, as well as the natural father and sibling, each having a proper right to respect for their private and family life. While the Court recognised the wide margin of appreciation of the Member States to decide how to balance interests between different parties under the umbrella of article 8, it also affirmed that the French authorities have balanced the interests of all concerned parties within the allowed limits, thus protecting mothers' and children's health at birth, and avoiding illegal abortions, and children being abandoned through an illegal procedure. The Court also observed that France introduced new legislation

[248] *Odièvre v. France*, European Court of Human Rights, No. 42326/98, judgment of 13.02.2003.

in 2002 which formed a National Council of Access to Information about Personal Origins whose aim is to facilitate investigations to collect information regarding the biological origin. Therefore it directed the applicant towards the possibility of obtaining identifying information regarding the mother on the condition that she consents. In this way, the Court found that France found a fair balance between the competing interests of all parties concerned with their own interests under the umbrella of article 8. The Court also did not find a violation of article 14 in conjunction with article 8, since the claim to inherit from the natural mother while also having adoptive parents was excessive and did not fall under the discrimination protection.

In the recent case of *Godelli v. Italy*,[249] similar to *Odièvre v. France*, the ECtHR did find a violation of article 8 due to failure of the Italian authorities to reveal information regarding the origins of a child abandoned at birth by the mother. The applicant was informed of her adoption when she was 10 by her adoptive parents. She claimed that ever since, she had suffered from a lack of identity due to the impossibility of finding information about her genetic roots, as the Italian law guaranteed secrecy in adoption cases as a way of primarily protecting the interests of the genetic mother. The ECtHR reaffirmed that article 8 also encompasses protection of the right to know the modus of conception as an integral part of personal identity and development. The Court also distinguished between the right to know the identity and the right to seek legal proceedings for establishing the parental link. The challenge in the case was to strike a fair balance among the competing interests of a child seeking to know identifying information, the mother's interests in preserving her anonymity, as well as the public interest to prevent illegal abortions and abandonment of children. Unlike the previous case, the Court found that the Italian system failed to balance the competing interests, giving automatic precedence to the mother's interests, without even considering the possibility of the child *as far as possible*[250] to disclose the mother's identity on condition of her consent. Even though the Court once again recognised that the interpretation of article 8 by the Member States still remains to a large extent a matter of discretion, it also referred to the necessity to introduce a system that balances fairly the interests of all concerned parties, thus providing access to either non-identifying information or identifying information (if the consent of the concerned party is provided) about one's origin.

In the case of *Jaggi v. Switzerland*,[251] the applicant claimed that he was barred from establishing the paternity of his alleged biological father because he was not allowed to have DNA tests performed on his alleged biological father's dead body. The ECtHR found violation of article 8, as an infringement of the applicant's private and family life, by the impossibility of obtaining DNA analysis

---

249 *Godelli v. Italy*, European Court of Human Rights, No. 33783/09, judgment of 25.09.2012.

250 And in concordance with article 7 of the Convention on the Rights of the Child, 1989.

251 *Jaggi v. Switzerland*, European Court of Human Rights, No. 58757/00, judgment of 13.07.2006.

of the mortal remains of his presumed father, without valid reasons for it (the DNA test was not considered to be particularly intrusive and the family did not hold any religious or philosophical objections). The applicant was informed by his mother about the identity of his father, which was also declared on his birth certificate. The applicant and the father had also established regular contact, but the presupposed father had always refused to submit to tests to establish his paternity. The applicant's claim for private DNA tests was rejected on grounds that at his age (60) he should have already developed his personality even in the absence of proof of certainty about the identity of his biological father. Even though the ECtHR acknowledged that establishing ancestry was of vital interest for developing personal identity, it also acknowledged the relativity of the right in regard to the rights of the other concerned parties. Once again, the Court emphasised the relational aspect of the rights (the rights of the third parties concerned with the eventual outcome, the right to respect for the dead body, as well as the public interest in the protection of legal certainty) as a reason why they cannot be claimed as individual absolute rights. On the other hand, the Court also acknowledged that the applicant had always been active in the search for the biological truth, which is an interest that does not diminish with age. On this basis, the reasons that relativise the applicant's right are counterfeit and not legally grounded. The Court also noted that "the protection of legal certainty alone could not suffice as ground to deprive the applicant of the right to discover his parentage".

In the case of *Gaskin v. the United Kingdom*[252] the right to private and family life under article 8 was challenged together with the right to seek information regarding the applicant's personal history under article 10 ECHR. The applicant also invoked articles 3 and 13 of the ECHR and article 2 of Protocol No. 1. After the death of his mother, the applicant was relocated under foster care by the local authorities. Complaining of the negligence to afford him proper foster parents, after reaching majority and ceasing to be under foster care, the applicant also took action to discover the records of his foster parents' history. Under the national rules, information of this kind is considered to be private and confidential; therefore he was refused access to the data. Following the decisions of the competent authorities, a resolution was adopted, which allowed disclosure of the information of the applicant's file, provided that consent was granted by the concerned party. Many contributors refused to waive confidentiality. Although they were not asked to give reasons for their decision, some stated that: "the third-party interests could be harmed, the contribution would be of no value if taken out of context, that professional confidence was involved, that it was not the practice to disclose reports to clients, that too great a period of time had elapsed for a letter of report to be in the contributor's recollection, and that it would be

[252] *Gaskin v. the United Kingdom*, European Court of Human Rights, No. 10454/83, judgment of 07.07.1989.

detrimental to the applicants' interests".[253] The UK Government claimed that its administrative system did not provide an absolute right to access case records in the applicant's situation and called upon the wide margin of discretion in such cases. On the contrary, the government stated that it managed to balance the competing interests: on the one hand, the public interest to provide an efficient childcare system, and on the other hand, the applicant's interest in having access to a coherent record of personal history.

The ECtHR held that the national authorities failed to secure access by the applicant to his records and thus failed to respect his private and family life under article 8 of the ECHR. The Court concluded that even though the case did not concern his genetic parents, it was still related to the applicant's basic identity built in his early childhood and formative years; thus the refusal to allow him access was an interference with his right to respect for private and family life under paragraph 2 of article 8. The Court considered that the interests of individuals seeking information necessary to understand their childhood and early development must be secured even when a contributor to the records is not available or improperly refuses consent. On the contrary, the principle of proportionality seeks an independent authority to be provided which will finally decide whether access should be granted, even in cases where the contributor refuses consent, so that the decision to disclose information is not solely under his authority.

In regard to article 10, the Court held that the Convention did not embody a positive obligation for the Member States to reveal information to the applicant, against the will of the local authority and thus did not find any violation.

In the dissenting opinions, several judges criticised the decision, claiming that there had not been any violation or that there had not been a proper balancing between the rights and interests of the concerned parties. Instead, they favoured the procedure followed by the United Kingdom authorities for determining which aspects of the applicant's file should be available, under the given circumstances, as representing a fair balance of interests of all concerned parties.

2.8.3.2. *Right of the child to be taken care of by both parents*

The right of the child to be taken care of by both parents as incorporated in the CRC is considered together with the right to be registered immediately after birth and the right to know the parents, as far as possible, and usually follows after the first two rights are realised.

In the ECtHR case law, the right of the child to be taken care of by both parents has been interpreted together with articles 7 and 3 of the CRC and article 8 of the ECHR mostly in (1) cases of attempts to legally recognise the other parent (as corresponding with the right to be registered); (2) cases of attempts

[253] *Ibid.* For more, see the facts of the case.

to know who the other parent is (as corresponding with the right to know the genetic parent); and (3) cases of custody where the child was separated by one of the already legally recognised parents (as corresponding with the right to be taken care of by both parents). All three rights as encompassed in article 7 CRC are interconnected and interdependent.

In cases of attempts to legally recognise the child from birth, the marital presumption was decisive and burdensome for children born out of wedlock as a parallel relationship to marriage in the following cases: *Kroon and Others v. the Netherlands*, *Chavdarov v. Bulgaria*, *Schneider v. Germany*, *Mizzi v. Malta*, and *Anayo v. Germany* as elaborated above.

The circumstances of being born out of wedlock invoked the impossibility of registering fatherhood such as in the cases *Camp and Bourimi v. the Netherlands*, *Mikulic v. Croatia* and *Yousef v. the Netherlands*. On the other hand, the recognition of parenthood out of wedlock is burdensome to prove the opposite, to rebut it, and thus to establish legal parenthood on the basis of a biological link later on after the birth of the child. Along these lines, in the cases of *Ahrens v. Germany* and *Kautzor v. Germany* the legal certainty of the already established family ties was safeguarded. The Court furthermore noted that a procedure for the sole purpose of establishing biological fatherhood without formally challenging legal fatherhood was not recognised in all Member States; therefore it treated it as a European consensus.

In cases of sperm donations to single women, the child will be registered as having a mother, while the father's name will be left blank on the birth certificate as the terms and conditions of the donation result in him being a *sperm donor* and not any form of *fatherhood*, thus treating the man who donates as a *donor* and not as a *father*. This is in line with the principle of informed consent, autonomy to decide, and individual responsibility for altruistic donations as stipulated in articles 5 and 6 of the UDBHR and article 5 of the Oviedo Convention. The donor has a right to remain anonymous if he consented to donate under circumstances of privacy and confidentiality as stipulated in article 9 UDBHR and article 7 UDHGHR. An important issue to be raised is if the information regarding the modus of conception and the modus of establishing the parental link (for instance, sperm donation, embryo donation or adoption) will be included in the birth certificate. If such information is provided, the later identifying information and the right to contact the genetic parent should depend on his consent, as the donor's private life and confidentiality should also be protected (article 10 Oviedo Convention).

A right to know the parent, as a right to disclose identifying information without also claiming the right to establish a parental link, has already been challenged in adoption cases: *Odièvre v. France* and *Godelli v. Italy*. In the second case, the Court distinguished between the right to know the identity and the right to seek legal proceedings to establish a parental link. Even though the Court reiterated that the interpretation of article 8 by the Member States still remains to a large extent a matter of discretion, it also referred to the need to introduce a system that balances fairly the interests of all concerned parties, thus providing access to either non-identifying information or identifying information (if the consent of the concerned party is provided) about one's origin. On the other hand, in the cases of *Mikulic v. Croatia* and *Jäggi v. Switzerland* the right to know the biological father was connected with a procedure to establish fatherhood.

In the cases of custody, the Court reached different judgments in *Morfic v. France*[254] and *Maumousseau and Washington v. France*[255] as compared to *Maire v. Portugal*[256] *and Monory v. Romania and Hungary.*[257] In the first two cases it demonstrated a will to appreciate the factual social role of being a parent and taking care of the child as important to protect private and family life. On the contrary, in the latter two cases it acknowledged the failure of the national authorities to provide the possibility of creating such ties at a young age with the child (even though they were lacking under the concrete circumstances). The Court reiterated that custodial cases require urgent handling, since a big time gap could cause irreversible consequences for the parent–child relationship, bearing in mind the age of the child.

Custodial cases, which presuppose already established parenthood, are different from cases attempting to establish parenthood in relation to children conceived by donor insemination, as the meaning of *donor* is different from the meaning of *parent* precisely due to the legal recognition. Nevertheless, one could question if the child could never claim a *right to be taken care of* by the other parent (in the case, the donor) due to circumstances of not having any familial reality with the donor, or the other way round, i.e. not having any familial history with the donor due to the national authorities' passivity in enabling contact between them. By allowing the child conceived by sperm donation a right to know their genetic origin, the donor does not have the right to contact him against his will. Even more, if such rights are afforded, they are usually allowed to be exercised by children once they turn 18, i.e. at the time when they are no longer children, but adults with an already built personal identity, and at the time when it is too late to establish family ties in order to qualify for protection of private and family life under article 8 ECHR.

In the above cases, the Court took different stands when it comes to examining if the genetic or the social reality are constitutional elements of the parent–child relationship, considering the different circumstances that in each case touch upon other legal issues. In the cases of *Mikulic v. Croatia* and *Jäggi v. Switzerland*, the ECtHR favoured genetic truth as being relevant to one's personal

254 *Morfis v. France*, European Court of Human Rights, No. 10978/04, judgment of 12.04.2007.

255 *Maumousseau and Washington v. France*, European Court of Human Rights, No. 39388/05, judgment of 06.12.2007.

256 *Maire v. Portugal*, European Court of Human Rights, No. 48206/99, judgment of 26.06.2003.

257 *Monory v. Romania and Hungary*, European Court of Human Rights, No. 71099/01, judgment of 05.04.2005.

identity and connected it with the proceedings for establishing a parental link. The stand is that the cases for examining biological reality without establishing a parental link are not to be afforded; thus the revealing of the biological link presupposes legal parenthood too. On the other hand, in the case of *Godelli v. Italy*, the Court favoured existing family life more than biological reality as a relevant factor for the parent–child relationship. The stand is that the right to know the identity of the genetic parent does not automatically encompass legal parenthood. In most cases, the Court weighed the biological truth and social reality of lived family life against the corrective measurement of the principle of the best interests of the child. The decisive power of legal certainty of the marital presumption was also examined in regard to its role as a ground for constituting family life *vis-à-vis* the uncertainty of extra-marital relationships and their legal inferiority in establishing family life and in relation to the state's capacity to deal with such cases within a reasonable time. Therefore not only biological truth *versus* social reality was confronted as relevant for establishing the affiliation, but in most of the cases, other legal circumstances contributed to case particularity. This was challenged in the cases: *Kroon and Others v. the Netherlands*, *Chavdarov v. Bulgaria*, *Scheider v. Germany*, *Mizzi v. Malta*, *Anayo v. Germany*, *Camp and Bourimi v. the Netherlands*, *Yousef v. the Netherlands*, *Ahrens v. Germany* and *Kautzor v. Germany*.

Article 7 of the CRC itself holds potentially conflicting truths: taking care of the child as encompassing activity in *doing* the parental role, and knowing the parent as striving to know who is *being* the genetic parent. The registration of the child from birth encompasses the necessity to establish care for the child from birth; thus the focus is on the active role of doing fatherhood, and primarily creating family life between the parent and child. The registration itself should provide a level of legal certainty of the private and family life, which develops based on mutual life, care, nutrition, affection and emotions which are more sensitive to later nullifications due to rebutting the parental role. The task to balance the genetic and biological realities should be taken with due respect for all concerned parties, and mostly the best interests of the child.

The legal impossibility of establishing the fatherhood of the donor of a child born by sperm donations to single women and therefore the right *to be cared for* by both parents does not lie in the rejected claims due to investigated and elaborated reasons, but due to the inadmissibility of such proceedings *per se*. This is an impediment of the legal evolution based on the case law in a rather novel field surrounded with many uncertainties. A society that faces the new biomedical challenges by allowing single women to procreate, without considering the consequences for the created child, thereby restricting the possibility for a court hearing, thus avoiding any responsibilities, does not respect the best interest of the child. Sperm donor children will firstly face the identity issue, posing questions and claims based on their right to know their genetic parent (which is currently topical, since the pioneers' children born by sperm donation are reaching maturity, and living the ignorant reality and thus raising awareness in the legal context and literature as well). Afterwards, the children (especially those predestined to be fatherless from birth as in the case of sperm donations to single women) will also challenge the possibility of meeting and establishing contact with the donor, calling upon their *right to be cared for by both parents*, even under the circumstances "as far as possible" or a right to establish a parental legal link after their maturity in a fair trial and on equal grounds as children conceived naturally.

2.9. EUROPEAN CONVENTION ON THE EXERCISE OF CHILDREN'S RIGHTS AND THE CONVENTION ON CONTACT CONCERNING CHILDREN

The European Convention on the Exercise of Children's Rights (ECECR) and the Convention on Contact concerning Children (CCC) deal exclusively with children's rights in the European context, particularly in the field of establishing the parental role, the scope of parental responsibility, as well as the right of the child to contact their parent and other persons with whom the child is related through family ties. In this respect, both Conventions are relevant to analyse the development of the regulations between parents and children, and also when the child is conceived by reproductive technology including more participants in the reproductive and parental project. Some authors have demonstrated disappointment with the rather ignorant attitude towards the Conventions by the Member States instead of their eager ratifications.[258] Critiques have also been directed towards the mechanisms for monitoring the Conventions' execution in Member States.[259] The ECECR in its article 16 provides for the creation of a Standing Committee in order to keep under review problems relating to the Conventions. The CCC has no direct monitoring mechanism but there is an obligation under article 11 to notify the Secretary-General of any appointment of a Central Authority.

The ECECR was open for signature in 1996, and at the time of writing has been ratified by the majority (28) of the Member States of the Council of Europe.[260]

---

258 Lowe N., "An Evaluation of the Council of Europe's Legal Instruments in the Field of Family Law, A Report for the Attention of the Committee of Experts of Family Law (CJ-FA)", *Cardiff Law School Research Papers, No. 2*, Presented to the 36th Plenary Meeting of the CF-FA, Strasbourg, 15–17 November 2006.

259 *Ibid.* p. 23.

260 European Convention on the Exercise of Children's Rights (ECECR), CETS No. 160, see online: http://conventions.coe.int/Treaty/Commun/ChercheSig.asp?NT=160&CM=&DF=&CL.=ENG. Last visited 25.07.2013. The Republic of Macedonia signed the Convention on 3 April 2001 and ratified it on 15 January 2002. The Convention entered into force on 1 October 2002.

Nevertheless, it was expected that the Convention would have attracted even wider ratification. The reasons for the fewer than expected countries ratifying the Convention are seen in the reluctance of the states to commit themselves to the costs of compliance even in three nominated fields of family cases.[261] Nevertheless, the standing principles of the Convention are encouraged for promotion as well as the efforts for securing more ratifications and accessions.[262]

Article 1(4) of the Convention requires Contracting States to "specify at least three categories of family cases before a judicial authority to which this Convention shall apply".[263] This formulation could be the subject of critique since it allows uniformity even among Contracting States on the scope of its application.[264]

The substantive part of the Convention is important in three major fields: (1) children's procedural rights; (2) the role of the judicial authorities (in consulting the child in appropriate cases, allowing the child to express his or her views and appreciating these views, the responsibility of acting speedily, and appointing a special representative for the child in cases in which there is a conflict between the child's and parents' interests); and (3) the role of representatives.[265]

Parents are considered as "holders of parental responsibilities" and not as "holders of parental rights", emphasising the modern child's oriented perspective.[266] The term refers not only to parents who are entitled to exercise parental responsibilities in full or partially, but also to other persons or bodies.

Article 3 regulates the right of the child to be informed and to express his or her views in proceedings envisaging the following rights: to receive all relevant information, to be consulted and to express his or her views, to be informed of the possible consequences of these views, and the possible consequences of any decision. The Explanatory Report to the Convention states that this article also includes the right of the child to receive necessary information even if he/she has not asked for any.[267] This could be applied in cases of adoption or when the child

---

261 Killerby M., "The Council of Europe's Contribution to Family Law (Past, Present and Future)", in Lowe N., Douglas G. (eds.), *Families Across Frontiers*, Martinus Nijhoff, 1996, p. 25.

262 Lowe N., "An Evaluation of the Council of Europe's Legal Instruments in the Field of Family Law, A Report for the Attention of the Committee of Experts of Family Law (CJ-FA)", *Cardiff Law School Research Papers, No. 2*, Presented to the 36th Plenary Meeting of the CF-FA, Strasbourg, 15–17 November 2006, p. 32.

263 In relation to this, the Republic of Macedonia declared that the "Convention shall apply to the following categories of family cases: adoption proceedings, cases concerning the custody of children, the proceedings while deciding on the custody and upbringing of children and proceedings concerning establishment of parental affiliation (paternity and maternity), as well as in the proceedings when parental affiliation is contested". See online: http://conventions.coe.int/Treaty/Commun/ListeDeclarations.asp?NT=160&CM=&DF=&CL=ENG&VL=1.

264 Lowe N., "An Evaluation of the Council of Europe's Legal Instruments in the Field of Family Law, A Report for the Attention of the Committee of Experts of Family Law (CJ-FA)", *Cardiff Law School Research Papers, No. 2*, Presented to the 36th Plenary Meeting of the CF-FA, Strasbourg, 15–17 November 2006, p. 14.

265 *Ibid.*

266 Article 2 of the ECECR.

267 Explanatory Report on the European Convention on the Exercise of Children's Rights, available online: http://conventions.coe.int/Treaty/en/Reports/Html/160.htm.

is conceived by donation of genetic material, regarding the information of the origin or the modus of conception.

Article 7 of the Convention stipulates the duty that national authorities shall act speedily in proceedings affecting a child in order to avoid unnecessary delay and enforcement.

The Convention on Contact Concerning Children originates from a recommendation of the Third European Conference on Family Law "Family Law in the Future" held in Cadiz, Spain in 1995. CCC builds upon the foundations set forth in the CRC (especially article 9 which promotes the right of the child to maintain personal relations and direct contact with both parents) and the above emphasised articles from the ECECR. The Convention was open for signature in 2003 and has currently been ratified by 18 Member States of the Council of Europe.[268]

The Convention goes beyond recognising the need for children to have contact with both parents, promoting also contact with certain other persons connected through "family ties". This category includes grandparents[269] or siblings based on law or on a *de facto* family relationship.[270] The novelty of the Convention is that it not only refers to parents or other family members recognised by the national laws, but also allows the possibility of other "legally not recognised" family members to have contact with the child under the umbrella of *de facto* family life.[271]

National authorities are free to determine which persons can be legally recognised as parents or as having family ties with the child, which are the best interests of the child, when the child is considered to have sufficient understanding, and whether contact is subject to the consent of the child.[272] Article 2 of the Convention defines the meaning of the term "contact" used in its three different forms: (1) direct contact ("personal" face-to-face contact), (2) indirect (not personal face-to-face contact but established over a distance *via*

---

268 Convention on Contact concerning Children, CETS No. 192, available online: http://conventions.coe.int/Treaty/Commun/ChercheSig.asp?NT=192&CM=8&DF=&CL=ENG. The Convention is not ratified by the Republic of Macedonia.

269 See, for instance, the decision of the ECtHR in the case of *Scozzari and Giunta v. Italy*, European Court of Human Rights, No. 39221/98, 41963/98, judgment of 13.07.2000 in which the Court recognised that family life as stipulated in article 8 ECHR includes also the ties between grandparents and grandchildren.

270 Article 2(d) ECCC.

271 The qualification of having family life between the grandparents and child has also been questioned by Nigel Lowe under the presupposition that the child is born out of wedlock while the interest/commitment requirement from the father is absent. See Lowe N., *A Study into the Rights and Legal Status of Children being Brought Up in Various Forms of Marital or Non-Marital Partnerships and Cohabitation*, A Report for the Attention of the Committee of Experts on Family Law, September 2009, p. 8.

272 Lowe N., "An Evaluation of the Council of Europe's Legal Instruments in the Field of Family Law, A Report for the Attention of the Committee of Experts of Family Law (CJ-FA)", *Cardiff Law School Research Papers, No. 2*, Presented to the 36th Plenary Meeting of the CF-FA, Strasbourg, 15–17 November 2006, p. 7.

telephone, letters, e-mail, etc.), and contact on a level of information (for instance sending recent photographs, medical reports, etc.).[273]

The Explanatory Report to the Convention affords national states the right to ascribe their meaning under the term "family ties". This could also include *de facto* family relationships (persons living in the same household, at the time being or in the past – for instance former foster parents, other relatives,[274] a parent's spouse or former spouse who is not the child's parent, or a person who has cohabited with the parent and the child).[275] The expression "having family ties" has been taken from the ECtHR and is used in most cases to distinguish between family life based on relationships outside marriage and within marriage. Nevertheless, the purpose of the term is also to acknowledge the acceptance of some other than legal factors that may indicate that a family relationship is existent and thus constituted.

The possibility of making specific arrangements in allocating contact for several persons is not only allowed but also encouraged in the Convention.[276] According to the case law of the ECtHR, Member States have an obligation to facilitate the exercise of the rights "in a manner calculated to allow these ties to develop normally".[277] Even though contact priority is given to legally recognised parents, persons other than parents, having family ties also have a right to apply for contact (even though it is not necessary for the application to be approved) in concordance with the best interests of the child.[278] This contact should be subject to the parents' and child's (having sufficient understanding) approval. In these terms, the judicial authorities should not refuse an application for contact if *de facto* family life exists with the child, but should consider the grounds and best interests of the child in granting such contact. In the context of sperm donation by a known donor to single women whom the child has met and established contact with already, the Convention allows application for temporal or permanent contact. Legalising a family tie in such a way may eventually lead to establishing the fatherhood of the donor if consent is obtained from the donor, the mother and the child.

With regard to the child's capacity to form and express their own views, the Member States are left to define the criteria to enable them to participate in matters when their interests are concerned. The right of the child to be informed

---

273 See the Explanatory Report on the Convention on Contact concerning Children, available online: http://conventions.coe.int/Treaty/en/Reports/Html/192.htm.

274 See, for instance, the case of *Boyle v. the United Kingdom*, European Court of Human Rights, No. 15680/90, judgment of 28.02.1999. The Court considered that the application of the uncle for contact with his nephew was admissible and a subject of procedural safeguard under article 8, paragraph 2 of the ECHR.

275 Explanatory Report on the Convention on Contact concerning Children, available online: http://conventions.coe.int/Treaty/en/Reports/Html/192.htm.

276 *Ibid*. p. 8.

277 *Ibid*. p. 11.

278 *Ibid*. p. 11.

and to express his or her views is regulated in article 6 of the Convention following articles 3 and 6 of the ECECR. The judicial authority of each Member State is under an obligation to enable the child to be informed, consulted and to express their own views, even though it is not under any obligation to accept them as absolute. On the contrary, the judicial authority should make the final decision based on the circumstances and what is considered to be the best interests of the child. Parents on the other hand are under an obligation to allow the exercise of the right to contact of the child with the other parent or the other persons with whom the child may have family ties. This elevates the child's right of contact to the level of a fundamental right with priority over parents' possible wishes to impose obstacles to the exercise of this right.[279]

The amount of national legislation that allows contact with third persons who are not biologically related to the child, if this is in the best interests of the child, has increased.[280] Some legal systems expressly mention persons with whom a "socio-familial" relationship exists,[281] while others refer to persons who have acted *in loco parentis*.[282] The purpose of this right is to appreciate and maintain a relationship with persons with whom the child has developed a significant emotional bond as a way of lifting the lived reality to an important level next to biology and genetics. Since legal affiliation as predominantly grounded in biology took precedence for a long period in the past, accepting the importance of social realities and integrating it into the legal system is developing gradually.[283] As such, there is a growing tendency to consider the right to contact as a right of the child and not primarily as a right of the parents. Thus, in much legislation nowadays the child's wishes are detrimental in the enabling and enforcing of contacts[284] or even vetoing legal orders.[285]

279 *Ibid.* p. 13.

280 Under different circumstances and conditions, it is present in the legislation of Austria, Belgium, the UK, the Netherlands, Serbia and Switzerland. See Schwenzer I., "Tensions Between Legal, Biological and Social Conceptions of Parentage", *Electronic Journal of Comparative Law*, Vol. 11, No. 3, 2007, p. 24, available online: www.ejcl.org/113/article113-6.pdf, p. 17.

281 For instance Germany. *Ibid.*

282 For instance Ireland. *Ibid.*

283 For instance see the case *Görgülüv. Germany*, No. 74969/01, [2004] ECHR 89 (26 February 2004), FamPra.ch 2005, 93 et seq. *Ibid.* pp. 17 and 18.

284 *Ibid.*, referring to the legislation of Belgium, Canada, Denmark and Switzerland.

285 *Ibid.*, referring to the legislation of Austria (14 years) and the Netherlands (12 years).

CHAPTER 3
OVERVIEW OF THE NATIONAL REGULATIONS IN TEN EUROPEAN COUNTRIES

3.1. GENERAL OVERVIEW

3.1.1. THE RIGHT OF SINGLE WOMEN TO USE ART

From the information gathered by the International Federation of Fertility Societies Surveillance 2010,[286] single women are allowed access to ART as a principle rule covered by statuses or guidelines in:

- EU Member countries: Belgium, Bulgaria, Denmark, Estonia, Finland, Greece, Hungary, Spain and the United Kingdom.
- Acceding EU countries: Iceland, Montenegro and Serbia.
- Other countries in the world: Canada, Israel, Russia, South Africa, USA, Belarus, Ghana, India, New Zealand, South Africa, Ukraine and Venezuela.

Single women have access to ART even though it is regulated neither by statutes nor by guidelines in: the Dominican Republic, Israel, Jamaica, Mexico, Nigeria, Uganda and Uruguay.

A rather political value was given to the issue of single women's access to ART in Slovenia where it was decided by referendum on 17 June 2001. After long debates, Slovenians decided that single women should not have access to ART with 72.36% of voters opposing and only 26.38% supporting it.[287]

From the European countries analysed below, single women cannot exercise their reproductive right by sperm donation in Italy, France, Germany and Sweden. They can apply for sperm donation and eventually conceive a child only under particular circumstances in the Republic of Macedonia, Republic of Croatia and Republic of Serbia. Single women are allowed access to ART without particular

[286] American Society for Reproductive Medicine, *International Federation of Fertility Societies Surveillance 2010*, Elsevier, 2010.

[287] See more Zerjav T., "The Politicization of Singlehood", *CEU eTD Collection*, 2012, p. 10.

conditions and on equal grounds to everybody in the Netherlands, Belgium and the United Kingdom.

3.1.2. THE RIGHT OF THE CHILD TO KNOW THE IDENTITY OF THE DONOR

Identifying information regarding the donor can be revealed (regulated by statutes or guidelines) in:

- EU Member countries: Germany, the Netherlands, Slovakia, Sweden, Finland and the United Kingdom.
- Acceding EU countries: Montenegro.
- Other countries in the world: Brazil, Australia, Hong Kong, Argentina, New Zealand, the USA and Vietnam.[288]

According to the Steering Committee of Bioethics, identifying the donor, initiated by the child, is also possible in Austria, Czech Republic, Estonia, Greece, Norway, Spain, Iceland, Georgia, Switzerland and Canada. Identifying information can also be available for the court only in Latvia, Russia, Slovakia, Ukraine and Israel.[289]

Identifying information regarding the donor can be revealed (even though regulation does not exist in statutes and/or guidelines) in Cameroon, Columbia, the Democratic Republic of Congo, El Salvador, Jamaica, Peru, Togo and Uruguay. The more recent *IFFS Surveillance* (2013) found that in general, the tolerance towards IVF practice is broadening, while the greater inclusiveness and disclosure of the identity of donors is increasing.[290] In this sense, the most recent modifications of the national laws reported in the domain of disclosure of identifying information about the donor were in Belarus, Belgium, Denmark, Hong Kong, Portugal, Russia and Switzerland.[291]

Non-identifying information regarding the donor is more common.

From the analysed European countries below, children do not have a right to know the donor in the Republic of Macedonia, Republic of Serbia, France, Germany and Belgium (Germany and Belgium are specific situations; see more below in the same chapter). Children do have the right to know the donor's identity in the Republic of Croatia, the Netherlands, the United Kingdom and Sweden.

---

288 *Ibid.* pp. 62–67.

289 See more in *Replies by the Member States to the Questionnaire on Access to Medically Assisted Procreation (MAP) and on the Right to Know their Origin for Children Born after MAP*, Steering Committee of Bioethics, CDBI/INF (2005) 7 REV 2, Strasbourg, 9 February 2012, p. 65.

290 Ory S., Devroey P. *et al.* (eds.), *IFFS Surveillance*, 2013 p. 148, available online: http://c.ymcdn.com/sites/www.iffs-reproduction.org/resource/resmgr/iffs_surveillance_09-19-13.pdf.

291 *Ibid.* p. 76.

3.1.3. LEGAL PROCEEDINGS FOR ESTABLISHING PATERNITY OF ART CONCEIVED CHILDREN

It is possible to contest the maternity and paternity of children conceived by ART in several countries. These possibilities, though, mostly represent the exception and not the rule and therefore are used to remedy other unexpected situations (such as a child conceived without the consent of the husband, revoked consent, the child was not born as a result of the ART procedure to which the consent referred, etc.). The possibility of contesting parenthood is available in Austria (although it is clearly stated that the donor is excluded by law from the possibility of being the legal father), Croatia (as an exception and related to misuse of the consent), Finland, Greece, Norway and Sweden (if it is not probable that the child was conceived by donor insemination or IVF), Switzerland (if the donor has knowingly donated sperm to a person without having a licence to carry out ART), Turkey (by DNA tests), Ukraine and Canada.[292]

In cases of single women conceiving children, the contestation of legal fatherhood is not an issue, because there is no candidate for the role. Nevertheless, a man has the possibility of recognising as his or adopting the child (if there is consent of the mother). The proceedings for establishing paternity, on the other hand, are mostly based on determining the exact genetic link between the father and child via the certainty of a DNA test. Therefore in most countries the proceedings for establishing the parental role are strictly related to the genetic link or existent *factual family life* with the child (*possession d'état*). Establishing the fatherhood of a donor who has consented to remain anonymous or not to build a family life with the child runs against the terms and conditions under which he donated at the time when the donation took place.

From the analysed countries below, the situation is as follows. The proceedings for establishing fatherhood in relation to ART conceived children are explicitly forbidden in the Republic of Macedonia (articles 62, 63 and 71 Family Law); Republic of Croatia (article 85 Family Law); Republic of Serbia (article 58 Family Law); Italy (article 9 Law on Medically Assisted Procreation, article 235 Civil Code); France (articles 311-19, 311-20 Civil Code), the Netherlands,[293] Belgium[294] and Sweden.[295]

---

292 *Replies by the Member States to the Questionnaire on Access to Medically Assisted Procreation (MAP) and on the Right to Know their Origin for Children Born after MAP*, Steering Committee of Bioethics, CDBI/INF (2005) 7 REV 2, Strasbourg, 9 February 2012, pp. 76–79.

293 Article 1:207 of the Dutch Civil Code a contrario. The donor is not to be assimilated with the "*verwekker*".

294 Article 2(p) and (q) of the Law on Medically Assisted Reproduction and the Allocation of Redundant Embryos and Gametes.

295 See more *Replies by the Member States to the Questionnaire on Access to Medically Assisted Procreation (MAP) and on the Right to Know their Origin for Children Born after MAP*, Steering Committee of Bioethics, CDBI/INF (2005) 7 REV 2, Strasbourg, 9 February 2012, p. 79.

The proceedings for establishing fatherhood in relation to ART conceived children are allowed, but their legal purpose is different and not related to establishing the fatherhood of the donor, in Germany, (sections 1599 and 1600 Civil Code) and in the United Kingdom (section 41 HEFA, section 4 Children Act).

The European national regulations that follow below are chosen on four grounds that correspond with the separate topics that are being examined: (1) the legal similarity and geographical vicinity with the Republic of Macedonia, (2) the varieties in between both extremes (restrictive and liberal) when it comes to exercising reproductive choices, (3) the varieties in between anonymous and non-anonymous donations as a concept of regulating sperm donations, and (4) the modus of how the countries in between both extremes and their varieties deal with the issue of civil proceedings for establishing fatherhood in relation to children conceived that way.

The first ground is the similarity of the legal tradition with the Republic of Macedonia. Namely, the Republic of Serbia and the Republic of Croatia are both successor countries from the Former Yugoslavian Republic, just as the Republic of Macedonia is, therefore originating from a common legal context. Nevertheless, they have developed similar, but also fundamentally different, regulations in the field of reproductive rights of single women. The geographic vicinity is also a reason why the restrictive regulation of exercising reproductive rights in one country can be noticed and influential in another, more liberal neighbouring country.

The second ground for choosing the legal overview of the national legislation of countries is the variety between both extremes – more conservative, and therefore restrictive, or more liberal, and therefore open when it comes to exercising reproductive choices. The rationale behind both regulations and the varieties in between could be rewarding for the research that tends to take an international perspective. An example of restrictive national regulation is Italy, in which even allogeneic donations are forbidden. Bypassing the ban on heterologous inseminations but still restricting the reproductive right to single women is a reason for looking at the regulations in France, Germany and Sweden. Examples of countries with more liberal regulations that allow (without any fundamental conditions) single women to exercise their reproductive rights include the Netherlands, Belgium and the United Kingdom.

Bearing in mind the novelty and actuality of the research questions, the third ground for the national context choices is the pioneering roles of those countries that introduced the concept of revealing the donor's identity and took a child-oriented stand. Along these lines, the aim is to introduce the problem of the impossibility of a child conceived by sperm donation to single women bringing proceedings for establishing fatherhood on a level that will allow comparison. In this way, it will be more evident and therefore possible to diagnose the drawbacks and problems as well as the advantages of and possible solutions fora more consistent application of ART.

The fourth ground is the essence of the research interest itself, namely how the countries within their systems of values and legal traditions appreciate the interests of the child conceived by sperm donation by allowing or not allowing the exercise of their right to civil proceedings for establishing fatherhood.

It has been noticed, though, that the national regulations cannot be categorised into groups because they differ not just with regard to these fundamental grounds, but also in the way they treat particular issues within particular grounds. Accordingly, what is considered a rule has many exceptions that sometimes even change or modify the rationale of the protection behind the rule. For instance, the countries that introduced the concept of revealing the donor's identity do have particular conditions regarding when and how to do so, without excluding the possibility of anonymous donations as well. Sweden is liberal when it comes to the rights of the child to know the donor, but explicitly forbids single women to found families by sperm donations. The Republic of Serbia allows single women to conceive a child by sperm donation only under very restricted conditions and administrative procedures that for some women makes it impossible to count on that option. The conclusion is that due to the novelty of the issues and the difficulty to foresee the future consequences in relation to the exercise of reproductive rights and the best interest of the child, the regulations are also "experimental". In this sense, the already adult children conceived by sperm donations with their right to know and be taken care of by both parents are re-examining and guiding the developmental path of the legal necessities for the present time and for the future.

3.2. REPUBLIC OF MACEDONIA

3.2.1. INTRODUCTION OF THE LEGAL CONTEXT IN APPLYING ART

The topic of artificial insemination (thus not covering the other reproductive technologies) has been regulated in the Socialist Federal Republic of Yugoslavia by the Health Measures in Exercising Freedom of Choice in Childbearing Act since 1977. The Act allows flexible interpretation of the issue of freedom of choice in childbearing and access to ART: while favouring couples, it does not explicitly exclude single persons. On the contrary, article 34, paragraph 1 in conjunction with article 32 stipulates that any adult, sane, healthy woman of reproductive age is entitled to medical help in reproduction if she has been proven to have problems conceiving, because of either her or her partner's infertility.[296]

[296] Zerjav T., "The Politicization of Singlehood", *CEU eTD Collection*, 2012, p. 10.

The independent Republic of Macedonia regulated assisted reproduction in the later Law on Bio-medically Assisted Fertilisation, enacted in April 2008.[297] The Law systematically covers the issues regarding the application of reproductive technologies, which had not been done before in the independent Republic of Macedonia. Even though the proposed draft of the law satisfied the need for a harmonised and modern law, it lacked a critical public review. Its approval was not preceded by a public debate, which in light of the sensitive issues it should have been and therefore the law proposal did not receive any serious criticism or suggestions. The fundamental principles of the Law are respect for human rights, and the dignity and privacy of individuals undergoing the medical procedure, as well as for the donors of genital cells and embryos.[298] The Law explicitly stipulates the reasons for implementing medical assistance: achieving insemination is possible if previous treatment or treatment with other methods was unsuccessful, and to protect against severe congenital diseases being transmitted to the children.[299]

The basic legal source for regulating family life and, among other issues, the relationship between parents and children, is the Family Law of the Republic of Macedonia.[300] This law continues the tradition of the family law regulations of the former Yugoslavia with the codification of the Republic of Macedonia in 1992.

3.2.2. THE RIGHT OF SINGLE WOMEN TO USE ART

The Macedonian Law on Bio-medically Assisted Fertilisation[301] allows realisation of single women's reproductive rights relating to the execution of the rights with certain conditions such as having had previous treatment or treatment using other methods that were unsuccessful, in accordance with the women's age and general parenting capability.[302]

With a regulation like this, theoretically, the possibility for a single woman to conceive without a partner may prove problematic from several points of view. Firstly, infertility is not the rationale behind a single woman's attempt to conceive using assisted reproduction. From a general point of view, it is not possible to

[297] Law on Bio-medically Assisted Fertilisation, Official Gazette of Republic of Macedonia, No. 37, 19.03.2008.

[298] Law on Bio-medically Assisted Fertilisation, article 2, paragraph 1.

[299] Law on Bio-medically Assisted Fertilisation, article 3.

[300] Family Law, Official Gazette of Republic of Macedonia 80/92, 22.12.1992.

[301] Law on Bio-medically Assisted Fertilisation.

[302] Law on Bio-medically Assisted Fertilisation, article 9, stipulates as follows: "Adult men and women having legal capacity, married or living under an extra-marital relationship, as well as unmarried women who are not in an extra-marital relationship shall have the right to use the assisted fertilisation procedure, provided that the previous treatment or the treatment using other methods was unsuccessful, and who in accordance with their age and general condition are capable of parenting."

apply the definition of infertility[303] since the single woman has not been engaged in unprotected intercourse for 12 months for the purpose of reproduction. It is also debateable how to apply the provision in law that she has the right to use assisted fertilisation if previous treatment was unsuccessful or treatment using other methods was also unsuccessful. Secondly, infertile single woman would not be able to conceive using sperm donations anyhow. Nevertheless, in practice, single women use ART to conceive without conditions. Moreover, many single women from neighbouring countries (such as Serbia, due to its rather complicated national administration for single women to use ART) travel to Macedonian medical facilities in order to undergo an ART procedure.[304]

3.2.3. THE RIGHT OF THE CHILD TO KNOW THE IDENTITY OF THE DONOR

The authorised health care institutions are obliged to provide protection of all personal, medical and genetic data of the donors, as well as to undertake all necessary measures not to reveal the identity of the donor and his/her family and vice versa.[305] All data regarding the donor's provenance, health biography and births resulting from the donation are to be afforded the utmost confidentiality in the Register of Donors in the authorised health care institutions for 30 years as from the date of their entry.[306] A child born by insemination with donated genital cells or embryos, 18 years of age and able to form an opinion on his/her own can request sight of the data regarding the health condition of the donor in the State Register of Bio-medically Assisted Fertilisation only for a medically justified reason and with previously obtained approval from the State Committee.[307] Nevertheless, this provision does not confront the accepted anonymity of the donor's identity which protects the donor's interests only and neglects the right of the child to know his/her genetic origin.

In this line, the Law on Bio-medically Assisted Fertilisation compromises the right of the child to know his/her genetic identity by prioritising the interests of donors and parents before the interests of the child, even though the former

---

303 *Infertility* is defined as a failure to conceive following 12 months of unprotected intercourse. Twelve months is the lowest reference limit for *time to pregnancy* by the World Health Organization. See also: De Melo-Martin, I., "On Cloning Human Beings", *Bioethics*, Vol. 16, No. 3, 2002, pp. 246–265; Cooper T.G., Noonan E., von Eckardstein S., *et al.*, "World Health Organization Reference Values for Human Semen Characteristics", *Human Reproduction Update*, Vol. 16, No. 3, 2010, pp. 231–245.

304 Mickovik D., Ristov A., "Bio-medically Assisted Fertilization in Republic of Macedonia", in Jansen B.C.S., Ignovska E. (eds.), *Law, Public Health Care System and Society. Macedonia – Social Policy, Legislation, Biomedicine and Ethics of Organ Transplantation, Fertilization and ART*, Academische Verlagsgemeinschaft, 2012.

305 Law on Bio-medically Assisted Fertilisation, article 7.

306 Law on Bio-medically Assisted Fertilisation, article 48.

307 Law on Bio-medically Assisted Fertilisation, article 57.

Yugoslavia and Republic of Macedonia as a successor country ratified the Convention on the Rights of the Child.[308]

3.2.4. LEGAL PROCEEDINGS FOR ESTABLISHING PATERNITY OF ART CONCEIVED CHILDREN

The parental responsibilities of the beneficiaries of bio-medically assisted fertilisation are derived from the informed written consent at the beginning of the procedure with the possibility of it being withdrawn before the implantation of the spermatozoids, the ova or the embryo into the woman's body.[309] The consent given has the legal significance of a statement for recognising parenthood after the child is born.

As harmonised with family law, donors do not have parental responsibilities in terms of rights or obligations towards the conceived child.

The Family Law provisions for establishing and rebutting parenthood do not apply when a child is conceived through assisted fertilisation or when a child is adopted. Namely, it is explicitly forbidden to claim or rebut paternity and maternity before the court if the child is conceived through artificial insemination.[310] The rationale behind this ban in the law lies in the accepted protection of the legal family of the child, but also in the protection of the privacy of donors.

Litigation with regard to establishing parenthood based on DNA proof concerning the biological/genetic relatedness with the child would threaten the accepted concept of anonymity of donors, and thus the secrecy surrounding biological/genetic parents in the case of assisted reproduction and adoption. It is also considered that it could endanger the already established family life of the child with the legal parents. Nevertheless, by protecting the anonymity of donors and the parents that gave the child up for adoption, as well as the later legal parents, the legislator infringes the right of the child to know his/her biological/genetic origins as stipulated in articles 7 and 8 of the CRC, and article 8 of the ECHR. This pattern of regulating legal affiliation places children in categories based on grounds of birth and offers different treatments, and accordingly, discriminates among them (confronting articles 12, 2 and 18 of the CRC).

---

308 See footnote 124.

309 Law on Bio-medically Assisted Fertilisation, article 12.

310 Family Law, 1992, articles 62, 63 and 71.

3.3. CROATIA

3.3.1. INTRODUCTION OF THE LEGAL CONTEXT IN APPLYING ART

Medically assisted procreation in Croatia has been regulated since 1978 by the Act of Exercising the Right to Free Decision of Giving Birth to Children.[311] The Croatian regulation on ART was among the pioneers in the field, bearing in mind that 1978 was the year of the first official test-tube baby.[312] The Act regulated three important parts of human reproduction: voluntary miscarriage, sterilisation and artificial insemination.[313] The name of the Act reflected the attitude of that time, according to which everybody had the right to decide freely the number and dynamics of their childbirths. As such, the right found a place in the Constitution of the former Socialistic Republic of Croatia of 1974.[314] After the political and constitutional changes in 1990, the reproductive right of individuals was restricted and ART became considered an exclusive right to couples (preferably married).[315] The consequences of the restrictions made the new regulation in the Medical Fertilisation Act 2009 controversial from the beginning.[316] Even though a new Law was enacted in 2012, the application of the medically assisted technologies and the consequences for family life are still a topic of ongoing public discussions.

---

311 Act for Exercising the Right to Free Decision of Giving Birth to Children, Official Gazette of the Republic of Croatia, 18/1978.

312 The history of artificial insemination for some authors can be traced back long before the first officially announced birth in 1978 in the UK. See more in Bartholomew GW., "The Development and Use of Artificial Insemination", *Eugenics Review*, Vol. 49, No. 4, 1958, pp. 187–195.

313 Korac A., "Draft of the Croatian Act on Medically Assisted Procreation – Balancing Procreative Rights", *Drustvena Istrazivanja*, God. 9, Br. 2-3, 1999, pp. 229–238.

314 Constitution of the Socialist Republic of Croatia, *Official Gazette* 8/1974.

315 Constitution of the Republic of Croatia, *Official Gazette* 56/90 and 135/97. The Croatian Parliament hesitated to give too great a liberty to the procreative rights of individuals at the constitutional level. See more Korac A., "Draft of the Croatian Act on Medically Assisted Procreation – Balancing Procreative Rights", *Drustvena Istrazivanja*, God. 9, Br. 2-3, 1999, p. 231.

316 Medical Fertilization Act, *Official Gazette of the Republic of Croatia*, No. 88/2009. History of the law (taken from: http://web.potpomognutaoplodnja.info/index.php?option=com_content&view=article&id=255:summary-of-the-croatian-art-law&catid=42&Itemid=85).

May 2009 – Law proposal first published and sent to the Parliament. The public discussion was centred on the legal problem of unmarried couples to use ART and not on medical aspects.

June 2009 – Croatian Society for Human Reproduction sent a negative opinion on the law to the Croatian Parliament.

July 2009 – The law was passed with 70 supporting votesout of 153 seats, after an amendment which permits access to ART to unmarried couples.

September 2009 – The patient association Roda filed suit before the Constitutional Court.

October 2009 – The parliament passed changes of the law by which the donors became anonymous and the extra-marital couples were facilitated to prove the existence of the factual relationship as a requirement to be ART beneficiaries.

3.3.2. THE RIGHT OF SINGLE WOMEN TO USE ART

The 1978 Act for Exercising the Right to Freely Decide on Giving Birth to Children clearly attributes reproductive freedom to everybody that can practise it at the level of a free decision. The Medical Fertilisation Act 2009 stipulated that the right to medical fertilisation primarily belongs to adults and capable men and women who are married and considering their age and general health condition are capable of performing parental responsibilities.[317] Unmarried couples' rights to use ART attracted controversies. Following human rights criticism over the criteria for couples to be entitled to treatment, the Law was amended in October 2009, therefore making it possible for unmarried couples to use ART. With the topical 2012 Law on Medically Assisted Fertilisation, couples can be beneficiaries of the ART procedure if their partnership is registered.[318] Single women can also be ART beneficiaries on the condition that they have undergone infertility treatments already or they do not have any other prospects of their infertility being cured.[319] This explicitly means that single women can reproduce using ART only if suffering from a medical condition. However, implicitly, single women without a partner who do not suffer from infertility are still barred from using ART.

3.3.3. THE RIGHT OF THE CHILD TO KNOW THE IDENTITY OF THE DONOR

The 1978 Act for Exercising the Right to Free Decision of Giving Birth to Children became insufficient and obsolete regarding affiliation in the ART context.[320] Under the first version of the Medical Fertilisation Act 2009, a child born by sperm donation was entitled to access the conception data records kept by the State Registry of Medical Fertilisation of the Ministry Responsible for Health Care only after approval of the National Committee for Medical Fertilisation and solely for medically justifiable reasons and taking into account the well-being of the child.[321] As part of the changes with the new law from 2012, ART conceived children are allowed to obtain identifying information about their biological parents once they turn 18, while their legal parents hold the responsibility to inform them of the modus of their conception before they reach maturity.[322] Nevertheless, donors do not hold any parental obligations or responsibilities

[317] Medical Fertilisation Act, 2009, article 6.

[318] *Predlog Zakona o Medicinski Potpomognutoj Oplodnji*, Vlada Republike Hrvatske, Zagreb, 2012, article 11, paragraph 1 and 3.

[319] *Ibid.* article 10, paragraphs 3 and 5.

[320] See more Korac A., "Draft of the Croatian Act on Medically Assisted Procreation – Balancing Procreative Rights", *Drustvena Istrazivanja*, God. 9, Br. 2-3, 1999, p. 230.

[321] Medical Fertilisation Act, 2009, article 10.

[322] *Predlog Zakona o Medicinski Pomognutoj Oplodnji*, 2012, article 15.

towards the conceived children.[323] They also do not hold a right to know the identity of the women or children for whom they are donating.[324]

3.3.4. LEGAL PROCEEDINGS FOR ESTABLISHING PATERNITY OF ART CONCEIVED CHILDREN

The new Law on Medically Assisted Fertilisation protects donors in relation to any possible parental responsibility that might be claimed in the future, remaining consistent with the Croatian Family Law that firmly forbids legal proceedings for rebutting and establishing both fatherhood and motherhood in relation to ART conceived children.[325]

3.4. SERBIA

3.4.1. INTRODUCTION OF THE LEGAL CONTEXT IN APPLYING ART

The affiliation of artificially conceived children was legally introduced in the Law on Marriage and Family Relations 1980.[326] After the political changes and prior to the current regulation, the matters regarding the application of ART were regulated by different legal acts and statutes.[327] The new Family Law of Serbia was enacted in 2005.[328] The assisted reproductive technologies are regulated by the Law on Infertility Treatment through a Procedure of Bio-medically Assisted Fertilisation 2009.[329] The Republic of Serbia was one of the last European countries to legally regulate assisted reproduction in one specific law. For some authors, the experiences of the other countries already regulating the field were not seized

---

323 *Ibid.* article 19, paragraph 5.

324 *Ibid.* article 19, paragraph 4.

325 *Obiteljski Zakon*, Broj: 01-081-03-2596/2, Zagreb, 16. Srpnja 2003, article 85.

326 Kovaček-Stanić G., "Porodicni Zakon Srbije iz 2005 godine u kontekstu planiranja porodice", *Zbornik Matice srpske za drustvene nauke*, br. 121, 2006, pp. 157–169, p. 164.

327 The Law for Health Care and Health Insurance, the Law on Pregnancy Interruption in Health Institutions in the Republic of Serbia, the Law on Conditions and Procedures for Pregnancy Interruptions in the Republic of Montenegro, the Law on Conditions and Procedures for Taking and Transplantation of Human Organs, as well as normative acts of health institutions. See more in *Replies by the Member States to the Questionnaire on Access to Medically Assisted Procreation (MAP) and on the Right to Know their Origin for Children Born after MAP*, Steering Committee of Bioethics, CDBI/INF (2005) 7 REV 2, Strasbourg, 9 February 2012.

328 Породични закон Србије, *Службен гласник Републике Србије* 18/05, 2005.

329 Закон о лечењу неплодности поступцима биомедицински потпомогнутог оплогења, *Службен гласник Републике Србије* 72/2009.

upon in a productive, systematic, theoretical or practical way to develop the new regulation.[330]

3.4.2. THE RIGHT OF SINGLE WOMEN TO USE ART

The title of the Law itself – Law on Infertility Treatment through a Procedure of Bio-medically Assisted Fertilisation – clearly depicts the main intention of the legislator and the context in which the law was drafted. The main goal of bio-medically assisted fertilisation is to assist procreation when it is not possible to cure infertility. Therefore the treatment addresses primarily couples (either married or living in an extra-marital relationship) for whom their infertility cannot be cured and who cannot conceive children in any other way.[331] Single women are addressed only under exceptional circumstances: living alone or having obtained consent from the Minister Responsible for Health and the Minister Responsible for Family Relations if there are justified reasons.[332] It is not precisely specified which reasons are considered "justified", and if single women are judged based on their infertility or partnerless status. For some authors, these legal provisions restrict rather than increase single women's reproductive freedom. Because of their complex administrative procedure, a number of women from Serbia travel to other countries to enforce their right to be beneficiaries of ART.[333]

Regardless of the possibility of single women using ART, even if under exceptional circumstances, some authors still consider that a solution of this kind is maleficent towards the child who will be condemned to be fatherless from the beginning, thus running against the right to be raised by both parents.[334]

3.4.3. THE RIGHT OF THE CHILD TO KNOW THE IDENTITY OF THE DONOR

The child does not have the right to know the identity of the donor in allogeneic inseminations. On the contrary, the purpose of the donation is mostly attributed

330 Kovaček-Stanić G., "Porodično pravni aspekt biomedicinski potpomognuto gplođenja u pravu Srbije i Evropskim pravima", *Zbornik Matice srpske za društvene nauke*, br. 131, 2010, pp. 415–430.

331 Закон о лечењу неплодности поступцима биомедицински потпомогнутог оплогења, 2009, article 26, paragraph 1.

332 *Ibid.* article 26, paragraph 3.

333 Mickovik D., Ristov A., "Bio-medically Assisted Fertilization in Republic of Macedonia", in Jansen B.C.S., Ignovska E. (eds.), *Law, Public Health Care System and Society.Macedonia – Social Policy, Legislation, Biomedicine and Ethics of Organ Transplantation, Fertilization and ART*, Academische Verlagsgemeinschaft, 2012.

334 Kovaček-Stanić G., "Porodičnopravni aspect biomedicinski potpomognutog oplođenja u pravu Srbije i Evropskim pravima", *Zbornik Matice srpske za društvene nauke*, br. 131, 2010, p. 418.

to conceiving a child in a heterosexual family, thus promoting natal policy, the children's stable family life, without interrupting their social and legal affiliation, while at the same time promoting the interest of donors in terms of their privacy. The information regarding the donor's identity is to be kept as a professional secret.[335] Furthermore, it is explicitly stated that donors hold neither any rights nor any obligations towards the conceived children who possess their genetic material.[336]

3.4.4. LEGAL PROCEEDINGS FOR ESTABLISHING PATERNITY OF ART CONCEIVED CHILDREN

The provisions that forbid ART conceived children from exercising their right to know the identity of the heterologous donor while him being clearly relieved from any rights and obligations towards them, are consistent with the Family Law which forbids legal proceedings for establishing fatherhood.[337]

When a child is conceived to a married or extra-marital couple, the possibility for rebutting the fatherhood of the presumed father (the husband) or the man that gave consent (the extra-marital partner) is due to the suspicion that the child was not conceived in the ART procedure to which they consented.[338] The other possibility for rebutting parenthood is when the mother's partner did not consent to ART treatment at all.[339] This regulation is similar to the one from the Law dated 1980.

According to Kovaček-Stanić, the legal consequences of proceedings for establishing parenthood in relation to ART conceived children operate against the essence and goal of sperm donation itself.[340]

---

335 Закон о лечењу неплодност и поступцима биомедицински потпомогнутог оплогења, 2009, article 48.

336 *Ibid.* article 51.

337 Породичнизакон Србије, 2005, article 58, paragraph 5.

338 *Ibid.* article 58, paragraph 4.

339 Kovaček-Stanić G., "Porodicni Zakon Srbije iz 2005 godine u kontekstu planiranja porodice", *Zbornik Matice srpske za društvene nauke*, br. 121, 2006, p. 164.

340 Kovaček-Stanić G., "Porodičnopravni aspect biomedicinski potpomognutog oplođenja u pravu Srbije i Evropskim pravima", *Zbornik Matice srpske za društvene nauke*, br. 131, 2010, p. 422.

3.5. ITALY

3.5.1. INTRODUCTION OF THE LEGAL CONTEXT IN APPLYING ART

Italy was the last country within the European Union in which more than 100 private clinics were performing ART without any regulation, control or even a minimum set of rules or guidelines.[341]

The controversial regulation in the Law on Medically Assisted Procreation and in the Guidelines on Medically Assisted Reproduction was passed in 2004, after more than a decade of long lasting debates and several different law proposals.[342] According to many authors, the restrictive regulation failed to meet expectations. Instead, it offered a legal framework that in most of the other European countries is considered malpractice.[343] Almost 10 years after the enactment of the Law, some authors even called the prohibition of heterologous fertilisation "a medical exodus" of Italian couples outside the Italian territory.[344] Bearing in mind the historical influence of the Catholic Church on the overall philosophy of the law claiming sanctity of human life from its conception, the law guarantees the rights of "all stakeholders, including the unborn child" as stipulated in its first article. In contrast to the Law on Abortion, dating from 1978, which allows suppression of post-implantation embryos within 90 days since the woman's last menstrual period, the Law on Medically Assisted Procreation forbids embryo cryoconservation and suppression in its article 14, paragraph 1.[345] The need for amending several parts of the Law was set forth in a 2005 Referendum, which rejected any amendments with 74% abstentions.[346]

The Civil Code regulates the persons and the family in its first book.[347]

---

341 Bohlen C., "Anything Goes in Italian Birth Science", *The Edmonton*, C6, 1995.

342 Rules on Medically Assisted Procreation, *Official Gazette*, No. 45, 24 February, 2004. See also online source: www.ieb-eib.org/en/pdf/loi-pma-italie-english.pdf. Guidelines on Medically Assisted Reproduction, *GazzettaUfficiale*, No. 191, 12 August, 2004.

343 See Benagiano G., Gianaroli L., "The New Italian IVF Legislation", *Reproductive BioMedicine Online*, Vol. 9, No. 2, 2004, pp. 117–125; Boggio, A., "Italy Enacts New Law on Medically Assisted Reproduction", *Human Reproduction*, Vol. 20, No. 5, 2005, pp. 1153–1157.

344 Parolin L.L., Metzler I., Schuster A., "(Not) Making 'Heternologous' Fertilization. The Italian ART Law and its Paradoxes", *Tecnoscienza, Italian Journal of Science & Technology Studies*, Vol. 4, No. 1, pp. 133–144, 2013.

345 Ibid. Boggio, A., "Italy Enacts New Law on Medically Assisted Reproduction", *Human Reproduction*, Vol. 20, No. 5, 2005, pp. 1153–1157.

346 *Replies by the Member States to the Questionnaire on Access to Medically Assisted Procreation (MAP) and on the Right to Know their Origin for Children Born after MAP*, Steering Committee of Bioethics, CDBI/INF (2005) 7 REV 2, Strasbourg, 9 February 2012, p. 11.

347 Il Codice Civile Italiano, *Gazzetta Ufficiale*, No. 79 del 4 aprile, 1942, Libro Primo – Delle Persone e della Famiglia.

3.5.2. THE RIGHT OF SINGLE WOMEN TO USE ART

According to the regulation on ART, both oocyte and sperm donation are forbidden. Article 4, paragraph 2 of the law stipulates that "it is prohibited to use technology on medically assisted procreation of heterologous type". This means that neither couples, nor single women may use sperm donation to conceive a child. Homologous (autologic) insemination though is allowed for heterosexual married or cohabiting partners who are alive and of a fertile age (article 5). For some authors,[348] this is against the Italian Constitution, which promotes the right to health care and equal protection, and also dislocates those seeking treatment into another, more ART liberal country.[349]

The first article of the Rules on Medically Assisted Procreation in its second paragraph stipulates the purpose of the ART treatment to be "removing causes of sterility or infertility only when there are no other effective treatment methods".[350] Consequently, article 4, paragraph 1 limits the use of ART to documented infertility proven and certified by medical procedure. These provisions also exclude single women as potential beneficiaries of the treatment, since the most common reason for using ART in single women cases does not have to be necessarily connected with infertility.

3.5.3. THE RIGHT OF THE CHILD TO KNOW THE IDENTITY OF THE DONOR

Allogeneic insemination is forbidden in Italy. Therefore, in principle, the genetic and legal fragmentation of fatherhood should not exist. In contrast, the genetic and intended parent should coincide in one father.

3.5.4. LEGAL PROCEEDINGS FOR ESTABLISHING PATERNITY OF ART CONCEIVED CHILDREN

Article 8 of the Law on Medically Assisted Procreation stipulates the juridical status of the newborn as a legitimate or recognised child of a couple, who have expressed the will to avail themselves of the techniques according article 6.

Therefore the law provides the same rights to ART children as to naturally conceived children. Nevertheless, the law predicts different treatment if the

---

348 Boggio, A., "Italy Enacts New Law on Medically Assisted Reproduction", *Human Reproduction*, Vol. 20, No. 5, 2005, pp. 1153–1157.

349 See also in the Italian Constitution, articles 3 and 29, *Gazzetta Ufficiale*, No. 298, 27 December 1948.

350 English translation available online: www.ieb-eib.org/en/pdf/loi-pma-italie-english.pdf.

compatibility between the natural and the legal parents is disturbed in cases of illegal fertilisations.

Article 9 of the same law forbids proceedings for establishing or rebutting parenthood when the provisions on forbidding allogeneic insemination are violated. Paragraph 3 continues that in the case of violation, the donor should not acquire legal parental responsibilities in concordance with article 235, paragraph 1 of the Civil Code and on appeal under article 263 of the Code. Therefore repudiation of paternity is prohibited even when illegal use is made of heterologous fertilisation. Gamete donors cannot have any legal parental ties with the born child.

3.6. FRANCE

3.6.1. INTRODUCTION OF THE LEGAL CONTEXT IN APPLYING ART

France regulated assisted reproduction in the Law on the Donation and Use of Elements and Products of the Human Body, Medically Assisted Procreation, and Prenatal Diagnosis (No. 94-654, 1994). This Law favours couples and does not provide treatment for single women without joint plans for parenthood with the donor.[351] The rationale behind this regulation is that children born with ART should have the right to live in two-parent families.[352] Consistent with this regulation, the later Bioethics Law (No. 2004-800, 2004) also includes the explicit requirement that access to ART should be given only to heterosexual couples, excluding homosexuals, as well as single women.[353] The treatment requirements are related to the inability to conceive a child due to a medical condition, thus automatically excluding homosexual couples and single women. This reproductive restriction is driven by the guiding principle of *projet parental* (parental project in terms of responsible parenthood), which primarily values children's rights over parents' rights. Along this line, only "appropriate good parents" are allowed to be engaged in the intentional creation of a family relation.[354] The French government

351 Lansac J., "French Law Concerning Medically-assisted Reproduction", *Human Reproduction*, Vol. 11, No. 9, 1996, pp. 1843–1847.

352 See more in: *Les lois de Bioéthique: Cinq ans après*, Étude adoptee par l'Assamblée générale du Conseil d'État le 25 novembre 1999, La Documentation française, Paris, 1999.

353 Act No. 2004-800 on Bioethics (codified in the Public Health Code, articles L. 1244-1 to L. 1244-4 for gametes donation and articles L. 2142 to L.2142-4 for medically assisted procreation). See more in *Replies by the Member States to the Questionnaire on Access to Medically Assisted Procreation (MAP) and on the Right to Know their Origin for Children Born after MAP*, Steering Committee of Bioethics, CDBI/INF (2005) 7 REV 2, Strasbourg, 9 February 2012, p. 8.

354 Cho C., "Defining Parenthood: Assisted Reproduction in France", *Yale Journal of Medicine & Law, (special edition) International Health Care*, Vol. 7, No. 2, 2011, p. 19.

has used *projet parental* to limit the term "optimal parenthood" to heterosexual couples.[355]

The recent scientific developments in the field of assisted reproduction imposed a need to update the Bioethics Law (2004). Following fierce and long debates, the French Parliament finally adopted the new Bioethics Law (2011-814 of 7 July 2011).[356] This new Law is inevitably linked, and therefore harmonised, with the Civil Code, Title VII (311-342-8) which regulates the affiliation between parents and children.

3.6.2. THE RIGHT OF SINGLE WOMEN TO USE ART

The Bioethics Law (2011)[357] follows the previous legal tradition. The Law authorises the exercise of the right to ART only in two cases: (1) in the case of a medically diagnosed infertility, or (2) in the case of a need to avoid transmission of a particularly grave illness to the child or to the partners, which want to conceive a child. Again, the Law excludes single women and homosexuals from the right to ART treatment and affords access to ART only to heterosexual couples.[358] The justification of the legislator for such a restrictive access is derived from the legal purpose of authorising ART, which is associated with medical and not social infertility.

3.6.3. THE RIGHT OF THE CHILD TO KNOW THE IDENTITY OF THE DONOR

The anonymity of sperm and ovum donations as an accepted principle since the Bioethics Law (1994) continues to be legal practice in the new Bioethics Law (2011).[359] However, this principle was challenged by the reality and position in which adults who had been conceived by ART found themselves. The debate that followed was fierce.[360] The first draft of the law amendments tried to combine the child's rights to know and the donor's rights to be anonymous by proposing a compromise: revealing the donor's identity only with their informed consent and if the matured child (18 years or older) initiates a legal procedure to reveal

355 *Ibid.*

356 Loi n° 2011-814 du 7 juillet 2011 relative à la bioéthique, *Journal Officiel*, 8 July 2011.

357 *Ibid.*

358 *Ibid.* article 33. The only change in this article is that the couple do not have to live together for two years as it was stipulated in the previous law.

359 *Ibid.* article 27.

360 Brunet L., Kunstmann J.-M., "Gamete Donation in France: the Future of the Anonymity Doctrine", *Medicine, Health Care and Philosophy*, No. 16, 2013, pp. 69–81. The authors enumerate some of the different standpoints in the debate: in favour of and opposing anonymity.

the information.[361] Nevertheless, the rules on donors' anonymity remained unchanged in the final version. The law refers to heterosexual couples only. The child is not even allowed to know the modus of their own conception. Sperm banks and clinics try to match donor and couple in order to achieve a resemblance making it less likely for the future offspring to question their biological roots. Some authors criticise the "imitating nature trend" calling the "fabrication of children" "the nearly perfect crime".[362] If single women were allowed access to ART, this "crime" would not be so perfect, since it would be evident that the child is fatherless. Nevertheless, revealing the identity of a donor registered in France is a criminal act liable to criminal prosecution (article 511-10 French Criminal Code).

Far away from promoting children's rights to know their parents' identity, mothers in France are still permitted to give birth anonymously,[363] while being informed of the right of the child to have their identity revealed.[364]

The right to know one's origin is different in the context of adoption. In this setting "the true parentage relationship" is balanced on individual bases with the "apparent status" (*possession d'état*) of factual emotional reality. The possession of states demonstrates belonging to the social family, making it impossible to initiate legal proceedings.[365] Therefore the adoption regulation is a "significant conceptual innovation which separated the idea of origins from the legal concept of parenthood", thus acknowledging that the right to know one's origin can be disassociated from the real, social and legal parental responsibilities.[366] According to Brunet, individuals' psychological identity should be independent of their civil identity. This author associates sperm donation with any other donation of parts and products of the human body. Accordingly, the doctrine of anonymity is a supreme expression of human solidarity, and the eventual revealing of the donor's identity should not result in any social or legal consequences.[367]

---

361 Bioethics Bill, No. 2911, French National Assembly, 20 October, 2010.

362 Brunet L., Kunstmann J.-M., "Gamete Donation in France: the Future of the Anonymity Doctrine", *Medicine, Health Care and Philosophy*, No. 16, 2013, pp. 69–81.

363 Article 316 of the Civil Code.

364 Article L. 222-6 of the Code de l'Action Socialeet des Families.

365 Brunet L., Kunstmann J.-M., "Gamete Donation in France: the Future of the Anonymity Doctrine", *Medicine, Health Care and Philosophy*, No. 16, 2013, pp. 69–81.

366 *Ibid.* See also Social Action and Families Code, articles L. 147 -1 and 147-7.

367 Brunet L., Kunstmann J.-M., "Gamete Donation in France: the Future of the Anonymity Doctrine", *Medicine, Health Care and Philosophy*, No. 16, 2013, pp. 69–81.

3.6.4. LEGAL PROCEEDINGS FOR ESTABLISHING PATERNITY OF ART CONCEIVED CHILDREN

The French Civil Code in Title VII, Section IV regulates the relationship between parents and children conceived by medically assisted procreation.[368] Article 311-19 stipulates that in a case of a medically assisted procreation with a third-party donor, no parental bonds can be established between the donor and conceived child. Article 311-20 continues in the same vein, stating that the consent given to ART prohibits any action for challenging parentage or claiming a status, unless under exceptional circumstances it can be proved that the child was not born out of ART or that the consent was deprived of effect.

The doctrine of "apparent status" usually presented in adoption cases has become a ground for a separate means of establishing paternity, valid as the certificate of birth or recognition, if supported by an affidavit.[369] In these terms, article 311-1 of the Civil Code stipulates that "apparent status shall result from a sufficient collection of facts showing a bond of parentage and relationship between an individual and the family to which the child belongs continuously". Furthermore, for greater legal certainty and stability, the facts are enumerated: the individual has always borne the name of those from whom he is said to descend; they have treated each other as if they were in a parental relationship; in their capacity the parents provided for his education, support and maintenance; and the child is recognised as such by the family, society, and the public authorities. If these conditions are fulfilled and presented in an affidavit on the initiative of the child or the parents, it is possible to become a modus for establishing the legal parenthood of the social parents holding "apparent status" with the child (article 311-3 of the Civil Code). Therefore the goal of these provisions is to promote a new balance between social and biological truth.[370]

3.7. GERMANY

3.7.1. INTRODUCTION OF THE LEGAL CONTEXT IN APPLYING ART

Assisted reproduction and the parental responsibilities that result from it are regulated in several legal documents: Act on the Protection of Embryos (*Embryonenschutzgesetz*) 1990/1991 in force; section 27a Social Code Book V

---

368 *Civil* Code, France. English Version (Légifrance), translated by Rouchette G., Berton A. (available online: www.legifrance.gouv.fr/content/download/1950/13681/.../Code_22.pdf).

369 Brunet L., Kunstmann J.-M., "Gamete Donation in France: the Future of the Anonymity Doctrine", *Medicine, Health Care and Philosophy,* No. 16, 2013, pp. 69–81, p. 75.

370 Brunet L., Kunstmann J.-M., "Gamete Donation in France: the Future of the Anonymity Doctrine", *Medicine, Health Care and Philosophy,* No. 16, 2013, pp. 69–81.

(*Sozialgesetzbuch* V) 2003/2004 in force; sections 1591 to 1600e, 1682, 1685 Civil Code (*Bürgerliches Gesetzbuch,* Reform in regard to Parents and Children 1997/1998 in force); section 9 Registration of Homosexual Partnership Act (*Lebenspartnerschaftsgesetz*) 2001/2001 in force; section 8b Transplantation Act (*Transplantionsgesetz*); and Tissues and Cells Regulation of the Transplantation Act (*TPG-Gewebeverordnung*) 2008/2008 in force.[371]

3.7.2. THE RIGHT OF SINGLE WOMEN TO USE ART

Only heterosexual couples with a physician's diagnosis confirming that treatment is necessary can be beneficiaries of an ART procedure. Single women are not allowed access to ART.[372]

3.7.3. THE RIGHT OF THE CHILD TO KNOW THE IDENTITY OF THE DONOR

Germany still upholds donors' anonymity (lacking relevant regulation), even though on a theoretical level (mostly referring to natural conception) it was one of the first countries to recognise the right to know one's origin.[373] The German Civil Code imposes a reciprocal duty of care among parents and children, including also a duty of the mother to inform the child of its genetic origin.[374] Persons may be obliged to comply with a court order to undergo parentage testing.[375] Therefore Germany has a unique position from a comparative perspective giving greater importance to biology unlike most of the other legal systems that rank bodily integrity higher on a scale of values than biological truth.[376]

The idea of a solely informational procedure (getting information regarding a child's origin without claiming any status) was launched with a debate on the desirability and legal feasibility of the so-called "isolated procedure" through a

[371] See more in *Replies by the Member States to the Questionnaire on Access to Medically Assisted Procreation (MAP) and on the Right to Know their Origin for Children Born after MAP*, Steering Committee of Bioethics, CDBI/INF (2005) 7 REV 2, Strasbourg, 9 February 2012, p. 9.

[372] *Ibid.* pp. 17 and 86.

[373] Blauwhoff J.R., *Foundational Facts, Relative Truths. A Comparative Law Study on Children's Right to Know their Genetic Origins*, Intersentia, 2009.

[374] German Civil Code, Section 1618a.

[375] German Civil Procedural Code, article 372a. See more in Blauwhoff, J.R., "Tracing down the Historical Development of the Legal Concept of the Right to Know One's Origins. Has 'To Know or Not To Know' Ever been the Legal Question?", *Utrecht Law Review*, Vol. 4, No. 2, 2008, p. 112.

[376] Frank R., "Compulsory Physical Examinations for Establishing Parentage", *International Journal of Law and the Family*, Vol. 10, No. 2, 1996, p. 21. See also Robertson J.A., "Reproductive Technology in Germany and the United States. An Essay in Comparative Law and Bioethics", *Columbia Journal of Transnational Law*, Vol. 43, No. 1, 2004, pp. 189–228.

court case in 1990.[377] As of 1 April 2008, the German Civil Code affords the right for determining biological parentage to the mother, the father and the child. If any of the family members refuses laboratory testing to determine the biological link, consent may be replaced by the family court, only if the test does not violate the best interests of the child.[378]

Bearing in mind the Civil Code, as well as the constitutional right of the child to know his/her origin on the one hand, and the existing donor anonymity on the other, Blauwhoff criticised the German legal inconsistency.[379] A recent case (6 March 2013) of a regional court of appeals in Hamm ruled the opposite, granting a child conceived by anonymous sperm donation the right to know the name of the genetic father.[380] Even though the terrain for revealing the donor's identifying information might not be clear yet (in terms of a non-existent national register of sperm donors' information),[381] the case might pave the way for future legal changes on behalf of ART conceived children, treating them the same as children conceived naturally.

3.7.4. LEGAL PROCEEDINGS FOR ESTABLISHING PATERNITY OF ART CONCEIVED CHILDREN

It is possible to challenge the paternity of a child conceived with ART only under particular circumstances.[382] The purpose of the proceedings is to defeat the argument that the child was born as a result of the ART treatment to which the parties consented. Since 2003 paternity may also be denied (among other cases) by the man who claims under oath that he had sexual intercourse with the mother during the conception period.[383] The consequences of these proceedings are broader than merely finding out the biological truth in terms of the identity of the progenitor and go on to establish his parental responsibilities. In these terms, the biological father could establish his own fatherhood in relation to the child, but only if he does not interrupt the already established factual social link between the child and the legal father (they behave and act as a family already), and only within a restricted time period (two years after he realised that he might be the potential biological father of the child).[384]

---

377 High Regional Court, Oldenburg, 17 July 1990, 1991 Fam. RZ. Pp. 351–352.

378 Blauwhoff, J.R., "Tracing down the Historical Development of the Legal Concept of the Right to Know One's Origins. Has 'To Know or Not To Know' Ever been the Legal Question?", *Utrecht Law Review*, Vol. 4, No. 2, 2008, p. 107.

379 Blauwhoff J.R., *Foundational Facts, Relative Truths. A Comparative Law Study on Children's Right to Know their Genetic Origins*, Intersentia, 2009, p. 351.

380 See www.bioethicsinternational.org/blog/2013/02/17/no-anonymity-for-sperm-donors-court-rules/.

381 *Ibid.*

382 Section 1599 ff German Civil Code.

383 Section 1600(1) German Civil Code.

384 Sections 1592(2) and 1600(1) German Civil Code.

Along this line, the father, the man who declares under oath that he had sexual intercourse with the mother of the child during the period of conception, the mother and the child can all initiate such a procedure.[385] If both parties of the couple have consented to the treatment, then the right to challenge the paternity is impossible. The proceedings neither refer nor are related to the proceedings for establishing the fatherhood of the donor.

3.8. THE NETHERLANDS

3.8.1. INTRODUCTION OF THE LEGAL CONTEXT IN APPLYING ART

The Dutch Civil Code from 1838 had huge French influence, therefore prohibiting paternity suits. The legislative reform of 1909 allowed the possibility for paternity suits from the mother claiming maintenance from the biological father.[386] Changes in the parentage law were brought about by the Family Law dating from 1998.[387] This law elevated biology and natural origins to a great extent.[388] Even though the Law did not regulate the right of the child to know his/her genetic parents, the direct application of article 7 of the CRC in the national legal system posed the question in several important cases and derived the right to know one's origin from the constitutional "personality right".[389] Non-anonymity of donors was introduced in 2004.[390] Assisted reproduction is regulated in several legal documents.[391] The central principle of the Dutch law on legal parenthood is

385 Section 1600(5) German Civil Code.

386 Act of 16 November 1909, Staatsblad 363.

387 Law of 24 December 1997, Staatsblad 772.

388 See more in Blauwhoff J.R., *Foundational Facts, Relative Truths. A Comparative Law Study on Children's Right to Know their Genetic Origins*, Intersentia, 2009, p. 123.

389 Rechtbank 's-Hertogenbosch, 27 March 1997, KG 1997, No. 147; Hoge Raad, 22 December 1995, NJ 1996, p. 419; NJCM 1996 21-3, pp. 426–427; Rechtbank Breda, 20 June 1989, 726; Rechtbank Breda, 5 March 1991, NJ 1991, 370. See more in Blauwhoff J.R., *Foundational Facts, Relative Truths. A Comparative Law Study on Children's Right to Know their Genetic Origins*, Intersentia, 2009, p. 123.

390 Dutch law: Wet donorgegevens kunstmatige bevruchting, 2002. See also Antokolskaia M., Boele-Woelki K., "Dutch Family Law in the 21st Century: Trend-Setting and Straggling Behind at the Same Time", *Nederlandse Vereniging Voor Rechtsvergelijking (Netherlands Comparative Law Association)*, Vol. 6, No. 4, December 2002. They refer to the Supreme Court decision in Hoge Raad, 15 April 1994, NJ 1994, 608, 3.4.3. in which the Court considered that the "personality right" conveys also the right of the child to know the identity of its parents. The Court furthermore considered that even though the right is a relative one, it should still prevail above the privacy rights of the mother, because of, among other reasons, her joint responsibility for the existence of the child.

391 See more in Janssens P.M.W., Simons A.H.M., Van Kooij R.J., Blokzijl E., Dunselman A.A.J., "A New Dutch Law Regulating Provision of Identifying Information of Donors to Offspring: Background, Content and Impact", *Human Reproduction*, Vol. 21, No. 4, 2006.

summarised as follows: "a child always has a mother, and may have a father".[392] Recent changes in the law allowed lesbian couples engaged in parental projects with the assistance of sperm donation to become legal parents without having to resort to step-parent adoption.[393]

3.8.2. THE RIGHT OF SINGLE WOMEN TO USE ART

The basic principle is equal access to ART for both single or lesbian women, even though some IVF centres apply a stricter policy than others.[394]

3.8.3. THE RIGHT OF THE CHILD TO KNOW THE IDENTITY OF THE DONOR

Following approximately 15 years of debate, a new law granting adults the right to access identifying information regarding the donor was enacted in June 2004.[395] In order to remain consistent with the previous donor-anonymous system, a dual system was introduced, thus allowing parents the possibility of choice between: *anonymous (A) donors* and *non-anonymous (B) donors*. After successful birth of a donor conceived child, the clinics are obliged to pass all the information[396] to the Central Register. The child after reaching 16 years of age may apply to the Foundation for Donor Data (FDD, an independent national foundation) which verifies if the child was conceived by donor insemination. Prior to revealing the donor-identifying information, the Foundation contacts the donor to acknowledge his willingness to disclose identifying information at the current time. If the donor objects to the identification, it is up to the Foundation to decide, based on the concrete circumstances, whose right should prevail, taking into consideration the best interests of the child in the first place. Even if donors are identified, there is no obligation that can bind them to establish contact with the child or to impose on them parental and financial responsibilities. Appreciating the non-retroactive enforcement of the new law, donors who donated gametes before 2004

---

392 Vonk M., *Children and their Parents. A Comparative Study of the legal Position of Children with Regard to their Intentional and Biological Parents in English and Dutch Law*, Intersentia, 2007, p. 53.

393 See more in Antokolskaia M., "Legal Embedding Planned Lesbian Parentage. Pouring New Wine into Old Wineskins", *Familie & Recht*, February 2014.

394 *Replies by the Member States to the Questionnaire on Access to Medically Assisted Procreation (MAP) and on the Right to Know their Origin for Children Born after MAP*, Steering Committee of Bioethics, CDBI/INF (2005) 7 REV 2, Strasbourg, 9 February 2012, p. 18.

395 Janssens P.M.W., Simons A.H.M., Van Kooij R.J., Blokzijl E., Dunselman A.A.J., "A New Dutch Law Regulating Provision of Identifying Information of Donors to Offspring: Background, Content and Impact", *Human Reproduction*, Vol. 21, No. 4, 2006.

396 Information regarding the identity of the women giving birth, the date and place of the treatment, and the identity of the donor (physical, social, psychological and medical).

(even if they were used after the new law) have the right to remain anonymous. The introduction of non-anonymous donations has led to a decreased number of donors. Consequently many couples started to look for donors themselves, and to make private arrangements with them.[397] These donors are often willing to take part in the child's life in a variety of ways from visits and contacts with the child to a wish to become a legal parent vested with shared parental responsibilities.[398]

3.8.4. LEGAL PROCEEDINGS FOR ESTABLISHING PATERNITY OF ART CONCEIVED CHILDREN

The general principle of the civil procedural law is that the court has unlimited discretion to assess the evidence submitted by the parties.[399] The court also holds discretion to order expert enquiries,[400] such as DNA-based parentage tests,[401] even though it is not obliged to do so. If the man refuses to cooperate with the court, it is possible to make adverse inferences against him, and establish his paternity. Not cooperating with a court order is in general in the Civil Code considered a violation of the right or breach of duty imposed by law by the father.[402]

Articles 1:199 and 1:207 of the Dutch Civil Code regulate the judicial determination of paternity. The first paragraph of article 1:207 stipulates that the paternity of a man can be determined even after his death if it is proven that he is the begetter (*verwekker*) of the child. A clear distinction has to be made between the *verwekker* and the "donor". The *verwekker* is the biological father of the child as a result of sexual intercourse with the mother, whereas the "donor" is the biological father but not the *verwekker*.[403] Paternity of the donor cannot be established by court decision. A sperm donor can recognise the child as his if he has gained the mother's consent. The court cannot replace the mother's consent after her refusal since the donor is not the *verwekker*.[404] Machteld Vonk criticised the Dutch regulation in cases of registered couples using assistance in reproduction with the man's own sperm in which case the resulting child will not be begotten in a natural way. According to the current regulation, in these cases, the unmarried father will be a second parent of the child only if the mother allows

397 Antokolskaia M., "Legal Embedding Planned Lesbian Parentage. Pouring New Wine into Old Wineskins", *Familie & Recht*, February 2014. See also Jänterä-Jareborg M., "Parenthood for Same-Sex Couples – Scandinavian Developments", in Boele-Woelki K., Fuchs A. (eds.), *Legal Recognition of Same-Sex Relationships in Europe* (2nd revised edition), Intersentia, Antwerp, 2012, p. 112.

398 *Ibid.*

399 Dutch Civil Procedure Code, article 152 in conjunction with article 150.

400 Dutch Procedural Code, article 194(1) in conjunction with article 150.

401 Dutch Procedural Code, article 194(1) in conjunction with article 150. Hoge Raad, 22 September 2000, NJ 2001, p. 647 with annotation JdB.

402 Dutch Civil Code, article 3:296 in conjunction with article 6:162.

403 Explanatory Memorandum, Kamerstukken II, 1995–96, 24649, no. 3, p. 8.

404 Article 1:204(3) in the fine print of the Dutch Civil Code.

him to be so, because he will be considered a sperm donor and not a begetter. According to this author, an alternative solution is to claim existence of *factual family life* with the child in order to establish paternity without being dependent on the mother's consent.[405] By analogy to this, one can draw the conclusion that if the unregistered partner is considered a sperm donor, then the sperm donor should also be entitled to institute legal proceedings for establishing his fatherhood. This could also apply in cases of single women conceiving a child with a known sperm donor if there is initial contact and possibly later established *family life* with the child. This should also be sufficient to ask the court for direct application of article 8 ECHR in the national law, which should eventually grant him the possibility of legal establishment of parental responsibilities (without depending on the mother's consent). The possibility of legal administration of the paternity of the donor has already been dealt with in practice, as opposed to the provisions stipulated in the law in the ECtHR case of *J.R.M. v. the Netherlands.*[406] Even though the case manifested legal sensitivity for the sperm donor to access proceedings, it considered that the consent of the mother is an important element of the rationale for granting him legal fatherhood.

The Dutch law allows division of parentage between more than two persons since those holding parental responsibilities do not have to necessarily coincide with the legal parents. This means that parental responsibilities are detached from legal parentage in a way that allows more persons to be engaged in the upbringing of the child.[407] Consequently, under the new legislation, if the birth mother gives consent for the child's recognition by the known sperm donor, the parentage will be split between three persons: the legal parents (the known sperm donor and the birth mother), and the holder of parental responsibilities (the partner of the birth mother).[408] Even though the status of a legal parent has a wider scope than the status of a holder of parental responsibilities, they both are entitled at least to the minimum right to maintain contact with the child.

---

405 Vonk M., *Children and their Parents, A Comparative Study of the Legal Position of Children with Regard to their Intentional and Biological Parents in English and Dutch Law,* Intersentia, 2007, p. 58.

406 *J.R.M. v. the Netherlands*, European Commission of Human Rights, No. 16944/90, Decision of 08.02.1993.

407 Antokolskaia M., "Legal Embedding Planned Lesbian Parentage. Pouring New Wine into Old Wineskins", *Familie & Recht*, February 2014, pp. 12 and 13.

408 *Ibid.*, referring to *Handelingen* II 2012/2013, 33 032, no. 13.

3.9. BELGIUM

3.9.1. INTRODUCTION OF THE LEGAL CONTEXT IN APPLYING ART

Assistance in reproduction has been regulated by the Law on Medically Assisted Reproduction and the Allocation of Redundant Embryos and Gametes since 6 July 2007. The law was followed by a technical revision in 2008.[409]

3.9.2. THE RIGHT OF SINGLE WOMEN TO USE ART

The Law regulating ART does not impose restrictions regarding access. The *commissioning parent* is defined in the Law as "any person who has decided to become a parent through medically assisted reproduction, regardless of whether or not the latter is achieved using his/her own gametes or embryos".[410] Nevertheless, each fertility centre is free to decide whether it will accept or refuse treatment either by specifying the medical reasons for the refusal or by invoking an objection of conscience.

3.9.3. THE RIGHT OF THE CHILD TO KNOW THE IDENTITY OF THE DONOR

Even though donor anonymity is a rule, non-anonymous donations are allowed if they are based on an agreement between the donor and recipient. If the rule is followed, then the fertility centre is legally bound to keep the secrecy regarding the identification of the donor. Article 2(i) of the law regulating ART in the definition of *embryo donors* encompasses the anonymity as a donation concept. Article 64 of the Law safeguards the privacy of the personal identifying information of the donor, allowing disclosure only of information regarding the medical state, physical characteristics of the donor, and information necessary for the application of the law to the single women/couple or to the general practitioner of the conceived child in the case of health-related issues. Furthermore, the information regarding the donor is qualified as a professional secret of the staff of the licensed clinics, making breach of the secrecy punishable under article 458 of the Penal Code.

---

409 Law of 19 December 2008, abolishing subsections 2 and 3 of article 3 of the Law of 6 July 2007.

410 Article 2(f) of the Law on Medically Assisted Reproduction and the Allocation of Redundant Embryos and Gametes, 2007.

3.9.4. LEGAL PROCEEDINGS FOR ESTABLISHING PATERNITY OF ART CONCEIVED CHILDREN

The parentage rules set out in the Civil Code afford the establishment of fatherhood through voluntary *acknowledgement*[411] or after judicial proceedings.[412] In the case of a sperm donation, the Law of 6 July 2007 states that the rules of the Civil Code have to be applied in favour of the commissioning parents to whom the donated gametes are donated.[413] This means that the man who gave his permission for the insemination of his partner by sperm from a donor will be able to acknowledge the child as his own even without the consent of the mother and even when there is proof before the court that he is not the biological father. *Judicial establishment* of paternity is based on the genetic link between the father and child[414] or if a situation of *possession d'état* can be proven, by treating the relationship between the child and the father as if they were affiliated.[415] Nevertheless, the possibility of proceedings to establish the fatherhood of the donor is excluded. Article 2(p) and (q) of the law regulating ART, while defining the gamete donor and receiver, clearly stipulates that "there should not be any possibility for the determination of a bond of affiliation between the gamete donor and the unborn child".

3.10. UNITED KINGDOM

3.10.1. INTRODUCTION OF THE LEGAL CONTEXT IN APPLYING ART

The English law regulates the family law issues in different Acts. Parental rights and duties are regulated in section 42(1) of the National Assistance Act 1948; section 6 of the Family Law Reform Act 1969 and, subsequently, the Family Law Reform Act 1987; the Guardianships of Minors Act 1971; Part I of the Guardianship Act 1973; Part II of the Children Act 1975 (amended 1989); and the Child Care Act 1980 (except Part I and sections 13, 24, 64 and 65).[416] Legal parenthood is as a general rule determined by biological facts.

After the birth of Louise Brown (the first officially born in vitro baby) in the United Kingdom in 1978, the growing need for regulating the impact of ART was canalised through the Committee formed in 1982 chaired by the philosopher Mary Warnock, which released the foundations for further regulation in the

411 Article 319 in conjunction with article 329 bis Civil Code.
412 Article 322 in conjunction with article 324 Civil Code.
413 Article 56, first subsection of the Law of 6 July 2007.
414 Article 324, second and third subsection Civil Code.
415 Article 324, third subsection Civil Code.
416 See more in Family Law Reform Act, 1987 c. 42, Part II Rights and Duties of Parents, available online: www.legislation.gov.uk/ukpga/1987/42/part/II/crossheading/parental-rights-and-duties-general.

so-called Warnock Report (1984).[417] The Committee proposed establishment of a regulatory authority that later on developed into the Human Fertilisation and Embryology Authority. The Warnock Report was at the time very influential (not only in the United Kingdom, but also worldwide, bearing in mind the novelty of the issue) and was a ground for the forthcoming Human Fertilisation and Embryology Act (HEFA, amended several times). Today, assisted reproduction (commonly regulated for England and Wales, Scotland and Northern Ireland) is regulated by the Human Fertilisation and Embryology Act (HEFA) 2008.[418]

3.10.2. THE RIGHT OF SINGLE WOMEN TO USE ART

The Warnock Report was restrictive towards single women (heterosexual or lesbian) using assistance of donor insemination and in vitro technology, arguing that it is better for children to be born into a two-parent heterosexual family.

Today, single women can be beneficiaries of ART, although clinics have different eligibility criteria. After examining the future plans of the woman willing to conceive, and her capability to parent, they can decide whether the treatment will be carried out or not.

The HEFA 1990 was restrictive towards single women, protecting the right of the child to have at least two parents (under English law, it is possible for the child to have more than two parents). Section 13 of the Act stipulated: "A woman shall not be provided with treatment services *other than basic partner treatment services* [part omitted in the HEFA 2008], unless account has been taken of the welfare of any child who may be born as a result of the treatment including the need of that child for a *father* [substituted with "supportive parenting" in the HEFA 2008]".

Nevertheless, a preferred option for granting treatment licences are couples (heterosexual or homosexual) with a reproductive project. In these terms, the HEFA uses the term "intended second parent" as referring to any man who agreed to the conditions of being a father, and any woman who agreed to be a second parent of the child conceived by ART.[419]

---

417 Warnock Report, 1984.

418 Initially regulated by the Human Fertilisation and Embryology Act, 1990; later on amended by the Human Fertilisation and Embryology Act, 2003.

419 See further Section 14 of HEFA 2008.

3.10.3. THE RIGHT OF THE CHILD TO KNOW THE IDENTITY OF THE DONOR

The Warnock Report recommended anonymous donations, considering that sperm donors will be less likely to donate if they are aware that their identity can be revealed.

In April, 2005 the Human Fertilisation and Embryology Act shifted existing donor anonymity to an open donor's non-anonymous status. Before the Act, the disclosure of identifying information was considered an offence. As from 2005, any child reaching 18 (therefore as from 2023) is able to ask the Human Fertilisation and Embryology Authority for identifying information.[420] Section 31ZA of the HEFA regulates the *Request for information regarding genetic parentage*. The Act allows information to be revealed regarding physical appearance even for anonymous donors to a child upon reaching 18 years of age. The Congenital Disabilities Act from 1976 allows disclosure of the identity of an anonymous donor if the child has developed an inheritable genetic condition.[421]

3.10.4. LEGAL PROCEEDINGS FOR ESTABLISHING PATERNITY OF ART CONCEIVED CHILDREN

The establishment of paternity is led by the marriage presumption, being rebuttable if the husband is not a biological father, only if the status provisions of the HEFA do not apply and therefore if the child is conceived via ART.

In section 41 (Persons not to be treated as fathers) of the HEFA, it is clearly stated that a donor who consented and therefore donated his sperm in a licensed clinic for the purpose of treatment services or non-medical fertility services is not to be treated as the father of the child. In contrast, section 26 of the Law Reform Act 1987 allows the court (either by its own motion or by an application of any other party) in any civil proceedings in which the parentage of any person fails to be determined to give a direction for the use of scientific tests to show the genetic parentage.

Section 4 of the 1989 Children Act regulates the acquisition of parental responsibilities by the father, in three cases: (1) if he becomes registered as the child's father; (2) if he and the child's mother make an agreement (a "parental agreement") that will grant him parental responsibilities; and (3) if the court on his application orders him parental responsibilities. Some authors interpret these provisions as if the English law allows known donors to apply for parental

420 *Replies by the Member States to the Questionnaire on Access to Medically Assisted Procreation (MAP) and on the Right to Know their Origin for Children Born after MAP*, Steering Committee of Bioethics, CDBI/INF (2005) 7 REV 2, Strasbourg, 9 February 2012, p. 63.

421 *Ibid*, p. 68.

responsibilities on the ground of being biological parents.[422] Following this logic, in cases of lesbian parental projects with a known sperm donor, his role (in terms of his consent) even determines that the co-mother must adopt the child and become a second legal parent. Moreover, all three parties are given the possibility to somehow participate in the child's upbringing whilst holding some level of parental status. Under the English law, the parental responsibilities may be attributed to more than two persons if it is in concordance with the best interests of the child. A possibility for an inclusive parental project for all interested parties (genetic, social and legal parents) for some authors is the most preferred legal solution.[423] Apart from being consistent with the international documents,[424] it could also solve the hypocritical attitude towards children conceived by sperm donation by acknowledging the reality and allowing full or partial parental responsibilities to more persons. Bearing in mind the history of integration of ART in affiliation law from the Warnock Report (which promoted two-parent families) until the present day, it can be concluded that when single women conceive children through ART, it should not only be possible but also recommended to attribute parental responsibilities to the known donor. A solution of this kind might satisfy both stakeholders: single women and their right to reproduce, while also providing a two-parent family for the child.

3.11. SWEDEN

3.11.1. INTRODUCTION OF THE LEGAL CONTEXT IN APPLYING ART

Assisted reproduction is regulated in the Act on Insemination (1984 Law No. 1140) and the In Vitro Fertilisation Act (1988:711, revised 2002).[425] Additionally, some aspects of ART are regulated by the Act on Ethics Review of Research Involving Humans (Law No. 460, 2003), and the Genetic Integrity Act (Law No. 351, 2006). The regulation of ART developed gradually from restrictive to more liberal.[426] Even though Sweden is perceived to be comparatively progressive in the field of

---

422 Vonk M., *Children and their Parents, A Comparative Study of the Legal Position of Children with Regard to their Intentional and Biological Parents in English and Dutch Law*, Intersentia, 2007, p. 196.

423 See, for instance, Bainham A., "The Rights and Obligations Associated with the Birth of a Child", in Spencer J.R., Du Bois-Pedain A. (eds.), *Freedom and Responsibility in Reproductive Choice*, Hart Publishing, 2006.

424 Such as articles 3 and 7 CRC and article 8 ECHR.

425 Adopted 1 March 1985, entered into 1 January 1989. See more in *Replies by the Member States to the Questionnaire on Access to Medically Assisted Procreation (MAP) and on the Right to Know their Origin for Children Born after MAP*, Steering Committee of Bioethics, CDBI/INF (2005) 7 REV 2, Strasbourg, 9 February 2012, p. 15.

426 Burell R., *Assisted Reproduction in the Nordic Countries: A Comparative Study of Policies and Regulation*, Nordic Committee of Bioethics, 2005.

the application of article 7 of the CRC, as being the first country in the world to allow access to donors' identifying information, the legal reality is different. In fact, under the Swedish law, there are many other restrictions and exceptions, such as the ban of oocyte donations[427] and embryo donations, surrogacy and single women's access to ART.[428] Even though sperm donation was allowed in 1985, for many years afterwards oocyte donation was forbidden.

3.11.2. THE RIGHT OF SINGLE WOMEN TO USE ART

Swedish legislation favours couples in a family project. It also provides a financial health package to married couples or those in stable relationships. Lesbian couples in a registered partnership or cohabiting were allowed access to ART in 2005. Nevertheless, single women are not. In February 2012, the Centre Party, Liberals and the Moderates started a campaign to promote and support changes in the Law in order to allow single women access to ART.[429] At the time of writing, no such changes have been achieved.

The legal relationship between parents and children is regulated by the Parental Code 1949 that has been subject to many amendments. Parental responsibility as a legal concept is encompassed in two other concepts: custody (Chapter 6) and guardianship (Chapters 9–15).[430] The provisions for establishing the paternity of ART conceived children are placed in Chapter I of the Parental Code, sections 5–9.[431]

3.11.3. THE RIGHT OF THE CHILD TO KNOW THE IDENTITY OF THE DONOR

Sweden was the first country in the world, in 1985, to give children conceived through the assistance of the reproductive technologies a legal right to know the identity of the sperm donor.[432] The legal discussion was bi-polar: on the one side were the supporters of the argument that there is no need of the child to know, accompanied with the priority to protect the non-genetic parent. On the other

427 Law No. 711, 1988. See more in Gunning J., "Oocyte Donation. The Legislative Framework in Western Europe", *Human Reproduction*, Vol. 13, No. 2, 1998, pp. 98–102, p. 101.

428 Svanberg A.S., Sydsjo G., Selling K.E., Lampic C., "Attitudes towards Gamete Donation among Swedish Gynaecologists and Obstetricians", *Human Reproduction*, Vol. 23, No. 4, 2008, pp. 904–911.

429 www.nomblog.com/19928/.

430 See more in: Jäntera-Järeborg M., Singer A., Sorgjerd C., *National Report: Parental Responsibility, Sweden*.

431 www.notisum.se/rnp/sls/lag/19490381.htm.

432 Ministry of Health and Social Affairs 1984:1140, *Law about insemination*. See more in Frith L., "Gamete Donation and Anonymity. The Ethical and Legal Debate", *Human Reproduction*, Vol. 16, No. 5, 2001, pp. 818–819.

side, there were the supporters of the truthfulness of the parent–child relationship accompanied with the best interests of children to receive relevant information regarding the foundations of their life, therefore safeguarding their personal integrity.[433] In addition, there has been a concern regarding the possibility of declination of the number of donors willing to donate. Some "aftermath" studies showed the opposite: an increasing number of donors despite the introduced non-anonymity.[434] This fact suggests that the donation decision does not have to be necessarily negatively influenced by the possibility of contacting the offspring in the future.[435]

At present, the first children after the novel regulation on donors' disclosure are already at the age to seek information regarding their genetic origin. The law does not indicate who is responsible for bringing the information regarding the modus of conception to the attention of the child, making the enforcement of the right to know of the child dependent on the willingness of its parents to reveal the truth.[436] Therefore the focus of the current discussions is mostly related to the compliance of the law with the reality of parents striving to make the decision regarding whether they should reveal the secret, and when and how to do so.[437] The exercise of the right to access the genetic origin information is related to the right to know and therefore the willingness (not an obligation) of the parents to tell. Thus the disclosure of the truth is a two-step process, including information on the fact of how the child was conceived, and information on the identity of the donor.[438] A number of studies show that the law's compliance with real family life is moderate. A small number of parents have told their children in comparison to those who intended to do so but never have.[439]

3.11.4. LEGAL PROCEEDINGS FOR ESTABLISHING PATERNITY OF ART CONCEIVED CHILDREN

Paternity as regulated in the Parental Code can be contested only if it is not suspect that the child was conceived by ART.[440]

---

433 Ministry of Health and Social Affairs 2001/02:89.

434 Daniels K., Lalos O., "The Swedish Insemination Act and the Availability of Donors", *Human Reproduction*, Vol. 10, No. 7, 1995, pp. 1871–1874.

435 *Ibid.*

436 Lalos A., Gottlieb C., Lalos O., "Legislated Right for Donor-Insemination Children to Know their Genetic Origin: A Study of Parental Thinking", *Human Reproduction*, Vol. 22, No. 6, 2007, pp. 1759–1768.

437 *Ibid.*

438 Svanberg A.S., Sydsjo G., Selling K.E., Lampic C., "Attitudes towards Gamete Donation among Swedish Gynaecologists and Obstetricians", *Human Reproduction*, Vol. 23, No. 4, 2008, pp. 904–911.

439 *Ibid.*

440 *Replies by the Member States to the Questionnaire on Access to Medically Assisted Procreation (MAP) and on the Right to Know their Origin for Children Born after MAP*, Steering Committee of Bioethics, CDBI/INF (2005) 7 REV 2, Strasbourg, 9 February 2012, p. 79.

PART II

THE LEGAL, ETHICAL AND SOCIOLOGICAL POSITIONS OF THE PARTICIPANTS

CHAPTER 4
ASSISTING SINGLE WOMEN TO FOUND FAMILIES

An international study in 16 countries has demonstrated that the majority of adults consider reproducing and rearing a child in the family to be necessary for their personal development.[441] A study in the United States found that more than 90% of women either have children or expect to have them in the future, while only 6% of women are voluntarily childless.[442] This shows an attitude that continuing the genes or a dream for a family with children is the prevailing choice for most people.

One of the most prominent feminists, Simone de Beauvoir, criticised the oppressiveness of normative femininity as subordinate to reproduction and motherhood as if it is the utmost desire in the women's domain.[443] She argued that women's reproductive bodies are a reason for their subordinate social status, while describing the strong emotional link between mother and child as "mutual and harmful oppression".[444] Thus, reproduction and its role in women's lives have led to disagreements among feminists regarding reproductive freedom and its interpretation – negative, as not to procreate, or positive, as to have children when wanted.[445] Striving for liberation, feminists' focus was set for a long time on the negative right promoting birth control, abortion and collective methods of childbearing. With the reproductive technologies revolution, feminists' politics changed. The new liberation took place on several levels. Firstly, the biological age limits were extended (allowing women professional opportunities). Secondly, changing women's reproductive nature with the artificiality of reproduction relieved the social reproductive pressure and silenced the voices that claimed

---

441 Gallup, Inc., *Global Study of Family Values*, 1997, available online: www.gallup.com/poll/9871/1997-global-study-family-values.aspx.

442 Chandra A., Martinez G., Mosher W., Abma J., Jones J., "Fertility, Family Planning, and Reproductive Health of U.S. Women. Data from the 2002 National Survey of Family Growth", *Vital and Health Statistics*, Vol. 25, 2005, pp. 1–160.

443 De Beauvoir S., *The Second Sex*, Parshley H.M. (trans.), Vintage Books, 1989. (The original title: *Le deuxième sexe*, Vols. 1 and 2, Gallimard, 1949).

444 *Ibid.*

445 Mottier V., "Reproductive Rights", in Waylen G., Celis K., Kantola J., Weldon S.L. (eds.), *The Oxford Handbook of Gender and Politics*, Oxford University Press, 2013, p. 215.

that women's intrinsic nature is above all to be a mother.[446] Nevertheless, what is similar to the current battle for individual positive reproductive rights is the struggle to separate between public and private spheres, as expressed in the feminist's second-wave slogan: "the personal is political".[447] As this wave aimed at minimising the gender differences, thus lobbying for gender-neutrality, the more recent trends aim at celebrating female differences, among others the ability to give birth to a child, thus claiming the moral superiority of women.[448] Moreover, treating women and men equally is a ground for injustice, bearing in mind their natural inequalities.[449]

The right to reproduce and thus to found a family is declared and protected as a human right in the UDHR (article 16)[450] and in the ECHR (article 12).[451] Both international human rights cornerstone documents associate the right to found a family with marriage. These definitions do not correspond with the reality any longer, even more so when the family is founded with the application of a new reproductive technology. Some aspects of the articles are so vague as to allow free interpretation by the national legislation depending on the political, legal, moral, religious and cultural background of the perception of family and privacy. Therefore the margin of appreciation for family law issues is wide, especially regarding the questions: is marriage a condition to found a family? To whom do the terms "men" and "women" refer: only to heterosexual partners or to homosexual too, or maybe to single women and single men as well (where surrogacy is an allowed practice)? Is reproduction a matter of dividing roles between genders and does it go together with asymmetrical reproductive rights and responsibilities?[452] Do men and women have to be of a certain age to conclude a marriage or to found a family as well? Finally, is the foundation of the family defined by the law, custom

446 Firestone S., *The Dialectic of Sex. The Case for Feminist Revolution*, Bantam Books, 1970, pp. 188, 193, 194.

447 Mottier V., "Reproductive Rights", in Waylen G., Celis K., Kantola J., Weldon S.L. (eds.), *The Oxford Handbook of Gender and Politics*, Oxford University Press, 2013, p. 225.

448 Kingdom E., "Birthrights. Equal or Special?", in Lee R., Morgan D. (eds.), *Birthrights, Law and Ethics at the Beginning of Life*, Routledge, 1989, p. 22. See also Eisenstein H., *Contemporary Feminist Thought*, Allen & Unwin, 1984, pp. 140–141.

449 Kingdom E., "Birthrights. Equal or Special?", in Lee R., Morgan D. (eds.), *Birthrights, Law and Ethics at the Beginning of Life*, Routledge, 1989, p. 25, referring to Wolgast E.H., *Equality*, Cornell University Press, 1980, p. 155.

450 (1) Men and women of full age, without any limitation due to race, nationality or religion, have the right to marry and to found a family. They are entitled to equal rights as to marriage, during marriage and at its dissolution. (2) Marriage shall be entered into only with the free and full consent of the intending spouses. (3) The family is the natural and fundamental group unit of society and is entitled to protection by society and the State.

451 Men and women of marriageable age have the right to marry and to found a family, according to the national laws governing the exercise of this right.

452 See, for instance, Sheldon S., "Reproductive Choice. Man's Freedom and Women's Responsibility", in Spencer J.R., Bois-Pedain A. (eds.), *Freedom and Responsibility in Reproductive Choice*, Hart Publishing, 2006, p. 176. Sheldon argues that biological asymmetry between genders does exist, suggesting that men's and women's responsibilities in the context of reproductive decision-making must also be asymmetrical.

or biology, and therefore is the family primarily a natural or a social construct? From here on, do the legal impediments to marry, cohabit with a partner and to found a family apply to blood relatives or only to legally recognised relatives? How can children conceived by sperm donation know their blood affiliation and does it matter?

What has changed from the time of enacting the documents on human rights until the current moment is the perception of the family unit. Today, the family is an extended concept as much as the national legal framework allows it to be.

The national public debates over reproduction are very often led by political ideologies, making the issues on reproduction a locus for shaping political positions.[453] For instance, single women families were severely criticised in a speech of Margaret Thatcher during a debate over the introduction of child support legislation.[454] With the purpose of firmly protecting heterosexuality in family life, the speech castigated other deviant forms for raising a child apart from "the real" heterosexual nuclear family.[455] This kind of imposed preference for family life also aimed at achieving economic goals (reducing the role of the state in providing welfare by chasing absent fathers to provide financially for their children), while also promoting moral messages that "parenthood is for life" and the importance of the "fathers' key role as a provider for their children".[456] The political discourse of transforming genders and identities, founding and ending relationships replaced the nuclear family with the "recombinant family".[457] This overwhelming diversity of new family forms has been a subject of interest of legal and sociological sciences investigating gender relations and independencies, intimacy and family policies.[458]

Thus, reproduction, access to ART for single women and the right of the child to a life in a two-parent heterosexual nuclear family are usually a matter of political decisions in particular societies. Accordingly, the private sphere of

---

453 Gal S., Kligman G, *The Politics of Gender after Socialism*, Princeton University Press, 2000.

454 See more in Donovan C., *Genetics, Fathers and Families. Exploring the Implications of Changing the Law in Favour of Identifying Sperm Donors*, Sage Publications, 2006, p. 496.

455 Brindle D., White M., "Thatcher Rounds on Absent Fathers", *Guardian*, 18 January 1990.

456 Donovan C., *Genetics, Fathers and Families. Exploring the Implications of Changing the Law in Favour of Identifying Sperm Donors*, Social & Legal Studies, Sage Publications, 2006. See also Millar J., "State, Family and Personal Responsibility. The Changing Balance for Lone Mothers in the United Kingdom", in Allen G. (ed.), *The Sociology of the Family. A Reader*, Blackwell, 1999, pp. 247–262.

457 Stacey J., *Brave New Families. Stories of Domestic Upheaval in the Late Twentieth Century*, Basic Books, 1990.

458 See more in Giddens A., Eichler M., *Family Shifts. Families, Policies, and Gender Equality*, Oxford University Press, 1997; Beck U., Beck-Gernheim E., *The Normal Chaos of Love*, Polity Press, 1995; Silva E.B., Smart C. (eds.), *The New Family?*, Sage, 1999; Jagger G., Wright C. (eds.), *Changing Family Values*, Routledge, 1999; Allen G., Hawker S., Crow G., "Family Diversity and Change in Britain and Western Europe", *Journal of Family Issues*, Vol. 22, No. 7, 2001, pp. 819–837; Beck-Gernheim E., *Reinventing the Family. In Search of New Lifestyles*, Polity Press, 2002; Scott J., Treas J., Richards M. (eds.), *The Blackwell Companion to the Sociologies of Families*, Blackwells Publishing, 2004.

family life is dragged away from home, and shifted to a level of political arena. This makes it possible for states not only to shape their political discourse within society, but also on these grounds to claim national jurisdiction in matters of family life as opposed to the notion of the universally accepted human right of the individual.

Yet, in most countries, the reproductive right does not derive from the family anymore. On the contrary, very often it is considered a genuine human right of each individual. Furthermore, the practice of the ECtHR and its interpretations of what classifies as Member States' jurisdiction within the margin of appreciation, with the assistance of the European standard rationale, evolved the national legal systems for recognising new human rights, such as the appreciation of the *individual* right to respect for one's private and family life and its content.[459] In these terms, constructing two-party families consisting of a single woman and child is a reality depending on whether it is *socially* and therefore *legally* acceptable or not. This is in contradiction to the claim that the reproductive right should be elevated to a natural right, since conceiving a child by oneself is naturally not possible as it is essentially related to another person (if cloning is not an option). Nevertheless, if it is viewed as *socially* and therefore *legally* possible it will also be technically feasible for single women to claim their right to conceive a child. Even with the assistance of technology, the allegedly absolute and natural character of the reproductive right is made misleading by the other participants holding interests in the same reproductive process – the other party that contributes genetic material and the resulting offspring. Even though the reproductive technologies were introduced with the purpose of overcoming couples' infertility, single women's right to reproduce using sperm donations has another dimension, which is the desire to experience motherhood without engaging in sexual intercourse and without sharing parental responsibility with a partner. Despite her *singleness*, at least three persons are still participating in the "reproductive project".

As the UDHR and ECHR associate the right to reproduce and to found a family with marriage, it becomes obvious that there is inconsistency between the indoctrination and single women's reproductive reality. John Harris recognised three family foundations depending on who is in the focus: (1) *society-centred* (the family is a fundamental unit of society and therefore the right to found a family is in the societal interest to ensure that there will be a next generation), (2) *adult-*

[459] See, for instance, Dobozi V., "The Right to Know One's Biological Identity", *The International Conference Challenges of the Knowledge Society* (7th edition), Bucharest, 17–18 May 2013, p. 512. The author argues that the case law of the ECtHR influenced and evolved the legal context in the UK in the domain of third party reproduction, integrating the right of any person to know his/her biological identity into the previous legal context (p. 516), thus announcing "the right to know one's biological identity" as a new human right.

centred (the right to found a family as a dimension of humans' freedom), and (3) *child-centred* view (securing the interests of the next generation, i.e. children).[460]

In the following text, the essence of the right to reproduce will be re-examined from the individual right to private and family life and marriage as a social construct directed by the state policies. Reproductive rights will be observed on two general levels: (1) as being "natural" and therefore classified as natural rights, and (2) as being "artificial", thus socially constructed and therefore socially dependent rights.

On the first level, the reproductive right will be observed from within its natural essence, thus an individual ontology, claiming it to be an *individual right* (1.1); and as a *right to privacy* (1.2.).

On the second level, the reproductive right will be observed from three perspectives: (1) from the family context, as a social construction of more persons, mostly but not necessarily related through *consanguinity*, therefore classifying it as a *right to family life* but also its compound element – *right to private life* (2.1.); (2) from the context of the wider political set of values to be protected and therefore the state policies that determine the extent of public interference in the right to privacy and family life as a *greater public good* (2.2); and (3) from the internationally accepted *principle of non-discrimination* as a goal towards treating equals equally and therefore as *a right to access ART* on equal grounds for everybody (2.3.).

The following text will examine (1) "nature" as an intrinsic human essence of an individual *versus* (2) "artificiality" as an imitation of the natural character typical of human agencies of the reproduction, in an attempt to investigate how absolute and how relative the right to reproduce is. In these terms, the natural rights will originate from within and will essentially and absolutely belong to the human agent, while the artificiality will originate from the outer social construction made by the norms of humans for regulating the nature of humans.

The binary approach of nature *versus* artifice of reproduction could be criticised by the argument that creating a child in both settings is the same, irrespective of the attempts to imitate nature or not. Furthermore, some authors consider that resemblance between natural heterosexuality and assisted reproduction is as hypocritical as placing family as a natural formation.[461] Warner derives the natural character of heterosexual reproduction in sexuality defining *reprosexuality* as "a relation to self that finds its proper temporality and fulfilment in generational transmission".[462] Assisted reproductive technologies have already absorbed the concepts of sexuality enabling separation of reproduction from sexual intercourse, thus endangering the heteronormative relations of natural

460 Harris J., "The Right to Found a Family", in Scarre G. (ed.), *Children, Parents and Politics*, Cambridge University Press, 1989.

461 Zerjav T., "The Politicization of Singlehood", *CEU eTD Collection*, 2012, pp. 30 and 44.

462 Warner M., "Introduction. Fear of Queer Planet", *Social Text*, No. 29, 1991, p. 9.

reproduction.[463] Accordingly, assisted reproduction has nothing to do with heterosexuality, allowing access to everyone irrespective of their sexuality, or singlehood.

On the other hand, some other authors criticise the location of parenthood and family in the realm of "rights talks".[464] They argue that these concepts are rather self-centred and encourage parental possessiveness while distorting the responsibility that attaches to the other concerned parties, as for instance the resulting child. The discussions over the right to parent or parental rights should always be seen as a "way of protecting the child's right to parental relationship".[465] Therefore the reproductive right and the right to parent are non-existent as individual human rights. Some other authors defocus the reproductive rights as making "reproductive choices talks" in its antipodes – "reproductive responsibilities talks".[466] In this focus, what matters are the consequences of having reproduced and not the exercise of the right to reproduce. In these terms, affording single women the right to reproduce by sperm donation should always be followed by non-anonymous donations. Otherwise, the right to reproduce is only instrumental in satisfying the adults' own needs and ends whilst being ignorant of children's interests.[467] On the contrary, disclosure of donors' identity is not intrusive to anybody. It does not interfere with women's right to use sperm donations and what is more makes it more legitimate and justified to form a family.[468]

4.1. THE "NATURE" OF THE REPRODUCTION

The founder of the discipline that tackles moral dilemmas of life and death – Van Potter – defined bioethics as a harmonic development between biology and ethics.[469] *Genetics* as a neologism that deals with *genes* and *ethics* should treat ethical problems approaching from the new possibilities to create and transform

463 Zerjav T., "The Politicization of Singlehood", *CEU eTD Collection*, 2012, p. 44.

464 Minow M., *Making All the Difference. Inclusion, Exclusion and American Law*, Cornell University Press, 1990; Fitzgerald W.A., "Maturity, Difference, and Mystery. Children's Perspectives and the Law", *Arizona Law Review*, Vol. 36, No. 11, 1994.

465 Richards J.L., "Redefining Parenthood. Parental Rights Versus Child Rights", *Wayne Law Review*, Vol. 40, 1993–1994, p. 1227.

466 Bainham A., "The Rights and Obligations Associated with the Birth of a Child", in Spencer J.R., Du Bois-Pedain A. (eds.), *Freedom and Responsibility in Reproductive Choice*, Hart Publishing, 2006.

467 McWhinnie A., "Gamete Donation and Anonymity. Should Offspring from Donated Gametes Continue to be Denied Knowledge of their Origins and Antecedents?", *Human Reproduction*, Vol. 16, No. 5, 2001, pp. 807–817.

468 Chestney E.S., "The Right to Know One's Genetic Origin. Can, Should, or Must a State that Extends the Right to Adoptees Extend an Analogous Right to Children Conceived with Donor Gametes?", *Texas Law Review*, Vol. 80, No. 2, 2001, pp. 365–391, p. 391.

469 Potter V.R., "Evolving Ethical Concepts", *Bioscience*, Vol. 27, No. 4, 1977, pp. 251–253.

life.[470] The foundations of genetics as a science were laid down in the 19th century by setting the rules for transmitting the units of information through generations from Gregor Mendel. The continuation of natural-evolutionary thought was followed by Darwinian "natural selection" of species in order to adapt to the environmental circumstances in order to survive (in *The Origin of Species by Means of Natural Selection*).

Adaptation to the environment by human beings is taking a less natural path, since humans have the capacity to reason and act, and therefore change the environment in which they live.[471] The human adjustment of reality is moral and not natural, since humans have the capacity to create new possibilities, unlike animals. Along these lines, the human adaptation of the environment in which they live is a human-created reality. With scientific technological progress, humans do hold the capacity to intervene in what was once a natural domain, and create, modify or enhance human genes or modes of reproduction. The origin of human life is no longer to such an extent a natural selection as selection of what is considered to be morally right and therefore legally permitted. Humans more than ever before are responsible for "natural selection" and the ways of conceiving future generations.

Rifkin and Perlas confronted the natural order as intrinsically given, by promoting the allogenic nature of humans which should use their capacity to manipulate nature as long it is fruitful for them.[472] Nevertheless, manipulating human nature does not necessarily mean that it is a good act *per se* for a particular person or for humanity in general. Therefore the responsibility to keep what is precious such as human dignity should prevail when making decisions.

The *Kantian categorical imperative* is a principle of minimum moral respect for human beings in relation to one another.[473] Treating human beings as objective ends in themselves and not just as a means to achieve higher goals, sets the deontological limits of the "all-mighty humans" and their unstoppable scientific progress. To follow the unstoppable beneficial development, but not to offend humans as an end in themselves could be accomplished by lifting up the deontological principles to norms which balance strict regulation with the permissiveness of exceptions depending on the particular circumstances. This is the only way that nature, scientific development and human society can coexist without suffocating or offending each other.

The definition of natural rights originates from the social contract developed by philosophers in the 16th and 17th centuries, which related the concept to the minimum protection that every individual should enjoy as part of their

470 Heyd D., *Genetics: Moral Issues in the Creation of People*, University of California Press, 1992, p. 23.

471 Zubiri X., *Sobre el Hombre*, Alianza Editorial, 1986, p. 346.

472 Rifkin J., Perlas N., *Algeny*, The Viking Press, 1983.

473 Kant I., "Grounding for the Metaphysics of Morals", in Cahn S.M. (ed.), *Classics of Western Philosophy*, Hackett Publishing Company, 1995, p. 1085.

inalienable human liberty. Hobbes defines natural law (*ius naturale*) as the liberty that each man has to use his own capacity, as he prefers, for the preservation of his own nature. Hobbes distinguishes the right (*ius*), referring to the liberty to act, from the law (*lex*), referring to the obligation to appreciate the limits of practising liberty. In these terms, the right and the law differ as much as do the liberty and obligation to refrain from it.[474] Therefore natural rights exist irrespective of the legal rules of the state, should have precedence over the state's regulation, and are universal and inalienable. In contrast, legal rights are those officially granted to the individual by a concrete legal system.

The family for Hobbes is an artificial and not natural institution, in which the father's right is strictly conventional, negotiable and contractual. For him, the father's right is purely conventional, i.e. it is based on force.[475]

For John Locke, three natural rights hold primacy over the legal rights of the state: (1) *life*, as everyone is entitled to live once is created; (2) *liberty*, as everyone is entitled to do what he/she wants as long as that does not conflict with the right to life; and (3) *property*, as everyone is entitled to own what one creates or gains through acquisition, gift, inheritance or trade as long as it is in concordance with the other two natural rights.[476]

Natural rights are usually associated with human rights because of their universality and the power beyond the national states' governments. Some authors, however, have fiercely argued against their absolute and inalienable nature[477] or strongly refused any identification between both rights.[478]

4.1.1. THE REPRODUCTIVE RIGHT AS AN INDIVIDUAL RIGHT

Proponents of the reproductive right look for its grounds in human freedoms, human dignity, free development and expression of one's own personality, personal and familial right to privacy and on the right to marry and found a family.

John Rawls, as a proponent of political liberalism, justifies individualistic reproductive logic, focusing on all values in the freedom of the individual and

[474] See more Hobbes T., *The Leviathan*, 1651, available online via Project Gutenberg: www.gutenberg.org/ebooks/3207.

[475] See more in the analyses of the patriarchal confusions in Pateman C., *The Sexual Contract*, Polity Press, 1988.

[476] Locke J., *Second Treatise of Government*, 1689, McPherson C.B. (ed.), *John Locke Second Treatise of Government*, Hackett Publishing Company, 1980.

[477] See more: Bentham J., "Critique of the Doctrine of Inalienable Natural Rights", *Anarchical Fallacies*, Vol. 2 of Bowring (ed.), *Works*, 1843; Burke E., *Reflections on the Revolution in France, and on the Proceedings in Certain Societies in London Relative to that Event. In a Letter Intended to have been sent to a Gentleman in Paris*, Dodsley, 1790.

[478] Jones P., *Rights, Issues in Political Theory*, Palgrave Macmillan, 1994, p. 73.

the commitment of society and public institutions to provide and guarantee the effectiveness of these freedoms.[479] He argues that a just society should provide a neutral framework of basic rights and liberties (without interference and with appreciation of others' rights and liberties) in order to enable individuals to pursue their own values and life plans.[480]

John Robertson describes "procreative liberty" as freedom in activities and choices related to procreation, only making a distinction between actions designed to avoid and those designed to cause procreation.[481]

As an individual right, reproduction can be observed as a *natural right* and a *right to privacy* to freely decide on enforcing the complex physiological construct of wishes, needs, and desires to rear, bear or beget a child. Article 8 of the ECHR treats jointly *the right to private and family life*. For the purposes of making a distinction between rights that originate from and belong to an individual, and those that originate from and belong to a group (family in the case), in this section *the right to privacy* and *the right to private life* will be tackled as rights of the individual irrespective of the belonging to a group or not.

If reproduction is observed as a process of continuing the human species, it seems reasonable to claim that the reproductive right is a natural right. As tackled by Plato, the desire for genetically related children is a natural desire for immortality: "mankind is immortal because it always leaves later generations behind to preserve its unity and identity for all time: it gets its share of immortality by means of procreation".[482]

But can it be claimed on solid legal grounds that not only reproduction as an intrinsic capacity and need of human beings, but also technical assistance to reproduce, should be available to everybody, even on an individual basis, and from these premises can a right that can be claimed be inferred? Since reproductive technologies have become available as a means for reproducing, it seems justified that access thereto should be available on equal grounds to everybody. Along this line, Sheila Maclean argues that once means are available they should not be distributed in a discriminatory way.[483] If the reproductive right is natural because it comes from within, supported by the concept of equality as a right to be claimed by everyone, it seems evident that it should be treated as a universal human right.

479 See more in Rawls J., *Theory of Justice* (revised edition), The Belknap Press of Harvard University Press, 1971, 1999; Rawls J., *Political Liberalism*, Columbia Classics in Philosophy, Columbia University Press, 1993, 1996, 2005.

480 See the interpretation of Rawls' Justice in De Melo-Martin I., *Making Babies. Biomedical Technologies, Reproductive Ethics, and Public Policy*, Kluwer Academic Publishers, 1998, p. 129.

481 Robertson J.A., "Noncoital Reproduction and Procreative Liberty. Embryos, Families, and Procreative Liberty. The Legal Structure of the New Reproduction", *Southern California Law Review*, Vol. 59, No. 5, 1986, pp. 939–1041, available online: www.public.iastate.edu/~jwcwolf/Papers/RobertsonPL.pdf, p. 249.

482 Plato, *The Laws*, Saunders T.J. (trans), Penguin, 1970, p. 183.

483 Maclean S., "The Right to Reproduce", in Campbell T. *et al.* (eds.), *Human Rights: from Rhetoric to Reality*, Blackwell, 1986, pp. 99–122.

Nevertheless, the possibility to claim it as a natural right does not seem so evident to those "who see the child as a gift from God, or a blessing on a marriage"[484] instead of seeing the child as part of their own private and family life.

Floyd and Pomerantz argue that the right to reproduce is not a natural right derived from intrinsic human nature for two reasons: (1) having a child involves other people, not only oneself, and therefore cannot be considered as an aspect of self-determination; and (2) reproduction creates a new person who is not consulted and therefore is not an aspect of the right to do with one's body as one wishes.[485] This is a strong argument to restrict individuals' liberty because it embeds reproduction in a network of conflicting interests between all the concerned parties in the reproductive process and not just the one who wants to reproduce. Locating the right to reproduce in a network, which by definition is a social construct of more than just one person, reduces the power to claim that each person holds a natural and absolute right to found a family. Therefore it is questionable how much the reproductive right has to do with nature and if this should be the strongest argument to claim its absolute character.

John Harris makes a point by locating the individual right in a network in which other individual rights conflict with each other, illustrating how the reproductive right is limited by the competing rights and freedoms of others.[486] The child as the significant "future other" should be treated with the utmost respect. John Stuart Mill argues that reproductive freedom should not only be restricted in regard to the best interest of the child, but it also should be considered a crime to conceive a child without prospects of being able to provide for him/her.[487]

The United Nations promotes the reproductive right as a basic human right of both the couple and the individual to freely decide on the number, spacing and timing of conceiving children in concordance with the definition of sexual and reproductive health. The exercise of the right should always go together with the responsibility towards living and future children, as well as towards the community.[488]

---

484 Chadwick R.F. (ed.), *Ethics, Reproduction and Genetic Control*, Routledge, 1990.

485 Floyd S.L., Pomerantz D., "Is there a Natural Right to Have Children?", in Arthur J. (ed.), *Morality and Moral Controversies*, Prentice-Hall, 1981, pp. 131–138.

486 Harris J., "The Right to Found a Family", in Scarre G. (ed.), *Children, Parents and Politics*, Cambridge University Press, 1989.

487 "It still remains unrecognized, that to bring a child into existence without a fair prospect of being able, not only to provide for its body, but instruction and training for its mind, is a moral crime, both against the unfortunate offspring and against society": Mill J.S., "On Liberty", Warnock M. (ed.), *Utilitarianism*, Fontana, 1972, p. 239.

488 *Report of the International Conference on Population and Development*, United Nations, Cairo, 1994, p. 40.

4.1.2. THE REPRODUCTIVE RIGHT AS A RIGHT TO PRIVACY

Within the individual framework for deriving the reproductive right, an alternative view of treating it as a natural right is to treat it as a right to privacy, or a right to a private life (article 8 ECHR). As such, the reproductive right is an aspect of the personal liberty freely to decide, without any governmental intrusion into matters that affect the private life of either married or single persons. In these terms, it is more related to liberty than to a right to be claimed[489] implying that other persons or the state should restrain from interfering in others' reproductive choices.[490]

The political theorist Philips has criticised the gender-biased concepts of public life as being associated with male political agency, and private and family life as a reserved female domain, arguing for detaching the genders from the concepts and leaving the choices to individuals.[491]

The right to privacy as a fundamental right of the individual and not of the family enjoys great recognition in the USA.[492] Apart from the great importance attributed to an individual, the health care system in a market-driven society treats patients as consumers with the utmost care to satisfy the private needs on the level of services.

In contrast, on more European soil, and at the beginning of opening the discussion on regulating access to ART, the Warnock Report argued that applying reproductive technology should not be considered a private matter since the resources are publicly financed and therefore the public has an interest in their proper allocation.[493] Reproduction is substantially associated with relations between parent and child, which for some authors are as profoundly private as they are eminently public ones. Therefore the interests of the child must be accessible to public scrutiny, because they are as public as anything in the history of civilisation has been.[494] Some other authors have associated access to ART with the harm done or avoided if the practice is allowed or restricted.[495]

---

489 Robertson J.A., *Children of Choice. Freedom and the New Reproductive Technologies*, Princeton University Press, 1994, Chapter 2, p. 22.

490 *Ibid.*

491 Philips A., *Endangering Democracy*, Polity Press, 1991.

492 In the case of *Eisenstadt v. Baird*, 405 U.S. 438, 1972, before the US Supreme Court, the judge ruled that that the right to privacy primarily envisages the right of the individual, married or single, to be free from unwarranted governmental intrusion into the decision-making process to bear or beget a child as considered to be fundamental for the person's liberty (the context was the right to use contraception on equal grounds for married as well as for unmarried couples in concordance with the equal protection clause of the Constitution).

493 Warnock Report, 1984.

494 Stoljar S.J., "Persons and Family", in Rheinstein M., Stoljar S.J. (eds.), *International Encyclopedia of Comparative Law*, Vol. 4, Mouton, 1973.

495 Hart H.L.A., *Law, Liberty and Morality*, Oxford University Press, 1963; Devlin P., *The Enforcement of Morals*, Oxford University Press, 1965.

It is indisputable that the early debates on access to ART looked for a solid argumentation in its therapeutic purpose, i.e. curing the infertility of a couple. The "luxury" of granting single women the right to a genetically related child is a rather new achievement. Many European countries gave the possibility to single women to conceive through ART only recently.[496] Despite the current very present liberalisation in Europe, the possibility for a single woman to be a beneficiary of the right to assisted fertilisation was and in many countries still is a controversial issue.[497] On another level, many studies relate the access to sperm donations for women as a modus for creating families by lesbian couples.[498]

Recent definitions of the meaning of what *private life* as part of article 8 of the ECHR encompasses also address the individual's physical and psychological integrity, personal or private space, personal information and identity, autonomy and sexuality, self-development as well as relation with others and reputation.[499] The case law of the ECtHR even announces that under the umbrella of article 8 of the ECHR, a potentially new human right – to know one's biological identity – may arise.[500]

496 Belgium, Bulgaria, Denmark, Estonia, Finland, Greece, Hungary, Iceland, Montenegro, Russia, Spain, Great Britain, Belarus, Serbia, Ukraine and Macedonia: Howard W.J. *et al.*, International Society of Fertilities Sciences, *IFFS Surveillance*, 2010, pp. 22–23.

497 For the situation in different countries, see more in Chapter 1.

498 Marina S., Marina F., Marina D., "Access to Fertility Treatment by Lesbian Couples", in Schenker J.G. (ed.), *Ethical Dilemmas in Assisted Reproductive Technologies*, Walter de Gruyter, 2011, p. 254; Haimes E., Weiner K., "'Everybody's Got a Dad …' Issues for Lesbian Families in the Management of the Donor Insemination", *Sociology of Health & Illness*, Vol. 22, No. 4, 2000, pp. 477–499; Flaks D. *et al.* "Lesbians Choosing Motherhood. A Comparative Study of Lesbian and Heterosexual Parents and their Children", *Developmental Psychology*, Vol. 31, No. 1, 1995, pp. 105–114; Chan R., Raboy B., Patterson C., "Psychological Adjustment Among Children Conceived via Donor Insemination by Lesbian and Heterosexual Mothers", *Child Development*, Vol. 69, No. 2, 1998, pp. 443–457; Brewaeys A., Ponjaert I., Van Hall E.V., Golombok S., "Donor Insemination. Child Development and Family Functioning in Lesbian Mother Families", *Human Reproduction*, Vol. 12, No. 6, 1997, pp. 1349–1359; Golombok S., Tasker F., Murray C., "Children Raised in Fatherless Families from Infancy: Family Relationships and the Socio-emotional Development of Children of Lesbian and Single Heterosexual Mothers", *Journal of Child Psychology and Psychiatry*, Vol. 38, No. 7, 1997, pp. 783–791.

499 Clayton, R., Tomlinson T., *The Law of Human Rights* (2nd edition), Oxford University Press, 2009.

500 *Research Report, Bioethics and the Case-law of the Court*, Council of Europe, European Court of Human Rights, 2012, pp. 44–50, available online: www.coe.int/t/dg3/healthbioethic/texts_and_documents/Bioethics_and_caselaw_Court_EN.pdf. The potentiality for recognizing specific human right to know one's biological identity is also interpreted as existent in some recent writings. See, for instance, Dobozi V., "The Right to Know One's Biological Identity", *The International Conference Challenges of the Knowledge Society*, Bucharest, 17–18 May 2013 (7th edition).

4.2. THE "ARTIFICIALITY" OF REPRODUCTION

The second two categories of re-observing the ontology of the reproductive right are related to its counterpart – *artificiality* as an attempt to contrive the natural model. They differ significantly from nature as a source of rights because they are "caused or produced by a human and especially social or political agency".[501] The initial title "artificial insemination" for technological assistance in the process of reproduction was precisely inspired by the capacity to imitate human nature by human achievement. In these terms, the reproductive right, and sometimes even obligation, are derived not from intrinsic human nature but from the social and political agency that strive to define and shape desirable against undesirable human practices and behaviour. As such, the reproductive right can derive from the family context, and in legal language is related to the *right to family life* (article 8 ECHR), or from the context of the wider political set of values to be protected in the name of the *public good*.

The *artifice* in artificial insemination is also described as a substitution of a mechanical procedure for "natural" intercourse.[502] Along these lines, "artificial insemination" is artificial because there are no parties engaged in intercourse, but still there is a conception of a child as if there was. What the artifice could not imitate though, is the substitution of the real father, who "does" the fatherhood, with the fictive donor who "is" a genetic father. From here on, the artifice in assisted reproduction mostly lies in fictive, imaginary fathers, which are results of an accepted social reproduction. Donor anonymity is a perfect example of "turning a blind eye" towards the needs of a child for a father. Therefore in cases of single women conceiving by sperm donation, the "artificiality" fails to imitate the nature of the parental relationship with a father.

4.2.1. THE REPRODUCTIVE RIGHT AS A RIGHT TO FAMILY LIFE

The right to family life depicts the social dimension of the family. Even though the affiliation laws are mostly built on the grounds of *consanguinity* connecting the familial chain with biological glue, family life as a lived reality is connected with emotional attachments (the factual mutual life, behaving and acting as a family). In these terms, the realisation of the need for a family life of single women could also be satisfied by adopting a child. Nevertheless, adoption could be the *artificial* substitution of satisfying the *right to family life* and not *the right to reproduce* genetically related offspring. Some authors have questioned fertility-preservation

[501] Merriam-Webster online dictionary, defining "artificial": www.merriam-webster.com/dictionary/artificial.

[502] Dewar J., "Fathers in Law", in Lee R., Morgan D. (eds.), *Birthrights, Law and Ethics at the Beginning of Life*, Routledge, 1989.

interventions as part of the societal dogmas.[503] Along these lines, if parenthood is an essential component of a person's life and makes people happier it would mean that genetically related families are preferred over those based on alternative ways of affiliating (such as adoption, donation of genetic material to substitute one's own, etc.).[504]

The right to claim existence of family life as *possession d'état/factual situation* is different from the right to claim a need to create family life. The fact that the child-wish and therefore the family wish are not purely physiological needs, but very often socially desirable and preferred practices has been outside the interest of many authors.[505] The social constraints of desirable human life in the past demanded the following of the "preferred template" of the woman as a mother and a wife, and of the man as a provider who passes on genes and inheritance as their expected contribution. This notion even had a greater political aim – building nation states through the perception of women as mothers of the nation, thus attributing to women a role even on the level of a national duty. Blaming women for decreasing birth rates in "aging nations"[506] are even nowadays political tools for building national policies.[507]

With women's emancipation, the social pressure on and expectances of the "all-mighty women" even increased. Nowadays, in Western societies, women are expected to play both roles: being economically independent, therefore family providers, as well as being caring mothers and possibly, but not necessarily, wives. With the possibility of conceiving alone with the assistance of ART, women are experiencing a second emancipation apart from economical, and that is emotional. It seems that independence of this kind leads to alienation of family life, and not a need for it. The burden of both emancipations is very tricky and as such analysed through the prism of the *theory of double bind*.[508] On these premises, it is difficult to distinguish whether the desire that develops into a need to have a

503 Pennings G., Mertes H., "Ethical Issues in Infertility Treatment", *Best Practice & Research Clinical Obstetrics & Gynecology*, Vol. 26, No. 6, 2012. The authors were examining the fertility-preservation interventions for people with cancer.

504 *Ibid.* See more in McLeod C., "Morally Justifying Oncofertility Research", in Woodruff T.K., Zoloth L., Campo-Engelstein L. *et al.* (eds.), *Oncofertility. Reflections from the Humanities and Social Sciences*, Springer, 2010, pp. 187–194; Asch A., "The Lessons of Oncofertility for Assisted Reproduction", in Woodruff T.K., Zoloth L., Campo-Engelstein L. *et al.* (eds.), *Oncofertility. Reflections from the Humanities and the Social Sciences*, Springer, 2010, pp. 181–186.

505 French M., *Beyond Power: Woman, Man and Morals*, Cape, 1985; Singer P., Wales D., *The Reproduction Revolution: New Ways of Making Babies*; Oxford University Press, 1987; Goodwin M., "Assisted Reproductive Technology and the Double Bind: The Illusory Choice of Motherhood", *Journal of Gender, Race and Justice*, Vol. 9, No. 1, 2005, pp. 1–54.

506 Nations in which mortality rates are higher than birth rates.

507 See more Anthias F., Yuval-Davis N., *Women-Nation-State*, St. Martin's Press, 1989; Peterson S.V., "Sexing Political Identities. Nationalism as Heterosexism", *International Feminist Journal of Politics*, Vol. 1, No. 1, p. 8; Kopac J., "Otrok, Zenin Dar Ocetu i Narodu (A Child, Wife's Gift to the Father and to the Nation)", *Sobotna Priloga Dela*, 2000.

508 Goodwin M., "Assisted Reproductive Technology and the Double Bind: The Illusory Choice of Motherhood", *Journal of Gender, Race and Justice*, Vol. 9, No. 1, 2005, pp. 1–54.

child is biological or social. Claiming that the desire to have a child is affected by social circumstances and that there is a social influence on the child-wish is not to say that the physiological desire is not urging or important. Nevertheless, its fundamental role as an essence natural to human beings just as life itself should be carefully evaluated.

Legally recognised family life as a lived practice encompasses many components: from emotional and custodial relationships to property-related relationships. In contrast to Plato's elaboration on the desire to continue the life circle towards endeavouring immortality, for some reproduction signifies legal continuation of the property as an appendix to the personality *mortis causa*. Moreover, for some the legal continuation of property is more important than the continuation of genes.

Therefore the *legitimation of a child* as a form of recognising an extra-marital child in the past, and recognising a child today as a way of creating legal acknowledgement of a future heir, could also prevail over the pure physiological or emotional need to have a child. Along these lines, the possibility of establishing the fatherhood of the sperm donor who donated to single women might be appealing to all of the concerned parties: the child, the donor and the woman. Inheritance as a motivation for establishing a legal parental link is likely to be a rationale for making a legal recognition or initiating a legal procedure, because the child is usually entitled to search for information regarding his/her origin only after reaching 18, when the emotional bonding or the parental responsibilities of the father will be to a great extent already exhausted. What could possibly remain from the legal effects of establishing *family life* among the father and the child is the acknowledgement of the biological reality (not only with the sperm donor, but also his and the child's family) and the property effects *mortis causa*, i.e. inheritance.

The problem appears on a level when one or two parties are against the idea of establishing the legal link, and the side-effects that arise. In these terms, women's need to found a family might not correspond with the idea of a *family life* for her child with the sperm donor and his family. The sperm donor might already belong to a family formation, without any need to expand either the emotional or the legal effects of another *family life*. The child's interests which should always prevail were already compromised from the moment of his/her conception as society has already reached a consensus not to have a voice in an adult's decision either altruistically to donate, or private and intimate to found a family. Namely, nobody asked the child if it agreed to be born under such circumstances. The child's echo is only heard afterwards, when reaching adulthood, going back and re-examining the rights and wrongs of the legal solutions of anonymous/non-anonymous donors assisting single women to reproduce.

At the present time and with the legacy of the legal solutions in the past, the *right to family life* as a positive right is confronted with the *right not to establish family life* as a negative right. The latter however has already been granted to the sperm donor, the woman and the child as a *conditio sine qua non* for realising the reproductive freedom of single women in the first place. As the foundation of family life has been conditioned, and as the conditions are more *contra* than *pro* with regard to establishing family life of the child, reconsiderations should be made on at least two levels: (1) if the single woman's right to found a family endangers the child's life to construct its own complete family narration, and (2) if the *conditio sine qua non* for single women's realisation of the right to family life are really tailored as if without them the idea of conceiving will no longer be possible (e.g. donors would abstain from donating).

Therefore another aspect is to pose the question if the donation conditions could be changed in order to respect and allow the possibility for future realisation of the *right to family life* of the child and the donor. Article 8 of the ECHR also encompasses the right to private and family life of the donor in relation to his human dignity and autonomy as a person donating to a health and social care institution.[509]

4.2.2. THE REPRODUCTIVE RIGHT AS A GREATER PUBLIC GOOD

Looking for the foundations of the right to reproduce in the outer political context as a doctrinarian set of values to be protected in the name of the *public/common good* goes back to the identification of the family with the state. According to Aristotle, the common good of the state (*πόλεις*) is a synthesis of the private interests of families (*οἶκος*), making the integrity of the family a private institution essential for the common life in the state.[510] On the other hand, an identification of this kind could be seen as an intrusion into the private and family life of the individual by the state. Very often the rationale for choosing one against another policy is mirrored by the global goals to be achieved (that may aim towards boosting or dropping the birth rate) as a public interest and not in the reflection of the particular individual liberty or right. Thus, other reasons (political, economic, religious and eugenic) which are beyond the individual through history have dominated the private and family domain dictating when, how and in what number people should procreate. The most influential example in the 18th century was the *Malthus theory on control of population growth* due to the estimated decrease of already scarce resources, and the possibility of overpopulation that

[509] No author, "Article 8: The Right to Respect for Private and Family Life, Home and Correspondence", *Human Rights Review*, 2012, p. 287, available online: www.equality humanrights.com/uploaded_files/humanrights/hrr_article_8.pdf.

[510] Provencal L.V., "The Family in Aristotle", *Animus*, Vol. 6, 2001, available online: www.mun.ca/animus/2001vol6/provencal6.htm#1.

might lead to famine, disease or war.[511] Some countries, such as China, have introduced the theory of population control in practice. The Chinese government adopted a one-child policy (unless particular circumscribed conditions obtained) in 1979.[512] These restrictions, in combination with cultural preferences for male children as ancestors of the family, led to severe practices of abortions for sex selection in both China and India.[513] In contrast, some other countries feared increased mortality and decreased birth rates and consequently promoted pro-natal policies as part of their strategy of growing nations. This was the case in France (introducing the most restrictive laws on abortion in Europe in 1920, as an attempt to recuperate for the lost lives during World War I),[514] Germany (the Nazis' rationale of increasing the population from 66 to 90 million in order to claim more territory)[515] and Italy (Benito Mussolini intended to grow worldwide power by growing the nation).[516] This was also noted in more recent years under the veil of maintaining political viability or seizing political dominance in the Middle East, Israel, Iran and Iraq.[517] Practices of this kind demonstrate that the use of the state's power to control reproduction and the private domain are not outdated in the domain of achieving other political goals. This is also an ongoing scenario in the Republic of Macedonia, manifesting in a form of constant promotion and subventions for families with more children, public governmental campaigns against abortion resulting in a recent change in the law on abortion,[518]

---

511 Malthus T., *An Essay on the Principle of Population*, London, 1798, available online: www.gutenberg.org/files/4239/4239-h/4239-h.htm.

512 See more in Croli E., Davin D., Kane P (eds.), *China's One-Child Policy*, New York, St. Martin's Press, 1985.

513 See more in Callahan J.C., "Introduction", in Callahan J.C. (ed.), *Reproduction, Ethics and Law. Feminist Perspectives*, Indiana University Press, 1995, p. 256.

514 *Ibid.* p. 255. Referring to McLaren A., *Sexuality and the Social Order. The Debate Over the Fertility of Women and Workers in France, 1770–1920*, Holms and Meier, 1983.

515 Callahan J.C. (ed.), *Reproduction, Ethics and Law. Feminist Perspectives*, Indiana University Press, 1995, p. 255, referring to Sanger M., *An Autobiography*, Norton, 1938, reissued Dover, 1971. It is also worthwhile mentioning that in this period Germany combined pro- and anti-birth policies, applying sterilisation laws to preclude reproduction by "inferiors" and intense propaganda to boost reproduction among "superiors", i.e. women of the desired heritage (Callahan J.C. (ed.), *Reproduction, Ethics and Law. Feminist Perspectives*, Indiana University Press, 1995, p. 257 referring to Field M.J., *The Comparative Politics of Birth Control. Determinants of Policy Variation and Change in the Developed Nations*, Praeger, 1983).

516 Callahan J.C. (ed.), *Reproduction, Ethics and Law. Feminist Perspectives*, Indiana University Press, 1995.

517 *Ibid.* p. 256.

518 Закон за прекинување на бременоста, *Службен весник на Република Македонија* (Law on Termination of the Pregnancy, *Official Gazette of the Republic of Macedonia*), 87/2013, 17.06.2013. After fierce public debate over the enactment of the changes in the law (more restrictive than before since it introduces mandatory counselling to women prior to abortions, as well as a time framework to re-evaluate their decisions), several non-governmental organisations for human rights and a university professor launched an initiative for evaluating the constitutionality of the Law before the Constitutional Court on the Global Day of Action for Access to Safe and Legal Abortion (28.09.2013). See: http://plusinfo.mk/vest/107490/HERA-Ustavniot-sud-da-go-zapre-zakonot-za-abortus. At the time of writing (05.05.2014), the process is still pending.

promoting family life as a preferred option against the selfishness of singlehood, and attempts to lift the heterosexual family as a constitutional category.[519] The legitimacy for imposing particular ways of family life is usually hypocritically grounded in other (than political) values which are closer to the individual and not to the state (so that the individual can identify him/herself on a personal level). That is how the individual right to family life melds with the dominantly accepted cultural values. The process of building values through different methods (one of which is continuous propaganda) and thus particular collective culture is long and persistent. Therefore carefully nurtured cultural values are imbedded not only in society but also in individual identification and integration within society. Consequently, they cannot fade away easily, but it is a long, time-consuming process for the change on both collective and private levels to occur. On the contrary, if states focus more on social and economic reforms instead of controlling reproduction,[520] a submissive individual may not feel suffocated in their exercise of reproductive choices in the collective culture. Nevertheless, it remains the case that matters of contraception, abortion, sexual freedom, parental choice and application of reproductive technologies are dependent on enforcement of morals, these being dictated by legitimate state interests.[521] This is especially important for the acceptance of the new reproductive technologies and the ways they are entering into the domain of family life and parenting, while questioning morality and human dignity. Ongoing re-evaluation of morality is a recent suggestion of the Human Fertilisation and Embryology Authority of the UK government to introduce a new way of life creation with DNA from three biological parents.[522] This possibility has already been contested as tantamount to eugenics. Nevertheless, the future will show if the UK will be the first country in the world to introduce this controversial IVF technique.

The field of family life is more sensitive to good practices of applying individual human rights, since it is lifted up to a level of community, considering it as "the smallest cell of the society"[523] and therefore a society in itself already. In these

519 Recent public discussion in the Parliamentary Commission for Constitutional Matters regarding the proposal to define the family as an exclusive union of one man and one woman in the Constitution (despite the already existent same definition in the Family Law) took place on 16 September 2013. See footnote 1493.

520 This is also suggested by Callahan J.C. (ed.), *Reproduction, Ethics and Law. Feminist Perspectives*, Indiana University Press, 1995, p. 258.

521 Cohwn S., Taub N. (eds.), *Reproductive Laws for the 1990s, Contemporary Issues in Biomedicine, Ethics, and Society*, Humana Press, 1989, p. 426.

522 Collins N., "Three Parents Babies "Incompatible" with Human Dignity", *The Telegraph*, 04.10.2013, available online: www.telegraph.co.uk/science/science-news/10356387/Three-parent-babies-incompatible-with-human-dignity.html.

523 In Aristotelian *Politics* I, the family is defined as a specific form of community which integrates individuals into a common life that enables them to become as members of the family also members of the political community, city-state). See more in Provencal L.V., "The Family in Aristotle", *Animus*, Vol. 6, 2001, available online: www.mun.ca/animus/2001vol6/provencal6.htm#1.

terms, it is questionable if a person belonging to a family formation is primarily an individual with rights or an individual with obligations and responsibilities.

The relational concept of personhood is ambiguous for several reasons. As a key element that launches all the other consequential misinterpretations is the context in which a person develops. By investigating cultural pro-attitudes, Prodanov distinguishes between individualists and collectivists, as related to Catholic, liberal and Western tradition on the one hand, and Orthodox, communitarian Eastern European tradition on the other hand. According to this author, while "the former sees the person as a bundle of rights", the latter perception of a person is identified with a "bundle of his social identities, affiliations and roles".[524] From this quotation, it is understandable why the actualisation of personhood in Western countries begins at the moment when one is entitled to acquire his own rights, and in Eastern countries only when one coexists in the group, class or community and consequently becomes a recognised subject, not as a holder of rights, but primarily as a holder of obligations. Therefore, if for *individualists* the human essence originates from within, as an inherited and self-sufficient element for individual development, for *communitarians* the same human essence is a substrate of social identities, affiliations and roles. Bearing in mind this historical background of development of thought and science, it is easy to understand why some authors hold firmly onto ontological properties, claiming individuality as a supreme value and promote observation over isolating oneself, while others always interrelate the individual with society, as a mutual mirror in which both the individual and society look upon and therefore shape themselves.[525]

For instance, it is questionable whether an individual single woman wanting to conceive a child by sperm donation in a country where the procedure for her is forbidden holds primarily an individual right to reproduce or an obligation to refrain from reproducing. It is also questionable whether such state intrusion into the field of family life is a harsh infringement of her individual human rights or a responsibility towards protection of the rights of the child to be brought up with two parents, or even beneficial for the higher public good.

In Western societies there are three major ethical traditions that are dominating and shaping the policy regarding the reproduction: (1) the *virtue-oriented tradition*, (2) the *social-utility tradition*, and (3) the *individual rights-oriented tradition* (as originating from *the deontological tradition*).[526]

524 Prodanov V., "Cultural Pro-Attitudes, Reproductive Ethics and Embryo Protection", in Evans D. (ed.), *Conceiving the Embryo, Ethics, Law and Practice in Human Embryology*, Martinus Nijhoff, 1996.

525 Taken from Ignovska E., "The Value of Life of the Embryo, the Argument of Potentiality to Develop, and the Context in which is Embedded", in Hongladarom S. (ed.), *Genomics and Bioethics: Interdisciplinary Perspectives, Technologies and Advancements*, 2011, p. 35.

526 Kaplan J.L., Tong R., *Controlling Our Reproductive Destiny. A Technological and Philosophical Perspective*, MIT Press, 1994.

The virtue-oriented tradition is mainly represented by the ancient Greek philosopher Aristotle. The *virtue of practical wisdom* or prudence encompasses the wisdom or intelligence with the practical thought as an ability to balance the rational with the emotional towards reaching a state of well-being or personal happiness (*εὐδαιμονία*).[527] Because people have different values, norms should guide the practices by objective rules, not by subjective ideals. Virtue-oriented ethicists recognise the heterogeneous society and therefore advocate extensive rules that grant individual character in each case, considering the particular circumstances. The particular individual good as the ultimate good (Epicurus, Spinoza, Nietzsche) can be measured through emotions that correspond with ethical or unethical actions. Thus, the feelings of content and joy or repulsiveness and sadness (David Hume, Baruch Spinoza); happ. or unhapp. (Aristotle, Socrates, Greek Stoics); self-fulfilled or not (Georg Wilhelm Friedrich Hegel and Francis Herbert Bradley) signify that the action is ethical or unethical.[528]

In contrast, the *social-utility tradition* seeks the maximum aggregate utility as the overall happiness of the group affected by the consequences of particular action rather than an individual happiness. Utilitarianism belongs to the consequentialism's branch. As a part of normative ethics, it guides human actions with normative rules that predict consequences which achieve overall maximum happiness and minimum suffering as an output. Consequences can only be calculated and anticipated by using the empirical knowledge of human behaviour through psychology, sociology and other sciences. A typical consequentialist's argument is "the welfare of the child", that takes into account the real effects of the protection of the best interest of the child.[529] Classic utilitarianism is represented by Jeremy Bentham and John Stuart Mill. Utilitarianism can be characterised as a quantitative approach to ethics that weighs up the good and bad practices in the final output and as such stands in contrast to deontological ethics, which does not regard the consequences of an act as a determinant of its moral worth. Utilitarianism has been criticised as a threat to individual rights, which are overruled by the majority in a democratic society that calculates only the aggregate utility.[530]

The *rights-oriented tradition* accepts the relativity of the rights and therefore claims that there have to be some circumstances that warrant the state's interference with an individual's procreative liberty. The rights actually derive from the duty or obligation, therefore representing the deontological tradition[531] as part of the normative ethics. According to deontology, an act is ethical if it

---

527 Aristotle, *Nicomachean Ethics*, Irwin T. (trans.) (2nd edition), Hackett, 1999.

528 Steinberg A., "The Foundations and Application of Medical Ethics", in Schenker J.G. (ed.), *Ethical Dilemmas in Assisted Reproductive Technologies*, Walter de Gruyter, 2011.

529 Pennings G., Martes H., "Ethical Issues in Infertility Treatment, Best Practice & Research", *Clinical Obstetrics & Gynecology*, Vol. 26, No. 6, 2012, pp. 853–863.

530 Riley J., "Utilitarian Ethics and Democratic Government", *Ethics*, Vol. 100, No. 2, 1990, pp. 335–348.

531 *"Deos"* in Greek means obligation.

complies with the positive normative rules that bind obligation or duty. As such, deontology contrasts with consequentialism. Immanuel Kant's deontological thought argues that what makes action right or wrong is not judged by the consequences but the motives of the person who undertakes the action. Therefore it is not solely important what consequences are caused by an action, but even more important are the reasons for which the action is taken. When claiming that an act is right, the rights-oriented tradition considers (1) whether the act is permitted for everyone on equal grounds, under the same circumstances and without discrimination; and (2) whether the act grants equal respect to the interests of everyone who will be affected by it. Making these conditions relevant for leaning towards a positivistic approach emphasises the drawbacks of the legal paternalism that impose the right choice of action, and consequently restricts the individual freedom to choose.

The rationale behind paternalism is an analogy with the parent–child relationship when an adult is unable to act voluntarily because he or she is ignorant of crucial information or is blocked by some form of internal or external coercion. The legal paternalistic approach considers that restricting liberties as an act of self-determination is not necessarily wrong. On the contrary, limited access to executing some liberties might prove to be beneficial for the person restricted and for the others affected by the action. Restriction of liberty cases have also been made against those who act immorally, where the term *immoral* is not equivalent to the term *illegal* (for instance in suicide cases).

Modern principles that guide medical ethics are: *autonomy* as a fundamental principle of making informed decisions about one's own health, *non-maleficence* as an obligation to restrain from hurting others and preventing potential harm, *beneficence* as an active obligation to do good and help others, and *justice* as related to equality and fair distribution of rights and obligations.[532]

The Warnock Report as one of the pioneers in the ethical deliberation on the use of ART suggests utilitarian reasoning and primacy of the common good in the application of assisted reproduction since the political choices will affect children and next generations in the long run. Warnock emphasises the consequentialism of her approach, taking a stance that the consequences are more important than the act itself. In her view, there are common values under which umbrella each individual should justify their own actions: "The question must ultimately be: what kind of society can we praise and admire? In what kind of society can we live with our conscience clear?".[533] Warnock refers to the political responsibility to make choices in the reproduction context that will have consequences in the future. Therefore regulating reproduction is not about creating positive law only, but about the capacity to anticipate the possible outcomes of a particular solution.

532 Beauchamp T.L., Childress F.J., *Principles of Biomedical Ethics* (5th edition), Oxford University Press, 2001.

533 Warnock M., *A Question of Life. The Warnock Report on Human Fertilization and Embryology*, Blackwell, 1985.

In these terms, if the consensus is achieved on a level that it is wrong to bring into the world a person who will not know and be parented by his/her father, most likely the possibility of this situation happening will be reduced in due course. On the other hand, if the consensus is achieved on a level that a child is not seriously harmed by not knowing or not being cared for by the genetic father, the possibility of seeing many children in the future sharing this particular destiny is very likely to become a reality. In the Report this was considered a threat to children, communities and society at large. At the current moment, ART interrupts the biological relationship with the donor in most countries as a policy. The link between begetting and rearing is broken through history by adoption too. Nevertheless, there is a difference between adopting and offering care and family to a parentless child in need of care, and voluntarily producing offspring sentenced to be parentless as a matter of policy. There is nothing wrong with adopting a child, but one could legitimately question if it is wrong to create a child for the purpose of giving it up for adoption. The donated gametes will turn into living examples of the policy of breaking the link between begetting and rearing. Donor conceived children are in a very different position than adoptive children within the family because they have not been abandoned by their genetic parents, and they are often biologically related to one member of the couple.[534]

From the ancient philosophers Plato and Aristotle, the family is in essence "a social association grounded in the human capacity to rationalise rather than a natural association grounded in the immediacy of sexual instinct and biological ties".[535] The definition of the nature of the family as such was not contested. What was a different interpretation of the family between Plato and Aristotle, however, originated from the very same discussion regarding the origins of the virtues of good and reaching happiness: the common good of the community as a whole *versus* the individual good. While Plato deduced the individual's particularity from the universality as a higher good of the state, Aristotle represented the opposite, inferring the good from the human essence of each individual to form associations which are founded in natural desire and necessities. By analysing Plato's and Aristotle's philosophies on families, Provencal concludes that it is natural to the human essence to form associations, either on a level of family or society, as a way of self-actualisation, lifting the family onto a spiritual level that aims towards realisation of ethical life of virtue and happiness.[536] St Thomas Aquinas also perceived family as a necessary community for meeting members' needs and gaining self-realisation.[537]

---

534 Frith L., "Gamete Donation and Anonymity. The Ethical and Legal Debate", *Human Reproduction*, Vol. 16, No. 5, 2001, p. 821.

535 Provencal L.V., "The Family in Aristotle", *Animus*, Vol. 6, 2001, available online: www.mun.ca/animus/2001vol6/provencal6.htm#1 (para. 63).

536 *Ibid.*

537 See, for instance, Gilby T., *The Political Thought of Thomas Aquinas*, University of Chicago Press, 1958.

Reproduction is a way of both self-realisation and realisation in the community. Some communitarian authors have criticised the extreme individualistic conceptions of the liberal traditions, moving reproduction from individual isolation as it involves and affects others.[538] Thus, locating individuals in a family makes the reproductive right of single women relative because of the rights and interests of the other concerned parties in the reproductive project. The reproductive right is diluted from its absolute character when against the rights and freedoms of the other concerned parties – the donor and the child. It is not disputable that reproduction is both natural and a social need of an individual. Nevertheless, an argument against its absolute realisation should promote the recognition and appreciation of others.

4.2.3. THE REPRODUCTIVE RIGHT AS A RIGHT TO ACCESS ART ON EQUAL GROUNDS FOR EVERYBODY – PRINCIPLE OF NON-DISCRIMINATION

The right to access particular goods or services is tackled by Aristotle, followed by Aquinas in terms of *distributive* (the relationship between the community and the individual and how the goods or services, but also the burdens are to be distributed) and *commutative justice* (the relationship between individuals in matters of exchange).[539] Associating distributive justice with equality in actions (because for Aristotle the justice is a virtue about actions and not about emotions) is vague itself. Does it encompass equality *per se* (every human person should be granted equal rights and liberties because they belong to the same kind, irrespective of the circumstances and the contribution), or proportional equality in terms of "to all its due" which is characterised mainly by differentiation of levels of merit and therefore treating equals equally, and unequals unequally? By posing the question of the right to access ART for single women we face a problem that is at the intersection between the relationship with the community and among different individuals. It is not only that the equality between every human person or women as a particular gender to access ART is concerned, but it is also the relationship between women, donors and children that makes the individual reproductive right itself more difficult to accept as an absolute one.

---

538 For a communitarian critique on liberal tradition, see Sandel M., *Liberalism and the Limits of Justice*, Cambridge University Press, 1982; Sandel M., *Liberalism and its Critics*, New York University Press, 1984; Rasmussen D. (ed.), *Universalism v. Communitarianism. Contemporary Debates in Ethics*, MIT Press, 1990; Avineri S., De-Shalit A. (eds.), *Communitarianism and Individualism*, Oxford University Press, 1992; Glandon M.A., *Rights Talk. The Impoverishment of Political Discourse*, Free Press, 1991.

539 Aristotle, *Nicomachean Ethics*, Book 3; Aquinas T., *Summa Theologica*.

The International Conference on Population and Development held in Cairo, 1994 recognised some reproductive rights as basic human rights. Paragraph 7.3 states: "these rights rest on the recognition of the basic right of all couples and individuals to decide freely and responsibly on the number, spacing and timing of their children and to have the information and means to do so, and the right to attain the highest standard of sexual and reproductive health. It also includes their right to make decisions concerning reproduction free of discrimination, coercion and violence, as expressed in human rights documents".[540]

The Fourth World Conference on Women held in Beijing in 1995 also confirmed the principles of non-discrimination and certain guarantees when it comes to the right to decide freely and responsibly about sexual and reproductive matters.

The Convention on the Elimination of All Forms of Discrimination Against Women guarantees the reproductive right of women as part of the basic human rights and freedoms, providing that every woman has the right to decide freely on the birth and number of children that she is going to bring up.[541]

The Ethics Committee of the American Society for Reproductive Medicine holds that it is an ethical obligation to treat unmarried and single persons equally with those who are married, even more so when it comes to the application of bio-medically assisted reproduction.[542]

The ECHR's article 14 secures the enjoyment of the rights and freedoms without discrimination on any grounds such as sex, race, colour, language, religion, political or other opinion, national or social origin, association with a national minority, property, birth or other status.

The emphasis on non-discrimination is also set forth in the first principle of the United Nations Report on Population and Development, as referring to the UDHR.[543] The same document also encourages and ensures women's control over their fertility as a cornerstone of population and development-related programmes.[544] Principle 8 recommends the state's responsibility to ensure universal access to (among others also) reproductive health services which include family planning and sexual health. The same principle affords reproductive rights to couples and individuals, as a basic right to decide freely and responsibly the number and spacing of their children, while also providing the information, education and means to do so. In these terms, the objectives aim

540 *Programme of Action of the International Conference on Population and Development*, Part One, Chapter VII, paragraphs 7.2. and 7.3, available online: www.unfpa.org/public/home/sitemap/icpd/International-Conference-on-Population-and-Development/ICPD-Programme#ch7.

541 Article 16, United Nations Convention on the Elimination of All Forms of Discrimination Against Women, 1979.

542 Ethics Committee of the American Society for Reproductive Medicine "Access to Fertility by Gays, Lesbians and Unmarried Persons", *Fertility and Sterility*, Vol. 92, No. 4, 2009.

543 *Report of the International Conference on Population and Development*, United Nations, Cairo, 1994.

544 *Ibid.* Principle 4.

towards ensuring access, affordability of a full range of reproductive healthcare services as well as other methods of personal choice for regulation of fertility that are not against the law to all users.[545]

From the prism of non-discrimination as a supreme principle for safeguarding human rights, should it be treated as constitutional[546] in the European democracies to forbid single, unmarried women to use ART? To deprive an unmarried, single woman, but not a lawful wife nor a woman in a couple, from using ART is a violation of the equal protection.

Once a possibility to conceive using assistance from a reproductive technology is introduced, should it be available to everyone and if not, what kind of arguments could be developed to justify the exclusion of certain categories of persons? In many European jurisdictions, still, single women are not allowed access to ART (see more in Chapter 1).

In circumstances of a wide palette of national attitudes from complete permissiveness to a complete ban on the use of sperm donations to single women, the concerns of the commissioning parents come down to the efforts of reproductive tourism or not. The ECtHR has already taken a stand when it comes to the wide margin of discretion of the Member States to decide on their own regarding permissiveness of gamete donations in the case of *S.H. and Others v. Austria*.[547] Thus, those who do not accept the regulation in their own country could always (if they are financially capable) turn to another more permissive country where they could eventually realise their goals.

Kaplan and Tong give four reasons why states may claim that they have legitimate grounds to limit ART to married woman only, while also offering four counterarguments.[548] The first reason is related to the state interests in population control, and countered by the argument of irrationality to focus population control on only one category (i.e. single women). The second reason is supported by the state interest in encouraging two-parent families, and countered by the statistical fact that two-parent families have already lost the battle following the high rate of divorce and separations. The third reason is represented by the state interest in discouraging poor income environments for children raised by one parent only, and countered by the fact that unmarried women who use ART are usually career women capable of supporting a child. The fourth reason is related to the state interest to prevent inbreeding when the donor is unknown, and countered by the argument that incestuous relationships could be better solved by a clear system for donor records. These authors furthermore treat human relationships,

545 *Ibid.* p. 41.

546 Since the Constitution is a harbour for the protection of human rights, safeguarding them as principles on which pillars of one democratic society rests and builds upon.

547 *S.H. and Others v. Austria*, European Court of Human Rights, No. 57813/00, judgment of 03.11.2011.

548 Kaplan J.L., Tong R., *Controlling Our Reproductive Destiny. A Technological and Philosophical Perspective*, MIT Press, 1994.

especially familial relationships, as profoundly important for making a life meaningful, no less so far women who have not found a man to found a family with. If a financially and emotionally secure woman is permitted to adopt a child, she should also be permitted to have a child by ART.

One of the most cited promotions of the right to reproduce was formulated by John Robertson in his book *Children of Choice*.[549] According to him, procreative liberty is the freedom to decide whether or not to have offspring. To deny procreative choice is to deny a crucial self-defining experience, thus infringing on the person's respect and dignity at the most basic level. According to Robertson, the right to reproduce protects both coital and non-coital reproduction, and ought to be given presumptive priority when conflicts arise. However, the right is not absolute and in the case of seeking restrictions, the burden of proof must be placed on those who want to infringe it. Robertson adds that "protection from unfit parenting requires that unfit parents do not rear, not that they do not reproduce".[550] Therefore the right is connected with reproducing as such rather than with the legal establishment of the parental relationship with the offspring. In this interpretation, the right to reproduce and the right to parent are not the same and an acknowledgement of the former does not necessarily entail an acknowledgement of the latter. It is the right to parent that is infringed by questioning or severing the relationship in cases of abuse and neglect, and not the right to reproduce. According to Robertson, persons have a right to have offspring, even if they do not or cannot rear. The reason why they have it is that denying them procreative choice denies them respect, dignity and in general a crucial self-defining experience. Nevertheless, it would be wrong if a child is created without assessing the reproductive responsibility of the one who ought to realise its reproductive right through medical assistance, due to the creation of a new person who should also be protected. If someone chose to reproduce in this way, it should be assumed that the rearing role and thus parenting was wanted. Especially in cases where third party is introduced into the process, the choosing parents and society should be responsible for the allowed and taken action. For instance, it cannot be ethically good to create a child via sperm donation and give it up for adoption after birth.

Therefore there is another perspective from which to observe reproduction – instead of invoking an indefensible right to become a parent, turning an eye to responsibilities of parenting and the welfare of the future child.[551] Accordingly, the gatekeeping should ensure that the prospective parents are ready to undertake the responsibilities in light of the best interests of the child. This also includes

549 Robertson J.A., *Children of Choice. Freedom and the New Reproductive Technologies*, Princeton University Press, 1994, p. 4.

550 *Ibid.* p. 31.

551 Asch A., "Licensing Parents, Regulating Assisted Reproduction", in Cutas D., Chan S. (eds.), *Families Beyond the Nuclear Ideal*, Bloomsbury Academic, 2012.

assisting the child to know and understand his/her origin, which is an extra responsibility attributed to ART parents in comparison to the other parents.[552]

It is a fact that the same level of legal scrutiny is not attributed to coital and non-coital reproduction. Even though the ethics of creating children should be the same, sexual reproduction is not a subject of scrutiny while assisted reproduction is.[553] An application for realising the reproductive right *via* sexual intercourse is not needed, while parenting by presumption, recognition or judicial determination is automatically included. Sexual reproduction is the only way to become a parent without fulfilling preconditions and being interfered with, until there is conflict between parents or proof of wrongdoing.[554] Nevertheless, assisted reproduction asks for proof of the future well-being of the child prior to conception. In these terms, conceiving a child by sperm donation does not happen spontaneously. It has to be a decision that is well thought out before being made, based on the adults' intentions and fair prospects for the well-being of the child. Therefore if donors are anonymous, accepting access to sperm donation for single women excludes the promised well-being perspective for the best interests of children. If others are to be concerned, the right to reproduce and access to ART could never be claimed on an individual basis.

The differentiation of what Robertson called the *right to reproduce* and the *right to parent* is what makes coital and non-coital reproduction enjoy different treatments. While in sexual reproduction, the right to reproduce cannot be denied, the right to parent can (if for instance the parents want to give the child up for adoption or they are unfit to parent). This cannot be allowed in non-coital reproduction since the prime intention of it is to parent (therefore it would be irrational to give birth to children and give them up for adoption, or claim to be an unfit parent afterwards). Along these lines, the responsibility to decide whom to allow access to conceive children *via* assistance is also greater. These children should be provided with better prospects, at least on a level of satisfying their fundamental rights, among which the right to know and be cared for by both parents[555] is also a matter of policy.

---

552 *Ibid.*

553 Cutas D., "The Right to Reproduce. Sex is Over-rated. On the Right to Reproduce", *Human Fertility*, Vol. 12, No. 1, 2009, pp. 45–52.

554 *Ibid.* Even though the State has had an interest in regulating sexuality at all times, from contraception to abortion, wrongdoing in this case is to be understood in terms of incest, teenage pregnancies or rape.

555 Articles 7 and 8 CRC.

4.3. INFERTILITY AS AN INABILITY TO CONCEIVE IN THE CONTEXT OF SINGLE WOMEN

The evaluation of the eligibility of the beneficiaries of ART treatment is usually connected to infertility.[556] This comes from the experience of couples, and as such it cannot be related to single women's application for sperm donation. As a medical condition, infertility is defined as a failure to conceive following 12 months of unprotected intercourse.[557] Twelve months is the lowest reference limit for *time to pregnancy* by the World Health Organization.[558] The definition, though, does not specify the frequency of the unprotected sexual intercourse. In one of the first reflections on the relationship between ART and infertility, the Warnock Report treats it as a disease or "malfunction" that needs treatment.[559] The definition of *health* that has not been amended since 1948 is rather wide in scope, encompassing "complete physical, mental, and social wellbeing and not merely the absence of disease or infirmity".[560] In these terms, single women not engaged in intercourse do not fulfil the condition of infertility to qualify for ART treatment, but do fulfil the condition of being unhealthy, thus deserving treatment. The assistance to reproduce does not heal infertility as a medical condition. It only assists in creating a baby; therefore it may heal the mental and social well-being of the beneficiaries.

Nevertheless, even fertile persons may opt to use reproductive technologies for different reasons such as timing, personal convenience, selection of characteristics of the offspring (a commonly forbidden practice, treated as tantamount to human

---

556 From pioneering international documents regarding human artificial procreations to recent national regulations. See, for instance, the *Report on Human Artificial Protection, Principles Set Out in the Report of the Ad Hoc Committee of Experts on Progress in the Biomedical Sciences (CAHBI)*, 1989 that as a condition to access assisted reproduction enumerates, *inter alia*, that "other treatments of infertility have failed or are not appropriate in the particular case or offer no prospect of success" (Principle 1(1)). Furthermore, Principle 7(1) stipulates that "a single person who is at risk of infertility or of another hazard that may impair his or her future procreative capacity may deposit his/her gametes for his or her own future use, provided that at the time of the artificial procreation all the requirements set out in the (these) principles are fulfilled".

557 See, for instance, De Melo-Martin, I., "On Cloning Human Beings", *Bioethics*, Vol. 16, No. 3, 2002, pp. 246–265.

558 See the medical definition of infertility from the WHO website: www.who.int/genomics/gender/en/index6.html. See also a medical study of its evaluation: Cooper T.G., Noonan E., von Eckardstein S. *et al.*, "World Health Organization Reference Values for Human Semen Characteristics", *Human Reproduction Update*, Vol. 16, No. 3, 2010, pp. 231–245.

559 Warnock M., *A Question of Life. The Warnock Report on Human Fertilization and Embryology*, Blackwell, 1985.

560 Preamble to the Constitution of the World Health Organization as adopted by the International Health Conference, New York, 19–22 June 1946; signed on 22 July 1946 by the representatives of 61 States (Official Records of the World Health Organization, No. 2, p. 100) and entered into force on 7 April 1948.

enhancement or eugenics),[561] avoidance of genetic defects[562] and protection against changed circumstances (for instance death or divorce).[563]

Another fallacy of legally prescribing ART only under the condition of infertility is that the condition might exist also without the practice of sexual intercourse for 12 months. Even though infertility is regularly connected with coitus, the condition as a failure to conceive asexually and with the assistance of ART is neglected. If infertility is understood without the second part of its definition, dropping the part of *unprotected intercourse*, it could also manifest by failure to conceive after perhaps several attempts of sperm donor inseminations. On the other hand, the sperm donor insemination of a woman in a couple is not a treatment to heal her medical condition (because she is fertile), but it is a treatment to heal the infertility of a particular couple. Accordingly, an infertile single woman would not need sperm donation because her condition does not allow her to conceive anyhow. She could only use sperm donation if she is fertile. Accordingly, curing infertility, or even overcoming infertility, is not a reason, or not the sole reason, to use ART. Even though in vitro fertilisation was introduced for the main purpose of overcoming infertility, for single women using ART, the reasons are usually of other nature such as: lack of partner, lesbian orientation, etc. Therefore calling ART a medical treatment (which is done in most European legislation, even in those which allow access to single women) is perhaps to refer to the other aspects of the definition of health, such as mental and social well-being, but not to physical or physiological treatment to cure illness or disease.

Paul Ramsey points out that medical science has taken a step in attempting to produce a baby, without first actually curing a woman's infertility.[564] Immaculada de Melo-Martin argues that infertility as an excuse to access IVF is overrated, since it underestimates the role of the social, ethical and political solutions, such as prevention in solving reproductive problems.[565] Leon Kass argues that infertility is more of a social disease than a disease that requires medical treatment: "it is not life threatening or crippling, nor does it lead to detectable bodily damage. To consider it a disease to a focus on an individual; yet infertility is a condition that

561 See more Sandal J.M., *The Case Against Perfection*, Harvard University Press, 2009.

562 See, for instance, the recent debates in the UK on the proposed therapy for parents at high risk of having children with conditions such as muscular dystrophy by the *Human Fertilisation and Embryology Authority* over the introduction of a third party in the reproductive process that will neutralise or diminish the risk of the condition: www.telegraph.co.uk/science/science-news/10356387/Three-parent-babies-incompatible-with-human-dignity.html.

563 See more in Schultz M.M., "Reproductive Technology and Intent-Based Parenthood. An Opportunity for Gender Neutrality", *Wisconsin Law Review*, Vol. 297, 1990, p. 313.

564 Ramsey P., "Shall we Reproduce? II Rejoinders and Future Forecast", *Journal of the American Medical Association*, Vol. 220, No. 11, 1972, pp. 1480–1485.

565 De Melo-Martin I., *Making Babies. Biomedical Technologies, Reproductive Ethics, and Public Policy*, Kluwer Academic Publishers, 1998, p. 125.

is located in a marriage, in a union of two individuals. If it is any kind of disease, it is a 'social disease'".[566]

One step further in treating infertility as a social disease in marriage is to treat it as a social disease of single women. In an attempt to establish an independent professional and economic position, women face a high probability rate of potential medical infertility later on in life, when they decide to found a family. It is a fact that women's fertility decreases with age and there is a large range of possibilities that might interfere with the later reproduction (e.g. endometriosis). Infertility is not a fixed and stable condition, but rather a gradual onset process developing after a certain age.[567] A number of studies show that women are at their reproductive peak after their young adulthood and through their late 20s. Fertility declines gradually in women's 30s and dramatically drops over the age of 35.[568] It is a notorious fact that as a woman ages, it becomes more difficult to conceive and maintain pregnancy. Problems in older women's reproductive projects are not only infertility, but also the possibility of chromosomal abnormalities,[569] higher chances of miscarriages or increased rates of Caesarean deliveries. Nevertheless, the choice of pursuing a professional career (earlier in life, while in the best reproductive stage) jeopardises a woman's choice to be a mother later on in life. The lust for women's economic independence could be explained by the long patriarchal history of dependency. As MacKinnon has put it, "patriarchy is the most effective ideology ever invented".[570] It is also practical to decide to found a family when women can ask for maternity leave and economically support the upbringing of their child. In these terms, the decision of women to postpone family arrangements is socially driven. The medical problems of facing infertility afterwards at a later age are a consequence of, not a reason for, women's choices. Therefore the social pressures to naturally distinguish between the genders are increasing infertility. On the other hand, if the idea is to cure or decrease infertility, a solution has to be found to make women's choices of career or family not exclusive to one another, and not treat ART as a medical treatment. Some feminists suggest better economical and professional possibilities of women so that they can concentrate on childbearing in their younger years.[571]

---

566 Kass L., "Babies by Means of In Vitro Fertilization. Unethical Experiments on the Unborn?", *New England Journal of Medicine*, Vol. 285, No. 21, 1971, pp. 1174–1179.

567 Garcia S.A., "Sociocultural and Legal Implications of Creating and Sustaining Life through Biomedical Technology", *Journal of Legal Medicine*, Vol. 17, No. 4, 1996, pp. 469–525.

568 London S., "Risk of Pregnancy-Related Death is Sharply Elevated for Women 35 and Older", *Perspectives on Sexual and Reproductive Health*, Vol. 36, No. 2, 2004.

569 *Ibid.* Chromosomal abnormalities occur in approximately 40–50% of pregnancies in women aged 30–35.

570 MacKinnon C.A., *Toward a Feminist Theory of the State*, Harvard University Press, 1989.

571 Berg F.B., "Listening to the Voices of the Infertile", in Callahan J.C. (ed.), *Reproduction, Ethics and the Law. Feminist Perspectives*, Indiana University Press, 1995; Goodwin M., "Assisted Reproductive Technology and the Double Bind: The Illusory Choice of Motherhood", *Journal of Gender, Race and Justice*, Vol. 9, No. 1, 2005, pp. 1–54.

Laura Purdy enlists at least two reasons why reproduction is an intersection between bioethics and feminist philosophy. The first relates to the fact that reproduction is the most obvious place where sex makes a difference. The second relates to the fact that the second feminist wave was born at the time of the development of reproductive biology. This author makes a connection between reproduction and bioethics, considering that having children is an undisputable part of morality, as it affects the children, the other intimates and society at large.[572]

Reproduction itself has been a source of discrimination between the genders in the past. The liberation of procreative dependence from sexuality shifted women's roles from mothers (primarily) to individuals (primarily). Sigmund Freud saw this separation between the natural sexual urge and the intentional and responsible act to procreate as one of the greatest triumphs of humanity.[573]

The reproductive decision-making process for women is tricky because of the biological specifics of the reproductive age which correlate with the age at which professional choices are also made. The burden of having them both at the same time is a heavy one, and very often the choice comes down to one of the two alternatives. Michele Goodwin argues that any decision will be the wrong one, since it will exclude the possibility of ever experiencing the other option (mothering or professional career). She used the *theory of double bind*[574] to depict the illusory choices that women think they might face. She criticises ART for deluding women that they can postpone their parental project in order to become more competent in the labour market, without emphasising the potential harm of a decision of that kind. The accompanying harm relates to difficulties in getting pregnant and possible infertility, as well as possible health problems for the mother (hormonal stimulation for ART purposes, failure of the process itself) and the child (multiple gestations are serious health risks).[575] For Goodwin, ART is falsely regarded as a back-up plan for women who want to postpone pregnancy as a way of avoiding discrimination in the labour market, therefore being not a women's free choice, but a socially constructed obstacle. She argues that assisted reproductive technology is mistakenly regarded as equitable accommodation for women and their families who wish to delay pregnancies in order to avoid discrimination. Therefore she claims that the social system fails to equitably accommodate women, families, and children by masquerading complex and even dangerous medical options as naturally positive alternatives.

---

572 Purdy L.M., *Reproducing Persons. Issues in Feminist Bioethics*, Cornell University Press, 1996.

573 Freud S., *Die Sexualität in der Ätiologie der Neurosen*, Psychanalyse.lu, 1898.

574 The Double Bind Theory was developed to describe "the psychological impasse created when contradictory demands are made on an individual with weaker power within a relationship or vulnerable social status", showing results that irrespective of what choice is made, it will always be the wrong one.

575 Green N.S., "Risks of Birth Defects and Other Adverse Outcomes Associated with Assisted Reproductive Technology", *Pediatrics*, Vol. 114, No. 1, 2004, pp. 256–259.

Because of the existence of the back-up plan to which women think they can turn later on in life, they are deluded more than ever before into thinking that they can postpone pregnancy. The necessity for economical independency comes rationally and together with a plan to raise and care for a child. On the contrary, early career women are often perceived as living a selfish life plan, thus not fulfilling their role as a caring mother of children. Still, women who delay pregnancies in order to provide steady income are later on confronted with reduced chances of successful conception.

This reality summarises women's choices as two alternatives: (1) working and delaying pregnancy or (2) becoming pregnant and mothering. Judith Warner disputes whether all choices in the context of mothering are truly objective, actionable opportunities.[576] She comments that in the context of working and mothering these are the choices that do not feel like choices at all. They are harsh realities of family life in a culture that has no structures in place to allow women and men to balance work and childrearing. Thus, she questions whether it is truly an unburdened option to either delay childbearing or become pregnant when a woman chooses, given that the results may be infertility.

Therefore the decision to establish an early career is driven by double bind choices and not by women's free will. Goodwin suggests that instead of making illusions of postponing women's biological clocks, it would be better if society provides positive discrimination in the labour market and reduces the later reliance on ART.[577] The criticism is of the social system that fails to accommodate women and spreads them in between the family and the current demanding labour market.

In contrast, a solution is usually sought in the possibility of oocyte preservation that for many women seems like a way to stop the biological clock from ticking. In addition, counting on the possibility of frozen gametes or embryos for later use, as well as egg and recently womb transplantation,[578] seem comforting in erasing the time pressure for becoming a parent. These technologies mean that reproductive life can be extended to a level that can even be realised *post mortem*. Using ART in this way does not necessarily mean that one has a fertility problem, but simply

576 Warner J., "Mommy Madness. What Happened When the Girls Who Had it All Became Mothers? A New Book Explores Why This Generation Feels so Insane", *Newsweek*, 21 February 2005.

577 Goodwin M., "Assisted Reproductive Technology and the Double Bind: The Illusory Choice of Motherhood", *Journal of Gender, Race and Justice*, Vol. 9, No. 1, 2005, pp. 1–54.

578 See more in: Rai N., *Revolutionary "Womb Transplant" Performed in Turkey – World's First*, 11.08.2011, available online: www.allvoices.com/contributed-news/9926041-revolutionary-womb-transplant-performed-in-turkey-worlds-first; "Nurse Hopes to have World's First Baby from a Transplant Womb Donated by her own Mother", *MailOnline*, 18.10.2011, available online: www.dailymail.co.uk/health/article-2050401/Married-nurse-hopes-worlds-baby-womb-transplant-donated-MOTHER.html; Grimez K., "Ethics around Womb Transplanttaion", *bionews.org.uk*, 10.03.2014, available online: www.bionews.org.uk/page_404116.asp?dinfo=0esSyGvLnIgvoXEHYEU8ANqO&PPID=404298.

that it prevents from one happening. If anything, it is in concordance with the notion of planned and responsible parenthood.[579]

Access to ART should not be driven by the condition of being infertile, since its purpose is not medical – to cure the condition. The possibilities for preventing and curing infertility should be sought elsewhere, in the programmes for locating resources primarily towards prevention, and secondarily towards curing it.[580] This should go together with social policies regarding women's labour and educational programmes towards re-constructing the stigmatised social responsibility of women to give birth for the family or the state.

Considering infertility as a medical condition that should be medically treated should refer to the well-being of the patient's health and not just be for the purpose of producing children. It is difficult to draw a line between what is medical and what is non-medical infertility. Non-medical infertility will encompass the impossibility of having children (whatever the reasons: social, homosexuality, etc.) and not only impossibility of conceiving them. It is important here to note the difference between *infertility* and *sterility* as the difference is not just conceptual but also functional, making the treatments and solutions to overcome it completely different. Apart from the medical treatment for curing the conditions, in the ART context, a woman not able to conceive and a woman not able to carry out pregnancy will be referred to egg donation or surrogacy respectively. Rochon noticed that the mixed usage, especially among medical and demographic contexts of both terms, might cause misunderstandings in practice.[581] Nevertheless, in the comparative literature a different usage of the terms is still present, treating *infertility* as an impossibility of conceiving, and *sterility* as an inability to produce or to carry out a pregnancy to term with the birth of a child and *vice versa*. For the purposes of the following, the term *infertility* will be used with the meaning of impossibility of conceiving, in concordance with the definition given above, while for explaining the inability to bear a child, an additional explanation will be given.

The pro-natal attitudes are very often not medical but culturally embedded and thus socially driven. Society places significance on involuntary infertility based on the gender roles, thus making the condition even more socially dependent. This is a phenomenon apparent in the developing as well as developed

579 As also being on the agenda of objectives and actions for Population and Development by the United Nations. See *Report of the International Conference on Population and Development*, United Nations, Cairo, 1995. The Report also improves the position of women in the labour market by urging feasibility for women to combine childbearing, breast-feeding and childrearing with participation in the workplace through laws, regulations and other appropriate measures (p. 23).

580 Pennings G., "Ethical Issues of Infertility Treatment in Developing Countries", *ESHRE Monographs*, Vol. 2008, No. 1, 2008, pp. 15–20.

581 Rochon M., "Sterility and Infertility: Two Concepts", *Cahiers Quebecois de Demographie*, Vol. 15, No. 1, 1986, pp. 27–56.

world.[582] The identification of the woman with the role of a mother as being her *reason for being* is not to be underestimated.[583] Consequently, childless women continue to be perceived in a pejorative light (i.e. as selfish). Frost pointed out that it can be a rational choice to have as well as not to have children.[584] Feminists fall in between two poles regarding women's realisation as a mother. On the one side are those which have understood childbirth as a way to affirm the uniqueness and power of women as a gender,[585] often taking inspiration from the tradition of goddess worship, which draws many images of power from a woman giving birth.[586] On the other side are those who argue that women should not be identified with the mother's role, therefore refusing to undertake the social pressure as a responsibility for mothering which is only one aspect of being a woman.[587]

The reproductive revolution caused a metamorphosis of motherhood in a way that returning is not possible anymore. Because of this, family narratives have changed and humans have lost their past identity of both individually and collectively identifying their family roles with a man – father and provider, and a woman – mother and housewife.[588] ART has offered another possibility for women's total independence: not just to choose not to reproduce, but also to choose when and under what circumstances (without a partner if necessary) to give birth and to mother a child.

Parenthood as one of the biggest transitions in the life roles of an adult man and woman means that the inability to conceive restricts the possibility of that transition happening. Therefore infertility is characterised as a transition in the life role because of realising that the parental project will not happen, and consequently, conciliation with the fact of not experiencing parenthood. The transition is defined as: "experiencing or not experiencing an event that changes the individual perception on one self and on the surrounding world, that inevitably imposes change in the behaviour that might lead to personal satisfaction or on the contrary, to depression due to non-fulfilment of the desired goal and need".[589]

582 Becker G., Nachtigall R.D., "Eager for Medicalisation. The Social Production of Infertility as a Disease", *Sociology of Health & Illnesses*, Vol. 14, No. 4, 1994, pp. 456–471.

583 Russo N.F., "The Motherhood Mandate", *Journal of Social Issues*, Vol. 32, No. 2, 1976, pp. 143–153.

584 Frost C., "Feminism and Infertility", *Resolve Inc. Newsletter*, 1980, p. 5.

585 Kittay E.F., "Womb Envy. An Explanatory Concept", in Treblicott J. (ed.), *Mothering. Essays in Feminist Theory*, Rowman & Allanheld, 1984.

586 Campbell J., Moyers B., "The Power of Myth", in Flowers B.S. (ed.), *The Power of Myth*, Doubleday, 1988.

587 See more in Overall C., *Ethics and Human Reproduction: A Feminist Analysis*, Allen & Unwin, 1987. Christine Overall argues that women have the right not to reproduce (entitled to abortion, contraception), but not the right to reproduce in terms of access to reproductive technologies, because that will, again, set the scene for potential exploitation of children and women's bodies.

588 Smith, P., "The Metamorphosis of Motherhood", in Callahan J.C. (ed.), *Reproduction, Ethics and Law. Feminist Perspectives*, Indiana University Press, 1995.

589 Koropatrick, S. *et al.*, "Infertility: A Non-event Transition", *Fertility and Sterility*, Vol. 59, No. 1, 1993, pp. 163–171.

Nevertheless, not everyone wants to have children. Infertility is only a disability that may lead to life deterioration when there is a child-wish to start with.

Infertility is usually a condition to claim realisation of the reproductive right with the assistance of ART. The strong need of the potential parents to have genetically related children is very often expressed in terms of reproductive freedoms and human rights.[590] The freedom to reproduce can be expressed positively as a right to reproduce, or negatively, as a right not to reproduce. According to Yvonne Denier, if someone has a reproductive right, then society and medical science have the obligation to provide that to which the person has a right.[591] If ART is available, it is discriminatory to claim that the assistance to realise the reproductive right belongs only to those who are infertile. For John Robertson, the right to reproduce is not an absolute right but ought to be given presumptive priority when conflicting with other rights. The burden of proof for limiting its realisation should be placed on those who are contesting it or tend to infringe it.[592] Along this line, procreative liberty is a crucial self-defining experience deserving respect and dignity at the most basic level.[593]

The United Nations' basis of action encompasses the definition of reproductive health as a "state of complete physical, mental and social well-being and not merely absence of disease and infirmity in all matters relating to the reproductive system and to its functions and processes".[594] Along these lines, everyone should be enabled to use the capacity to decide if, when and how often to reproduce. In concordance with the definition of health, reproductive health care is defined as "the constellation of methods, techniques and services that contribute to reproductive health and well-being by preventing and solving health problems".[595]

Single women conceiving without a partner under the current dominant regulations is problematic from at least two perspectives. Firstly, formally, infertility (as a normative condition to use ART in most European countries) is not the rationale behind a single woman's attempt to conceive using assisted reproduction. From a general point of view, it is not possible to apply the definition of infertility since the single woman has not been engaged in unprotected

590 Chan, S., Quibly M., "Frozen Embryos, Genetic Information and Reproductive Rights", *Bioethics*, Vol. 21, No. 8, 2007, pp. 439–448.

591 Denier, Y., "Need or Desire? A Conception and Moral Phenomenology of the Child Wish", *International Journal of Applied Philosophy*, Vol. 20, No. 1, 2006, pp. 81–95. According to Denier, the positive right is generally defined as "a right to". Consequently, to this right corresponds the obligation to provide and secure that to which the person holds as a "a right to". In contrast, the negative right is "the right not to realize the optional right". To this right corresponds the obligation to protect any obstruction in the liberty to choose one's own actions.

592 Robertson J.A., *Children of Choice. Freedom and the New Reproductive Technologies*, Princeton University Press, 1994.

593 *Ibid.* p. 4.

594 *Report of the International Conference on Population and Development*, United Nations, Cairo, 1994, p. 40.

595 *Ibid.* p. 40.

intercourse for 12 months for the purpose of reproduction. It is also arguable how the provision in many laws across Europe that single women have the right to use assisted fertilisation if the previous treatment is unsuccessful or treatment with other methods is also unsuccessful should be applied.[596]

The theory has already attributed new meaning to infertility that the normative language has to follow, so to make the afforded freedom of single women to conceive using ART more feasible. The term "psychological infertility", meaning the inability of women to conceive a child due to the women's aversion to the natural procreative act in heterosexual coitus, is promoted by lesbian groups.[597] As such, the term sheds light on another aspect of infertility, which is beyond the scope of its definition.

Another solution for improving the legal terminology and avoiding legal misinterpretations and therefore restrictions on the conditions to use ART is to replace the word *infertility* with the wider concept of *inability to conceive*.

The concept of infertility as an inability to conceive should be divided into three branches as to the reasons for reproductive failure: (1) *medical* (as a medical condition of a couple trying to conceive), (2) *presumed* (as for those who do not engage in heterosexual intercourse – single women, lesbian couples), or (3) *medical infertility caused by social factors* (infertility caused by postponing the reproductive process due to different reasons – realising women's professional goals, and thus economic independency, lacking a partner or other set of circumstances).

Another aspect of infertility arises after the birth of the first child. In these terms, there is a difference between a *primary infertility* (i.e. childless individuals/ couples), or *secondary infertility* (i.e. individuals/couples which have one child, but are unable to have another one), etc.

Secondly, the more problematic aspect of treating single women's inability to conceive a child without a partner is the possible harm towards the child conceived that way.[598] Women's reproductive right should not be observed in isolation. Since the conception affects another future life (that of the child), the right of single women to the treatment should be seen in the relational context with the child and the donor.

---

596 For instance, in the Republic of Macedonia.

597 See more in Dargan F., "New IVF Rules to Include Lesbians", *The Herald Sun*, Vol. 12, No. 2, 2001.

598 The threats towards the child will be discussed in depth in Chapter 6: Children conceived by sperm donors' assistance to single women.

4.4. THE REPRODUCTIVE RIGHTS AND THE CORRELATIVE RESPONSIBILITIES OF THE COUPLE

4.4.1. RIGHTS

Reproductive rights, more than any other rights, should be observed in a relation, thus investigating the correlative responsibilities that accompany it. The freedom to reproduce does come with responsibility that is attached not only to the partner, but even more so to the progeny.

The Proclamation of Teheran from 1968 states: "Parents have a basic right to decide freely and responsibly on the number and spacing of their children and a right to adequate education and information in this respect".[599]

Planned and responsible parenthood as a key goal of the United Nations Population and Development Strategy inevitably includes both individuals in the decision-making process of conceiving a child. The aim of family planning is to enable both couples and individuals to decide freely and responsibly about the number, spacing and timing of making informed reproductive choices. Consequently, family planning is in concordance with the promotion of optimum health, respect for the dignity of all persons, and family well-being.[600] The enablement of free and informed choices should offer a variety of methods depending on the age, parity, family size preference and other factors to ensure access to proper effective family planning methods.[601]

There are three forms of coexisting in a couple and thus contexts in which reproduction can take place: marriage, extra-marital relationship (registered or recognised by law with a particular set of rights and obligations between the partners),[602] and unregistered relationship (neither registered nor recognised by law). Related to these three contexts, procreation can happen *via* intercourse (planned, thus intentional; or not planned, thus not intentional), and *via* the assistance of the reproductive technology (planned, thus intentional). Therefore in the assisted reproduction context, contestation of fatherhood is only possible if the partner of the mother did not consent to the treatment, or if the child was not born as a result of the assisted reproduction.[603] On the contrary, in a

[599] Proclamation of Teheran, International Conference on Human Rights, 1968.

[600] *Report of the International Conference on Population and Development*, United Nations, Cairo, 1994, p. 44.

[601] *Ibid.* p. 45.

[602] For instance, in the Republic of Macedonia, an extra-marital relationship is recognised by the law as a heterosexual community of mutual life that lasts for more than one year. As such (even though without any official registration), the relationship produces the same legal consequences as marriage in the scope of the mutual maintenance and property regime acquired during its existence. This is stipulated in article 13 from Family Law, 1992.

[603] As a European standard accepted in most of the Member States that regulate assisted reproduction in couples. See also article 8 regulating Contesting parental affiliation in cases of medically-assisted procreation, "Appendices III and IV, Draft Recommendation on the

natural procreation context, the consent to intercourse of the partner is taken as consent to eventual procreation. Along these lines, in the first scenario, the consent to reproduce can be withdrawn after being given and prior to sperm/ embryo implantation into the woman's uterus.[604] The reproductive right in the ART context is dependent on the informed consent of the beneficiaries. It encompasses a twofold right of parenthood: the positive one of being a parent, and the negative one of not imposing parenthood on a person who does not want to experience it.[605]

On the other hand, in the second scenario, the situation is different since gametes are implemented in the woman's uterus *via* coitus. On the ground of her bodily integrity, the reproductive decision is later on left to the woman, even though one may criticise the miniscule role of her partner as a co-author of the reproductive project.[606] As a "joint reproductive responsibility" one may question whether both partners should be equally responsible, therefore granting men the right to choose too.[607] In the US *Casey* case before the Supreme Court, the judge ruled: "it cannot be claimed that the father's interest in the foetus welfare is equal to the mother's protected liberty".[608] In another case in the UK the man wanted his female partner to keep the pregnancy against her wish to abort the foetus.[609] It has been argued publicly that accepting that men have "feelings" over the decision regarding abortion is not a strong enough ground to think that their feelings take precedence over women's.[610] The issues of contraception and abortion are related to the negative reproductive right, i.e. the right not to reproduce.

Even though the partner may not have intentionally embedded reproduction into the sexual act, his biological paternity may be legally challenged before the Court.[611]

On the other hand, both genetic fathers may be restricted from recognising the child as their own as a way of establishing their parental roles resulting from exercising their right to reproduce or their right to donate reproductive material

Rights and Legal Status of Children and Parental Responsibilities, CJ-FA, 2011, RAP 5 prov., Committee of Experts on Family Law Task to Draft One or More Legal Instruments on the Rights and Legal Status of Children and Parental Responsibilities, CJ-FA, Draft Report of the Fifth Meeting, Strasbourg, 25–27 May 2011, p. 42.

604 See, for instance, the case of *Evans v. the United Kingdom*, European Court of Human Rights, No. 6339/05, judgment of 10.04.2007.

605 Green Y., "Informed Consent for Treatment of Fertility", in Schenker J.G. (ed.), *Ethical Dilemmas in Assisted Reproductive Technologies*, Walter de Gruyter, 2011.

606 Gibbs N., "A Man's Right to Choose", *Time US*, 15.03.2006, available online: www.time.com/time/nation/article/0,8599,1173414,00.html.

607 *Ibid.*

608 *Ibid.*

609 See, for instance, Moore S., "Does a Man have the Right to Decide on Abortion?", *Mail Online*, 17.08.2013, available online: www.dailymail.co.uk/news/article-33265/Does-man-right-decide-abortion.html.

610 *Ibid.*

611 See, for instance, the case of *Mikulic v. Croatia*, European Court of Human Rights, No. 53176/99, judgment of 07.02.2002.

for others (in cases of donations). The genetic father conceiving through coitus could be restricted for several reasons, among which: (1) an already existing marital presumption or family life of the child with another social parent,[612] (2) rejected consent from the mother and/or the child, and (3) in cases in which the conception occurred as a result of rape[613] or incestuous relationship.[614] Nevertheless, this father has the option of resorting to the court for paternal proceedings. The donor can also recognise the child as his with the consent of the mother and the child. Nevertheless, in the case of refusal, he cannot resort to the court to establish his fatherhood solely on the grounds of being a genetic parent.[615]

The realisation of reproductive rights and correlative responsibilities is different depending on the context. In natural procreation a man can be declared a father against his will and intention, while not being able to interfere with the woman's decision to terminate the pregnancy.[616] In the context of assisted reproduction, the relevant factor for becoming a parent is the expressed intention in a form of consent. Furthermore, all three contexts of bringing a child into existence have a different legal modus for establishing the parental link, thus parental responsibilities creating different consequences for children from the moment of birth.

It remains the case that the reproductive project can be carried out only by the couple together and not on the level of an individual right. In these terms, neither one of the couple can procreate naturally or reproduce with the assistance of bio-medical technology without the contribution or consent of the other party (rape is excluded from this observation).[617] Therefore the existence of the individual right to procreate in a couple is absurd.

---

612 See, for instance, the cases *Chavdarov v. Bulgaria*, European Court of Human Rights, No. 3465/03, judgment of 21.11.2010; and *Schneider v. Germany*, European Court of Human Rights, No. 17080/07, judgment of 15.09.2011.

613 See more Appendices III and IV CM/Rec (2011) RAP 5 prov., *Committee of Experts on Family Law Tasked to Draft One or More Legal Instruments on the Rights and Legal Status of Children and Parental Responsibilities (CJ-FA), Draft Report of the Fifth Meeting*, Strasbourg, 25–27 May 2011 (hereafter Draft Recommendation), p. 37. Article 14 stipulates the establishment of paternal affiliation by voluntary recognition. Paragraph 2 allows States to impose conditions or restrictions on voluntary recognition in cases of rape or incest. See also article 23, defining parents, p. 46.

614 *Ibid.* See also Ignovska, E., Verschelden, G., "De rechterlijke toetsing van het belang van het kind bij het onderzoek naar het vaderschap", case-note by the Constitutional Court no. 30/2013, 7 March 2013, *Tijdschrift voor Jeugd en Kinderrechten*, Vol. 2, pp. 155–164. The Belgian case of the Constitutional Court No. 169/2003, judgment of 25.08.2011 considered that the absolute impossibility to establish paternal affiliation judicially violates article 10 (enjoyment of rights and freedoms without discrimination) and article 11 (Belgians are equal before the law) of the Constitution when it comes to an incestuous child regarding which the judge rules that the affiliation bond is in the best interests of the child.

615 See, for instance, the case of *J.R.M. v. the Netherlands*, European Commission of Human Rights, No. 16944/90, decision of 08.02.1993.

616 Gibbs N., "A Man's Right to Choose", *Time US*, 15.03.2006, available online: www.time.com/time/nation/article/0,8599,1173414,00.html.

617 Draft Recommendation on the Rights and Legal Status of Children and Parental Responsibilities, CJ-FA, 2011, p. 37.

4.4.2. RESPONSIBILITIES

Reproductive responsibilities correlating with reproductive rights are primarily attached to the child and thus are parental responsibilities. A number of studies show that it is better for the psychological development of the child as well as for its prospects to be raised in a two-parent family, instead of being raised by one parent only.[618]

Reproductive obligations towards the partner are not related to an obligation to procreate. They are related to the co-parenting role towards the child. In order to execute the parental role, the prerequisite is to examine the conditions for attributing the legal parental affiliation. The principles set out in the White Paper suggest three possibilities for establishing the paternal link: by presumption, which correlates with marriage, and by recognition and by judicial decision, which correlate with the concepts of an extra-marital relationship and an unregulated relationship. The exceptions are only allowed if determined by law and consistent with the best interests of the child.[619] The Draft Recommendation on the Rights and Legal Status of Children and Parental Responsibilities (Draft Recommendation) also suggests the same three forms of attributing the paternal link, additionally extending the application of the presumption to cases of registered partnerships and cohabiting different-sex couples.[620]

To overcome the discrimination against children based on their birth, the Draft Recommendation suggests a tripartite division of couples' mutual life: marriage, registered partnership of different-sex couples, and cohabiting different-sex couples. The purpose of making this trichotomy is to delineate a wider scope of application of the paternal presumption. Therefore it is recommended that the notorious marital presumption extends *mutatis mutandis* to the mother's registered partner (in registered partnerships – article 11), and to the mother's cohabiting partner (in unregistered partnerships – article 12). Nevertheless, if national laws of the Member States do not accept the wider scope of the paternal presumption, there is still a possibility to establish the paternal affiliation by recognition or by a decision of a competent authority (usually the court in civil proceedings). In cases of medically assisted procreation, the rule of informed consent of both partners applies as a prerogative for recognising the parental role after the birth of the child. This rule applies equally to all forms of unions: marriage and registered or non-registered (cohabiting partners) partnerships.

---

618 Schenner J.G., "Assisted Reproduction Practice in Europe: Legal and Ethical Aspects", *Human Reproduction Update*, Vol. 3, No. 2, 1997, p. 176; Dunn J., Deater-Deckard, Pickering K., O'Connor T.G., Golding J., ALSPAC Study Team, "Children's Adjustment and Prosocial Behavior in Step-, Single-Parent, and Non-Stepfamily Settings. Findings from a Community Study", *Journal of Child Psychology and Psychiatry*, Vol. 39, No. 8, 1998, pp. 1083–1095.

619 *Report on Principles Concerning the Establishment and Legal Consequences of Parentage – White Paper*, Committee of Experts on Family Law, 2006.

620 Draft Recommendation on the Rights and Legal Status of Children and Parental Responsibilities, CJ-FA, 2011.

This means that relevant facts for rebutting the parental role can only relate to the fallacy of the given consent from the partner or to situations where the child was not born as a result of the procedure (article 18).

Comparing the establishment of fatherhood (thus the attribution of the role after the realisation of the reproductive right) in natural and assisted reproduction for couples amounts to presumption (with the possibility of being rebutted on grounds of biology) or recognition, and intention (which can only be rebutted on grounds of its fallacy). In the case of natural procreation, fatherhood can be imposed (in court proceedings) on the biological father (even if he does not want to accept the role). In the case of assisted reproduction, fatherhood is a matter of legally binding intention expressed prior to the implantation of the sperm/embryo into the woman's body; thus it cannot be imposed against the prospective father's will.

4.4.3. MARRIAGE

Marriage still holds precedence as a preferred place where reproduction takes place. Both the UDHR and ECHR link the reproductive right and the right to found a family to marriage.

The reproductive right is broader than mere reproduction. It also encompasses the right to be legally constituted as a parent of the child as a result of the reproduction. Even though the ways of establishing parenthood will be elaborated in more detail in a later chapter, a conceptual framework will be given in the following for the purposes of linking the parental reproductive right with the right/responsibility to attribute legal parenthood.

For mothers it has been a general rule that the woman who gives birth to the child is to be considered a legal mother *regardless of the genetic connection.*[621] The mere fact of giving birth irrespective of the legal framework of the partnership (if any) is sufficient to qualify a woman as the mother of the child.[622] For fathers though, it is a bit trickier. Usually, the marital presumption presumes that the father of the child is the married husband of the mother if the child was born during the marriage or 300 days (presumed period for pregnancy) after the marriage dissolution. The Draft Recommendation allows the application of the

621 Especially stressed because ithas been a novelty after the introduction of the surrogacy agreements. See more Draft Recommendation on the Rights and Legal Status of Children and Parental Responsibilities, CJ-FA, 2011, p. 34.

622 The rule that the affiliation link between the mother and the child should be established as from the moment of birth is also acknowledged by the ECtHR in the cases: *Marckx v. Belgium*, No. 6833/74, judgment of 13.06.1979; *Kearns v. France*, No. 35991/04, judgment of 10.01.2008; *Kroon and Others v. the Netherlands*, No. 1835/91, judgment of 27.10.1994. A possibility of exception as for example in cases of anonymous births and giving the child up for adoption is also afforded by the ECtHR in the case of *Odièvre v. France*, No. 42326/98, 13.02.2003.

presumption to be determined by national laws when it comes to the time limits and the particular regulation on factual and legal separations of the spouses.[623]

Institutionalising the reproductive project in the legal framework of marriage supported by the marital presumption of paternity is in line with the child's protection under article 7 of the CRC providing the child with the right to registration, name, nationality and known fatherhood from the time of birth.

The marital parental presumption for husbands conceiving a child naturally is a practical tool to found the affiliation link with the child. The White Paper enumerates five situations related to the marital presumption in which the husband should be presumed to be a father: (1) conceived before the marriage and born during the marriage; (2) conceived and born during the marriage; (3) conceived during the marriage and born after the end of the marriage; (4) conceived during a first marriage of the mother and born during a second marriage of the mother; and (5) conceived before the marriage and born after the end of this marriage.[624] It can be a matter of national regulations of the Member States how they will apply it in cases where the child is born in a second marriage soon after the dissolution of the previous.[625] The marriage can also be a cradle of doubt since the marital presumption can be decisive as regards the genetic link of the husband. Therefore the presumption should not be understood as a definite rule on establishing paternity. On the contrary, a possibility of being rebutted before a competent authority should be available as a remedy for a false presumption.[626]

For husbands of mothers inseminated by sperm from a donor, the marital context is a place for safely and calmly establishing the legal fatherhood of the social parent. The early attitude to assisted reproduction regarded sperm donation as fundamentally wrong, for a number of reasons.[627] First, it was considered a breach of marriage in that it introduced a third party into the procreative process, and was thus analogous to adultery. The secrecy and deceit were also perceived as having potentially harmful effects on the child. It was also considered to amount to a fraud on society in that it involved withholding information concerning "questions of kinship, inheritance and actual identity". Along these lines, sperm donations were considered to present danger for all parties involved – the recipients, the donor, the child and the medical practitioner, while also posing a danger to society at large by weakening the institution of marriage, deceiving

---

623 Draft Recommendation on the Rights and Legal Status of Children and Parental Responsibilities, CJ-FA, 201, p. 18.

624 White Paper, Principle 2, p. 10.

625 See also article 3 of the Draft Recommendation on the Rights and Legal Status of Children and Parental Responsibilities, CJ-FA, 2011.

626 Presumptions should be subject to effective re-examination with a possibility to be rebutted and not to be understood as a *de facto* rule. This has also been confirmed in the case of *Kroon and Others v. the Netherlands*, European Court of Human Rights, No. 18535/91, judgment of 27.10.1994.

627 *Artificial Human Insemination, The Report of a Commission Appointed by His Grace the Archbishop of Canterbury*, London, SPCK, 1952.

children, and by "substituting an anonymous and mechanical procedure for an intimate personal relationship". Some instances of sperm donations were regarded as clearly worse than others, for example the insemination of single women.

The Warnock Committee resolved that the child's status depends on the father's consent, making the husband's consent to the treatment a ground for establishing fatherhood in relation to the child born in marriage. In the context of anonymous sperm donations, marriage as a source to supply the legal link between the father and the child leads to peculiar consequences. These are inconsistent with both the ideology of marriage as a union of parents and children, and the state's policy of accepting an ignorant attitude towards children as members of the family. As a medium of paternal rights over children, and as a legitimate form for infertile fathers to have children and to hide their infertility, it illustrates the extent to which society has decided to be manipulative towards children and the intimacy of the family cradle. The initially intended protective function of the marital paternal presumption in cases of hidden truths regarding the act of conception is infringing article 8 of the CRC and the right of children to preserve their identity as an official record of their genetic ties. ART clearly depicts the constructed notion of paternity as a form of social reproduction. This retreat into marriage both as the medium of paternal rights over children and as a convenient shroud for male infertility illustrates the extent to which sperm donations both cast confusion and threaten to undermine the notion of fatherhood.

John Harris assumes that marriage is morally and biologically irrelevant to claims that may legitimately be made about the foundation of a family. This author ignores the institution except insofar as it figures in the articulation of prejudices that should be dismissed.[628]

The fact that the marital presumption for establishing fatherhood and/or the lack of it can very often be decisive has also been acknowledged by the ECtHR in several rulings.[629] Therefore it is necessary to provide for an additional legal possibility of establishing parental affiliation.[630] A possible solution is recommended in the Draft Recommendation stipulating parental presumption not only in marriage but also in all three forms of sharing mutual life among heterosexual couples (registered partnership and unregistered cohabiting couples).

The right to reproduce thus goes hand in hand with the parental right/obligation. This is an owed obligation in the relationship with the mother (the

628 Harris J., "The Right to Found a Family", in Scarre G. (ed.), *Children, Parents and Politics*, Cambridge University Press, 1989.

629 See, for instance, *Rozanski v. Poland*, European Court of Human Rights, No. 55339/00, judgment of 18.05.2006; *Shofman v. Russia*, European Court of Human Rights, No. 74826/01, judgment of 24.11.2005; *Mizzi v. Malta*, European Court of Human Rights, No. 10699/05, judgment of 10.10.2006.

630 Article 6 of the Draft Recommendation on the Rights and Legal Status of Children and Parental Responsibilities, CJ-FA, 2011 p. 33.

holders should be encouraged to exercise the rights jointly)[631] and more importantly with the child, and is therefore referred to as parental responsibility.[632] As such, there should be a distinction between *allocation (attribution)* and *exercise* of the parental responsibilities.[633] The prerequisite for the latter is the fulfilment of first: the exercise of the parental responsibilities can be performed only after they are attributed to the parents. Therefore the first and foremost responsibility to the father, mother and mostly to the child is the allocation of the parental responsibilities to its holders. This is in line with articles 7 and 8 of the CRC. The *exercise* of the parental responsibilities is beyond the scope of this discussion and therefore will only be elaborated when relevant for the attribution itself.

The "ideology of familialism" – two parents and child/children[634] – may be a preferred context for the child's development, but does not correspond with the diverse realities. The underlying concern of the nuclear family is to provide all children with a father. A child born after sperm donation to a married couple has a presumed father unless the presumption is disturbed. Determining the paternity of these children is a compromise between the policy of locating the child in a two-parent family and the right of the child to know and be taken care of by his parents from the moment of birth. In cases of anonymous donations, article 7 of the CRC is compromised by the parent's wish for secrecy regarding the conception. Nevertheless, the increasing national legislative acceptance of disclosure of the identities of the donors balances the right of the child to know, be taken care of by his/her parents, and above all to be born (with assisted reproduction for parents facing reproductive problems).

The ECtHR interpreted respect for family life (article 8) of the ECHR as an existence of a legal safeguard that will enable the child's integration into his/her

631 Article 29 of the Draft Recommendation on the Rights and Legal Status of Children and Parental Responsibilities, CJ-FA, 2011.

632 The term "parental responsibility" (as singular) is used in the Council Regulation Concerning Jurisdiction and the Recognition and Enforcement of Judgments in Matrimonial Matters and the Matters of Parental Responsibility (EC) No. 2201/2003 of 27.11.2003 (repealing Regulation (EC) No. 1347/2000 and the Hague Convention on Jurisdiction, Applicable Law, Recognition, Enforcement and Cooperation in Respect of Parental Responsibility and Measures for the Protection of Children. The plural version of it – "parental responsibilities" – is used in the other Council of Europe instruments: Recommendation on Parental Responsibilities No. R (84) 4, the "White Paper" on Principles Concerning the Establishment and Legal Consequences of Parentage, and the Draft Recommendation on the Rights and Legal Status of Children and Parental Responsibilities.

633 Draft Recommendation on the Rights and Legal Status of Children and Parental Responsibilities, CJ-FA 2011, article 19.A distinction between the terms *attribution* and *exercise* of parental responsibilities is recognised in the Brussels II bis Regulation and in the Hague Convention on Jurisdiction, Applicable Law, Recognition, Enforcement and Cooperation in Respect of Parental Responsibility and Measures for the Protection of Children. The White Paper also makes a distinction between *to whom parental responsibilities should belong* and *who should exercise them.* See more in Boele-Woelki K. *et al.*, *Principles of European Family Law Regarding Parental Responsibilities*, Intersentia, 2007, p. 66.

634 As called by Barett M., Macintosh M., *The Anti-Social Family*, Verso, 1985.

family as from the moment of birth.[635] The same article allows exceptions if the execution of the right itself offends the principles of lawfulness, public order and the rights and freedoms of others. It is in the child's best interests to establish parentage as from the moment of birth, giving stability to his/her development.

The legal presumption that the married husband is the father of the child depicts solely the legal effects of a child born under circumstances of marital community. The presumption as initially triggered by the probability of the biological connection between the father and the child encompasses also the intention-based fatherhood when sperm donation is the case. Thus, not only the genetic contribution, but also family life as a presupposed element in a marital relationship (even if the child and the parent are physically not living together), grants a ground for the legal entitlement of parenthood. The ECtHR also reaffirmed this in a case in which married partners did not share the same household. Nevertheless, the family life as a factual state between the child and father was established.[636]

Children conceived by sperm donation to a couple face different problems from those conceived to single women. Firstly, a social father has already taken these children under his care. On this level, a substitute father is present in their lives. What they may lack is information about their origin, since many fathers choose not to share that information because they are reluctant publicly to admit their infertility.

Secondly, like other children situated in a marital community, they also may experience dissolution of the marriage or death of one of the parents. In these situations, children in the later single-parent families or re-constructed families suffer greater harm. The most influential factor in the sense of the incidence of behavioural problems with children after divorce seems to be the exposure to parental conflict.[637] Divorce is usually accompanied by depression and anxiety of the mothers[638] that very often is associated with psychological disorders of their children as well.[639]

Another environment for raising children conceived by sperm donation is in within lesbian-couple families. This is an alternative formation of fatherless

635 See more in *Marckx v. Belgium*, European Court of Human Rights, No. 6833/74, judgment of 13.06.1979; *Johnston and Others v. Ireland*, European Court of Human Rights, No. 9697/82, judgment of 18.12.1986.

636 *Berrehab v. Netherlands*, European Court of Human Rights, No. 10730/84, judgment of 21.06.1988.

637 Amato P., "Children's Adjustments to Divorce: Theories, Hypothesis and Empirical Support", *Journal of Marriage and Family*, Vol. 55, No. 1, 1993, pp. 23–38.

638 Hetherington E.M., Stanley-Hagan, M.M., "Parenting in Divorced and Remarried Families", in Bornstein M.H. (ed.), *Handbook of Parenting*, Vol. 3, 2002, Lawrence Eribaum Associates, pp. 287–315.

639 Dunn J., Deater-Deckard, Pickering K., O'Connor T.G., Golding J., ALSPAC Study Team, "Children's Adjustment and Prosocial Behavior in Step-, Single-Parent, and Non-Stepfamily Settings. Findings from a Community Study", *Journal of Child Psychology and Psychiatry*, Vol. 39, No. 8, 1998, pp. 1083–1095.

but not single-parent families. Making access to sperm donations exclusive to heterosexual and not to homosexual women is discriminatory and a breach of the most fundamental human right. Allowing single women to reproduce using ART also encompasses allowing lesbian women to reproduce using ART. The acceptance of lesbian parents having a child proved to be more controversial than the acceptance of homosexual marriages, because it breaks down at least three boundaries: (1) the ideological, because it endangers the father figure, (2) the structural, because it advocates either one parent or two-mother families, and (3) biogenic, because of the avoidance of coitus.[640] In circumstances like these and in countries that allow lesbians to co-parent, many problems[641] that face single mothers are solved by raising the child in a two-parent family. Even the early studies on lesbian families and their interactions have shown that children raised in these environments did not show emotional, behavioural or gender-development problems, lower self-esteem or difficult peer adjustment.[642] A number of later studies have shown that children of lesbian mothers have the same gender development as children of heterosexual mothers.[643] In countries where homosexual partnerships are not legally recognised (for instance in the Republic of Macedonia), the possibility of having a partner for lesbian women at the time of the conception or later on in life that could apply to be a second parent of the child is excluded as an option.

A vast number of studies show that children in two-parent lesbian families do not differ from children in two-parent heterosexual families with respect to psychological adjustment and suggest that it is the number of parents rather than the gender of parents that is important for children's development.[644]

640 Haimes E., Weiner K., "'Everybody's Got a Dad ...' Issues for Lesbian Families in the Management of the Donor Insemination", *Sociology of Health & Illness*, Vol. 22, No. 4, 2000, pp. 477–499.

641 The fear of losing one of the parents, financial problems, and organisational framework regarding the household and the care of the child. See also Marina S., Marina F., Marina D., "Access to Fertility Treatment by Lesbian Couples", in Schenker J.G. (ed.), *Ethical Dilemmas in Assisted Reproductive Technologies*, Walter de Gruyter, 2011, p. 254.

642 Golombok S., Spencer A., Rutter M., "Children in Lesbian and Single-Parent Households. Psychosexual and Psychiatric Appraisal", *Journal of Child Psychology and Psychiatry*, Vol. 24, No. 4, 1983, pp. 551–572; Green R., Mandel J.B., Hotvedt M.E., Gray J., Smith L., "Lesbian Mothers and their Children. A Comparison with Solo Parent Heterosexual Mothers and their Children", *Archives of Sexual Behavior*, Vol. 15, No. 2, 1986, pp. 167–184; Kirkpatrick M., Smith C., Roy R., "Lesbian Mothers and their Children. A Comparative Survey", *American Journal of Orthopsychiatry*, Vol. 51, No. 3, 1981, pp. 545–551.

643 Goldeberg A.E., "Lesbian and Gay Parents and their Children", *Washington, DC. American Psychological Association*, 2010; Patterson C.J., "Children of Lesbian and Gay Parents. Psychology, Law and Policy", *American Psychologist*, Vol. 64, No. 8, 2009, pp. 727–736.

644 In the United States: Flaks D. *et al.*, "Lesbians Choosing Motherhood. A Comparative Study of Lesbian and Heterosexual Parents and their Children", *Developmental Psychology*, Vol. 31, No. 1, 1995, pp. 105–114; Chan R., Raboy B., Patterson C., "Psychological Adjustment Among Children Conceived via Donor Insemination by Lesbian and Heterosexual Mothers", *Child Development*, Vol. 69, No. 2, 1998, pp. 443–457. In Belgium: Brewaeys A., Ponjaert I., Van Hall E.V., Golombok S., "Donor Insemination. Child Development and Family Functioning in Lesbian Mother Families", *Human Reproduction*, Vol. 12, No. 6, 1997, pp. 1349–1359. In

Accordingly, a number of studies have shown that the mothers were manifesting affection, care and responsiveness just the same as heterosexual mothers.[645]

Reproductive responsibilities in marriage are automatically parental responsibilities due to the marital presumption. The husband/partner of the woman who has given birth is automatically presumed to be the father/second parent and is thus deemed to be the legal parent.[646] It is within the national legislation to decide the scope to which they will extend the presumption.[647] A reasonable solution is the one suggested in the Draft Recommendation that extends the presumption to the registered partnerships and to cohabiting different-sex couples.[648]

4.4.4. EXTRA-MARITAL RELATIONSHIP

The reproductive right as exercised in an extra-marital relationship is similar to the one in marriage. Consent from both partners is required for both natural and medically assisted reproduction. The only difference is that when natural conception takes place, it is, again, up to the woman to decide regarding the pregnancy that takes place under her bodily jurisdiction. In the case of medically assisted reproduction, the consent of both parties prior to implantation of the sperm/embryo into the woman's uterus has significance for granting parenthood.

Regarding the reproductive, thus parental, responsibilities, extra-marital relationships in most national regulations need an additional action to establish the link between father and child as opposed to marriage as a nest for automatically and legally gluing family ties. Nevertheless, the responsibility owed to children born in this setting is tantamount to those born in marriage in the international documents and case law of the ECtHR.[649] Thus the child born in an extra-marital

the UK: Golombok S., Tasker F., Murray C., "Children Raised in Fatherless Families from Infancy: Family Relationships and the Socio-emotional Development of Children of Lesbian and Single Heterosexual Mothers", *Journal of Child Psychology and Psychiatry*, Vol. 38, No. 7, 1997, pp. 783–791.

645 Golombok S., Spencer A., Rutter M., "Children in Lesbian and Single-Parent Households. Psychosexual and Psychiatric Appraisal", *Journal of Child Psychology and Psychiatry*, Vol. 24, No. 4, 1983, pp. 551–572; Kirkpatrick M., "Clinical Implications of Lesbian Mother Studies", *Journal of Homosexuality*, Vol. 14, No. 1–2, pp. 201–211, 1987; Mucklow B.M., Phelan G.K, "Lesbian and Traditional Mothers' Responses to Child Behavior and Self-Concept", *Psychological Reports*, Vol. 44, No. 3, pp. 880–882; 1979.

646 This principle is confirmed and cases of possible overlap with another relationship are delineated in article 9 of the Draft Recommendation on the Rights and Legal Status of Children and Parental Responsibilities, CJ-FA, 2011.

647 *Ibid.* article 9.

648 *Ibid.* articles 11 and 12.

649 As stipulated in the European Convention on the Legal Status of Children Born Out of Wedlock, Council of Europe, ETS No. 085, with entry into force on 11 August 1978. It was also confirmed in the ECtHR case law that a child born in a relationship where the father and

relationship could be voluntarily recognised or granted fatherhood by a court.[650] The introduction of a parental presumption to extra-marital relationships is suggested by the later Draft Recommendation.[651]

An extra-marital relationship can be registered (*registered partnership of different-sex couples* to which the Draft Recommendation refers) or non-registered (while still on some level equal to, marital relationship as in the Republic of Macedonia,[652] or *cohabiting different-sex couples* to which the Draft Recommendation refers).

The Draft Recommendation offers novelty in this field, lifting the application of the presumption also to cases of registered partnerships of different-sex couples.[653] Furthermore, it clearly notes that it should only apply to states that allow different-sex couples to enter into registered partnerships, while being of facultative nature and left to the particular state to decide its application.[654] The paternal presumption also applies in the cases of *cohabiting couples*. The term refers to "couples who are in marriage-like relationship who may or may not be living in the same place of residence".[655] In these terms, a relationship in which partners do not necessarily cohabit but have grown a relationship with a sufficient consistency to be called a *de facto* family can also qualify to be recognised as such. Consequently, there is an analogy of the application of the affiliation provisions in cohabiting different-sex couples even without regulation of cohabitation on national level.[656] The Draft Recommendation affords application of the parental

the mother are living together outside marriage is *ipso iure* part of that family unit due to the fact of the birth and from the moment of the birth of the child. See more in the cases: *Keegan v. Ireland*, European Court of Human Rights, No. 16969/90, judgment of 07.04.1994; *Lebbik v. the Netherlands*, European Court of Human Rights, No. 45582/99, judgment of 01.06.2004.

650 See Principles 6 and 7 from the White Paper.

651 Draft Recommendation on the Rights and Legal Status of Children and Parental Responsibilities, CJ-FA, 2011, articles 11 and 12.

652 The form given to extra-marital relationships in the Republic of Macedonia resembles more the form of cohabiting different-sex couples given in the Draft Recommendation.

653 Draft Recommendation on the Rights and Legal Status of Children and Parental Responsibilities, CJ-FA, 2011.

654 This is a better solution than the current one in the case of the Republic of Macedonia. Namely, existence of a *de facto* relationship that partially causes consequences similar to marriage without being formally registered can be manipulated in many possible scenarios. For instance, an extra-marital relationship can exist next to marriage without being considered bigamy. Another possibility is that an extra-marital relationship can exist among close blood-related relatives, thus being incestuous. Concerning the establishment of the paternal role, a child can be born in an extra-marital relationship existing next to marriage. In this sense, the proposed presumption in the Draft Recommendation cannot apply in the cases of non-registered extra-marital relationships. For more on the European regulations on extra-marital relationships as well as recommendations for changing the regulation in the Republic of Macedonia, see Мицковиќ Д., "Вонбрачната заедница во земјите на Европската унија", *Centre for Regional Research and Cooperation Studiorum*, 25 December 2013; Мицковиќ Д., Ристов А., "Реформите во наследното и семејното право и ингеренциите на нотарите", Нотариус, бр. 19, p. 75, available online: www.nkrm.org.mk/dokumenti/notarius/84_426597554.pdf.

655 Draft Recommendation on the Rights and Legal Status of Children and Parental Responsibilities, CJ-FA, 2011, article 12.

656 *Ibid.*

presumption in these *de facto* family unions. As such, the presumption cannot be called "marital" anymore. Marriage is losing its supremacy of being a reproductive nest throughout the European countries in which there is growing interest in informal cohabitations.

4.4.5. NOT REGULATED RELATIONSHIP

The term *not regulated relationship* has different use in the text in comparison to *extra-marital relationship*. The intention is to depict situations in which a child is born without planning and without the wish of the couple/one of the partners to maintain either the relationship or the child. As such, it is broader than both extra-marital relationships, i.e. the *registered partnership* and the factually *cohabiting different-sex couples* from the Draft Recommendation, in the sense that it neither includes any form of registration with the official authorities, nor shared dwelling of the parents in the present or intentions for it in the future.

Children born outside any legal formation of the couple still enjoy the same treatment as other children.[657] The modus of establishing their fatherhood though is different. Since there is no possibility of invoking a presumption in this case, fatherhood can be recognised (by the biological or the social father – the future partner of the mother) or challenged before the court or other competent authority.

Not only the biological father, but also the later partner of the mother, can voluntarily recognise the child as his.[658] This determination once again confirms the prevalence of social over biological factors in the establishment of the paternal role. Nevertheless, preferences are that the voluntary recognition should be conditional on the child's and/or the mother's consent.

In cases in which such voluntary will does not exist, the Draft Recommendation directs the parties to establish paternal affiliation with the competent authority.[659]

Parental responsibilities in a couple (in all three forms) are legally enabled to be satisfied in relation to the child with regard to the right protected under article 7 of the CRC in both contexts of reproduction – natural and medically assisted (on condition of enforcing disclosure of the donor's identity). They are, however, more controversial in cases in which single women conceive a child by sperm donation. In the second case, the possibility of the child being taken care of by a second parent (either genetic or social) is excluded from the moment of birth.

---

[657] Convention on the Legal Status of Children Born Out of Wedlock, Council of Europe, ETS No. 085, article 2 and article 3. See also the case *Marckx v. Belgium*, European Court of Human Rights, No. 6833/74, judgment of 13.06.1979.

[658] Draft Recommendation on the Rights and Legal Status of Children and Parental Responsibilities, CJ-FA, 2011, article 14.

[659] Draft Recommendation on the Rights and Legal Status of Children and Parental Responsibilities, CJ-FA, 2011, article 15.

In most national regulations, the possibility for a civil procedure for establishing legal fatherhood of children conceived by sperm donation to single women is excluded.

4.5. THE INDIVIDUAL REPRODUCTIVE RIGHTS AND CORRELATIVE RESPONSIBILITIES OF SINGLE WOMEN

4.5.1. RIGHTS

There is vast literature on the reasons and consequences of the phenomenon of living as a single person.[660] Much of it is concentrated on the sociological context that underpins the lifestyle as opposed to living in a couple. Along these lines, the antonyms appeared as singled/coupled, singlehood/coupledom, where the latter is the norm against which all deviations are measured.[661] The definitions of what a solo parent is differ. Lone parent could refer to people who do not live with a partner but with dependent children. For other authors, solo mothers are those who decided to be such from the moment they decided to use sperm donation, as opposed to teenage pregnancies or older mothers who adopted.[662]

A starting point of emergence of singlehood is the decreasing incidence of marriage and the increasing rates of divorce.[663] This came as another consequence of liberating women from being household hostages brought by the changes in the labour market as well as by the increased urge for individualisation.[664] Consequently, the gender roles changed dramatically and the possibility for identification with the family model in which the partners were raised was diminished. The individualisation and primacy of personal happiness incited many rebellions against family life. The "irretrievable breakdown of marriage" as a ground for divorce facilitated the feasibility of legal dissolution more than ever before.

Initially, single parent families were a product of separation, divorce or death of one of the parents. Since the rate of divorces has increased from the 1960s up

660 See more in Stein P., "Singlehood. An Alternative to Marriage", *The Family Coordinator*, Vol. 24, No. 4, pp. 489–503, 1975; DePaulo B.M., Morris W.L., "Singles in Society and in Science", *Psychological Inquiry*, Vol. 16, No. 2, 2005, pp. 57–83; DePaulo B.M., Morris W.L., "The Unrecognized Stereotyping and Discrimination Against Singles", *Current Directions in Psychological Science*, Vol. 15, No. 5, pp. 251–254, 2006; Keiser C.R., Kashy D.A., "The Contextual Nature and Function of Singlism", *Psychological Inquiry*, Vol. 16, No.2, 2005, pp. 122–126; Giddens A., *The Transformation of Intimacy. Sexuality, Love and Eroticism in Modern Societies*, Polity Press, 1993.

661 Zerjav T., "The Politicization of Singlehood", *CEU eTD Collection*, 2012, p. 52.

662 Murray C., Golombok S., "Going it Alone. Solo Mothers and their Infants Conceived by Donor Insemination", *American Journal of Orthopsychiatry*, Vol. 75, 2005, pp. 242–253.

663 See more in Beck U., Beck-Gernsheim, E., *The Normal Chaos of Love*, Polity Press, 1995.

664 *Ibid.*

to the present time, the number of single parent families has increased as well. According to a study on lone parent families in 1992, 29% of single parents were registered in the USA, while the percentage varied in the European Union states from higher (in the Nordic countries and in the UK, being highest in Denmark at 34.4%) to lower in the southern countries (being lowest in Spain at 13.4%).[665] This trend of lone parents corresponds with the divorce or separation rates.[666] Some more recent studies show that the percentage of single-mother families has increased throughout Europe, mainly during young and middle adulthood.[667] The percentage of single mothers aged over 40 increased in Belgium from 9% to 13% between 1987 and 2002, and in Spain from 3% to 6%. Still, single mothers are not a common phenomenon in Europe.[668]

The trend of becoming a single mother by choice and not because of separation from a partner is a recent phenomenon. Singlehood is not to be confused with asexuality. On the contrary, it can be considered a transitional phase (of those seeking a partner, but who have not found one yet) or a permanent decision (of those who favour living alone instead of living as a couple).[669] Asexuality and singlehood as alternatives to sexuality and sexual relationships are challenging the nature of reproduction in a heterosexual setting.[670] Treating single women differently from other women is not due to their desire to reproduce, but the state of being single because of a lack of a partner. Voluntarily single mothers have made the decision to have children without cohabiting with any affective sexual partner. In these terms, "single" is not a phase but a condition at a certain stage in life when a woman decides to adopt or conceive and give birth without cohabitation with any affective sexual partner.[671] The analogy with nature as not being natural to reproduce alone is not to be confused with the natural need to reproduce irrespective of the status of being a single woman or not.

There are two kinds of one-parent families: (1) voluntarily composed (adoption or fertilisation – sexual or assisted by a sperm donor), and (2) involuntarily composed (due to denial of parenthood or death of the other parent, or separation or divorce of the parents). While the first kind of families are intended and planned, the second kind usually are not. The main difference between children from different kinds of families is the fact that those in the first

665 European Observatory on National Family Policies, *Policy and the Employment of Lone Parents in 20 Countries, the University of York*, 1996, pp. 16–17.

666 European Observatory on National Family Policies, *A Synthesis of National Family Policies*, 1994, pp. 33 -34 referring to table on *Divorce*, Council of Europe, 1994, Eurostat 1995, and *One Person Households*, Eurostat, 1995.

667 Fokkema T., Liefbroer A.C., "Trends in Living Arrangements in Europe. Convergence or Divergence?", *Demographic Research*, Vol. 19, 2008, pp. 1351–1471.

668 *Ibid.*

669 Zerjav T., "The Politicization of Singlehood", *CEU eTD Collection*, 2012, p. 32.

670 *Ibid.*

671 See the provisional definition of the object of study in Jordana-Pröpper O., "An Anthropological Approach to Voluntarily Single Motherhood in Barcelona", *Journal of Comparative Research in Anthropology and Sociology*, Vol. 4, No. 1, 2013.

category are often not allowed access to the complete family history, while those in the second are provided with that privilege.

Feminists are the fieriest supporters of the reproductive right of the single woman, mainly because they strive for women's choices. For Shalev, the reproductive choice means "the right of women to choose whether or not to reproduce, including the right to decide whether to carry or terminate an unwanted pregnancy and the right to choose their preferred method of family planning and contraception".[672]

According to Laura Purdy, reproduction is the intersection between bioethics and feminist philosophy for two reasons: (1) reproduction is the most obvious place where gender does make a difference, and (2) the second feminist wave was born approximately at the same time as the development of reproductive biology.[673]

The transformation from two-parent to single-parent families came about for several reasons: women's education and emancipation, the desire for individuality and the increased divorce rates, conceiving a child out of wedlock without a later father's recognition,[674] and the women's decision to procreate with the assistance of a sperm donor.[675] Single-parent families can thus be divided according to many criteria and can belong in many categories, among which are: (1) single-mother or single-father families (according to the fact of who has the role of single parent); (2) single parent by circumstances (divorce, separation, death) or single parent by choice;[676] and (3) single-parent families from the beginning or becoming one over time (depending on whether the family was composed of two parents when the child was born or not).

4.5.2. RESPONSIBILITIES

The reproductive right in terms of the right to marry and to found a family has been elaborated extensively. The reproductive responsibility, though, in terms of responsible parenthood with regard to the reproductive choices towards the

---

672 Shalev C., "Rights to Sexual and Reproductive Health. The ICPD and the Convention for the Elimination of All Forms of Discrimination against Women", *Health and Human Rights*, Vol. 4, No. 2, 2000, pp. 52–53.

673 Purdy L.M., *Reproducing Persons. Issues in Feminist Bioethics*, Cornell University Press, 1996.

674 The SFRY Constitution, 1946 (as part of the legal tradition of the Republic of Macedonia) recognised children born out of wedlock as equal with children born in marriage solely in relation to their parents. The later SFRY Constitution 1963 granted them full equal status regarding their inclusion in the affiliation system and inheritance.

675 Fisher S.N., Markovic K., Radat J. Ogresta, "'Za' i 'O' Jednoroditeljskim Obiteljima", Zagreb, *Udrugaza Unapredgenje Kvaliteta Zivljena, LET*, 2006.

676 See more Novakov M., "Jednoroditeljske Porodice", *Socioloski Pregled*, Vol. XLVI, No. 3, 2012, pp. 387–399. This author also doubts the appropriate use of the term *single parent by choice*, since usually the choice comes down to single motherhood or restraining from motherhood, and not to complete or incomplete families (in terms of one or two parents), p. 390.

child, especially in single-women cases, has been tackled less.[677] It was only in recent history that the concept of parental responsibilities replaced the concept of bundle of parental rights and stressed a child-oriented perspective.[678] Therefore the reproductive responsibilities seek at least minimum standards to be met before bringing a child into existence.

Joel Feinberg's "plausible moral requirement" concerns birth rights of the future children.[679] He asserts that the child's interests and well-being should be protected before it is born. If not, the child becomes a victim of violation of its own rights by the parents.[680] Accordingly, future parents should have constraints before procreating as a minimum threshold condition for being suitable for the parenting role. For Harris, this adult reproductive constraint is the fate of the children who will constitute the family.[681] For Freeman, the parental responsibility is derived from the autonomous decision-making process of the parents. Along these lines, he states: "to exercise parental responsibility is to plan parenthood sensibly and with the empathy for the needs of the child".[682]

Responsibility accompanies all human agents as intrinsically linked with human agency.[683] Therefore responsibility should be an integral part of any decision-making process and should precede the ethical choice when embedded in a relationship with another human agent. This should especially be the case when the future generations of children are concerned. Annemie Dillen argues that to be responsible and to take up one's responsibility is not the same.[684] Responsible parenthood does not relate only to the planning of the child's birth (the number and dynamic of childbirths in the domain of family planning), but should go much further into the parental responsibilities owed to satisfy the child's right to an indissoluble relationship with his/her parents.[685] Thus, Dillen concludes that children are the primary object of responsibility of their parents. This does not originate from documents on children rights (which are interpretations of nature

677 See more in Freeman M., *The Moral Status of Children. Essays on the Rights of the Child*, Martinus Nijhoff, 1997.

678 *Ibid.* Freeman locates the shift from the concept of *parental rights* to *parental responsibilities* in 1975 Justice Report, *Parental Rights and Duties and Custody Suits*, Justice, 1975.

679 Feinberg J., *Harm to Others. The Moral Limits of the Criminal Law*, Oxford University Press, 1984.

680 *Ibid.* pp. 99–102.

681 Harris J., "The Right to Found a Family", in Scarre G. (ed.), *Children, Parents and Politics*, Cambridge University Press, 1989, p. 133.

682 Freeman M., *The Moral Status of Children. Essays on the Rights of the Child*, Martinus Nijhoff, 1997.

683 Levinas E., *Otherwise than Being, or Beyond Essence*, Martinus Nijhoff, 1981.

684 Dillen A., "Foundations of Responsibility for Children", *International Journal of Children's Spirituality*, Vol. 13, No. 1, 2008, pp. 51–61.

685 *Ibid.* Referring to the work of the pedagogue Han Van Crombrugge over the concept of "parental promise". See more in Van Crombrugge H., "'Ik zal er zijn voor jou'. Van Huwelijksgezin naar contractueel gezin: het instituut van het opvoedingscontract en de cultuur van de belofte" ("'I will be there for you'. From marital family to contractual family: the institute of the educational contract and the culture of promise"), *Rondom Gezin* 25, 2005, pp. 32–50.

based on experiences and empirical research and therefore a social construct) but is primordial and intrinsic nature of any human relationship.

Reproductive choices debates excessively focus on reproductive *rights*. Their primary concern should be reproductive *responsibilities* that go along whenever humans embed in a relationship, and especially when the other human is a child.

4.5.3. SINGLE WOMEN AS INVOLUNTARILY SINGLE PARENTS

Single-parent families are often associated with the difficulty of the single parent to provide for the children alone, usually accompanied by stress and financial insecurity.[686] As a result, they are connected with side-effects that children experience in their development such as cognitive, emotional and behavioural problems.[687] Children of divorced parents or children whose parent died can also suffer more discomfort and stress in comparison to those who never had to face such a loss. In some recent studies, the absence of a father figure has shown to be both very relevant[688] and irrelevant for the child's development of gender roles.[689]

A number of studies examining the coordinates of psychological adjustment and development, anxiety, depression and hostility of children have shown that single-parent families in financially stable homes can raise children even better than in nuclear families.[690] Some other studies regarding children raised in homosexual families countered the idea of the heterosexual nuclear family as a

686 McLanahan S., Sandefur G., *Growing up with a Single Parent. What Hurts, What Helps*, Harvard University Press, 1994; Coleman L., Glenn F., *When Couples Part. Understanding the Consequences for Adults and Children*, One Plus One, 2009.

687 Amato P., "The Impact of Family Formation on the Cognitive, Social and Emotional Well-Being of the Next Generation", *Future of Children*, Vol. 15, No. 1, 2005, pp. 75–96.

688 Yeung W.J., Sandberg J.F., Davis-Kean P.E., Hofferth S.L., "Children's Time with Fathers in Intact Families", *Journal of Marriage and Family*, Vol. 63, No. 1, 2001, pp. 136–154; Hawkins D., Amato P., King V., "Parent-Adolescent Involvement. The Relative Influence of Parent Gender and Residence", *Journal of Marriage and Family*, Vol. 68, No. 1, 2006 pp. 125–136; Lamb M.E., "How do Fathers Influence Children's Development? Let me Count the Ways", in Lamb M.E. (ed.), *The Role of the Father in Child Development*, John Wiley & Sons, 2010; Blankenhorn D., *Fatherless America. Confronting Our Most Urgent Social Problem*, Basic Books, 1995; Popenoe D., *Life Without Father. Compelling New Evidence that Fatherhood and Marriage are Indispensable for the Good of Children and Society*, Free Press, 1996.

689 Biblarz T., Stacey J., "How does the Gender of Parents Mater?", *Journal of Marriage and Family*, Vol. 72, No. 1, 2010, pp. 3–22.

690 See more in Golombok S., Badger S., "Children Raised in Mother-Headed Families from Infancy. A Follow up of Children of Lesbian and Single Heterosexual Mothers at Early Adulthood", *Human Reproduction*, Vol. 25, 2010, pp. 150–157; Golombok S., Tasker F., Murray C., "Children Raised in Fatherless Families from Infancy: Family Relationships and the Socio-emotional Development of Children of Lesbian and Single Heterosexual Mothers", *Journal of Child Psychology and Psychiatry*, Vol. 38, No. 7, 1997, pp. 783–791; Golombok S., MacCallum F., "Children Raised in Fatherless Families from Infancy. A Follow up of Children of Lesbian and Single Heterosexual Mothers at Early Adolescence", *Journal of Child Psychology and Psychiatry*, Vol. 45, 2004, pp. 1407–1419.

preferred matrix for raising children, proving that the child's well-being depends more on parenting abilities than on the structure of the family.[691]

On the other hand, a number of studies have shown the opposite – single-parent families experience financial hardship and are at the edge of poverty.[692] This is not surprising since it has always been more difficult to raise a child alone as compared to raising a child in a couple. In London in 1974, one-third of poor families were single-mother families. In Germany, 70% of single mothers were at the edge of poverty, while in Russia according to a survey in 1996, 40% of single mothers were below the edge of poverty. In Croatia 11.2% of social welfare is granted to single-parent families, while in the Republic of Serbia single-parent families manifest an attitude of isolation.[693] Manifested in different ways from distant, disappointed and stressed parents trying to provide and care for the household, to lack of care and attention, children in these circumstances can also experience difficulties throughout their childhood. A comparative study of 24 countries showed that children's living conditions have implications for their development.[694] Accordingly, single-parent families have lower material resources and poorer health in comparison to two-parent families. Some studies show that single mothers suffer a great deal of stress and discomfort in comparison to mothers raising a child together with a partner.[695] Other studies have associated the poor quality of parenting shown by single women to the higher rates of psychological problems, mostly depression related to singlehood and the increased responsibilities of dealing with it alone. Due to depression, the parent's emotional availability, control and discipline over their children deteriorate.[696]

In contrast, many other studies have shown that children growing up in single-parent families have a normal development without being deprived of a proper childhood nor experiencing psychological disadvantages.[697]

Some authors have recognised the overload of responsibilities, financial problems and the difficulty to reconcile work, family and personal life as the main problems for single mothers. This shows another aspect of the problem that seeks another kind of solution – national social policies that will facilitate single

691 Patterson C., "Children of Lesbian and Gay Parents. Psychology, Law and Policy", *American Psychologist*, Vol. 64, 2009, pp. 727–736; Biblarz T., Stacey J., "How does the Gender of Parents Mater?", *Journal of Marriage and Family*, Vol. 72, No. 1, 2010, pp. 3–22.

692 See more Novakov M., "Jednoroditeljske Porodice", *Socioloski Pregled*, Vol. XLVI, No. 3, 2012, p. 393.

693 *Ibid.*

694 Laftman S.B., "Family Structure and Children's Living Conditions. A Comparative Study of 24 Countries", *Child Indicators Research*, Vol. 3, 2010, pp. 127–147.

695 Dziak E., Janzen B.L., Muhajarine N., "Inequalities in the Psychological Well-Being of Employed, Single and Partnered Mothers. The Role of Psychological Work Quality and Work-family Conflict", *International Journal for Equity in Health*, Vol. 9, No. 6, 2010.

696 Cummings E.M., Davies P.T., "Maternal Depression and Child Development,", *Journal of Child Psychology and Psychiatry*, Vol. 35, No. 1, 1994, pp. 72–112; McLanahan S., Sandefur G., *Growing up with a Single Parent. What Hurts, What Helps*, Harvard University Press, 1994.

697 See Golombok S. Her different studies show different aspects of how children in single-mother families are not deprived of proper care, affection and financial stability.

mother's parenting. The possible solution may vary from tax relief, financial bonuses and benefits to better social services, kindergartens, medical assistance and so on.

4.5.4. SINGLE WOMEN AS PARENTS BY POSTHUMOUS REPRODUCTION

A way of "voluntarily choosing"[698] single motherhood but with approval in the form of a written consent from a deceased partner is to conceive a child *post mortem* of the father. The attitude towards posthumous use of a man's gametes for reproductive purposes varies in different European countries from not regulated to regulations that explicitly forbid or allow the practice.[699] It is up to the national authorities to decide if and under which conditions they will practise the conception after the death of the father.[700] If allowed, the only request is for the Member States to provide the consent of all concerned parties, and to make explicit rules regarding the consequences of the child's status in relation to the deceased father. It is also up to the states to decide if they afford any succession rights from the father to the child. This means that the states are permitted to treat a deceased person as the legal parent, but not necessarily to confer any consequent succession rights.[701] This is consistent with the Roman law and continental law acceptance of the inheritance principles that only alive persons can possibly inherit. Some authors criticise different treatments of children on grounds of the way they were conceived, considering posthumous conceptions as discriminatory.[702] Since posthumously conceived children are no different from other children, they should not be victims of a failure to synchronise law with

698 The term "voluntarily choosing" single motherhood by posthumous reproduction is stressed because it is questionable if it is a matter of choice or a question of not having another option to conceive a child with the beloved partner (bearing in mind that the death of the partner is not a preferred choice and therefore parenting without a partner is also not a matter of choice but a matter of circumstance).

699 For a comparative scope of different regulations in Europe, see Lowe N., *A Study into the Rights and Legal Status of Children being Brought Up in Various Forms of Marital or Non-Marital Partnerships and Cohabitation*, A Report for the Attention of the Committee of Experts on Family Law, September, 2009, p. 13.

700 See more in the Draft Recommendation on the Rights and Legal Status of Children and Parental Responsibilities, CJ-FA, 2011, p. 41.

701 *Ibid.*

702 See, for instance, Suppon J.M.F., "Life after Death: the Need to Address the Legal Status of Posthumously Conceived Children", *Family Court Review*, Vol. 48, No. 1, 2010, pp. 228–245. This author suggests a model statute promoting legal parenthood of posthumously conceived children and their deceased parents. Consequently, these children should be entitled to inheritance rights if provided in the form of a will stating that the deceased parent intended to be a parent, there is an existence of genetic relationship between the parent and the child, and the child is born within three years from the death of his or her deceased parent (p. 228).

technology.[703] Automatically denying rights to posthumously conceived children is in contradiction to the promotion of the child's best interests.

Children conceived posthumously and by sperm donation to single women are in a similar position. A widowed woman will be a single mother intentionally, and the child will not meet the father, let alone have the possibility of being taken care of by him.

4.5.5. SINGLE WOMEN AS PARENTS BY CHOICE

The Convention on the Elimination of All Forms of Discrimination Against Women guarantees the reproductive right of women as part of the basic human rights and freedoms providing that every woman has the right to decide freely the birth and number of children that she is going to bring up.[704] The Ethics Committee of the American Society for Reproductive Medicine holds that it is an ethical obligation to treat unmarried and single persons equally to those who are married, even more so when it comes to the application of bio-medically assisted reproduction.[705] United Nations' goals on population and development confirmed the WHO definition of *health,* embedding it in the context of reproduction defining *reproductive health* as "a state of complete physical, mental, and social well-being and not merely absence of disease or infirmity in all matters relating to the reproductive system and to its functions and processes". Thus, infertility is not just a medical but also a social condition, promoting access to available reproductive technologies not only to couples but also to single women.

In the category of "single women by choice" belong dominantly heterosexual women in their 30s and 40s who are well educated and financially independent.[706] These women do not necessarily reject the ideals of the nuclear family. In contrast, they are usually balancing their biological clocks with their prospects, trying to salvage at least some of it by hoping that their partner and father figure will appear later on in life.[707] On the contrary, perceptions of single mothers by choice

[703] *Ibid.* p. 249.

[704] Article 16, United Nations Convention on the Elimination of All Forms of Discrimination against Women, 1979.

[705] Ethics Committee of the American Society for Reproductive Medicine "Access to Fertility by Gays, Lesbians and Unmarried Persons", *Fertility and Sterility*, Vol. 92, No. 4, 2009.

[706] See more in Murray C., Golombok S., "Going it Alone. Solo Mothers and their Infants Conceived by Donor Insemination", *American Journal of Orthopsychiatry*, Vol. 75, 2005, pp. 242–253; Hertz R., *Single by Chance, Mother by Choice. How Women are Choosing Parenthood without Marriage and Creating the New American Family*, Oxford University Press, 2006.

[707] Graham S., "Choosing Single Motherhood? Single Women Negotiating the Nuclear Family Ideal", in Cutas D., Chan S. (eds.), *Families – Beyond the Nuclear Ideal*, Bloomsbury Academic, 2012.

often correspond with a pejorative image of divergents from "normal" two-parent families, and therefore as being unnatural and bad.[708]

A number of studies have shown that choosing to be a single parent intentionally is not a matter of choice, but instead it is a constrained decision to found a family in the absence of prospects for it (fertility decreasing while not having a loving partner).[709] Some surveys have showed that women even feel grief when deciding to take "the last train" to establish themselves as sole mothers due to the lack of a partner rather than pursuing the nuclear family ideal. For many, decisions of that kind are of temporary nature until they meet the partner with whom they can raise their already conceived children.[710]

In the comparative literature, single mothers by choice have been condemned for several reasons. *Inter alia*, they have been condemned for purposely undermining the nuclear family (thus depriving the child of a father intentionally, not merely as a result of a dysfunctional family or circumstances), and for opening the doors to reproductive consumerism (such as ordering or buying a baby, choosing a father according to personal preferences from a catalogue of sperm donors, etc.).[711]

According to some proponents of single women's right to determine their reproductive destiny as much as possible, they are eligible to be single parents at least on four grounds: age, responsibility, emotional maturity and financial capability.[712] These four grounds also grant them different legitimacy than single parents conceiving wrongly in their teenage years or those who are dependent on social care institutions.[713] The purpose of the differentiation is to strengthen the argument of their social justification.

708 Correia H., Broderick P., "Access to Reproductive Technologies by Single Women and Lesbians. Social Representations and Public Debate", *Journal of Community & Applied Social Psychology*, Vol. 19, No. 4, pp. 241–256, 2009; Fineman M., *The Sexual Family. Family and Queer Legal Theory. Intimate Encounters, Uncomfortable Conversations*, Ashgate, 2009.

709 Graham S., "Choosing Single Motherhood? Single Women Negotiating the Nuclear Family Ideal", in Cutas D., Chan S. (eds.), *Families – Beyond the Nuclear Ideal*, Bloomsbury Academic, 2012; Mannis V.S., "Single Mothers by Choice", *Family Relations*, Vol. 48, No. 2, 1999, pp. 121–128; Bock J., "Doing the Right Thing? Single Mother by Choice and the Struggle for Legitimacy", *Gender and Society*, Vol. 16, No. 1, 2000, pp. 62–86; Hertz R., *Single by Chance, Mother by Choice. How Women are Choosing Parenthood without Marriage and Creating the New American Family*, Oxford University Press, 2006; Jadva V., Badger S., Morrissette M., Golombok S., "'Mom by Choice, Single by Life's Circumstance …' Findings from a Large-scale Survey of the Experiences of Single Mothers by Choice", *Human Fertility*, Vol. 12, No. 4, 2009, pp. 174–84.

710 Graham S., "Choosing Single Motherhood? Single Women Negotiating the Nuclear Family Ideal", in Cutas D., Chan S. (eds.), *Families – Beyond the Nuclear Ideal*, Bloomsbury Academic, 2012.

711 *Ibid.* Also see Soiseth A., *Choosing You. Deciding to have a Baby on my Own*, Seal Press, 2008.

712 Bock J.D., "Doing the Right Thing? Single Mother by Choice and the Struggle for Legitimacy", *Gender and Society*, Vol. 14, No. 1, 2000, pp. 62–86.

713 *Ibid.*

On the other hand, condemning the child to be fatherless from birth, but even more so not to know his/her own genetic origin, is for many authors morally wrong and a reason why single women should be banned access to ART.[714]

Some authors demonstrated moral panic about the prospects of fatherless families when debates about introducing the possibility to conceive alone started.[715] Political leaders also expressed their unwillingness to support future failures of the expectations of children conceived that way to fair access to family history.[716]

Up until 2010, many European countries gave single women the possibility of conceiving through ART: Belgium, Bulgaria, Denmark, Estonia, Finland, Greece, Hungary, Iceland, Montenegro, Russia, Spain, Great Britain, Belarus, Serbia, Ukraine and the Republic of Macedonia.[717] Despite the current very present liberalisation in Europe, the possibility for a single woman to be a beneficiary of the right to assisted fertilisation was and in many countries still is a controversial issue. The French Code of Public Health stipulates that only couples have the right to use ART,[718] supporting the view that a child born with ART has the right to live in a family composed of two parents.[719] In Slovenia, the right was decided through a referendum in which 80% of voters supported the exclusive possibility to conceive through assisted reproduction for couples only.[720] The Republic of Serbia has chosen the middle ground: while couples have the possibility to exercise their reproductive right as a principle rule, single women's right to reproduce through ART is allowed as an exception: if there are justified reasons and if there is consent from the Ministers responsible for Health and Family Relationships.[721] Due to the restrictions and conditional exercise of the reproductive right based on fulfilling certain criteria (among others, women below a certain reproductive age) the doors of "reproductive tourism" were opened to its neighbour – the Republic of Macedonia. Nowadays, many women from Serbia come to Macedonia

---

714 Velleman D., "Family History", *Philosophical Papers*, Vol. 34, No. 3, 2005, pp. 357–378.

715 Walker K., "1950s Family Values v. Human Rights: In Vitro Fertilization, Donor Insemination, and Sexuality in Victoria", *Public Law Review*, Vol. 11, No. 4, pp. 292–307; Cannold L., "DNA tests, Paternity 'Fraud' and Moral Panic about Single Women and Lesbians forming Families with Donor Sperm", *Journal of Professional and Applied Ethics*, Vol. 4, No. 2, 2003.

716 Dempsey D., "Donor, Father or Parent? Conceiving Paternity in the Australian Family Court", *International Journal of Law, Policy and Family*, Vol. 18, 2004, p. 80.

717 Howard W.J. *et al.*, International Society of Fertilities Sciences, *IFFS Surveillance*, 2010, pp. 22–23.

718 Article L. 2141-2, Code de la Sante publique, amendment Loi n. 2011-814 du juillet 2011 – article 33.

719 *Les Lois de Bioéthique. Cinq ans après*, Étude Adoptee par l'Assamblée générale du Conseil d'État le 25 novembre 1999, La Documentation Française, Paris, 1999.

720 Gordon, K., van Houten, N., IFFS Surveillance 07, *Fertility & Sterility*, Vol. 87, No. 4, 2007, pp. 7–18.

721 Article 26, Law on Infertility Treatment through a Procedure of Bio-medically Assisted Fertilisation, Republic of Serbia.

to undergo an ART procedure.[722] Macedonian Law on Bio-medically Assisted Fertilisation allows the realisation of single women's reproductive right relating to the execution of the right on certain conditions such as having had previous treatment or treatment with other methods that was unsuccessful, and in accordance with women's age and general condition regarding their capability to parent.[723]

A study of the reactions and consequences of older single mothers conceiving a child by sperm donation found tolerably normal socio-emotional development of the children.[724] Nevertheless, the study also discovered hardship on the part of the single women regarding their health (since they were conceiving at an older age, had many miscarriages and other additional problems with conceiving and bringing the pregnancy to term). Many women also experienced financial hardship in conjunction with the problem of who to leave their children with while they were working extra hours. As a result, the conclusion followed that older single mothers assisted by sperm donation present a rather complex situation regarding their family realities.

A later study, regarding the satisfactions, concerns, problems and ways of dealing with them in single-mother families assisted by sperm donation, found a diversity of reactions. While mothers mostly demonstrated great satisfaction with conceiving a child, they were mostly concerned that in case of illness, there will be no one to take care of the child.[725] They were also concerned about their older age that in comparison with their children's peers' mothers was obvious. All the children in the examined sample desired a father. The information given, irrespective of its identifying or not character, meant a lot to them. In the absence of a real father figure, they were looking for a father's identification in the most present male person in their life, very often blaming the mother for the lack of it. In the conclusion of the same study, all single-mother families needed an enlarged family formation. The mothers needed help from their elderly mothers, friends or relatives. The children needed company from a male figure and from another sibling to save them from loneliness.[726]

---

722 See Mickovikj D., Ristov A., "Bio-medically Assisted Fertilization in the Republic of Macedonia", in Jansen B.E.S., Ignovska E. (eds.), *Law, Public Health Care System and Society*, Vol. 8, 2012.

723 Article 9, Law on Bio-medically Assisted Fertilisation, 2008 stipulates as follows: "Adult man and woman having legal capacity, married or living in extra-marital relationship, as well as unmarried woman who is not in an extra-marital relationship shall have the right to use the assisted fertilisation procedure, provided that the previous treatment or the treatment with other methods is unsuccessful, and who in accordance with their age and general condition are capable of parenting."

724 Weissenberg R., Landau R., Madgar I., "Older Single Mothers Assisted by Sperm Donation and their Children", *Human Reproduction*, Vol. 22, No. 10, 2007, pp. 2784–2791.

725 Weissenberg R., "Are Two A Family? Older Single Mothers Assisted by Sperm Donation and their Children Revisited", *American Journal of Orthopsychiatry*, Vol. 82, No. 4, 2012, pp. 523–528.

726 *Ibid.*

There have been a number of studies focusing on the effects of the lack of a father figure for the cognitive, social and emotional development of the child, showing negative outcomes.[727] There have also been a number of studies that showed negative outcomes when it comes to the health of the mothers.[728]

The route that women take to motherhood without relying on a male "provider" can take different dimensions such as adoption, known donor pregnancies, anonymous donor insemination or "accidental" pregnancies.[729] In most of the investigated studies that deal with the family life created in each form it has been argued that mothers and children are doing fine. For some authors, the rationale behind these decisions is very logical and practical as a reaction to what is believed to be "irresponsible men's behaviour when it comes to long-term commitments to childbearing".[730] As a response, women demonstrate that it is possible to found a family without making compromises and playing the submissive role as compensation for a biological and economic provider.[731] For these authors, women engaging in this kind of scenario are being creative in finding solutions to care for all aspects of their family. They also consider that the choices they make from the beginning (which eventually affect children's future possible kinship with the father) balance in a way to serve the child's well-being.[732] Especially interesting for the foundation on which fatherhood rests and its impossibility of being established is the situation of conceiving a child with a known sperm donor. As some authors have investigated, the initial consent to donating just the sperm and nothing more than that has proved to change over time, as the known donor (usually a friend) meets the child.[733] Often, it happens as a love at first sight with their own progeny. Even if the affection is not so strong at

727 McConachie H., "Psychological Correlates of Depressive Symptoms among 12–14 year old Norwegian Adolescents", *Child: Care, Health and Development*, Vol. 30, No. 2, 2004, p. 184; Weitoft G.R., Hjern A., Haglund B., Rosen M., "Mortality, Severe Morbidity, and Injury in Children Living with Single Parents in Sweden. A Population Based Study", *The Lancet*, Vol. 361, 2003, pp. 289–295.

728 Franz M., Lensche H., "Psychosocial Distress and Symptoms of Single Mothers and their Children in a Large Community Sample", *Z Psychosomatic Medicine and Psychotherapy*, Vol. 49, No. 2, 2003, pp. 115–138; Roos E., Burstrom B., Saastamoinen P., Lahelma E., "A Comparative Study of the Patterning of Women's Heal by Family Status and Employment Status in Finland and Sweden", *Social Science & Medicine*, Vol. 60, No. 11, 2005, pp. 2443–2451; Whitehead M., Burstroom B., Didericksen F., "Social Policies and the Pathways to Inequalities in Health. A Comparative Analysis of Lone Mothers in Britain and Sweden", *Social Science & Medicine*, Vol. 50, No. 2, 2000, pp. 255–270.

729 Hertz R., Ferguson I.T.F., "Kinship Strategies and Self-Sufficiency Among Single Mothers by Choice. Post Modern Family Ties", *Qualitative Sociology*, Vol. 20, No. 2, 1997.

730 *Ibid.* See also Gerson K., *No Man's Land. Man's Changing Commitments to Family and Work*, Basic Books, 1993; Stacey J., *Brave New Families. Stories of Domestic Upheaval in the Late Twentieth Century*, Basic Books, 1990.

731 *Ibid.* Hertz R., Ferguson I.T.F., "Kinship Strategies and Self-Sufficiency Among Single Mothers by Choice. Post Modern Family Ties", *Qualitative Sociology*, Vol. 20, No. 2, 1997.

732 *Ibid.* p. 190.

733 *Ibid.* p. 197. See also the case of *J.R.M. v. the Netherlands*, European Commission on Human Rights, No. 16944/90, decision of 09.02.1993.

the beginning, many women and their sperm providers do actually stay in touch for the purposes of contact between the child and the genetic father.[734] These contacts create over time a relationship between the father and the child. If the idea of the parenthood has changed and all parties agree with the status, the sperm donor also has the possibility of recognising the child as his. As such, this will create a new relationship between the father and the child, while the relationship with the mother can remain the same. In the Australian context for instance, even though the donor has no rights or liabilities towards the conceived child, it is possible for the Family Court to make a parenting order in favour of an interested person that will eventually constitute that person as a legal parent.[735] Some authors have developed parenting manuals constructing possibilities for known sperm donors who donated to lesbian couples gradually to develop continuing contact with the child that will result in co-parenting arrangements.[736] Others claimed that a known donor's degree of social contact with the child and how he/his family will be known is subject to negotiation.[737] This situation, though, contradicts the situations of accidental pregnancies. There, the father (if he knows), the mother or the child (later on) can apply for court proceedings to establish parenthood. What is different is that even though not every consent to sexual intercourse envisages consent to parenthood, it is taken as a package and cannot be divided. Thus in the first case, the consent explicitly rejects the parental role, while in the latter, the consent to sexual intercourse is not separated from the responsibility to parent, nor is it a subject for negotiation.[738]

---

734 *Ibid. J.R.M. v. the Netherlands*, European Commission on Human Rights, No. 16944/90, decision of 09.02.1993.

735 The Australian Family Law Act, sections 61D, 64B, 64C. See also the way the Court dealt with the case of *Re Patrick* in which the possibilities for socially recognising the kinship status of "known donors" were challenged. The judge found a socially viable kinship connection between the father and the child that existed external to the commissioning lesbian mothers' perceived boundary of what a homo-nuclear family should look like. The decision of the Court was interesting in that it brought a new distinction between "social parenthood" and "social fatherhood". A father was considered the man with whom a child has frequent contact in which the status of the biological ties for the social relationship is made apparent, rather than a man who exists primarily for the child as a potential source of knowledge about his origins. See more in Dempsey D., "Donor, Father or Parent? Conceiving Paternity in the Australian Family Court", *International Journal of Law, Policy and Family*, Vol. 18, 2004, pp. 84–91.

736 Saffron L., *Challenging Conceptions: Pregnancy and Parenting Beyond the Traditional Family*, Cassell, 1994; Martin A., *The Lesbian and Gay Parenting Handbook*, Harper Perennial, 1993.

737 Donovan C., "Who Needs a Father? Negotiating Biological Fatherhood in British Lesbian Families Using Self-Insemination", *Sexualities*, Vol. 3, No. 2, 2013, pp. 149–164; Dunne G.A., "Opting into Motherhood: Lesbians Blurring the Boundaries and Transforming the Meaning of Parenthood and Kinship", *Gender and Society*, Vol. 14, No. 1, 2000, pp. 11–25; Haimes E., Weiner K., "'Everybody's Got a Dad ...' Issues for Lesbian Families in the Management of the Donor Insemination", *Sociology of Health & Illness*, Vol. 22, No. 4, 2000, pp. 477–499.

738 See also Schultz M.M., "Reproductive Technology and Intent-Based Parenthood. An Opportunity for Gender Neutrality", *Wisconsin Law Review*, Vol. 297, 1990, p. 324. The author elaborates that the grounds for imposing a status-based parental regime in conceptions *via* ART are weaker than in conceptions that occur because of sexual intercourse. The justification of such outcomes can be traced to the presumed intention between coital partners. On the

4.6. DISCUSSION OF THE POSITION OF SINGLE WOMEN USING ASSISTANCE BY SPERM DONORS TO REPRODUCE

Judith Stacey defined the postmodern family as "not a new model of family life, not the next stage in orderly progression of family history, but the stage when the belief in a logical progression of stages breaks down"[739] in the 1990s. It seems that this definition is still applicable and is the only one that can never fade away. Evolutionary models of family history are rupturing. The post-modern family lurches forward and backward into an uncertain future including both experimental and nostalgic elements. Even the idea of seeing it as transitional is not precise enough to depict the changes because there is no expectancy of uniform family models in the future. On the contrary, it has to be accepted that each family is a model of its own, as each individual is a holder of the right to found it independently.

A judicial investigation of paternity proceedings in Portugal (where the right to paternity is almost considered a human right),[740] resulted in a conclusion that there is still social disgust regarding single-mother families.[741] The author argued that on the one hand, it is assumed that single-mother families are indispensable due to the limited economic resources they can possess. On the other hand, these families represent potential sources of deviant behaviour in the absence of adequate socialisation of their members, which occurs precisely due to the father's absence.[742]

The core problem in single women exercising their right to reproduce and found a family lies in the binary of what Zerjav calls *perfect* and *imperfect families*.[743] Two opposing rights frame the discourse: those of single women to exercise their reproductive right without discrimination, and those of children to know and be raised by their parents as in concordance with their best interests. Imperfect families do not provide the child with the ideal of being brought up by two parents. In this framework, imperfections are also foreseen for two-parent homosexual families, since then the natural character of reproducing is not imitated and therefore its purpose not valid. According to this standard, single-women families are even more deviant from the ideal norm of family life.

---

other hand, the intention to reproduce with assisted technology cannot be presumed, but necessarily has to be explicit and factual.

739 Stacey J., *Brave New Families. Stories of Domestic Upheaval in the Late Twentieth Century*, Basic Books, 1990.

740 See footnote 1123.

741 Machado H., "Biologising Paternity, Moralizing Maternity.The Construction of Parenthood in the Determination of Paternity through the Courts in Portugal", *Feminist Legal Studies*, Vol. 16, No. 2, 2008, pp. 215–236.

742 See also Narayan U., Bartkowiak J.J. (eds.), *Having and Raising Children: Unconventional Families, Hard Choices and the Social Good*,Pennsylvania State University Press, 1999.

743 Zerjav T., "The Politicization of Singlehood", *CEU eTD Collection*, 2012, p. 40.

Summarising the debate about the natural and artificial character of reproduction and family, three arguments can be extrapolated in single women's cases. Firstly, lack of a partner in creating family is not natural; therefore unequal treatment of single women is justified. Its counterargument offers another perspective: having a partner is not always possible and not necessarily related to the need to have a child; therefore unequal treatment of single women is not justified. Secondly, a heterosexual two-parent family is a natural environment for raising a child; thus single women should not be encouraged to have children. The counterargument is that single mothers can provide a better environment for the child than dysfunctional heterosexual families; thus they should be enabled to have children. Thirdly, assisted reproduction is a medical treatment to cure infertility; thus single women cannot prove that they are eligible for the treatment. Its counterargument reveals another aspect: single women can also be medically infertile, even though they are surely socially infertile; thus they should be entitled to infertility treatment.[744]

Family laws are at an intersection between individual rights and communitarian rights (as a member of a family as a community). Perceptions depend on the prevailing aspect in the observation – individual choices and liberty or communal responsibility as a member of the family. Therefore, different interpretations are present in the comparative literature. Some authors argue that family law regulations should, as a priority, guide the needs of the individuals and not principally structure their behaviour.[745] The changing family laws should aim towards guiding individuals in their choices, increasingly varied, by providing a legal framework for their personal development, and not structure society by assigning a single way of life.[746] On the other hand, other authors take the responsibility towards the other members of the family as a guiding principle in regulating family. In these communitarian terms, and following the best interests of the child argument, assisted reproduction should cover only couples.[747] Even though the reproductive right of the woman should be guaranteed, it should not compromise the right of the child to have two parents. The legal regulation of treatments for infertility should balance the reproductive autonomy of the adults (in this case – single women), and the welfare of the children.[748]

If the emphasis is on individual reproductive autonomy, then it will follow that society has a rights-based duty to provide that to which one has a right.

744 *Ibid.* Zerjav categorises the main arguments of the access to ART in the construction of the heterosexual norm through the deviancy and normalcy of single women using the Fairclough structure of argument. See also Fairclough N., *Analysing Discourse*, Routledge, 2003, p. 8.

745 Leleu Y.H., "The Great Shift in Belgian Law", *Reflexions*, Université de Liège, available online: http://reflexions.ulg.ac.be/cms/c_11968/the-great-shift-in-belgian-law.

746 *Ibid.*

747 Mickovikj D., "Дилемите во врска со Законот за био-медицинското потпомогнато оплодување", *Pravnik*, 2008.

748 Storrow R.F., "The Bioethics of Prospective Parenthood. In Pursuit of the Proper Standard for Gatekeeping in Infertility Clinics", *Cardozo Law Review*, Vol. 28, No. 5, 2007, p. 101.

This will also include a positive right to a child and prevention from involuntary childlessness. In this light, procreation is seen primarily through the lenses of the progenitors – those who strive to fulfil their own child wish. As such, the role of the child is merely instrumental towards satisfying someone else's wishes and desires.[749] Contrary to that, this should not imply that such desire has to be fulfilled at all costs, in particular when it might harm others. If fair prospects were given to children conceived by assisted reproduction to exercise their rights on the same level as other children prior to lobbying for procreation as personal fulfilment, the consensus of exercising reproductive rights may have been reached earlier. The decision to procreate and form a family is a basic and intimate human prerogative that requires consensus between the parties involved. It is also fundamental to the very existence and survival of the human species. Interests between participating parties (single women, donors and children) are still conflicting. It is necessary for these interests to be reconciled in such a way as to offer certainty in the anticipation of the consequences of undertaken actions, and therefore legal stability. In these terms, the bioethical and legal conflicts need to be solved in order to claim that each person from the relationship enjoys protection of its own.

The issue of allowing reproductive freedom to single women is questioned by the best interests of the child to have a father. It is very clear that one option excludes the other. On the one hand, there is condemnation of single women's reproductive liberty due to ignorance towards the child's need for a father. On the other hand, there is justification for making such reproductive choices in the desirability of the child to be born in the first place. Some authors criticise the "life after birth" of children having to live with the lifelong injuries and consequences of their parents' pre-birth choices.[750] Depriving children of one of their fundamental rights (that should be protected as their constitutional right because deprivation originated when the child was *in utero*) would be tantamount to declaring children second-class citizens.[751]

The common feature of international recommendations[752] and national family regulations in Europe is that provisions for establishing fatherhood do not

---

[749] Denier, Y., "Need or Desire? A Conception and Moral Phenomenology of the Child Wish", *International Journal of Applied Philosophy*, Vol. 20, No. 1, 2006, pp. 81–95.

[750] See Goodwin M., "A View from the Cradle. Tort Law and the Private Regulation of Assisted Reproduction", *Emory Law Journal*, Vol. 59, 2010, pp. 1040–1099. Citing the judgment in the case of *Thornawell v. United States*, 471 F. Supp. 344, D.D.C. 1979 at 353.

[751] *Ibid.*

[752] Article 17 of the Draft Recommendation clearly stipulates that gamete or embryo donors are not considered legal parents. The definition of "parents" is understood as "persons considered as parents according to the national law" (article 2). Thus, for donors article 23 does not apply which stipulates that parental responsibilities should belong to both parents irrespective of the relationship between them, referring to cases in which the other parent refuses to execute parental responsibilities. It goes on to state that: "In cases where only one parent has parental responsibilities by the operation of law, States should make procedures available to the other parent to have an opportunity to acquire parental responsibilities unless it is contrary to

apply in cases in which the conception occurred through assisted fertilisation. If the context of intentionally conceiving the child by sperm donation is within the couple's family, the harm done by the absence of the genetic father in the child's life is partially amortised by the presence and the active parental role of the social father. Nevertheless, there is no such substitution in single women's contexts of intentionally conceiving a child by sperm donation. Sperm donors are not considered parents, and this is difficult to challenge in court. Regulations of that kind compromise articles 2, 6(1), 7, 8, 12 and 18 of the CRC. Procedural rules of each state should allow a child born with the assistance of reproductive technology and capable of forming his/her own views to be heard in judicial and administrative proceedings affecting him/her.[753] In these terms, proceedings to establish paternity or at least to be acquainted with the genetic father affects a child born with the assistance of reproductive technology just as it affects a child born in marriage or a recognised child. The different treatment of children depending on their birth and status is discrimination in the CRC. It is an obligation of the state signatories of the Convention to respect and ensure the rights of each child within their jurisdiction without discrimination of any kind, irrespective of, among others, the child's birth or other status.[754] It is also an obligation of the state signatories to use their efforts to ensure recognition of the principle that both parents have joint responsibilities for the upbringing of the child.[755] Even though the Convention does not determine the difference between uses of the term 'parent' (with its biologic/genetic, legal or social meaning) in the case of conception of a child by a single woman, there is no other father apart from the donor.

A common feature that should be equally valued in single-women and couple families constituted by sperm donations is the right of the child to know his/her genetic origins. A child who has donors intruding into parentage will be cut off from their genetic heritage and part of his/her kinship (brothers, sisters and other relatives.[756] If genes play an important role in the physical and intellectual characteristics of a person[757] and identity is considered a complex construct that operates on psychological, political, personal and social levels that takes shape

the best interests of the child. Lack of consent or opposition by the parent having parental responsibilities should not as such be an obstacle for such acquisition". On this level, it seems that donor-conceived children are entitled to fewer rights due to the choices of their genetic parents, and because of protecting their intentions they do not have a legal modus for establishing their fatherhood or partial parental responsibilities.

753 Article 12 CRC.

754 Article 2(1) CRC.

755 Article 18(1) CRC.

756 See more in Callahan S., Monagle E.J., Thomasma C.D (eds.), *Medical Ethics: A Guide for Health Care Professionals*, Aspen Publishers, 1987.

757 See more in Landau R., Weissenberg R., "Disclosure of Donor Conception in Single-mother Families: Views and Concerns", *Human Reproduction*, Vol. 25, No. 4, 2010, pp. 942–948.

by contemplating difference and sameness,[758] then the denial of knowledge of a genetic parent can have psychological implications for the donor's offspring who may feel deprived of information that they need to develop a full sense of identity.[759] In addition, a potential risk of not knowing the genetic family is the possibility of transmission of genetic disorders,[760] as well as the possibility of incest through a relationship between siblings unaware of their genetic connection.[761] To have a right to access the genetic data does not exclude the right not to access the genetic data. If the possibility of a choice is given to those who are affected the most by this decision, a curiosity unfolds towards questioning if it is justified to introduce an action solely designed to ascertain genetic parentage without creating any possibility for establishing a legal relationship. This is especially questionable in cases where single women conceive a child by sperm donation in which the father's role is not yet taken.

The same issue regarding the right to know or establish the paternal link with the progenitor is identified when sperm donation is used for inseminating women in a couple. Nevertheless, reasons why the scope of this research is limited to single women only are twofold.

Firstly, single-women families are the manifestation of how assisted reproductive technologies are changing family laws by making it feasible to conceive a child on one's own (without a partner). This shifts us into a new era of conceptualisation of family life.

Secondly, the issues are treated differently due to the different contexts surrounding both families: (1) lacking (single-mother families), and (2) not lacking (couple families) a father in the child's life. Two parents will raise the child conceived in the second context, even though the father will be the child's social and legal but not genetic parent. The child conceived in the first context is destined to be fatherless from the beginning. Promoting or criticising the right to know one's own genetic history, and/or the right to proceedings for establishing fatherhood will however apply to both cases. In most European countries, the two-parent family is the preferred model, which means that the child cannot have more than one father. Nevertheless, a possibility of having more persons as holders

758 Richards B., "What is Identity?", in Gaber I., Aldridge J. (eds.), *The Best Interests of the Child, Culture, Identity, and Transracial Adoption*, Free Association Books, 1994.

759 Baran A., Pannor R., *Lethal Secrecies: the Psychology of Donor Insemination, Problem and Solution*, Amistead Press, 1993.

760 There is a recent case of "Donor 7042" who passed a potentially severe genetic disorder to at least five of the children conceived from his sperm (while 43 children were conceived with his sperm through 14 different fertility clinics worldwide) after the fertility clinic failed to detect the mutation. See more in Hsu C., "Denmark Tightens Sperm Donation Law After 'Donor 7042' Passes Rare Genetic Disease to 5 Babies", *Medical Daily*, 25.10.2012, available online: www.medicaldaily.com/denmark-tightens-sperm-donation-law-after-donor-7042-passes-rare-genetic-disease-5-babies-242737.

761 Morton M., Irving M.A., "Common Questions that Arise in Adoption", in Turnpenny P. (ed.), *Secrets in the Genes: Adoption, Inheritance and Genetic Disease*, British Agencies for Adoption and Fostering, 1995.

of parental responsibilities is also present in some national and international regulations (for instance in the UK and in the Draft Recommendation).[762]

The debates caused by assisted reproduction are a "struggle to find a balance between biological and emotional reality".[763] By acknowledging the genuine desire of couples or single women who want to realise their wish for a child, society should not restrain from revealing the genetic truth to a child who requests the identifying data. Legislation that regulates assisted reproduction should appreciate both the genetic origin of the child and at the same time, the social reality of parenthood.

Kinship is more a matter of culture than biology. Assisted reproduction just highlights the social aspect of affiliation by negotiating the legal family. We acquire kin through marriage and cohabitation as well as reproduction and adoption. It is social understanding rather than the biological fact of reproduction that governs kinship.[764] Therefore, it is a matter of social compromise: either allowing single women to reproduce by sperm donation and bear the consequences of conceiving initially fatherless children, or not allowing it at all. A balance in between could be achieved if the concept of donations is open, thus allowing children to receive identifying information about the donors that may lead to possible contact and/or establishing family life. In any event, due weight should be given to the consent of the donor, which makes the legal establishment of paternity a matter of intention.

---

762 Draft Recommendation, CJ-FA, 2011, Article 22. See also Vonk M., *Children and their Parents, A Comparative Study of the Legal Position of Children with Regard to their Intentional and Biological Parents in English and Dutch Law*, Intersentia, 2007.

763 Doek J.E., "The Nuclear Family: Who are the Parents?", in Eekelaar J., Nhlapo T. (eds.), *The Changing Family: International Perspectives on the Family and Family Law*, 1998, p. 550.

764 Richards M., "Genes, Genealogies and Paternity: Making Babies in the Twenty-first Century", in Spencer J.R., Bois-Pedain A. (eds.), *Freedom and Responsibility in Reproductive Choice*, Hart Publishing, 2006, pp. 53–54.

CHAPTER 5

SPERM DONORS AS ASSISTANCE TO REPRODUCTION FOR SINGLE WOMEN

The political as opposed to natural constitution of ancient families for some authors is associated with the fiction of patriarchy.[765] This had a meaning of a form of political power that when introduced only referred to the sexual domination of the rule of husbands and fathers in the smallest cell of society. Only afterwards did the fiction of patriarchy take on the broader meaning of class domination, and thus a universal feature of human society. Accordingly, the representatives of this stream associate the father's role in the family as strictly conventional (i.e. imposed by force) and thus the family only as an artificial institution that negotiates the roles of its members, just as society does.[766] In these terms, the patriarchal family is not based on biology or natural ties, but on "legal fiction".[767] While the mother's biological participation is always certain as the one who physically gives birth to the child, paternity has to be discovered or invented, therefore becoming only human creation. This fiction though, served the political role of keeping the family together. Thus, the "fiction of adoption" and the "reality of kinship" were considered equal as long as the family formation was maintained.[768] By analogy, ancient families are not much different from the contemporary families founded by adoptions or by sperm donations. Again, the role of the father is negotiated – the "legal fiction" of the husband as being present when sperm is donated to couples, and his non-existence when sperm is donated to single women. Despite genetics, lacking social and legal fathers in children's lives could be an experience of single-mother families founded naturally too. Nevertheless, lacking both a genetic and social father is exclusively ascribed to single women – parents by choice. Is fatherhood so unimportant?

In the comparative literature, there has been much less interest in investigating men as fathers and their experiences in reproductive rights and

---

765 Pateman C., *The Sexual Contract*, Polity Press, 1988, p. 19.

766 *Ibid.* p. 26, referring to Hobbes T.

767 *Ibid.* p. 27 referring to the term "legal fiction" as used by Sir Maine in Maine H.J.S., *Ancient Law*, J.M. Dent and Sons Limited, 1917, 1861, p. 76, available online via the Gutenberg project, Chapter II: www.gutenberg.org/files/22910/22910-h/22910-h.htm.

768 *Ibid.* p. 27.

policies in comparison to women as mothers.[769] Reproduction, family life and child rearing have traditionally been considered to belong to the women's domain. Consequently, males' reproductive choices, sexuality, child rearing and family identifications have been neglected. As such, the lack of literature that deals with the reproductive experiences of men as begetters, donors or social parents makes the topic a rather ambiguous field for making assumptions or conclusions.

A recent study offers a systematic review of the literature dealing with the demographic characteristics, attitudes, motives and experiences of sperm donors, also suggesting that the psychological needs and experiences of the donor, and their follow up and counselling, are largely neglected.[770] The same study has also noticed that most of the research and related literature comes from Western societies (mainly from the United Kingdom and the Scandinavian countries), therefore offering only Western interpretation of sperm donors' attitudes. Accordingly, other European countries with Latin heritage, developing countries or countries with predominantly Eastern or African ideologies are not represented.[771] A common general feature from the existing literature is that the donor is neglected as a person and as a stakeholder, treated merely as a means towards an end. Reasons for these kinds of attitudes are to a large extent associated with the priority given to the other stakeholders (participants) in the reproductive project, therefore treating the donor merely as someone who altruistically gives something for somebody else without any expectations in return. Since the other participants have other interests, the focus has always been on them. Some authors suggest that turning an eye on the donor as a person (a visible and not invisible man with rights and responsibilities) by supporting follow-up research on his attitudes and behaviour, as well as counselling after the donation, may solve the puzzle regarding the legal and moral gaps in donation practice, bearing in mind its multidimensional nature.[772] On the contrary, the focus of the comparative research is mostly on institutional factors related to legislation and recruitment of donors because donors are considered important for enabling assisted reproductions for others and not for themselves.[773]

---

769 An anthropological research on reproductive experiences found more than 150 volumes dedicated to women, and very few dedicated to men. See more in Inhorn M.C., "Defining Women's Health. A Dozen Messages from More than Ethnographies", Medical Anthropology Quarterly, Vol. 20, No. 3, 2006, pp. 345–378; la Cour Mosegaard M., "Stories of Fatherhood. Kinship in the Making", Inhorn M.C., Tjørnhøj-Thomsen T., Goldberg H., la Cour Mosegaard M. (eds.), *Reconceiving the Second Sex. Men, Masculinity and Reproduction*, Berghahn Books, 2009.

770 Van den Broeck U., Vandermeeren M., Vanderschueren D., Enzlin P., Demyttenaere K., D'Hooghe T., "A Systematic Review of Sperm Donors. Demographic Characteristics, Attitudes, Motives and Experiences of the Process of Sperm Donation", *Human Reproduction Update*, Vol. 19, No. 1, 2012, pp. 37–51, p. 37.

771 *Ibid.* p. 51.

772 *Ibid.* pp. 50–51.

773 *Ibid.* p. 50.

Worldwide the demand for sperm donors is much higher than the offer (i.e. availability of men willing to donate).[774] This refers mainly to the shortage of male donors and not to their willingness for multiple donations. It is important to limit the number of created offspring *per* donor for the purposes of avoiding complicated affiliations and increased possibilities of incest. This relates to the parameters of the country concerned, such as the size, density and mobility of the country's population.[775]

There have been many reasons for the scarce donor supply. The most important is associated with the recent trend of revealing the donor's identity.[776] The countries that introduced the non-anonymous system initially faced a decrease of the number of donors willing to donate.[777] Nevertheless, many studies show that this number has increased once again after some time,[778] associating the problem with scarce sperm resources to the recruitment strategies.[779] Studies investigating donor recruitment indicate that the media and advertising are most efficient in attracting donors.[780] By accepting new strategies for their recruitment, the fault for decreasing their number, mainly ascribed to the switch to non-anonymous donation systems, will be minimised or at least neutralised.

The "crisis in the family" as the nuclear heterosexual family for some authors was ascribed to the neglected role of the fathers and thus associated with the "crises of the fatherhood".[781] This, in addition to the best interests of children to know and be raised by both parents, resulted in a reconfiguration of the concept of fatherhood and parental responsibilities that go along with it. The interest of investigating fathers' roles in children's begetting and rearing increased even more once the sperm donations interrupted family units, thus once fatherhood was fragmented into genetic and social fatherhood, and as such investigated in the domain of becoming legal. The donor's participation in family life was accompanied by

---

774 *Ibid.* p. 38.

775 Gong Z., Zheng Li., "Sperm Donation and Sperm-Bank Management", in Schenker J.G. (ed.), *Ethical Dilemmas in Assisted Reproductive Technologies*, Walter de Gruyter, 2011.

776 Van den Broeck U., Vandermeeren M., Vanderschueren D., Enzlin P., Demyttenaere K., D'Hooghe T., "A Systematic Review of Sperm Donors. Demographic Characteristics, Attitudes, Motives and Experiences of the Process of Sperm Donation", *Human Reproduction Update*, Vol. 19, No. 1, 2012, p. 38.

777 *Ibid.* p. 38.

778 See, for instance, in the UK: Shukla U., Deval B., Jansa M.P., Hamoda H., Savvas M., Narvekar N., "Sperm Donor Recruitment, Attitudes and Provider Practices – 5 Years After the Removal of Donor Anonymity", *Human Reproduction*, Vol. 28, No. 3, 2013, pp. 676–682, p. 676; *Human Fertilisation and Embryology Authority. Human Fertilisation and Embryology Act,* HEFA, 2008, Chapter 22.

779 Van den Broeck U., Vandermeeren M., Vanderschueren D., Enzlin P., Demyttenaere K., D'Hooghe T., "A Systematic Review of Sperm Donors. Demographic Characteristics, Attitudes, Motives and Experiences of the Process of Sperm Donation", *Human Reproduction Update*, Vol. 19, No. 1, 2012, p. 38.

780 *Ibid.* p. 45.

781 Collier R., "Men, Heterosexuality and the Changing Family. (Re)constructing Fatherhood in Law and Social Policy", in Jagger G., Wright C. (eds.), *Changing Family Values*, Routledge, 1999, pp. 38–58.

conservation of the truth in obscurity, treating it as "material from an anonymous testis" and them as "non-persons"[782] in order to protect heterosexual nuclear families with infertility problems. This notion was nourished by "reaching a psychological point of view of his non-existence"[783] which included keeping secrecy in the family and hiding the donor's identity in absolute obscurity.[784] The shift to introducing the donor as a person with his own intentions, thoughts and feelings started to develop gradually in the literature in the mid-1970s.[785] Thus, the donor's personality became important for commissioning parents in terms of reflecting his characteristics to their offspring. From a practice of total ignorance of the existence of the donor as provider of gametes, we are currently experiencing the transition tension towards his recognition as a procreator and as person who wants to establish contact with his progeny and possibly family life.[786] Studies in the field of donors' attitude vary in both extremes. While some studies have shown that most donors are not interested,[787] others (although fewer) have revealed that most donors are interested in the outcome of their donation, especially regarding the issue whether the donation was successful.[788]

In the narrations of women wanting to conceive a child by sperm donation there is recognition of the preferred father for their child. Many sperm banks allow access to a catalogue for choosing a donor that will fit the personal preferences for a father and not just sperm. From medical and family histories to physical appearances and recorded tapes of what the possible father may look like, single women conceiving by sperm donation opt for the most father-like figure.[789] The possibility of choosing is also being ethically condemned for its eugenic nature, eventually leading to human enhancement, as well as for the commercialisation of

782 Glezerman M., "Two Hundred and Seventy Cases of Donor Insemination. Management and Results", *Fertility and Sterility*, Vol. 35, 1981, pp. 313–319.

783 *Ibid.*

784 In concordance with early assumptions that donors should be kept a family secret. See more in Finegold W.J., *Artificial Insemination*, Charles C. Thomas, 1964.

785 Daniels K., "The Semen Providers", in Daniels K., Haimes E. (eds.), *Donor Insemination. International Social Science Perspectives*, Cambridge University Press, 1998, pp. 76–104.

786 See more in Grace V.M., Daniels K.R., Gillett W., "The Donor, the Father, and the Imaginary Constitution of the Family. Parents' Construction in the Case of Donor Insemination", *Social Science & Medicine*, Vol. 66, 2008, pp. 301–314. The authors analyse the narratives of 41 couples from New Zealand (a country that introduced non-anonymous sperm donations) finding tensions within their conflicting opinions regarding the donor, from negating to recognising him as a person. The authors suggest a new framework of thinking regarding donations, stressing the procreative role of the donor in the specific reproductive project. This, according to them, will be a landmark of the future families.

787 Pedersen B., Nielsen A., Lauritsen G.J., "Psychosocial Aspects of Donor Insemination", *Acta Obstetricia et Gynecologica Scandinavia*, Vol. 72, No. 9, 1994.

788 Jadva V., Freeman T., Kramer W., Golombok S., "Sperm and Oocyte Donors' Experiences of Anonymous Donations and Subsequent Contact with Their Donor Offspring", *Human Reproduction*, Vol. 26, No. 3, 2011, pp. 638–645.

789 Graham S., "Choosing Single Motherhood? Single Women Negotiating the Nuclear Family Ideal", in Cutas D., Chan S. (eds.), *Families – Beyond the Nuclear Ideal*, Bloomsbury Academic, 2012; Kirkman M., "Saviours and Satyrs. Ambivalence in Narrative Meanings of Sperm Provision", *Culture, Health & Sexuality*, Vol. 6, No. 4, 2004, pp. 319–335.

the process of reproducing.[790] Nevertheless, the wish of the mother to choose the characteristics of the donor cannot be perceived solely in the light of reproducing a perfect baby. On the contrary, it could also be seen from a perspective of a wish to choose a person who looks like a proper father.[791] This illusion of choosing a father also changed the idea of the donations itself. Emphasising the role of procreation of the sperm donations and introducing non-anonymous donations also elevated the responsibility of the donors.

On the other hand, many see the donor and the genetic contribution as irrelevant to the reproductive project since the role of being a father should not be confused with "the doing part" as a constitutive element of the concept of legal fatherhood.[792] Therefore, many women opt for an anonymous donor who should never be personified with the idea of being a father and thus allowed to have a role in "the doing part" as well.[793] For these reasons (among others), ever since non-anonymous donations were introduced in some European countries, many women had Denmark as their destination for reproductive tourism. There, anonymity is still preserved, considered by most donors to be very important for their contribution.[794] The newspapers keep on writing about the possibilities offered by the Danish clinics to women or couples worldwide. Denmark is even considered a mecca for foreign women who want to conceive by ART.[795] Out of the three most frequent categories of persons using the facilities of the Danish sperm banks – lesbian couples, heterosexual couples and single women – the last category is growing by far the fastest. The Danish Department of Health registered in 2008 2,694 and in 2010 4,665 foreign women undergoing medically assisted treatment in their clinics.[796] In addition, national beneficiaries use the sperm donations. Research has suggested that the biological father of approximately 5–8

790 See Sandal J.M., *The Case Against Perfection*, Harvard University Press, 2009; Hanson F., "Donor Insemination. Eugenic and Feminist Implications", *Medical Anthropology Quarterly*, Vol. 15, No. 3, 2001, pp. 287–311; Pennings G., "The Right to Choose your Donor. A Step Towards Commercialization or a Step Towards Empowering the Patient?", *Human Reproduction*, Vol. 15, No. 3, 2000, pp. 508–514.

791 Scheib J., Riordan M., Schaver P., "Choosing between Anonymous and Identity-release Sperm Donors. Recipient and Donor Characteristics", *Reproductive Technologies*, Vol. 10, 2000, pp. 50–58.

792 See, for instance, CJ-FA, RAP 5, 2011, p. 20, Article 17, paragraph 1(a) stipulating that gamete or embryo donors are not considered legal parents.

793 Graham S., "Choosing Single Motherhood? Single Women Negotiating the Nuclear Family Ideal", in Cutas D., Chan S. (eds.), *Families – Beyond the Nuclear Ideal*, Bloomsbury Academic, 2012.

794 Ernst E., Ingerslev H.J., Schou O., Stoltenberg M., "Attitudes Among Sperm Donors in 1992 and 2002. A Danish Questionnaire Survey", *Acta Obstetrica et Gynecologica Scandinavica*, Vol. 86, No. 3, 2007, p. 332.

795 Henley P., "Business Booms for Danish Sperm", *BBC News*, Copenhagen, 19 May 2011, available online: www.bbc.co.uk/news/world-europe-13460455.

796 *Ibid.*

of all Danish children is not the person stated on the official birth record.[797] The choice between anonymity and non-anonymity shows the importance one grants to family relationships and actual parenting as opposed to the genetic link.[798]

In recent years, it has been noted that the interest in the fathers' recognition and contribution in the family is increasing. From the past tendencies of fathers to evade responsibilities, nowadays there is an increasing interest for them to assert rights towards their children.[799] In this light, both the advantages of the child's well-being and the father's personal growth are emphasised as resulting from their greater involvement.[800] From the extensive literature analysed in this part, the impression is that there is also a growing interest in recognising the donor's contribution to the family. By recognising him as a person with identity and opening the possibility of contacting him, his role is shifting from "being a donor" to "being a genetic father". This is not just a terminological shift, but also a meaningful one in changing attitudes towards him. As such, only the circumstances of establishing factual family links with the child will distance him from the role of being not just genetic but also possibly a legal father too, therefore not just *being* the father but also *doing* the father's role. Empirical studies found a diversity of roles given to known sperm donors from (1) male figures with which children have a relationship but not parental status – "a symbolic father", (2) an embodied human referent that the child may identify as his or her progenitor, and (3) a "parent" as a figure with a significant caregiver role.[801]

5.1. "THE NATURE" AND "THE ARTIFICIALITY" OF SPERM DONATION

The nature of sperm donations is multidimensional.[802] In order to understand the attitudes of the donors, as explained in the existing literature, some authors have

---

797 Ernst E., Ingerslev H.J., Schou O., Stoltenberg M., "Attitudes Among Sperm Donors in 1992 and 2002. A Danish Questionnaire Survey", *Acta Obstetrica et Gynecologica Scandinavica*, Vol. 86, No. 3, 2007, p. 327.

798 Pennings G., "The 'Double Track' Policy for Donor Anonymity", *Human Reproduction*, Vol. 12, No. 12, 1997, p. 2839. See also Haimes E., "Gamete Donation and the Social Management of Genetic Origins", in Stacey M. (ed.), *Changing Human Reproduction*, Sage, pp. 119–147, 1992.

799 Sheldon S., "Reproductive Technologies and the Legal Determination of Fatherhood", *Feminist Legal Studies*, Vol. 13, No. 3, 2005(a), p. 355. This author refers to the media's reporting in the UK in the 1980s that mostly discussed support liability and criticism of those "deadbeat dads" who sought to avoid fatherhood. In contrast, nowadays, the media is overwhelmed by the activities of fathers' rights activists protesting their lack of access to their children.

800 See more research on this issue referring to the effects of paternity proceedings to both children and fathers used in Moulton R., "Who's Your Daddy?: The Inherent Unfairness of the Marital Presumption for Children of Unmarried Parents", *Family Court Review*, Vol. 47, No. 4, 2009, pp. 703 and 704.

801 Kelly F., "(Re)forming Parenthood: The Assignment of Legal Parentage Within Planned Lesbian Families", *Ottawa Law Review*, Vol. 40, 2008, p. 188.

802 Van den Broeck U., Vandermeeren M., Vanderschueren D., Enzlin P., Demyttenaere K., D'Hooghe T., "A Systematic Review of Sperm Donors. Demographic Characteristics, Attitudes,

suggested a distinction between: (1) *potential sperm donors* (as candidates of sperm donation, currently in the recruiting process); (2) *actual sperm donors* (which have contacted a centre and are currently donating sperm), with a possibility of being further divided into four sub-categories: (a) anonymous, (b) non-anonymous, (c) those who are, and (d) those who are not paid for their donation; and (3) *non-donors* (people in the general population).[803]

Sperm donations can be associated with their reasons (like where the idea for the donation comes from) and purposes (like where the donation is going or what the expectation of it is). These differentiations are not just linguistic, but also substantially important for conceiving children assisted by third parties. Firstly, they relate to the number of donors willing to donate, thus providing material for the recipients and beneficiaries of ART. Secondly, they relate to solving the legal issues of the future progeny. For instance, the reasons for the donation could be altruistic or lucrative (threat of commodification),[804] while the purposes (as expected ends to be achieved) could encompass simple donation or procreation.

Another group of authors enumerated the donors' most mentioned reasons for donations.[805] The most common are: financial compensation and altruism (including empathy, knowing the infertile couple/single person and willingness to help them), procreation (including having as many children as possible and passing on genes or experiencing immortality),[806] and evaluating one's own fertility by undergoing a physical and biochemical examination. The rearmost reasons are the desire to parent a child, not wanting one's own child, curiosity and the desire to contribute to science. These authors also list two reasons that have not been or have only been restrictively tackled – sexual satisfaction and detached procreation.[807] From these reasons, they categorise arguments *contra* and *pro* sperm donation from donors' perspectives.[808] In the first category, they list the compromises between the normative and moral liberations related to oneself, one's spouse, the child, and society. In the second category, they relate sperm donation

Motives and Experiences of the Process of Sperm Donation", *Human Reproduction Update*, Vol. 19, No. 1, 2012, p. 38.

803 *Ibid.* p. 40.

804 A threat because very often commodification is associated with devaluation of human life as values of humans are measured with money and their lives as means towards other ends (i.e. conceiving a child for somebody else). See, for instance, some of the early critics on commercial surrogacies: Radin M.J., "Market-Inalienability", *Harvard Law Review*, Vol. 100, 1987, pp. 1849–1937. Radin criticises commercial surrogacy by showing concerns that the market concepts endanger personhood (p. 1877).

805 Bossema E.R., Janssens P.M.W., Landwehr F., Treucker R.G.L., Kor Van Duinen, Nap A.W., Geenen R., "A Taxonomy of Possible Reasons For and Against Sperm Donation", *Acta Obstetricia et Gynaecologica Scandinavica*, 2012, p. 680.

806 Plato, *The Laws*, Saunders T.J. (trans), Penguin, 1970, p. 183. Plato associates procreation with the wish to transcend beyond one's life into the next generation's lives, thus becoming immortal.

807 Bossema E.R., Janssens P.M.W., Landwehr F., Treucker R.G.L., Van Duinen K., Nap A.W., Geenen R., "A Taxonomy of Possible Reasons For and Against Sperm Donation", *Acta Obstetricia et Gynaecologica Scandinavica*, 2012, p. 684.

808 *Ibid.* p. 679.

to selfishness (including narcissism and procreation) and psychosocial drives (including altruism, detached procreation and sexual/financial satisfaction).

From the comparative spectrum of conducted studies and as a summary of the large amount of possible reasons for donations, four different types of donors' motivation can be extracted: (1) altruism, (2) financial compensation, (3) procreation or genetic fatherhood, and (4) examination of the donor's own fertility status.[809] Most of the surveys from the comparative literature consider that the motivation of the donors is multifaceted. Furthermore, the motivation also depends on the states' policies regarding anonymity since these changes influence changes in the profile of sperm donors.[810]

The discrepancies between the reasons and the purposes may lead to problems since purposes may change over time or expectations may not be met,[811] for instance if an anonymous sperm donor feels guilty about having a genetic child with no possibility of contact. Alternatively, a non-anonymous donor (or an anonymous donor in the case of breach of confidentiality) may find himself pursued by a child with whom he wants no relationship. Alternatively, he may experience the opposite, his resemblance and attachment with the child he contacted, willing to be more than a name in the child's life, thus conflicting with the rearing parents who oppose frequency in their meetings.[812] It may even be possible for sperm donors to try to find their child and not – as mostly expected – the child to start investigating his/her origin. Many authors stress that donors should refrain from initialising contact with their offspring, considering it not just their moral but also their legal responsibility.[813] Nevertheless, changes of donors' attitudes *prior* to and after donation show a dose of confusion of the donors' perceptions and expectations about their donations. Even though most donors consider that they are fully aware of what they have got themselves into, some evidence also suggests that not all donors are aware of their motivations and the further implications of the donation.[814] This suggests that psychological counselling prior to and after the donations could be useful in meeting the reasons and purposes of the donors in improving their future legal security. Moreover, unpredictable and complex

---

809 Van den Broeck U., Vandermeeren M., Vanderschueren D., Enzlin P., Demyttenaere K., D'Hooghe T., "A Systematic Review of Sperm Donors. Demographic Characteristics, Attitudes, Motives and Experiences of the Process of Sperm Donation", *Human Reproduction Update*, Vol. 19, No. 1, 2012, p. 42. Also see more in-depth studies on p. 45.

810 Hedrih A., Hedrih V., "Attitudes and Motives of Potential Sperm Donors in Serbia", *Vojnosanitetski Pregled*, Vol. 69, No. 1, 2012, pp. 49–57, p. 55.

811 Kaplan J.L., Tong R., *Controlling Our Reproductive Destiny. A Technological and Philosophical Perspective*, MIT Press, 1994, p. 234.

812 Gong Z., Zheng Li., "Sperm Donation and Sperm-Bank Management", in Schenker J.G. (ed.), *Ethical Dilemmas in Assisted Reproductive Technologies*, Walter de Gruyter, 2011.

813 Van den Broeck U., Vandermeeren M., Vanderschueren D., Enzlin P., Demyttenaere K., D'Hooghe T., "A Systematic Review of Sperm Donors. Demographic Characteristics, Attitudes, Motives and Experiences of the Process of Sperm Donation", *Human Reproduction Update*, Vol. 19, No. 1, 2012, p. 49.

814 *Ibid.* p. 50.

consequences may appear bearing in mind that assisted reproduction involves more persons and their families.

The sperm donor's family (wife or children) may also be challenged by the information on the fact that their husband or father has other genetically related children. A number of studies evaluated the factors that influenced the decision-making process of donors behind the donation. Most of the studies reported that a minority of donors involved their partners in the decision-making process.[815] In contrast, a study in Sweden reported that the majority of donors considered that their partners' opinion was important, although their companions were mostly enthusiastic or neutral.[816] In one study approximately 25% of the donors felt that they needed permission from their partner.[817] As a summary of the evaluation of the surveys, partners' involvements in the decision-making process is welcomed, but the donors do not feel that they need consent from their partners for the donation.[818] The probability that they will not tell their present or future partners remains great, leaving more space for inconveniences later on in life if the information comes as a surprise.

The past donation practice in the USA and Europe differed precisely in the reasons for donations. While in the USA, most of the donors were associated with a rationale of "earning some money" for the service (which in turn raised issues over commodification),[819] in Europe it is a common rule that donations have to be altruistic (if reasonable costs for the donation itself, i.e. travel expenses, loss of earnings or medical costs related to the medical procedure and possible side-effects are not calculated).[820] Twenty-five Member States of the Council of Europe

---

815 *Ibid.* p. 46.

816 *Ibid.* p. 46. See also. Lalos A., Daniels K., Gottlieb C., Lalos O., "Recruitment and Motivation of Semen Providers in Sweden", *Human Reproduction*, Vol. 18, No. 1, 2003, pp. 212–216.

817 Van den Broeck U., Vandermeeren M., Vanderschueren D., Enzlin P., Demyttenaere K., D'Hooghe T., "A Systematic Review of Sperm Donors. Demographic Characteristics, Attitudes, Motives and Experiences of the Process of Sperm Donation", *Human Reproduction Update*, Vol. 19, No. 1, 2012, p. 46. See also Thorn P., Katzorke T., Daniels K., "Semen Donors in Germany: A Study Exploring Motivations and Attitudes", *Human Reproduction*, Vol. 23, No. 11, 2008, pp. 2415–2426.

818 Van den Broeck U., Vandermeeren M., Vanderschueren D., Enzlin P., Demyttenaere K., D'Hooghe T., "A Systematic Review of Sperm Donors. Demographic Characteristics, Attitudes, Motives and Experiences of the Process of Sperm Donation", *Human Reproduction Update*, Vol. 19, No. 1, 2012, p. 46.

819 See, for instance, Mahlstedt P.P., Probasco K.A., "Sperm Donors, Their Attitudes Towards Providing Medical and Psychosocial Information for Recipient Couples and Donor Offspring", *Fertility and Sterility*, Vol. 56, No. 4, 1991, pp. 747–753. Some other studies in the USA have demonstrated that even though the financial aspect is the primary motive, it often coincides with more altruistic reasons to donate. See more in Schover L.R., Rothman S.T., Collins R.L., "The Personality and Motivation of Semen Donors. A Comparison with Oocyte Donors", *Human Reproduction*, Vol. 7, No. 4, 1992, pp. 575–579.

820 See Yannakoudakis M., *Report on Voluntary and Unpaid Donation of Tissues and Cells*, 2011/2193 (INI), European Parliament, Committee on the Environment, Public Health and Food Safety, 29 June 2012, Chapter – Non-Remuneration, Consent and Safeguarding Health, paragraph 6. In the Explanatory Statement, the Rapporteur takes the position that altruism is vital when donating tissues and cells, available online: www.europarl.europa.eu/sides/

have binding rules concerning voluntary and unpaid donation of tissues and cells in their national regulations, while only Ireland and Liechtenstein have no legal regulation regarding this field.[821]

Without material compensation for the donation, it was unlikely to maintain the willingness of donors and it was expected that the number of donations would decrease. Proof of the opposite is the largest sperm bank in Europe – located in Denmark.[822] This has also been confirmed in a recent study that discovered that the number of donors in the UK has more than doubled following the change in legislation regarding the openness of the system of donations.[823]

Studies researching donors' motivation to donate have shown that an altruistic desire to assist infertile couples without financial contribution (apart from the reimbursement of expenses) is the main driving force behind donations.[824] Factors that facilitate their decision to donate are the personal

---

getDoc.do?type=REPORT&reference=A7-2012-0223&language=EN; the Second Report from the Commission to the European Parliament, the Council, the European Economic and Social Committee and the Committee of the Regions on Voluntary and Unpaid Donation of Tissues and Cells (COM(2011)0352), 17.06.2011, p. 3. See also Directive 2010/53/EU of the European Parliament and of the Council on Standards of Quality and Safety of Human Organs Intended for Transplantation of 7 July 2010 (OJ L 207, 06.08.2010, p. 14); Directive 2004/23/EC of the European Parliament and of the Council on Setting Standards of Quality and Safety for the Donation, Procurement, Testing, Processing, Preservation, Storage and Distribution of Human Tissues and Cells of 31 March 2004 (OJ L 102, 07.04.2004, p. 48); *World Health Organization's Guiding Principles on Human Cell, Tissue and Organ Transplantation*, Guiding Principle 5 (p. 5), available online: www.who.int/transplantation/Guiding_Principles Transplantation_WHA63.22en.pdf (even though the latter explicitly excludes their application for transplantation of gametes, ovarian or testicular tissue or embryos for reproductive purposes).

821 Second Report from the Commission to the European Parliament, the Council, the European Economic and Social Committee and the Committee of the Regions on Voluntary and Unpaid Donation of Tissues and Cells (COM(2011)0352), 2011, p. 3. and Figure III p. 5.

822 The Danish sperm bank Cryos that started working in 1987 is the world's largest today. In these years, the bank has registered more than 30,000 births and more than 2,000 babies a year, exporting sperm to over 70 countries. Together with some other similar companies (like the European Sperm Bank), Denmark has become the sperm capital of the world. Cryos alone possesses 170 litres of sperm (equal to around 130,000 sperm samples) and a waiting list of 600 donors. The founder of Cryos notes that the reasons for donations are mostly not financial (since it only costs around £54, and once the price increased, it was not followed by an increased number of donors) but a mix of altruism and a desire to earn "pocket money" since many of the donors are students. The recipients on the other hand pay for the sperm samples from around £30 to £350 per vial depending on whether the donor is anonymous (three-quarters of the donors are anonymous) or whether they have provided an extended profile (from basic details of height and weight to baby photographs, an extended personality profile and even recorded messages where they explain why they have chosen to donate). See more in Sarfraz M., "Come Inside: The World's Biggest Sperm Bank", *The Guardian*, 02.11.2012, available online: www.theguardian.com/society/2012/nov/02/worlds-biggest-sperm-bank-denmark.

823 Shukla U., Deval B., Jansa M.P., Hamoda H., Savvas M., Narvekar N., "Sperm Donor Recruitment, Attitudes and Provider Practices – 5 Years After the Removal of Donor Anonymity", *Human Reproduction*, Vol. 28, No. 3., 2013, pp. 676–682, p. 680.

824 See, for instance, Riggs D.W., Russell L., "Characteristics of Men Willing to Act as Sperm Donors in the Context of Identity-Release Legislation", *Human Reproduction*, Vol. 26, No. 1, 2010, pp. 266–272. See also Hedrih A., Hedrih V., "Attitudes and Motives of Potential Sperm Donors in Serbia", *Vojnosanitetski Pregled*, Vol. 69, No. 1, 2012, pp. 49–57.

relationships with the persons willing to procreate and the support from the partner.[825] Recommendations have been made for campaigns for promotion of the donations and public awareness of the consequences of the donations.

Negative estimations of the possibility of decreasing numbers of future donors were also made when non-anonymous donations appeared on the scene. Then, the fear of losing donors became not just fiction but reality as shown by the statistics and numbers.[826] Thus, the purposes of the donations also started to matter – solely giving away genetic material, with expectations of not having any information about or contact with the future progeny (depersonalisation);[827] or the opposite of it – awareness of the reproductive outcome, and therefore expectations of revealing their identity, followed by possible contact with their progeny in the future (identification and possible parenthood).[828] Some authors have suggested that it is of utmost importance to know how to read the difference between father, parent and a known donor in the pre-conception period and afterwards.[829] Others argue that parenthood is central to human experience and that the feelings accompanying it are rather unpredictable and uncontrollable,

---

825 Sharon R.C., "The Invisible Man. Artificial Insemination by Donor and the Legislation on Donor Anonymity: A Review", *Journal of Family Planning and Reproductive Health Care*, Vol. 30, No 4, 2004, p. 273. See also Daniels K.R., "Semen Donors in New Zealand: Their Characteristics and Attitudes", *Clinical Reproduction and Fertility*, Vol. 5, No. 4, 1987, pp. 177–190.

826 Frith L., "Gamete Donation and Anonymity. The Ethical and Legal Debate", *Human Reproduction*, Vol. 16, No. 5, 2001, p. 823. In Sweden both the number of donors and recipients decreased after introducing non-anonymous systems in 1984, although the decline was reversed later on (see Daniels K., Lalos O., "The Swedish Insemination Act and the Availability of Donors", *Human Reproduction*, Vol. 10, No. 7, 1995, pp. 1871–1874). In the Netherlands, this trend was repeated (Weber W., "Dutch Sperm Donors will Remain Anonymous for Another Two Years", *The Lancet*, Vol. 355, No. 9211, p. 1249). During 15 years of debate on the abolition of donor anonymity the number of donors decreased by 70%, and the number of semen banks by 50% (Janssens P.M.W., Simons A.H.M., Van Kooij R.J., Blokzijl E., Dunselman A.A.J., "A New Dutch Law Regulating Provision of Identifying Information of Donors to Offspring: Background, Content and Impact", *Human Reproduction*, Vol. 21, No. 4, 2006, p. 852). In Western Australia, the number of donors decreased 90% after the introduction of an open system of donations (*Select Committee on the Human Reproductive Technology Act Report*, Parliament of Western Australia, 1999). Some other studies have shown that the number of donors will also decrease if anonymity is lifted (Cook R., Golombok S., Bish A. *et al.*, "Disclosure of Donor Insemination Parental Attitudes", *American Journal of Orthopsychiatry*, Vol. 65, No. 4, pp. 549–559, 1995). Donors prefer to have an option to choose about the amount of information they are willing to reveal to their future progeny (Daniels K., Lewis G., Carson R., "Information Sharing in Semen Donation. The Views of Donors", *Social Science and Medicine*, Vol. 44, No. 5, 1995, pp. 673–680).

827 As it has been called by Marjorie Maguire Schultz. Schultz M.M., "Reproductive Technology and Intent-Based Parenthood. An Opportunity for Gender Neutrality", *Wisconsin Law Review*, Vol. 297, 1990, p. 333.

828 As, for instance, the Australian Court reasoned in the case *Re Patrick*. The judge found the mother's de-personalising attitude towards the known sperm donor irrational, unreasonable and fanciful. See more in Dempsey D., "Donor, Father or Parent? Conceiving Paternity in the Australian Family Court", *International Journal of Law, Policy and Family*, No. 18, 2004, p. 91.

829 Dempsey D., "Donor, Father or Parent? Conceiving Paternity in the Australian Family Court", *International Journal of Law, Policy and Family*, No. 18, 2004, pp. 93 and 94.

that any binding commitments should not be enforced.[830] This has proven to be true especially in surrogacy cases. The first and therefore cornerstone case on surrogacy was that before the New Jersey Supreme Court *In re Baby M*.[831] The case emphasised precisely the impossibility of anticipating human behaviour when it comes to making decisions to reproduce for others, since the surrogate mother withheld her contracted obligation to give the child to the commissioning parents after giving birth. Accordingly, some authors reflected upon it that as emotions cannot be conserved in rational boxes of contracts, thus they cannot be foreseen in binding frameworks.[832]

One may condemn the analogy between surrogacy and sperm donation contracts. Nevertheless, in both cases women and men participate through their genetic and biological or just biological/genetic contribution respectively. While in the first case, women usually have the possibility of withdrawing their decisions a short while after childbirth,[833] in the second case donors do not have that option.[834] Schultz describes this as an "underlying nature of the decision that confronts a prospective father as compared to a prospective mother".[835] Therefore, it emphasises the social compromise that the "physical and emotional connections

830 See Schultz M.M., "Reproductive Technology and Intent-Based Parenthood. An Opportunity for Gender Neutrality", *Wisconsin Law Review*, Vol. 297, 1990, p. 348. See also Suh. M.M., "Surrogate Motherhood. An Argument for Denial of Specific Performance", *Columbia Journal of Law and Social Problems*, Vol. 22, 1989, pp. 357–396.

831 *In re Baby M*, 537 A.2d 1227, 109 *N.J.* 396 (02.03.1988).

832 See, for instance, Schultz M.M., "Reproductive Technology and Intent-Based Parenthood. An Opportunity for Gender Neutrality", *Wisconsin Law Review*, Vol. 297, 1990, p. 350 as referring to the concept of bounded rationality, even though in a different field a vendor of nuclear reactors gave an excuse for the non-performance of contracting obligations for reasons of commercial impracticability; see Joskow P.L., "Commercial Impossibility, the Uranium Market and the Westinghouse Case", *Journal of Legal Studies*, Vol. 6, No. 1, 1977, pp. 119–176.

833 This is differently regulated in different countries that regulate surrogacies. One modus of regulation is to treat women which give birth as mothers, and only afterwards to transfer the motherhood through court orders to the intended mothers. This is the case in the UK, making it similar to the procedure for giving the child up for adoption, which also allows a possibility for the surrogate mother to change her intention and not surrender the child for adoption. The other modus of regulation is through binding agreements authorised by the court before the transfer of a fertilised ova into the body of another woman (article 1458 of the Greek Civil Code), thus granting the commissioning parents the legal parenthood right after the birth of the child (as an exception to the rule *mater semper certa est*) in Greece (article 1464 of the Greek Civil Code). A similar solution is also provided in the Family Code of Ukraine. See more in Natzis N.A., "The Regulation of Surrogate Motherhood in Greece", *Social Science and Research Network*, 2010, pp. 3 and 6, available online: http://papers.ssrn.com/sol3/papers.cfm?abstract_id=1689774; and Lowe N., *A Study into the Rights and Legal Status of Children being Brought Up in Various Forms of Marital or Non-Marital Partnerships and Cohabitation*, Report for the Attention of the Committee of Experts on Family Law, September, 2009, p. 10.

834 In most of the international documents regarding the establishment of the legal paternity in cases of sperm donor-assisted conceptions, it is explicitly emphasised that donors are not to be considered parents. See, for instance, in the Draft Report CJ-FA, 2011, RAP 5, p. 20, article 17, paragraph 1(a). This excludes their possibility to withdraw their decision to be only donors in the child's life after the birth of the child.

835 Schultz M.M., "Reproductive Technology and Intent-Based Parenthood. An Opportunity for Gender Neutrality", *Wisconsin Law Review*, Vol. 297, 1990, p. 351.

between a prospective child and a mother up to the time of birth are different from those of a father in ways that make differentiation in the abidingness of their decisions appropriate".[836] Therefore, Schultz argues that there is a natural gender difference in the underlying essence of the decisions that confront a prospective father as compared to a prospective mother related to the physical and emotional connections between a prospective child up to the time of birth, thus related to the gestation period in the woman's body.[837] Since men and women have biologically different parts to play in the process of reproduction, both the burdens and benefits of it are not proportional.[838] The applicant in the case of *M.B. v. the United Kingdom*[839] claimed gender discrimination on the grounds that natural mothers do not have to seek legal recognition and registration of their parenthood because they gain it automatically. In contrast, natural fathers must obtain a parental responsibility agreement with the mother or a parental responsibility order from a court if the child is born out of wedlock. The Commission rejected this reasoning, however, arguing that the difference in treatment is objective and reasonable having regard to the scope of possible circumstances in which conception can possibly take place (from casual, unintentional or violent to conception in a stable relationship). Thus, the requirement that the natural father undertakes additional action to establish his fatherhood is for purposes of appreciating the flexibility in response to the differing situations, having regard to the paramount principle of the child's welfare.

This seems to emphasise the stereotypes over the gender roles, claiming that "women are appropriately dominant in the realm of children and that men will remain secondary because of their biological roles in procreation".[840] Consequently, it seems like the policies that focus more on roles ascribed beforehand tend to limit equality and freedom rather than enhance them. Equality will be achieved once the perception of men in the reproductive process changes in the direction of mutual sharing of the responsibilities and values in the domain in which women have predominated for a long period.[841] Thus, determining parenthood exclusively based on biology for women, and based on biology augmented and constrained by social and legal convention for men, strengthens the gender biological differences.[842] Some other authors suggest closer equalisation between the mother's and father's roles, relating the source of parental responsibilities for both genders to the birth of the child.[843] In these terms, sperm donations come closer to surrogacies – just as the woman who gives birth to the child (the

836 *Ibid.* p. 352.
837 *Ibid.* p. 352.
838 *Ibid.* p. 384.
839 See footnote 227.
840 *Ibid.* p. 394.
841 *Ibid.* p. 395.
842 *Ibid.* p. 398.
843 See more in Weinberg R., "The Moral Complexity of Sperm Donation", *Bioethics*, Vol. 22, No. 3, 2008, pp. 166–178.

surrogate mother) holds parental responsibility for the child from the moment of birth, the same should apply to the sperm donor. The enablement of further transfer of the same parental responsibilities towards the commissioning parents should be dependent upon their explicit withdrawal after the birth of the child. According to this author, parental responsibility starts from the birth of the child for donors as well as for accidental fathers, thus also equalising "artificial" and "natural" procreations.[844]

The reproductive technologies divide sexuality and reproduction. For some authors sex is an activity of intrinsic value apart from its procreative potential.[845] To that end, sex should be freed from the risk of reproduction, while procreation should be planned. Ordinary coital reproduction has lost the exclusivity for conceiving children, replaced by a rational and planned reproductive project that takes place in a laboratory. Yet this does not make children conceived by "artificial" insemination less natural than the others, nor change the blood affiliation between them and their ascendants and descendants, as well as their siblings. Consequently, individual intentions (purpose and choice) become grounds for reproducing, establishing parenthood and founding families. Thus, based on the willingness to undertake parental responsibilities, the interest of the child is also protected on conventional grounds.[846] These negotiated grounds may also include introduction of the sperm donor and his genetic history in the child's life in order to substitute what the artificial project could not imitate – natural affiliation.

Legal parenthood and not natural parenthood are substantial and long-term activities. The role of care for the upbringing of the child (which is substantial for the child's development) attributes to the legal and not the genetic parent.[847] As made feasible by the use of ART, it includes rationally thoughtful and wanted experience in adults' lives.

Yet, in order to make parenthood an ongoing relationship, it should be given a chance. There is a difference in introducing the father's presence in the child's life when naturally or artificially conceived. In the first case, some authors have questioned if the mother's negative attitude towards the father's presence in the child's life should be a determent for his exclusion.[848] The case of *Lehr v. Robertson*

844 *Ibid.* p. 166.

845 Luker K., "Abortion and the Politics of Motherhood", *University of California Press*, 1984, pp. 175–186.

846 "Conventional grounds" is used in a sense of conforming or adhering to accepted standards in contracts established by the consent of the parties.

847 See also Weinberg R., "The Moral Complexity of Sperm Donation", *Bioethics*, Vol. 22, No. 3, 2008, p. 167. This author argues that parental responsibility (as a content of legal parenthood) most fundamentally entails the responsibility to raise and nurture a child.

848 Shanley M.L., "Father's Rights, Mother's Wrongs? Reflections on Unwed Fathers' Rights, Patriarchy, and Sex Equality", in Callahan J.C., *Reproduction, Ethics and the Law. Feminist Perspectives*, Indiana University Press, 1995, p. 225.

in the USA[849] urged for better recognition of the role of the genetic father (who wanted to block the adoption of his child by his stepfather) *vis-à-vis* the genetic mother (who wanted to pursue the adoption). Even though the majority held that Lehr did not make sufficient contact to establish a parental right, declaring that a genetic father's rights are tangible and subject to affirmative responsibilities towards the offspring, the Supreme Court recognised that the state did not apply the equal protection clause regarding the legal parental rights of both parents.[850] Thus, mothers' unwillingness to cooperate may cause fathers to refrain from the possibility of making contact with their progeny that should qualify them to establish parental rights. The ECtHR has dealt with similar cases too.[851] For some authors, all fathers should be given a chance to express their interest in developing a parent–child relationship.[852] Some others even go further arguing that all unwed fathers should have a right to be notified by the state of the existence of their offspring and be heard before any adoption can proceed, making the mother obliged to identify the biological father.[853] This follows the rationale of the different biological roles that men and women take in human reproduction. Therefore the law should recognise the necessity that both the mother and the father must be permitted to demonstrate commitment to their child in different

849 *Lehr v. Robertson*, 463 U.S. 248, 1983. See also the following cases in the USA: *Stanley v. Illinois*, 405 U.S., 645, 1972, *Quilloin v. Walcott*, 434 U.S. 246, 1978, *Caban v. Mohammed*, 442 U.S. 380, 1979; *Michael v. Gerald D.*, 491 U.S. 110, 1989.

850 *Lehr v. Robertson*, 463 U.S. 248, 1983, at 268.

851 See, for instance, the case of *Schneider v. Germany*, European Court of Human Rights, No. 17080/07, judgment of 15.09.2011 in which there was not a factual family life of the child with the genetic father due to the marital presumption and shared life of the child with the husband of the mother; *Anayo v. Germany*, European Court of Human Rights, No.20578/07, judgment of 21.12.2010 in which the genetic father from an extra-marital relationship was refused any contact with his twins on grounds that he did not hold any parental responsibilities, while also not having any factual social and family life; *Ahrens v. Germany*, European Court of Human Rights, No. 450071/09, judgment of 22.03.2012 in which Mr Ahrens assumed that he was the genetic father of a child whose mother had a common household relationship with another man who recognised the child as his. The German Court of Appeal constituted that the fact of already established family life between the child and the legal father was stronger than merely the genetic connection; *Kautzor v. Germany*, European Court of Human Rights, No. 23338/09, judgment of 22.03.2012 in which Mr Kautzor was precluded from civil proceedings for rebutting legal paternity on grounds of already established social, legal and family life with the legal father; *Yousef v. the Netherlands*, European Court of Human Rights, No. 33711/96, judgment of 05.11.2002 in which the biological father of a child born out of wedlock was not allowed to recognise the child as his later on in life because it could distance the child from the family with whom it was already living. The Committee of Experts on Family Law also recognised the need to balance between "the biological truth" reflecting primarily biological and genetic parentage, and "the social parenthood", reflecting the fact with whom the child is living and who is taking care of him or her (referring to the case of *Nylund v. Finland*, European Court of Human Rights, No. 27110/95, judgment of 29.06.1999). See more in the White Paper, 2006, p. 7.

852 Shanley M.L., "Father's Rights, Mother's Wrongs? Reflections on Unwed Fathers' Rights, Patriarchy, and Sex Equality", in Callahan J.C., *Reproduction, Ethics and the Law. Feminist Perspectives*, Indiana University Press, 1995, p. 226.

853 *Ibid*, p. 226. See also Hamilton J.R., "The Unwed Father and the Right to Know of his Child's Existence", *Kentucky Law Journal*, Vol. 76, pp. 949–1009, 1988.

ways.[854] From these premises is derived the responsibility to tell the man that he has a child. Resolving parental responsibilities can only come afterwards. For some authors (as mentioned earlier), these rules should also apply to the sperm donor since he should be a holder of parental responsibilities from the moment of birth of the child, leaving the further transfer for afterwards.[855]

5.2. THE RIGHTS AND CORRELATIVE OBLIGATIONS OF SPERM DONORS DONATING TO COUPLES AND SINGLE WOMEN

An important problem that was not properly addressed when initially donor inseminations were accepted was the one related to the ambiguity of the rules governing the rights and duties of donors, recipients and children. This in turn led to the possibility of medical malpractice, medical products liability, and new interpretations of rights and responsibilities of participants and recipients of sperm donations.[856] The need to reduce uncertainty and safeguard decisions regarding the reciprocal expectations and reliance is especially important.[857]

Some authors have differentiated between sperm donations for couples and single women arguing that the identity and parental rights of donors are not the same in both cases.[858] While in the first one, they will disappear or be less important (due to the donor's substitution by the partner of the role of father), in the latter they may be treated as of crucial importance in the child's life.[859]

The world's most famous sperm bank Cryos has noticed recently that there is an increasing trend of new types of clients – lesbian couples and single women.[860] This, supported by other recent studies, suggests that next to heterosexual couples suffering from infertility, lesbian couples and single women are also primary

---

854 Shanley M.L., "Father's Rights, Mother's Wrongs? Reflections on Unwed Fathers' Rights, Patriarchy, and Sex Equality", in Callahan J.C., *Reproduction, Ethics and the Law. Feminist Perspectives*, Indiana University Press, 1995, p. 236.

855 Weinberg R., "The Moral Complexity of Sperm Donation", *Bioethics*, Vol. 22, No. 3, 2008, p. 166.

856 Kaplan J.L., Tong R., *Controlling Our Reproductive Destiny. A Technological and Philosophical Perspective*, MIT Press, 1994, p. 237.

857 Schultz M.M., "Reproductive Technology and Intent-Based Parenthood. An Opportunity for Gender Neutrality", *Wisconsin Law Review*, Vol. 297, 1990, p. 324.

858 Kaplan J.L., Tong R., *Controlling Our Reproductive Destiny. A Technological and Philosophical Perspective*, MIT Press, 1994, p. 239 referring to the feminist Gena Corea.

859 The author supports this claim by giving an example of two "exceptional" cases before the Courts in the USA (New Jersey in 1977 and California Supreme Court in 1980) related to sperm donations to friends in which the genetic fathers were granted visitation rights on grounds that "every child should have a father in his everyday life". See *ibid.* p. 239.

860 Sarfraz M., "Come Inside: The World's Biggest Sperm Bank", *The Guardian*, 02.11.2012, available online: www.theguardian.com/society/2012/nov/02/worlds-biggest-sperm-bank-denmark.

recipients of donor sperm nowadays.[861] Some studies have demonstrated that donors are more willing to donate to single women than to lesbian couples (the proportion of actual donors that would donate for lesbian couples and for single women varied from 50 to 68% and from 40 to 64% respectively).[862]

In a situation of absence of clear regulation of sperm donations (which was the case when sperm donations were introduced), the donor may be assigned the same rights and responsibilities as those of a father[863] just by applying the same rules for establishing fatherhood as to the other children. It remains that the father is a legal fiction even more in contemporary than in the ancient families, where the roles are negotiated on grounds of intentions and not biology. If genes were determinant in establishing legal affiliations, treating children born naturally and with the assistance of sperm donors would have been considered not just differently but also discriminatory.

5.2.1. ANONYMOUS SPERM DONOR

The anonymity of donors was for a long period after introducing sperm donations the only possible scenario for assisting the process of reproduction. In the past, very much importance was attached to secrecy in sperm donation projects. For instance, some authors claim that some fertility clinics would mix the sperm of more than one donor before inseminating a woman, so that no one could know who the genetic father of the child was.[864] This practice was known as artificial insemination by combination, referring to the combination of a donor's sperm and the husband's sperm.[865] A commonly used justification to maintain the anonymity of the donors was to protect those involved from perceived societal disapproval and stigma.[866] The recent initiative in the UK to mix genetic material from three parents (the mother's and from another woman) in order to avoid the

---

861 Van den Broeck U., Vandermeeren M., Vanderschueren D., Enzlin P., Demyttenaere K., D'Hooghe T., "A Systematic Review of Sperm Donors. Demographic Characteristics, Attitudes, Motives and Experiences of the Process of Sperm Donation", *Human Reproduction Update*, Vol. 19, No. 1, 2012, p. 38.

862 *Ibid*, p. 47, see also Ernst E., Ingerslev H.J., Schou O., Stoltenberg M., "Attitudes Among Sperm Donors in 1992 and 2002. A Danish Questionnaire Survey", *Acta Obstetrica et Gynecologica Scandinavica*, Vol. 86, No. 3, 2007.

863 *Ibid*. p. 240.

864 See in Johnston J., "Mum's the Word: Donor Anonymity in Assisted Reproduction", *Health Law Review*, Vol. 11, No. 1, 2002, p. 51.

865 Clapshaw D., "Legal Aspects of Artificial Human Reproduction: Can the Law Afford to Play Ostrich?", *Auckland University Law Review*, Vol. 4, No. 3, 1982, p. 254.

866 Johnston J., "Mum's the Word: Donor Anonymity in Assisted Reproduction", *Health Law Review*, Vol. 11, No. 1, 2002, p. 51. See also Landau R., "The Management of Genetic Origins: Secrecy and Openness in Donor Assisted Conception in Israel and Elsewhere", *Human Reproduction*, Vol. 13, 1988, p. 3272.

risk of the mother passing on inherited defects may also cause complex genetic identification.[867]

In the late 80s and early 90s most of the studies revealed the negative attitudes of donors towards the removal of anonymity.[868] Even recent studies show that maintaining anonymity is still important. A survey regarding donors' attitude towards the anonymity of donation in Denmark demonstrated that donors were becoming more resistant to the idea of disclosure of their identity that may lead to contact with their genetic offspring as the years go by.[869]

Those who support the anonymity of donors still consider that it is beneficial for all concerned parties – the donor (and his present or future private and family life), the family to whom the sperm is donated or single women (thus, hiding the infertility problem or excluding the possibility of third party interference),[870] and the child (considering that it suffers harm with the information of the modus of conception).[871]

From a donor's perspective, preserving anonymity may be an important element to which they consented at the beginning, and to which they prefer and expect the others to remain loyal. Informed consent as a principle of bioethics encompasses full information prior to any medical treatment for persons making

---

867 See in Collins N., "Three Parent Babies 'Incompatible' with Human Dignity", *The Telegraph*, 04.10.2013, available online: www.telegraph.co.uk/science/science-news/10356387/Three-parent-babies-incompatible-with-human-dignity.html.

868 Daniels K.R., "Semen Donors: Their Motivation and Attitudes to their Offspring", *Journal of Reproductive and Infant Psychology*, Vol. 7, No. 2, 2007, pp. 121–127; Schover L.R., Rothman S.T., Collins R.L., "The Personality and Motivation of Semen Donors. A Comparison with Oocyte Donors", *Human Reproduction*, Vol. 7, No. 4, 1992, pp. 575–579; Cook R., Golombok S., "A Survey of Semen Donation: Phase II – The View of the Donors", *Human Reproduction*, Vol. 10, No. 4, 1995, pp. 951–959.

869 Ernst E., Ingerslev H.J., Schou O., Stoltenberg M., "Attitudes Among Sperm Donors in 1992 and 2002. A Danish Questionnaire Survey", *Acta Obstetrica et Gynecologica Scandinavica*, Vol. 86, No. 3, 2007, pp. 327–333.

870 Thus, mimicking natural family and giving the impression that the child is genetically related to both parents (in a couple), so to avoid severe social and psychological problems. See Frith L., "Gamete Donation and Anonymity. The Ethical and Legal Debate", *Human Reproduction*, Vol. 16, No. 5, 2001, p. 822.

871 See, for instance,in the research study of Golombok S., "New Families, Old Values. Considerations Regarding the Welfare of the Child", *Human Reproduction*, Vol. 13, No. 9, 1998, pp. 2342–2347. Another study in the UK found that the majority (80%) of the mothers of children conceived by sperm donation did not want to reveal the secrecy under justification of protecting their children from societal stigma and preserving the children's bond with the infertile birth father, see Cook R., Golombok S., Bish A. *et al.*, "Disclosure of Donor Insemination; Parental Attitudes", *American Journal of Orthopsychiatry*, Vol. 65, 1995, pp. 552 and 553. Similar attitudes of couples towards sperm donors were reported in Sweden (see Gottlieb C., Lalos O., Lindblad F., "Disclosure of Donor Insemination to the Child, The Impact of Swedish Legislation on Couples' Attitudes", *Human Reproduction*, Vol. 15, 2000, pp. 2052–2056) and in the Netherlands (see Brewaeys A., Golombok S., Naaktgeboren N., "Donor Insemination: Dutch Parents' Opinions About Confidentiality and Donor Anonymity and the Emotional Adjustment of their Children", *Human Reproduction*, Vol. 12, No. 7, 1997, pp. 1591–1597).

decisions to participate.[872] The doctrine of informed consent has the purpose of obliging the physician to provide his or her patient with sufficient information that will enable an informed judgment related to giving or withholding consent to a medical procedure.[873] Thus, the information given to the patient also should include the nature and probability of the risks involved, the benefits to be reasonably expected, as well as the inability of the physician to predict the results.[874] Even though the concept of informed consent refers mostly to the relationship between the physician and the patient, in the context of sperm donations (which, however, are not considered medical treatments), consent to being a donor also encompasses responsibilities towards the recipients and the resulting children. These can differ depending on the circumstances under which the sperm is given – anonymity, thus restraining from any future information disclosure or contact with the progeny, or non-anonymity, thus with responsibility to provide information and/or establish contact with the child. As such, the given consent (for a particular donation arrangement) is related to legal liability for those who do not respect the rights and correlative responsibilities they have bonded themselves into when they consented. Therefore it serves largely also to achieve social and legal security and maintain order. For these reasons, the countries that shifted from anonymous to non-anonymous systems allowed a transition period not to influence already made donations. For instance, in the Netherlands and in the UK it is explicitly stipulated that the new regulation will not apply to donations made prior to its enactment.[875] This is meant to protect donors who donated under the previous circumstances.

Schultz argued that contracts in the field of reproduction and parental projects are prone to changed circumstances that can take place in the latter phase and not prior to the birth of the child – giving the child up for adoption, voluntary

---

872 See more in Beauchamp T.L., Childress F.J., *Principles of Biomedical Ethics* (5th edition), Oxford University Press, 2001, Part II, Respect for Autonomy, p. 57.

873 Stoddard J.C., Fox J., "Egg Donation Consent Forms", in Seibel M.M., Crockin S.L. (eds.), *Family Building through Egg and Sperm Donation. Medical, Legal, and Ethical Issues*, Jones and Bartlett Publishers, 1996, p. 158.

874 *Ibid.*

875 In the Netherlands, for instance, it is clearly stated that donors who donated gametes before the new law in 2004 have the right to remain anonymous even in cases where their gametes (stored in cryobanks) are used after the enactment of the new law. In order not to confuse the donors' and recipients' expectations, the Dutch Society of Semen Banks and Doner Insemination advises its members to restrain from use of semen from anonymous donors donated prior to 2004. See more in Janssens P.M.W., Simons A.H.M., Van Kooij R.J., Blokzijl E., Dunselman A.A.J., "A New Dutch Law Regulating Provision of Identifying Information of Donors to Offspring: Background, Content and Impact", *Human Reproduction*, Vol. 21, No. 4, 2006, p. 854. In the UK as from the changes in the law introducing identifiable donors from 1 April 2005, all new donors have been required to provide identifying information. Those who donated previously may re-register to be identifiable and thus be entered in the HEFA register. Nevertheless, there is no formal obligation or encouragement for them to change their status. See more in Blyth E., Frith L., Jones C., Speirs M.J., "The Role of Birth Certificates in Relation to Access to Biographical and Genetic History in Donor Conception", *International Journal of Children's Rights*, Vol. 17, 2009, pp. 207–233, p. 210.

termination of parental rights or acknowledgement of paternity.[876] This opens the door to unpredictable reactions of the progenitors towards their progeny. Even though it has been noted more often in the cases of surrogate mothers, it has also been questioned in the context of sperm donor inseminations.[877] A number of studies have investigated the changing attitudes before and after donation.[878] Some have reported up to 37% of donors that changed their attitude towards anonymity.[879] Out of these, more than half felt unsure about anonymity before, while one of four were prepared to be more open about themselves after the donation.[880] Other studies have reported that donors' attitudes towards revealing non-identifying information is much higher than towards revealing identifying information.[881] Nevertheless, changing attitudes leave the parties in an ambiguous situation that endangers their legal certainty. Schultz questions whether contracts are an appropriate framework for regulating relationships between the contracting parties in procreative arrangements, bearing in mind that emotions may prevail over reason.[882] On the other hand, this author argues that determining legal parenthood on grounds of agreements that appreciate personal intentions will eventually lead to gender-neutral avenues to parenthood that will focus primarily on responsible parenthood (irrespective of the gender) and therefore protect the best interests of the children.[883] Other authors do not mind appreciation of personal intentions if they are expressed at a later stage – after (and not prior to) the birth of the child attributing automatically parental responsibilities even

876 Schultz M.M., "Reproductive Technology and Intent-Based Parenthood. An Opportunity for Gender Neutrality", *Wisconsin Law Review*, Vol. 297, 1990, p. 351.

877 Some studies show that donors may also have different feelings about their donations after a certain period. See Ethics Committee Report, "Interests, Obligations and Rights of the Donor in Gamete Donation", *Fertility and Sterility*, Vol. 91, No. 1, 2009, p. 24. See also Daniels K., Blyth E., Crawshaw M., Curson R., "Short Communication. Previous Semen Donors and their Views Regarding the Sharing of Information with the Offspring", *Human Reproduction*, Vol. 20, No. 6 2005, pp. 1670–1675.

878 Van den Broeck U., Vandermeeren M., Vanderschueren D., Enzlin P., Demyttenaere K., D'Hooghe T., "A Systematic Review of Sperm Donors. Demographic Characteristics, Attitudes, Motives and Experiences of the Process of Sperm Donation", *Human Reproduction Update*, Vol. 19, No. 1, 2012, p. 46. See also Daniels K., Blyth E., Crawshow M., Curson R., "Short Communication: Previous Semen Donors and Their Views Regarding the Sharing of Information with Offspring", *Human Reproduction*, Vol. 23, No. 6, 2005, pp. 1670–1675; Frith L., Blyth E., Farrand A., "UK Gamete Donors' Reflection on the Removal of Anonymity Implications for Recruitment", *Human Reproduction*, Vol. 22, No. 6, 2007, pp. 1675–1680.

879 Daniels K., Blyth E., Crawshow M., Curson R., "Short Communication: Previous Semen Donors and Their Views Regarding the Sharing of Information with Offspring", *Human Reproduction*, Vol. 23, No. 6, 2005, pp. 1670–1675.

880 *Ibid.*

881 See more in Van den Broeck U., Vandermeeren M., Vanderschueren D., Enzlin P., Demyttenaere K., D'Hooghe T., "A Systematic Review of Sperm Donors. Demographic Characteristics, Attitudes, Motives and Experiences of the Process of Sperm Donation", *Human Reproduction Update*, Vol. 19, No. 1, 2012, p. 46.

882 Schultz M.M., "Reproductive Technology and Intent-Based Parenthood. An Opportunity for Gender Neutrality", *Wisconsin Law Review*, Vol. 297, 1990, p. 355.

883 *Ibid*, p. 398.

to sperm donors.[884] According Weinberg, parental responsibilities start at the moment we accept to be the beginning of human personhood for the child, since then the child needs parental care and protection.[885] Consequently, if we accept that personhood occurs at conception, at the time of activation of the brain and therefore the capacity to reason, at viability or at the time of birth, the parental responsibilities will then respectively occur.[886] They can only cease if there is explicit (or implicit – if the child is abandoned) intention. Only then can they be transferred to other parents or custodial institutions that will replace them. Louw also follows the same line of reasoning, arguing that the child only becomes a legal subject at birth, thus from that moment on is in need and therefore has a right to parental care.[887]

In the international arena, most countries endorse anonymous gamete donations nowadays.[888] Moreover, many countries, as for instance France, Denmark and the Republic of Macedonia, do not allow any information regarding the conception. In the United States, there is no explicit regulation either on state or federal level, leaving the matter in the domain of non-legally binding professional guidelines. From the previous preference of anonymity as a concept for donation,[889] the new trend is moving towards a more open non-anonymous system of donations.[890] The practice though still differs, and both anonymous and non-anonymous donations are executed by the clinics.[891] The consequences of donor anonymity endanger the opportunity of the child to decide over the importance of knowing not only the genetic father, but also relatives with whom they share a genetic connection, while allowing this decision to be made for them by their legal parents and the legal system.[892] Furthermore, this situation will continue throughout their lives and affect future generations.[893]

884 Weinberg R., "The Moral Complexity of Sperm Donation", *Bioethics*, Vol. 22, No. 3, 2008, p. 177.

885 *Ibid.*

886 *Ibid.*

887 Louw A., "The Constitutionality of a Biological Father's Recognition as a Parent", *Potchefstroom Electronic Law Journal*, Vol. 13, No. 3, 2010, pp. 188–189.

888 Frith L., "Gamete Donation and Anonymity. The Ethical and Legal Debate", *Human Reproduction*, Vol. 16, No. 5, 2001, p. 818.

889 Ibid p. 819 referring to: American Society for Reproductive Medicine, "Ethical Considerations of Assisted Reproductive Technologies", *Fertility and Sterility*, suppl. 3.4.

890 Ethics Committee Report, "Interests, Obligations and Rights of the Donor in Gamete Donation", *Fertility and Sterility*, Vol. 91, No. 1, 2009, p. 27.

891 Frith L., "Gamete Donation and Anonymity. The Ethical and Legal Debate", *Human Reproduction*, Vol. 16, No. 5, 2001, p. 819 and Ethics Committee Report, "Interests, Obligations and Rights of the Donor in Gamete Donation", *Fertility and Sterility*, Vol. 91, No. 1, 2009, p. 24.

892 See Cohen S.R., "The Invisible Man. Artificial Insemination by Donor and the Legislation on Donor Anonymity: A Review", *Journal of Family Planning and Reproductive Health Care*, Vol. 30, No. 4, 2004, pp. 270–273, p. 271; Johnston J., "Mum's the Word: Donor Anonymity in Assisted Reproduction", *Health Law Review*, Vol. 11, No. 1, 2002, pp. 51–55.

893 McWhinnie A., "Ethical Dilemmas in the Use of Donor Gametes", *Medicine and Law*, Vol. 17, No. 3, 1998, pp. 311–317.

The prognosis for the future inclines towards changing this attitude, thus enabling greater access of children to identifying information regarding the sperm donor.[894]

5.2.2. NON-ANONYMOUS SPERM DONOR

Non-anonymous donations are approaching the international arena slowly but surely. In recent years, there has been growing interest in recognising the right of the child to know his/her origins, not just as a declaration or an ideal which if circumstances allow the national regulations should ensure, but as a fundamental interest of human beings. Thus, the main arguments for removing donor anonymity focus on children's best interests and the notion that denial of knowledge regarding one's genetic origin can be in contradiction to one's human rights and personal dignity.

Those who support the non-anonymity of donors also consider it beneficial for all concerned parties: the donor (and his present or future private and family life, provided that no extra responsibilities are imposed against his will),[895] the family to which sperm is donated or single women (thus appreciating openness and honesty over deception and secrecy that may lead to stress and anxiety within the family)[896] and the child (many authors consider that not knowing the origin is not only harmful towards personal identity, but is also equivalent to degradation of human dignity and human rights).[897] Once open systems are introduced, the concept of the right of the child to know their biological identity should prevail over adults' interests (if related to anonymity). Therefore, some authors have been more pragmatic in finding ways to overcome the potential conflict of the perceived interests with those of the child's parents.[898] To start with, there has to

---

894 Freeman T., Jadva V., Kramer W., Golombok S., "Gamete Donation: Parent's Experiences of Searching for Their Child's Donor Siblings and Donor", *Human Reproduction*, Vol. 24, No. 3, 2009, pp. 505 and 514.

895 Cohen S.R., "The Invisible Man. Artificial Insemination by Donor and the Legislation on Donor Anonymity: A Review", *Journal of Family Planning and Reproductive Health Care*, Vol. 30, No. 4, 2004, p. 272 referring to an interview with Dr Mohamed Taranissi, the Medical Director of the Assisted reproduction and Gynecology Centre in London. See "Call to End Sperm Donor Anonymity", *BBC News Online*, 14 May 2002, available online: http://news.bbc.co.uk/2/hi/health/1986683.stm.

896 Turner A.J., Coyle A., "What Does it Mean to be a Donor Offspring? The Identity Experiences of Adults Conceived by Donor Insemination and the Implications for Counseling and Therapy", *Human Reproduction*, Vol. 15, No. 9, 2000, pp. 2041–2051.

897 Frith L., "Gamete Donation and Anonymity. The Ethical and Legal Debate", *Human Reproduction*, Vol. 16, No. 5, 2001; Turner A.J., Coyle A., "What Does it Mean to be a Donor Offspring? The Identity Experiences of Adults Conceived by Donor Insemination and the Implications for Counseling and Therapy", *Human Reproduction*, Vol. 15, No. 9, 2000, pp. 2041–2051.

898 *Ibid.* p. 822.

be a mechanism of informing the child of the circumstances of the conception[899] (and not to leave this solely to the parents' willingness to tell, as it is a common policy even in countries that have introduced open systems of donations).[900] One of the suggestions is to have a policy of recording the donations on the birth certificate.[901]

Initially, there was scepticism around the possibility of revealing the identities of donors mostly due to the fear that donors will not be willing to donate under these circumstances, and thus assisted reproduction would become heavily burdened. Donors were considered discouraged from donating if they knew that their offspring might contact them in the future. This showed to be true from the practical experience of introducing non-anonymous donations in the pioneering countries: Sweden, the Australian province of Victoria, England, New Zealand and the Netherlands.[902] In reality, the number of donors decreased in the UK, and this in turn led to reproductive tourism to countries that keep the promise of anonymity, such as Denmark.[903]

The fear that the number of donors will decrease in the long run after the introduction of non-anonymous donors is gradually fading away. On the contrary, a number of studies show that the interest in donation will not decrease if the concept of disclosure of identity is introduced.[904] According to Doek, even if there was a risk of fewer donors in the future due to shifting the concept from anonymous to its opposite, this should be dismissed as irrelevant to the child's rights.[905]

Furthermore, in the recent literature a new trend is recognised. Donors have started to accept the procreative role of the donation rather as a fact than merely as a future illusion they will never encounter. Thus, they move beyond the conception of their donation as a gift of "a thing" or a collection of sperm

---

899 See Shenfield F., Steele S., "What are the Effects of Anonymity and Secrecy on the Welfare of the Child in Gamete Donation?", *Human Reproduction*, Vol. 12, No. 2, 1997, pp. 392–395.

900 See Frith L., "Gamete Donation and Anonymity. The Ethical and Legal Debate", *Human Reproduction*, Vol. 16, No. 5, 2001, p. 822. See also Council of Europe, *Medically Assisted Procreation and the Protection of the Human Embryo. Comparative Study on the Situation in 39 States*, 1998.

901 Frith L., "Gamete Donation and Anonymity. The Ethical and Legal Debate", *Human Reproduction*, Vol. 16, No. 5, 2001, p. 822 referring to Warnock M., "The Good of the Child", *Bioethics*, Vol. 2, 1987, pp. 141–155.

902 Bernstein G., "Regulating Reproductive Technologies. Timing, Uncertainty and Donor Anonymity", *Boston University Law Review*, Vol. 90, 2010, pp. 1189–1219; Carbone J., Gottheim P., "Markets, Subsidies, Regulation, and Trust. Building Ethical Understandings into the Market for Fertility Services", *Journal of Gender, Race, and Justice*, Vol. 9, No. 3, 2006, pp. 509–548.

903 See, for instance, Gill C., "Why I'm Happy to Tell my Child I Don't Know who Her Father Is", *MailOnline*, 14.03.2011, available online: www.dailymail.co.uk/femail/article-1365913/sperm-donors-why-im-happy-tell-child-I-dont-know-father-.html.

904 Crawshaw M., "Prospective Parents' Intentions Regarding Disclosure Following the Removal of Donor Anonymity", *Human Fertility*, Vol. 11, No. 2, 2008, pp. 95–100.

905 See Doek J.E., "The Nuclear Family: Who are the Parents?", in Eekelaar J., Nhlapo T. (eds.), *The Changing Family: International Perspectives on the Family and Family Law*, 1998, p. 546.

as initially perceived.[906] A number of studies associate the reasons for donations with their age, concluding that younger donors (below 25) are more inclined to donate if there is a financial incentive, while older donors (above 25) are more altruistically driven.[907] It has been suggested that removal of a financial reward will attract older donors in stable relationships, rather than younger donors.[908] In Sweden, the sperm donor's profile has shifted from young students to mature family men.[909] The acceptance of a non-anonymous donation programme in both Sweden and Victoria showed that donors became more often not just more mature and older, but also married.[910] The possible threat here, though, may be the sperm quality and the higher risk of congenital abnormalities.[911]

From comparative surveys, another subgroup emerges, composed of single men and/or homosexual men, which turn to be more strongly motivated by procreation and passing on genes. For this smaller group, identifying information, potential contact and even a father role towards the offspring is not a burden, but a stimulation to donate.[912]

The overall number of donors has not experienced a severe decline in the long run, suggesting that the possibility for meeting offspring in the future is not so threatening after all in relation to making the decision to donate.[913] This goes along with accepting the responsibility of the parents to reveal the modus of the conception and the possibility of the donor to be contacted by the child. A number of studies examine the preferred time in the life of the child when the

---

906 See, for instance, Grace V.M., Daniels K.R., Gillett W., "The Donor, the Father, and the Imaginary Constitution of the Family. Parents' Construction in the Case of Donor insemination", *Social Science & Medicine*, Vol. 66, 2008.

907 Cook R., Golombok S., Bish A. *et al.*, "Disclosure of Donor Insemination; Parental Attitudes", *American Journal of Orthopsychiatry*, Vol. 65, 1995, pp. 951–959.

908 Daniels K.R., Hall D.J., "Semen Donor Recruitment Strategies – A Non Payment Based Approach", *Human Reproduction*, Vol. 112, No. 110, 1997, pp. 2330–2335.

909 Cohen S.R., "The Invisible Man. Artificial Insemination by Donor and the Legislation on Donor Anonymity: A Review", *Journal of Family Planning and Reproductive Health Care*, Vol. 30, No. 4, 2004, p. 271.

910 Frith L., "Gamete Donation and Anonymity. The Ethical and Legal Debate", *Human Reproduction*, Vol. 16, No. 5, 2001, p. 823. See also Glover J., *Fertility and the Family. The Glover Report on Reproductive Technologies to the European Commission*, Fourth Estate, London, 1989.

911 Frith L., "Gamete Donation and Anonymity. The Ethical and Legal Debate", *Human Reproduction*, Vol. 16, No. 5, 2001, p. 823. See also Asada H., Sueoka K., Hashiba T. *et al.*, "The Effect of Age and Abnormal Sperm Count on the Nondisjunction of Spermatozoa", *Journal of Assisted Reproduction and Genetics*, Vol. 17, No. 1, 2000, p. 51.

912 Van den Broeck U., Vandermeeren M., Vanderschueren D., Enzlin P., Demyttenaere K., D'Hooghe T., "A Systematic Review of Sperm Donors. Demographic Characteristics, Attitudes, Motives and Experiences of the Process of Sperm Donation", *Human Reproduction Update*, Vol. 19, No. 1, 2012, p. 49.

913 Daniels K., Lalos O., "The Swedish Insemination Act and the Availability of Donors", *Human Reproduction*, Vol. 10, No. 7, 1995, pp. 1871–1874.

information should be revealed.[914] They seem to conclude that children told about the modus of conception and the identity of the donor at an earlier age accept the information better than those told later on in life.

Furthermore, donors' attitude has changed towards wanting contact with their own genetic offspring. Even though the vision of "ideal donor" goes hand in hand with the vision of "ideal family", i.e. someone who is just willing to give with an intention of helping others and without any expectations of being involved in the recipient family, non-anonymous donations have attracted another kind of donor – those who may want to be overly involved in the child's life.[915] Some authors anticipate possible concerns because of this, since the non-anonymous donor will be at disposal to the child's call for contact, but not able himself to initiate access to the child's life. This in turn makes the relationship not mutual.

A Dutch study that focused on the variation of donor-type choices by the prospective parents' sexual orientation showed that significantly more lesbian (98%) than heterosexual (63%) future parents chose an identity-registered donor.[916] The intention of most of them (93%) was to inform the child about the modus of conception. A greater percentage (80%) of lesbian couples were found in comparison to heterosexual couples (18%) to look for a known donor among friends and family prior to conceiving their child.

Changing the previous anonymous to non-anonymous system of donations also involves mandatory counselling for all the parties participating in the process – the donors and the recipients of the genetic material. This way the possible consequences that parties may face in the future become predictable and thus expected with due responsibility. Such practices make the assisted reproductive process meet the expectations of the reality without having anybody left behind due to conspiracy over the act of conception.

The parents of donor conceived children usually worry that revealing information regarding the sperm donor conception may harm their relationship with the child.[917] Thus, they fear that the donor may interfere in their private and family life sometime in the future.[918] Nevertheless, open-identity policies impose

---

914 Jadva V., Freeman T., Kramer W., Golombok S., "The Experiences of Adolescents and Adults Conceived by Sperm Donation. Comparison by Age of Disclosure and Family Type", *Human Reproduction*, Vol. 24, No. 8, 2009, pp. 1909–1919.

915 Pennings G., "The 'Double Track' Policy for Donor Anonymity", *Human Reproduction*, Vol. 12, No. 12, 1997, p. 2843.

916 Brewaeys A., De Bruyn J.K., Louwe L.A., Helmerhorst F.M., "Anonymous or Identity-Registered Sperm Donors? A Study of Dutch Recipients' Choices", *Human Reproduction*, Vol. 20, No. 3, 2005, pp. 820–824.

917 Burr J.A., Reynolds P., "Thinking Ethically about Genetic Inheritance. Liberal Rights, Communitarianism and the Right to Privacy for Parents of Donor Insemination Children", *Journal of Medical Ethics*, Vol. 34, No. 4, 2008, pp. 281–284.

918 Brewaeys A., De Bruyn J.K., Louwe L.A., Helmerhorst F.M., "Anonymous or Identity-Registered Sperm Donors? A Study of Dutch Recipients' Choices", *Human Reproduction*, Vol. 20, No. 3, 2005, pp. 820–824; Vanfraussen K., Ponjaert-Kristoffersen I., Brewaeys A., "An Attempt to Reconstruct Children's Donor Concept. A Comparison Between Children's and

an obligation to build a relationship with the child on the premises of truthfulness, openness and transparency.[919] Therefore, there is an obligation for the donor himself to reveal his identity to the child once asked. The donation system in the Netherlands is a good example of appreciating both the donor (asked if he is willing to disclose identifying information when the child requests it) and the child (after reaching 16 years).[920] This obligation corresponds with the informed consent given at the time of the donation, highlighting that sperm donations procreate children, not merely altruistically contribute to some other persons to establish their child wish. Along these lines, the obligation also changes the donation intentions – from altruistic to procreative.[921] Some studies found that men are likely to be motivated to donate by a desire to procreate.[922]

Children's rights seem to have invaded the academic discussions over their interests in conceptions assisted by sperm donations. Much less attention has been paid to the interests of the donors themselves (regarding the selection of recipients, the outcomes of the resulting pregnancies and contact with the offspring). Accepting the concept of non-anonymity also encompasses a twofold relationship that goes in two directions. If children are afforded the right to know the identity of their genetic parent, it should be reasonable to assume that the donor would also have the same interest in a form of right to know his progeny. This goes hand in hand with the given possibility introduced with the open donations that will only manifest in the future.[923] This is a legitimate ground

Lesbian Parents' Attitudes Towards Donor Anonymity", *Human Reproduction*, Vol. 16, No. 9, 2001, pp. 2019–2025.

919 Ravelingien A., Pennings G., "The Right to Know your Genetic Parents. From Open Identity Gamete Donation to Routine Paternity Testing", *American Journal of Bioethics*, Vol. 13, No. 5, 2013, pp. 33–41.

920 Janssens P.M.W., Simons A.H.M., Van Kooij R.J., Blokzijl E., Dunselman A.A.J., "A New Dutch Law Regulating Provision of Identifying Information of Donors to Offspring: Background, Content and Impact", *Human Reproduction*, Vol. 21, No. 4, 2006, p. 853.

921 See, for instance, the statement of a non-anonymous donor at *Cryos* expressing happiness if a child as a result of his sperm donation contacts him in the future after turning 18 years: Sarfraz M., "Come Inside: The World's Biggest Sperm Bank", *The Guardian*, 02.11.2012, available online: www.theguardian.com/society/2012/nov/02/worlds-biggest-sperm-bank-denmark. See also Janssens P.M.W., Simons A.H.M., Van Kooij R.J., Blokzijl E., Dunselman A.A.J., "A New Dutch Law Regulating Provision of Identifying Information of Donors to Offspring: Background, Content and Impact", *Human Reproduction*, Vol. 21, No. 4, 2006, p. 855. They argue that in the Netherlands, the 2004 legislation that made donors traceable brought a change in the motives of the recruited donors, shifting from altruistic to procreative motivations for donations. They explain this by the fact that donors motivated by a desire to procreate appear to find it less of a problem that the offspring might discover their identity and possibly contact them.

922 Riggs D.W., Russell L., "Characteristics of Men Willing to Act as Sperm Donors in the Context of Identity-Release Legislation", *Human Reproduction*, Vol. 26, No. 1, 2010, pp. 266–272.

923 See also Ethics Committee Report, "Interests, Obligations and Rights of the Donor in Gamete Donation", *Fertility and Sterility*, Vol. 91, No. 1, 2009, p. 22.

to ask whether current concepts for gamete donations are addressing donors as participants with a set of responsibilities but also rights in the process.[924]

Donors' interests in gamete donation vary from proper conditions for them to donate and their protection in the process, as well as fair material contribution for the costs they experienced to protection of imposed responsibilities against their will, and enforceability of their possible intention to have contact with the progeny.[925]

The open system of donations poses another donor dilemma, namely should they be open solely regarding identifying information or also to establishing contact with the progeny? In the comparative literature, both opposite poles are noted. A number of studies report the prevalence of donor closure towards contact with their offspring, even though they accept the disclosure of their identity.[926] It has also been noted that potential donors with children were more reluctant to meet their progeny than those without.[927] In contrast, a study in Sweden demonstrated that donors were, in the majority, willing to meet their progeny, even though in their understandings, the meetings did not include any moral responsibilities.[928]

The Ethics Committee of the American Society of Reproductive Medicine (ASRM) grouped gamete donor information sharing into four levels: (1) *non-identifying information* – where the donor only provides non-identifying medical or biographical information (at the time when he donates without giving a possibility to be contacted for that purpose again in the future), (2) *non-identifying contact for medical updates* – where the donor agrees to be contacted with anonymity intact through the programme for medical updates and further information if requested,[929] (3) *non-identifying personal contact* – where the donor

924 *Ibid.* p. 24. See also Fortescue E., "Gamete Donation – Where is the Evidence that there are Benefits in Removing Anonymity of Donors? A Patient's Viewpoint", *Reproductive Biomedicine Online*, Vol. 7, No. 2, 2003, p. 703; Blyth E., "Gamete Donation – Where is the Evidence that there are Benefits in Removing Anonymity of Donors? A Patient's Viewpoint", *Reproductive Biomedicine Online*, Vol. 7, No. 6, 2003, p. 704–705.

925 Ethics Committee Report, "Interests, Obligations and Rights of the Donor in Gamete Donation", *Fertility and Sterility*, Vol. 91, No. 1, 2009, p. 22.

926 See, for instance, Mahlstedt P.P., Probasco K.A., "Sperm Donors, Their Attitudes Towards Providing Medical and Psychosocial Information for Recipient Couples and Donor Offspring", *Fertility and Sterility*, Vol. 56, No. 4, 1991, pp. 747–753; Cook R., Golombok S., Bish A. *et al.*, "Disclosure of Donor Insemination; Parental Attitudes", *American Journal of Orthopsychiatry*, Vol. 65, 1995, pp. 549–559; Godman K.M., Sanders K., Rosenberg M., Burton P., "Potential Sperm Donors' and their Partners' Opinions Towards the Release of Identifying Information", *Human Reproduction*, Vol. 21, No. 11, 2006, pp. 3022–3026.

927 See, for instance, Riggs D.W., Russell L., "Characteristics of Men Willing to Act as Sperm Donors in the Context of Identity-Release Legislation", *Human Reproduction*, Vol. 26, No. 1, 2010, pp. 266–272.

928 Lui S.C., Weaver S.M., Robinson F., Debono M., Nieland M., Killich S.R., Hay D.I.M., "A Survey of Semen Donor Attitudes", *Human Reproduction*, Vol. 10, No. 1, 1995, pp. 234–238.

929 In the Republic of Macedonia this is the only possible information to be obtained regarding the donor. Article 57, Law on Bio-medically Assisted Fertilisation, 2008. The Article stipulates that a child born with gamete or embryo donation, 18 years old and with capacity to reason, can

agrees to have non-identifying contact when the child reaches a certain age and both agree to the disclosure, and (4) *identifying personal contact* – where the donor agrees to have identifying information shared with the offspring when the child reaches the age of maturity and both agree to the disclosure.[930]

In the Netherlands, the law of 25 April 2002 (entered into force on 1 June 2004) introduced a dual system, giving parents a choice between (1) so-called *A donors* (anonymous semen donors – those who already donated under circumstances of guaranteed privacy), and (2) so-called *B donors* (donors that can be traced if the child should, at a later date, request information regarding the identity of the donor). In the second category belong both *initially anonymous donors*, but agreeing to be identified after a request from the child in the future (used for multiple women), and *initially known donors* who donated for a particular woman and whose identity is known to the parents from the beginning (so-called *private donors*).[931] Other information that does not lead to identification, such as medical information could be requested by the general practitioner of the child or by the child (after reaching 12 years of age) or by his/her parents.[932]

The Ethics Committee of the American Society for Reproductive Medicine suggests a list of donors' interests and rights as well as their responsibilities that accompany their donations of which they should be at least informed *prior* to their engagement in the process. In the domain of their rights, they should be informed of the possibility (if any) to remain anonymous or to be revealed later on. Accordingly, they should know the consequences that follow each of their choices: giving up any paternal rights or maybe even the possibility of meeting their progeny in the future (bearing in mind that there are scarce sources regarding the long-term emotional and psychological aspects of gamete donations).[933] They should also be informed of the possibility of having children – half-siblings (in their family and in the recipient family), which in turn may cause complex blood

---

ask for access to information regarding the health condition of the donor (after an approval from the State Commission on grounds of medically justified reasons). This is also stipulated in article 10 of the Oviedo Convention as a restriction to the respect for privacy while still consistent with article 8 of the ECHR as respect for private and family life. Thus, the article stipulates: "Everyone has the right to respect for private life in relation to information about his or her health. Everyone is entitled to know any information collected about his or her health. However, the wishes of individuals not to be informed shall be observed. In exceptional cases, restrictions may be placed by law on the exercise of the rights contained in paragraph 2 in the interests of the patient".

930 Ethics Committee Report, "Interests, Obligations and Rights of the Donor in Gamete Donation", *Fertility and Sterility*, Vol. 91, No. 1, 2009, p. 24.

931 Janssens P.M.W., Simons A.H.M., Van Kooij R.J., Blokzijl E., Dunselman A.A.J., "A New Dutch Law Regulating Provision of Identifying Information of Donors to Offspring: Background, Content and Impact", *Human Reproduction*, Vol. 21, No. 4, 2006, pp. 852, 853 and 854.

932 *Ibid.* p. 853. See also Wet van 25 april 2002, houdende regels voor de bewaring, het beheer en de verstrekking van gegevens van donoren bij kunstmatige donorbevruchting (Wet donorgegevens kunstmatige bevruchting), *Stbl.* 2002, 240.

933 Ethics Committee Report, "Interests, Obligations and Rights of the Donor in Gamete Donation", *Fertility and Sterility*, Vol. 91, No. 1, 2009, p. 24.

affiliation.[934] Apart from the children in their family, who may also want to know about the existence of their blood ties elsewhere, their partner (present or future) also may have an interest in knowing the truth and the consequences of it. In this context, Guido Pennings enumerated three possible partners' interests (the author mentions "marital interests" but they do not have to necessarily be related to marital partners): (1) sexual exclusivity and adultery, (2) family composition, and (3) procreational exclusivity.[935] He defines "procreational partners" as persons who decide together about their fertility and family planning (including the decision to remain childless or to adopt a child).[936] From here, the author extracts the *prima facie* right of the partner to participate in all decisions about gamete transactions meant for procreation. Sperm donations, though, differ to a large extent from oocyte donations (for which most of the clinics still ask for consultation of the donor's partner).[937] Yet, Pennings concludes that the obligation to inform the partner of the donations cannot be a legal obligation (in these terms, to be an obligation of the donor to tell the partner, or even more, the possibility of one partner vetoing the procreative liberty of the other).[938] Nevertheless, the obligation to inform or consult the partner prior to donation has more of a moral nature, still leaving it to the donor to decide what kind of relationship he wants to develop with his partner.

The donor himself also may have preferences to know about the outcome of his donation, such as to be informed of the outcome of the cycle, whether the donation resulted in a born child, or whether the child is healthy or not.[939] A number of studies have dealt with the interests of the donors in the outcome of their donation.[940] On the contrary, their responsibilities once again relate to

---

934 For instance, the world's greatest sperm bank Cryos reported that the average donor can assume he has fathered 25 or even more children. Thus, the probability of complicated blood relations in one country, or around the world is even bigger. See more in Sarfraz M., "Come Inside: The World's Biggest Sperm Bank", *The Guardian*, 02.11.2012, available online: www.theguardian.com/society/2012/nov/02/worlds-biggest-sperm-bank-denmark. After the controversial "Donor 7042" case because of the genetically transmitted mutations that the donor passed to at least to five out of 43 children conceived with his sperm donation (that he donated in 14 different fertility clinics worldwide), Denmark tightened the rules on sperm donations, allowing a maximum of 12 inseminations from a single donor as from October, 2012. See more in Hsu C., "Denmark Tightens Sperm Donation Law After 'Donor 7042' Passes Rare Genetic Disease to 5 Babies", *Medical Daily*, 25.10.2012, available online: www.medicaldaily.com/denmark-tightens-sperm-donation-law-after-donor-7042-passes-rare-genetic-disease-5-babies-242737.

935 Pennings G., "Partner Consent for Sperm Donation", *Human Reproduction*, Vol. 11, No. 5, 1996, p. 1132.

936 *Ibid.* p. 1135.

937 *Ibid.* p. 1132.

938 *Ibid.* p. 1136.

939 Ethics Committee Report, "Interests, Obligations and Rights of the Donor in Gamete Donation", *Fertility and Sterility*, Vol. 91, No. 1, 2009, p. 26.

940 Van den Broeck U., Vandermeeren M., Vanderschueren D., Enzlin P., Demyttenaere K., D'Hooghe T., "A Systematic Review of Sperm Donors. Demographic Characteristics, Attitudes, Motives and Experiences of the Process of Sperm Donation", *Human Reproduction Update*, Vol. 19, No. 1, 2012, p. 44.

the level of responsibilities they will undertake prior to the donation. Therefore if they accept the non-anonymous donor's role, they should also be willing to accept the invitation call to meet the progeny in the future. The Ethics Committee of the American Society for Reproductive Medicine concludes that it is an underestimation of the role of the donations if they see it solely through the prism of transfer of gametes and not to its fullness, i.e. part of a method of family building that involves a complex interchange of emotions and psychological needs of all concerned parties (the donor, the recipient, the offspring and potentially the donor's family).[941] A recent pioneering case in British Columbia, Canada crossed the line when it comes to the known donor's recognition in the child's life by recognising the possibility of the child to have three parents on the birth certificate: the commissioning lesbian couple and the donor himself. Even though the case was described as enhancing the best interests of the child by allowing involvement of all concerned parties, some others have also warned that the effect of a triple-parent relationship on children is unknown.[942] The birth certificate in British Columbia has space for up to four persons to be listed as legal parents of the child allowing donors to be listed as additional parents if the parents sign a written agreement before conception.[943]

5.3. DISCUSSION OF THE POSITION OF SPERM DONORS ASSISTING SINGLE WOMEN TO REPRODUCE

5.3.1. DIFFERENCES AND SIMILARITIES BETWEEN THE LEGAL POSITIONS OF SPERM DONORS DONATING TO COUPLES AND SINGLE WOMEN

There is already a widely accepted consensus that family life overrules the biological/genetic contribution as to affording legal paternity. The methods for proving the genetic connection are precise and near to certainty. Still, the law has opted in reality to neglect that fact as irrelevant not only in cases of adoption[944]

941 Ethics Committee Report, "Interests, Obligations and Rights of the Donor in Gamete Donation", *Fertility and Sterility*, Vol. 91, No. 1, 2009, p. 27.

942 Cassidly P., "Canada: Three Parents Listed on Baby's Birth Certificate", *bionews.org.uk*, 17.02.2014, available online: www.bionews.org.uk/page_396795.asp. See also http://guardianlv.com/2014/02/british-columbia-baby-has-three-different-parents-on-her-birth-certificate/; www.christianpost.com/news/canadian-group-responds-to-case-of-baby-with-three-legal-parents-114567/.

943 See www.cbc.ca/news/canada/british-columbia/della-wolf-is-b-c-s-1st-child-with-3-parents-on-birth-certificate-1.2526584.

944 As adoption is considered to be "an avenue to parenthood through legally recognised intention rather than through biological connection". See more in Schultz M.M., "Reproductive Technology and Intent-Based Parenthood. An Opportunity for Gender Neutrality", *Wisconsin Law Review*, Vol. 297, 1990, p. 320.

and donations (as a matter of policy stipulated in law), but also in cases in which children are conceived *via* sexual intercourse (not as a matter of policy, but more as a result of the practice of the courts). This has been proven in a number of cases before the ECtHR,[945] as well as in the US courts.[946] In this aspect and with an additional interpretation of the norms by the courts, it seems like both ways of establishing paternal links (naturally and artificially) equalise and thus favour the familial *prior* to the genetic ties. Consequently, sperm donations to couples will create the same consequences – the partner of the mother who consents to the donation will be the father of the conceived child, initially as a matter of legal fiction, and later as a matter of family life, thus excluding the donor from the family portrait. Accordingly, the new concepts of parenthood underline the intentions of the adults to become parents with the application of ART;[947] thus, founding families becomes a matter of consent.

If analogy is made to single-women cases conceiving a child by sperm donations, it could still be possible to maintain donors' ignorance towards their progeny (if these were the conventional rules under which he initially consented to donate), and therefore to keep him aside from the child's life in terms of parental rights and responsibilities. Nevertheless, if the other scenario of non-anonymous donors willing to establish contact with their progeny takes place, a development of familial links with the child may be inevitable. Thus, not on grounds of genetics, but on grounds of established family relations, the donor may claim paternal affiliation with the child, irrespective of the nature (sexual or platonic) of the relationship with the mother. This would encompass the mother's consent from the beginning in allowing the contact in the first place if she evaluates them in the context of the best interests of the child.[948] Nevertheless,

945 Specifically 853 cases.

946 See, for instance: *Lehr v. Robertson*, 463 U.S. 248, 1983 in which the Supreme Court protected the new intact family in a claim of the genetic unwed father who contested parental rights in relation to a child against a now-married mother's husband. The Court reasoned that the mere existence of a biological link does not merit equal protection as in cases where the natural father grasps the opportunity to develop a relationship with his child (*Caban v. Mohammed*, 441 U.S. 380, 392) making the putative father not capable of imposing what the best interest of the child is (pp. 256–263). In the case of *Michael H. and Victoria D. v. Gerald D.*, 491 U.S. 110, 1989 the Court reasoned that biology is irrelevant to legal paternity (p. 2340) and afforded the mother (now in a new "loving family home") to decide if the natural father should have visitation rights in relation to the daughter (pp. 132–136).

947 European Parliament, Directorate General for Internal Policies, Policy Department C: Citizens' Rights and Constitutional Affairs, Legal Affairs, *Recognition of Parental Responsibility: Biological Parenthood v. Legal Parenthood, i.e. Mutual Recognition of Surrogacy Agreements: What is the Current Situation in the MS? Need for EU Action?*, 2010, p. 13.

948 The opposite resulted in the above mentioned case of *J.R.M. v. the Netherlands*, European Commission on Human Rights, No. 16944/90, decision of 08.02.1993. In the case, the applicant agreed to donate his sperm in order to enable a lesbian couple to become parents. The couple preferred a known donor, so that they could afford to the child a right to know the biological father's identity. The applicant had regular visits to the couple and the child during the pregnancy and after birth. After a while, he expressed his wish to establish a certain visiting arrangement, which was unacceptable for the couple. Consequently, he requested

the consent and intention from the mother have to persist in order to allow the possibility of family life to develop.

In these terms, the concept of parenthood comes closer to the definitions of sexual and reproductive health and the norms on planned and responsible parenthood, promoting rational decisions to parent over emotional/impulsive spontaneity of conceiving children *via* sexual intercourse without reproductive intentions. It seems like sexuality loses its precedence in the domain of reproduction. Reproductive medicine has already divided these two aspects in the process of procreation. Consequently, intentions become more valid grounds to reproduce, establish parenthood and found families. Thus, parents willing to undertake parental responsibilities will also be willing to protect the best interests of the child.

Children in both cases – couples and single women conceiving with the assistance of sperm donations, irrespective of the accepted conventions of anonymity or non-anonymity of the sperm donors – may have interests in information on the identity of or establishing contact with donors. This could only be realised with the mutual consent of the donors and the legal parents as authors of the conventional reproductive project. As a reality of that kind, it does not differ much from the cases in which the father of the naturally conceived child does not want to establish any personal relationship with his progeny.[949] Even though most of the legislation protects the interests of the child to establish a paternal link with the genetic father (considering it as eligible for restrictions to the *respect of privacy* of the genetic father),[950] in reality it is not possible to impose fatherhood on someone who has no intentions to parent, and even firmly opposes any contact or responsibilities.

If the other scenario is taking place, i.e. donors want to meet and establish contact with the child, it should be dependent on the decision of the couple/the

the Dutch Juvenile Court to determine an arrangement concerning his access to the child. The application was admissible due to the fact of the combination of biological connection and weekly contact with the child. Nevertheless, the Court refused the applicant's request for contact and access to the child considering it against the best interests of the child in the particular circumstances of disagreement of the legal parents. Furthermore, the child already had two legal parents. This judgment may also mean that if the circumstances were different in the sense of an existing agreement of the parents regarding regular contact of the donor with the child, the donor might have been granted particular visiting arrangements. This could mean that the possibility of granting parental responsibilities to the donor is not excluded if several factors are in favour of it, one of which (lacking in the case) is the intention and consent of all concerned parties. If the circumstances were like that, the Court might have ruled in favour of granting him access/regular contact with the child that may even lead to eventually gaining parental responsibilities.

949 See, for instance, *Mikulic v. Croatia*, European Court of Human Rights, No. 53176/99, judgment of 07.02.2002.

950 Article 10 of the Oviedo Convention reaffirmed its consistency with article 8 of the ECHR as respect for private and family life. Nevertheless, it also allowed restrictions to the respect of privacy, for instance, in cases where the judicial authority orders tests to identify and/or determine the affiliation link as an exception based on the principle of protection of the rights of the others.

single mother to approve/disapprove such relations.[951] The conventions of the relationship as explicitly set from the beginning exclude the donor from any future demands he may impose on the family in the future.[952] Therefore, it should be up to the couples/single women to decide whether they will introduce the donor in the family, as parents are entitled to decide on the best interests of their children. This approach was used in adoption cases, considered as protecting the welfare of all concerned parties for a long period.[953] Adoption took precedence over the legal secrecy of the genetic parents in terms of prohibiting disclosure of their personal information. Moreover, it was seen as a promotion of an integrated family, without interference from the birth parents, while protecting the adoptee from the stigma of illegitimacy.[954] Nevertheless, the rules of "dangerous secrets" in adoptive families changed as a matter of policy[955] (even though they remain largely dependent on national regulations) due to the recognition of the acclaimed right of the child to know the genetic origin after the introduction of the CRC in 1989.[956] The possibility of disclosure of the birth parents to the adopted children was especially the subject of interest in the comparative literature in the 90s.[957] This in turn did not provoke many controversies over the establishment of parenthood of genetic parents once they have withdrawn from parental responsibilities and given the child up for adoption. Much of the evidence on the harm caused to children that did not have the possibility to know their genetic origin in conceptions with gamete donations was extracted from adoption cases and soon after received scepticism due to the inappropriateness

951 See, for instance, *J.R.M. v. the Netherlands*, European Commission on Human Rights, No. 16944/90, judgment of 08.02.1993.

952 See, for instance, in the Draft Report, CJ-FA, 2011, RAP 5, p. 20, article 17, paragraph 1(a), which explicitly stipulates that gamete or embryo donors are not considered legal parents. Also in the previously mentioned case of *J.R.M. v. the Netherlands* the judge considered that the fact of sperm donation in itself is not a sufficient basis for creation of family life within the meaning of article 8 of the ECHR and that agreements on rights and duties concerning the child are null and void. This is not the case in Canada though. See footnotes 942 and 943.

953 Schultz M.M., "Reproductive Technology and Intent-Based Parenthood. An Opportunity for Gender Neutrality", *Wisconsin Law Review*, Vol. 297, 1990, p. 320 referring to Churchman D., "The Debate Over Open Adoption", *Public Welfare*, Vol. 44, No. 11, 1986.

954 Schultz M.M., "Reproductive Technology and Intent-Based Parenthood. An Opportunity for Gender Neutrality", *Wisconsin Law Review*, Vol. 297, 1990, p. 320 referring to the "Open Adoption Records Movement", *Journal of Family Law*, Vol. 26, pp. 397–398.

955 See article 22 (Access to and disclosure of information), paragraph 3 from the European Convention on the Adoption of Children (revised), Council of Europe, Strasbourg, 27 November 2008 stipulating "the adopted child shall have access to information held by the competent authorities concerning his or her origins. Where his or her parents of origin have a legal right not to disclose their identity, it shall remain open to the competent authority, to the extent permitted by law, to determine whether to override that right and disclose identifying information, having regard to the circumstances and to the respective rights of the child and his or her parents of origin. Appropriate guidance may be given to an adopted child not having reached the age of majority".

956 Article 7 CRC.

957 See, for instance, Berry M., "Risks and Benefits of Open Adoption", *The Future of Children, Adoption*, Vol. 3, No. 1, Spring 1993, pp. 125 and 133.

of their comparison.[958] A set of partial responsibilities for all concerned parties (if there is an intention) is possible, however, in countries that allow more than two persons to hold parental responsibilities (for instance in the UK).

Single women can also adopt a child in most countries. Nevertheless, this should not be confused with the treatment assisting them to conceive a child by sperm donation. Apart from the different purposes of both adoption and sperm donation conceptions, as related to taking care of an already conceived child and conceiving a genetically related child, there should be a difference in the attitudes of the genetic fathers (under the presupposition that they were consulted on the adoption or consented in a licensed clinic to the donation). Accordingly, they suspended and surrendered their parental rights when they gave up the child for adoption (after the birth of the child) or when they donated (*prior* to its conception). Parents that have either recognised or surrendered their parental rights and responsibilities (in terms of giving consent to adoption, or the consent was not necessary because they were already deprived permanently of their parental responsibilities) cannot reverse or change their decision after a certain period.[959] This is consistent with the protected legal certainty of all concerned parties in the future. There is a difference, though, between surrendering already existent parental responsibilities (in adoption cases) – an active deed – and consenting that no rights or responsibilities will be claimed in the future (in sperm donation cases) – obliging to a passive deed. In these

---

[958] Shentfield F., "Filiation in Assisted Reproduction. Potential Conflicts and Legal Implications", *Human Reproduction*, Vol. 9, No. 7, 1994, pp. 1348–1354. See also Golombok S., "New Families, Old Values. Considerations Regarding the Welfare of the Child", *Human Reproduction*, Vol. 13, No. 9, 1998, pp. 2342–2347.

[959] See, for instance, in the Family Law of the Republic of Macedonia article 59 (paragraph 1) stipulating that the statement for recognition of fatherhood and the consent of the mother and the child for the recognition cannot be reversed (they can only be declared null and void if it is proven that they were given under coercion, because of fraud or misconception (paragraph 2), and article 103 stipulating the consent of the parents to give the child up for adoption, and the cases in which the consent is not necessary *prior* to the adoption because the parental responsibilities are deprived permanently as in cases of: (1) deprivation of the legal capacity, (2) deprivation of the parental right, (3) parent of unknown address for more than one year, (4) child under custody of someone else in relation to which the parent did not show any interest for more than six months from the time when he was obliged to take the child under his protection, (5) the parent to whom the mother referred as the genetic father of the child born out of wedlock did not recognise the child nor initiate proceedings to establish fatherhood within a period of three months after the birth of the child. See also in the CJ-FA, White Paper, p. 13 referring to article 4 of the European Convention on the Legal Status of Children Born Out of Wedlock, which stipulates: "the voluntary recognition of paternity may not be opposed or contested in so far as the internal law provides for these procedures unless the person seeking to recognise or having recognised the child is not the biological father" (proposing exceptions in cases of medically assisted reproduction), and p. 20 dealing with the consent of the genetic parents *prior*to adoption. See also the more recent Draft Report, CJ-FA, 2011, RAP 5, p. 37, article 14, regarding the establishment of paternal affiliation by voluntary recognition, suggesting that the person that can recognise the child as his does not have to be necessarily the biological father, but can also be the partner of the mother (who is not genetically related to the child), and p. 47, article 25, paragraph 1(b) dealing with the termination of parental responsibilities.

terms, there is no obstacle to allow a known sperm donor who has established contact and a relationship with his progeny, that resemble family life (which also presupposes allowance from the mother to enable such contact), to ask (or at least to be asked by the child) for legal establishment of his paternity before the court. A legal obstacle may only be if the national legislation explicitly does not allow access to civil proceedings in cases where the child is conceived with the assistance of medically assisted reproduction.[960] Also in cases of conceiving a child naturally out of wedlock, passivity from the genetic father's side will not induce any changes. His activity, though, at a later stage may also not produce any changes (if there is already established fatherhood in relation to the child from a man that later recognises or adopts the child). Nevertheless, the genetic father from natural conception is allowed to seek for recognition/protection (if one claims that the parental right starts from the moment that the child is born) of his right before the court. The purpose of the exclusive legal solutions for donor conceived children is to enhance the legal certainty, and not to impose parental responsibilities on unwilling sperm donors, as well as to protect already established families. Nevertheless, there is no justification why this should not be a matter of decision in legal proceedings to which the parties should at least have access (as in concordance with article 6(1) of the ECHR). It is a matter of weighing up conflicting rights, interests and responsibilities in deciding if the decision will be constitutional (in terms of constituting a new right, i.e. parental right/responsibility) or not. The rationale for forbidding paternal proceedings for children conceived by assisted reproduction can be traced to the non-allowance of changed circumstances that imposed the conflict of rights in the first place. Namely, only conflicting rights can appear before the civil court. If all parties agree (the known sperm donor, the mother and the child), there is no conflict of rights and interests among them. In order to achieve the same consequences (if establishing parenthood of the sperm donor is their goal), they always have the possibility to allow administrative recognition of the child. Nevertheless, it remains open if changed circumstances (from the initial consent of the donor to restrain from parental responsibilities to his later willingness to establish a legal parental bond with the child) that infringe the right of couple-parents or single mothers are eligible to challenge confront paternal proceedings before the court.

960 As for instance in the Republic of Macedonia. For more see in the first part. (The conclusion is that in "natural" conceptions, in most countries and as a matter of principle, the parental responsibilities of the genetic parents start immediately after the birth of the child for both of them. What happens to them later on is another issue. This is why adoptions in the White Paper are under the section of "Change of parenthood" meaning that parenthood was once established (at the time of the birth) but changed only afterwards. Nevertheless, this also makes "natural" conceptions different from "artificial" ones, because in the latter, the parental responsibilities of the genetic parents (i.e. donors) do not start after childbirth. Donors have withdrawn and given up their parental responsibilities even before the conceptions have taken place. This is why in "artificial" conceptions there is no change of parenthood. The donor never gains parental responsibilities automatically merely due to the fact of being the genetic parent at the time of the birth of the child.)

Besides, the application for access to legal proceedings for establishing fatherhood in relation to a child conceived by sperm donation to a single woman may not come from the donor. It could also be possible that another man (for instance, the future factual partner of the mother) on grounds of factual family life with the child (not genetics) would like to claim paternal responsibilities towards the child, against the mother's will.[961]

Paternal proceedings will be the subject of scrutiny in the following part.

5.3.2. DIFFERENCES AND SIMILARITIES BETWEEN THE LEGAL POSITIONS OF ANONYMOUS AND NON-ANONYMOUS SPERM DONORS

The concept of sperm donations under anonymity is strict, rigid and clear. As such, it does not allow much turbulences and changing attitudes among the parties, due to their changed emotions or circumstances. This is also consistent with the *principles of privacy and confidentiality,*[962] *informed consent, autonomy to decide and individual responsibility*[963] of the donor. Thus, it should be easier to match the reasons and purposes as expectations of the donation for both parties – the donors and recipients. The child as a third party, though, is omitted and therefore his/her interests are neglected. Nevertheless, the position of the donor vanishes from any possible further consequences, his role is forgotten and he is not in any way related to the resulting offspring.

Non-anonymous donors may have different expectations towards the meaning of what the revealing of their identity encompasses. Even though in most cases both anonymous and non-anonymous donors do not mind if information regarding their medical history is revealed, identity disclosure is

961 This is also consistent with the Draft Report, CJ-FA, 2011, RAP 5, p. 37, article 14, regarding the establishment of paternal affiliation by voluntary recognition, suggesting that the person that can recognise the child as his does not have to be necessarily the biological father, but could also be the partner of the mother (who is not genetically related to the child). It follows (as in the other cases of paternal recognition) that if the consent of the mother is not gained, then her partner could refer to a competent authority to establish paternal affiliation (article 15, p. 38).

962 Article 9 UDBHR stipulates: "the privacy of the persons concerned and the confidentiality of their personalinformation should be respected. To the greatest extent possible, such informationshould not be used or disclosed for purposes other than those for which it wascollected or consented to, consistent with international law, in particular international human rights law." Article 7 UDHGHR stipulates: "genetic data associated with an identifiable person and stored or processed for the purposes of research or any other purpose must be held confidential in the conditions set by law".

963 As stipulated in article 5 ("the autonomy of persons to make decisions, while taking responsibility for those decisions and respecting the autonomy of others, is to be respected ..."), and article 6, paragraph 1 ("any preventive, diagnostic and therapeutic medical intervention is only to be carried out with the prior, free and informed consent of the person concerned, based on adequate information. The consent should, where appropriate, be express and may be withdrawn by the person concerned at any time and for any reason without disadvantage or prejudice").

usually associated with future contact.[964] There is a difference between the types of contact with the offspring from a one-time meeting to close and family types of relations. From analyses of comparative studies, a general summary leads to the presupposition that donors prefer that the first step towards contact with the child should be taken by the child him/herself (and not be initiated by the donor or by the parents).[965] For some donors, it is even considered a moral responsibility not to seek contact with the child after the conception. Most of the donors in non-anonymous systems feel uncertain about their anonymity, suggesting that pre- and post-donation counselling might be beneficial to them.

Systems that still practise anonymous donations are simple to administer. Those who introduced non-anonymous donations had two options: to find a way to transit from the previous to the new system (so that the new system could prevail over time but without major discrepancies),[966] and to accept parallel existence

---

964 Van den Broeck U., Vandermeeren M., Vanderschueren D., Enzlin P., Demyttenaere K., D'Hooghe T., "A Systematic Review of Sperm Donors. Demographic Characteristics, Attitudes, Motives and Experiences of the Process of Sperm Donation", *Human Reproduction Update*, Vol. 19, No. 1, 2012, p. 49.

965 *Ibid.* p. 49.

966 As, for instance, in the Netherlands in which since the enactment of the new law (brought in 2002, in force from 2004) a dual system was introduced, giving parents a choice between (1) so-called *A donors* (anonymous semen donors – those who donated under circumstances of guaranteed privacy), and (2) so-called *B donors* (donors that can be traced if the child should, at a later date, request information regarding the identity of the donor). In the second category belong both *initially anonymous donors*, but agreeing to be identified after a request from the child in the future (used for multiple women), and *initially known donors* who donated for a particular woman and whose identity is known to the parents from the beginning (so-called *private donors*). To avoid discrimination among children and to take maximum account of and address possible child wishes to know, an autobiographical document should be provided and added to the files. This will allow children who know or suspect that they have been conceived with sperm donation to ask for and obtain information from the *Foundation for Donor Data* after they reach 16 years of age. Subsequently, the Foundation contacts the donor to ask permission for the transfer of identifying information to the child. This allows the acceptance of new circumstances and changed opinions of the donor regarding the disclosure. Nevertheless, even if the donor objects to the identification, the Foundation has an authority, after weighing up the pros and cons to decide if the identifying information should be given to the child. The wish of the donor offspring is taken as precedence, unless there are strong counterarguments from the donor's side (what is a strong argument is not specified in the law, but should encompass, among other arguments, *A donors* who donated *prior* to the new law, while their sperm was used after its enactment). In the case of a conflict or difficulty to make a decision, the Court may intervene. This means that the donation system in the Netherlands has counted on all possible aspects, allowing possibilities of donors to remain anonymous and the parents to choose (even though the Dutch Society of Semen Banks and Donor Insemination advises its members to refrain from the use of semen from anonymous donors in order to minimise the ambiguity), while still keeping priority of the right of the child to know, especially for the future donations. Even if the information of the donor's identity is revealed that does not oblige him to necessarily establish contact with the child, or to undertake any legal or financial obligations. Nevertheless, if contact is established, it may be from a superficial to an intimate long-lasting relationship. See more in Janssens P.M.W., Simons A.H.M., Van Kooij R.J., Blokzijl E., Dunselman A.A.J., "A New Dutch Law Regulating Provision of Identifying Information of Donors to Offspring: Background, Content and Impact", *Human Reproduction*, Vol. 21, No. 4, 2006, pp. 852, 853 and 854.

of both systems as a possibility of choice of donors and recipient parents (thus still accepting anonymous and non-anonymous donations and administration of information and contact with the child respectively).

The second system has several fallacies and severe critics. Once again, the problem related to the protection of children is not solved. Moreover, children are treated differently depending on the preferences of the adults (the donors to donate and the parents to choose). Consequently it comes down to matching the preferences of those who are undertaking the reproductive project, offering only selective justice to children whose parents will allow them to exercise their right to know their genetic origin.

Guido Pennings suggested a double-track policy for donor anonymity in 1997 based on some already established practices (such as in the USA and the Netherlands).[967] According to his proposal, the best way to balance the rights of donors, recipients and donors' offspring is to offer the possibility to all concerned parties to choose between anonymous and non-anonymous donations. Thus, the donors' possibility to choose would be at the time of their donation, while the recipients would be able to choose when they apply for assistance to the fertility clinic. The palette of choices could vary from identifying information (of the donor, his progeny or the parents), donors' possibility to contact the child,[968] donors' preferences of the donation recipients (heterosexual couples, single or lesbian women), donors' possibility to be asked about the disclosure and the contact at a later time (postponed choices), etc. This would mean that the donations should mostly depend on the intentions of the participants made on a rational level, with precise rights and responsibilities, as well as possible flexibility in their modifications over time. This model also takes the relativity of the different perspectives into consideration, without favouring anybody. It is also related to a written, binding (obliging) contract among the parties, appreciating their intentions and preferences.[969] According to this author, that and not the legal imposition of a formal contract should be a solid ground for its later appreciation.

The severe fallacy of this system was also recognised by the Royal Commission on New Reproductive Technologies in Canada that anticipated possible discrimination among children if a dual system of donation were to be introduced. It would in practice mean that some children would have a right to information about their genetic origins, while some others would not. In addition, this is not due to their choice, but due to the mutual choice of their sperm donor and parents. Pennings suggests that if children's equality is the primary consideration, then secrecy should not even be considered as an option. Nevertheless, he also suggests

[967] Pennings G., "The 'Double Track' Policy for Donor Anonymity", *Human Reproduction*, Vol. 12, No. 12, 1997, p. 2839.

[968] *Ibid.* p. 2840, referring to a sperm bank in the USA where the donor consented to meet the child at least once.

[969] For more on contracts in the field of reproduction, see footnote 1474.

that some minimal requirements should be imposed on the relationship between the donor and the child.[970]

Another fallacy of the system ascribes to the time-distance period between the donation and the maturity of the child (being capable of seeking information, even though the years could be differently regulated depending on the national systems). This is a mutually problematic relationship placing both donors and recipient-parents in a confusing position since their attitudes may change over time. Pennings recommends that it is very important that the original agreement remains constant for the purposes of legal certainty. He also suggested choosing more reliable donors such as married ones or those in relationships. This, though, should be combined with another aspect with priority to be regulated – setting the donors' age limit in order to minimise the risk of abnormalities. The preferred age for sperm donors should be less than 40, since increased male age is associated with a progressive increase in the prevalence of aneuploid sperm.[971]

Imposing the requirement of a stable relationship and a family with children is already preferable for women engaging in surrogacy. Making an analogy here may be as inappropriate as much as it is to compare the surrogate woman's and the donor's contribution. Their physical contributions are very different, making this also a reason why surrogate women usually have the possibility to change their mind after the birth of the child (for instance in the UK), while this is not a common nor expected possibility for sperm donors. An absurd situation like that will also endanger the willingness of donors to donate and recipients to engage in such reproductive project. A better solution, though, may be if the parties are re-evaluated if interest persists for both anonymity and disclosure at a later time. This has already been executed as another policy of double-tracking in New Zealand and Australia. There, identifiable donors are allowed to be identified either from the time of the donation or from the time the child reaches the capacity to ask for information (that is when the donor is contacted for information on his intention to be disclosed or not).[972]

The third fallacy is related to the restriction of the disclosure related to a change of attitudes or refusal from the beginning (even though they agreed on non-anonymous donation) by the child's parents to tell the child. This could be solved, though, if additional mechanisms are introduced, such as noting the modus of conception on the birth certificate,[973] or allowing each child (who knows

[970] Pennings G., "The 'Double Track' Policy for Donor Anonymity", *Human Reproduction*, Vol. 12, No. 12, 1997, p. 2840.

[971] American Society for Reproductive Medicine, Ethics Committee, 2006.

[972] Pennings G., "The 'Double Track' Policy for Donor Anonymity", *Human Reproduction*, Vol. 12, No. 12, 1997, pp. 2841 and 2842 referring to Daniels K.R., "Gamete Donation and Its Impact on Relationships", *Western Australia Reproductive Technology Council Annual Report*, 1996, and Bennett B., "Gamete Donation, Reproductive Technology and the Law", in Petersen K. (ed.), *Intersections: Women on Law, Medicine and Technology*, Ashgate, 1997, pp. 127–144.

[973] As suggested in the Warnock Report for purposes of making the information of the modus of conception available also to children conceived by gamete donation. See more in the Warnock

or suspects that he has been conceived by sperm donation) after a certain age to have access to a special register of data regarding birth information (as is the case in the UK[974] and in the Netherlands).[975]

A number of studies show that the parents' choices from among different types of donors closely relate to their intention to tell or not to tell the truth to their children. Most of the parents who choose non-anonymous donors do tell their children, while those who choose anonymous donors are more prone to keep secret the modus of conception. A study in the USA on families assisted by sperm donations revealed that around 93% of parents that agreed to non-anonymous donations told their children about the modus of conception, including 70% of heterosexual couples.[976] Similarly, a study in the Netherlands found that 63% of heterosexual and 98% of lesbian couples had chosen non-anonymous (identifiable) donors, while major differences were discovered among those who opted for anonymous and non-anonymous (identifiable) donors.[977] Out of those who chose anonymous donors, 83% did not want to inform their child, while out of those who chose non-anonymous (identifiable) donors secrecy towards the child was not an option.[978]

The main conceptual difference between anonymous and non-anonymous donations is the way donations are perceived – merely as a gift of an object, thus treated as a means to someone else's end (the donor – whatever his reasons are, and the recipient parents – with a reason to found a family), or as a part of the

---

Report, p. 194. Even though this proposal was never implemented, more than 20 years later, a Joint Committee of the House of Lords and House of Commons recommended the use of birth certificates as means of enabling donor-conceived persons to learn the nature of their conception. See more in Blyth E., Frith L., Jones C., Speirs M.J., "The Role of Birth Certificates in Relation to Access to Biographical and Genetic History in Donor Conception", *International Journal of Children's Rights*, Vol. 17, 2009, p. 207. The authors suggest that birth certificates should be revised offering a workable model to promote disclosure without compromising privacy concerns.

974 After the foundation of the Human Fertilisation and Embryology Authority in 1991, a Register of Information was introduced containing confidential information on all donors and recipients. The purposes for it were: (1) the donor could be traced and further donations prevented if a child was found to have a hereditary disorder, (2) after reaching 18 years of age, children could ask for information if they were born by gamete donation, (3) those intending to marry could find out whether they were related to their intended spouse. See more in Cohen S.R., "The Invisible Man. Artificial Insemination by Donor and the Legislation on Donor Anonymity: A Review", *Journal of Family Planning and Reproductive Health Care*, Vol. 30, No. 4, 2004, p. 270.

975 See, for instance, in the Janssens P.M.W., Simons A.H.M., Van Kooij R.J., Blokzijl E., Dunselman A.A.J., "A New Dutch Law Regulating Provision of Identifying Information of Donors to Offspring: Background, Content and Impact", *Human Reproduction*, Vol. 21, No. 4, 2006, p. 853.

976 Schelb J., Riordan M., Rubin S., "Choosing Identity-Release Sperm Donors: The Parents' Perspective 13–18 Years Later", *Human Reproduction*, Vol. 18, No, 5, 2003, pp. 1115–1127, paragraph – Openness about using DI, available online: http://humrep.oxfordjournals.org/content/18/5/1115.long.

977 Brewaeys A., De Bruyn J.K., Louwe L.A., Helmerhorst F.M., "Anonymous or Identity-Registered Sperm Donors? A Study of Dutch Recipients' Choices", *Human Reproduction*, Vol. 20, No. 3, 2005, p. 820.

978 *Ibid.*

reproductive process, thus creating a child with its own rights and interests, among which the minimum is the right to know his/her own genetic history.

Non-anonymous donations represent children as active agents with their own rights. This is opposite to the patriarchal view in a broader sense that their parents know what their best interest is and how to protect it. For this reason, it is very likely that identifiable donations will prevail over time. The donor's participation in the reproductive project should be recognised and acknowledged in its full capacity – assisting others in procreating children. Genetics becomes a less important ground to establish legal fatherhood in competition with social fatherhood in factual family life. As such, there is no harm to anybody if the veil of secrecy is lifted and if the family connection with the child is developed based on mutual empathy, care and nutrition for the child, which *per se* describes parental responsibilities.

Sperm donations have already intruded into families, causing fragmentations of the fathers' roles into genetic, social and legal. The right of the child to know his/her origin and to be taken care of by both parents is the preferred scenario for the child's development.[979] Sperm donors' participation in couples' family projects partially satisfies these criteria as long as it is not hidden under a veil of secrecy, and parental roles of biological fathers are substituted by social, thus legal fathers. Nevertheless, this is not the case in voluntarily single women's reproductive projects.

Two recent cases in Germany show different attitudes for donors depending on the accepted conditions for donation (anonymity or known identity).[980] In the first one, a single woman inseminated with sperm donated by an anonymous donor in Denmark claimed child support on grounds of impossibility to receive it from the other parent. Her claims were rejected by the Federal Administrative Court in Leipzig, under argumentation as follows: "The granting of support as a replacement service should be the exception in the case where the resort to the other parent is not possible".[981] The German law explicitly stipulates that the state will not pay child support if the mother refuses to identify the father, under which category anonymous donations also belong. The other case referred to granting the possibility of a known sperm donor to a lesbian couple to challenge the fatherhood of the later legally recognised father.[982] By this, the court in Karlsruhe allowed paternal proceedings for rebutting (and possibly establishing) fatherhood in relation to a child conceived by non-anonymous sperm donation. Thus, the difference of allowing or not the possibility to pose any paternal inquiries relates to the concept of donation – anonymous or not.

---

979 Incorporated in article 7 of the CRC.

980 See in "No Child Support if Dad is Anonymous Sperm Donor", *The Local* (Germany's News in English), 17 May 2013, available online: www.thelocal.de/20130517/49763.

981 *Ibid.*

982 *Ibid.*

Recent legislative policies give precedence to the truth about the act of conception. Disclosure of the donor's identity has shifted changes also in donors' attitudes, making them aware of the possibility of meeting the child in the future, and possibly establishing regular contacts that may look like "family life".[983] Consequently, the number of donors initially decreased. Those still willing to donate are more frequently associated with reproductive and not solely altruistic intentions. Thus, reproduction becomes not just separated from sexual intercourse, but also from parental responsibilities. This is the current sperm donor's reality, promoting that sperm donations create children, but family relations create family bonds. If national legislation accepts this reality, the fear of facing conflicting interests in paternal proceedings before the court would be overcome. As such, both ways of conceiving children – "naturally" or "artificially" – will equalise in their eligibility to paternal proceedings. In both cases, the decision will depend on weighing, on the one hand, biology and genetics, and, on the other hand, intention, social reality and established factual family life.

[983] In the context of article 8 of the ECHR.

CHAPTER 6

CHILDREN CONCEIVED BY SPERM DONORS' ASSISTANCE TO SINGLE WOMEN

The CRC defines a child as "every human being below the age of eighteen years unless under the law applicable to the child, majority is attained earlier".[984] This construction leaves the beginning of childhood open, for purposes of not confronting the everlasting debate when human life and personhood starts, thus not endangering its universal ratification.[985] Nevertheless, the Preamble of the Convention shows continuation of the tradition of the 1959 Declaration on the Rights of the Child,[986] and explicitly takes over the statement that "the child by reason of his physical and mental immaturity needs special safeguards and care, including appropriate legal protection before as well as after birth". This, though, should not interfere with the interpretation of the definition of the child as provided in article 1, leaving it up to the State Parties to decide how they will regulate abortions and family planning.[987]

The term "child" could also be used in relation to the link with the parents and not solely in relation to age.[988] In this sense, the child never ceases to be a child in relation to his/her parents. Nevertheless, it also never becomes the case that a possibility of establishing the link is not provided. Therefore, the issues of parenthood and parental responsibilities are irretrievably related to the child's legal position.[989] As related to its age, the child is entitled in its full capacity to act as an agent for itself after reaching majority, i.e. after ceasing to be a child in the general sense. During discussions of the CRC Committee regarding the

---

984 Article 1 CRC.

985 Hodgkin R., Newell P., *Implementation Handbook for the Convention on the Rights of the Child*, UNICEF, United Children's Fund, 2007, p. 105, referring to CRC/C/2/Rev.8, p. 1.

986 Declaration of the Rights of the Child, adopted by the UN General Assembly Resolution 1386 (XIV) of 10 December 1959.

987 Hodgkin R., Newell P., *Implementation Handbook for the Convention on the Rights of the Child*, UNICEF, United Children's Fund, 2007, p. 2.

988 This is how it is used in part I of Appendix IV of the Draft Recommendation on the Rights and Legal Status of Children and Parental Responsibilities dealing with the position and status of children. See p. 29 of the Draft Recommendation.

989 Lowe N., *A Study into the Rights and Legal Status of Children being Brought Up in Various Forms of Marital or Non-Marital Partnerships and Cohabitation*, A Report for the Attention of the Committee of Experts on Family Law, September 2009, p. 4.

concept of the child's evolving capacities it was pointed out that its purpose is not to overpower the child but to emphasise parental responsibilities over their authority.[990] The concept of a child as an active subject of rights (related to articles 5, 12 and 16 CRC) was meant to strengthen the rights of the entire family.[991] Therefore the focus of evolving capacities should not only be on the children's growing autonomy in relation to their parents, but also on their own process of development (articles 6, 27 and 29 CRC).[992]

For some authors, children's rights usually only come into play when they conflict with their parents' or prospective parents' rights.[993] When they conflict, the fact that children are vulnerable and cannot speak for themselves seems to weigh heavily in the balance. The most common type of conflict with children's rights under article 8 of the ECHR is the one between a parent's right to family life and children's best interests in the same context of family life.[994] Along these lines, children's best interests, as a principle, should overrule the conflict of rights between them. Nevertheless, the complexity of the relationship, especially in cases of children conceived by assisted reproduction, is never binary. On the contrary, it usually needs additional investigation of the facts and circumstances in order to balance conflicts of fundamental rights between adults (parents or prospective parents) and children. Other authors have also dealt with the issue of striking a balance between the child's autonomy and the need for protection.[995] The holders of parental responsibilities should legally represent the child in matters concerning the child's person and property, but this legal representation should not take place in cases of conflict among them. Furthermore, the child should have the right to self-representation in legal proceedings concerning him or her, having regard to the child's age and maturity.[996] Even though of other nature

990 Hodgkin R., Newell P., *Implementation Handbook for the Convention on the Rights of the Child*, UNICEF, United Children's Fund, 2007, p. 2, referring to Burkina Faso CRC/C/SR.136, paras. 51 and 53.

991 Hodgkin R., Newell P., *Implementation Handbook for the Convention on the Rights of the Child*, UNICEF, United Children's Fund, 2007, p. 79.

992 *Ibid.* p. 80.

993 Ieven A., "Privacy Rights in Conflict: In Search of the Theoretical Framework Behind the European Court of Human Rights' Balancing of Private Life against Other Rights", in Brems E. (ed.), *Conflicts Between Fundamental Rights*, Intersentia, 2008, p. 48.

994 *Ibid.*

995 Boele-Woelki K. *et al.*, *Principles of European Family Law Regarding Parental Responsibilities*, Intersentia, 2007, p. 40.

996 Principle 3:24 of the *Principles on European Family Law regarding Parental Responsibilities*. In all European jurisdictions (surveyed for the purpose of drafting the principles) the right and the duty to legally represent the child are an aspect of parental responsibilities. The attribution of a special representative in cases of conflict of interests among the parents and the child is, though, administrated differently in each national legislation. *Ibid.* pp. 159 and 160. Principle 3:38 deals with the appointment of a special representative for the child, stipulating: "in proceedings concerning parental responsibilities in which there could either be a serious conflict of interests between the child and the holders of parental responsibilities or in which the welfare of the child is otherwise at risk, the competent authority should appoint a special representative for the child". *Ibid.* p. 253.

(between two adults), and therefore avoided in the further discussion, it has to be noted that the conflict may also happen on another level – between the parents not being able to agree on an important decision regarding their mutual child.[997]

Throughout history, the child has been seen as weak and incompetent, and therefore inferior to and dependent on adults that should represent his/her interests. Despite the view of perceiving the child as the weak party or potential victim, children in Western societies are seen as active subjects ("agents").[998] Philipp Aries introduced the idea that the concept of childhood is socially constructed as influenced in a particular cultural and historical context and therefore is relative.[999] For this author, childhood is a relatively new concept emerging in the 17th century. Due to the non-existence of chronological birth registers, the age of individuals was not known. Thus, based on appearance, habits and behaviour persons were considered infants or adults. As depicted by medieval artists, children's appearance was often represented (clothes, gestures) as if they were adults. According to Aries, it was only after the 17th century that the interest and thus affection and attention towards children developed the concept of childhood. Even though Aries' views on the history of childhood remain a cornerstone of the development of the concept of childhood, they have also been a subject of numerous critiques, especially regarding the negation of the concept of childhood prior to the 17th century.[1000]

In contemporary times, and especially after the specific international regulation of children's rights in the CRC, the child has a central position. Children's interests should have priority and as such are protected by their parents, the state policies and national legislation. Only once they gain legal

---

997 In many national legal systems both parents have to agree over important decisions that regard the child. In many countries, there is a presumption that each parent acts with the agreement of the other parent (e.g. in Belgium, the presumption applies to all acts, even though it can be rebutted regarding *bona fide* actions towards third parties (article 373, second subsection of the Civil Code). In France and Spain the presumption applies only to routine decisions, while in Russia it applies only to decisions which are not of great importance). In other countries each holder of parental responsibilities is entitled to act alone, except for matters of great importance (e.g. Denmark, England and Wales, Poland, Greece, Ireland, Italy, and Lithuania). Conflicts may appear when important issues (e.g. education, change of residence, medical treatment) have to be dealt with jointly by both holders of parental responsibilities. Then, some countries provide for additional mechanisms for solving the problem (veto, time limits for agreement, etc.). Principle 3:14 of the *Principles of European Family Law regarding Parental Responsibilities* suggests a modus for resolving conflicts between parents regarding the exercise of their parental responsibilities by introducing a third party – competent authority. See more in Boele-Woelki K. *et al.*, *Principles of European Family Law Regarding Parental Responsibilities*, Intersentia, 2007, p. 88.

998 Dillen A., "Foundations of Responsibility for Children", *International Journal of Children's Spirituality*, Vol. 13, No. 1, 2008, pp. 51–61.

999 Aries P., *Centuries of Childhood. A Social History of Family Life*, Baldick R. (trans.), A Vintage Giant, 1962.

1000 See, for instance, Adrian W., "The Infancy of the History of Childhood", *An Appraisal of Philipp. Aries, History and Theory. Studies in Philosophy of History*, Vol. 19, No. 2, 1982, pp. 132–153; Hendrick H., "Children and Childhood", *Refresh*, Vol. 15, Autumn 1992.

capacity do they become eligible agents to protect their own rights themselves. Nevertheless, just as their maturity is not automatically gained only after they blow out the birthday cake candles on their 18th birthday, their legally recognised capacity to reason, express opinions and be heard by official authorities in cases that concern them also, develops gradually. In these terms, the CRC Committee has emphasised that "adolescents up to 18 years old are holders of all the rights enshrined in the Convention, they are entitled to special protection measures, and, according to their evolving capacities, they can progressively exercise their rights (article 5)".[1001] The Convention used the concept of "evolving capacities" for purposes of avoiding arbitrary age limits of definitions of maturity regarding particular issues, thus acknowledging that children's development towards decision-making capacity and independent adulthood must be respected and promoted throughout childhood.[1002] The CRC Committee has recognised this as a new social contract that marks an era of full appreciation of children as right-holders who are not only entitled to receive protection but also hold the right to participate in all matters affecting them. As such, it implies long-term changes in political, social, institutional and cultural structures.[1003] The Committee has detected that the gravest obstacles for accepting the child as a right-holder are traditional and cultural attitudes that are already rooted in different national contexts.[1004] Thus, the Committee has asked for State Parties, among other measures, to amend the procedural civil codes to ensure that children are heard in judicial proceedings affecting them.[1005] Furthermore, the Committee has indicated that reservations on articles of the Convention that challenge full recognition of the child as a subject of rights should be reconsidered for withdrawal.[1006]

This is related to article 12 of the Convention which obliges State Parties to assure to the child who is capable of forming his or her own views, in accordance with his/her age and maturity, the right to express them freely in all matters

1001 Hodgkin R., Newell P., *Implementation Handbook for the Convention on the Rights of the Child*, UNICEF, United Children's Fund, 2007, p. 3, referring to CRC/GC/2003/4, para. 1.

1002 Hodgkin R., Newell P., *Implementation Handbook for the Convention on the Rights of the Child*, UNICEF, United Children's Fund, 2007, p. 77. See also Committee on the Rights of the Child, General Comment No. 7, 2005, CRC/C/GC/7/Rev.1, para. 5.

1003 Committee on the Rights of the Child, *Report on the forty-third session*, September 2006, Day of General Discussion, Recommendations, Preamble. For the full text, see www.ohchr.org/english/bodies/crc/discussion.htm. See also Extract from Committee on the Rights of the Child, General Comment No. 7, "Implementing child rights in early childhood", 2005, CRC/C/GC/7/Rev.1, para. 14.

1004 Hodgkin R., Newell P., *Implementation Handbook for the Convention on the Rights of the Child*, UNICEF, United Children's Fund, 2007, p. 150. See also in the Committee's Concluding Observations on States' Reports. Chile CRC/C/15/ Add.173, para. 29; Burkina Faso CRC/C/15/; Morocco CRC/C/15/Add.211, para. 30; India CRC/C/15/Add.228, para. 36; Algeria CRC/C/15/Add.269, para. 33; Hungary CRC/C/HUN/CO/2, para. 24; United Republic of Tanzania CRC/C/TZA/CO/2, para. 2.

1005 Mexico CRC/C/MEX/CO/3, para. 28.

1006 Committee on the Rights of the Child, *Report on the forty-third session*, September 2006, Day of General Discussion, Recommendations, para. 14.

affecting him/her (paragraph 1). The child should in particular be provided with the opportunity to be heard in any judicial and administrative proceedings affecting him/her, either directly or through a representative or appropriate body, in a manner consistent with the procedural rules of the national law (paragraph 2). The CRC Committee has marked the fundamental importance of article 12 as a general principle that should safeguard all other aspects for implementation of the Convention.[1007] Furthermore, this article emphasises that human rights extend towards the child which should be regarded as an active subject with their own views and feelings.[1008] To that extent, other human rights documents also address children as active subjects. The UDHR in article 19 affords the right to everyone to freedom of opinion and expression without interference. The ICCPR prescribes the right to hold opinions without interference to everyone (article 19(1)), the European Charter on Fundamental Rights (article 24(1)) stipulates that children "may express their views freely", and "such views shall be taken into consideration on matters which concern them in accordance with their age and maturity". The same provision is also stipulated in article II-84 of the Draft Treaty for a European Constitution, 2003. The Convention on the Exercise of Children's Rights in its article 1 grants children procedural rights in family law proceedings, in particular those involving parental responsibilities. Article 3 safeguards any child that has sufficient understanding according to the national laws, the right to: (1) receive all relevant information, (2) to be consulted and express his or her views, and (3) to be informed of the possible consequences and compliance with these views and the possible consequences of any decision. The Convention on Contact Concerning Children categorises rights that belong to children based on their sufficient understanding into: (1) the right to receive all relevant information, (2) right to be consulted, and (3) the right to express his or her views.

The phrase "any judicial ... proceedings affecting the child" covers a wide range of civil proceedings, including parental disputes in which the child's interests are tackled. This article, taken together with article 2 of the CRC, should at least provide access to children conceived by assisted means of conception to proceedings for challenging parenthood, irrespective of what the outcome would be. The ECtHR has already taken a stand to evolve the rights stipulated in the ECHR by its interpretation, taking the particularities of each case on an individual basis (even in cases that are socially sensitive, such as prevention from tracing one's origins).[1009] Thus, the fear of revealing secrets or imposing parenthood on otherwise unwilling sperm donors should be at least a subject that

---

1007 Hodgkin R., Newell P., *Implementation Handbook for the Convention on the Rights of the Child*, UNICEF, United Children's Fund, 2007, p. 149. See also France CRC/C/15/Add.240, paras. 21 and 22; China CRC/C/CHN/CO/2, paras. 37 and 40; Belgium CRC/C/15/Add.178, paras. 21 and 22; Lebanon CRC/C/LBN/CO/3, paras. 35 and 36.

1008 *Ibid.*

1009 *European Court of Human Rights: The ECHR in 50 Questions*, July 2012, available online: www.echr.coe.int/Documents/50Questions_ENG.pdf, pp. 3 and 11.

could be questioned in a judicial system open for every child on equal terms and conditions. The CRC Committee also affirmed that the right of the child to be heard in judicial and administrative proceedings applies to all relevant settings without limitations.[1010] It has also stressed that appropriate measures should be taken in order to address discrimination against vulnerable or marginalised children in order for all children to fully enjoy the rights enshrined in article 12.[1011]

Children are attributed active legal rights to act as subjects themselves in a number of cases: (1) adoption cases (article 21(a) that addresses the informed consent of persons concerned with the adoption); (2) cases of deprivation of liberty, torture or other cruel, inhuman or degrading treatment or punishment (article 37 that suggests a right to initiate court action rather than just to be heard); and (3) cases of children being accused or recognised as having infringed the penal law (article 40, that stresses the juvenile's right to an active capacity in legal proceedings). Children are attributed active rights to express their views, with due weight being given to them when it comes to exercising the parental rights and responsibilities of their parents as a matter of principle (21 and 25, paragraph 2) in the White Paper.[1012]

Calling children "young persons" has a political notion just as the concept of personhood has. It invokes an aspect of treating persons equally and attributing them the same capacities. Treating children both as dependants in need of parental care and at the same time as holders of their own rights as equals to their caregivers has been associated with their superior treatment.[1013] Nevertheless, it remains open how the conflicts between their interests (if it is possible to generalise what their best interests should be) and the interests of their parents are to be solved before they are conceived. These conflicting rights also touch upon the decisions of their parents after they are conceived and before they are born (abortion, pre-genetic diagnosis for different purposes), as well as the decisions of their parents about what should be considered their best interest after they are born (adoption, the way parents care for the upbringing of the child and bring decisions that regard them, etc.). The CRC Committee in its Guidelines for Periodic Reports adopted in 1996,[1014] requested State Parties to provide relevant information with respect to article 1, *inter alia* regarding the possibility of access to information about the child's biological origin.[1015] Hence, even in the definition

1010 Committee on the Rights of the Child, *Report on the forty-third session*, September 2006, Day of General Discussion, Recommendations, paras. 34–36 and 38.

1011 *Ibid.* paras. 8 and 10.

1012 White Paper, Principle 21, p. 25.

1013 Ruddick W., "When Does Childhood Begin", in Scarre G., *Children, Parents and Politics*, Cambridge University Press, 1989, p. 32.

1014 United Nations, CRC, *General Guidelines for Periodic Reports*, 11/20/1996, CRC/C/58, para. 24, available online: www.unhchr.ch/tbs/doc.nsf/%28Symbol%29/CRC.C.58.En?Opendocument.

1015 Hodgkin R., Newell P., *Implementation Handbook for the Convention on the Rights of the Child*, UNICEF, United Children's Fund, 2007, p. 4 (referring to CRC/C/58) and p. 11.

of the child, the importance of article 7 was emphasised in regard to adopted children and children born through assisted reproductive means of conception. It was also stressed that States that do not allow such information are breaching article 7, while the implementation of this right depends on sufficient information being included in the registration of the child's birth and on how the information is accessible to the child.[1016]

The identity issues usually become apparent in adolescent years.[1017] Therefore it is very likely that children will experience the urge to know and meet their genetic father later on in life. This depends to a large extent on the parents' decision regarding disclosure, as well as the nationally accepted strategies to enable or disable the enforcement of it. Knowing and meeting one's parent may also be accompanied by a desire for an ongoing relationship. Even though it is tricky to interpret children's rights in the sphere of their right to full genetic history having its peak of inconsistency in sperm donations to single women, restrictive norms that do not allow further investigation of the developed circumstances (as for instance ban of paternal proceedings for children conceived *via* assisted reproduction) are adding more to the problem than solving it. Thus, how can the corrective wide principle of the best interests of the child be implemented and is it possible to decide what is the children's best interests in advance and for every child (as a matter of policy that does or does not allow children access to information and contact with the genetic parents)?[1018] In each different situation the child will be faced with different interests, making it difficult to impose standards based on general presumptions on what the child's best interests might be.[1019]

6.1. CHILDREN CONCEIVED "NATURALLY"

Legal affiliation (in terms of legally attributing parenthood) of naturally conceived children was for a long period of time (and in some countries even nowadays) governed by the Roman law principles of *mater semper certa est* and *pater est quem nuptiae demonstrant.* Family laws are gradually changing in this domain, and thus on a general level are characterised as undergoing a state of transition. Nuclear families are losing their primacy, being more often replaced with intentional parentage. Since the transitional period is still weighing the tensions between the old Roman law presumptions and the new social tendencies

---

1016 *Ibid.* pp. 11, 105 and 107.

1017 Coleman J.C., Hendry L., *The Nature of Adolescence* (3rd edition), Routledge, 1999.

1018 Comparatively, the best interests of the child may be regarded as the "guiding principle" (France, Germany, Hungary, Spain and Switzerland), or the "primary" or "paramount consideration" (England and Wales, Finland, Ireland, Norway, Portugal and Sweden). See more in Boele-Woelki K. *et al.*, *Principles of European Family Law Regarding Parental Responsibilities*, Intersentia, 2007, p. 37.

1019 Steinbock B., "Defining Parenthood", in Spencer J.R., Bois-Pedain A. (eds.), *Freedom and Responsibility in Reproductive Choices*, Hart Publishing, 2006.

(high divorce rates, alternative nests for founding families apart from marriage, recomposed, medically assisted, homosexual families, etc.), it is more common than before for parent–child relationships to be assessed on the facts of the individual case, rather than on general rules.[1020]

Today, parentage can be grounded on four facts: (1) the genetic link between the adult and the offspring, (2) the contract (including marital) or intent-based parenthood (as a consent given prior to insemination, for recognising or adopting a child), (3) the social link (as proven commitment to the child in terms of doing fatherhood), and (4) the best interests of the child as a correcting and balancing principle that prioritises children's rights over adults' rights.[1021]

Naturally conceived children hold different rights and responsibilities owed to them by their parents when it comes to establishing their affiliation links depending on the national state regulations and the contexts in which they were born or are raised: (1) in wedlock or outside it, (2) in step families,[1022] and (3) given up for adoption and adopted. The CRC Committee identified several grounds for discrimination that State Parties should try to avoid, including the status of non-marital children (born out of wedlock) and children of single-parent families.[1023] It also requested that a State Party review the domestic legislation in order to abolish the discriminatory classification of "illegitimate children" and to secure their right to equal treatment, including the right to equal inheritance.[1024]

Since the term *parental rights* has faced a widely accepted shift to *parental responsibilities*, for the purpose of stressing the role of the parents primarily to take care of their children and not to exercise rights over them, it may be obsolete to discuss children's obligations towards their parents, even more so in the field of attributing parental status. This is to be differentiated from the obligation which children (may)[1025] have towards their parents under an already legally recognised relationship (both moral and legal, such as maintenance of parents in need).[1026] Since children have rights to know their parents, to have contact and to be taken care of by them (article 7 CRC), attributed due to their vulnerable position, it

1020 Schwenzer I., "Tensions Between Legal, Biological and Social Conceptions of Parentage", *Electronic Journal of Comparative Law*, Vol. 11. 3, 2007, p. 24, available online: www.ejcl.org/113/article113-6.pdf. See also Sheldon S., "Reproductive Technologies and the Legal Determination of Fatherhood", *Feminist Legal Studies*, Vol. 13, No. 3, 2005(a), p. 349.

1021 Shanley M.L., *Making Babies, Making Families, What Matters Most in an Age of Reproductive Technologies, Surrogacy, Adoption, and Same-Sex and Unwed Parents*, Beacon Press, 2001.

1022 Foster families will be excluded from the discussion since their role is usually limited to serving particular roles towards the child for a limited period of time without intention of extending the quality of the relationships in terms of gaining parental responsibilities (as it is for instance in the Swiss law or in the English law; for more see in Schwenzer I., "Tensions Between Legal, Biological and Social Conceptions of Parentage", *Electronic Journal of Comparative Law*, Vol. 11, No. 3, 2007, available online: www.ejcl.org/113/article113-6.pdf, p. 14).

1023 Hodgkin R., Newell P., *Implementation Handbook for the Convention on the Rights of the Child*, UNICEF, United Children's Fund, 2007, pp. 24 and 25.

1024 *Ibid.* p. 31, referring to Philippines CRC/C/15/Add.259, para. 21.

1025 Since it is differently regulated in different national legislation. White Paper, p. 28.

1026 See, for instance, Principle 26, paragraph 2 from the White Paper.

becomes meaningless to elaborate on the obligation of the child owed to the parent to know them, to have contact with them or to be taken care of by them.

Motherhood has always been considered less problematic to be acknowledged in comparison to fatherhood. Therefore, for a long time it has been taken as a constant that does not need any reform.[1027] From the comparative analyses of different national regulations the conclusion is that even the establishment of motherhood is in transition.[1028] In these terms, aside from the fact of giving birth, the status of a mother can be legally attributed either by designation in the birth register,[1029] by recognition[1030] or by proof of the virtue of the so-called *possession d'état* – the lived-out mother–child relationship in judicial proceedings.[1031] Furthermore, in France, a woman can avoid attribution of legal motherhood after birth of a child if she decides to give birth anonymously (an *accouchement sous X*).[1032] This practice has been approved by the ECtHR as complying with the ECHR in the case of *Odièvre v. France*,[1033] even though comparatively it is still not considered a preferred scenario for bringing a child into the world.[1034]

In contrast to motherhood, comparatively fatherhood has been and still is to a large extent negotiated and dependent on the status (for instance, in or out of wedlock with the mother at the time of the birth of the child).

6.1.1. CHILDREN BORN IN AND OUT OF WEDLOCK

Before the introduction of medical assistance to family creation, the legal issues surrounding parenthood were related to the struggle to treat all children equally irrespective of the form of the relationship between their parents. The term "illegitimate" children referred to those born outside a formal marital relationship of the genetic father with the genetic mother as they failed to comply with the

1027 See, for instance, article 2 in the Convention on the Legal Status of Children Born Out of Wedlock. Paragraph 3 from the same article shows a connection with the Convention of the International Commission of Civil Status (ICCS) relating to the establishment of maternal affiliation of natural children from 12 September 1962.

1028 Schwenzer I., "Tensions Between Legal, Biological and Social Conceptions of Parentage", *Electronic Journal of Comparative Law*, Vol. 11, No. 3, 2007, available online: www.ejcl.org/113/article113-6.pdf, p. 3. Referring to National Reports from Austria, Belgium, Canada, China/Macau, Croatia, Denmark, England, Germany, Japan, the Netherlands, Serbia and Switzerland.

1029 Articles 310-3(1) and 311-25 of the French Code Civil, article 312 § 1 j.° article 57, 2° of the Belgian Code Civil.

1030 Articles 310-3(1) and 316 of the French Code Civil and article 313 of the Belgian Code Civil.

1031 Articles 310-3(1) and 311-25 of the French Code Civil and Article 314, subsection 4 of the Belgian Code Civil.

1032 Article 326, French Code Civil.

1033 *Odièvre v. France*, European Court of Human Rights, No. 42326/98, judgment of 13.02.2003.

1034 Schwenzer I., "Tensions Between Legal, Biological and Social Conceptions of Parentage", *Electronic Journal of Comparative Law*, Vol. 11, No. 3, 2007, available online: www.ejcl.org/113/article113-6.pdf, p. 3.

marital presumption for attributing fatherhood, thus failed to be "legitimate" or recognised by the law. The revolutionary shift towards eliminating grounds for discrimination among children based on their birth and their parents' relationship gradually through international human rights treaties[1035] and changes in national regulations[1036] has been followed by Court decisions.[1037] Now there is a widespread European consensus that all children should be treated equally irrespective of the circumstances that may bar their eligibility to enjoy equal rights as other children. Because of this, and for purposes of creating conditions for children to enjoy their rights (from *inter vivos* rights – care for their upbringing that goes along with their parents' parental responsibilities – to *mortis causa* – inheritance rights) towards their fathers, it is essential to create conditions for legally recognising their relationship. Thus, children born outside marriage (as a state regulated form of coexisting in a relationship) can also establish their link with their (genetic) father with two additional mechanisms. The first one is recognition by the father and acceptance of this recognition by the other concerned parties, primarily the mother, thus achieving consensus over taking roles. The second one is in cases of disputes over the willingness to recognise, thus making it subject to civil proceedings before the Court. The nature of disputes before the civil law courts is related to the existence of contested petitions among the parties which in family law matters are related to their status. Thus, family law proceedings for establishing fatherhood in relation to naturally conceived children can constitute or not a new status for the concerned parties which in turn changes the quality of the relationship of the whole family (the mother, the father and the child). From the lessons learned in the past and from the notion for overcoming discrimination

---

1035 From more general articles that promote non-discrimination on grounds of birth or other status of the parents (article 2 and 7 UDHR, article 14 ECHR, article 2(2) CRC) to more specific regulation in the Convention on the Legal Status of Children born Out of Wedlock, or the Preamble of the ECECR affording to children an opportunity to exercise their rights in particular in family proceedings affecting them.

1036 For instance, the equal status of marital and extra-marital children in the Federative Yugoslavian Republic was established in the 1946 Constitution. See article 26(5), Устав Федеративне Народне Републике Југославије, available online: http://sr.wikisource.org/wiki/%D0%A3%D1%81%D1%82%D0%B0%D0%B2_%D0%A4%D0%B5%D0%B4%D0%B5%D1%80%D0%B0%D1%82%D0%B8%D0%B2%D0%BD%D0%B5_%D0%9D%D0%B0%D1%80%D0%BE%D0%B4%D0%BD%D0%B5_%D0%A0%D0%B5%D0%BF%D1%83%D0%B1%D0%BB%D0%B8%D0%BA%D0%B5_%D0%88%D1%83%D0%B3%D0%BE%D1%81%D0%BB%D0%B0%D0%B2%D0%B8%D1%98%D0%B5_%281946%29. From a comparative overview, it can be concluded that the regulation of equalisation of the treatment of children on grounds of their birth in the Federative Yugoslavian Republic was among the first ones in Europe. In most European countries the equalisation happened after the Second World War (Germany in 1949, Hungary in 1945, Italy in 1948, the Netherlands in 1947) even though in some countries the father's rights were superior to those of the mother (Belgium and Portugal). The discrimination between the parents from a married community persisted until 1970 in France, and 1983 in Greece. In most jurisdictions, if the child was born out of wedlock the parental responsibilities belonged to the mother, thus excluding the father. See more in Boele-Woelki K. *et al.*, *Principles of European Family Law Regarding Parental Responsibilities*, Intersentia, 2007, p. 46.

1037 *Marckx v. Belgium*, European Court of Human Rights, No. 6833/74, judgment of 13.06.1979.

and treating children equally irrespective of the marital status of their mothers, the main element for constituting a new status or not was accepted to be the scientific medical proof of matching DNA between the father and the child. DNA tests can identify a genetic parent with accuracy that amounts to certainty. Nowadays, it is also possible to undergo paternity tests during pregnancy, even though the technique is considered to carry a small risk of causing a miscarriage.[1038] Paternity tests involve extracting DNA from the white cells in a blood sample, or from cells from a cheek swab, even though any cellular material from the body (hair roots, semen stains, saliva) could also be sufficient.[1039] This means that taking a sample for DNA tests can also be done without any prior consent of the person under investigation (for instance from the cells left on a glass after drinking water). Testing the DNA compliance of the father and the child in order to examine the genetic link can be done in a regulated manner (civil proceedings for establishing fatherhood) or in a non-regulated, private do-it-yourself manner. In cases of coital procreation where civil proceedings for establishing fatherhood are a common practice, two rights might conflict: the one of the child to know and automatically establish the fatherhood of the genetic parent, and the one of the father that might not be willing to comply with the DNA testing. In some countries, non-consensual DNA analysis is considered a criminal offence. For instance in the UK, the Human Tissue Act 2004 stipulates in section 45(1) that: "A person commits an offence if (1) he has any bodily material intending (i) that any human DNA in the material be analysed without qualifying consent, and (ii) that the results of the analysis be used otherwise than for an excepted purpose (which is in the cases of forensic or clinical use)".[1040] On the other hand, the practice of the ECtHR in the case of *Mikulic v. Croatia*, recognised negligence on the part of State authorities for failing to enable the child to realise the right to a fair trial within a reasonable time, when the father refused to undertake medical tests.[1041] Aside from the question of whether paternity examination is intrusive in relation to the alleged father's privacy and bodily integrity, a positive DNA test is to be considered constitutional in terms of constituting the status of the father. In contrast to this civil law practice, the more recent practice of the ECtHR delivers a different message when it comes to the relevance of genes in establishing the constitutional status of the father.[1042] From the analysed cases it seems that the factual family life with the child is granted higher value than genetics in attributing constitutional status to a father. Thus, the constitutional status of becoming a legal father is not related to constituting a totally new situation that did not exist

---

1038 See more in Richards M., "Genes, Genealogies and Paternity: Making Babies in the Twenty-first Century", in Spencer J.R., Bois-Pedain A. (eds.), *Freedom and Responsibility in Reproductive Choice*, Hart Publishing, 2006, p. 68.

1039 *Ibid.*

1040 Human Tissue Act, 2004. Taken from the legislation.gov.uk: www.legislation.gov.uk/ukpga/2004/30/section/45.

1041 *Mikulic v. Croatia*, European Court of Human Rights, No. 53176/99, judgment of 07.02.2002.

1042 See footnote 851. For a similar practice in US courts, see footnote 946.

before, but is more related to affirming the situation that in reality already existed, while only giving it legal acknowledgement. This is only possible in cases in which there are competing persons for the father's role in the child's life. In paternity cases in which the child was conceived naturally outside wedlock, but there is no competition between genetics and factual family life with another man, the situation is usually considered to be clearer. Thus, for purposes of achieving equality of children born outside wedlock and those protected by the automatic marital recognition, most of the national regulations are in favour of appreciating the accuracy of DNA tests. This sensitivity towards not discriminating against children born within and outside marriage is also related to the rationale that children should be taken care of by both parents. It is also associated with the concept of planned and responsible parenthood. Even though engagement in sexual intercourse is not always associated with procreation, civil proceedings based on DNA tests that attribute parental responsibility to the genetic father do consider coitus as a source of procreational responsibility.[1043] This would mean that unplanned fatherhood can be imposed on the genetic father. On the other hand, assisted reproductions are always planned and then intention (consent) rather than genetics is to be considered as a source of procreational responsibility. Nevertheless, this was also challenged in the UK case *In Re D.*[1044] Even though none of the nationally accepted grounds to establish fatherhood were fulfilled, the applicant claimed that he held the right to be a father of the child he was planning. He stated that the whole process of choosing a donor that looks like him makes the child a product of two and not of one person only.[1045] The sole idea of planning a child is already associated with living future reality accompanied by

1043 About the concept of "procreational responsibility" as introduced by Vonk, see more in footnote 1177.

1044 An unmarried man who initially gave consent for sperm donation and insemination of his partner, lodged paternity proceedings for the child born after they separated. The actual insemination took place after the separation and without his knowledge. The lapse of time between the given consent and the actual insemination, following the separation, deprived the validity of the consent due to the changed circumstances of their relationship. The woman misused the trust of the initially given consent without reporting the changed circumstances to the clinic before the insemination. After the man found out about the birth of the child, he claimed that even though he did not fulfil any of the requirements to ground his legal parentage, he considered that the misused consent (deemed invalid) afforded him parental responsibilities as from the time of the birth. The Court considered that the applicant did not possess grounds to claim paternity since he was neither the genetic father, nor had a relationship with the mother or a social family bond with the child. Therefore, it refused to grant him the status of a legal parent claiming that it takes an ongoing joint project to create a child. Nevertheless, through the case, the judge showed sympathy towards fostering contact between the man and the child, suggesting that the existence of more than one party interested in sharing the parenthood is not necessarily a bad thing. See in *In Re D,* Contact: Human Fertilisation and Embryology Act, Judge Hedley, p. 250. See also Sheldon S., "Reproductive Technologies and the Legal Determination of Fatherhood", *Feminist Legal Studies*, Vol. 13, No. 3, 2005(a), p. 359.

1045 Sheldon S., "Reproductive Technologies and the Legal Determination of Fatherhood", *Feminist Legal Studies*, Vol. 13, No. 3, 2005(a), p. 356.

emotional investment. For some authors the "emotional investment" is a ground to found fatherhood.[1046] Cases like this prove that even though parenthood is one concept that should equally apply to "natural" and "artificial" conceptions, the parental fragmentation caused by the use of the reproductive technologies is more complex than the law can possibly foresee. Therefore, access to paternal legal proceedings on an individual case-by-case basis should not only be afforded, but also supported.

Some authors have criticised the concept of not conferring automatic, inherent parental rights to biological fathers on the same basis as mothers as a form of discrimination.[1047] This raises the question of whether biological parents should have the constitutionally guaranteed right to assume parental responsibilities on equal grounds and without discrimination on grounds of gender, birth and marital status.[1048] In the South African discrimination-sensitive context, the Children's Act offers additional modes for acquiring parental responsibilities by a biological father who is not married to the mother. These are grouped depending on whether he was living with the mother in a permanent life-partnership at the time of the child's birth (when he gets full parental responsibilities automatically) or regardless of this, if he consents to be identified, contributes or has attempted in good faith to contribute to the child's upbringing and maintenance for a reasonable period.[1049]

The use of discrimination in this context is differentiation-aware, taking into account the social and economic disparities between groups and individuals,[1050] thus designed to protect or advance persons, or categories of persons disadvantaged by unfair discrimination.[1051] Therefore in evaluating whether the right falls under the discrimination domain, several relevant factors are considered: the nature of the right, the importance and the purpose of the limitation, the nature and the extent of the limitation, the relation between the limitation and its purpose, and the availability of less restrictive means to achieve the purpose.[1052] The purposes of the limitation to treat unwed men as fathers from the moment of birth has been associated with important societal goals – encouraging the preservation of the family unit for the benefit of the

1046 Laqueur T., "The Facts of Fatherhood", in Hirisch M., Keller F.E. (eds.), *Conflicts in Feminism*, Routledge, 1990, pp. 205–221.

1047 Louw A., "The Constitutionality of a Biological Father's Recognition as a Parent", *Potchefstroom Electronic Law Journal*, Vol. 13, No. 3, 2010, p. 156.

1048 *Ibid.* pp. 159 and 160.

1049 *Ibid.* p. 160. See more in the South African Children's Act, section 21(1).

1050 Currie I., De Waal J., Erasmus G., *The Bill of Rights Handbook* (5th edition), Juta, 2001, pp. 233–234.

1051 *Harksen v. Lane,* 1998, 1 SA 300 (CC) para 324C-D.

1052 Louw A., "The Constitutionality of a Biological Father's Recognition as a Parent", *Potchefstroom Electronic Law Journal*, Vol. 13, No. 3, 2010, p. 163. See also the South African Constitution, section 36(1).

children and discouraging or punishing men for irresponsible procreations.[1053] Nevertheless, the limitation reflects the different attitudes towards children based on their parents' behaviour. Having this in mind, the author (Louw) still argues that in the South African context, there is an infringement of the parents' right to equality in terms that it discriminates against both biological mothers and fathers on grounds of sex, gender and marital status. It also discriminates against children as far as social origin and birth (out of wedlock), right to dignity, right to parental care, and right to supremacy of his/her best interests are concerned.[1054] Allowing the mother a superior position means also allowing manipulations in the child's relationship with the father.[1055] The necessity for equal treatment for both genetic parents could be supported by the importance of the role they have in the upbringing of their children.[1056] Therefore laws should reflect a "fundamental premise of equality between parents"[1057] and should allow both parents to acquire parental rights and responsibilities automatically at the birth of the child.[1058] Article 16(1)(d) of the CEDAW stipulates unequivocally that men and women have the "same rights and responsibilities as parents". Nevertheless, this is not the case in attributing parental status since women become mothers (usually) by the fact of giving birth while unmarried fathers do so only by additional legal action (recognition with the mother's consent or judicial decision without the mother's consent, often having to prove, apart from their genetic contribution, an interest in contributing to the maintenance and upbringing of the child). Therefore the question is whether the differentiation between committed and uncommitted fathers can be considered unfair discrimination.[1059] Since sex and gender are listed grounds for discrimination, the author concludes that fathers are not treated equally to mothers in attributing parental responsibilities to them since they have to additionally pass the screening test (by showing the necessary commitment to either the mother or the child).[1060] This disables them from developing a family life (in terms of article 8 ECHR) with both the mother and the child. When the father is not aware of his paternity or was disabled by the mother from forming an attachment with the child, it can be argued that his not-automatic recognition as a father from the time of the child's birth impairs his

[1053] Louw A., "The Constitutionality of a Biological Father's Recognition as a Parent", *Potchefstroom Electronic Law Journal*, Vol. 13, No. 3, 2010, p. 178. Referring to Preiss J. in *Fraser v. Children's Court*, Pretoria North, 1997, 2 SA 218 (T), para. 234H.

[1054] *Ibid.* p. 162.

[1055] Eckhard B., *Toegangsregte tot buite-egtelike kinders – behoort die wetgewer in te gryp?*, TSAR, 1992, p. 129.

[1056] Sinclair J.D., "Legal Personality", in Van Heerden B. *et al.* (eds.), *Boberg's Law of Persons and the Family* (2nd edition), Juta, 1999, p. 27.

[1057] Sinclair J.D., "Family Rights", in Van Wyk D. *et al.* (eds.), *Rights and Constitutionalism: The New South African Legal Order*, Juta, 1994, p. 540.

[1058] Louw A., "The Constitutionality of a Biological Father's Recognition as a Parent", *Potchefstroom Electronic Law Journal*, Vol. 13, No. 3, 2010, p. 195.

[1059] *Ibid.* p. 175.

[1060] *Ibid.* p. 165.

dignity and is discriminatory as compared with the parental attribution of the mother.[1061] Consequently, the burdens accompanying civil proceedings (financial expenses, time-consumption, etc.) have the potential either to force the father to surrender in the fatherhood battle or to reject his application on grounds of detachment, and, as a result, the best interests of the child are neglected.[1062] On the other hand, if the civil proceedings are seen as an alternative legal remedy for the father to establish what he should be granted from the moment of the child's birth, then the discrimination is even more emphasised since the same burdens of proof do not apply to mothers. The attitude of positive discrimination towards women is primarily associated with the fact of their bodily integrity that is connected with the act of giving birth, but also with the notion of treating them as a vulnerable group in society, disadvantaged by unfair discrimination in the past.[1063] Mothers' overpower could be misused in several ways – from exclusion of the father in the family, to his inclusion solely in the financial sector. This in turn manifests an attitude of treating the child as an object of negotiations between his/her parents.[1064] In these terms, the automatic paternal attribution to the father is perceived as a limitation of women's autonomy to fully decide on the issues related to her child in order to share it with the other parent. If the focus is on the other aspect of parental rights, perceiving them as parental responsibilities, it will also mean that they will share the burden of the upbringing of the child. Thus, the married mother shares parental rights and responsibilities with the father, while an unmarried mother takes all the rights but also has to bear all the burdens alone. This should be considered as discriminatory for both unmarried men and women.[1065] Therefore the suggestion for avoiding discrimination between married and unmarried mothers goes in the direction of treating mothers and fathers equally when it comes to their allocation of parental responsibilities.[1066] The current situation of automatically attributing roles to mothers but not to fathers not only stresses the natural difference between the genders when it comes to birth, but also supports the stereotypes that a child's care is a mother's duty, which fathers are not suited to perform.[1067] It also perpetuates the image of both natural fathers as disinterested in their children,[1068] or lesser parents with deficient parenting skills,[1069] and mothers as capable of legal parenthood just because of

---

1061 *Ibid.* p. 177.

1062 Kruger J.M., *Die toegangsbevoegdhede van die ongetroude vader – Is die finale wordgespreek? B. v S., 1995 3 SA 571 (A)*, THRHR, 1996, p. 519.

1063 As argued in the case *Brink v. Kitshoff*, 1996, 4 SA, 197 (CC) para 44.

1064 Van Onselen D., *TUFF – the Unmarried Fathers' Fight*, De Rebus, 1991, p. 500.

1065 Louw A., "The Constitutionality of a Biological Father's Recognition as a Parent", *Potchefstroom Electronic Law Journal*, Vol. 13, No. 3, 2010, p. 167.

1066 *Ibid.* p. 168.

1067 *Ibid.* p. 169.

1068 Goldberg V., *The Right of Access of a Father of an Extramarital Child: Visited Again*, SALJ, 1993, p. 274.

1069 Mosikatsana T.L., *Is Papa a Rolling Stone? The Unwed Father and his Child in South African Law – a Comment on Fraser v. Naude*, CILSA, 1996, p. 152.

their biological link with the child.[1070] Apart from seeing this as discrimination against adult parents, the more striking damage is caused towards the child's right to parental care by both the mother and the father. Thus, children whose father is not married to their mother or who has not committed to the child (irrespective of the reasons, one of which is possibly not even being aware of the birth of the child) are going to be unfairly treated differently to children with legally responsible parents as from the moment of birth. Therefore the differentiation between mothers and fathers as far as the acquisition of parental responsibilities is concerned constitutes an infringement of a child's right to parental care.[1071] Moreover, it perpetuates during their whole life, including when they cease to be children in the general sense (when it comes to their inheritance rights). As such, the differentiation has already been qualified as discrimination by the ECtHR.[1072]

The CRC Committee recommends that the States should facilitate the establishment of legal paternity for children born out of wedlock where the biological father does not want to legally recognise the child as his by creating accessible and expeditious legal and other assistance.[1073]

Even though from a comparative overview all legal systems still appreciate the marital presumption for establishing fatherhood, there are already some legal systems that follow the lived reality of families by acknowledging equal treatments of children irrespective of the status of the parents (married or not).[1074] For instance, in Canada the (marital) presumption is extended to apply to heterosexual registered partnerships.[1075] Some other countries (Belgium, Denmark, France and Norway) regulate more closely how the presumption will be modified in the case of separation of the mother and the husband.[1076] France even allows married mothers to decide if they will acknowledge the father's presence on the birth certificate in cases of non-existence of an actual relationship with the child.[1077] Some countries (the USA, Canada, Australia, Belgium, France and Croatia) already apply the marital presumption also to the man who cohabits with the mother or has already established social family life with the child.[1078] This is also recommended by the Draft Recommendation on the

[1070] Louw A., "The Constitutionality of a Biological Father's Recognition as a Parent", *Potchefstroom Electronic Law Journal*, Vol. 13, No. 3, 2010, p. 183.

[1071] *Ibid.* p. 187, referring to section 28(1)(b) of the South African Constitution.

[1072] In cases *Marckx v. Belgium*, European Court of Human Rights, No. 6833/74, judgment of 13.06.1979, and *Inze v. Austria*, European Court of Human Rights, No. 8695/79, judgment of 28.10.1987.

[1073] Hodgkin R., Newell P., *Implementation Handbook for the Convention on the Rights of the Child*, UNICEF, United Children's Fund, 2007, p. 106 referring to Antigua and Barbuda CRC/C/15/Add.247, paras. 33 and 34.

[1074] Schwenzer I., "Tensions Between Legal, Biological and Social Conceptions of Parentage", *Electronic Journal of Comparative Law*, Vol. 11, No. 3, 2007, available online: www.ejcl.org/113/article113-6.pdf, p. 4.

[1075] *Ibid.* p. 5, referring to article 314 Code Civil, from the National Report Canada, I.B.1.a.

[1076] *Ibid.* p. 5, referring to the national reports of Belgium, Denmark, France and Norway.

[1077] *Ibid.* p. 5.

[1078] *Ibid.* p. 7.

rights and legal status of children and parental responsibilities.[1079] Nevertheless, in most countries, the establishment of fatherhood in relation to a child born out of wedlock is only possible with additional legal action (recognition or civil proceedings). This makes legal affiliation the only legal field that still encounters significant differences between children born in and out of wedlock.[1080] This field is even more challenged and urged to attain better harmonisation when children are conceived by medically assisted technology. On a level of equalising children's rights irrespective of their parents' choices or contexts in which they were conceived, one could legitimately question if the equal treatment should also be attributed to children conceived by sperm donation to single women. If paternal proceedings for children conceived with medical assistance are not allowed, there is an obvious exclusion of a group of misfortunate ones.

The purpose of the marital presumption is to facilitate the establishment of fatherhood, followed usually by a possibility to be challenged (therefore if contested, it should not be considered final). In most legal systems, the *pater est* rule is allowed to be challenged by the mother[1081] (apart from Japan and Switzerland), the child (even though this is often conditional, depending upon the child's age or the ongoing living relationship),[1082] the biological father[1083] and the mother's husband himself.

The recent tendencies, supported by the right to know one's genetic origin, lead to extending the marital presumption to cohabiting couples and to extending the possibilities for challenging fatherhood.

6.1.2. CHILDREN LIVING IN STEPFAMILIES

Stepfamilies as a second category in which children conceived naturally may find themselves purely touch upon social parenthood. The position of the stepfather can be dependent on whether the child already has a legal father or not (since in

1079 Article 11 of the Draft Recommendation regulates the application of the presumption to registered partnerships of different-sex couples. See Draft Recommendation, pp. 35 and 36.

1080 Schwenzer I., "Tensions Between Legal, Biological and Social Conceptions of Parentage", *Electronic Journal of Comparative Law*, Vol. 11, No. 3, 2007, available online: www.ejcl.org/113/article113-6.pdf, p. 10.

1081 *Ibid.* p. 6. This is not allowed in Japan and Switzerland. The ECtHR, though, has affirmed this right to the mother in the case of *Kroon v. the Netherlands*, European Court of Human Rights, No. 18535/91, judgment of 27.10.1994.

1082 As, for instance, in Switzerland and Belgium. For more, see in Schwenzer I., "Tensions Between Legal, Biological and Social Conceptions of Parentage", *Electronic Journal of Comparative Law*, Vol. 11, No. 3, 2007, available online: www.ejcl.org/113/article113-6.pdf, p. 6.

1083 Most countries place restrictions on this possibility. The time framework is relevant, for instance, in Greece, the USA, Denmark, the UK, the Netherlands, Belgium and Serbia. The existence of a social relationship between the child and the putative father is relevant, for instance, in Germany, France and Belgium. See more in Schwenzer I., "Tensions Between Legal, Biological and Social Conceptions of Parentage", *Electronic Journal of Comparative Law*, Vol. 11, No. 3, 2007, available online: www.ejcl.org/113/article113-6.pdf, p. 6.

most countries, the child can only have two legal parents, and moreover whether the parental responsibilities can belong to two persons). There are three general practices regarding the treatment of stepparents in children's lives: (1) no parental responsibilities towards the child, (2) limited parental responsibilities afforded simply by their status of being a stepparent, (3) full parental responsibilities following legal action of adoption of the child of their partner. The level of acceptance of the concept of social fatherhood can be measured by the significance that is given to the relationship between the stepparent and the child during the relationship and especially after its dissolution. There are only a few legal systems that take social parenthood seriously by treating these parents the same way as genetic parents once the relationship breaks down, thus governing custody issues on grounds of the best interest of the child and not dependent on the way the parenthood was established.[1084] This notion is also reflected in the Draft Recommendation that supports legislation to allow the partner of the mother (which is a genetically unrelated man) to voluntarily recognise the child as his.[1085]

Even though biological or at least presumed biological ties still prevail over social ties, marriage is losing power as the preferred context where fatherhood is established. There is a growing tendency of affording greater appreciation to the factual family realities than presumptions.[1086] The most recent developments manifest a significant reduction of the relevance of legal parental status, appreciating social parentage more than ever before. This is in contrast to the still prevailing concept of dominance of the genetic ties worldwide.

6.1.3. CHILDREN GIVEN UP FOR ADOPTION AND ADOPTED

Adoption as a third category of attributing parental status has a primary intention of offering care and protection to naturally conceived children which are abandoned by their genetic/biological parents. This fact makes adoptions substantially different when it comes to attributing paternal status in comparison to conceptions *via* sperm donations. The latter are initiated by the realisation of an adult's reproductive right to conceive; thus the focus is on the parent and not the child.

Irrespective of the genes investment, once the child enters into a family there is an unbreakable bond of psychology and history that develops between

1084 Schwenzer I., "Tensions Between Legal, Biological and Social Conceptions of Parentage", *Electronic Journal of Comparative Law*, Vol. 11, No. 3, 2007, available online: www.ejcl.org/113/article113-6.pdf, p. 14.

1085 Draft Recommendation, article 14, p. 37.

1086 Schwenzer I., "Tensions Between Legal, Biological and Social Conceptions of Parentage", *Electronic Journal of Comparative Law*, Vol. 11, No. 3, 2007, available online: www.ejcl.org/113/article113-6.pdf, p. 15.

the parents and the child. This way of developing family-life realities is for many authors interpreted as stronger than genes, and thus more important for children's lives.[1087] On the other hand, many authors suggest that if the adults are willing to cooperate, contact with the family of origin may be beneficial for the child.[1088] A number of studies argue that for older children, continuation of contact with the families of origin is rather a protective than destabilising factor.[1089]

As a general concept, adoption is widely accepted. The range of eligible adoptees is another issue. On the one hand, couples are the preferred scenario for the child's best upbringing environment. Even though most countries allow only heterosexual couples to adopt,[1090] there is a growing tendency of extending the concept to homosexual partnerships as well. The most liberal positions concerning joint adoptions are in Canada (Quebec) and the Netherlands. These countries allow practically any two persons who want to assume joint responsibilities for a child to adopt jointly.[1091] On the other hand, single-parent adoptions are provided for in most legal systems. Nevertheless, their full actualisation is often conditional, among the other general restrictions, additionally on the marital status of the person who is adopting. This aggravates adoptions for instance of the partner who wants to establish a legal link with the child of his/her partner.[1092] Therefore, stepparent adoptions are often considered as a special category thus allowed if the couples are married[1093] or rarely if they are merely cohabiting.[1094] A special case is when the child already has legal parents and the parental responsibilities cannot

---

1087 Charo R.A., "And Baby Makes Three – or Four, or Five, or Six: Redefining the Family After the Reprotech Revolution", *Wisconsin's Women's Law Journal*, Vol. 7, No. 1, 1992, pp. 1–23.

1088 See more in Sykes M.R., "Adoption with Contact: A Study of Adoptive Parents and the Impact of Continuing Contact with Families of Origin", *Journal of Family Therapy*, Vol. 23. No. 3, 2001, p. 300 referring to the studies of Wallerstein J.S., Kelly K.B., *Surviving the Breakup*, Grant McIntyre, 1980, and Mitchell A., *Children in the Middle London*, Tavistok, 1985.

1089 *Ibid.* referring to studies of Borland M., O'Hara G., Triseliotis J., *Adoption & Fostering: The Outcome of Permanent Family Placements in 2 Scottish Local Authorities*, Scottish Office, 1991; Fratter J., Rowe J., Sapsford D., Thoburn J., *Permanent Family Placements: A Decade of Experience*, BAAF, 1991; Wedge P., Mantle G., *Sibling Groups and Social Work*, Gower, 1991; Ryburn M., "Contact After Contested Adoptions", *Adoption and Fostering*, Vol. 18, 1994, pp. 30–37.

1090 As, for instance, in the Republic of Macedonia and prevailing in Eastern Europe.

1091 Schwenzer I., "Tensions Between Legal, Biological and Social Conceptions of Parentage", *Electronic Journal of Comparative Law*, Vol. 11, No. 3, 2007, available online: www.ejcl.org/113/article113-6.pdf, p. 19.

1092 For instance in Austria, Croatia, Romania, Switzerland and Germany. See more in Schwenzer I., "Tensions Between Legal, Biological and Social Conceptions of Parentage", *Electronic Journal of Comparative Law*, Vol. 11, No. 3, 2007, available online: www.ejcl.org/113/article113-6.pdf, p. 19.

1093 For instance in Austria, Belgium, Denmark, Canada, China/Macau, Romania and Switzerland. See more in Schwenzer I., "Tensions Between Legal, Biological and Social Conceptions of Parentage", *Electronic Journal of Comparative Law*, Vol. 11, No. 3, 2007, available online: www.ejcl.org/113/article113-6.pdf, p. 20.

1094 For instance in China/Macau. See more in Schwenzer I., "Tensions Between Legal, Biological and Social Conceptions of Parentage", *Electronic Journal of Comparative Law*, Vol. 11, No. 3, 2007, available online: www.ejcl.org/113/article113-6.pdf, p. 20.

be attributed to third persons. For reasons of enabling the stepparent to act as such in the family, the Netherlands allows him/her to hold joint parental responsibility with the natural parent without the need for the stepparent to adopt the child.[1095] A similar solution is also provided in the French legal system.[1096]

Comparing adoptions and families assisted by sperm donations could shed new light on the moment that we consider parental responsibilities should start from. The European Convention on the Adoption of Children[1097] stipulates the consents to adoptions in its article 5. For the purposes of the Convention, "father" and "mother" are the persons who according to the national law are the parents of the child (paragraph 6). If they are not holders of parental responsibilities in respect of the child, the law may provide that it should not be necessary to obtain their consent (paragraph 4). In the case of pending proceedings for the establishment of paternity, or, where such a procedure exists, adoption procedures should be suspended to await the results of the parentage proceedings (article 16).

For married parents that give their child up for adoption, it is commonly accepted that both of them have to consent to the transfer of parental responsibilities, since due to the marital presumption, they are already considered holders of parental responsibilities (article 5(1)(a)). It may turn out to be problematic when a child born out of wedlock is given up for adoption but the father is not known. Nowadays, many countries' legislation requires consent even from the unmarried father. Only when the consent cannot be obtained can it be dispensed with.[1098]

This would mean that, in general, parental responsibilities start from the time of birth for natural parents. Only once they withdraw from their responsibilities afterwards (and not before, like in sperm donations), can parental responsibilities be transferred to the new commissioning parents. Nevertheless, the donor could also be considered an unknown father, who did not show interest in the child for a certain time period after its birth. Based on this ground, his parental responsibilities could be considered as ceasing to exist, thus making the mother the only responsible parent.

Even though in most countries adoptions are still considered to be closed and confidential, the recent trend of recognition of the right of the child to know his/her origin is in the direction of allowing a more open attitude towards the

1095 *Ibid.*

1096 Article 343(1) French Code Civil. See more in Schwenzer I., "Tensions Between Legal, Biological and Social Conceptions of Parentage", *Electronic Journal of Comparative Law*, Vol. 11, No. 3, 2007, available online: www.ejcl.org/113/article113-6.pdf, p. 20.

1097 European Convention on the Adoption of Children (revised), Council of Europe, Strasbourg, 27 November 2008.

1098 See more in Schwenzer I., "Tensions Between Legal, Biological and Social Conceptions of Parentage", *Electronic Journal of Comparative Law*, Vol. 11, No. 3, 2007, available online: www.ejcl.org/113/article113-6.pdf, p. 20.

information regarding the natural parents.[1099] In contrast to the past, nowadays there is a growing interest in the adoptive family protecting the biological family relationship to the greatest extent possible.[1100]

The CRC Committee has reiterated its concern over the practice of keeping the identity of biological parents of the adoptee secret. In this regard, the Committee suggests that "adoption laws should guarantee the right of the child to know his or her origin and to have access to information about the background and vital medical history of both the child and biological parents".[1101]

Issues surrounding secrecy in procreation were first encountered in the adoption context. Some authors draw an analogy between revealing secrets in adoptions and in medically assisted procreations, arguing that the latter should benefit from the first in terms of already gained interest in defining blurred origins in children's lives.[1102] The analogy is driven by the similarities between the situations in which both the donor offspring and the adoptee are placed in connection with the family law's emphasis on the child's best interests and their interest in knowing their origins.[1103] The main difference between them can be found in the relationships of the adoptee which usually has no genetic relationship to each parent (if the adoption is not from the stepparent) whereas the donor offspring is usually related to one custodial parent.[1104] Despite the differences,[1105]

1099 For instance in Austria, Belgium, Canada, Romania, Croatia, Serbia, Greece, England, Germany and Switzerland. See more in Schwenzer I., "Tensions Between Legal, Biological and Social Conceptions of Parentage", *Electronic Journal of Comparative Law*, Vol. 11, No. 3, 2007, available online: www.ejcl.org/113/article113-6.pdf, p. 22. In the USA adoptees can access non-identifying information about their biological parents in 35 states, mutual consent registers are introduced in 19 states, access to identifying information without mutual consent is allowed in four states and intermediary service to facilitate reunions is introduced in 19 states. Nevertheless, the claim to elevate the right to know the identity of the birth parents to a constitutional level is destined to fail. The Courts refuse to recognise a privacy right from the First Amendment and thus for adoptees a right to receive information about the biological family on an equal footing as non-adoptees. See more in Chestney E.S., "The Right to Know One's Genetic Origin. Can, Should, or Must a State that Extends the Right to Adoptees Extend an Analogous Right to Children Conceived with Donor Gametes?", *Texas Law Review*, Vol. 80, No. 2, 2001, pp. 368 and 376.

1100 Schwenzer I., "Tensions Between Legal, Biological and Social Conceptions of Parentage", *Electronic Journal of Comparative Law*, Vol. 11, No. 3, 2007, available online: www.ejcl.org/113/article113-6.pdf, p. 15. This is taken from National Reports of Austria, Germany and the Netherlands.

1101 Hodgkin R., Newell P., *Implementation Handbook for the Convention on the Rights of the Child*, UNICEF, United Children's Fund, 2007, p. 106 referring to Armenia CRC/C/15/Add.225, para. 38. See also Russian Federation CRC/C/RUS/CO/3, paras. 40 and 41, Uzbekistan CRC/C/UZB/CO/2, paras.40 and 41.

1102 Chestney E.S., "The Right to Know One's Genetic Origin. Can, Should, or Must a State that Extends the Right to Adoptees Extend an Analogous Right to Children Conceived with Donor Gametes?", *Texas Law Review*, Vol. 80, No. 2, 2001, p. 366.

1103 *Ibid.* pp. 368 and 380.

1104 *Ibid.* p. 375.

1105 Some authors consider that the similarities and points of convergence are far more important than the differences and points of divergence in arriving at conclusions. See more in Garrison M., "Law Making for Baby Making: An Interpretative Approach to the Determination of Legal Parentage", *Harvard Law Review*, Vol. 113, No. 4, 2000, p. 880. In contrast, some others

some authors argue that if from a comparative and international perspective it is widely accepted that the knowledge of the child's genetic origins is in the child's best interest, more than the most consistent family law policy would be if access to information to both adoptees and donor offspring is enabled.[1106]

In addition to this, the other internationally safeguarded children's rights (1) to be heard in any judicial or administrative proceedings (including adoption proceedings),[1107] (2) to "informed consent" of all persons concerned with the adoption (including children),[1108] and (3) ensuring their best interest as a paramount consideration,[1109] imply that there is an obligation to respect the children's views irrespective of the modus of conception and administration of their parents' parental responsibilities on a national level.[1110]

6.2. CHILDREN CONCEIVED "ARTIFICIALLY"

Non-coital reproduction produces babies and not parents.[1111] This means that the purpose of conceiving a child by sperm donation is to produce a baby for the mother, without at the same time imposing the necessity to produce a father to the child. This is the rationale behind different treatments of children conceived "naturally" and "artificially" when it comes to the judicial protection affecting the child as opposed to the principle of his/her best interests, even though they are both guaranteed in the same documents.[1112] Despite the notorious discrimination against children on grounds of the method of their conception, the compromise to discard the biological and genetic reality in order to bring the child into the world prevails in the worldwide national family law regulations. This, furthermore, confirms that kinship and parenthood are social institutions, and as such are politically negotiated based on the accurate estimations as being preferred or less

consider that due to differences between adoption and assisted reproduction, the treatment between children, accordingly, should also be different. See more in Cahn N., Singer J., "Adoption, Identity, and the Constitution: The Case for Opening Closed Records", *Journal of Constitutional Law*, Vol. 2, No. 1, p. 188.

1106 Chestney E.S., "The Right to Know One's Genetic Origin. Can, Should, or Must a State that Extends the Right to Adoptees Extend an Analogous Right to Children Conceived with Donor Gametes?", *Texas Law Review*, Vol. 80, No. 2, 2001, p. 380. See also Garrison M., "Law Making for Baby Making: An Interpretative Approach to the Determination of Legal Parentage", *Harvard Law Review*, Vol. 113, No. 4, 2000, p. 898.

1107 Article 12(2) CRC.

1108 Article 21(a) CRC.

1109 Article 3(a) CRC.

1110 See the Committee on the Rights of the Child, *Report on the forty-third session*, September 2006, Day of General Discussion, Recommendations, para. 44.

1111 Richards M., "Genes, Genealogies and Paternity: Making Babies in the Twenty-first Century", in Spencer J.R., Bois-Pedain A. (eds.), *Freedom and Responsibility in Reproductive Choice*, Hart Publishing, 2006.

1112 Convention of the Right of the Child and the European Convention on the Exercise of Children's Rights.

preferred forms of affiliation. The best interests of the child in terms of the right to be taken care of by both parents in the context of planned and responsible parenthood of single mothers by choice is intentionally overlooked. If children's rights area point of reference when it comes to developing family law policies that appreciate individual reproductive rights, at least the paternal proceedings should be accessible for further investigation.[1113] It is easily foreseen that the individual reproductive right of a single woman excludes the right of the child to have a father. Therefore regulations opting for individual reproductive freedom have made a compromise already by interpreting the best interests of the child in the notion to be born above all, and very certainly not in the notion to be taken care of by both parents. As far as the ideal of having two parents is far from the reality, single women's choices to found a family alone seem not to infringe anyone's rights and freedoms. The more disturbing legal disconsolation is the ignorant treatment towards children solely on the grounds of their parents' reproductive choices. National legal systems that do not allow paternity to be challenged through the judicial or administrative authorities for all children and on equal grounds lack internal legal consolidation. It should be accepted that parenthood is not just a matter of genetics, and that the accuracy of DNA tests cannot be the only ground for attributing parental roles. On the contrary, the combination of all grounds that symbolise the passive (being) and the active (doing) role of parenthood could be a determent for bringing decisions regarding paternal status. Once consolidation is achieved on this level, the fear of challenging parenthood (and thus, the fear of challenging the harmony of established national rules) would be overcome.

The introduction of sperm donations was followed by their availability to couples only, in most national legal systems. The rationale behind this kind of regulation is associated with the protection of the child and the ideal of having two parents. Consequently, even in the cases of heterologous (allogeneic) inseminations, the child has a substitute for the genetic father, and that is his/her intentional – and later on – social and legal father. Even though both partners of a couple should equally possess the right to reproduce, the reproductive project can be carried out only by the couple together and not on the level of an individual right. In these terms, neither individual of a couple can procreate naturally or reproduce with the assistance of bio-medical technology without contribution or consent by the other party. Reproductive technologies already have a well-supported case law and potential to confuse and disrupt the already existing concepts of parenthood.[1114] Two UK cornerstone cases show different attitudes of the

1113 This is disputable though. For some authors establishing parentage is not necessarily important. What may be more important, though, is that there is someone who acts as a father and a mother towards the child. See more in Eriksson A., Saldeen A., "Parenthood and Science-Establising and Contesting Parentage", in Eekelaar J., Sarcevic P. (eds.), *Parenthood in Modern Society: Legal and Social Issues for the Twenty-First Century*, Martinus Nijhoff, 1993.

1114 Sheldon S., "Reproductive Technologies and the Legal Determination of Fatherhood", *Feminist Legal Studies*, Vol. 13, No. 3, 2005(a), p. 349.

presumed fathers in joint reproductive projects towards their children conceived by homologous (autologic) and heterologous (allogeneic) sperm donations. The first one of *Evans v. the UK* also came before the ECtHR.[1115] It represented a battle for realising the individual reproductive right of a woman against the man who donated sperm for their mutual reproductive project but withdrew his consent after their divorce, rejecting any potential paternal responsibilities towards the eventual child. In contrast, the second case of *In Re D*[1116] represented a battle for the parental responsibilities of a man from an unwed relationship who consented to sperm insemination from a donor to his partner. He pledged parental responsibilities for the resulting child after the relationship broke down, even though he did not hold any ground to qualify as a father (apart from the given consent that was considered as having already expired since the relationship was terminated). These two cases raise two specific problems. First is the meaning of obtaining treatment services together in a couple, while only the woman and not also the man receives any "positive" treatment of any kind. Second is the timing relevant for the treatment to be considered a joint or individual project given that infertility treatment may be a long and protracted process.[1117] Another potential problem may be the interpretation of the medically assisted project that is pursued by a woman only, without either consent or willingness from her partner (for instance if she is married). How then should the marital presumption be interpreted? Or perhaps should the woman be eligible to be inseminated by sperm donation only under a condition of terminating the relationship? From here, it becomes clear that the realisation of an individual reproductive right to found a family within a family (marital community or partnership) is impossible.

From the perspective of the child, the only difference between the contexts of the conceptions (couple or single woman) is that the social care and substitution for the father's role when conceived as a joint project of two will be satisfied from the time of birth. The child, though, in both cases will still have the same urges (and, if recognised, rights) to know his/her genetic origin, to express his/her own opinions in administrative and judicial proceedings, and potentially establish fatherhood of the genetic or another social father in the future.

1115 See footnote 212.

1116 See footnote 1044.

1117 Sheldon S., "Reproductive Technologies and the Legal Determination of Fatherhood", *Feminist Legal Studies*, Vol. 13, No. 3, 2005(a), p. 354.

6.3. DISCUSSION OF THE POSITION OF CHILDREN CONCEIVED BY SPERM DONATION TO SINGLE WOMEN

Many studies show that children want to know the donor and genuinely yearn for information and possibly contact.[1118] A recent study has shown that parents' willingness to disclose the modus of conception has increased,[1119] but still the predominant reality is different. The right to know the origin is dependent on the right to know the modus of conception. On this level, it has been argued that there should exist a mandatory disclosure mechanism, such as recording the donor conceptions on birth certificates, formal linking with the information to the birth certificate registers[1120] or even mandatory DNA tests.[1121] The latter suggests DNA paternity tests routinely on each newborn. This would create reliable registers of birth, enable the child to know the truth without efforts to find it out later on in life and prevent false paternity in cases where parenthood is established via presumption while the family life bond with the child has already been created.[1122] The mandatory tests at birth or shortly after are already reality in Portugal,[1123] and are under consideration as a proposal in some states in the

---

1118 Jadva V., Freeman T., Kramer W., Golombok S., "Experiences of Offspring Searching for and Contacting their Donor Siblings and Donor", *Reproductive BioMedicine Online*, Vol. 20, No. 4, 2010, pp. 523–532; Turner A.J., Coyle A., "What Does it Mean to be a Donor Offspring? The Identity Experiences of Adults Conceived by Donor Insemination and the Implications for Counseling and Therapy", *Human Reproduction*, Vol. 15, No. 9, 2000, pp. 2041–2051; Machado H., "Biologising Paternity, Moralizing Maternity.The Construction of Parenthood in the Determination of Paternity through the Courts in Portugal", *Feminist Legal Studies*, Vol. 16, No. 2, 2008, pp. 215–236.

1119 Daniels K., Gillett W., Grace V., "Parental Information Sharing with Donor Conceived Offspring. A Follow-up Study", *Human Reproduction*, Vol. 24, No. 5, 2009, pp. 1099–1105.

1120 See more in Ravelingien A., Pennings G., "The Right to Know your Genetic Parents. From Open Identity Gamete Donation to Routine Paternity Testing", *American Journal of Bioethics*, Vol. 13, No. 5, 2013, pp. 33–41; Cahn N., "Necessary Subjects. The Need for a Mandatory National Donor Gamete Databank", *DePaul Journal of Health Care*, Vol. 12, No. 1, 2008, pp. 203–224; Frith L., "Beneath the Rhetoric, The Role of Rights in the Practice of Non-anonymous Gamete Donations", *Bioethics*, Vol. 15, No. 15/16, 2001, pp. 473–484; McGee G., Brakman S.V., Gurmankin A.D., "Gamete Donation and Anonymity. Disclosure to Children with Donor Gametes should not be Optional", *Human Reproduction*, Vol. 16, No. 10, 2001.

1121 For a discussion of mandatory or not-mandatory paternity tests, see more in Ravelingien A., Pennings G., "The Right to Know your Genetic Parents. From Open Identity Gamete Donation to Routine Paternity Testing", *American Journal of Bioethics*, Vol. 13, No. 5, 2013, pp. 33–41; Turney L., Wood P., "'Paternity Fraud' and the Invisible Child", *Australian Journal of Emerging Technologies and Society*, Vol. 5, No. 2, 2007, pp. 119–131.

1122 *Ibid.* Ravelingien A., Pennings G., "The Right to Know your Genetic Parents. From Open Identity Gamete Donation to Routine Paternity Testing", *American Journal of Bioethics*, Vol. 13, No. 5, 2013, pp. 33–41.

1123 *Ibid.* See also Machado H., "Biologising Paternity, Moralizing Maternity. The Construction of Parenthood in the Determination of Paternity through the Courts in Portugal", *Feminist Legal Studies*,Vol. 16, No. 2, 2008, pp. 215–236, p. 221. The Portuguese family law changes were introduced in 1966, providing for an "unofficial inquiry of paternity" that occurs in court and investigates the paternity of any minor under the age of two whose birth record does not show the identity of the father. Article 1864 of the Portuguese Civil Code states: "at any time that

USA.[1124] Secrecy, on the other hand, could damage the communication between parents and children, and create a hostile relationship of hatred, guilt and mistrust.[1125] Some authors have differentiated between *secrecy* as not knowing that genetic and social parentage have been separated and *anonymity* as related to anonymous progenitors.[1126] In these terms, secrecy is a much darker concept than anonymity. Both concepts have firstly been investigated in the field of adoptions. There, *secrecy* was considered a deceit over an important matter, excluding the child and evoking a sense of being an outsider, while *anonymity* was related to the genealogical and personal information regarding the development of a positive sense of identity and of the whole self.[1127] Thus, some authors consider the desire to know the genetic history a psychological need in the quest for the child's own roots and reunions,[1128] while considering secrecy as interfering with the child's security of attachment.[1129] Others have criticised this model as pathological, claiming that the "social identity" of the adopted child is more relevant for his/her

---

a minor's birth register is made in which only the maternity is established, the clerk is bound to forward an unabridged register certificate to the court so that the father's identity may be unofficially investigated". The purpose of the changes was to protect the essential rights of the child whose paternity is not legally determined, such as "the rights to personal identity", and "the development of personality", generally seen as associated to "the right to paternity". Thus, in the Portuguese legal system the determination of paternity is even considered a human right. The cited author considers that under the theoretical veil of protection of children's rights, in practice, the reality is different. Namely, the access to DNA tests, and therefore paternal proceedings is restricted only to children with "well-behaved" mothers (those who are examined and the court concludes that their sexual behaviour allows further investigation of the father), thus making it socially controlled in a subordinate and sexualised manner (p. 223). The author associates this with the ideology of a breadwinning mate: the mother is asked about her sexual life so that she can identify the father, while the putative father is asked about his willingness to provide financial support (p. 227).

1124 Friedman M., "N.J. Legislator Proposes Bill Requiring Genetic Testing for all Newborns, Parents to Verify Paternity", *NJ. Com*, 1 March 2012, available online: www.nj.com/news/index.ssf/2012/03/nj_legislator_proposes_measure.html.

1125 Daniels K., "Donor Gametes. Anonymous or Identified?", *Best Practice & Research Clinical Obstetrics and Gynecology*, Vol. 21, No. 1, 2007, pp. 113–128; Shehab D., Duff J., Pasch L.A., MacDougall K., Scheib J.E., Nachtigall R.D., "How Parents Whose Children have been Conceived with Donor Gametes make their Disclosure Decision. Contexts, Influences, and Couple Dynamics", *Fertility and Sterility*, Vol. 89, No. 1, 2008, pp. 179–187.

1126 O'Donovan K., "What Shall We Tell the Children? Reflections on Children's Perspectives and the Reproduction Revolution", in Lee M., Morgan D. (eds.), *Birthrights, Law and Ethics at the Beginning of Life*, Routledge, 1989, p. 98.

1127 O'Donovan K., "What Shall We Tell the Children? Reflections on Children's Perspectives and the Reproduction Revolution", in Lee M., Morgan D. (eds.), *Birthrights, Law and Ethics at the Beginning of Life*, Routledge, 1989, p. 99. See also Bok S., *Secrets*, Vintage, 1984, Chapter 3.

1128 O'Donovan K., "What Shall We Tell the Children? Reflections on Children's Perspectives and the Reproduction Revolution", in Lee M., Morgan D. (eds.), *Birthrights, Law and Ethics at the Beginning of Life*, Routledge, 1989, p. 100. See also Triseliotis J., "Obtaining Birth Certificates", in Bean P. (ed.), *Adoption: Essays in Social Policy, Law, and Sociology*, Tavistock, 1984, pp. 38–39, 41–42.

1129 Lycett E., Daniels K., Curson R., Golombok S., "Offspring Created as a Result of Donor Insemination: A Study of Family Relationships, Child Adjustment, and Disclosure", *Fertility and Sterility*, Vol. 82, No. 1, 2004, pp. 172–179.

proper development instead of the "ego identity".[1130] In these terms, the adoptive family could provide for the child to build his/her own identity as a concept that develops through his/her lifetime. Thus, the concepts of secrecy and anonymity were familiar when they were transferred to the field of gamete donations later on. In this new field, secrecy also arises from the stigmatisation of infertility and illegitimacy, but it also serves to preserve certain perceived standards of morality and normality.[1131]

On the other hand, the premises that overrule genetics due to the importance of factual family life consider DNA as overrated. Some authors criticise the overestimation of DNA as it provides limited input to personal identity while at the same time empowering ethical and social disturbances that may lead to eugenics.[1132] Some others have considered the ethical questions regarding the role of DNA-based paternity testing, and social and policy questions about the role that biological links play in grounding parental responsibilities.[1133] Three cultural currents are extrapolated from the current behaviour over the meaning of knowing one's origins: (1) a pre-modern interest in a naturalistic account of personal identity (referring to "genetic essentialism", as a given personal identity rather than socially constructed, (2) a modern passion for science (the naturally given identity as discovered by science), and (3) a post-modern emphasis on radical individual self-determination (as exposed on the internet).[1134] Regarding the recent trends in affiliation laws in Europe, three common elements are: (1) equalisation (since the primary object of reforms was to eliminate the discrimination between children on grounds of birth, (2) liberalisation (in terms of suppressing numerous restrictions on the establishment and contestation of affiliation), and (3) modernisation (in terms of modernising affiliation laws by adapting them to new medico-genetic technologies).[1135]

Some early studies introduced the term "genealogical bewilderment" to describe a family where one of the "natural" parents was unknown.[1136] Sants raised awareness of the importance of origins with his clinical observations of

---

1130 O'Donovan K., "What Shall We Tell the Children? Reflections on Children's Perspectives and the Reproduction Revolution", in Lee M., Morgan D. (eds.), *Birthrights, Law and Ethics at the Beginning of Life*, Routledge, 1989, p. 101 referring to Haims and Timms, *Adoption*, p. 98.

1131 O'Donovan K., "What Shall We Tell the Children? Reflections on Children's Perspectives and the Reproduction Revolution", in Lee M., Morgan D. (eds.), *Birthrights, Law and Ethics at the Beginning of Life*, Routledge, 1989, p. 107.

1132 Nordgren A., "Personal Genomics. Consumer Genomics Companies and their Rhetoric", in Tupasela A., (ed.), *Consumer Medicine*, TemaNord, Nordic Council of Ministers, 2010.

1133 Rothstein M.A., Murray T.H., Kachnick G.E., Majumder M.A. (eds.), *Genetic Ties and the Family, Baltimore*, Johns Hopkins University Press, 2005.

1134 *Ibid.* p. 38.

1135 Senaeve P., "The Reform of Affiliation Law in France and in Benelux Countries", in Eckelaar J., Sarcevic P. (eds.), *Legal and Social Issues for the Twenty-First Century*, Martinus Nijhoff, 1993.

1136 Sants H., "Genealogical Bewilderment in Children with Substitute Parents", *The British Journal of Medical Psychology*, Vol. 37, No. 2, 1964, pp. 133–141.

the "genealogical bewilderment" described by adoptees.[1137] This term was often used to explain the possible identity problems that adopted children may face since the right to know one's genes was firstly tackled in the context of adoption. Even though adoptions should be elaborated separately from sperm donations, it seems reasonable to make a connection as long as the identity part is concerned. Since the battle for adopted children to know their origin in some countries won, the analogy with the right to know the parents of the children conceived by sperm donation was inevitable.[1138] The different treatment between adopted children and children conceived by anonymous sperm donation was ruled to be discriminatory in a case before the Canadian Supreme Court.[1139] Some authors have tried to link the natural and artificial conceptions *via* their right to know the genetic origin.[1140] Others have argued that, regardless of the context, all children should have the right to test paternity if it is misattributed or if it is hidden.[1141]

Even though the right of the child to know his/her origins as stipulated in article 7 of the CRC is unique in the sense that it is not stipulated in the same manner in the other international conventions, some parts of it can be identified, or can be upheld in the right to identity as embodied in article 8, and the child's right to maintain regular contact with his or her parents as provided in article 4 of the Convention on Contact Concerning Children.[1142] From a comparative study of European national legislation as well as ECtHR jurisprudence, it became evident that a right to identity is largely an undeveloped concept. Its controversy is related to its relational aspects putting the right in a position to be balanced with the rights and interests of third parties.[1143]

1137 Sykes M.R., "Adoption with Contact: A Study of Adoptive Parents and the Impact of Continuing Contact with Families of Origin", *Journal of Family Therapy*, Vol. 23. No. 3, 2001, p. 298.

1138 See also Chestney E.S., "The Right to Know One's Genetic Origin. Can, Should, or Must a State that Extends the Right to Adoptees Extend an Analogous Right to Children Conceived with Donor Gametes?", *Texas Law Review*, Vol. 80, No. 2, 2001, pp. 365–391.

1139 *Pratten v. British Columbia* (Attorney General), BCSC 656, 2011 (see www.cbc.ca/bc/news/bc-110519-pratten-sperm-donor-ruling.pdf). See also Motluk A., "Canadian Court Bans Anonymous Sperm and Egg Donation", *Nature News*, 27 May 2001.

1140 Cohen G., "Response. Rethinking Sperm-Donor Anonymity. Of Changed Selves, Non-Identity, and One-Night Stands", *Georgetown Law Journal*, Vol. 100, No. 2, 2013, pp. 431–447.

1141 Ravelingien A., Pennings G., "The Right to Know your Genetic Parents. From Open Identity Gamete Donation to Routine Paternity Testing", *American Journal of Bioethics*, Vol. 13, No. 5, 2013, pp. 33–41.

1142 Lowe N., *A Study into the Rights and Legal Status of Children being Brought Up in Various Forms of Marital or Non-Marital Partnerships and Cohabitation*, A Report for the Attention of the Committee of Experts on Family Law, September 2009, p. 10. See also Van Bueren G., *Child Rights in Europe*, Council of Europe, Strasbourg, 2007, p. 64.

1143 Lowe N., *A Study into the Rights and Legal Status of Children being Brought Up in Various Forms of Marital or Non-Marital Partnerships and Cohabitation*, A Report for the Attention of the Committee of Experts on Family Law, September, 2009, p. 36.

6.3.1. CONFLICTING RIGHTS IN CONCEPTIONS BY SPERM DONATIONS TO SINGLE WOMEN

Children's rights as protected in the international documents oppose single women's reproductive right to be considered solely as their individual human right. Firstly, children's right to be registered from birth (article 24(2) ICCPR and article 7 CRC) is supported by the right to know and be taken care of by both parents (article 7 CRC) as related to their personal identity (article 8 CRC) as well as the ideal of what family should look like. In addition, articles 9(3) and 18(1) CRC compel State Parties to "respect the right of the child who is separated from one or both parents to maintain personal relations and direct contact with both parents on a regular basis, except if it is contrary to the child's best interests" and "to use their best efforts to ensure recognition of the principle that both parents have common responsibilities for the upbringing and development of the child".

Secondly, the right of the child not to be discriminated against on grounds of birth and other status (articles 2 UDHR, 2 CRC, 24(1) ICCPR) as well as for reasons of parentage (article 10(3) ICESCR) also conflicts with single women's absolute reproductive right. Unequal treatment is followed by a less favourable position of children born with medical assistance in comparison to those born without when it comes to the options available for discovering the genetic history, requesting DNA tests for purposes of matching compatibility and rebutting or establishing parenthood in the Court.

Thirdly, the best interests of the child as protected and enforced by legal/administrative authorities (article 3 CRC)[1144] in conjunction with the right to

[1144] The best interests of the child apart from occupying a significant place in the CRC, as a consideration is also present in other international instruments: CEDAW (article 16(1)(d) guaranteeing equal status of men and women as parents in all matters related to family relations considering their children's interests of paramount importance); European Charter on Fundamental Rights (article 24(2)), the Draft Treaty for a European Constitution, 2003 (article II-84(2)) stipulating that in all actions taken by public authorities or private institutions that are related to children, their best interests must be a primary consideration. Even though this principle is widely accepted, comparatively, the interpretation of conflicting situations regarding parents' rights to decide for their children and the enforcement of children's rights to decide for themselves is slightly different. For instance, in Italy and Lithuania, it is emphasised that issues concerning parental responsibilities must be decided exclusively in the interests of the child, whereas others, such as Bulgaria, England and Wales, Poland, and Russia stress that the holders of parental responsibilities ultimately decide, outside of litigation, which are the child's best interests. Nevertheless, there always will be situations in which children's will oppose parents' rights and this is not only dependent on the societal values but also the individual relationship and particularity of the case. The best interests principle should be interpreted as giving priority to children in relation to their parents when there is a clash between their interests. See more in Boele-Woelki K. *et al.*, *Principles of European Family Law Regarding Parental Responsibilities*, Intersentia, 2007, pp. 37 and 38. The best interests of the child in terms of the child's right to be informed, consulted and to express his or her opinion in all matters that concern him or her in proceedings before a competent authority to determine the allocation of parental responsibilities, and in resolving disputes about the exercise of parental responsibilities is also safeguarded in the Draft Recommendation, article 21.

a fair trial (article 6(a) ECHR and article 10 UDHR) which in many national regulations is overlooked (among which, in the Republic of Macedonia, it is explicitly and deliberately disregarded).[1145]

The CRC Committee emphasised the necessity of a registration system accessible to all and free of charge, so that all children can be registered at birth without discrimination of any kind.[1146] Even though the Convention does not explicitly stipulate which information must be registered, it is suggested that minimum requirements should be considered: the child's name at birth, sex, date and location of birth, and the parents' names, addresses and nationality statuses.[1147]

The CRC frames the family affiliation in terms of rights: the right of the child to know and be cared for by its parents, "as far as possible"[1148] (article 7), and the right of the child to preserve his or her identity, including family relations as recognised by law without unlawful interference (article 8).

The national regulations of the State Parties have responded differently to this challenge in the field of children's rights. The United Kingdom interprets parents as only those who are treated as such as a matter of national law. This also includes cases when the child has only one parent, irrespective of the reasons – adopted by one person, or conceived with gamete donation to one person.[1149] In view of the expected problems with the practice of secret adoption, the former Union of Soviet Socialist Republics objected to a more absolute definition upholding "secret" adoptions.[1150] To prevent the controversies that article 7 may cause regarding anonymous donations or adoptions, several countries – the Czech Republic,[1151] Poland and Luxembourg – have entered reservations.[1152] The Norwegian Committee on the Rights of the Child acknowledged the possible contradiction between the child's right to know his or her genetic origins and the policies of State Parties "in relation to artificial insemination namely in keeping

1145 See footnote 310.

1146 Committee on the Rights of the Child, General Comment No. 7, 2005, CRC/C/GC/7/Rev.1, para. 25.

1147 Hodgkin R., Newell P., *Implementation Handbook for the Convention on the Rights of the Child*, UNICEF, United Children's Fund, 2007, p. 101.

1148 The words "as far as possible" were incorporated into the Convention as insisted on by the delegations of the United States and Germany in response to the original draft submitted by a few countries (Algeria, Egypt, Iraq, Jordan, Kuwait, Libyan, Arab Jamahiriya, Morocco, Oman, Pakistan and Tunisia). For a commentary on the CRC, see Ziemele I., *A Commentary on the United Nations Convention on the Rights of the Child. Article 7 – The Right to Birth Registration, Name and Nationality, and the right to Know and Be Cared for by Parents*, Martinus Nijhoff, 2007, p. 153.

1149 Hodgkin R., Newell P., *Implementation Handbook for the Convention on the Rights of the Child*, UNICEF, United Children's Fund, 2007, p. 105, referring to CRC/C/2/Rev.8, p. 42.

1150 *Ibid.* p. 105, referring to E/CN.4/1989/48, pp. 18–22.

1151 The Czech Republic expressed reservations with respect to both artificial insemination and secret adoption. See more in *ibid.* p. 105 referring to the Czech Republic, CRC/C/2/Rev.8, p. 20.

1152 Ziemele I., *A Commentary on the United Nations Convention on the Rights of the Child. Article 7 – The Right to Birth Registration, Name and Nationality, and the right to Know and Be Cared for by Parents*, Martinus Nijhoff, 2007, p. 154.

the identity of donors secret".[1153] Permitting mothers to give birth anonymously in France and Luxembourg was interpreted as deemed to be in the best interests of the child, and thus not endangered by article 7.[1154] Nevertheless, seeing no obstacle regarding children born anonymously (under X) was not seen enthusiastically. On the contrary, it was encouraged for the State Parties to take all necessary measures to prevent and eliminate the practice.[1155]

The CRC Committee has objected to national laws which do not allow children which are adopted or conceived by gamete donations to find out who their biological parents are.[1156] It also recommended that "the State Party should ensure, as far as possible[1157] respect for the child's right to know his or her parents' identities".[1158] From such commentaries it may be inferred that the right contained in articles 7 and 8 may indeed include knowledge of genetic parentage and that the words "as far as possible" should be interpreted as requiring a significant effort on the part of State Parties to enable children to have access to such information, regardless of the way in which they have been conceived, the circumstances under which they have been born or the form of their legal parents' relationship.[1159]

It has been suggested that these rights should be observed in the context of three other rights stipulated in: article 5, which also includes the members of the extended family or community as provided for by local custom; article 9, which requires that children should not be separated from their parents against their will, except when such separation is in their best interests; and article 18 which stipulates the joint responsibility of both parents for the care of their children.[1160]

For some authors, the child's genuine personal, legal and familial identity is wide in scope, including also siblings, grandparents and other relatives who appear to be important in the child's life.[1161] Article 7 promotes an established

[1153] *Ibid.* p. 108.

[1154] *Ibid.* p. 105 referring to CRC/C/2/Rev.8, p. 28.

[1155] *Ibid.* p. 106 referring to Luxembourg CRC/C/15/Add.250, paras. 28 and 29.

[1156] Ziemele I., *A Commentary on the United Nations Convention on the Rights of the Child. Article 7 – The Right to Birth Registration, Name and Nationality, and the right to Know and Be Cared for by Parents*, Martinus Nijhoff, 2007, p. 27 referring to the CRC Committee, *Concluding Observations: Kazakhstan Un Doc. CRC/C/15/Add.213, 2003, Estonia UN Doc. CRC/C/15/Add.196*, 2003. See also Hodgkin R., Newell P., *Implementation Handbook for the Convention on the Rights of the Child*, UNICEF, United Children's Fund, 2007, p. 106 referring to Armenia CRC/C/15/Add.225, para. 38. See also Russian Federation CRC/C/RUS/CO/3, paras. 40 and 41, Uzbekistan CRC/C/UZB/CO/2, paras. 40 and 41, and Norway CRC/C/15/Add.23, para. 10.

[1157] For a discussion of the interpretation of the term "as far as possible", see more in the text to footnotes 144, 148, 150, 151, 152 and 153.

[1158] See Switzerland CRC/C/15/Add.182, paras. 28 and 29.

[1159] See also Pluym L., "Het recht van het kind om zijn ouders te kennen (art. 7.1 IVRK) na heterologe medisch begeleide voortplanting, adoptie en draagmoederschap in België", *Tijdschrift voor Jeugd en Kinderrechten*, p. 9, March 2012.

[1160] Hodgkin R., Newell P., *Implementation Handbook for the Convention on the Rights of the Child*, UNICEF, United Children's Fund, 2007, p. 108.

[1161] Hodgkin R., Newell P., *Implementation Handbook for the Convention on the Rights of the Child*, UNICEF, United Children's Fund, 2007, p. 114.

relationship that should be nurtured, fostered and preserved.[1162] The right of an established relationship and thus to be taken care of is immediately dependent on the right to establish contact. The Convention on Contact concerning Children of the Council of Europe[1163] defines "family ties" as "a close relationship such as between a child and his or her grandparents or siblings, based on law or on a *de facto* family relationship".[1164] This means recognition of both legal and social family relations, as a prerequisite for furthermore establishing contact. Article 4 entitles both the child and the parent to obtain and maintain regular contact with each other (paragraph 1), allowing exceptions only when the best interests of the child make it a necessity (paragraph 2). Article 5 goes even further, extending the right to contact of the child also to the other persons which have family ties with the child. Principle 3:5 of the *Principles on European Family Law regarding Parental Responsibilities* deals with the contact of the child with the parents and the other persons (close relatives or other persons with whom the child has close personal relations).[1165] Once again, the application of these articles depends on who is considered to be a parent: the genetic, the legal or the social parent and how the family tree ramification (legally recognised or not) develops from here on.

The most closely related to article 7 is article 8 that suggests to the State Parties to respect the right of the child to preserve his or her identity, including family relations as recognised by law without unlawful interference. In its paragraph 2, it goes even further in suggesting that in cases where the child is illegally deprived of some or all of the elements of his or her identity, they should provide assistance and protection with a view to speedily re-establish his or her identity. Other aspects of the child's identity are addressed in other articles (article 16 insofar as it protects against arbitrary interference in privacy, family and home; article 30, as it provides to enjoy culture, religion and language; and article 20, as it provides that children deprived of their family environment should, where possible, have continuity of upbringing, particularly with regard to their ethnic, cultural and linguistic background).[1166] The use of "family relations as recognised by law" in article 8 is left rather vague after discussions on the relevancy of the "genuine personal family identity" for the "family identity as recognised by the law".[1167]

1162 *Ibid.*

1163 Convention on Contact Concerning Children, Council of Europe, ETS No. 192, Strasbourg, 15 May 2003.

1164 Article 2(d) Convention on Contact Concerning Children.

1165 Boele-Woelki K. *et al.*, *Principles of European Family Law Regarding Parental Responsibilities*, Intersentia, 2007, p. 164.

1166 Hodgkin R., Newell P., *Implementation Handbook for the Convention on the Rights of the Child*, UNICEF, United Children's Fund, 2007, p. 113.

1167 As the article initially suggested by Argentine had an idea of including more than just legal forms of identity. See more in Hodgkin R., Newell P., *Implementation Handbook for the Convention on the Rights of the Child*, UNICEF, United Children's Fund, 2007, p. 114, referring to E/CN.4/1986/39.

On the other hand, the phrase "speedily re-establish" the child's identity should also encompass an understanding that the child might have also developed another cultural and social identity in the environment where it was placed. Thus, removing him/her from the new environment could be treated as a second deprivation of identity, and unacceptable in terms of the child's best interests.[1168] This could be troublesome for parents who have been illegally separated from their children, but it could also cause serious hardship and harm to parents who still do not have that status for different reasons (for instance, when the genetic father of a child is not informed by the mother regarding the birth, or he is informed but barred from rebutting the fatherhood of her legal husband to whom the marital presumption of being a father applies). These practices are not unfamiliar to the ECtHR. As a matter of fact, the Court has been more in favour of protecting the new established social reality than preserving the genetic identity.[1169]

Separation from parents as stipulated in article 9 could be due to a variety of reasons, one of which is custom-related when the child is conceived out of wedlock.[1170] Another could be related to the contact given to the non-resident parent following parental separation in countries that do not recognise the concept of joint parental responsibilities.[1171] Article 9 in conjunction with article 18 guarantees the right to the child to be cared for by both parents who should share common responsibility for its upbringing, development and best interests. The CRC Committee has made it clear that a State Party should establish precise criteria for limiting the parent–child relationship and the parental rights. It also recommends that the State Parties should take all necessary measures to ensure that both parents and children are given an opportunity to participate in the proceedings and make their views known in accordance with article 9.[1172]

The United Nations Standard Minimum Rules for the Administration of Juvenile Justice (the so-called "Beijing Rules") extend the scope of the rules to care and welfare proceedings, stressing the need for privacy, speed, the child's right to representation, to the presence of parents, appeal procedures, powers to discontinue proceedings, good record keeping and research-based policy.[1173] In addition, the CRC Committee has acknowledged that family law practice should be accessible to everybody, and that family law procedures should be conducted without undue delay.[1174] Furthermore, it is important that "all interested parties be given an opportunity to participate in the proceedings and make their views

[1168] *Ibid.* p. 117.

[1169] See footnote 851.

[1170] For this, the Committee on the Rights of the Child has already given encouragement to the Sri Lanka authorities to give full support to mothers who wish to keep their children born out of wedlock. See more in Sri Lanka CRC/C/15/Add.40, para. 34.

[1171] As for instance, in the Republic of Macedonia. See in Family Law, articles 80, 81 and 82.

[1172] Lithuania CRC/C/LTU/CO/2, para. 40.

[1173] Hodgkin R., Newell P., *Implementation Handbook for the Convention on the Rights of the Child*, UNICEF, United Children's Fund, 2007, p. 129.

[1174] Nicaragua CRC/C/15/Add.265, para. 37.

known".[1175] This means that even a non-resident father or a parent who is absent for a certain period of time should be given an opportunity to show care and affection towards the child. Even though a definition is not given of the scope of persons who could qualify as "interested parties" and the interpretation is left to the domestic legislation, it could be expected that it should include any family member related to the child up to a particular line. This in conjunction with article 12(2) means that the child should be directly engaged (personally or through representative) in any judicial and administrative proceedings that affect his/her interests.

Article 9(3) promotes ongoing personal relationships and direct contact with both parents on a regular basis, unless contrary to the child's best interests. The article refers to the relationship with the parent from whom the child is separated, thus encompassing only legally recognised parents to whom custody is granted. Nevertheless, the CRC Committee recognised that statusless fathers of children born out of wedlock may be deprived from this possibility, and urged State Parties to provide for the possibility to request custody.[1176] Seeking custody for genetic fathers of children born out of wedlock assumes their status as a father already. This in a context of sperm donations could be interpreted as if the donor is already a father who could ask or not for custody, and thus status as a father.

Regarding these conflicting rights, some authors suggest a greater shift from parent-centred to child-centred national family laws.[1177] According to Vonk, the dignity of every child (also when born in an atypical family) deserves respect departing from the notion that all children should have the most favourable position in life.[1178] The author associates this with a new concept of procreational responsibility both before and after conception.[1179] In the first context, the personal integrity of the child to be conceived entails ensuring that the child's genetic/biological history is available for the child at a later date considering the roles of the participants when known sperm donors are used. In the second context, the procreational responsibility entails care for the child during its life and is a basis for attributing legal parenthood to the parent. From here, the author develops two systems of legal parenthood in cases of donor-assisted families: (1) legal parenthood for intentional parents without evaluating the donor's intentions, and (2) legal parenthood for intentional parents with regard

1175 Hodgkin R., Newell P., *Implementation Handbook for the Convention on the Rights of the Child*, UNICEF, United Children's Fund, 2007, p. 129.

1176 Liechtenstein CRC/C/LIE/CO/2, paras. 18 and 19.

1177 See, for instance, Vonk M., 'Towards a New Concept of Parenthood: Procreational Responsibility", Boele-Woelki K., Sverdrup T. (eds.), *European Challenges in Contemporary Family Law*, Intersentia, 2008, p. 131. This author tackles the concept of parenthood and procreational responsibility on the basis of the notions that (1) a child's family situation deserves legal protection, and (2) a child should have the possibility to acquire two legal parents.

1178 *Ibid.* p. 132.

1179 *Ibid.* p. 146.

to the intentions of the donor.[1180] Other authors argue the moral component of the parenthood claiming that not only that it is possible, but also it is sometimes necessary to distinguish parenthood as a genealogical (i.e. biological) category from parenthood as a moral category. As such, in cases of necessary conflict, parenthood as a moral commitment should take priority over parenthood as a biological patrimony. Accordingly, an attribution parent in the moral sense is the permanent commitment to unconditionally love and care for the physical, emotional, moral and spiritual welfare of the child.[1181]

On the other hand, conflicting rights could also be observed from a perspective of human rights as protected in the constitution or as interpreted by the ECtHR. In this light, other authors suggest that conflicts of fundamental rights should be observed beyond their paradigm value, dignity or utility on a level of constitutionally entrenched rules (as a permission to do or to refrain from doing something).[1182] As such, they have identifiable right-holders and assignable duty-bearers; thus the court is empowered to invalidate action taken by parliament and compensate them for any possible damage.[1183] Zucca suggests that the constitutionally protected liberties should be viewed in terms of Rawls' system of basic liberties as mutually and not just individually adjusted, thus allowing constitutional constructivism which expands into creating a system for the resolution of difficult questions.[1184]

Other authors criticise too much delegation of the human rights conflicts by the ECtHR to national legislation under the "excuse" of the doctrine of margin of appreciation. Namely, whenever the Court encounters policy or other sensitive issues for which there is not a consensus among the Member States, it uses the margin of appreciation doctrine, thus leaving the balancing up to the domestic authorities.[1185] Even though some mechanism of weighing exists and some rights are given priority over others (for instance the right to life over the right to private life, or children's rights over adults' rights), still some aspects of children's rights are protected more than others just because of greater consensus among the Member States (for instance there is a greater level of consensus when it comes to custody cases as compared to access to information cases).[1186] Apart from these, there is a lack of explicit rules concerning conflict resolution that would increase

---

1180 *Ibid.* pp. 149 and 150.

1181 Berkman J., "Virtuous Parenting and Orphaned Embryos, Human Embryo Adoption, Bioetechnology, Marriage, and the Right to Life", in Berg T.V., Furton E.J. (eds.), *Human Embryo Adoption: Biotechnology, Marriage, and the Right to Life*, The National Bioethics Center and the Westchester Institute for Ethics and the Human Person, 2006.

1182 Zucca L., "Conflicts of Fundamental Rights as Constitutional Dilemmas", in Brems E. (ed.), *Conflicts Between Fundamental Rights*, Intersentia, 2008, p. 21.

1183 *Ibid.*

1184 *Ibid.* pp. 33 and 34. See also Rawls J., *A Theory of Justice*, Harvard University Press, 1989 (revised edition), Rawls J., *Political Liberalism* (2nd edition), Columbia University Press, 2005.

1185 *Ibid.* p. 53.

1186 *Ibid.* p. 53.

legal certainty, rule of law, justice and equality in treating similar cases alike on a universal level.[1187]

Principle 3:7 of the *Principles of European Family Law regarding Parental Responsibilities* also deals with the conflict of interests between the child and the holders of parental responsibilities.[1188] The notion that the child's best interests have to be always considered as "a primary consideration" resolves the conflicts in favour of the child as a principal rule. This is enabled by, firstly, recognising the child's right to autonomy (Principle 3:4) and, secondly, introducing mechanisms for the child to access the information necessary to participate in the decision-making process that concerns him or her (Principle 3:6). Next to these two prerequisites, the child may need an independent representative who will protect his/her rights when they are in conflict with the holders of the parental responsibilities.[1189]

The right to private life as protected by the ECHR is, by definition, never absolute,[1190] thus is prone to be the subject of conflict between different holders. The second paragraph of article 8 lists a number of goals which legitimise interferences with the protected right in the first paragraph, including protection of the rights and freedoms of others. Certain personal relationships which do not strictly qualify as family life (because of lack of legal or "actual" family ties) have already been resumed under the umbrella of private life by the ECtHR due to their potential to become one (as in the cases of potential future children conceived through IVF or adopted after birth).[1191] On the other hand, the notion of *private life* could conflict with other persons' *privacy rights*, in terms of their decisional freedom, which also falls under the scope of private life.[1192] The ECtHR already encountered such conflicts in cases of requests for access to identifying information about descent on condition of his confidentiality,[1193] obtaining a paternity test from a person against his will (and his protected bodily integrity)[1194] or identifying information about a mother who gave birth anonymously.[1195] From the Court's reasoning it seems that the interpretation of *private life* in different legislative contexts depends on the qualification of whether balance is achieved at

1187 *Ibid.* p. 52.

1188 Boele-Woelki K. *et al.*, *Principles of European Family Law Regarding Parental Responsibilities*, Intersentia, 2007, p. 56.

1189 Article 4(1), Convention on the Exercise of Children's Rights. Other documents that favour the child's position in a conflict with parents are: the CRC (article 3), the European Charter on Fundamental Rights (article II-84, paragraph 2), the Draft Treaty for a European Constitution 2003 (article II-84, paragraph 2).

1190 Ieven A., "Privacy Rights in Conflict: In Search of the Theoretical Framework Behind the European Court of Human Rights' Balancing of Private Life against Other Rights", in Brems E. (ed.), *Conflicts Between Fundamental Rights*, Intersentia, 2008, p. 40.

1191 *Ibid.* p. 40.

1192 *Ibid.* pp. 44 and 45.

1193 *Gaskin v. the United Kingdom*, European Court of Human Rights, No. 10454/83, judgment of 07.07.1989.

1194 *Mikulic v. Croatia*, European Court of Human Rights, No. 53176/99, judgment of 07.02.2002.

1195 *Odièvre v. France*, European Court of Human Rights, No. 42326/98, judgment of 13.02.2003.

a point at which the national institutions stayed within or exceeded the margin of appreciation afforded to it under article 8.[1196]

6.3.2. HARMONISING DIFFERENCES BETWEEN CHILDREN CONCEIVED "NATURALLY" AND "ARTIFICIALLY"

The idea of equality for all human beings deserving respect and dignity of equal worth is connected with the idea of liberty: "to respect the equal worth of persons is, among other things, to promote their ability to fashion a life in accordance with their own view of what is deepest and most important".[1197] As such, this respect should not be endangered by characteristics attributed by the whims of fortune.[1198] It is the dignity of the child born into an atypical family (in this case, comprising a mother and a child only) that deserves respect. Placing a category of children in a position less favourable than the majority of their peers through no action or choice of their own is obvious inequality.

The discussions over the position of children conceived by sperm donation to single women in an attempt to bring them closer to those conceived "naturally" are centred on the following issues.

6.3.2.1. The reasons why children should have a right to access the data on their genetic origin

As has been shown in the previous text, there is evidence that the majority of children conceived through donor insemination wish to know the donor's identity. There is also evidence suggesting the opposite.[1199] The main arguments supporting the right of the child to know their genetic origin are connected with the right to personal identity. According to some authors, genes play an important role in the physical and intellectual characteristics of a person.[1200] Some others define identity as a complex construct that operates on psychological, political, personal and social levels taking shape by contemplating difference and sameness.[1201] Denial of

1196 Ieven A., "Privacy Rights in Conflict: In Search of the Theoretical Framework Behind the European Court of Human Rights' Balancing of Private Life against Other Rights", in Brems E. (ed.), *Conflicts Between Fundamental Rights*, Intersentia, 2008, p. 47 referring to the ECtHR statement in the case of *Evans v. the United Kingdom*, para. 91, judgment of 10.04.2007.

1197 Nussbaum M.C., *Sex and Social Justice*, Oxford University Press, 1998, p. 5.

1198 *Ibid.*

1199 Janssens P.M.W., Simons A.H.M., Van Kooij R.J., Blokzijl E., Dunselman A.A.J., "A New Dutch Law Regulating Provision of Identifying Information of Donors to Offspring: Background, Content and Impact", *Human Reproduction*, Vol. 21, No. 4, 2006, p. 854.

1200 Ladau R., Weissenberg R., "Disclosure of Donor Conception in Single-Mother Families: Views and Concerns", *Human Reproduction*, Vol. 25, No. 4, 2010, pp. 942–948.

1201 Richards B., "What is Identity?", in Gaber I., Aldridge J. (eds.), *The Best Interests of the Child, Culture, Identity, and Transracial Adoption*, Free Association Books, 1994.

knowledge of a genetic parent can have psychological implications for the donor's offspring who may feel deprived of information they need to develop a full sense of identity.[1202] The other arguments that support the right to know where one comes from are related to the possibility of transmission of genetic disorders, as well as the possibility of incest through a relationship between siblings unaware of their genetic connection.[1203] To have the right to access the genetic data does not exclude the right not to access the genetic data. Nevertheless, from the evidence on children's interests, the possibility of a choice should be given to those who are affected the most by this decision.

6.3.2.2. The reasons why children's parents/the state should have a right to make the genetic origin a non-accessible secret

A number of studies suggest that the reason why single mothers by choice want to keep the genetic data of their offspring secret is derived from their wish for parental exclusivity, preventing interference with their family by a strange, unknown man.[1204] The reason why some fathers (being because their partner was inseminated by sperm donation) support secrecy is the fear of rejection of their paternal role and the fear that the donor might take over.[1205] In a study regarding the factors associated with the parents' decision on revealing the biological truth, five dominant tendencies were found: (1) the impact of secrecy on them as parents, (2) the reason why they wanted to reveal the secret afterwards, (3) their anxiety regarding the secrecy, (4) the wish that they could have had disclosed it much earlier, and (5) the recalled comments from their children that they suspected the secret about their family origin.[1206]

Existent data in the international literature show that the majority of parents who used a semen donor intend to, or actually do, tell their offspring that they were conceived by donor insemination. The number of those who intend to tell, though, is higher than those who actually do.[1207] Most of the national states' regulations are still falling behind in accepting the fragmentation of parenthood

---

1202 Baran A., Pannor R., *Lethal Secrecies: the Psychology of Donor Insemination, Problem and Solution*, Amistead Press, 1993.

1203 Morton M., Irving M.A., "Common Questions that Arise in Adoption", in Turnpenny P. (ed.), *Secrets in the Genes: Adoption, Inheritance and Genetic Disease*, British Agencies for Adoption and Fostering, 1995.

1204 See, for instance, Landau R., Weissenberg R., "Disclosure of Donor Conception in Single-mother Families: Views and Concerns", *Human Reproduction*, Vol. 25, No. 4, 2010, p. 944.

1205 Daniels K.R., Grace V.M., Gillett W.R., "Factors Associated with Parents' Decisions to Tell Their Adult Offspring about the Offspring's Donor' Conception", *Human Reproduction*, Vo. 26, No. 10, 2011, p. 2787.

1206 *Ibid.* p. 2785.

1207 Janssens P.M.W., Simons A.H.M., Van Kooij R.J., Blokzijl E., Dunselman A.A.J., "A New Dutch Law Regulating Provision of Identifying Information of Donors to Offspring: Background, Content and Impact", *Human Reproduction*, Vol. 21, No. 4, 2006, p. 854 referring to the studies of Rumbar and Adair (1999); Gottlieb *et al.* (2000); Schein *et al.* (2003); Cook *et al.* (1995); Golombok *et al.* (2004).

caused by gamete donations in their affiliation laws, and consequently in their parental proceedings. This is again associated with the fear of unpredicted situations that may disturb the already established grounds for legal certainty in family matters. In the pioneering countries that have introduced an open-identity system, the motives of the donors changed from strictly altruistic to procreative. Some authors explain this with the fact that donors motivated by a desire to procreate appear to find it less problematic that their offspring might discover their identity and possibly contact them.[1208]

6.3.2.3. The reasons why children conceived "naturally" and "artificially" are treated differently by law

It is evident that there is a difference in the treatment of children depending on the context in which they are born. One could question the legitimacy of introducing an action solely designed to ascertain genetic parentage without a possibility of creating any legal relationship in cases of artificial conceptions.[1209] This is in contrast to paternal proceedings that grounded on biological facts of DNA tests force establishment of the genetic father, granting mandatory legal relationship in cases of natural conceptions.[1210]

The ECtHR has never safeguarded the notion that the child has a right to a relationship with the father as from the time of birth (apart from in marital cases). On the contrary, it has always been a question to investigate whether there is a family life relationship upon which the legal parenthood could be grounded. This opposes the supremacy of genetics in legal affiliations. Even more, the practice of the Court has shown more sympathy towards the social bond established later on with the partner of the mother that inclines towards doing the caring role for the child as in contrast to favouring genetic ties.[1211]

If national regulations on legal affiliation and paternal proceedings incorporate the fact that biological/genetic, social and legal parents do not overlap in one person in cases of donor inseminations, it should be more evident to determine the limits of the actions towards establishing parenthood. It should be clear that "biology" is only one "fundament", next to "intention", to base legal parentage upon.[1212]

1208 *Ibid.* p. 855.

1209 See more in footnotes 951 and 952.

1210 See more in footnote 240.

1211 See more in the cases of *Söderbäck v. Sweden*, European Court of Human Rights, No. 24484/97, judgment of 28.10.1998; *Kroon v. the Netherlands*, European Court of Human Rights, No. 18535/91, judgment of 27.10.1994; *Lebbink v. the Netherlands*, European Court of Human Rights, No. 45582/99, judgment of 01.06.2004.

1212 Vonk M., *Children and their Parents, A Comparative Study of the Legal Position of Children with Regard to their Intentional and Biological Parents in English and Dutch Law,* Intersentia, 2007, p. 267.

The comparative legal experience of countries discussing the anonymity of donors implies that there are arguments that support the right of donors to anonymity, especially in terms of personal property of their own genetic material as well as privacy of their reproductive choices. Nevertheless, the recent tendencies towards promoting child-centred family policies support the right of the child to know his/her origin and override the interests of donors and legal parents. These can be listed as follows:

1. Promoting equality of all children without any discrimination concerning the nature of their conception and the reproductive choices of their parents;
2. Promoting the best interests of the child when medical information about the genetic hereditary construction is important;
3. Prevalence of the right to personal identity as a complex construct in the context of family life, familial kinship and affiliation over the desires and wishes of anonymous donors and parents who claim exclusivity of their parenthood;
4. Prevalence of the concept that treats children as active subjects and appreciates their views as important in matters that affect them as in contrast to the paternalistic approach of parents to bring choices in advance on behalf of them;
5. The importance of knowing the genetic links can prevent incestuous relationships by blood relatives and inbreeding, which can increase the chances of the offspring being affected by recessive or deleterious traits and;
6. Psychological security of children, donors and legal parents as an anxiety relief connected with keeping a secret.

If we accept the presumption that it is in the best interests of all children to be registered, to know, and to be taken care of by both parents, while at the same time promoting the most favourable position for all children, then the practice of single women conceiving with anonymous sperm donations under rigid circumstances that ban any future paternal inquiries is hypocritical. Not only does the realisation of the individual reproductive right not go together with the right of the child conceived that way to have two parents, but moreover they exclude each other. Therefore national regulations that allow single women to reproduce without additionally paying attention to the right of the child to know and possibly have two parents promote adults' individual rights over children's rights. An example of a more child-sensitive approach that tries to balance the rights of the concerned parties in the reproductive project is the regulation of New Zealand that considers the child's interests to derive from sperm donations as important for appreciation. The New Zealand Law Commission in the Discussion Paper on Legal Parenthood before considering the possibility to introduce a concept with more parents in the child's life[1213] underlined several principles:

1. Children have a right to know the circumstances of their conception and birth.
2. Persons raising children should have the legal responsibilities and rights necessary to nurture and rear the child.
3. A child can have a number of committed and co-operative adults involved in his or her upbringing, provided that these people always have clear lines of responsibility and mechanisms for dealing with conflict (collaborative and autonomous parenthood should be facilitated by legal process).
4. Children are to be equal and they and their families not disadvantaged by the circumstances of their creation or form of family.[1214]

A number of authors promote an inclusive legal concept of multiple parenthood that includes all possible parents in the child's life.[1215] According to definitions in recent international instruments, the term "holder of parental responsibilities" can be attributed to more than two persons, encompassing some or all parental responsibilities.[1216] Principle 19 of the *White Paper* states that the parental responsibilities should as a principle belong to both parents. Principle 20 (paragraph 3) allows a person other than a parent to exercise some or all parental responsibilities in addition to or instead of parents upon a decision being made by a competent authority. The Brussels II bis Regulation (Article 2(8)) under the term "holder of parental responsibilities" encompasses any person having parental responsibility over a child.[1217] This would mean a possibility of all interested parties participating with full or partial responsibilities for the upbringing of the child. The formula does not impose choosing between the two possible parents but acknowledging that the child might have interests and rights in securing a relationship with both.[1218] It would represent the prerogative of the child's best interests the most in the context of the socially stigmatised practice of assisted

1213 See more in the 2005 New Zealand Law Commission's Report, No. 88 on New Issues in Legal Parenthood, available online: www.lawcom.govt.nz/sites/default/files/publications/2005/04/Publication_91_315_R88.pdf.

1214 See more in the *Law Commission Preliminary Paper 54, New Issues in Legal Parenthood. A Discussion Paper*, Wellington, New Zealand, 2004, pp. 5–7.

1215 See, for instance, Vonk M., *Children and their Parents, A Comparative Study of the Legal Position of Children with Regard to their Intentional and Biological Parents in English and Dutch Law*, Intersentia, 2007; Bainham A., "The Rights and Obligations Associated with the Birth of a Child", in Spencer J.R., Du Bois-Pedain A. (eds.), *Freedom and Responsibility in Reproductive Choice*, Hart Publishing, 2006.

1216 Article 2(b), European Convention on the Exercise of Children's Rights, Council of Europe, 1996.

1217 See footnote 136.

1218 Bainham A., "The Rights and Obligations Associated with the Birth of a Child", in Spencer J.R., Du Bois-Pedain A. (eds.), *Freedom and Responsibility in Reproductive Choice*, Hart Publishing, 2006.

reproductions. It would also show greater appreciation of the international documents such as article 7 of the CRC and article 8 of the ECHR. As such, it should be regarded seriously as an obligation to be implemented by Member States and not as an optional choice of national regulations.[1219]

[1219] *Ibid.*

PART III

LEGAL WAYS OF ESTABLISHING FATHERHOOD

CHAPTER 7

ESTABLISHING FATHERHOOD THROUGH AN INTERNATIONAL PRISM

The growing interest in giving children a central position with a legal emphasis on their autonomy and priority of their rights has led to their procedural rights, but also to greater complexity in court proceedings concerning attribution and exercise of parental responsibilities in Europe[1220] and in the USA.[1221]

The history of international regulations dealing with the establishment or contestation of a parent–child relationship in Europe can be traced to the activities of the International Commission on Civil Status (ICCS)[1222] and its consequential conventions: the Convention Extending the Competence of Authorities Empowered to Receive Declarations Acknowledging Natural Children (Rome, 14 September 1961),[1223] the Convention on the Establishment of Maternal Descent of Natural Children (Brussels, 12 September 1962),[1224] the Convention on Legitimation by Marriage (Rome, 10 September 1970)[1225] and the Convention on the Voluntary Acknowledgement of Children Born Out of Wedlock (Munich, 5 September 1980).[1226] The identity status in terms of name and forename, extracts from civil status records concerning (*inter alia*) the birth of the child, and the international exchange of information relating to it have been regulated in the following conventions and recommendations: the Convention on Changes of Surnames and Forenames (Istanbul, 4 September 1958),[1227] the Convention on the Law Applicable to Surnames and Forenames (Munich, 5 September 1980),[1228] the

---

1220 Lowe N.V., Douglas G. (eds.), *Bromley's Family Law* (10th edition), Oxford University Press, 2007.

1221 Bainham A., *Children: The Modern Law* (3rd edition), Jordan Publishing, 2005; Guggenheim M., *What's Wrong with Children's Rights?*, Harvard University Press, 2005.

1222 The ICCS is an intergovernmental organisation with an aim to facilitate international co-operation in civil-status matters and to improve the operation of national civil-status departments. For more see: www.dialogueuroafricainmd.net/web/uploads/activity/civil_registry/more_documents/Supporting-Documents-ICCS.pdf, p. 1.

1223 http://ciecl.org/Conventions/Conv05Angl.pdf.

1224 http://ciecl.org/Conventions/Conv06Angl.pdf.

1225 http://ciecl.org/Conventions/Conv12Angl.pdf.

1226 http://ciecl.org/Conventions/Conv18Angl.pdf.

1227 www.refworld.org/pdfid/3decd4747.pdf.

1228 http://ciecl.org/Conventions/Conv19Angl.pdf.

Convention on the Recognition of Surnames (Antalya, 16 September 2005),[1229] the Convention on the Issue of Certain Extracts from Civil-Status Records for Use Abroad (Paris, 27 September 1956),[1230] the Convention on the International Exchange of Information Relating to Civil Status (Istanbul, 4 September 1958)[1231] and its Additional Protocol (Patras, 6 September 1989), the Recommendation Relating to the Publicity of Civil-Status Registers and Records (Lisbon, 10 September 1987), the Recommendation Relating to the Harmonisation of Civil-Status Records (Lisbon, 10 September 1987), and the Recommendation on the Harmonisation of Extracts from Civil Status Records (Madrid, 7 September 1990).[1232]

The Commission on European Family Law (CEFL) was established in 2001 comprising approximately 26 distinguished experts in the field of family and comparative law from all European Union Member States and other European countries.[1233] The main goal was to launch a pioneering theoretical and practical ground on the path towards harmonising family laws in Europe. This was done by comparative research on family laws on national levels in an attempt to explore possible common core principles that cover several legal problems: divorce and maintenance, parental responsibilities, and property relations. As a result, a set of *Principles of European Family Law* was created that was a serious starting point and a basis for potential harmonisation of family law within Europe.[1234] The set aims and objectives were addressed to national legislators in their quest to modernise their national laws. Nevertheless, they also had a role as a source of inspiration for both European and international legislature.[1235] The Council of Europe also recognised the need for comparative surveys and research in the field of family law, taking into account both the peculiarities of the concept of private and family life in national legislation, but also the nature of it that goes beyond national borders (in cross-border family relationships, for instance, in the cases of international marriages or custody issues).[1236] This resulted in several activities through meetings and consequently reports and draft recommendations of the CJ-FA Working Group No. 3 on the new legal instrument on the rights and legal

1229 www.ciecl.org/Conventions/Conv31Angl.pdf.

1230 http://ciecl.org/Conventions/Conv01Angl.pdf.

1231 http://ciecl.org/Conventions/Conv03Angl.pdf.

1232 For more see in: www.dialogueuroafricainmd.net/web/uploads/activity/civil_registry/more_documents/Supporting-Documents-ICCS.pdf, p. 6.

1233 The other (potential future European Union Member States) countries were also included in the survey in order to contribute to the process of harmonisation of the family law on a European level, thus making the application of the principles more universal. See more on the website of the CEFL: http://ceflonline.net/history/.

1234 The *Principles of European Family Law* consist of 39 principles based on 22 national reports and the relevant international and European documents in the field.

1235 Boele-Woelki K. *et al.*, *Principles of European Family Law Regarding Parental Responsibilities*, Intersentia, 2007, Preface, p. v.

1236 Council of Europe, Human Rights and Rule of Law, Family, available online: www.coe.int/t/dghl/standardsetting/family/Introduction_en.asp.

status of children and parental responsibilities. The most relevant for the purposes of establishing parenthood, therefore, for this book are the Report on Principles Concerning the Establishment and Legal Consequences of Parentage (the White Paper),[1237] and the more recent Draft Report of the fifth meeting drafting also Recommendation on the Rights and Legal Status of Children and Parental Responsibilities (the Draft Recommendation)[1238] following after the Guidelines on Child-friendly Justice, adopted by the Committee of Ministers in 2010.[1239] These documents do not have to be formally signed or ratified by the Member States. Consequently, there are no sanctions against their "non-compliance". Nevertheless, the Council of Europe prescribes them relevancy to some extent by requesting Member States' governments to monitor their implementation and to inform on the actions taken accordingly.[1240] Their utility has been located in: (1) assisting Member States to implement existing conventions, (2) providing international encouragement to Member States to ensure that their national laws comply with the recommendations, and (3) enriching the practice of the ECtHR when determining the extent to which a particular legal solution has been commonly embraced in the Member States.[1241] The Draft Recommendation explicitly restricts its scope to exclude private international law issues. In these terms, the instrument does not oblige *stricto sensu* states to recognise a status accepted by another state (for instance registered partnerships, extra-marital relationships, etc.).[1242] The flexible nature of family issues depending on the systems of values surrounding different national contexts still presents obstacles for harmonisation of the family laws on a European or international level (as elaborated earlier).[1243]

1237 *Report on Principles Concerning the Establishment and Legal Consequences of Parentage – White Paper*, Committee of Experts on Family Law, 2006, available online: www.coe.int/t/dghl/standardsetting/family/CJFA_2006_4e%20Revised%20White%20Paper.pdf.

1238 *Draft Report of the Fifth Meeting*, Committee of Experts on Family Law tasked to draft one or more legal instruments on the Rights and Legal Status of Children and Parental Responsibilities, Strasbourg, 25–27 May 2011. The text mostly refers to the resulting Draft Recommendation on the Rights and Legal Status of Children and Parental Responsibilities. For the purposes of elaborating on the Draft Recommendation, Ursula Kilkelly's Report and Nigel Lowe's Explanatory Memorandum are used which are attached in the same document. Available online: www.coe.int/t/dghl/standardsetting/family/CJFA%20_2011_%20RAP%205%20E%2013%207%202011%20-rev%20cg-.pdf. In the process of drafting the recommendation, references were made to the *White Paper*. Nevertheless, due to many legal, social and scientific developments since then, there are a number of significant differences. See p. 29 of the same document.

1239 Available online: https://wcd.coe.int/ViewDoc.jsp?Ref=CM/Del/Dec%282010%291098/10.2abc&Language=lanEnglish&Ver=app6&Site=CM&BackColorInternet=C3C3C3&BackColorIntranet=EDB021&BackColorLogged=F5D383. The Guidelines contain references to various Council of Europe conventions and recommendations, and invite States to speedily ratify the relevant documents in order to safeguard justice for all children.

1240 Article 15 of the Statute of the Council of Europe. See more in Lowe N., "An Evaluation of the Council of Europe's Legal Instruments in the Field of Family Law, A Report for the Attention of the Committee of Experts of Family Law (CJ-FA)", *Cardiff Law School Research Papers No. 2*, Presented to the 36th Plenary Meeting of the CF-FA, Strasbourg, 15–17 November 2006, p. 4.

1241 *Ibid.*

1242 Draft Report, p. 30.

1243 See Chapter 2, International regulations.

Furthermore, a necessity to revise and update family laws has emerged due to the rapid development of science in the field of reproduction, creating new ways of founding families. As a result, the new generations of conceived children should not be victims of the failure to synchronise law with technology. Therefore the chosen modus for interpreting family law issues and offering recommendations towards further enhancement and possible harmonisation seems to be the most feasible one for the time being.

The field of parental responsibilities was chosen as a second working field of the CEFL shortly after its establishment in 2001. The focus on parental responsibilities followed naturally after the focus on divorce and maintenance between the former spouses, being a consequence of custody disputes over children, and therefore associated with parental status.[1244] A more pertinent reason was the increasing international unification (since the European countries are bound to respect the international child conventions) of the laws related to the protection of children including all civil matters from attribution, exercise and delegation to restriction and termination of parental responsibilities. The Preamble of the CEFL's *Principles of European Family Law* recognises both the existing diversities of the family law systems, as well as the growing convergence of laws. This is used as a starting point of the CEFL's attempt to contribute to their harmonisation and further facilitation of the free movement of persons within Europe.[1245] Even more, nowadays, having sperm donations as a modus of conceiving families, the importance of finding universal principles that go beyond national legislation is derived from human rights.

From the beginning, the CEFL recognised the necessity for the States to update their laws so that they can provide greater legal certainty regarding the legal status of all children.[1246] This can only be provided if the principles that govern the establishment and legal consequences of parentage are safeguarded in a consistent manner. The definition of the concept of parenthood, encompassing the terms *parents* and *parental responsibilities* as a starting point for the further elaboration is clarified at the beginning of both the White Paper and the Draft Recommendation.[1247] Even though they refer to legal parenthood only, efforts have been made to achieve a balance between the genetic and social reality in the parental constitution. Some authors warn about possible dangers if science is used as evidence in paternity suits causing inconsistencies between the sociological, psychological and legal truth.[1248] The practice of the ECtHR has

1244 See more in Boele-Woelki K. *et al.*, *Principles of European Family Law Regarding Parental Responsibilities*, Intersentia, 2007, pp. 2 and 3.

1245 *Ibid.* p. 7.

1246 White Paper, p. 6.

1247 See footnotes 33, 34 and 36.

1248 Eriksson A., Saldeen A., "Parenthood and Science-Establising and Contesting Parentage", in Eekelaar J., Sarcevic P. (eds.), *Parenthood in Modern Society: Legal and Social Issues for the Twenty-First Century*, Martinus Nijhoff Publishers, 1993; European Commission, Directorate General XII, Office for Official Publications of the European Communities, Luxembourg,

already given some interpretation regarding the striving for balance between biology and the fact of existent family life. Even though these interpretations differ depending on the circumstances of individual cases, it is important that the parental responsibilities are established sooner than later. This is for the purpose of enhancing legal certainty and avoiding further conflicts, having concern primarily for the best interests of the child. It is also very important that decisions by competent authorities and the enforceable agreements concerning parental responsibilities are recognisable and enforceable immediately.[1249]

The White Paper contains 29 principles grouped around three areas: (1) establishment of legal parentage,[1250] (2) legal consequences of parentage,[1251] and (3) legal consequences where parentage has not been established.[1252] It explicitly refrains from questions regarding biological parentage, considering it a matter of biology and medicine, and therefore of a different nature. Consequently, legal parentage for the purposes of the principles is to be understood as a parentage established in a manner prescribed by law.[1253]

The White Paper underlined firstly that it is in the best interests of the child to establish parentage as from the moment of birth, and secondly that it is important to give stability over time to the established parentage.[1254] This means that matters relating to parentage are one of the main issues when dealing with the legal status of children. Rendering as far as possible integration of the child in a family also encompasses the second premise of giving stability over time to the established family life.[1255] Consequently, this would embrace appreciation of the private and

Science, Research, and Development, Studies on the Socio-Economic Impact of Biotechnology: Genetic Fingerprints, Scientific Truth and Affiliation Law, OOPEC, 1997.

1249 More generally, Principle 3:39 of the *Principles of European Family Law regarding Parental Responsibilities* deals with enforcement. More particularly, the Brussels II bis Regulation deals with the recognition and enforcement of judgments in matrimonial matters and matters of parental responsibility (articles 23 and 28). It also offers a list of reasons for eventual refusal of recognition, which also applies to enforceability (article 23). In order to ensure that the child will maintain contact with both parents continuously, some access rights are directly recognised and enforceable.

1250 This part contains 17 principles regarding the establishment of maternal affiliation, the establishment of paternal affiliation, the cases of medically assisted procreation in the establishment of paternal affiliation, contestation of parentage and the change of parentage. This part is of the utmost importance for the purposes of this doctoral thesis.

1251 This part contains 11 principles regarding parental responsibilities, maintenance, the family name of the child, the nationality of the child, succession and the right of the child to know his or her origins.

1252 This part contains one principle regarding the possible consequences when the parentage cannot be established allowing certain aspects of it to be a subject of exception if additional legal action is taken, approved by a competent authority.

1253 White Paper, p. 6.

1254 White Paper, pp. 6 and 7.

1255 The respect for family life, according to the interpretation of the ECtHR, implies that there should be rules in the domestic law to render possible integration of the child in his/her family as from the moment of birth. This was affirmed in the cases of *Marckx v. Belgium*, European Court of Human Rights, No. 6833/74, judgment of 13.06.1979, paras. 15 and 31, and *Johnston*

family life on a higher level than the determination of the biological facts.[1256] Hence, the White Paper leaves room for social factors to prevail over biological factors if circumstances so favour: "the law may opt not to allow the parentage to be established on the basis of biological affiliation, for instance in cases of medically assisted procreation with an anonymous donor of sperm" or "where the child is born as a result of an incestuous relationship".[1257] Nevertheless, it also holds that the non-establishment of parentage does not necessarily preclude the child from obtaining information relating to his/her biological parents.[1258] Its Principle 28 stipulates: "the interest of a child as regards information on his or her biological origin should be taken into account in law". The discussion of the Working Party of the White Paper confirmed the controversial nature of this subject, particularly due to the ongoing discussions in some Member States and the inconsistency of the interpretation of article 7 of the CRC.[1259] Because of this reason, it refrained from drafting a principle that would attribute an absolute right of the child to access information about his/her origins. It also recognised that for the sake of protection of classified information and confidentiality of public records "in certain situations, the best interest of the child or of other persons involved may justify withholding from the child such information or certain parts of it".[1260] The Draft Recommendation goes the extra mile in this field, affording to children a general right to access information concerning their origin.[1261] Principle 29 of the White Paper anticipates possible consequences where parentage has not been established due to legal impossibility. It stipulates that "in cases where the law does not allow parentage to be established between a certain person and a child, States may permit exercise of some parental responsibilities by that person upon decision of a competent authority". Even though from the explanation this principle exemplifies the impossibility of establishing fatherhood due to the legal impediments of an incestuous relationship where the father is known, it does not restrict its scope solely to such case.[1262] It could also be interpreted as encompassing cases of known sperm donors. This is particularly because analogy between these two scenarios has already been given when referring to the allowance of the State Parties not to establish fatherhood on the basis of biological affiliation.[1263] In the second scenario, the case may be even stronger

and Others v. Ireland, European Court of Human Rights, No. 9697/82, judgment of 18.12.1986, para. 72.

1256 See the case of *Nylund v. Finland*, European Court of Human Rights, No. 27110/95, judgment of 29.06.1999.

1257 White Paper, p. 7.

1258 White Paper, p. 32.

1259 White Paper, p. 31.

1260 White Paper, p. 31.

1261 Draft Recommendation, article 4. See also footnote 1266.

1262 White Paper, p. 32.

1263 See footnote 1257.

if the biological facts are accompanied with contact between the known sperm donor and the child, creating in that way the social fact of existent family life.

The latter Draft Recommendation on the Rights and Legal Status of Children and Parental Responsibilities took into consideration several documents in the field including *inter alia*: (1) Recommendation No. R (84) 4 on Parental Responsibilities, (2) Recommendation No. R (97) 5 on the Protection of Medical Data, (3) Recommendation No. R (98) 8 on Children's Participation in Family and Social Life, (4) Recommendation Rec (2006) 19 on the Policy to Support Positive Parenting, (5) Recommendation CM/Rec (2007) 17 on the Gender Equality Standards and Mechanisms, (6) Recommendation CM/Rec (2010) 5 on the Measures to Combat Discrimination on Grounds of Sexual Orientation or Gender Identity, (7) Guidelines on Child-Friendly Justice of the Committee of Ministers of the Council of Europe, as well as (8) the White Paper and (9) the Principles of European Family Law Regarding Parental Responsibilities, developed by the Commission of European Family Law. The content of the Draft Recommendation is divided into three parts dealing with: (1) the position and status of children, (2) parental affiliation, and (3) parental responsibilities.

For the purposes of preparing the Draft Recommendation, Dr Ursula Kinkelly prepared a Report based on a survey conducted on children from six different countries.[1264] The children reached a consensus on the issues of their right to know their origin and contact their biological parents. In the adoption cases, most of the children felt that they should be told as early as possible about their adoption as it is a major issue of their identity. Children of "socially less acceptable families" – LGBT (lesbian, gay, bisexual and transgender) – in the case perceived a lack of legal recognition of their lives and development. The response to these results was a recommendation to strengthen the obligation to consider the views of children, and their recognition in the process of decision-making, especially when it comes to issues related to identity and origins. Along these lines, the Appendix to Recommendation CM/Rec (2011)[1265] in its article 4 stipulates that "children should have access to information concerning their origins". It even goes further in its paragraph 2 stating that: "where the persons who procreated the child have a legal right not to have their personal information disclosed, it shall remain open to the competent authority, to the extent permitted by national law, to determine whether to override the right and disclose relevant information, particularly non-identifying information, having regard to the circumstances and to the respective rights of the child and the persons involved". This paragraph appreciates children's right to know at least the medical history of the donor, but also their identity if a national authority recognises that it is

1264 The survey was conducted on the following issues: family name, parental responsibilities, decision-making, family origin and legal representation. The consulted children were from Azerbaijan, Croatia, France, Ireland, Lithuania and Serbia. See more in *Draft Report of the Fifth Meeting*, 2011, p. 3.

1265 *Ibid.* Appendix to Recommendation CM/Rec (2011), CJ-FA, RAP 5 prov, p. 17.

in the child's best interest. Thus, the right of the child to know overrules the interests of the other participants in the reproductive project, which still hold relevancy but only of secondary nature. Consequently, the absolute nature of the right is reduced since the idea is to strike a fair balance between the child's right to know and the biological parent's right to anonymity. Therefore the decision is left to a competent authority on a case-by-case basis.[1266] This, however, should not to be identified with the issues of mandatory legal parentage associated with biological ties. The Draft Recommendation also introduces a novel perspective and enhancement of the legal proceedings that regard the relationship between children and parents. Therefore it will be taken together with the White Paper and used as a point of reference for parental proceedings in order to clarify the legal affiliation of children conceived by sperm donation to single women in this part. The establishment of paternal affiliation in both the White Paper and Draft Recommendation is regulated in a manner that covers all children as a principle rule. Principle 2 of the White Paper recommends that the law should always provide for the possibility to establish paternal affiliation by presumption,[1267] recognition[1268] and judicial decision. Article 6 of the Draft Recommendation also safeguards that a legal possibility for establishing parental affiliation should always be at disposal. This is in concordance with the ECtHR's case law reasoning in a number of cases affirming that having no legal mechanism to establish or challenge paternity is a violation of article 8 of the ECtHR in a number of cases.[1269] Nevertheless, the relativity of this right was also affirmed in another case in which the Court allowed restriction of its exercise, on condition of its proportionality to the legitimate aims being pursued, its justification, and prevention from discrimination and pointless time limits.[1270]

There is a growing tendency that the marital presumption for establishing parenthood extends towards cohabiting partners in both the White Paper and Draft Recommendation.[1271] The possibility of recognising the child is always an option for the genetic father (for the relevance of this work, including the sperm donor) conditional on consent from the mother and/or the child. There is also a growing tendency for the recognition to extend towards the non-genetic father.[1272]

1266 *Draft Report*, p. 31.

1267 Meaning the achieved legal effects by simple operation of law. See more in White Paper, p. 9.

1268 Meaning the established paternal affiliation on the basis of will before an administrative authority (civil register) in a protocol before a court or administrative authority, by written agreement between parents or by joint signature of birth registration. See more in White Paper, p. 9.

1269 *Różański v. Poland*, European Court of Human Rights, No. 55339/00, judgment of 18.05.2006, *Shofman v. Russia*, European Court of Human Rights, No. 74826/01, judgment of 24.11.2005, *Paulik v. Slovakia*, European Court of Human Rights, No. 10699/05, judgment of 10.09.2006, and *Mizzi v. Malta*, European Court of Human Rights, No. 26111/02, judgment of 12.01.2006.

1270 *Znamenskaya v. Russia*, European Court of Human Rights, No. 77785/01, judgment of 02.06.2005.

1271 Principle 5, the White Paper, and articles 11 and 12, Draft Recommendation.

1272 See footnote 1337.

Access to civil proceedings, though (if the consent is not obtained), is not extended to cover every situation nor is provided for every child. Excluded from this possibility are situations in which the child is conceived with an anonymous sperm donor and when it is conceived in an incestuous relationship.[1273] The establishment of the paternal affiliation may also be prohibited in the so-called "exceptional circumstances" determined by law when the best interests of the child so require (Principle 2, paragraph 2 of the White Paper). This again leaves it up to the national legislation to decide what exceptional circumstances are considered on a general level and as a matter of rule that do not comply with the best interests of the child. Taking into account the necessity of all children to be treated in an equal manner and not to be discriminated against on the grounds of their birth, the following text will distinguish between "natural" and "artificial" parenthood in order to demonstrate that different treatment does exist even though it is not proclaimed as a general rule, but only as an exception.[1274]

7.1. "NATURAL" CONCEPTIONS – BIOLOGICAL/ GENETIC FATHERHOOD AS A PRINCIPLE RULE

Parenthood is attributed to persons who are considered to be parents of the child according to national law.[1275] Therefore the legal attribution of paternity is important for a person to be a holder of parental responsibilities. There are three general ways of establishing fatherhood in the various national legislation as well as supported on a level of principles and recommendations in the White Paper and in the Draft Recommendation that apply on equal level to all naturally conceived children without exception: (1) by marital presumption, (2) by recognition, and (3) by judicial decision.[1276] When it comes to the contestation of the paternal affiliation for naturally conceived children, the general ground is the biological link since it is considered that legal fatherhood can be contested if the child has not been procreated by the father.[1277] With regard to this, though, there are exceptions that differ among the various national legislation and such differentiation is allowed by the practice of the ECtHR. Namely, the European Commission on Human Rights has been contradictory when it comes to the appreciation of the DNA tests for purposes of establishing fatherhood. On the one hand, it considered that such tests are in the best interests of the child, and

1273 White Paper, p. 7.

1274 Even though it is stated that Principle 2 of the White Paper is a general principle that applies regardless of the fact if the child was born as a result of medically assisted procreation or not. See more White Paper, p. 7.

1275 Draft Recommendation, 2011, article 1.

1276 Principle 2 of the White Paper, and article 6 of the Draft Recommendation.

1277 Principle 11, paragraph 2, the White Paper, p. 14.

do not violate the father's rights resulting from article 8 of the ECHR.[1278] In the cases of *Mikulic v. Croatia*[1279] and *Jäggi v. Switzerland*,[1280] the ECtHR valued the genetic truth as important for one's personal identity and connected it with proceedings for establishing a parental link. In the case of *Kalacheva v. Russia*, the Court reasoned that if the national system gives priority to genes while DNA tests prove almost to certainty that the father of the child born out of wedlock is a person who does not want to establish fatherhood, then the system fails to respect private and family life by not providing adequate means for the establishment to take place.[1281] The Court considered that in the given circumstances, the domestic authorities' approach disappointed with regard to the handling of the applicant's case in concordance with the obligation of the States to strike a fair balance between the competing interests of the parties with due regard to the best interests of the child.[1282]

In the case of *Kroon and Others v. the Netherlands*, it even considered that the biological and social reality should prevail over legal presumptions and the quest for legal certainty of relations, so that any presumptions of paternity had to be effectively capable of being rebutted and not amount to a *de facto* rule.[1283] The case of *Tavli v. Turkey* concerned the impossibility to disclaim paternity because the scientific progress was not incorporated in the Turkish Code of Civil Procedure. In this case, the Court concluded that "a fair balance has not been struck between the general interest of the protection of legal certainty of family relationships and the applicant's right to have the legal presumption of his paternity reviewed in the light if the biological evidence".[1284] On the other hand, it also considered that "the choice of the means calculated to secure compliance with article 8 of the

---

1278 White Paper, p. 20. The case of *Van der Velden v. the Netherlands*, European Court of Human Rights, No. 29514/05, judgment of 07.12.2006 considered, though, that taking a mouth swab, in order to obtain cellular material, amounts to interference in the right to respect for private life.

1279 *Mikulic v. Croatia*, European Court of Human Rights, No. 53176/99, judgment of 07.02.2002. In this case, the connection with *DNA tests* and *paternal proceedings* was the part in which the Court concluded that while a person cannot be forced to undergo DNA testing (allowing this decision to be left to the discretion of the Courts), the national system has to secure the interests of the persons seeking the establishment of paternity in another manner.

1280 *Jäggi v. Switzerland*, European Court of Human Rights, No. 58757/00, judgment of 13.07.2006, paras. 36, 37 and 38. The case concerned preclusion from being compelled to be available for DNA testing in conflict with the right to receive information about the genetic origin. The Court assured that "the State obligation will depend on the particular aspect of private life that is at issue", as well as on the very nature and interests concerned. In this regard, it considered that the right to know one's parentage is an integral part of the notion of private life, and as such, it asked for particular scrutiny when weighing up competing interests.

1281 *Kalacheva v. Russia*, European Court of Human Rights, No. 3451/05, judgment of 07.06.2009, in particular paras. 29, 30, 32, 34 and 36.

1282 *Ibid.* paras. 37 and 38.

1283 *Kroon and Others v. the Netherlands*, European Court of Human Rights, No. 18535/91, judgment of 27.10.1994, para. 40.

1284 *Tavli v. Turkey*, European Court of Human Rights, No. 11449/02, judgment of 09.11.2006, para. 36.

ECHR in the relation of individuals between themselves is in principle a matter that falls within the States' margin of appreciation".[1285] In another case, it was reasoned that the State Parties are not required to make such tests compulsory.[1286] In the case of *Nylund v. Finland* that dealt with a conflict of presumptions, the Court reasoned that a paternity claim that emphasises mere biological paternity is directed towards obliging the parties to undergo blood tests.[1287] Nevertheless, it also recognised the rationale behind the national law that does not allow a possibility to acknowledge mere biological links without additional legal action (since such claim was impossible under the national law). Accordingly, the Court concluded that the establishment of biological paternity would not as such create any rights and obligations for those concerned, while having as a consequence disturbance of the already created family life of the child.[1288] On the other hand, the impossibility of contesting the link made on grounds of presumption notwithstanding the medical proof of matching DNA was considered to be violation of, *inter alia*, articles 8 and 6 of the ECHR.[1289]

Some authors consider that there is selective use of DNA testing in paternity cases that is often based on the evaluation of the moral character of the child's mother.[1290] As such, the exact certainty of the DNA tests is used restrictively depending on the already accepted sets of values of the dominant social groups. Consequently, scientific knowledge both embeds and is embedded in social identities, institutions, representations, and discourses.[1291]

Contestation of parenthood on biological grounds is usually not possible if the child was given up for adoption. This is the field where, historically, the factual family life with the child has started to matter more than biology as a ground to establish legal parenthood. Biological parents have a possibility to renounce their parental responsibilities and allow other willing parents to take over. This is also where the intentions to parent (expressed in a legally prescribed way) become significant and therefore distanced biology from the legal concepts of parenthood. Both parents have to withdraw parental responsibilities after the birth of the child.[1292] The national law, though, may dispense with the need for consent if the

1285 *Ibid.* para. 36.

1286 As, for instance, in the case of *M.B. v. the United Kingdom*, European Commission of Human Rights, No. 22920/93, judgment of 06.04.1994.

1287 *Nylund v. Finland*, European Court of Human Rights, No. 27110/95, judgment of 29.06.1999.

1288 See more in *Working Party on the New Legal Instrument(s) on the Rights and Legal Status of Children and Parental Responsibilities*, Committee of Experts on Family Law, CJ-FA-GT3, 2010, p. 5.

1289 See, for instance, the cases of *Shofman v. Russia*, European Court of Human Rights, No. 74826/01, judgment of 24.11.2005, and *Mizzi v. Malta*, European Court of Human Rights, No. 26111/02, judgment of 12.01.2006.

1290 Machado H., "Biologising Paternity, Moralizing Maternity.The Construction of Parenthood in the Determination of Paternity through the Courts in Portugal", *Feminist Legal Studies*, Vol. 16, No. 2, 2008, pp. 215–236, p. 219.

1291 Jasanhoff S. (ed.), *States of Knowledge: The Co-Production of Science and Social Order*, Routledge, 2004.

1292 Following the European Convention on the Adoption of Children, article 5.

parents are not holders of parental responsibilities,[1293] if the consent cannot be obtained[1294] (in particular if the whereabouts of the parents are unknown or they cannot be found or are dead)[1295] and if they have been deprived of their parental responsibilities.[1296] In most national legislation the parental responsibilities of the natural mother are gained immediately after birth (apart from the States that regulate surrogacies in a manner in which the surrogate mother is not to be considered as a mother from the time of the birth, for instance, Greece and Ukraine).[1297] For fathers in marital relationships the parental responsibilities are also gained immediately after birth due to the marital presumption.[1298] While this is not the same for fathers from an extra-marital relationship, the case law of the ECtHR in the case of *Keegan v. Ireland*[1299] showed sensitivity towards appreciating the genetic father as a relevant man to consent to the adoption of his child born out of wedlock in the context of protection of his family life under article 8 of the ECHR.

Consequently, the conclusion is that in "natural" conceptions, in most countries and as a matter of principle, the parental responsibilities of the genetic parents start immediately after the birth of the child for both of them.[1300] What happens to them later on is another issue. This is why adoptions in the White Paper are under the section "Change of parenthood", meaning that parenthood was once established (at the time of the birth) but changed only afterwards. Nevertheless, this also makes "natural" conceptions different from "artificial" ones, because in the latter, the parental responsibilities of the genetic parents (i.e. donors) do not start after childbirth. Donors have withdrawn and given up their parental responsibilities even before the conceptions have taken place. This is why in "artificial" conceptions there is no change of parenthood. The donor never

1293 The White Paper underlined that the reference to "fathers" in the provisions related to adoptions shall be understood as a reference to the man who is a holder of parental responsibilities. White Paper, p. 21.

1294 This does not include cases in which the person is not capable of giving consent due to mental disability, therefore legal incapacity. See, for instance, the case of *E.P. v. Italy*, European Court of Human Rights, No. 31127/96, judgment of 16.11.1999. This case concerned violation of articles 8 and 6(1) regarding a mother who was incapable to grant consent, whose child was given up for adoption without her permission.

1295 Principle 15 of the White Paper. See White Paper, p. 20.

1296 Article 5, paragraph 3 of the European Convention on the Adoption of Children. See also the case of *Söderbäck v. Sweden*, European Court of Human Rights, No. 24484/97, judgment of 15.12.1997 that considered an adoption of a child granted to the mother's husband, without the consent of the natural father.

1297 See footnote 835. This is in concordance with article 7 of the Draft Recommendation that allows States having legislation governing surrogacy arrangements to introduce special rules regarding such cases (apart from the general rule *mater semper certa est*).

1298 The European Convention on the Adoption of Children of 1967 requires the consent of the father of the child to an adoption if the child is born in wedlock.

1299 *Keegan v. Ireland*, European Court of Human Rights, No. 16969/90, judgment of 26.05.1994.

1300 This is especially the case if the child is born in marriage. Even if the child is not born in marriage, the genetic father has the possibility to gain (or it can even be imposed on him) parental status that will count retroactively as from the time of birth.

gains parental responsibilities automatically merely due to the fact of being the genetic parent at the time of the birth of the child.[1301]

7.1.1. MARRIAGE

The marital presumption is based on the probability that the biological paternity coincides with the legal paternity grounded in the civil law institution of marriage.[1302] In most legal systems even if a biological tie does not exist between the child and the mother's husband, the law considers the mother's husband to be a legal father, thus imposing a necessity to take civil proceedings in order to remove the presumption.[1303] As such, this was recognised in the ECtHR case of *Berrehab v. the Netherlands*, confirming that there is a family life relationship between the child and the father from a marital community as from the moment of birth just by the very fact of it, even if the parents are not living together.[1304] A number of other cases before the ECtHR have also confirmed that the presumption applies when the child is conceived or born during the marriage.[1305]

To scrutinise the situations in which the marital presumption can apply, the White Paper listed five scenarios related to the possibilities when a child is conceived: (1) before the marriage and born during it, (2) during the marriage and born during it, (3) during the marriage and born after it, (4) during a first marriage of the mother and born during her second marriage, (5) before the marriage and born after the end of it. In all these cases, the paternal presumption should apply when the child is born during the marriage (unless by exception the spouses are separated) or within the normal period of gestation after the end of the marriage. Nevertheless, this formula does not solve cases of conflicting paternity when the child was conceived and born during the marriage by another partner of the mother (adulterous relationship). The ECtHR has dealt with a

1301 For a suggestion to equalise the position between "natural" and "artificial" conceptions, see *infra* the text under Chapter 8, section 8.3.

1302 White Paper, p. 9. The marital presumption, the possibility for its exception in cases of factual or legal separation of the spouses, and the time limits of its application are regulated in articles 9 and 10 of the Draft Recommendation.

1303 Machado H., "Biologising Paternity, Moralizing Maternity. The Construction of Parenthood in the Determination of Paternity through the Courts in Portugal", *Feminist Legal Studies*, Vol. 16, No. 2, 2008, pp. 215–236, p. 216.

1304 *Berrehab v. the Netherlands*, European Court of Human Rights, No. 10730/84, judgment of 21.06.1988. The fact of factual family life is gaining more significance nowadays, irrespective of the fact of marriage. Along these lines, and bearing in mind that certain national laws prohibit the marital presumption after *de facto* or legal separation of the spouses, both the White Paper and the Draft Recommendation also allow exceptions if the child was born after the factual or legal separation of the spouses.

1305 See, for instance, the cases of *Kroon and Others v. the Netherlands*, European Court of Human Rights, No. 18535/91, judgment of 27.10.1994; and *Anayo v. Germany*, European Court of Human Rights, No. 20578/07, judgment of 21.12.2010.

number of cases of the same or similar nature.[1306] The Draft Recommendation supports States to provide rules in their national law to solve situations resulting from the conflict of presumptions.[1307] Along these lines, the second ground for establishing fatherhood – by recognition – can also appear once fatherhood has already been established by virtue of the marital presumption. Nevertheless, most national legal systems do not allow the child to have more than two parents. Therefore if the place of the father is already taken, the third person can only recognise the child after having contested the existent parenthood, activating the third mechanism – judicial proceedings. For purposes of allowing flexibility and avoiding contestation of fatherhood, the second paragraph of Principle 4 of the White Paper allows State Parties to enforce exceptions in cases of dissolution of marriage by annulment or divorce (if the reasons are doubted fatherhood).[1308] This, however, is not a solution, especially in the cases where the husband has already established a family link with the child before realising that there is not a genetic link between them. Acknowledging the difficulties of properly addressing all possible conflicts related to the presumption, the White Paper (Principle 6) delegates the issue to the State Parties to deal with in their national regulations.

The dissolution of marriage (or other formal relationship) and the legal or factual separation of parents do not affect already attributed parental responsibilities.[1309] This is accepted in most European national legislation with some exceptions regarding the content of the parental responsibilities.[1310] It is accepted as a principle on a European level that parents having parental responsibilities should have an equal right and duty to exercise them jointly, whenever possible.[1311]

1306 See, for instance, the cases in footnotes 1283, 1287, and 1289.

1307 Draft Recommendation, article 13. This article encourages States to provide for solutions in their national laws for cases where the application of presumptions may lead to contradicting results, for instance, if the woman remarries and gives birth to a child shortly after the death of her husband.

1308 This is inspired by some national laws that prohibit the presumption of paternity after annulment or divorce in order to protect the possibility for the biological father to recognise the child without the need for first contesting the paternal affiliation in judicial proceedings. See more in White Paper, p. 11.

1309 Principle 3:10 of the *Principles of European Family Law Regarding Parental Responsibilities*. See Boele-Woelki K. *et al.*, *Principles of European Family Law Regarding Parental Responsibilities*, Intersentia, 2007, pp. 79 and 80.

1310 For instance, in Lithuania, the right to administer the child's property remains with the parent with whom the child will continue to live. In Austria and Switzerland, sole parental responsibilities are attributed by a court order to the parent with whom the child will reside, unless the parents' request for continuation of their joint responsibility. A more extreme case is Hungary where the attribution of the parental responsibilities does not continue automatically after the relationship dissolution, but a court has to decide. See also Boele-Woelki K. *et al.*, *Principles of European Family Law Regarding Parental Responsibilities*, Intersentia, 2007, pp. 79 and 80.

1311 Principle 3:11 of the *Principles of European Family Law Regarding Parental Responsibilities*.

7.1.2. EXTRA-MARITAL RELATIONSHIPS

Most national legislation does not have legitimacy presumption statuses for unmarried couples.[1312] This is considered to be a lack of equality between children born in different contexts, but also between parents founding families in different contexts.[1313] As a consequence of the rapid recent social changes and the slower path of the legislators to follow, the courts have been sources of law, by their interpretations of the grounds to base the legal parentage upon.[1314]

This resulted in informal recognition of multiple parenting arrangements in legal practice, demonstrating again that family law matters are very case-sensitive and are to be solved on an individual basis. Thus, the paternity statuses have been tailored also by other than biology facts, such as: enduring psychological relationships, living arrangements and the best interests of the child. Some authors have differentiated between (1) legal parents,[1315] (2) parents by estoppel,[1316] and (3) *de facto* parents.[1317] Moulton upholds the American Law Institute (ALI) Principles of the Law of Family Dissolution suggesting that the presumption of legitimacy similar to the marital presumption should also apply in cases where the child has been born out of wedlock and has lived with the alleged father for more than two years. This should make it less possible for another third party to

[1312] For a comparative overview of how this is regulated in different countries in Europe, see Lowe N., *A Study into the Rights and Legal Status of Children being Brought Up in Various Forms of Marital or Non-Marital Partnerships and Cohabitation*, A Report for the Attention of the Committee of Experts on Family Law, September 2009, p. 14.

[1313] Moulton R., "Who's Your Daddy?: The Inherent Unfairness of the Marital Presumption for Children of Unmarried Parents", *Family Court Review*, Vol. 47, No. 4, 2009, p. 698.

[1314] *Ibid.* p. 699. See also DiFonzo J.H., "Toward a Unified Field Theory of the Family: The American Law Institute's Principles of the Law of Family Dissolution", *Brigham Young University Law Review*, 2001, p. 930.

[1315] A legal parent should be recognised as such under the national law (either according to the marital presumption or adoption). See more in Moulton R., "Who's Your Daddy?: The Inherent Unfairness of the Marital Presumption for Children of Unmarried Parents", *Family Court Review*, Vol. 47, No. 4, 2009, p. 700.

[1316] This corresponds with the legal concept of "parent by estoppel" suggested in the *ALI Principles* that can be established in three cases: (1) when someone enters into an "implicit or explicit agreement" to provide financial support to a child, (2) when a man was married to or cohabiting with a mother when she gave birth to the child, or (3) when the "child was conceived pursuant to an agreement" between two people in which they both agreed to share responsibilities for and be parents to the child. Consequently, a parent by estoppel can be a man who has lived with the child for more than two years in good faith that he was the child's father, therefore exercising the parental responsibilities.

[1317] An individual other than a legal parent or a parent by estoppel who lived with the child and regularly performed the majority of the caretaking functions for the child, pursuant to an agreement with the legal parent or as a result of the legal parents' inability to perform such functions. This person has to fulfil other requirements, such as proving that he already had performed caretaking functions equal to or greater than those performed by the legal parent with whom the child primarily lived for reasons other than financial compensation for a period of no less than two years. Moulton R., "Who's Your Daddy?: The Inherent Unfairness of the Marital Presumption for Children of Unmarried Parents", *Family Court Review*, Vol. 47, No. 4, 2009, p. 701. See also ALI Principles, 2.03.

launch a non-paternity suit against the psychological and social parent.[1318] The evaluation of the circumstances to qualify as a parent by estoppel or *de facto* parent should be based on the estimation of the quality and duration of the parent-child relationship. This creates another alternative standard for establishing fatherhood that is taken away from a mere biological connection to the child.[1319] The critics of the ALI Principles mainly pointed towards their alleged threat to the constitution by prioritising "legal strangers"[1320] as psychological parents over biological parents.[1321] Nevertheless, the American legal practice is also familiar with cases in which the courts have recognised that the psychological parent holds the right to establish private and family life with the child on grounds other than biology.[1322] Some authors find the Principles a valuable contribution precisely due to what the critique was about, in addition to the corrective requirements for providing equality between children conceived in and out of wedlock. The quality and the duration of the father–child relationship should be relevant for children born in both contexts.[1323]

The growing tendency that the marital presumption for establishing parenthood should extend toward cohabiting partners is in concordance with the ideal of treating children equally irrespective of the context of their birth or their parents' relationship, thus avoiding the status of "illegitimate children".[1324]

1318 Moulton R., "Who's Your Daddy?: The Inherent Unfairness of the Marital Presumption for Children of Unmarried Parents", *Family Court Review*, Vol. 47, No. 4, 2009, pp. 699 and 700. See also American Law Institute, *Principles of the Law of Family Dissolution*, 2.03(1)(a), 2.03(1)(b), 3.02(1).

1319 *Ibid.* pp. 705 and 706.

1320 People who lack an adoptive or biological tie to the child.

1321 Moulton R., "Who's Your Daddy?: The Inherent Unfairness of the Marital Presumption for Children of Unmarried Parents", *Family Court Review*, Vol. 47, No. 4, 2009, p. 706 referring to Meyer D.D., "Partners, Care Givers, and the Constitutional Substance of Parenthood", in Wilson R.F. (ed.), *Reconceiving the Family: Critique on the American Law Institute's Principles of the Law of Family Dissolution*, 2006, p. 47.

1322 See, for instance: *Quilloin v. Walcott,* 434 U.S. 246, 249, 1978, dealing with a stepfather who was trying to adopt his stepson with whom he was living in opposition to his biological parent; *Lehr v. Robertson*, 463 U.S. 248, 1983, in which the Court reasoned that there is a difference between actual and potential relationships, considering the biological relationship only as a potential invitation for the father to avail himself of a more enduring relationship with the child, *Caban v. Mohammed*, 442 U.S. 380, 1979, in which the Court was willing to protect the unwed biological father's rights when willing to develop a relationship with the child on equal terms as the mother. See also their interpretation in Moulton R., "Who's Your Daddy?: The Inherent Unfairness of the Marital Presumption for Children of Unmarried Parents", *Family Court Review*, Vol. 47, No. 4, 2009, p. 707.

1323 Moulton R., "Who's Your Daddy?: The Inherent Unfairness of the Marital Presumption for Children of Unmarried Parents", *Family Court Review*, Vol. 47, No. 4, 2009, pp. 708 and 709.

1324 Principle 5 of the White Paper and articles 11 and 12 of the Draft Recommendation. The latter differentiates between *registered partnerships* (article 11 stipulates: "States permitting different sex couples to enter into registered partnership are free to apply *mutatis mutandis* the presumptions contained in articles *9* and *10* to the mother's registered partner"), and (not-registered) *cohabiting different sex couples* (article 12 stipulates: "States are free to apply *mutatis mutandis* the presumptions mentioned in articles *9* and *10* to the mother's cohabiting partner"). This is also suggested in the Proposed European Convention on Family Status (article 17). See Lowe N., *A Study into the Rights and Legal Status of Children being Brought Up*

The identification of family-life relationships between married and cohabiting partners and the establishment of an affiliation link with their child as from the moment of birth was acknowledged and dealt with in ECtHR cases *Keegan v. Ireland*[1325]and *Lebbink v. the Netherlands.*[1326] A possible drawback of their equalisation is the burden of proof that the mutual life existed at the time of birth (if the cohabitation was not registered). The Draft Recommendation uses the term "cohabiting couple" meaning a couple in a marriage-like relationship who may or may not be living in the same place of residence.[1327] Some States, for instance the Republic of Macedonia, look for similarities of the extra-marital with the marital relationship in order to prove the existence of the "alternative to marriage" family life.[1328] The ECtHR has also made a decision confirming that family life can be existent even if the relationship is not officially registered, and consequently approved by the State in the form of a marriage.[1329] A number of other cases dealt with non-discrimination on grounds of birth of children born of adulterous relationships or out of wedlock with regard to their inheritance rights.[1330] This too is related to the constitution of status, because only children in relation to whom legal parenthood is established can possibly qualify as heirs.[1331]

In most national legislation, formalised relationships that are not marriage (registered partnerships, civil unions, extra-marital relationships) do not attribute parental responsibilities automatically (as marriage does).[1332] The establishment of the filiation can follow by additional legal action making it relevant for the attribution of parental status. In some countries, though, this additional legal action (in the form of recognition or acknowledgement) can also happen after conception and prior to the birth of the child.[1333] This is also a possibility

in Various Forms of Marital or Non-Marital Partnerships and Cohabitation, A Report for the Attention of the Committee of Experts on Family Law, September 2009, p. 47.

1325 *Keegan v. Ireland*, European Court of Human Rights, No. 16969/90, judgment of 26.05.1994.

1326 *Lebbink v. the Netherlands,* European Court of Human Rights, No. 45582/99, judgment of 01.06.2004.

1327 From the Explanatory Memorandum of the Draft Recommendation, p. 36.

1328 Article 13, Family Law of the Republic of Macedonia.

1329 *Kroon v. the Netherlands*, European Court of Human Rights, No. 18535/91, judgment of 27.10.1994.

1330 *Marckx v. Belgium*, European Court of Human Rights, No. 6833/74, judgment of 13.06.1979; *Mazurek v. France*, European Court of Human Rights, No. 34406/97, judgment of 01.02.2000; *Camp and Bourimi v. the Netherlands* , European Court of Human Rights, No. 28369/95, judgment of 03.10.2000.

1331 See also article 5 of the Draft Recommendation that refers to the right of succession of children.

1332 Belgium, the Czech Republic, France, Lithuania, Portugal, Russia and Spain. See more in the Boele-Woelki K. *et al.*, *Principles of European Family Law Regarding Parental Responsibilities*, Intersentia, 2007, p. 63.

1333 In Belgium, as stipulated in article 328, the second part of the Belgian Civil Code. Acknowledgment of fatherhood during pregnancy is also possible in Estonia, Lithuania, Norway, Russia, Sweden (see more in Lowe N., *A Study into the Rights and Legal Status of Children being Brought Up in Various Forms of Marital or Non-Marital Partnerships and Cohabitation*, A Report for the Attention of the Committee of Experts on Family Law, September 2009, p. 11) and in the Republic of Macedonia (see more in footnote 1471).

anticipated in the Draft Recommendation (article 14(3)). Some countries have already made efforts to change their laws to equalise, as much as possible, the position of children born in registered partnerships with the position of those born in marriage, as well as the position of women and men in the relationships.[1334]

State regulations that do not extend the marital presumption to an extra-marital relationship, but also those which do (when the paternal affiliation is not established by a presumption) should provide a possibility of establishing paternal affiliation by voluntary recognition.[1335] It is up to the national regulations to estimate whether the recognition should be conditional on the consent of the mother, the child (alone or through a representative) and/or a competent authority for purposes of evaluating if the requirements are met by the person who recognises the child as his (paragraphs 2 and 3 of Principle 7 and paragraph 2 of article 14 of the Draft Recommendation).[1336] The Draft Recommendation has another novelty in this field, allowing the possibility for another person apart from the biological father to recognise the child as his, for instance if the recognition is by the latter partner of the mother (i.e. a genetically unrelated man).[1337] This is already a possibility in some national legislation,[1338] while it should be distinguished from the possibility to adopt the partner's child (if the child does not have already a

---

1334 For instance, in the Netherlands, the Dutch Civil Code (article 1:253aa) attributes joint parental responsibilities to both partners for a child born during their registered partnership, without additional recognition of the father, unless legal family ties already exist between the child and another parent. See more in Boele-Woelki K. *et al.*, *Principles of European Family Law Regarding Parental Responsibilities*, Intersentia, 2007, p. 63. See also footnotes 1357 and 1358.

1335 Principle 7 of the White Paper; article 14 of the Draft Recommendation.

1336 This comes from the dissenting opinions and arguments regarding the necessity for the consent of the mother and the child, since it may also be considered as a burden for establishing fatherhood. See more in White Paper, p. 13. The fear of overpowering mothers to hold exclusivity over parental responsibilities by consenting to the biological fatherhood of the assumed father is neutralised by the possibility of civil proceedings. On the other hand, empowering mothers to consent regarding who they are going to share the parental responsibilities with is in concordance with the notion of intentional parenthood. The Draft Recommendation (article 14, paragraph 3) has a novelty in this field allowing voluntary recognition during the mother's pregnancy which has effect from birth. This means a possibility for children conceived out of wedlock to have their fatherhood established as from the time of their birth.

1337 See Article 14 of the Draft Recommendation and its interpretation on p. 37.

1338 For instance, in Bulgaria. In contrast, in Lithuania, the partner can recognise the child of the mother only if he is the child's biological parent. In Denmark, the spouse or the parent with sole parental authority can be attributed parental authority by agreement with the parent and additional approval by a competent authority. In England and Wales this can be done through a residence order and in Finland through a court order. In Austria, a stepparent (from a formalised or informal relationship with the parent) may apply to the court for the transfer of parental responsibilities from the previous holder (if granted, the latter loses them). In France, the court may grant a stepparent some personal rights regarding the child, such as a right to contact, but not full parental responsibilities. In Germany and Switzerland the law recognises "limited parental responsibilities" regarding daily matters for the parent's partner. In the Netherlands, the court may allow the partner of the parent joint parental responsibilities in exceptional circumstances. See Boele-Woelki K. *et al.*, *Principles of European Family Law Regarding Parental Responsibilities*, Intersentia, 2007, pp. 70 and 71.

legally recognised other parent), which is present in many national legislation.[1339] The Draft Recommendation explicitly extends the application of the marital presumption to registered and cohabiting *different-sex couples*, while it does not mention whether the recognition could apply to the partner of a homosexual registered relationship too.[1340] Restrictions on the possibility of voluntary recognition can be afforded in particular cases in which recognition is considered inappropriate (e.g. rape or incest). In the event the concerned parties do not agree and oppose recognition, the person that recognised the child should still has the possibility of challenging fatherhood in judicial proceedings.[1341] This is where the legal ways of establishing (but also contesting)[1342] fatherhood in relation to children in different settings – "naturally" and "artificially" conceived – differs. Namely, in most legal systems the legal possibility to challenge the fatherhood of the donor (known or unknown) is not allowed. This is mostly due to the fact of accepting the exclusivity of the biological fact as relevant and determinant in paternity proceedings. Legislation that allows combination of biology and family life in national paternal proceedings consider known sperm donors' applications admissible.[1343] The results of the proceedings, however, (in terms of constituting status or rejecting the claim) are dependent on the way biology and family life are evaluated in the context of the concrete circumstances of the individual case.

This brings us to another significant difference between "naturally" and "artificially" conceived children on a level of how their parenthood is decided upon. Principle 14 of the White Paper promotes the use of the medical and genetic techniques, as well as the use of the information resulting from them for the purposes of proving or contesting fatherhood before competent authorities. The explanation goes even further in exemplifying the possible usage: (1) making blood or DNA tests compulsory for the parties, (2) burden of proof – introducing rules according to which a refusal to undergo a relevant test is evidence against

1339 For instance, in a registered partnership in Belgium, Denmark, Germany, the Netherlands, and Sweden, or in a relationship that is not registered in Portugal, Russia, Spain, and Lithuania. See Boele-Woelki K. *et al.*, *Principles of European Family Law Regarding Parental Responsibilities*, Intersentia, 2007, p. 69.

1340 This is related to still very different practices in Europe regarding the recognition of homosexual partnerships.

1341 Principle 8, White Paper, and article 15, the Draft Recommendation. Even though the latter allows a not genetically related person to recognise the child as his, in the following explanation it does not include him among the persons eligible for judicial proceedings after contested recognition. Paragraph 3 of article 15 enlists persons with a right to initiate legal proceedings: the mother, the man claiming to be the biological father, other persons justifying a specific interest (as for example descendants or ancestors of the person claiming to be the father or the mother), and public authorities.

1342 Article 16 of the Draft Recommendation stipulates that: "Paternal affiliation may be contested on the grounds that the child has not been procreated by the person who is considered to be the legal father".

1343 *J.R.M. v. the Netherlands*, European Commission on Human Rights, No. 16944/90, decision of 08.02.1993.

the refusing party, (3) in cases of need, providing financial support for blood tests or providing to meet them through the system of legal aid.[1344]

It was affirmed that the obligation to undergo paternity testing does not infringe the father's rights in the context of article 8 of the ECHR.[1345] Nevertheless, it was also affirmed that there is no obligation on the State Parties to make compulsory testing available.[1346]

Judicial proceedings are not solely tailored to fit the requirements of the person who wants to contest the already established link, so that they can take place afterwards. On the contrary, they are primarily designed to address the child (alone[1347] or through a representative) with concern for his/her best interests in the light of knowing and being taken care of by both parents (article 7 CRC). Other persons may also hold interests in initiating proceedings of this kind: the mother, other persons justifying a specific interest (e.g. descendants, ancestors), and the public authorities (e.g. social services).[1348] Nevertheless, challenging parenthood at any time can also have drawbacks with regard to the respect for legal certainty. This is where the already developed social reality is to be lifted to a higher level than, for instance, the possibility to challenge parenthood on biological grounds. Principle 8 of the White Paper in the third paragraph suggests to the States to specify time limits for instituting legal proceedings for the purposes of giving stability to the family situation of the persons involved over time.[1349] This is how the legal certainty should not infringe all concerned parties, having regard also for them and not only the child. There should especially be a focus of limitation after the child reaches 18 years, when it thus becomes a mature adult and not a child anymore. Allowing for the possibility of eventual changes in his/her affiliation at this level could be motivated by other reasons (property, inheritance, etc.) and not care for them and protection of their upbringing. The time limits for the same reason of legal certainty are also stipulated when it comes to the contestation of affiliation.[1350]

Article 5 of the Draft Recommendation stipulates equal rights to succession of all children to the estate of each of their parents and of those parents' families, regardless of the circumstances of their birth. In the case of *Camp and Bourimi v.*

1344 White Paper, p. 19.

1345 White Paper, p. 20.

1346 *M.B. v. the United Kingdom*, European Commission of Human Rights, No. 22920/93, judgment of 6.4.1994.

1347 In regard to article 3 of the European Convention on the Exercise of Children's Rights that entitles the child with sufficient understanding (as considered by the internal law) to have a right to be informed and to express his or her views. As such, this could be considered the bedrock of the Draft Recommendation, promoting above all the child's best interests and the right of the child to be informed, consulted, and to express his or her opinions in all matters concerning him or her. Draft Recommendation, p. 29.

1348 Principle 8 of the White Paper and article 15 of the Draft Recommendation.

1349 White Paper, p. 14.

1350 Principle 13, White Paper.

the Netherlands,[1351] the ECtHR found violation of article 14 in conjunction with article 8, due to discrimination against a child born out of wedlock to inherit from the father who died before the child's birth. In this case, the child was not recognised (was only proclaimed legitimate two years after the death of the father) nor could a marital presumption for establishing parenthood have been applied. Nevertheless, the Court found the fact that the father died before the child was born as not a valid reason to take a different approach between children born out of wedlock who had and children who did not have an opportunity to be recognised by a living father. Therefore, the Court found discrimination between persons in similar situations based on birth.

7.1.3. NOT REGULATED RELATIONSHIPS

Two ways of establishing fatherhood in relation to a child born out of a not regulated relationship are again feasible: recognition and judicial decision. Once the parental responsibilities are established, their content does not differ from the content in regulated relationships under circumstances of separation or dissolution of the relationship of the parents. The purpose of Principle 23 of the White Paper is to underline that irrespective of the parents' relationship, once the legal parentage has been established, the attitude towards their children should be the same (making joint attribution and exercise of parental responsibilities an ideal situation for the child).[1352] Even more, the White Paper stresses that beyond the discrimination against children based on their parents' relationship, their parents should also be protected from discrimination concerning the attribution and exercise of the parental responsibilities (Principle 25, paragraph 1). This is in light of the provisions for non-discrimination (or prohibition of discrimination) based on gender or other status as a fundamental human right in all international human rights documents.[1353] This would also mean that the genetic father of a naturally conceived child would have a right to be informed by the mother about the birth. This is for reasons of enabling him (equally as the mother) to use the available ways of establishing his fatherhood (recognition or civil proceedings) based on that information.

Both the White Paper and Draft Recommendation support the notion that parental responsibilities should as a principle belong to both parents.[1354] The latter

---

1351 *Camp and Bourimi v. the Netherlands*, European Court of Human Rights, No. 28369/95, judgment of 03.10.2000.

1352 White Paper, p. 25.

1353 For instance, article 14 of the Convention for the Protection of Human Rights and Fundamental Freedoms, article 2(1) of the CRC. The article of non-discrimination is at the forefront of the Draft Recommendation (article 1 defines the principle that extends to article 2 – discrimination based on parentage, and article 20 that also extends towards the other holders of parental responsibilities).

1354 Principle 19 of the White Paper and article 23 of the Draft Recommendation.

stipulates: "in cases where only one parent has parental responsibilities by the operation of law, states should make procedures available for the other parent to have an opportunity to acquire parental responsibilities, unless it is contrary to the best interests of the child. Lack of consent or opposition by the parent having parental responsibilities should not as such be an obstacle for such acquisition". The idea behind these provisions is that joint parental responsibilities are considered to be an ideal situation for children and consequently fit their best interests the most. In this light, they do not make a distinction between married and unmarried parents. When only one parent has parental responsibilities by the operation of law, the other parent should have at least a possibility of acquiring them too, unless that is against the best interests of the child.[1355]

Through the lenses of a comparative observation, most countries nowadays consider parental responsibilities a consequence of filiation between the child and the parent, and not the relational status of their parents.[1356] For children born out of wedlock motherhood is usually established by the fact of the birth, while the biological necessity imposes that fatherhood is established by additional action.[1357] Only then (even though not on equal grounds) will both parents hold parental responsibilities towards the child. Some countries differ in this field, making the establishment of parenthood in relation to the child born out of wedlock equal for both the mother and the father,[1358] or attribute joint parental responsibilities only if the parents live together.[1359]

A person other than the parent can also exercise some or all of the parental responsibilities in addition to or instead of the parents upon a decision by a competent authority.[1360] This means that different persons may be in charge of the whole or of a part, fully or to a certain degree of the content of the parental responsibilities. In this context, it is important to make clear that different terminology (or different content of it) is often used in different national systems.

1355 Boele-Woelki K. *et al.*, *Principles of European Family Law Regarding Parental Responsibilities*, Intersentia, 2007, p. 60.

1356 Belgium, Bulgaria, the Czech Republic, France, England and Wales, Greece, Hungary, Italy, Lithuania, Poland, Russia and Spain. See more in Boele-Woelki K. *et al.*, *Principles of European Family Law Regarding Parental Responsibilities*, Intersentia, 2007, p. 61.

1357 This could also differ from: (1) an agreement with the mother (in Austria, Denmark, England and Wales, and Germany), (2) a registration of joint request at an official Register (in the Netherlands and Portugal), or registration on the child's birth certificate (in England and Wales), (3) a joint petition to the guardianship authority which can confer joint parental responsibilities to unmarried parents (in Switzerland), and (4) a court order or registration with the tax authority (in Ireland and Sweden). See more in Boele-Woelki K. *et al.*, *Principles of European Family Law Regarding Parental Responsibilities*, Intersentia, 2007, p. 62.

1358 For instance, France and Italy require an unmarried mother to recognise her child or the court to determine the maternity, just the same as for the father. Boele-Woelki K. *et al.*, *Principles of European Family Law Regarding Parental Responsibilities*, Intersentia, 2007, p. 61.

1359 As it is, for instance, under Hungarian and Italian law. See more in Boele-Woelki K. *et al.*, *Principles of European Family Law Regarding Parental Responsibilities*, Intersentia, 2007, p. 61.

1360 Principle 20 (paragraph 3) of the White Paper, Principle 3:9 of the Principles of European Family Law regarding Parental Responsibilities, article 24 of the Draft Recommendation.

Therefore it is important at least to distinguish between the use of the terms *attribution* and *exercise* of the parental responsibilities.[1361] The Brussels II bis Regulation defines parental responsibility as "all rights and duties to the person or the property of the child which are given to a natural or a legal person by judgment, by operation of law or by agreement having legal effect" (article 2(7)). Accordingly, the term "holder of parental responsibilities" encompasses any person having parental responsibility over a child (article 2(8)).[1362] This would mean a possibility of all interested parties to participate with full or partial responsibilities in the upbringing of the child. The White Paper attributes parental responsibilities primarily to the child's parents who should exercise them jointly. Nevertheless, it also allows that they can be exercised in full or in part by third persons (Principles 19, 20(1), and 20(3)). The Draft Recommendation in its articles 22 and 24 under the term "holders of parental responsibilities" encompasses the child's parents, and the other persons or bodies having parental responsibilities in addition to or instead of the parents. The CRC (article 3(2)) obliges the State Parties "to ensure the child such protection and care as is necessary for his or her well-being, taking into account the rights and duties of his or her parents, legal guardians, or other individuals legally responsible for him or her". It goes even further by stipulating that "parents, or where applicable, the members of the extended family or community, as provided by local custom, legal guardians or other persons legally responsible for the child" should provide guidance and direction to the child to exercise its rights afforded by the Convention. The participation of the extended family in the child's life has been also incorporated (directly or indirectly) in many international documents and interpreted in the light of the respect for private and family life (article 8 ECHR).[1363] Principle 3:9 of the *Principles of European Family Law regarding Parental Responsibilities* deals with the *attribution* of parental responsibilities to three groups of persons (apart from the parent's partner) who enjoy priority, due to the best interests of the child: (1) the child's grandparents, (2) foster parents, and (3) other persons who have close family ties or other ties with the child.[1364] Comparatively, the scope of persons given priority to exercising parental responsibilities with regard to the

1361 See footnote 633.

1362 See footnote 138.

1363 The Hague Child Abduction Convention, 1980 (article 3), the Convention on Recognition and Enforcement of Decisions concerning Custody, 1980 (article 4(1)), the Hague Child Protection Convention, 1996 (article 1(2)), the Convention on the Exercise of Children's Rights, 1996 (article 2(b)), the European Charter of Fundamental Rights, 2000 (article 7), the Draft Treaty for a European Constitution, 2003 (article II-67), and the Convention on Contact Concerning Children, 2003 (articles 5(1) and 5(2)). See also the case of *Scozzari and Guinta v. Italy*, European Court of Human Rights, No. 39221/98, 41963/98, judgment of 13.07.2000 in which the Court recognised some aspects of the parental responsibilities (right to contact with the child) to be attributed and exercised by the grandparents.

1364 Boele-Woelki K. *et al.*, *Principles of European Family Law Regarding Parental Responsibilities*, Intersentia, 2007, p. 72.

child differs.[1365] On the other hand, Principle 3:17 deals with the *exercise* of some or all parental responsibilities in addition to or instead of the parents. This does not mean neither transfer nor attribution of the parental responsibilities to third persons. On the contrary, it regards temporary entrustment of some aspects of it to a specially appointed person (such as a guardian), without infringing the parents' parental authority and without the child being necessarily separated from them.[1366]

On the other hand, a close relative (e.g. grandparent, sibling) and third person (who is not a relative, but to whom the child has significant, close emotional ties) may also have a right to contact with the child. This group mainly includes stepparents, foster parents or former partners of the holder of parental responsibilities. Comparatively, some countries ask for proof of the significant affectionate relationship (e.g. Belgium),[1367] "socio-familial relationship" (Germany),[1368] social parental relationship with a close personal relationship (the Netherlands)[1369] or close relationship in respect of the child (Spain).[1370] Some other countries do not recognise the right to contact of third persons (Bulgaria, Denmark, Finland, Hungary, Italy, Lithuania and Russia).[1371] The content of the contact comprises the child staying for a limited period with or meeting a parent or a person other than a parent with whom he or she is not usually living, as well as any communication between the child and such person.[1372] The right to contact with the child may develop into regular contact that after a certain period

1365 In Austria, the court can entrust one or both grandparents or foster parents with parental responsibilities. As foster parents can be considered stepparents, relatives or other persons with close ties with the child, who can on a permanent basis take care for the child, the court can entrust one or both grandparents or foster parents. In France, the grandparents have priority in taking on the parental responsibilities when parents are deprived of it. In other countries (e.g. Belgium, Bulgaria, Greece, the Czech Republic and Germany), third persons (guardians, foster parents) can take on the role of temporary care but not the parental responsibilities. In some other countries, when the parents are not capable or are relieved of their parental responsibilities, third persons can take on the parental responsibilities (Hungary, Italy, Lithuania, Poland and Portugal). In another group of countries, a third person's attribution to parental responsibilities is an addition to and not a substitution of the existing parental responsibilities (in England and Wales, Finland and exceptionally in Lithuania). This means that these countries allow the existence of three or more parallel holders of parental responsibilities in the child's life. Some other countries do not allow parental responsibilities to be transferred unless their parents have died (Norway), or they are given up for adoption (Russia and Switzerland). Boele-Woelki K. *et al.*, *Principles of European Family Law Regarding Parental Responsibilities*, Intersentia, 2007, pp. 74 and 75.

1366 *Ibid.* pp. 110 and 114.

1367 See article 375*bis* of the Belgian Civil Code requiring for third persons a special affective bond (*bijzondere affectieve band, lien d'affection particulier*) with the child.

1368 German Civil Code, article 1685, paragraph 2.

1369 Dutch Civil Code, article 1:377.

1370 Spanish Civil Code, article 160.

1371 Boele-Woelki K. *et al.*, *Principles of European Family Law Regarding Parental Responsibilities*, Intersentia, 2007, p. 170.

1372 Principle 3:26, *Principles of European Family Law regarding Parental Responsibilities*. This is similarly regulated in the Convention on Contact Concerning Children (article 2(a)). It can include any form of communication (from intensive to less frequent), visiting rights,

may also be interpreted as private and family life (article 8 ECHR), and therefore ground to attribute parental responsibilities to a parent who is not genetically related to the child.

Even though most of the civil jurisdictions empower courts to rule on parental issues, some national jurisdictions restrict that power by moderating the time framework in which the right to a fair trial regarding the constitution of the status can be exercised.[1373] This seems logical if the reasons for constituting parental status are found in the primary role of the parent to take care of the child (while still being a child, and not when the child will become an adult), accompanied by the need to safeguard legal certainty.

7.2. "ARTIFICIAL" CONCEPTIONS – SOCIAL AND LEGAL FATHERHOOD AS A PRINCIPLE RULE

The initial stand coming from the pioneering Principles regarding human artificial procreation and their impact on paternal proceedings was clear, stating: "donor means a person, other than the surrogate mother, who provides his/her gametes or an embryo for the benefit of another person",[1374] continuing: "no filial relationship may be established between the donor of the gametes and the child conceived as a result of artificial procreation. No proceedings for maintenance may be brought against a donor or by a donor against a child".[1375]

In the European comparative context, it is commonly accepted that the sperm donor is not to be considered the legal father. Instead, the father is to be considered the mother's husband or the mother's male[1376] or same-sex cohabitant[1377] (on condition that they consented for the treatment).[1378] Therefore in contrast to "natural" conceptions, for "artificial" ones, biology is irrelevant. What matters is the legalisation of the ties *via* intention or social fact of family life with the child.

communication via phone, fax, mail, etc. See more in Boele-Woelki K. *et al.*, *Principles of European Family Law Regarding Parental Responsibilities*, Intersentia, 2007, p. 178.

1373 For instance, in Bulgaria paternal proceedings can be initiated by the child within three years of attaining majority, or by the mother within three years of the child's birth. In Finland paternal proceedings can be initiated only if the child is not 15 years or over and objecting. See more in Lowe N., *A Study into the Rights and Legal Status of Children being Brought Up in Various Forms of Marital or Non-Marital Partnerships and Cohabitation*, A Report for the Attention of the Committee of Experts on Family Law, September, 2009, p. 11.

1374 *Report on Human Artificial Protection, Principles Set Out in the Report of the Ad Hoc Committee of Experts on Progress in the Biomedical Sciences (CAHBI)*, 1989, Scope and definitions.

1375 *Ibid.* Principle 14(3).

1376 For instance, in Austria, Estonia, France, Greece, the Netherlands, Norway, Spain, Sweden and the United Kingdom.

1377 For instance, in Norway, Spain, Sweden and the United Kingdom.

1378 See more in Lowe N., *A Study into the Rights and Legal Status of Children being Brought Up in Various Forms of Marital or Non-Marital Partnerships and Cohabitation*, A Report for the Attention of the Committee of Experts on Family Law, September 2009, p. 12.

The three general ways of establishing fatherhood elaborated above should apply on equal level to all children irrespective of the modus of their conception or the context in which they were born.[1379] In these terms, the White Paper supports equal application of the paternal presumption (including the conflicts arising from it) also for medically assisted conceptions in marital and extra-marital relationships (Principle 9). It also affords the possibility of application of the principles regarding voluntary recognition and the judicial decision. The idea behind this is to equalise as much as possible the legal positions of children in both contexts: conceived "naturally" and "artificially". It goes even further by recognising that all stages of the procedure for establishing parenthood should be available, including civil proceedings if there is a disagreement regarding the recognition. What should differ though is the merit that will be taken as relevant to decide if the legal parenthood will be granted on grounds of intention or biology. Along these lines, the partner of the mother who consents to the treatment cannot oppose his parenthood, because for him, the intention expressed in the form of written consent is the relevant fact for establishing his fatherhood.[1380] Consequently, the sperm donor cannot claim his fatherhood on biological grounds in the same case, because he lacks the fact of positive intention expressed in the written consent.[1381] This has also been affirmed in the case of *J.R.M. v. the Netherlands* in which the Court concluded that the sperm donor does not hold the right to family life with the child just because he is a biological father.[1382] This could only apply in legal systems that allow up to two parents to be registered on the birth certificate, as do most European positive family laws. The situation would be different for instance in British Columbia (Canada) where the new Family Law Act allows up to four persons to be registered on the birth certificate, which has already resulted in the first child with three parents.[1383] On the contrary, in the European context with predominantly two-parent families as the template, the White Paper does not address the peculiarities of conceptions with the assistance of sperm donation to single women. They do belong to a special category for several reasons. Firstly, the child does not have any competing father (social, biological or legal). Secondly, a known sperm donor may also express an intention to recognise the child as his. Thirdly, if the recognition is consented to

1379 Article 2(1) of the ICCPR, article 14 of the ECHR, article 12 of the Treaty Establishing the European Community, 1975, article 2 of the CRC, article 21 of the European Charter of Fundamental Rights, 2000, article II-81, Draft Treaty for a European Constitution 2003.

1380 Article 17 (paragraphs 1(b), 1(c), 2), the Draft Recommendation.

1381 *Ibid.* Article 17, paragraph 1(a) stipulates: "gamete or embryo donors are not considered as the legal parents".

1382 *J.R.M. v. the Netherlands*, European Commission on Human Rights, No. 16944/90, Decision of 08.02.1993.

1383 See footnotes 944 and 945. Another similar case of a gay man who donated sperm to his lesbian former wife through a licensed clinic, seeking greater parental access but contrary to the mother's wishes, was also dealt with in the UK. See more in Wijlaars L., "Gay Man Who Donated Sperm to Lesbian Ex-Wife Seeks Parental Access", *bionews.org.uk*, 13.02.2012, available online: www.bionews.org.uk/page_124417.asp.

by the mother, his claim for fatherhood could be approved or rejected by the Court with a judicial decision grounded on a combination of facts: genes, intentions and family life with the child. A case of known sperm donor (former partner of the later single woman) being granted parental responsibilities has already been dealt with in the Australian context.[1384]

When it comes to the contestation of fatherhood, the grounds differ significantly in cases of medically assisted procreations. The White Paper elaborates the need to distinguish between the two in this particular domain due to the relevance of the genes that have always been a priority in paternity proceedings for "natural" conceptions.[1385] The Draft Recommendation has different rules for contestation of the fatherhood of "naturally"[1386] and "artificially"[1387] conceived children. Namely, in the latter case, the contestation of the paternal affiliation is only possible if one of the following grounds is satisfied: (1) the father consented to medically assisted procreation but the child was not born as a result of such treatment, (2) the father consented to medically assisted procreation with the use of his sperm, but the sperm of a third person was used, and (3) the father did not consent at all to the treatment.[1388] Therefore in cases of "artificial" inseminations, the legal father cannot contest his paternal affiliation on grounds that he is not the biological father. The ECtHR has also accepted restrictions on contestation in the case of *Rasmussen v. Denmark*.[1389] The White Paper affords the right to contestation to the father, the child/representative, the mother or to other persons holding a specific interest (for instance, the person claiming to be the father). It also affords a possibility for the States to opt not to allow contestation of paternity if they consider that it is in the child's best interests (for instance in the cases of

1384 Even though under the Victorian State Law, known sperm donors are not to be considered as legal fathers. In this particular case, the judge explained that the federal law that holds the presumption of legal parentage for biological progenitors (not rebutted in the case) suppressed the state provisions, supported by the notion that the law envisages two parents. See more in Blackburn-Starza A., "Australian Known Sperm Donor Granted Parenthood", *bionews.org.uk*, 24.06.2013, available online: www.bionews.org.uk/page_315706.asp.

1385 White Paper, p. 17. This is being harmonised with the regulation in the European Convention on the Legal Status of Children Born Out of Wedlock (article 4) that allows contestation of voluntary recognition only if the person seeking to recognise or having recognised the child as his is not the biological father.

1386 Article 16, paragraph 2 of the Draft Recommendation allows biology to be the only ground for contestation. The Proposed European Convention on Family Status has the same solution in article 23(2)(b). See Lowe N., *A Study into the Rights and Legal Status of Children being Brought Up in Various Forms of Marital or Non-Marital Partnerships and Cohabitation*, A Report for the Attention of the Committee of Experts on Family Law, September, 2009, p. 49.

1387 Article 18, paragraph 1, of the Draft Recommendation suggests the States to provide appropriate rules for contestation of fatherhood when the child is conceived by medically-assisted procreation and the fatherhood is grounded on other facts and not genetic contribution (i.e. validity of the given consent for the treatment). Paragraph 3 of the same article also allows a ban of contestations of parental affiliations in cases where this is in the best interest of the child.

1388 For purposes of comparison see footnote 1277.

1389 *Rasmussen v. Denmark*, European Court of Human Rights, No. 8777/79, judgment of 28.11.1984.

medically assisted procreations or where the father recognised and cared for the child being aware that the child is not biologically related to him).[1390] This goes along with the strive to achieve legal certainty and security of already established family relationships. It has also been safeguarded in a number of cases before the ECtHR.[1391] Nevertheless, the contestation does not apply when the child was conceived by sperm donation to a single woman simply because there is no fatherhood to be contested in the first place.

The concept of "family life" as enlisted in article 8 ECHR is a developing concept, demonstrating the dynamic and progressive nature of families, taking account of the social change and acting as a catalyst for further change.[1392] At the present time, the general situation as summarised by Nigel Lowe is as follows: (1) the mother–child relationship is considered a "family" irrespective of the context in which the child is born,[1393] (2) the married father–child relationship is also considered a "family", (3) unmarried fathers, though, need to establish family life with the child, i.e. a sufficient interest in and commitment to the child.[1394] In medically assisted reproductions, legal fathers have also to consent to the treatment, as a form that grants them acknowledged status and therefore capacity to further show sufficient interest and commitment to the child. This clearly shows that proving fatherhood is not solely dependent on matching DNA. As such, there is no excuse to ban access to paternal proceedings due to fear of revealing secrets and biology interrupting already created families.

7.2.1. MARRIAGE

The marital presumption in cases of sperm donations to couples affirms legal fatherhood of the social father (i.e. the partner of the woman who was inseminated) as from the moment of her giving birth to the child. In terms of the

1390 White Paper, p. 17.

1391 In the case of *M.B. v. the United Kingdom*, European Commission of Human Rights, No. 22920/93, judgment of 06.09.1994 the Commission considered that there were sound reasons of legal certainty and security to refuse DNA tests to be conducted on the husband that require a good cause before allowing the marital presumption to be disturbed. See footnote 230. Restriction to contestation where the circumstances were not in favour of the child's best interests was noted in the cases of *Nylund v. Finland*, European Court of Human Rights, No. 27110/95, judgment of 29.06.1999, and *X, Y and Z v. the United Kingdom*, European Court of Human Rights, No. 21830/93, judgment of 22.04.1997.

1392 Lowe N., *A Study into the Rights and Legal Status of Children being Brought Up in Various Forms of Marital or Non-Marital Partnerships and Cohabitation*, A Report for the Attention of the Committee of Experts on Family Law, September, 2009, p. 7. See also Van Bueren G., "Child Rights in Europe", Council of Europe, Strasbourg, 2007, p. 118.

1393 This would be true only if an exception to the principle *mater semper certa est* does not apply (as, for instance, in surrogacy cases in Greece).

1394 Lowe N., *A Study into the Rights and Legal Status of Children being Brought Up in Various Forms of Marital or Non-Marital Partnerships and Cohabitation*, A Report for the Attention of the Committee of Experts on Family Law, September 2009, p. 7.

White Paper's meaning of legal parent,[1395] the marital presumption assumes legal fatherhood and not biological fatherhood. Therefore it would be inappropriate to contest this legal fatherhood grounded on intention (in the sense of consent prior to the treatment that marks the fact that the reproductive project was mutual with the partner) supported by the social fact of family life with the child, due to the rationale of acknowledging biological fatherhood.[1396] Paragraph 2 of Principle 10 of the White Paper also forbids the mother's husband or companion who gave his consent to the treatment to oppose the establishment of his paternity, unless the court finds that the child was not born as a result of the treatment he consented to. It should be clear that legal parenthood can have several sources including both biological and social ties. Since they are equally legitimate to claim legal parentage, they cannot compete among each other based on the fact of which one should prevail or should be given greater value. On the contrary, they can only compete with and contest against each other once the other circumstances are evaluated, which is dependent on the specificities of a particular case. This is a more relevant reason why the possibility for challenging parenthood in relation to children conceived by sperm donations to single women should be allowed. The possibility does not mean that fatherhood will be established. It will only allow an access to evaluate the grounds, and therefore access to justice for everyone as in concordance with article 6 of the ECHR.

7.2.2. EXTRA-MARITAL RELATIONSHIPS

The European Convention on the Legal Status of Children Born Out of Wedlock does not allow fatherhood, once recognised, to be opposed or contested, for purposes of safeguarding legal certainty. Nevertheless, it allows an exception in cases when the person who recognised the child as his is not the biological father.[1397] The Convention does not address conceptions assisted by third persons for whom fatherhood cannot be grounded in biology but in intention given in the form of consent prior to the treatment. In cases of reproductive projects for partners in extra-marital relationships, the consent to the treatment is usually taken as recognition or as a ground to establish fatherhood after the birth of the child. On these grounds, and not on grounds of biology, the given consent cannot be withdrawn, opposed or contested.

1395 See footnote 1253.

1396 This is also in concordance with the White Paper, which reasons that "the law may opt not to allow the parentage to be established on the basis of biological affiliation, for instance in cases of medically assisted procreation with an anonymous donor of sperm". White Paper, p. 7.

1397 Article 4 from the European Convention on the Legal Status of Children Born Out of Wedlock stipulates: "the voluntary recognition of paternity may not be opposed or contested in so far as the internal law provides for these procedures unless the person seeking to recognise or having recognised the child is not the biological father".

7.2.3. SINGLE WOMEN – PARENTS BY CHOICE

International documents deal very scarcely with the sole exercise of parental responsibilities, even less with the cases of voluntarily single mothers. This is due to the ideal attributed to two-parent families as best fitted to satisfy the best interests of the child. Article 8 of the European Convention on the Legal Status of Children Born Out of Wedlock stipulates: "where the father or mother of a child born out of wedlock does not have parental authority over or the custody of the child, that parent may obtain a right of access to the child in appropriate cases". Even though this provision was tailored to refer to "natural" conceptions, it reflects the preferable scenario for children having the possibility to establish filiations with both parents irrespective of the circumstances surrounding their birth.

Principle 3:15 of the *Principles on European Family Law regarding Parental Responsibilities* allows the sole exercise of parental responsibilities if in conformity with the child's best interests and if both parents have agreed followed by a competent authority.[1398] Even though this principle does not refer to situations where the child is intentionally born fatherless, it could be interpreted as if both parents agreed (if the consent of the donor and of the mother to the treatment is considered an agreement). Similarly, this is also afforded in Principle 20 of the White Paper. Even though both principles refer to *exercise* and not to *attribution* of parental responsibilities (while the difference is not clear in many national legal systems), it is also questioned if it should be afforded, having account for the proclaimed right of the child to have and to be taken care of by both parents.[1399] The agreements for sole parental responsibilities by the parents (in the countries in which this is available) are usually scrutinised by a competent authority that should pay attention to the best interests of the child.[1400] Nevertheless, from a comparative spectrum of the European countries, the sole exercise of parental responsibilities after irreversible breakdown of the relationship between the parents is not a rule, but usually an exception. Only a few countries, under certain circumstances entitle one parent to be the sole holder of parental responsibilities after dissolution of the child's parents' relationship followed by disagreement regarding the mutual exercise.[1401] It has to be underlined, though, that this is exceptional and not a general rule.

Principle 3:16 of the *Principles of European Family Law regarding Parental Responsibilities* anticipates situations where only one parent has parental responsibilities (either *ex lege*, when parenthood has been established only in relation to one parent, or in exceptional circumstances when it has been

1398 Boele-Woelki K. *et al.*, *Principles of European Family Law Regarding Parental Responsibilities*, Intersentia, 2007, p. 100.

1399 *Ibid.* p. 101.

1400 See more in *ibid.* p. 102 and 103.

1401 For regulation in different European countries, see *ibid.* p. 103.

established in relation to both of them, while one of them is not capable or is deprived of exercising them). This Principle, though, does not explicitly refer to the situation when the child has been conceived by a single woman by choice. From the explanation of it, it refers to cases when the child as a matter of circumstances has established the parenthood of one parent only (for instance in cases of children born out of wedlock while not recognised by the father).[1402] Nevertheless, the point is that when there is only one parent as holder of parental responsibilities, that parent can exercise them in their full capacity without the need for consent or agreement by anybody else.

A tricky issue that tackles single parents by choice and their children that has not been elaborated much when discussing the individual reproductive right is the situation when something happens to the sole parent that disables further exercise of the parental responsibilities. Principle 3:31 of the *Principles on European Family Law regarding Parental Responsibilities* deals with the death of the parents. Paragraph 2 stipulates that "if a parent having sole parental responsibilities dies, responsibilities should be attributed to the surviving parent (not having in mind single-parents-by-choice cases) or a third person upon a decision by the competent authority". Principle 23 of the White Paper has similar content, adding in its paragraph 3 also: "where there is no longer any parent still living, the competent authority should take a decision concerning the attribution of parental responsibilities. The national legislation may provide that these responsibilities may be given to a member of the family or to a stepparent or to a person designated by the surviving parent unless the interests of the child require other measures". Comparatively, in most of the countries, after the death of one parent the full parental responsibilities are transferred to the surviving one.[1403] Unfortunately, this is not possible in the cases of single-women-parents-by-choice, which also makes the position of the children born into this kind of family a bit more fragile. Nevertheless, in the event that both parents die (and there is no remaining parent to transfer the parental responsibilities to), they are usually replaced by another institution (usually guardianship, subject to the court's supervision), or rarely another person (usually a family member, a friend, a married couple with a close personal relationship with the child). In some countries there is a possibility for a declaration (in the form of designation for a guardian) to be made before a competent authority.[1404]

The term "holders of parental responsibilities" is inspired by article 2(b) of the 1996 European Convention on the Exercise of Children's Rights. Article 23 of the Draft Recommendation sets as a general principle that parental responsibilities should belong to each parent irrespective of the relationship between the parents. It also suggests the states provide legal procedures by which the other parent will

1402 Boele-Woelki K. *et al.*, *Principles of European Family Law Regarding Parental Responsibilities*, Intersentia, 2007, p. 101.
1403 *Ibid.* p. 204.
1404 For how it is regulated in different European countries, see further *ibid.* p. 207.

also be given the possibility to acquire such responsibilities. Article 24 allows that other (third) persons should also (if necessary or in the best interests of the child) have the possibility to be attributed parental responsibilities. The purpose of this is to enable stepparents to have a factual and legal possibility to exercise parental responsibilities. This would allow situations in which three persons can be holders of parental responsibilities (for instance, where the child already has a mother and a father, there is a possibility for parental responsibilities to be given to the mother's later partner), or a situation in which the initially fatherless child can establish a link with the later partner of the mother. Family life in the light of article 8 of the ECHR is based on the existence of regular contacts between the family members. The child's right to continuous contact is also provided in the CRC (article 9) and the Convention on Contact concerning Children (article 4(1)). If this is taken *mutatis mutandis*, the contact as a mutual right of the parent and the child of an already established relationship, could also serve as a source to constitute the status, once it is exercised on a regular basis.

A child with a level of maturity that allows reflection on the decision regarding the attribution of parental responsibilities should be allowed active participation.[1405] This includes the child's right to be informed, consulted and to express his or her opinion in all matters that concern him or her in proceedings before a competent authority to determine the allocation of parental responsibilities and in resolving disputes about the exercise of parental responsibilities.[1406] Some authors have investigated the discrepancies between the declarations of this right and its real application in practice, concluding that the latter differs markedly from the theory outlined formally in the law.[1407]

From a comparative overview of the recognition of the child's right to be heard in proceedings concerning parental responsibilities, it was observed that the great majority of jurisdictions do impose a duty on the court to hear the child, directly or by delegating the hearing to a suitable person or body,[1408] while some others have the possibility of the discretion of the court to decide if it will hear the child.[1409] Three interrelated (often emerging in consecutive order) parts of the right of the child to participate in matters that concern him/her can be

1405 Principle 3, *ibid.* See also Principle 2, Recommendation No. R (84) 4 on Parental Responsibilities.

1406 Article 21 Draft Recommendation. For more on the right of the child to actively participate in matters that concern him/her, see Chapter 6, Children conceived by sperm donors' assistance to single women.

1407 See more in Resetar B., Emery R.E., "Children's Rights in European Legal Proceedings: Why are Family Practices so Different from Legal Theories?", *Family Court Review*, Vol. 46, No. 1, 2008, p. 73. See also Woodhouse B.B., "Child Custody in the Age of Children's Rights: The Search for a Just and Workable Standard", *Family Law Quarterly*, Vol. 33, No. 3, 1999, pp. 815–832.

1408 Austria, Bulgaria, the Czech Republic, Denmark, England and Wales, Finland, Germany, Greece, Hungary, Lithuania, the Netherlands, Norway, Poland, Portugal, Russia, Spain, Sweden, and Switzerland. From a survey done in Boele-Woelki K. *et al.*, *Principles of European Family Law Regarding Parental Responsibilities*, Intersentia, 2007, p. 50.

1409 Belgium, France, Ireland and also the Republic of Macedonia. See *ibid.* p. 51.

differentiated: (1) the child's right to receive information, (2) the child's right to be consulted, and (3) the child's right to express his or her opinion.[1410] The rationale behind this differentiation is to enable the child firstly to receive the information and to be consulted as a prerequisite that will enable him/her fully and truly to take part in the decision-making process. If the responsible person decides not to hear the child, they have to elaborate the reasons, making the participation of the child a general rule, while non-participation an exception.[1411] The hearing could take place directly (before the competent authority), or indirectly (before a person or body appointed by the competent authority). Due weight should be given to the child's age and maturity.

The child's active involvement in any (administrative and) judicial proceedings affecting him/her covers a wide range of civil (and administrative) proceedings, including parental disputes in which their interests are at stake. Articles 2, 3 and 12 of the CRC taken together with article 6(1) of the ECHR, should at least provide access for children conceived "artificially" to proceedings for challenging parenthood, irrespective of what the outcome would be. The ECHR becomes a vivid instrument that lives with the evolving reality enabled by the interpretations from the ECtHR. This is how even issues that were initially considered ethically, traditionally and nationally sensitive became over time elevated to a level of universal principles (such as the right to family life of the factual, and not solely of the biological parent, as well as the growing recognition of the right to know one's origins).[1412] Thus, the attribution of fatherhood also has to be examined on an individual level, enabled by equal access to paternal proceedings for both children and parents irrespective of the contexts of conceptions. The peculiarities of each case individually will have to balance different grounds for constituting the legal concept of parenthood. The CRC Committee also affirmed that the right of the child to be heard in judicial and administrative proceedings applies to all relevant settings without limitations.[1413] It has also stressed that appropriate measures should be taken in order to address discrimination against vulnerable or marginalised children in order for all children to fully enjoy the rights enshrined in article 12.[1414] This implies the creation of a new concept for attribution of paternal responsibilities that will not discriminate against parents (based on their mutual relationship), and children (based on the circumstances of their conception and birth). On the contrary, the new concept should harmonise

---

1410 Principle 3:6 of the European Family Law Principles.

1411 See Principle 3:37 of the European Family Law Principles that explicitly deals with the participation of the child in hearings before competent authorities concerning parental responsibilities.

1412 *European Court of Human Rights: The ECHR in 50 Questions*, July 2012, available online: www.echr.coe.int/Documents/50Questions_ENG.pdf, pp. 3 and 11.

1413 Committee on the Rights of the Child, *Report on the Forty-Third Session*, September 2006, Day of General Discussion, Recommendations, paras. 34–36 and 38.

1414 *Ibid.* paras. 8 and 10.

the legal ways of establishing fatherhood and should apply irrespective of the context of conception.

7.3. EXTRAPOLATING A UNIVERSAL CONCEPT FOR PATERNAL ATTRIBUTION

From the above elaborated documents that deal with the ways of establishing fatherhood, there is an evident discrepancy between the two contexts of conceptions: "natural" and "artificial". Even though the documents try to merge both contexts of conceiving children in the field of establishing parenthood, they also accept their limits by making restrictions and exceptions or even separate headings for medically assisted conceptions.[1415] Accepting the international proclamations, given the priority *inter alia* afforded to non-discrimination against children and parents (based on grounds of their status or birth),[1416] the right of the child to know his/her origins and as far as possible to be taken care of by both parents,[1417] the right to express his/her own opinions in matters that affect him/her,[1418] including the right to a fair trial in civil proceedings[1419] with regard to the respect for private and family life,[1420] several points for adapting the concept of paternal attribution are suggested.

As a starting point, it should be considered that establishing paternity as from the moment of birth and the tendency of giving stability over time is important for children and parents.[1421] This should encompass that parenthood should start for the genetic parents (both the mother and the father in both contexts "natural" and "artificial") as from the time of birth. Up to this moment, the genetic relation between the child and the parent should be of paramount importance as it corresponds with the genetic reality and the nature of procreations. From this moment on, possible changes in terms of withdrawal from parental responsibilities and their later transfer to the commissioning parents should activate the other side of the parental concept – intentions and responsible parenthood – as an artifice that creates family life as lived reality. This being clarified, a neutral terrain will be paved for accepting both realities – genetic and social – acknowledging that both are relevant up to some level to be taken as grounds for paternal attribution in parental proceedings. Furthermore, this should reduce the fear of meeting both realities once they are contested in civil proceedings, making access to justice available for all parties to the relationship.

1415 See, for instance, footnotes 1386 and 1387.
1416 See footnote 1035.
1417 Article 7 of the CRC.
1418 Articles 3 and 12 of the CRC.
1419 Article 6(1) of the ECHR.
1420 Article 8 of the ECHR. For more on the rights of the child, see Chapter 6, Children conceived by sperm donors' assistance to single women.
1421 See footnote 1257.

Thus, donors should be considered genetic parents of their live progeny at the time of birth and accordingly notified of this fact. Once they are notified, they should resign their parental responsibilities that will bar any further inquiries from them in the domain of exercising them. This will prevent further contestations in court, and will also regulate in advance the limits up to which the donors' liabilities can extend. This will also demonstrate a more serious attitude towards sperm donor conceptions. Firstly, they will engage themselves in donations being aware that their sperm sample is not just a number in the laboratory. By acknowledging the donor from the birth of his genetically related child, he will at least be acquainted with the results of the donation. This should also reduce the number of procreated children by one sperm donor, since the numbers will be replaced with existent children with their existence (or identity) known to the donor. An obligation of the donor to withdraw from his paternal responsibilities should derive from a pre-agreement to which he should have consented in a formal procedure executed by a licensed clinic. Any further conflicts regarding the rights and duties undertaken under this pre-agreement should be dealt with between the contracting parties – the clinic and the donor. This would bring sperm donations closer to surrogacies and adoptions, harmonising the parental concept and enabling uniform application of the procedural rules regarding attribution and exercise of parental responsibilities. This would also reduce any further conflicts between the genetic and the social grounds for establishing parenthood, or at least, make them solvable on fairly balanced facts. Thus, paternal proceedings should be available for every child and parent irrespective of the context of the conception, if it is accepted that there are other grounds apart from biology to deal with the merit of such cases, and thus to found the legal parentage. Therefore the already available ways of establishing parenthood should not make a difference between the contexts of conceptions. Presumption, recognition and judicial decision should be available legal possibilities at the disposal of every child.[1422] Nevertheless, this should not interfere with the child's right to know his/her origins and the resulting genetic information as facts. Even more, the clear-cut difference between genetics and the social aspects of family life should break through eventual illusions and place the expectations on a more realistic terrain. Shifting anonymous to non-anonymous concepts of donations should make it clear to the donors that their progeny may want to know their identity and possibly meet them in the future. Article 4 of the Draft Recommendation goes a step further by suggesting that even when anonymity is guaranteed, it should be open to the competent authority to override the rights and disclose relevant information.[1423]

Secondly, accepting the extension of the marital presumption to extra-marital relationships is an acknowledgement that grounds other than biology,

[1422] See the text to footnotes 1267, 1269, and 1270.

[1423] Referring to the text related to footnote 1265.

such as enduring psychological relationship and living arrangements, are relevant for the parent–child relationship.[1424] This also shows greater response of the law to synchronise not just with the emerging technologies, but also with the emerging social changes, accepting the increasing interest to found families outside the marital institution. Thus, a more appropriate term to replace the *marital presumption* becomes *paternal presumption* (since it applies to the establishment of the paternal link irrespective of the relationship between the parents).

Thirdly, accepting the possibility of recognition as a way of establishing fatherhood should also apply to others apart from genetically related men with their children. This will demonstrate an attitude that accepts other than biological facts for the paternal constitution. It will also enable a possibility for children conceived by sperm donations to single women potentially and eventually to have a person exercise the father's role engaged in their upbringing. As this is conditional on an additional consent from the mother and/or the child, and/or other authorities, the child's best interests will be evaluated with due scrutiny.[1425] Nevertheless, the harmonisation of the paternal concept would mean that even this man (genetically unrelated but socially closely related to the child) should have a possibility of constituting legal paternity before the court, once the consent from the concerned parties is not gained. It is up to the court to measure the relevant facts of the relationship, taking into account also the enduring psychological relationship, living arrangements, affection and care as part of the family life with the child (as encompassed under article 8 of the ECHR). This again shows that family law matters, maybe even more than others, are surrounded with circumstances that can differ on a case-by-case basis. Therefore they should be reconsidered on individual bases and a possibility of that kind should be available. Since the constitution (or rejection of the claim) of recognised but contested parenthood is traditionally challenged before the court, judicial proceedings should be accessible to children and parents irrespective of the context of the conception. It is another issue if these proceedings should/could be delegated to other authorities such as social institutions, mediators, etc.

Fourthly, and in concordance with what has been said so far, the extension of access to civil proceedings as a third way of determining parenthood should also be afforded to children conceived by medically assisted conceptions. The rationale could be located in the grounds upon which contestations of already established parenthood are afforded. Firstly, the marital presumption is usually challenged on genetic grounds as proved by the accuracy of scientific DNA tests. The legal parenthood established *via* adoptions is not allowed to be challenged on genetic grounds, because the intentions leading to a caring relationship and family life with the child are considered to matter more. Nevertheless,

---

1424 Apart from being a way to equalise the positions of parents and children in and out of formal marital arrangements.

1425 See the text related to footnotes 1335, 1336, 1337, 1338 and 1339.

in adoption cases it is considered that the parenthood was already challenged at the time when the genetic parents withheld their parental responsibilities and consequently transferred them to the adoptive parents. That is why adoptions are listed under the section of change of parenthood in the White Paper.[1426] If donors are also asked to withdraw from their parental responsibilities after the birth of the child, their position would be made equal to men giving their child up for adoption. Therefore for them, paternity is also to be considered already challenged perhaps not as a *res judicata* but substantially challenged regarding its constitution. Challenging paternity would be even less possible if the child has already established family life with two parents. Cases of single mothers by choice that have adopted a child or given birth themselves to a child conceived by sperm donation encompass situations of an empty place for the father. At this level, there is nothing conflicting with it. The child may want to know the identity of the genetic parent and should have mechanisms available to do so. Nevertheless, accepting the fact that the parental concept encompasses much more than mere genetic links should guide the further possible inquiries in eventual paternal proceedings. Knowing the genetic origins could also result in the development of perpetual contact that if followed by expressed intention and willingness from the concerned parties could create factual family life. In contrast, the content of the right to know one's genetic origins could also be exhausted at that stage, taking into account that it is a separate and not always integrated part of the concept of legal parenthood. This is how the law will acknowledge, accept and sync with the consequences of the scientific participation in the family creations and the resulting fragmentation of parenthood.

Lastly, going back to the first point, giving stability to established fatherhood over time would mean that certain time limits should apply to the possibility for access to proceedings for challenging parenthood in order to ensure a decent level of legal certainty.[1427]

[1426] See the text related to footnotes 1300.

[1427] See the text related to footnotes 1347, 1348, 1349 and 1350.

CHAPTER 8

APPLYING THE RESULTS OF THE ANALYSIS IN THE CASE OF THE REPUBLIC OF MACEDONIA

8.1. MAPPING THE TERRAIN FOR THE DISCUSSION

The lenses for the perception of reproduction in the Western and Eastern European countries are different.[1428] While in general the Western countries consider the project of having children as a matter of personal choice made by individuals or couples, in the Eastern countries, reproduction can also be perceived as a social obligation, providing continuity on a small scale of the family name,[1429] and on a large scale of the nation.[1430] Therefore, in the Eastern

1428 Van Balen F., Inhorn M.C., "Introduction: Interpreting Infertility. A View from the Social Sciences", in Inhorn M.C., Van Balen F. (eds.), *Infertility Around the Globe*, University of California Press, 2002, pp. 3–32.

1429 See more in: Sutton D.E., "Local Names, Foreign Claims: Family Inheritance and National Heritage on a Greek Island", *American Ethnologist*, Vol. 24, No. 2, 1997, pp. 415 and 429. The article connects the local-level kinship practices with the significance they give to the name, in an attempt to explain the Greeks' "hysteria over history" in relation to the international controversy – the naming of the "Former Yugoslav Republic of Macedonia". The author reasons that a denial of accepting the right of choosing a name for one international subject is justified by the attempt to rationalise the irrational naming practice by relating it to possessions (i.e. ownership through inheritance), and history (i.e. ownership through heritage). The case study suggests how anthropologists can use kinship to make a unique contribution to current studies of nationalism "from the bottom up". The relatedness between kinship and nationalism comes from their joint features – they are both culturally constructed ideologies with claims to natural, biological self-evidence, and they both need to be deconstructed and understood as powerful meaning-giving systems. In this sense, kinship and nationalism interpenetrate and overlap cultural domains with sometimes similar but also sometimes conflicting messages. Other authors also argue that it is important to analyse kinship as "one among a number of potential, interpenetrating classificatory systems (race, caste, ethnicity) that are part of the process of nation building". See also Williams B., "Classification Systems Revisited. Kinship, Caste, Race, and Nationality as the Flow of Blood and the Spread of Rights", in Yanagisako S., Delaney C. (eds.), *Naturalizing Power: Essays in Feminist Cultural Analysis*, Routledge, 1995, p. 206.

1430 *Ibid.* p. 416, arguing that interest in studies over kinship in the Western world was lost in the 1970s and 1980s due to the theoretical shift from concerns about the local societies to that of nation-states and global processes. Its significance in the study of modern nation-states has been underplayed because the absence of kinship turned out to be one of the defining characteristics of the Western view of itself. In this sense, kinship remained a mere metaphor,

European countries parenthood has deeper social roots that go along with more severe consequences of involuntary childlessness.[1431] A pronatalist society usually has the justification for such policy in the wider nation-state ideology, instead of individual well-being and self-fulfilment.[1432] This is consistent with Foucault's premises that reproductive sexuality has turned into a domain of collective anxiety and state intervention due to the fact that the future of our species and our nation depends on it.[1433] The policy of prioritising the greater public good over the individual is covered by linking a person's social and moral worth to reproduction.[1434]

On a general level, the perception is that sperm and oocyte donation are more easily available in the Eastern European than in the Western European countries. This perception makes the Eastern European countries be considered favourable

---

while nation-states now run on principles of so-called rational bureaucracy. Nevertheless, whether seen as practice or metaphor, they are still important for understanding both the national discourse and its local ramifications. See also in Herzfeld M., *The Social Production of Indifference. Exploring the Symbolic Roots of Western Bureaucracy*, Berg, 1992, p. 68.

1431 Pennings G., "Ethical Issues of Infertility Treatment in Developing Countries", *ESHRE Monographs*, Vol. 2008, No. 1, 2008, pp. 15–20.

1432 See, for instance, the recent speech of the Prime Minister of the Republic of Macedonia in which he emphasised that above all the greatest problem that the country is facing is the decreasing demography and depopulation, leading to recession of the nation. See more in the brief from the speech: "Груевски: наталитетот е особено загрижувачки", *Глас на ВМРО-ДПМНЕ*, 23.11.2013, available online: http://glas.mk/2012/10/gruevski-natalitetot-e-osobeno-zagrizuvacki/. For more see also http://daily.mk/cluster/efd1242f4a9db38755c37cb77418784d. He called upon the demographic statistics showing that only approximately 22,000 children were born in 2011 as opposed to 40,000 in 1980, a drop of almost 50%, while the population is rapidly aging, with a ratio of employed people to pensioners of 1.7 to 1, as opposed to 5 to 1 in 1980. He also stressed that the current fertility rate is 1.4 children per mother which is far below the minimum of 2.1 needed to maintain the population. (For more accurate information on the national demography see the official State's statistics website: *Државен завод за статистика, население*, www.stat.gov.mk/OblastOpsto.aspx?id=2). The Prime Minister concluded that the country is facing a demographic crisis that poses a greater existential threat than the global economic crisis. Consequently, soon after, other political parties came up with certain controversial solutions to the problem, one of which (greatly contested), was the introduction of an annual tax in the amount of one average monthly salary for unmarried males above 35 and for females above 30 years. While this proposal was firmly opposed, the Social Affairs Minister announced a new set of other measures to combat the decreasing birth rate including "activities in the educational system, migration and infrastructure policies, economic development and fight against poverty and social exclusion". Some other past measures, though, were also controversial. For instance, in 2009, the government initiated a new modus for boosting the population growth by financial incentives to mothers with more than one child. In April the same year, the court discarded that provision on the grounds that it was discriminatory, envisaging state help only for mothers living in mainly ethnic Macedonian areas with a low average birth rate. Other local NGOs (e.g. "Coalition for Life") in the meantime organised marches aimed at "raising awareness amongst the youth about the importance of marriage and child birth". See more in Marusic S.J., "No Extra Tax for Macedonia's Bachelors, *BalkanInsight*, 05.11.2012, available online: www.balkaninsight.com/en/article/no-extra-tax-for-macedonia-s-bachelors.

1433 Foucault M., *The History of Sexuality, Vol. 1, An Introduction*, Hurley R. (trans.), Vintage Books, 1990.

1434 Ulrich M., Weatherall A., "Motherhood and Infertility: Viewing Motherhood through the Lens of Infertility", *Feminism & Psychology*, Vol. 10, No. 30, 2000, pp. 323–336.

destinations for those seeking cross-border reproductive treatments.[1435] Some studies have recorded large numbers of patients from Austria, Italy, Germany and the UK travelling to more recently joined European Union Member States such as Czech Republic and Slovenia (2004) to seek medical care.[1436] The reasons are associated with favourable legislative environment, accompanied with implemented EU Directives for quality and safety, as well as the lower prices for medical care. Another reason for putting Eastern European countries on the map for cross-border reproductive tourism for these authors is the firmly accepted anonymity of the donors (five countries allowing non-identifying information, while only three countries allow identifying information of the donors).[1437] For some other authors, the most common reasons for travelling for reproductive purposes is law evasion when the technique is either forbidden *per se* or when a particular group is excluded from treatment. There may also be some other access limitations, such as long waiting lists, poor quality or expensive treatments.[1438]

Even though generalisations are usually accompanied with stereotyping and prejudices (even more, in this particularly novel field where changing developments emerge as we speak), one argument holds as a fact – the regulation and practice of donations and the disclosure of identifying information in Western and Eastern European countries are different.[1439] For some authors, this should be changed in the process of European integrations since the Eastern European health care facilities should prepare for the potential requests for donor identification in the future.[1440] The change is justified by the psychological welfare of the child to know their personal identity and family belonging as being crucial for its own integrity and personality, and its increasing recognition by the ECtHR.[1441] As such, it is considered that regulations paying attention only to the physical aspects of the ART procedure (for instance, transmitting viral or genetic disease, thus allowing non-identifying information only regarding the medical file of the donor), while not paying attention to the psychological welfare of the child do not appreciate the

1435 Shenfield F, De Mouzon J., Pennings G., *et al.*, "ESHRE Task Force on Cross-Border Reproductive Care. Cross-Border Reproductive Care in Six European Countries", *Human Reproduction*, Vol. 25, No. 6, 2010, pp. 1361–1368.

1436 *Ibid.*

1437 *Ibid.*

1438 Shenfield F., Pennings G., De Mouzon J., Ferraretti A.P., Goossens V., on behalf of the ESHRE Task Force Cross Border Reproductive Care (CBRC), "ESHRE's Good Practice Guide for Cross-Border Reproductive Care for Centers and Practitioners", *Human Reproduction*, Vol. 26, No. 7, 2001, p. 1.

1439 Jones H.W., Cohen J., Cooke I., Kempers R. (eds.), "IFFS Surveillance 07", *Fertility and Sterility*, Vol. 87, Supp. 1, 2007, pp. 28 and 33. Ory S., Devroey P. *et al.* (eds.), *IFFS Surveillance*, 2013, pp. 15 and 58.

1440 Dostal J., "Specific Ethical and Legal Aspects of ART Practice in Eastern European Countries", in Schenker J.G. (ed.), *Ethical Dilemmas in Assisted Reproductive Technologies*, Walter de Gruyter, 2011.

1441 Shenfield F., Surreau C., "The Welfare of the Child. Whose Responsibility?", in Shenfield F., Surreau C. (eds.), *Contemporary Ethical Dilemmas in Assisted Reproduction*, Abingdon, 2006.

best interests of the child. These interests, though, are protected and integrated in the European Commission Directives.[1442]

The European Union is bound to respect children's rights from two perspectives: (1) as an integral part of the human rights, being subject to the Millennium Development Goals, the European Convention on Human Rights and Fundamental Freedoms as well as the European Charter of Fundamental Rights (especially in its article 24), and (2) as a self-standing set of concerns and not simply subsumed into wider efforts to mainstream human rights in general, being subject to the CRC and its Optional Protocols. This is recognised as appropriate by the European Commission due to the fact that certain rights have an exclusive or particular application to children, such as the right to maintain relations with both parents.[1443] The question of identity has also to a great extent been recognised as an important element of building children's protection mechanisms across Europe.[1444] On the agenda for the rights of the child is also reviewing legislation that will facilitate the recognition and enforcement of decisions on parental responsibilities. As indicated by the Euro-barometer surveys, 76% of children interviewed were not aware that they have rights and 79% did not know who to contact in case of need. Therefore one of the European actions highlighted for the period 2010–2015 for creating child-friendly justice under the European Union Agenda for the Rights of the Child is to turn the promises into practical reality mainly by evaluating and re-evaluating the EU and national legislation on, among others, enforcement of decisions on parental responsibilities.[1445] Along this line, full recognition of the rights of the child means that children must be given a chance to voice their opinions and participate in the decision-making in matters that affect them. This is stipulated in article 24(1) of the Charter that requires the European Union to take children's views into consideration in accordance with their age and maturity.[1446] The Member States (of the Council of Europe) are also bound to respect on the one hand, the ratified universal international documents, and, on the other hand, the decisions of the ECtHR that concern the practice of the national courts.[1447]

1442 European Commission Directives 2004/23/EC, 2006/17/EC and 2006/86/EC.

1443 Communication from the Commission – *Towards an EU strategy on the rights of the child* {SEC (2006) 888} {SEC (2006) 889} COM/2006/0367 final, available online: http://eur-lex.europa.eu/legal-content/en/ALL/;jsessionid=8vlVTxjKjthhvD40pbF21N3wV7lCt8chyGGsc3cxC0dvzRcYRFpD!-639655971?uri=CELEX:52006DC0367.

1444 *Ibid.* p. 2.

1445 Communication from the Commission to the European Parliament, the Council, the European Economic and Social Committee and the Committee of the Regions. An EU Agenda for the Rights of the Child, COM/2011/0060 final.

1446 *Ibid.* p. 4.

1447 Article 400 of the Law on Litigation Procedure (Закон за парнична постапка, *Службен весникна Република Македонија*. бр. 79/05, 21.09.2005. See the English unofficial translation: Law on Litigation Procedure, consolidated text) of the Republic of Macedonia regulates the repetition of proceedings due to a final decision of the ECtHR as follows: "(1) When the European Court of Human Rights confirms violation of certain human right or of the fundamental freedoms anticipated in the European Convention for the Protection of Human

The legal tendency of the Republic of Macedonia is to follow the best practice regulations of the European Union Countries and to implement the Directives in order to harmonise the national legal system for the purposes of accession. Still, the level of discussions and flexibility to follow the development of the science in the field of ART and family life is considered to be more neglected in the Eastern in comparison to the Western European countries.[1448] It has also been acknowledged that setting forth a uniform practice of medically assisted technologies on an international level is impossible, due to the diversity of traditions, political situations and medical practices. Because of this, and being aware of this, most national legislation does not forbid reproductive tourism. An international consensus, at this time, can only reflect the lowest common denominator.[1449]

Another critique regarding the performance of ART in the Eastern European countries is that they do not, or do so less, assess the issues regarding the moral status of human embryos. Therefore the discussions over definitions of the beginning of human life or the meaning of a human person are more neglected in the academic and in the political arena in comparison to the related discussions in the Western European countries.[1450]

The act of conception and the issue of defining the particular moment of gestation when the zygote starts to acquire features of a human embryonic life worthy of legal protection is a subject of sharp debate and serious discussions around the world. Despite the disagreements, a legal compromise has been achieved that has not yet been regarded as universal, nor has it reconciled the differences between ethical, religious and professional groups concerned by the various national legislation. For the sake of the proposed discussion, which does not focus on the ethical deliberation of embryonic life, a legal compromise has also been set in the Macedonian Law on Bio-medically Assisted Fertilisation. Article 29 of the Law forbids extra-corporal development of an embryo older than 14 days, which means after the development of the primary notch and thereafter claims gradual level of protection of the embryo, transferring the ethical

Rights and Fundamental Freedoms and its additional protocols, ratified by the Republic of Macedonia, the party can, in a period of 30 days as of the final verdict of the European Court of Human Rights, file a request to the court in the Republic of Macedonia, having tried in the first instance in the procedure wherefore the decision violating some human right or fundamental freedom is adopted, to amend the decision violating such right or fundamental freedom. (2) The provisions on repeating the procedure shall accordingly apply to the procedure referred to in paragraph (1) of this Article. (3) In the repeating of the procedure the courts shall be obliged to obey the legal opinions stated in the final verdict of the European Court of Human Rights confirming the violation of the fundamental human rights and freedoms".

1448 Dostal J., *Ethical and Legal Aspects of Assisted Reproduction.Situation in the Member States that Joined the European Union in 2004* (1st edition), Olomouc Palacky University, 2007.

1449 Jones H. W., Cohen J., Cooke I., Kempers R. (eds.), "IFFS Surveillance 07", *Fertility and Sterility*, Vol. 87, Supp. 1, 2007, p. 67.

1450 Dostal J., "Specific Ethical and Legal Aspects of ART Practice in Eastern European Countries", in Schenker J.G. (ed.), *Ethical Dilemmas in Assisted Reproductive Technologies*, Walter de Gruyter, 2011, p. 82.

dilemmas of the value of its life into the domain of abortion, once the embryo is in the woman's body.[1451]

On the other hand, in the international academic arena there is a misconception that the regulation and application of ART in the Republic of Macedonia is almost non-existent.[1452] This is mainly due to a lack of scholarship that will conduct research and surveys, resulting in deficiency of written material for the greater international audience. In contrast, national authors consider that the legislation and practice are in parallel with the scientific development, and moreover that the application of the bio-medically assisted technologies is more liberal than in the other surrounding Balkan countries, or in the wider European context.[1453] The liberal nature of the topical law is associated with the fact that both homologous and heterologous donations of sperm and ova have been given the green light, as well as posthumous reproductions, and research on embryos under strict conditions. Even though surrogate motherhood is

---

1451 The Law on Termination of Pregnancy (Закон за прекинување на бременоста,*Службен весник на Република Македонија*, бр. 87, 17.06.2013) stipulates that as a general rule, termination of pregnancy can be performed up until the tenth week from the time of conception (article 3). As an exception, termination of pregnancy can also be performed after the tenth week from the time of conception under several conditions, *inter alia*, if it is confirmed that (1) the pregnancy endangers the health and life of the woman (article 4, paragraph 2); (2) she may experience severe personal, familial, financial or other hardships that will affect her health (including disturbed marital and familial relationships, asocial familial environment, financial instability, disturbance of the health of the other members of the family and the number of the children in the family – article 4, paragraphs 4 and 5); and (3) there are certain expectations that the child will have severe physical or psychological disturbances (article 4, paragraph 3). This means that legal life does not start at conception. Accordingly, the parental responsibilities are not related to the act of conception. The legal consequences of personhood start at the time of birth when the legal capacity of being a natural person is gained. Therefore the parental responsibilities also start at the time of birth. An exception exists in the Law on Inheritance, following the Roman law principle – *nasciturus pro iam nato habetur, quotiens de commodis eius agitur ius* – which presumes that the foetus will be considered as already born for purposes of inheritance, and therefore is treated as a natural person before being born. The Inheritance Law (article 122) stipulates that only an "alive person at the time of activating the legal consequences of the inheritance (the death of the deceased) has the capacity to be a heir (paragraph 1). Already conceived child at the time of the death, will be considered as if it is born already, if is born alive later on" (paragraph 2). For more on the ethical and legal status of embryos, see Ignovska E., "The Value of Life of the Embryo, the Argument of Potentiality to Develop, and the Context in which is Embedded", in Hongladarom S. (ed.), *Genomics and Bioethics: Interdisciplinary Perspectives, Technologies and Advancements*, 2011; Mickovikj D., Ristov A., "Bio-medically Assisted Fertilization in the Republic of Macedonia", in Jansen B.E.S., Ignovska E. (eds.), *Law, Public Health Care System and Society*, Vol. 8, 2012.

1452 See, for instance, Dostal J., "Specific Ethical and Legal Aspects of ART Practice in Eastern European Countries", in Schenker J.G. (ed.), *Ethical Dilemmas in Assisted Reproductive Technologies*, Walter de Gruyter, 2011; *Reply by the Member States to the Questionnaire on Access to Medically Assisted Procreation (MAP) and on the Right to Know about Their Origin for Children Born after MAP*, Steering Committee of Bioethics, Strasbourg, 9 February 2012.

1453 In terms of introducing liberal solutions in the first systematic Law on Bio-medically Assisted Fertilisation from 2008. See also Mickovikj D., Ristov A., "Bio-medically Assisted Fertilization in the Republic of Macedonia", in Jansen B.E.S., Ignovska E. (eds.), *Law, Public Health Care System and Society*, Vol. 8, 2012.

regulated but strictly forbidden,[1454] there is currently an ongoing discussion regarding amendments/a new law for its allowance.[1455] There is a growing interest in regulating surrogacies worldwide.[1456] In this context, one of the concerns that will need to be addressed in due course is also the right of the child to know his/her origin.

This topic has been neglected previously, because the starting point for the regulations has always been confidentiality.[1457] Consequently, the topical Family Law and the Law on Bio-Medically Assisted Fertilisation are compromising the right of the child to know his/her genetic identity in prioritising the interests of the donors and parents before the interests of the child, even though the former Yugoslavia and the Republic of Macedonia as a successor country, respectively, ratified the CRC.[1458]

As a consequence, both laws will have to undergo changes in the field of affiliation in order to harmonise with the international documents and the practice of the ECtHR, as well as on a national legal level.

1454 Article 27 of the Law on Bio-medically Assisted Fertilisation explicitly forbided surrogacies (during the time when this book was written). Surrogacies were introduced by amending the Law on Bio-medically Assisted Fertilisation on 9 October 2014 (Offical Gazette of the Republic of Macedonia, No. 149). Nevertheless, the contested issues argued here (for instance the right of the child to know his/her genetic identity) were not changed.

1455 At the time of writing (15.02.2014), there were no draft proposals yet. It was only on a level of public discussion that started by gathering experts from different fields – gynaecologists, psychologists, sociologists, ethicists, and lawyers to discuss the context and the climate for introducing it legally. See, for instance, www.dnevnik.mk/?ItemID=A0A1BEBD942CDB4A8CD10ADA49EBD5B2; http://mk.voanews.com/content/article/1836062.html;http://tocka.com.mk/1/116521/debata-na-tema-surogat-majcinstvo.

1456 See more in International Surrogacy and Donor Conceived Persons, "Preserving the Best Interest of Children", Call for Action by the International Social Service Network, July 2013, available online: http://iss-ssi.org/2009/assets/files/maternite-substitution/ISS%20call%20for%20action%20-%20Surrogacy%20-ENG.pdf; *A Preliminary Report on the Issues Arising from International Surrogacy Arrangements*, Hague Conference on Private International Law, March 2012, available online: www.hcch.net/upload/wop/gap2012pd10en.pdf; Blyth E., Crawshaw M., Van den Akker O., "What are the Best Interests of the Child in International Surrogacy?, *bionews.org.uk*, 17.02.2014, available online: www.bionews.org.uk/page_397263.asp.

1457 See, for instance, in the context of donations, article 17 of the Law on Bio-medically Assisted Fertilisation, and in the context of adoptions article 123-a of the Family Law.

1458 See footnote 124. See also the explanation of the Law on Bio-medically Assisted Fertilisation explicitly stating that one of the aims of the law is to undertake necessary measures to keep the confidentiality of the information regarding the donor, including his identity and to prevent traceability to him or his family, the child and its family. See more in Влада на Република Македонија, *Предлог за донесување на Закон за биомедицинско потпомогнато оплодување со предлог на закон*, Скопје, јануари, 2008, стр. 29, available online: www.sobranie.mk/default.asp?pSearch=%D0%B1%D1%80%D0%B0%D0%BA+&x=0&y=0. See also the Criminal Code that regulates the unauthorised disclosure of secret information in its article 150, stipulating that a lawyer, notary, barrister, doctor, delivery nurse, any other health care employee, psychologist, religious minister, social worker or any other person that within its job duties will reveal a secret (that should be regarded as confidential) without authorisation will be fined or imprisoned. Criminal Code (Кривичен законик, *Службен весникна Република Македонија*, бр. 37/96, 80/99, 4/2002, 43/03 , 19/04 и Одлукана Уставен суд: Службен весник 48/01 г.).

The following text will, firstly, give an overview of *de lege lata* affiliation, diagnosing the discrepancies and problems on a national level.[1459] This is for the purposes of examining the internal consistency of the legal presumptions on affiliation for establishing parenthood in cases of medical assistance and the competing biological/genetic, legal and social criteria for becoming a parent when they conflict before the court.

Secondly, the text will offer suggestions *de lege ferenda*, or how the law should comply with the national and international challenges of harmonising the practice of sperm donations with the concept of affiliation and family life. This will be conducted from an international perspective of (1) the right to private and family life (article 8 ECHR) and the ways of establishing parental responsibilities, and therefore creating families, (2) the right of the child to know his/her genetic origin (article 7 CRC) as originating from the right to identity (article 8 CRC) on the way to belonging to a particular family, and (3) the right to a fair trial (article 6(1) ECHR) in parental proceedings on equal grounds for parents and children irrespective of the contexts of conceptions, and their interpretations from the *ECtHR*.

8.2. *DE LEGE LATA* AND CONSIDERING *DE LEGE FERENDA*

The Constitution of the Republic of Macedonia affords special protection to the family, children (with parents and even more so parentless) and motherhood.[1460] It is a human right to decide freely on procreation, thus to decide on founding families.[1461] The Republic undertakes the role of leading human population policy in line with balanced economic and social development.[1462] The right to respect and protect private life, as well as personal and family life, dignity and reputation is guaranteed.[1463] Every citizen holds a right to submit inquiries and petitions to the state authorities and the other public services and to receive a response.[1464] Every citizen also holds the right to ask for protection of the rights and freedoms as protected in the Constitution before the Constitutional Court.[1465]

Two legal pillars will be used as a point of reference in the following part: (1) the Family Law, as being a basic legal source of the family life regulation

1459 Mostly regulated in the Family Law and in the Law on Bio-medically Assisted Fertilisation, but also in other related laws in the Republic of Macedonia.

1460 Articles 40 and 42, the Constitution of the Republic of Macedonia, *Official Gazette of the Republic of Macedonia*, No. 52, 22.11.1992.

1461 *Ibid.* article 41, paragraph 1.

1462 *Ibid.* article 41, paragraph 2.

1463 *Ibid.* article 25.

1464 *Ibid.* article 24.

1465 *Ibid.* article 50.

and the relationship between parents and children,[1466] and (2) the Law on Bio-medically Assisted Fertilisation, as regulating for the first time in a systematic legal document the practice of ART, therefore also interrupting and influencing the legal affiliation.[1467] Other laws and the Constitution will also be called upon in the fields that are of interest for the discussion.

8.2.1. THE FAMILY LAW

8.2.1.1. Family

The law defines *family* as a living community of parents, children and other relatives if they live in a mutual household.[1468] This definition represents only the extended family[1469] aiming at the nuclear family, shedding no light on other family forms such as single-parent families, reconstructed families or families founded with an intervention of a third party as in the case of assisted donation of sperm/ovum or embryo.

A family can be founded by birth or adoption of a child; consequently, parenthood can be established by the fact of birth or adoption.[1470] This means that as a principle rule the fact of birth creates consequences of parenthood for both the mother and the father from that moment on. If the birth happens out of wedlock, additional action of recognition or judicial proceedings will be retrograde with the legal consequences of parenthood as if they had started from the time of the birth of the child. The father has the possibility of recognising the child as his after as well as prior to birth, with legal effect only after the birth of the child.[1471] Adoption is the only exception that follows a later fact (and not the birth itself) to constitute the family. This makes the foundation of families assisted by donations follow the fact of birth, negotiated to exclude the genetic parent before the insemination even takes place. Accordingly, consent to treatment has

1466 Family Law, 1992. This law continues the family law tradition of the former Yugoslavia with its own codification dating from 1992. See further Chapter 3, section 3.2, Republic of Macedonia.

1467 Law on Bio-medically Assisted Fertilisation. See also Chapter 3, section 3.2, Republic of Macedonia.

1468 Law on Bio-medically Assisted Fertilisation, article 2.

1469 As a family that includes other relatives of the nuclear family if they live in one household. See more in Andersen M.L., Taylor H.F., *Sociology: Understanding a Diverse Society*, Thomson Wadsworth, 2008, p. 396.

1470 *Ibid.* article 7. See also the Law on Inheritance, article 122 that stipulates the capacity to inherit, stating that a heir can only be a person that is alive at the time of the death of the deceased (when the inheritance is open) – paragraphs 1 and 2. If the child is conceived but not born yet at that moment, he/she would qualify as a heir only if born alive – paragraph 3.

1471 Article 53 of the Family Law. The father also has a possibility to recognise the child as his during the paternal proceedings against him initiated by the other legitimate parties before the court. In that case, the proceedings stops and it is considered as if he has recognised the child as his. See the case before the Supreme Court – Пресуда на Врховниот суд на Република Македонија, Рев. Бр. 957/98, 25.06.1998.

significance for recognition of the child not only before birth but indeed before insemination, with legal effect only after the birth of the child.[1472] This could be interpreted as if the law allows other than biological facts to constitute families if at the time of birth parenthood was already negotiated *via* a contract of free wills expressing the intention to parent.[1473] Contracts in the field of family law and reproduction are controversial in their nature.[1474] The issue is related to the

[1472] Article 12, paragraph 2 of the Law on Bio-medically Assisted Fertilisation.

[1473] For some authors the consent is at the heart of any valid contract, including in the field of reproduction. If conceptions are intentional and the goal is to increase the voluntariness of the decision, then attention should be paid to the parties' negotiations before conception. This is how they can exercise their freedom of choice (by expressing intentions before conception) with respect to the individual's reproductive capacity. See in Shanlev C., *Birth Power: The Case for Surrogacy*, Yale University Press, 1989, pp. 11, 12, 96 and 103.

[1474] They are also controversial under the Macedonian legal system. The later text will refer to provisions from the Law on Obligations (Закон за облигационите односи, *Службен весник на Република Македонија*, бр. 18, 05.03.2001) and the Law on Ownership and Other Real Rights (*Law on Ownership and Other Real Rights* – Закон за сопственост и други стварни права, *Службен весник на Република Македонија*, бр. 18, 05.03.2001) to relate the reproductive arrangements to the concept of contracts. Nevertheless, they (gamete donations, more specifically – sperm donations for the reproductive purposes of other parties) are legally derived from the "free written consent" in the form of a "written statement" verified by a notary (article 15, paragraphs 1 and 2 of the Law on Bio-medically Assisted Fertilisation). The consent refers to, firstly, donation of the donor's sperm, and secondly, to withdrawing of his eventual parental responsibilities (article 15, paragraph 4). Consequently, the donor holds obligations from the given consent: firstly, an active obligation – to donate (*dare*), and secondly, a passive obligation – to restrain from parental responsibilities (*non facere*). These obligations correspond to the rights of the commissioning parents which also give "free written consent" with a significance of a statement for accepting fatherhood (or motherhood) after the child is born, as transferred from the donor. In this light, analogy with contracts could be at least considered. The considerations derive from the importance we attribute to the embodiment in our understandings of the "self" and its freedom, as well as the tension between promoting freedom to dispose of it through contracts and the preservation of non-contractual human relationships. For Shanley, the contractarian theories that ignore the limits to the freely willed self run the risk of confusing broadly conceived human freedom and dignity with a narrow notion of freedom of contract (*infra* Shanley M.L., pp. 619 and 635). Nevertheless, as some authors have argued "at some point contracts must be embedded in social relations that are non-contractual" (Held V., "No-Contractual Society: A Feminist View", *Canadian Journal of Philosophy*, Vol. 17, Suppl. 1, Special Issue: Suppl. Vol. 13, *Science, Morality & Feminist Theory*, 1987, pp. 124 and 125). For more on the contract in the field of reproduction, but in the context of surrogacies, see Shanley M.L., "'Surrogate Mothering' and Women's Freedom: A Critique of Contracts for Human Reproduction", *Signs*, Vol. 18, No. 3, 1993, pp. 618–639. This author distinguishes three poles of authors that elaborate the contracts in the field of surrogacies as a service for others: (1) those who support contract pregnancies because women should have the right to enter a contractual arrangement to bear a child and receive money for the service (the opposite would be an infringement of their autonomy and self-determination); (2) those who focus on the desire for a child for the commissioning parents, arguing that a prohibition on pregnancy contracts violates their right to procreate; and (3) those who oppose pregnancy contracts, particularly if the surrogate woman enters into obligations out of direct economic needs or is forced to fulfil the contract against her will (see more on p. 618). For some others, contracts in the field of reproduction are usually vague. Even if they are clear, their validity and enforceability is a matter of controversy since the legal rules on parentage usually cannot be overruled by private arrangements. See more in Antokolskaia M., "Legal Embedding Planned Lesbian Parentage. Pouring New Wine into Old Wineskins", *Familie & Recht*, February 2014, p. 5. Yet the Dutch Supreme Court applied tort law and contract law principles of justice and

status that the law attributes to parts or products of the human body. If they are considered property, then the person owning and possessing them could easily dispose of them for a reasonable financial or other contribution in the exchange.[1475] If they are not considered property, then they are considered to be outside the commercial market (*res extra commercium*), and therefore impossible to dispose of.[1476] There is a difference between the American (more market-driven), and the

---

equity in family law matters – protecting functional parent-child relationships, for instance, when it comes to the "consent to acknowledgment" cases. See more in Kleijkamp G.A., *Family Life and Family Interests, A Comparative Study on the Influence of the European Convention of Human Rights on Dutch Family Law and the Influence of the United States Constitution on American Family Law*, Kluwer Law International, 1999, pp. 365 and 366. In the USA the support of firm, strict written agreements that set out the rights and expectations of the parties in reproductive arrangements is higher. See, for instance, Garcia M.A., "In with New Families, Out with Bad Law: Determining the Rights of Known Sperm Donors Through Intent-Based Written Agreements", *Duke Journal of Gender Law & Policy*, Vol. 21, 2014, p. 221 and 224. In some provinces of Canada, despite the controversies, strict contracts are practised. An example of a clearly articulated contract in writing is the one in the Canadian case of *W.W. v X.X. and Y.Y.*, ONSC 879, 2013 where the sperm donor explicitly signed over any and all parental rights to any children created with the use of his donated sperm. He stated that he withdrew from any rights to see, visit, claim, request custody of any children or even to share information regarding the conception with them, having in return no responsibilities to pay support of any kind. In addition to this, it was also stated that the legally binding contract could not be changed or revoked without the consent and agreement of the mother and the other adoptive parent. Despite all the strictly regulated aspects of the relationship, the donor tried to rebut the validity of the contract by claiming, later on, that he signed it under duress. This is an example of how contracts in the field of family law are rather tricky to be evaluated later on, especially the part that is related to children, as it may be considered contrary to public policy. See more Kelly F., "Equal Parents, Equal Children: Reforming Canada's Parentage Laws to Recognize the Completeness of Women-led Families", *University of New Brunswick Law Journal*, Vol. 64, 2013, pp. 263, 264, and 265.

1475 This is regulated in Section I, Part I: Contracts of the Macedonian Law on Obligations.

1476 This is regulated in the Law on Ownership and Other Real Rights. See, especially, articles 9 and 12. The first regulates the general restrictions on ownership stipulating that the owner gains the right of ownership depending on the nature and the purpose for using the thing, as well as the general interest prescribed by law. It is forbidden to exercise the right of ownership contrary to the purpose recognised by law, the morals of society or for purposes of causing harm to another person, or restricting another person from exercisinghis own rights. The second regulates the subject of the right to property, excluding things that according to their nature or the law hold restrictions in their exercise. Article 43 of the Law on Obligations regulates the allowed grounds (if they are consistent with the Constitution, the law, and the good customs) for contractual rights and obligations. The objects of a contractual pledge have to fulfil two conditions: (1) to be owned by the pledge debtor, and (2) the object to be in the legal traffic. If the second condition is not satisfied, then the ownership cannot be transferred from one person to another. Despite this, it is not certain how the fruits of the *resextra commercium* are to be treated. According to some authors, regardless of the fact that the object is not dispensable and therefore outside the rules of the legal market, the fruit of the object may fall under the domain of a contractual pledge after its separation. It is another issue if products (fruits) of the human body can be considered as objects. See more in Przeska T., "Things that May be Object of Contractual Pledge in the Legal System of Republic of Macedonia", *Iustinianus Primus Law Review*, Vol. 1, No. 1, 2010, p. 1. See also Gavella N., Stvarno Pravo, Svezak 2, Narodne Novine, 2007, p. 180. Along this line, other authors also argue that: "our bodies are factories: they produce things like blood, skin, hair … Self ownership gives us the title to these, and protects our liberty to dispose of them." See Steiner H., *An Essay on Rights*, Blackwell, 1994, p. 233. Other authors, in an attempt to investigate the "investment of genetic material" of

European (less market-driven and more driven by altruistic reasons) approach to this issue. The European approach[1477] promotes altruistic donations, in relation to which sole contribution to the expenses (in terms of efforts, time spent, costs and lost salary) is supported. This in reality is a bit more than just "fair expenses" or "pocket money", since if it were otherwise, the interest of the donors would have been drastically reduced. A line should be drawn to differentiate between donations of organs, tissues and cells,[1478] and gametes that can be used for reproductive purposes.[1479] While the first ones save lives, but and are extracted from one's already created body, and therefore are related to one's bodily integrity, the second ones create lives, but are not part of one's body, but products of it.[1480] Donations are regulated with expression of free will in the form of consent,[1481] which as such could fall under the domain of contracts that consequently produce rights and obligations for the contracting parties.[1482] In the case of sperm donation, the obligation of the donor is more than giving up possession of his sperm. He also gives up the consequent progeny and parental responsibilities that follow. His obligation correlates with the right of the commissioning parents. On the contrary, his rights are related to the material satisfaction of his expenses,

---

the progenitors, and consequently their share in the "joint creation", have distinguished two conceptual components with which the progenitors participate in the newly formed embryo: (1) physical, made out of tissue samples, cells, DNA and the atoms that make the nucleic acid molecules that hold genetic code as unique genes, and (2) informational – the code itself, the particular arrangement of atoms that make the DNA sequence that forms the individual genome. According to them, physical components might be a subject of property rights and from here on, they support the "property-based approach" as an answer to the question "what rights over embryos arise from property in genetic material?". See also Ignovska E., "The Value of Life of the Embryo, the Argument of Potentiality to Develop, and the Context in which is Embedded", in Hongladarom S. (ed.), *Genomics and Bioethics: Interdisciplinary Perspectives, Technologies and Advancements*, 2011.

1477 As envisaged in the Oviedo Convention, article 21 stipulating that "the human body and its parts shall not, as such, give rise to financial gain".

1478 In the Republic of Macedonia regulated by the Law on Extracting and Transplanting Human Body Parts for Medical Treatment (Закон за земање и пресадување на делови од човечкото тело заради лекување, *Службен весник на Република Македонија*, бр. 47, 08.04.2011. Article 2, paragraph 2 of the Law makes it clear-cut, stipulating that "the provisions of this law will not apply on reproductive organs and tissues, organs and tissues of embryos or fetuses, blood and blood derivatives". For more on this law, see Deanoska-Trendafilova A., Cadikovski V., "Legal and Medical Issues Concerning the Transplantation of Human Body Parts for Treatment in the Republic of Macedonia", in Jansen B.C.S., Ignovska E. (eds.), *Law, Public Health Care System and Society. Macedonia – Social Policy, Legislation, Biomedicine and Ethics of Organ Transplantation, Fertilization and ART*, Academische Verlagsgemeinschaft, 2012, pp. 27–81.

1479 In the Republic of Macedonia regulated by the Law on Bio-medically Assisted Fertilisation.

1480 Regarding the treatment of the products of the body, see footnote 1476.

1481 Article 15 of the Law on Bio-medically Assisted Fertilisations and article 20 of the Law on Obligations.

1482 If sperm donations are considered altruistic and not tradable for financial or other gain, then they would be considered gifts. Again, gifts in law are related to property and possessions of things (article 555 of the Law on Obligations stipulates that the contract for gift envisages an obligation of the giver (donor) to give (donate) to the receiver (recipient) a certain object, or to transfer a certain right, cease to exist certain debt or to take over a debt without contribution).

and the preservation of his privacy (if he is anonymous), or disclosure of his identity and/or contact with the progeny (if he is not anonymous – this is not an option in the Republic of Macedonia). These premises are usually regulated in the mutual contract that follows the free disposition of the contracting parties.[1483] The contracts in the field of reproduction, though, have been much more developed in the domain of surrogacies. There, the role of the surrogate mother is limited to her role of "renting" her uterus for the commissioning parents, making her just biologically (due to the gestation) and not necessarily also genetically related to the child she will give birth to.

If on the one hand it is accepted that contracts can constitute families before birth, and before conceptions or inseminations, it becomes absurd to claim exclusivity of the relevance of accurate DNA tests proving biological ties in parental proceedings in cases of conflict later on.[1484] The main reason why the law has opted not to challenge parental inquiries in civil proceedings is due to its inconsistency in accepting both the biological but also the social reality of family lives.[1485] If gamete donation is treated as a second exception next to adoption, then the donor would be considered a parent at the time of the birth.[1486] Accordingly,

---

1483 Law on Obligations, article 3 regards the freedom of regulating mutual obligations in concordance with the Constitution, the law and good customs, and article 14 regulates the dispositive character of the law. For more on the donor's rights and obligations from the relationship see Part II under Chapter 5, section 2.2, The rights and correlative obligations of sperm donors donating to couples and single women.

1484 The scientific proofs of matching genetic links between the parent and the child are stipulated in article 61 of the Family Law that stipulates that a father of the child born out of wedlock will be the mother's sexual partner in a time period of 180 to 300 days before the birth of the child, unless the opposite is proven. For this purpose, the Court is entitled to take into account also the mutual relationship between and habitat of the mother and the defendant before and after birth, as well as the medical and other proofs that do not exclude the defendant as a father.

1485 The Family Law forbids (1) parental proceedings if the parental relationship has been established by adoption (article 75), (2) contestation of fatherhood if the mother has been inseminated by sperm donation following consent by her marital partner (article 71 – this article has not been harmonised with the Law on Bio-medically Assisted Fertilisation that allows inseminations of extra-marital partners as well as single women (article 9)), and (3) establishment of fatherhood if the child has been conceived using artificial insemination (article 62). Nevertheless, these articles infringe the right to a fair trial as stipulated in article 6(1) of the ECHR, and restrict access to examination of the family life of children conceived artificially or adopted (article 8 of the ECHR), which in turn is discriminatory on grounds of birth.

1486 For instance, in Quebec, Canada a new chapter on "Filiation of Children Born of Assisted Procreation" was incorporated into Title Two – "Filiation" of the Civil Code of Quebec. This was interpreted by some authors as a third distinctive model of affiliation next to blood and adoption. Article 538 of the Civil Code defines the parental project as a project involving assisted procreation from the time that a person or a couple decides, in order to have a child, to resort to the genetic material of a person who is not party to the parental project. This could include any kind of assistance from medical to "friendly" for purposes of assisting others to have a child. Article 538.2, paragraph 1 allows the donor, who agreed to assist reproduction by sexual intercourse, to establish his paternity within one year after the birth of the child. This bars the partner of the birth mother from claiming her own filiation on grounds of factual family life or *possession d'état* with the child during that period of time. See more in Leckey R., "'Where the Parents Are of the Same Sex': Quebec Reforms to Filiation", *International Journal for Law, Policy and the Family*, Vol. 23, 2009, p. 66 and 75.

he would be obliged by a pre-contract to reject the parental responsibilities and to transfer them to the commissioning parents at a later stage (similar to surrogacy contracts).[1487] This way the parenthood would start at the time of birth for both genetic parents, but the family would be constituted later on through additional legal action. It has already been discussed that families are more social than natural constructions. Consequently, the law has to follow this reality, just as it has created it.

On the other side of the spectrum of mixing genetic and social facts in composing families are the newly parental contracts for co-parenting among known mothers and fathers that match each other solely for the reproductive purposes of having a mutual child.[1488] This resembles sperm donation by a known donor, with the exception of the fact that it does not treat the man as a donor but as a father. In these terms, the interests of all parties are satisfied (normally without conflicts): (1) the single woman and her child-wish, but also a father, while not necessarily a partner; (2) the man and his child-wish together with a mother, but not necessarily a partner; and (3) the child and his/her interests in having both a mother and a father. Since these arrangements are rather new and unexplored in practice, the applicable law will be the positive law of the nation state that refers to children conceived out of wedlock. The parental contract does not even have to be concluded, nor does the practice have to be performed in a licensed clinic since the parental responsibilities will follow according to the law, by additional recognition or judicial proceedings. One of the concerns is that they will suspend families as we know/knew them and will introduce parental contracts without parental relationships. The positive aspect of it, as well as protecting the right of the child to know and be taken care of by both parents, is that the conflicts between the parents will be solved on a rational basis without the emotional disturbances that go along with the eventual breakdown of the parents' relationship. Since this is a rather new phenomenon, other future research could possibly analyse the future consequences of arrangements of such kind.

[1487] A pre-contract in the Law on Obligations (article 37, paragraph 1) is defined as a contract to undertake an obligation to conclude another, later, main contract. The pre-contract is binding if it integrates the substantial parts of the main contract (article 37, paragraph, 2). The court may order the obliged party to act upon the obligation and conclude the main contract upon the request of the interested party within a particular time frame (article 37, paragraph 4). The pre-agreement loses its obligatory nature if the circumstances surrounding its conclusion change to the extent that the pre-contract would have never been concluded had they existed at the time of its conclusion (article 37, paragraph 6). Nevertheless, it should be noted that contracts and pre-contracts, as stipulated in the law, are related to the obligations *dare*, *facere*, *non facere*, and *pati*, that should be possible, allowed, determined or determinable (article 38 of the Law).

[1488] Al Jazeera English, "Family on Your Own Terms", *The Stream*, 24.02.2014, available online: http://stream.aljazeera.com/story/201402242305-0023501.

8.2.1.2. Marriage

Marriage is defined as a legally regulated union between a man and a woman in which the interests of the marital partners, the family and society are established.[1489] The Law on Prevention and Protection from Discrimination refers to, *inter alia*, also gender, belonging to a marginalised group, personal and social status, family and marital status and any other ground stipulated in the law or an internationally ratified document as discriminatory treatment.[1490] The law defines equality as a principle according to which everyone should be treated equally in terms of rights and obligations, encompassing also differences that should also be afforded equal treatment.[1491]

Nevertheless, it also explicitly accepts the same definition of marriage as in the Family Law.[1492] There was a recent attempt to include this definition in the Constitution, making a statement that homosexual partnerships are not favoured, and are a threat to the family and to the proper development of children.[1493] Therefore the initiatives for changes in the Constitution aimed to strengthen and safeguard the exclusive position of marriage as a heterosexual nest, even though the same provisions already exist in the positive national regulation under the Family Law.[1494]

[1489] Family Law, article 6.

[1490] Law on Prevention and Protection from Discrimination (Закон за спречување и заштита од дискриминација), *Official Gazette of the Republic of Macedonia*, No. 50, 13.04.2010, article 3.

[1491] Law on Prevention and Protection from Discrimination, article 5, paragraph 6.

[1492] Law on Prevention and Protection from Discrimination, article 5, paragraph 5.

[1493] See more in the notes of the Parliamentary debate over the proposal for changes in the Constitution of the Republic of Macedonia: *Стенографски белешки од 72-та седница на Собранието на Република Македонија*, одржана на 23 септември, 2013, стр. 4, available online: www.sobranie.mk/default.asp?pSearch=%D0%B1%D1%80%D0%B0%D0%BA+&x=0&y=0. Very recent similar behaviour was noticed in Croatia, which is worthwhile mentioning for purposes of comparing patterns of countries that share the same legal heritage from the past (as part of former Yugoslavia). Namely, in Croatia the issue of defining marriage as a union between a man and a woman in the Constitution was decided by a referendum (the third in the country, after the decisions on the issues of independence and EU accession). The initiative was taken by the organisation *U imeobitelji* (*In the name of the family*) that collected signatures necessary for a referendum (more than 740,000). The results were also overwhelming since a large majority of the population (more than 65%) voted for the exclusivity of marriage to heterosexual couples. See online: www.slobodnaevropa.org/content/u-hrvatskoj-referendum-o-ustavnoj-definiciji-braka/25185749.html;www.tportal.hr/vijesti/hrvatska/302015/Ovo-su-ekstemni-rezultati-referenduma.html.

[1494] The rationale was that if the exclusivity of heterosexual marital community is given at a constitutional level, not just at a level of law, it will be more difficult for the left oriented opposition when it gains a majority in Parliament to change the law and introduce homosexual partnerships in the future. The idea is to make it as difficult as possible for the time being and for the future to recognise family life for homosexual partners as marriage as well as other sorts of partnerships (see more in *Стенографски белешки од 72-та седница на Собранието на Република Македонија*, одржана на 23 септември, 2013, стр. 4, available online: www.sobranie.mk/default.asp?pSearch=%D0%B1%D1%80%D0%B0%D0%BA+&x=0&y=0, p. 5). This is in contrast to what happened in Croatia. Namely, several days after the referendum that defined marriage as an exclusively heterosexual community, an initiative to ensure protection of the right to family life to unions that are not marriage arose. Amendments in

Homosexual partnerships/unions/cohabitations are regulated neither in the Family Law nor in any other law in the Republic of Macedonia, thus making the climate not homosexual-friendly, thus significantly different from other legislation in Western Europe. Therefore the provisions on affiliation in the Family Law do not trigger the parenthood of homosexual couples.

8.2.1.3. Extra-marital relationships

Extra-marital relationship is a legal term that generates legal consequences. It is defined as a community of mutual life between a man and a woman with a continuity of more than one year. Its constitution is related to the mere fact of joint habitation and not with any formal requirement to be registered. The non-registration status creates problems in proving its existence in practice, supported by the legal vacuum when it comes to the legal obstacles for initiating the relationship,[1495] and the mutual inheritance.[1496] One of the legal impediments is close affiliation (either by blood or by the fact of family life).[1497] While the second is evident, the first is not, especially in systems that practise anonymous gamete donations. Consequently, the law omits to regulate on equal grounds the legal obstacles for establishing marital and extra-marital relationships, while the problem of legalising inbreeding for both relationships when the partners are blood related without (under rules of anonymous donations) or with (under rules

the Constitution are meant to introduce a balance and eliminate a feeling of inequality among gay couples because of the new definition of marriage. See more in New Indian Express, "Croatia's Government Proposes Law on Gay Partnership", 12.12.2013, available online: www.newindianexpress.com/world/Croatias-government-proposes-law-on-gay-partnership/2013/12/12/article1942238.ece#.UvuTYxA1CiU.

1495 By analogy to marriage, legal obstacles for concluding a valid marriage are: (1) existence of another marital community of one/both of the partners (article 17 of the Family Law); even more bigamy is treated also as a criminal offence (article 195 of the Criminal Law stipulates that a person who concludes a marriage while being in a marriage already, and/or a person who concludes a marriage while being aware of the fact that the other person is already in a marriage will be punished with imprisonment of three months up to three years), (2) legal incapacity to reason (article 18 of the Family Law), (3) the validity of the consent – given under threat or misconception (article 19 of the Family Law), as well as (4) the affiliation ties, i.e. (a) by blood including all relatives in *linea recta*, and up until the second degree of blood relatedness in *linea lateralis* (article 20, paragraph 1 of the Family Law, while article 194 of the Criminal Law criminalises the action with imprisonment of the perpetrator from three months up to three years), and (b) by shared family life including affiliation by adoption (article 20, paragraph 1 of the Family Law), affiliation by belonging to the same extended family (here approved exceptions under justified reasons by the court in extra-procedural proceedings are allowed – article 21 of the Family Law), and affiliation from extra-marital relationships (article 22 of the Family Law).

1496 It is not clear if the partners from the extra-marital relationship will inherit from each other since the Family Law explicitly stipulates that the legal consequences of the extra-marital relationship are the same as those of the marital relationship in the domain of mutual maintenance and joint property, intentionally or not dropping the issue of inheritance, and therefore leaving it up to the interpretation of the judges/notaries. See article 13, Family Law.

1497 *Ibid.*

of known donations) the knowledge of that fact remaining. Nevertheless, the extra-marital relationship has the same legal regime as the marriage itself when it comes to the right of mutual maintenance, and the division of mutual property.[1498] The once established rights and responsibilities of parents and other relatives towards their children and *vice versa* are equal regardless of the marital/extra-marital relationship of their parents.[1499] However, the establishment of parental rights and responsibilities is not the same. In marriage, the marital presumption assumes fatherhood automatically, while in extra-marital relationships the parental status of the father has to be additionally acquired. The Draft Recommendation and White Paper suggest application of the marital presumption in both scenarios.[1500] Replacement of the term "marital presumption" with "paternal presumption" is more adequate in the sense of appreciating the fact that the marriage is not the only place where families can be founded, while considering the automatic attribution of fatherhood after birth as a preferable scenario for children.

8.2.1.4. Affiliation and establishment of parental responsibilities

The Family Law uses the term "parental right" to depict what in most European countries and international documents is referred to as "parental responsibilities".[1501] In this sense, the term "parental right" encompasses the rights and obligations of the parents to care for the personality, rights and interests of their children.[1502] Bearing in mind the CRC and the primary obligation of the parents to care for their children, instead of exercising rights over them, the term "parental right" should be replaced with the term "parental responsibilities". Consequently, the text will use the term "parental responsibilities", with the meaning of "parental right" as used by the Family Law, for purposes of consistency.

Parental responsibilities of the father are to be established differently depending on the context in which the conception occurred: (1) without or (2) with the assistance of reproductive technology.

In the first case, the establishment of the parenthood depends on the marital/extra-marital relationship of the parents. If the child is born within a marital relationship, the parenthood can be established on the ground of the legal presumption: "the husband of the mother is the father of the child born during the marriage or 300 days after the dissolution of the marriage".[1503] The presumption can be rebutted before the court by the husband, the mother or the child under certain circumstances and within certain time limits on grounds of biological/

[1498] Family Law, article 13.
[1499] Family Law, article 9.
[1500] See footnote 1324.
[1501] See more in footnote 632.
[1502] Family Law, article 44.
[1503] Family Law, article 50.

genetic relatedness.[1504] The law omits including the genetic progenitor (if different from the husband) as an active party able to initiate court litigation to rebut paternity based on the ground of presumption (as a first step towards establishing his own fatherhood). The progenitor's legal affiliation can only be established if the mother or the child initiate court litigation and rebut the paternity of the married husband, after which the recognition of the genetic parent may follow. This means that the law favours protection of family life as constituted in marital cohesion over genetic bonds. The rationale is derived from two premises: (1) marriage has been perceived as a preferable medium for founding and raising families throughout history and even nowadays, (2) it promotes legal protection of already established familial links and therefore legal certainty.[1505]

On the other hand, the establishment of fatherhood in relation to a child born out of wedlock (not necessarily an extra-marital relationship) is associated with the act of recognition.[1506] Such a recognition would result in legal parenthood only if there is consent by the mother, the guardian (if the mother is not alive or missing) and the child is older than 16.[1507] If the recognition is followed by consent, both statements cannot be withheld.[1508] If the consent for the recognition is not provided, the person who claims fatherhood may seek judicial recognition of his genetic link with the child, which eventually will establish him as a father.[1509] The same request for judicial recognition of fatherhood may also be launched by the mother, the guardian of the child or the child (from 18 to 21

1504 Family Law, articles 64–67. The time limits for the husband to launch proceedings to rebut his fatherhood are rather restrictive – three months after he receives the information regarding the fact of the birth of the child (article 64, paragraph 1). Nevertheless, he is allowed to request from the Supreme Court an extension of the time period and new validity date for his petition (up to the time of the child gaining majority) if he has revealed new facts and proof that deny his genetic paternity (article 65). In this context, the Supreme Court made a decision explicitly stating that the suspicious mind and accordingly, the psychological and health-related consequences are not *per se* a sufficient ground to accept the petition and extend the due date. See more in the Decree of the Supreme Court – Решение на Врховниот суд на Република Македонија, бр. 38/98, 16.12.1999. The purpose of the restrictive terms for challenging the genetic relatedness that derive from the marital presumption can be explained by the fact that the law firstly prioritises genes as important in the relation, and, only secondly protects the already established family link with the child.

1505 Other European legislation is also familiar with this legal solution. For instance, in the Netherlands, a third party (apart from the marital partners) cannot dispute the legal fatherhood of the mother's husband, even if the third party can prove that he (not the husband) is the child's biological father. Furthermore, under the Dutch law, a married man can only under very strict circumstances, recognise a child as his begotten with a woman who is not his wife. In England, on the other hand, both cases are possible: a third party outside the marriage may recognise the child as his, and a married man may recognise a child as his begotten with a woman who is not his wife. See more in Vonk M., *Children and their Parents. A Comparative Study of the Legal Position of Children with Regard to their Intentional and Biological Parents in English and Dutch Law,* Intersentia, 2007, p. 65. Under the national Macedonian legislation, there is no prohibition on a married man recognising another woman's child as his.

1506 Family Law, article 51.

1507 Family Law, articles 56 and 57.

1508 Family Law, article 59.

1509 Family Law, article 58.

years old) if the biological father does not recognise the child as his himself.[1510] The legal presumption for establishing fatherhood in relation to a child born outside a marital relationship supposes that the father of the child is the person with whom the mother had sexual intercourse in the framework between 180 and 300 days before the child was born, unless the opposite is proven.[1511] Therefore in deciding the paternity of the child, the court prioritises medical proof of an existing biological/genetic link with the child, as well as the relationship and the mutual life between the mother and the defendant. Nevertheless, the existing presumption does not apply to conceptions as a result of assisted reproduction in extra-marital relationships, and therefore it is impossible to initiate proceedings for establishing parenthood.

From the above-cited provisions in the Family Law, it follows that if the child is not conceived through assisted fertilisation or adopted, the father of the child will be the genetic parent as a principal rule. An exception to this principle is envisaged in two cases: (1) the existent marital presumption was never rebutted, but the husband of the mother was not the genetic parent, and (2) the child of an extra-marital relationship was recognised by a person other than his genetic father. Once the parenthood is established, children are treated equally irrespective of their birth or the relationship of their parents.[1512]

When it comes to the establishment of motherhood in relation to a child conceived naturally and without the use of assisted reproduction, the Family Law has accepted the Roman law principle of *mater semper certa est*. Therefore the mother of the child is the woman who gives birth to the child except in the case of adoption (which is not an exception *per se* because the transfer of the status happens only afterwards). Motherhood can also be rebutted but only if it is proven that the registered mother on the birth certificate is not the mother who gave birth to the child. Bearing in mind that the contestation of motherhood can be invoked only if the child was not adopted, once again, the conclusion follows that the biological/genetic mother will be the mother of the child as a principal rule.[1513] Following the current debates over introducing surrogacies, there are two possibilities for their future regulation: (1) to change the principle and consider the surrogate mother a delivery, surrogate woman, and the commissioning mother a mother from the time of the birth (as, for instance, in Greece), and (2) to keep the principle and apply the same rules as in adoption.[1514] If the time of birth is accepted as a moment that generates legal consequences of parentage, then the second option will be more adequate.

1510 Family Law, article 60.

1511 See footnote 1484.

1512 Family Law, articles 8 and 9, the Law on Inheritance (Закон за наследувањето, *Службен весник на Република Македонија*, бр. 08/95, 15.02.1995), article 4 (stating explicitly that in order to qualify the child as heir, the affiliation has to be established in a legally prescribed manner).

1513 Family Law, article 75.

1514 See footnote 833.

Parental proceedings are special civil proceedings under the jurisdiction of the Law on Litigation Procedure, integrated in the Family Law.[1515] Their peculiarity is reflected in the fact that the court has authority (unlike in other civil law disputes) to question the facts upon which the parties rely in their petition if they refer to their mutual juvenile children, even if they are not contested among the parties themselves.[1516] The nature of their peculiarity is related to the priority of protection of the child's interests, even when they are in conflict with their parents' interests. If the child and the parent (that is a legal representative – legal guardian of the child) have conflicting interests, a special institution (Centre for Social Affairs) will appoint for the child a guardian *ad litem* for specific cases.[1517] The data regarding the birth of the child, his/her parents, eventual later recognition of the fatherhood, establishing and rebutting of the fatherhood or motherhood, adoption, appointing a guardian for the child and the termination of his/her temporal role are to be noted in the Register of Births (*Матична книга на родените*).[1518]

The provisions for establishing and rebutting parenthood analysed above do not apply when the child is conceived with bio-medical assistance or when the child is adopted. Namely, it is forbidden to claim or rebut paternity and maternity before the court if the child is conceived through artificial insemination.[1519]

The rationale behind this ban in the law derives from the accepted protection of the legal family of the child, but also from the attributed primacy of the biological criterion for establishing parenthood before the court. The litigation for establishing parenthood based on DNA evidence regarding the biological/genetic relatedness to the child would threaten the accepted concept of the anonymity of donors, thus the secrecy surrounding biological/genetic parents in the case of assisted reproduction and adoption. It is also considered that it could endanger the already established family life of the child with the legal parents. Nevertheless, by protecting the anonymity of donors and the parents that gave the child up for adoption, or the later legal parents, the legislator infringes the right of the child

1515 Article 1 of the Law stipulates: "this Law shall regulate the rules of the procedure on basis of which the court contends and decides upon the basic rights and obligations of the person and citizen in the disputes within the field of personal and family relations, labor relations, as well as property and other civil relations of natural persons and legal entities, unless it is envisaged, by a special law, that the court decides upon some of the listed disputes according to the rules of another procedure". Закон за парнична постапка, *Службен весникна Република Македонија.* бр. 79/05, 21.09.2005. See the English unofficial translation: Law on Litigation Procedure, consolidated text, unofficial translation. See also part VIII of the Family Law that regards civil proceedings, article 222. The proceedings for establishing and rebutting paternity and maternity are placed between articles 262 and 272 of the Family Law.

1516 See article 270 in conjunction with article 257 of the Family Law.

1517 Article 266 of the Family Law.

1518 Article 4, Law on Registers of Birth (Закон за матичната евиденција, Службен весник на Република Македонија, бр. 08/95, 15.02.1995).

1519 Family Law, articles 62, 63 and 71. There is inconsistency between the usage of the terminology in the Family Law (using the term "artificial insemination"), and the Law on Bio-medically Assisted Fertilisations (using the term "bio-medically assisted fertilisation").

to know his/her biological/genetic origins as stipulated in articles 7 and 8 of the CRC, and in article 8 of the ECHR.[1520]

Parental responsibilities should normally be exercised mutually by both parents.[1521] If the parents do not live together,[1522] or after dissolution of the marriage or termination of the extra-marital relationship, they continue to exist for both of them. Nevertheless, only one of them will have custody and will be fully entitled to live in the same household and care on a daily basis for the welfare and upbringing of the child.[1523] This means that the concept of joint parental responsibilities for both parents after the dissolution of their relationship as in most of the other European countries, and as stipulated in article 9 of the CRC, is not appreciated in its full capacity. There are numerous complaints before the European Commission of Human Rights and the European Court of Human Rights where applicants have alleged violations of the right to respect for family life under article 8 of the ECHR due to denial of the right to custody or access after separation or divorce.[1524] The European Commission and the European Court are clear that the breakdown of a couple's relationship does not destroy the right to family life either parent enjoys concerning the children born/adopted in that relationship.[1525] Furthermore, any act by a State authority aimed at the removal of children from parental care leads to an interference with the exercise of the right to protect family life under article 8 of the ECHR.[1526] Nevertheless, this does not exclude the possibility of the State's withdrawal of custody from one of the parents if it is in the best interests of the child, and if it is in accordance with the limitation clause in article 8, paragraph 2 of the ECHR.[1527] Thus, harmonising with the already accepted international documents and in terms of article 9 of the CRC and article 8 of ECHR, the Macedonian legislator should consider the possibility of introducing the concept of shared parental responsibilities after the dissolution of the relationship of the parents.

Apart from birth and adoption, affiliation can also be established between the child and the stepparent following a (re)marriage of one of the parents (father or mother) of the child. The stepparent does not take over the parental

1520 See, for instance, footnotes 1141 and 1216, as well as the analyses of Kleijkamp G.A., *Family Life and Family Interests, A Comparative Study on the Influence of the European Convention of Human Rights on Dutch Family Law and the Influence of the United States Constitution on American Family Law*, Kluwer Law International, 1999, p. 26.

1521 Family Law, article 76.

1522 Family Law, article 79 stipulates that the parents can agree among each other about the content of their relationship with the child, or the Centre of Social Work can decide for them.

1523 Family Law, article 80, decided by the court in separate civil litigation regulated in articles 272–273.

1524 See more in Cohen J., "Respect for Private and Family Life", in MacDonald R.S.J., Matscher F., Petzold H. (eds.), *The European System for the Protection of Human Rights*, Martinus Nijhoff, 1993, pp. 405–444.

1525 See Gomien D. *et al.*, *Law and Practice of the European Convention on Human Rights and the European Social Charter*, 1996, pp. 242–244.

1526 *Ibid.*, p. 243.

1527 *Ibid.*

responsibilities of the child's other parent, even though in reality he/she will have the role of a social parent. Nevertheless, the stepparent can gain the responsibility of maintenance of a child who is a minor only if the child does not have any other relatives (not just parents) obliged by the law and capable of undertaking maintenance.[1528] The stepparent can also assume parental responsibility for the child by adopting the child, if the child does not have another registered parent, and if the other criteria for adoption are fulfilled.[1529] The Draft Recommendation also affords the right of the stepparent to recognise the child as his own.[1530]

The legal recognition of factual family life between persons sharing a common habitat without officially claiming affiliation status among them is integrated in the Law on Inheritance. Article 29 of the law stipulates that the "person under care" and the "caregiver",[1531] the stepparent and the stepchild, the mother and father-in-law, and the wife/husband of their child, as well as the other blood relatives that live together in "permanent community",[1532] do inherit from each other under certain circumstances.[1533]

8.2.2. THE LAW ON BIO-MEDICALLY ASSISTED FERTILISATION

8.2.2.1. Beneficiaries of bio-medically assisted fertilisation and the establishment of parental responsibilities

The Law on Bio-medically Assisted Fertilisation in its article 9 sets the scene for the beneficiaries of the right to assisted fertilisation: the adult man and woman having legal capacity, married or living in an extra-marital relationship, as well as the unmarried woman who is not in an extra-marital relationship shall have the right to use the assisted fertilisation procedure, provided that previous treatment or treatment with other methods is unsuccessful, and who in accordance with their age and general condition are capable of parenting.

The possibility for a single woman to be a beneficiary of the right to assisted fertilisation is problematic under the current legal context from several points of view.

1528 *Ibid.* article 182.

1529 *Ibid.* articles 95–134.

1530 See footnote 1337.

1531 A "person under care" for the purposes of the law is a child taken care of by another person without establishing an affiliation link among them (article 19, paragraph 4).

1532 "Permanent community" for the purposes of the law is defined as a community of continuous joint habitation for at least five years before the death of the *de cuius* (article 29, paragraph 3).

1533 If the deceased does not have a living marital partner and other heirs from the first succession order, then they inherit the whole inheritance in equal shares. If the deceased has a living marital partner, then the persons sharing a common habitat would inherit one half of the inheritance in equal shares (article 29, paragraphs 1 and 2).

Firstly, infertility is not the rationale behind a single woman's attempt to conceive using assisted reproduction. From a general point of view, it is not possible to apply the definition on infertility since the single woman has not been engaged in unprotected intercourse for 12 months for the purpose of reproduction. It is also debateable how to apply the provision in the law that she has the right to use assisted fertilisation if previous treatment is unsuccessful or treatment with other methods is also unsuccessful. Furthermore, the validity of the provision that relies on infertility while depicting the right to access ART is not just outdated, but also wrong taking into account the fact that an infertile woman would not be able to use sperm donations to conceive a child anyhow.

Secondly, from a perspective of the rights of the child, it is debateable whether under the current anonymous context of donations it is in the child's best interests to be born intentionally without a father, neither biological/genetic nor legal, and further without knowing the facts surrounding the conception.

According to Mickovikj, under the present circumstances assisted reproduction in the Republic of Macedonia should cover only couples. Even though the reproductive right of the woman should be guaranteed, it should not compromise the right of the child to have two parents.[1534] This author's rationale arises from the premises that it is better for the psychological development of the child to be raised in a family, instead of being raised by one parent only,[1535] supported by the argument that the legal regulation of treatments for infertility should balance the reproductive autonomy of the adults (in this case single women) and the welfare of the children.[1536] Nevertheless, if there is an effort to achieve a balance, it can be seen in the attempt of allowing single women to conceive children to whom they will give fair prospects of eventually getting to know their genetic father.

The law prohibits the use of donated spermatozoids/ova for insemination with ova/spermatozoids from a blood-related woman/man with whom the donor is not allowed to conclude a marriage. It is also prohibited to use a donated embryo for insemination of a woman with whom it is prohibited for the donor of the spermatozoids used to create the embryo to conclude a marriage, or for insemination of a woman who is related in the first line with the woman whose ovum is used to create the embryo.[1537] The prohibition on using donated cells due to blood relation is, however, incomplete. Namely, article 22 stipulates that implantation of an embryo created from the ovum of a woman who is related in the second line with the woman in whom the embryo is implanted. This means that sisters related in the second line can donate ova to each other. This practice

1534 Mickovikj D., "Дилеми во врска со Законот за био-медицинско потпомогнато оплодување", 2008.

1535 *Op. cit.* 1997, p. 176.

1536 Storrow R.F., "The Bioethics of Prospective Parenthood. In Pursuit of the Proper Standard for Gatekeeping in Infertility Clinics", *Cardozo Law Review*, Vol. 28, No. 5, 2007, p. 101.

1537 Article 22 CRC.

will eventually lead to a situation where the sister of the mother (the aunt of the child) will be the child's biological/genetic parent. Therefore the first cousins of the child will actually be his/her *consanguinei uterini* – brothers or sisters by the same mother. The complex kinship of that kind should not be allowed. Mickovikj also considers that sisters should not donate ova to each other. This author anticipates the presupposed risk of psychological trauma of such complex affiliation if the child finds out that his/her aunt is actually his/her mother, while his/her cousins are his/her brothers or sisters.[1538] In most European countries (with the exception of Germany, Finland and the Netherlands) it is forbidden for close relatives to donate genetic material to each other.[1539]

Paragraph 3 of article 22 should be changed in view of prohibiting the insemination of a woman who is related in the second line with a woman whose ovum is used to create the embryo. One reason is the complicated affiliation and disturbances of the accepted Roman law system of consanguinity in the continental law and in the Macedonian law on succession. The current article is problematic under the current context of "hidden truth", since the child will most probably not know the blood-related relatives and therefore the legal prohibition of insemination between persons subject to legal obstacles to concluding marriage will not apply to him/her in the future.[1540]

The current article will also be problematic if the child gains (in the future) the right to know his/her genetic origins and the consequences that might arise if the child finds out that his/her biological aunt is his/her biological mother.

Another controversial issue from the above provisions is the donation of the embryo. Since no single beneficiary of the assisted reproduction will be genetically related to the child, the donation of an embryo resembles adoption of the embryo. The only biological difference to an adoption is the gestational role, and the fact of giving birth by the "mother to be". This is similar to the role of the surrogate mother in the child's life only without the intention of "the mother to be". Mickovikj also holds the opinion that the legal provisions about embryo donation should be reconsidered and furthermore elaborated considering their problematic nature.[1541] Because of the controversies, the donation of an embryo is forbidden in Austria, Germania, Sweden, Norway, Denmark, Italy, Slovenia, Switzerland and Turkey, while it is permitted only in eight European countries.[1542]

1538 Mickovikj D., "Дилеми во врска со Законот за био-медицинско потпомогнато оплодување", 2008.

1539 Schenner J.G., "Assisted Reproduction Practice in Europe: Legal and Ethical Aspects", *Human Reproduction Update*, Vol. 3, No. 2, 1997, p. 176.

1540 Ignovska E., "The Impact of Assisted Reproduction on Affiliation within the Family Law of the Republic of Macedonia", in Jansen B.C.S., Ignovska E. (eds.), *Law, Public Health Care System and Society.Macedonia – Social Policy, Legislation, Biomedicine and Ethics of Organ Transplantation, Fertilization and ART*, Academische Verlagsgemeinschaft, 2012, p. 206.

1541 Mickovikj D., "Дилеми во врска со Законот за био-медицинско потпомогнато оплодување", 2008.

1542 *Ibid.*

Surrogate motherhood was (at the time of writing) forbidden by law in the Republic of Macedonia. The contract for giving birth in lieu of somebody else, followed by giving away the child after birth for financial compensation, or for no compensation, was null and void.[1543] Nevertheless, surrogacies were introduced (after completing this work and therefore they are not profoundly elaborated here) by amending the Law on Bio-medically Assisted Fertilisation on 9 October 2014.

On the other hand, Macedonia's regulation of posthumous insemination is one of the most liberal in Europe. A man and a woman, who, based on medical acknowledgments or experience of medical science, are threatened with infertility due to health reasons can preserve their spermatozoids, ova and ovum or testis tissue for the purpose of their own usage. In the event of the death of the man and with his previous written consent posthumous insemination is allowed to be performed one year after the day of his death, at the utmost.[1544]

Setting the limits and boundaries in law should correspond with certain values aimed at being protected. In the case of surrogacy, the bodily integrity of the surrogate woman was a strong argument for protection at the time of opting for its ban.[1545] In the case of posthumous insemination, the interest of the planned and wanted child to be born above all is also a strong argument for protection. Nevertheless, there may be consequences of, on the one hand, the strict ban on the surrogacy and, on the other hand, the liberal regulation of posthumous insemination, for affiliation (at the time of writing), or allowed surrogacies used by a woman who wants to mother a posthumously born child (after surrogacies were introduced).[1546]

Under the current legal constellation, there is consideration about the possible abuses of the law.

One possibility for abusing the law by introducing hidden surrogacy arrangements (when they were banned) or applying surrogacies (after their allowance) with a purpose they were not meant for, could happen in the realm of the allowed and regulated practice of posthumous fertilisation. The law regulates the consent of the man as the only requirement for posthumous insemination of the woman for which he gave the consent, without stating explicitly whether this consent refers to fertilisation of his married wife, extra-marital partner or any other woman. In other words, the posthumous fertilisation could be realised

---

1543 Law on Bio-medically Assisted Fertilisation, article 27.

1544 Law on Bio-medically Assisted Fertilisation, article 33.

1545 This is again related to the question if the parts of the human body can be disposed of on the market like commodities and therefore "rented" for financial contribution. Even authors who consider that self-determination should be elevated, do not support pregnancy contracts for financial gain. Substitution for the lost wage also encompasses "proprietary self" suggesting that it is possible to separate labour capacities from the person "like pieces of property". See more in Shanley M.L., "'Surrogate Mothering' and Women's Freedom: A Critique of Contracts for Human Reproduction", *Signs*, Vol. 18, No. 3, 1993, pp. 624 and 627, and Pateman C., *The Sexual Contract*, Polity Press, 1988, p. 150.

1546 Note: the text does not trigger the other controversies behind the regulation of surrogacy and posthumous reproduction apart from those that affect affiliation.

with the sole purpose of the deceased and his parents continuing his genes, using a woman in a secret/public agreement who would agree to be fertilised with the genetic material of the deceased with the intention of giving up the child after birth. Practices of this kind will ultimately lead to a traditional form of surrogacy despite the official ban (the new amendments in the law refer to gestational form of surrogacies while explicitly forbid traditional form), and despite the *a priori* condemnation of the child not having a mother and a father.

Another fictive scenario, if the concept of anonymous donations is changed in the future, concerns concealed surrogacy by an intimate (internal) agreement between a single woman using sperm or embryo donation and the known donor and his partner. The concern is that the mother may opt to give her child up for adoption to the donor and his partner afterwards. These two scenarios, for some couples, may be the only way to conceive a genetically related child in legal surroundings that ban surrogacies/traditional surrogacies or surrogacies for same-sex partners making the legal system inconsistent.

Surrogate motherhood in the "grey zone" could lead to insecurity and uncertainty amongst its participants and even more complicated affiliation. In relation to these considerations, the intended parents of the child could be subject to blackmail by the child's gestational mother who may claim exclusivity to exert the maternal right or may threaten abortion.

Apart from the above scenarios, there is always the possibility of "reproductive tourism" as a practice of travelling to another country for fertility treatment.[1547] The problem of "reproductive tourism" in the Macedonian context through the prism of affiliation is introducing surrogacy arrangements despite their inconsistency with both the Family Law (the mother of the child is the woman who gives birth to the child), and the Law on Bio-medically Assisted Fertilisation (before the amendments, ban on surrogacy; and after the amendments, surrogacy arrangements available only to heterosexual married partners). Apart from this, "reproductive tourism" could be available only to those who are willing and can afford to pay for it, thus raising ethical concerns about disparity.

There is no doubt that unpredictable situations could arise which cannot be anticipated in advance. Nevertheless, the legislator should investigate the rationale behind the beneficiaries of the assisted fertilisation, bearing in mind the possibilities for abusing the purpose of the law, and not necessarily the law itself.

[1547] Mattoras R., "Reproductive Exile *versus* Reproductive Tourism", *Human Reproduction*, Vol. 20, No. 12, 2001, p. 3571. See also Inhorn M.C., Patrizio P., "Rethinking Reproductive 'Tourism' as Reproductive 'Exile'", *Fertility and Sterility*, Vol. 92, No. 3, 2009, pp. 904–906.

8.2.2.2. The right of the child to know his/her genetic origins

As harmonised with the Family Law, donors do not hold any parental responsibilities, in terms of rights or obligations in relation to the conceived child. The authorised health care institutions are obliged to provide protection of all personal, medical and genetic data of donors, as well as to undertake all necessary measures not to reveal the identity of the donor and his/her family and vice versa.[1548] All data regarding the donor's provenience, health biography and births resulting from the donation are to be kept in the utmost confidentiality in the Register of Donors in the authorised healthcare institutions for 30 years as from the date of their entry.[1549] A child born by insemination with donated genital cells or embryos, when 18 years of age and able to form an opinion on his/her own can request sight of the data regarding the health condition of the donor in the State Register of Bio-medically Assisted Fertilisation only due to a medically justified reason and with a previously obtained approval from the State Committee.[1550] However, this provision does not confront the accepted anonymity of the donor's identity which only protects donors' interests and neglects the right of the child to know his/her genetic origins.

In the context of legally prescribed anonymity in the Republic of Macedonia, the definition of the conflict can be framed in terms of priority of rights: those of the child to know his/her origin and those of the donor and legal parents of respect for their privacy. The right of the child to know his/her origins cannot be exhausted by the right to information about his/her conception without revealing the identity of the donor. The right to information about the circumstances of the conception on the one hand will not necessarily infringe the right of the donor to privacy, but on the other hand will not satisfy the child's right to know his/her genetic origins.

8.3. CONCLUSION: HARMONISING RIGHTS

The family law provisions for establishing fatherhood of the Republic of Macedonia do not apply in cases in which the conceptions occurred through assisted fertilisation. This pattern of regulating legal affiliation places children in categories on grounds of birth and offers different treatments, and accordingly discriminates among them (confronting articles 12, 2 and 18 of the CRC). Under the current regulation, the procedural rules of the national law do not allow a child born with the assistance of reproductive technologies and capable of forming his/her own views to be heard in judicial and administrative proceedings affecting

1548 Article 7 CRC.
1549 Articles 47 and 48 CRC.
1550 Article 57 CRC.

him/her.[1551] Paternal proceedings and access to information regarding genetic origins affect a child born with the assistance of reproductive technologies just as they affect a child born in marriage or a recognised child. It is an obligation of the State signatories of the Convention to respect and ensure the rights of each child within their jurisdiction without discrimination of any kind, irrespective of, among others, the child's birth or other status.[1552] It is also an obligation of the State signatories to use their efforts to ensure recognition of the principle that both parents *have* (this could be interpreted also as at least *could have*) joint responsibilities for the upbringing of the child.[1553]

Consequently, a single woman's reproductive right to conceive without a partner should be guaranteed only if the child has the right to know the circumstances of the conception, and its biological/genetic origins, as a prerequisite for eliminating the fear that this information may endanger the legal parentage later on before the court. Once it is clear that finding out the genetic origins is not automatically connected with establishing affiliation links, there will be no legally sound reason to ban paternity proceedings for children conceived by medically assisted fertilisation or adopted.

The concept of open identity in reproductive matters should be introduced in the Macedonian Family Law and in the Law on Bio-medically Assisted Fertilisation. The act of assisted reproduction should take a child-oriented perspective, promoting the best interests of the child before the interests and preferences of the parents and donors. The term *parent* should have a precise meaning in order to differentiate the diverse roles that a person might have in a child's life. Defining the difference between the biological and legal parent correlates with the reality of conception with donated genetic material. Once the difference is established, it should be less difficult to discover something as fundamental as one's origin. Persons have a vital interest in receiving the necessary information to know and understand their childhood and early development. This information can also prevent inbreeding, legal misunderstandings and vague disputes over paternity. Therefore the right to information about personal identity should not be covered up by the adults' stigmatisation of the act of reproduction.[1554]

This encompasses an active obligation of the Member States to create a system in which the interests of the individual seeking access to records relating to his/her private and family life must be secured when a contributor to the records either is not available or improperly refuses consent.[1555] Following the most

1551 Article 12 CRC.
1552 Article 2(1) CRC.
1553 Article 18(1) CRC.
1554 Ignovska E., "The Impact of Assisted Reproduction on Affiliation within the Family Law of the Republic of Macedonia", in Jansen B.C.S., Ignovska E. (eds.), *Law, Public Health Care System and Society.Macedonia – Social Policy, Legislation, Biomedicine and Ethics of Organ Transplantation, Fertilization and ART*, Academische Verlagsgemeinschaft, 2012, p. 228.
1555 *Gaskin v. the U.K.*, European Court of Human Rights, No. 10454/83, judgment of 07.07.1989, para. 49.

recent developments in changing family laws according to the changes in society, the Draft Recommendation also supports a general right to access information concerning one's origin.[1556] Correspondingly, the concept of secrecy in the Macedonian legal system in both adoptions and gamete donations should be overruled. Since the right to know one's personal origins as derived from family history is increasingly regarded as a fundamental human right, the national legal context will have to take action to create conditions that promote human dignity on both individual and family level.

The protection safeguarded by article 8 is conditional on the prerequisite of already established private and family life.[1557] Even though it is stimulated to legally establish and thus protect family life from the time of birth,[1558] it is not solely the legally recognised family life entrenched from infringement of respect for it or from interference by a public authority regarding its exercise. Family life could also be characterised as a bundle of behaviour, attitudes, emotions, rights and responsibilities that form the basis of a caring and loving relationship over time among genetically or not genetically related affiliates. The protection of article 8, as interpreted by the ECtHR, also refers to this lived reality of family life that has to be evaluated based on the circumstances of each individual case.[1559] Respect for family life requires that biological and social reality prevail over a legal presumption.[1560] In the dissenting opinion of the decision in the case of *Kroon v. the Netherlands*, Judge Bonnici argued that family life cannot exist between parties who have intentionally excluded it.[1561] This is related to the existence of

---

1556 Draft Recommendation, article 4. See also footnote 1266.

1557 Kleijkamp G.A., *Family Life and Family Interests, A Comparative Study on the Influence of the European Convention of Human Rights on Dutch Family Law and the Influence of the United States Constitution on American Family Law*, Kluwer Law International, 1999, p. 28.

1558 See footnotes 1254, 1255, 1256.

1559 The Court has upheld several times that "the existence or non-existence of 'family life' is essentially a question of fact depending upon the real existence in practice of close personal ties". See the cases of *Hokkanen v. Finland*, European Court of Human Rights, No. 19823/92, judgment of 22.10.1994, paras. 54 and 58; *Brayer v. Germany*, European Court of Human Rights, No. 3545/04, judgment of 28.05.2009, para. 30; *Lebbink v. the Netherlands*, European Court of Human Rights, No. 45582/99, judgment of 01.06.2004, para. 36; *K. and T. v. Finland*, European Court of Human Rights, No. 25702/94, judgment of 12.06.2001, para. 150.

1560 *Kroon v. the Netherlands*, European Court of Human Rights, No. 18535/91, judgment of 27.10.1994, para. 40.

1561 *Ibid.* para. 3 of the dissenting opinion of judge Mifsud Bonnici stating as follows: "'family life' necessarily implies 'living together as a family'. The exception to this refers to circumstances related to necessity, i.e. separations brought about by reasons of work, illness or other necessities of the family itself. Forced or coerced living apart, therefore, is clearly an accepted exception. But, equally clearly, this does not apply when the separation is completely voluntary. When it is voluntary, then clearly the member or members of the family who do so have opted against family life, and against living together as a family. And since these are the circumstances of the instant case where the first two applicants have voluntarily opted not to have a 'family life', I cannot understand how they can call upon Netherlands law to respect something which they have wilfully opted against. The artificiality of this approach is in strident contradiction to the natural value of family life which the Convention guarantees. The judgment moreover fails to explain how 'a relationship [which] has sufficient constancy to create ... family ties' can

intention to establish and maintain a relationship. As such, it could also refer to sperm donations where the participants have explicitly excluded any creation of family life.

In these terms, article 8 of the ECHR encompasses obligations of the Member States associated with its negative aspect of refraining from interferences with private and family life, but also its affirmative aspect of taking action to create conditions that promote human dignity on both individual and family level.[1562] Accepting the fact that circumstances in society change and that the domestic laws have to follow, and thus continuously evolve,[1563] both "illegitimate" as well as "legitimate" families should enjoy equal protection.[1564] The difference between them, acknowledged as discrimination in the cases of *Marckx v. Belgium*, *Keegan v. Ireland*,[1565] and *Johnston and Others v. Ireland*[1566] could by analogy be compared with the difference in treatment between "natural" and more contemporary "artificial" families to whom the laws still owe evolution. In legislation where the donor is not to be considered a legal father under any circumstances due to a ban on access to paternal proceedings exclusively for such cases, these "illegitimate" children (genetic but not legal) will be discriminated against in comparison to "legitimate" children (children with a possibility of being legal towards their genetic parent). The Commission (in its first case regarding ART) held the opinion that the donor in himself does not hold a right to respect for his family life with the child. Yet it also accepted that the situation could have been different if contact over a longer period existed between them, supported by any contribution (financial or otherwise) to the child's upbringing.[1567] Thus the Commission included close personal ties in addition to parenthood as relevant to qualifying

be made equivalent to 'a relationship which has sufficient constancy to create family life', as manifestly these two propositions are by no means the same or equivalent."

1562 Conelly A.M., "Problems of Interpretation of Article 8 of the ECHR", *International and Comparative Law Quarterly*, Vol. 35, No. 3, 1986, p. 572. See also Kleijkamp G.A., *Family Life and Family Interests, A Comparative Study on the Influence of the European Convention of Human Rights on Dutch Family Law and the Influence of the United States Constitution on American Family Law*, Kluwer Law International, 1999, p. 44.

1563 *Marckx v. Belgium*, European Court of Human Rights, No. 6833/74, judgment of 13.06.1979, para. 41 of the judgment.

1564 *Ibid.* stating as follows: "As regards Belgium itself, the statement stresses that the differenceof treatment between Belgian citizens, depending on whether theiraffiliation is established in or out of wedlock, amounts to a"flagrant exception" to the fundamental principle of the equality ofeveryone before the law" (Article 6 of the Constitution).

1565 *Keegan v. Ireland*, European Court of Human Rights, No. 16969/90, judgment from 26.05.1994.

1566 *Johnson and Others v. Ireland*, European Court of Human Rights, No. 9697/82, judgment of 18.12.1986, para. 75 stating that: "Examination of the third applicant's present legal situation, seen as a whole, reveals, however, that it differs considerably from that of a legitimate child; in addition, it has not been shown that there are any means available to her or her parents to eliminate or reduce the differences. Having regard to the particular circumstances of this case and notwithstanding the wide margin of appreciation enjoyed by Ireland in this area ... the absence of an appropriate legal regime reflecting the third applicant's natural family ties amounts to a failure to respect her family life".

1567 *J.R.M. v. the Netherlands*, European Commission on Human Rights, No. 16944/90, decision of 08.02.1993, Decision and Reports 74, p. 120.

for protection under article 8 of the ECHR. The affirmative aspect of States' obligations in the realm of family life, emphasised by the ECtHR, encompasses the necessity for their pro-active role in enabling family ties to develop normally,[1568] including also the ties between near relatives as they may play a considerable part in family life.[1569] If this is not provided, the Court discerns "no objective and reasonable justification for the differences of treatment".[1570] Even though the Court accepted that the "support and encouragement of the traditional family is in itself legitimate and praiseworthy", it also affirmed that this should not be done in a manner to prejudice the "illegitimate" family from the guarantees of article 8.[1571] Admittedly, it recognised that the "tranquillity" of legitimate families may be disturbed from an "illegitimate" child, but this alone should not be a motive that justifies depriving the child of fundamental rights.[1572] Furthermore, it considered that leaving the child's fundamental right to family life up to the parents' initiative to adopt him/her later on in life to be plain discrimination.[1573] On the contrary, a uniform way of addressing legal parenthood should apply to all parents, irrespective of their mutual relationship,[1574] and all children irrespective of the modus of their conception.

1568 *Marckx v. Belgium*, European Court of Human Rights, No. 6833/74, judgment of 13.06.1979, para. 45 stating as follows: "'Respect' for a family life so understood implies an obligation for the State to act in a manner calculated to allow these ties to developnormally". See also the case of *Johnson and Others v. Ireland*, ECtHR, No. 9697/82, judgment of 18.12.1986, para. 74, referring to the former case stating as follows: "the normal development of the natural family ties between thefirst and second applicants and their daughter requires, in the Court's opinion, that she should be placed, legally and socially, in aposition akin to that of a legitimate child". Paragraph 75 goes further: "the absence of an appropriate legal regime reflecting the applicant's natural family ties amounts to a failure to respect her family life".

1569 *Ibid.* stating as follows: "In the Court's opinion, "family life", within the meaning of Article 8 (art. 8), includes at least the ties between near relatives, for instance those between grandparents and grandchildren, since such relatives may play a considerable part in family life".

1570 *Ibid.* para. 48.

1571 *Ibid.* para. 40.

1572 *Ibid.* para. 48.

1573 *Ibid.* para. 55.

1574 As recognised in the cases of *Eriksson v. Sweden*, European Court of Human Rights, No. 11373/85, judgment of 22.06.1989, paras. 24 and 58; *Keegan v. Ireland*, European Court of Human Rights, No. 16969/90, judgment of 26.05.1994, para. 50; and *Kroon v. the Netherlands*, European Court of Human Rights, No. 18535/91, judgment of 27.10.1994, para. 30. The Court reiterated that family life as safeguarded in article 8 of the *ECHR* does not only encompass marriage-based relationships but also other *de facto* family ties where the parties live out of wedlock (e.g. the case of *Keegan v. Ireland*) or do not live together but there are other factors that create *de facto* family ties (e.g. *Kroon v. the Netherlands*). Consequently, the child born in such a relationship should be part of that family merely by the fact of birth, even if the parents separate later on. Even more, it recalled that the mutual enjoyment by parent and child of each other's company constitutes a fundamental element of family life in concordance with article 7 of the CRC affording to the child, as far as possible, the right to be cared for by his or her parents (see also *McMichael v. the United Kingdom*, European Court of Human Rights, No. 16424/90, judgment of 24.02.1995, para. 86, and *Johansen v. Norway*, European Court of Human Rights, No. 17383/90, judgment of 07/08/1996, para. 52). This view is also upheld in the White Paper, Principle 25, paragraph 1.

Discrimination as stipulated in article 14 of the ECHR exists if three premises can be proved in consecutive order: (1) there is a distinction or difference in treatment granted to different groups in the enjoyment of one of the rights guaranteed by the Convention, (2) the groups enjoying different treatment are in an analogous position, and (3) the distinction does not have an objective and reasonable justification, or is not proportionate to the aim meant to be achieved (irrespective of its legitimacy).[1575] If article 14 is viewed as complementary to another substantive provision of the ECHR (in this case, article 8) this would mean that it should provide protection from discrimination only with regard to that particular right. Thus, even though one of the complementing rights has not been violated separately, the facts may demonstrate breach of them together (in this case, article 8 in conjunction with article 14).[1576] Following this formula for evaluating discrimination, the case of children conceived by sperm donation to single women seem to be eligible for claiming their case.

Firstly, there is an evident and notorious distinction or difference in the treatments granted to "naturally" and "artificially" conceived children in the enjoyment of their right to private and family life (taken alone or together with articles 7 and 8 of the CRC), as barred from protection in a fair trial before the court (article 6(1) of the ECHR).

Secondly, when the fundamental rights to be registered immediately after birth, to know and be cared for by both parents, as far as possible (article 7 CRC) and to preserve the child's own identity and family relations as recognised by law without unlawful interference (article 8(1) CRC) as part of the child's own private and family life (article 8 ECHR) are barred from being realised or challenged either in a fair trial before the court or in administrative proceedings, it means that the State Party has failed to ensure the implementation of these rights (article 7(2) CRC) or failed to provide appropriate assistance and protection for re-establishing speedily the identity of the "artificially" conceived child (article 8(2) CRC). "Naturally" conceived children in an analogous situation normally have access to information regarding their origins (adoption is differently regulated in different countries, even though the trend of revealing information is increasing)[1577] and have procedural rights to challenge or establish parenthood before the court as a last instance once the other ways (presumption or recognition) are exhausted (adoption again is not endangered from parental proceedings if it is clear that the social parenthood coincides with the legal parenthood due to the parties' intentions).

[1575] Kleijkamp G.A., *Family Life and Family Interests, A Comparative Study on the Influence of the European Convention of Human Rights on Dutch Family Law and the Influence of the United States Constitution on American Family Law*, Kluwer Law International, 1999, p. 53.

[1576] *Ibid.* p. 54.

[1577] In the case of the Republic of Macedonia, adoptions too are in the "secrecy zone" regarding the information related to the genetic origins of the child. The proposed changes should also change this practice.

Thirdly, the distinction in treatment for the pursuit of the aim to keep the donors' identity unrevealed or to maintain the unity of the created "artificial" families for the sake of legal certainty is not proportional to the harm done to children and their fundamental rights.[1578] On the contrary, children are taken as means employed to satisfy the needs of a single woman (or other women in a family) to have children, while not violating their other subsidiary instrumental means – the donor (if he consents to donate solely under conditions of secrecy). If legal proceedings that challenge parenthood do not have an intention to hide the truth over the act of conception, while also balance the "natural" (genetics) over "artificial" (social) facts of parenthood, it would not be necessary to compromise children's rights by the rights of the adults. "Artificially" conceived children should also on the same grounds as "naturally" conceived children be able to challenge parenthood before the court. It is the State's task to allow access to justice for everyone and adapt family laws to the evolutive path of medicine and society. This provided, it is the national court's task to weigh up the proportionality of genetics and factual family life facts, given the priority afforded to the best interests of the child on an individual case basis. Consequently, the aim could be achieved through an open judicial system that accepts both realities and judges them accordingly, where no one feels deprived of their fundamental rights guaranteed in the Convention. The scope of the margin of appreciation will vary according to the circumstances, the subject matter and its background. One of the relevant factors is also the European consensus among the Member States.[1579] Since the legal solutions to the issue are very diverse in different European countries, it will be difficult to extrapolate a common ground for harmonising the laws. Nevertheless, the increasing trend shows that in most countries the identity of donors is unveiled for the purposes of appreciating children's right to a narrative regarding their origins.[1580] This is also accompanied by a sensitive approach regarding access and administration of such cases before the courts.[1581] The

1578 Some authors argue the opposite: children conceived by sperm donation to single women or to lesbian couples are discriminated against because their family stability and security are not the same as of those conceived to heterosexual couples, if the possibility of the donor to claim parental rights in judicial proceedings is left up to the discretion of the judges. This only comes as a further reaction from the Canadian system (some not all provinces, including Quebec, Alberta, British Columbia, Prince Edward Island and Manitoba) that is already steps ahead in terms of allowing known donors to compete for parental responsibilities (see further footnote 1585) as in comparison to the European context. See more in Kelly F., "Equal Parents, Equal Children: Reforming Canada's Parentage Laws to Recognize the Completeness of Women-led Families", *University of New Brunswick Law Journal*, Vol. 64, 2013, pp. 253 and 254.

1579 See, for instance, *Rasmussen v. Denmark*, European Court of Human Rights, No. 8777/79, judgment of 28.11.1984, para. 40.

1580 See more in Chapter 3, section 3.1.2, The right of the child to know the identity of the donor.

1581 *J.R.M. v. the Netherlands*, European Commission on Human Rights, No. 16944/90, Decision of 08.02.1993. In this case, the application of the sperm donor to the Dutch Juvenile Court and later on, the Court of Appeal and the Supreme Court was considered admissible, but was rejected because the Dutch Courts reasoned that "family life" requires, apart from biological fatherhood, the existence of additional circumstances. As the case was brought before the

ECtHR has already formed an opinion rejecting access to national authorities when a person considers that his/her rights have been violated and is considered as a violation of article 13 of the ECHR.[1582]

Otherwise, children's role is evidently instrumental in the adults' reproductive projects (since they were never asked if they agreed to be born under conditions that restrict them from certain procedural rights) as a scholarly example of violating the Kantian categorical imperative. The ECtHR has not yet dealt with a case that prohibits access to paternal proceedings in relation to a child conceived by sperm donation to a single woman. Cases like this or related to the meritum of the Court's decision are present in the Canadian legal system.[1583] Nevertheless, the proportionality between the means employed and the aims sought to be achieved in the realm of articles 8 and 6(1) for the purposes of investigating discrimination has been measured in a number of cases.[1584]

The Court's decision can be constitutional (constituting status) as well as not constitutional (confirming the situation as it is and not granting parental status). If the aim of the parental proceedings is to constitute status and there

---

European Commission of Human Rights, the Commission considered that "the situation in which a person donates sperm only to enable a woman to become pregnant through artificial insemination does not of itself give the donor a right to respect for family life with the child". The Commission went on further: "With regards to the applicant's complains under Article 13 in conjunction with Article 6 para. 1 and Article 8 (Art. 13+6-1+8) of the Convention that the Dutch courts refused to declare his request to have access to the child admissible, the Commission recalls that an applicant who has an arguable claim that his rights guaranteed by the Convention have been violated must have an effective remedy before a national authority for that claim. The word 'remedy' in this sense does not mean that the applicant's claim must be vindicated and that the applicant must 'win'. He must have an opportunity to have his claim examined by a national authority conforming to the requirements of Article 13 (Art. 13), which is able to examine the merits of his complaint (No. 10496/83, Dec.14.5.84, D.R. 38 p. 189)". With regard to the complaints of the applicant related to article 14 and the alleged discrimination in comparison to that against a legitimate father, the Commission did not find the two situations comparable and analogous, and therefore rejected the possibility of discrimination. See also footnotes 1269 and 1270.

1582 *Ibid. J.R.M. v. the Netherlands.*

1583 For instance, on the one hand, cases of lesbian couples assisted by sperm donors in Quebec: *S.G. v. L.C.*, RJQ 1685 (QCCS) [SG], 2004; *L.O. v. S.J.*, QCSC 302, 2006; *A. v. B, C and X*, QCCA 361, 2007; cases in Ontario: *M.A.C. v. M.K.*, ONCJ 18, 2009; A.A. v. B.B., ONCA 2 [A.A.], 2007; *W.W. v. X.X. and Y.Y.*, ONSC 879, 2013. On the other hand, cases of single mothers by choice conflicting known donors: *Johnson-Steeves v. Lee*, 6 WWR 608 (ABQB), 1997; *Caufield v. Wong*, ABQB 732, 2007; *L.B. & E.B. c. G.N.*, QCCS 348 [L.B.], 2011. Out of these cases a clear trend has emerged: known donors have been declared parents in almost all applications, while judges held uniformly their position that it is in the child's best interests to have access to his or her biological father, independent of the circumstances or structure of the child's family. See Kelly F., "Equal Parents, Equal Children: Reforming Canada's Parentage Laws to Recognize the Completeness of Women-led Families", *University of New Brunswick Law Journal*, Vol. 64, 2013, p. 257 as well as footnote 1578.

1584 See, for instance, in the cases of *Marckx v. Belgium*, European Court of Human Rights, No. 6833/74, judgment of 13.06.1979, paras. 31, 33, 34 and 43; *Rasmussen v. Denmark*, European Court of Human Rights, No. 8777/79, judgment of 28.11.1984, paras. 38 and 39; *McMichael v. the United Kingdom*, European Court of Human Rights, No. 16424/90, judgment of 24.02.1995, paras. 95, 97, 98 and 99.

is an existent factual family life between the child and the known donor, there is also a possibility for the donor to recognise the child as another means to achieve the same goal. This would signify that there is an intention among them, accompanied by the fact of genetics overlapping with social reality. Nevertheless, the recognition may be obstructed by the mother's consent for which the initial intention to be a sole mother (or at least not to parent together with the donor) remains.[1585] If recognition were a sufficient instrument for establishing relationships between parent and child, judicial parental proceedings would have never been introduced. On the contrary, complicated situations may arise among the concerned parties in both contexts of conceptions – "natural" and "artificial". Therefore the availability of the Court to judge cases of conflicting interests between parties should be afforded on the same grounds to everyone on the same subject matter.

In recent years, the notion of family life has been viewed in a more sociological and functional than moralistic light, with the main emphasis placed on the protection of children's interests.[1586] The ECtHR through its decisions reflects the spirit of the existing family laws: equality and paedo-centrism.[1587] The fundamental principle of affiliation law has always been legal certainty and the protection of already established families. This is especially evident in proceedings that impose time limits for challenging parenthood. The predominantly biological criterion as the determent for establishing parent–child relationships is losing ground next to the social mandate for the determination of what constitutes a legal family life.[1588] For these reasons, the time limits for challenging parenthood tend to legally secure the position of the already established parent who "does" the parenting when confronted with the person who merely "is" a genetic contributor. The same applies when a person recognises as his a child born out of wedlock for which solely the consent of the mother is required and not necessarily proof of his genetic contribution. The Dutch solution to the matter shows the significance of such recognition by replacing the word "acknowledgment" with "acceptance" of fatherhood, stressing the fact that the man intends to father the child and

1585 On the issue whether the mother's consent to the father's acknowledgment of the child as his is necessary or not in cases where the man is a biological father while also having established links that can qualify as "family life", see the Decision of the Dutch Supreme Court HR 8 April 1988, *NJ* 1989, 170, r.o. 3.3; HR 18 May 1990, *NJ* 1991, 374 and 375; HR 8 November 1991, *NJ* 1992, 440 cited in Kleijkamp G.A., *Family Life and Family Interests, A Comparative Study on the Influence of the European Convention of Human Rights on Dutch Family Law and the Influence of the United States Constitution on American Family Law*, Kluwer Law International, 1999, pp. 165 and 170.

1586 Kleijkamp G.A., *Family Life and Family Interests. A Comparative Study on the Influence of the European Convention of Human Rights on Dutch Family Law and the Influence of the United States Constitution on American Family Law*, Kluwer Law International, 1999, p. 140.

1587 Almeida S., "The Right to Respect for (Private and) Family Life in the Case-Law of the ECtHR; the Protection of New Forms of Family", *Academia.edu*, p. 25, available online: https://www.academia.edu/2269426/The_right_to_respect_for_private_and_family_life_in_the_case-law_of_the_European_Court_of_Human_rights_the_protection_of_new_forms_of_family.

1588 *Ibid.* p. 298.

not necessarily to acknowledge his biological fatherhood, making it clear that acknowledgment is a legal act and not necessarily an act of biological truth.[1589]

Therefore not only children conceived with gamete donations can be parented by a person who is not genetically related to them. On the contrary, "naturally" conceived children can also have a social and legal parent that does not coincide with their genetic parent and they also may have an interest in knowing their origins. This, however, does not mean that they will necessarily have to establish legal bonds with them. The affiliation law's developments manifest an obvious paradox: on the one hand, there is an increasing emphasis on biological truth,[1590] while on the other hand parental rights and responsibilities are increasingly granted to persons other than the biological parents.[1591] These conflicts between genetic and social reality could apparently exist in both contexts of conceptions. What is employed in the context of "natural" conceptions for the purposes of safeguarding legal certainty is the time limit that restricts the genetic parent from coming back into the child's life whenever he/she wants and therefore interrupting the already created social family unit. A problem may appear, though, if the genetic father is never informed of the birth of his child or he is informed/finds out only after the expiry of the restricted time limit. If birth registers in "natural" conceptions prescribe the genetic link between the parent and the child as from the time of birth, as far as possible (if the mother can identify the genetic father), that would mean that mothers' responsibility to identify the father should increase. If birth registers in "artificial" conceptions prescribe the genetic reality of the parents as from the time of birth, as far as possible (if the donor is not anonymous), this would mean that the donor will have to withdraw from his parental responsibilities as in concordance with his consent given prior to conception. This would make all children equal in relation to their chances of knowing their genetic origins and all parents regarding their chances of establishing legal family ties with their children. The only difference would be the presumed affirmative consent of the natural father (*procreator – verwekker* as in the Dutch legal system) to parent his child born as a result of sexual intercourse, as opposed to the explicit negative consent of the donor not to parent his genetically related child conceived with the assistance of medicine.[1592] This would additionally

---

1589 *Ibid.* p. 171.

1590 *Ibid.* pp. 364 and 365.

1591 *Ibid.* p. 299. See also *Shofman v. Russia*, European Court of Human Rights, No. 74826/01, judgment of 24.11.2005. This case regarded the time limits for the presumed father that restricted him from rebutting his legal paternity.

1592 An exception of *presumed affirmative consent* of the genetic father who procreated via sexual intercourse or *presumed negative consent* of the donor is the regulation in Quebec in cases of "parental projects" (which include transfer of genetic material of one person for the purpose of another party/parties' reproductive project). The Civil Code of Quebec (SQ c. 64, article 538.2, 1992) stipulates that if the genetic material is provided by way of sexual intercourse, a bond of filiation may be established, in the year following birth, between the contributor and the child. Nevertheless, if there is no "parental project" among the parties, the situation falls under the rules of blood filiation. The case of *L.B. & E.B. c. G.N.* QCCS 348 [L.B.], 2011 before the court in

equalise the positions between the genders (the genetic mother and father) in terms of equal opportunities for establishing the parenthood of their genetically related child. If it is accepted that parents are persons genetically related to the child and become so only after the child is born, i.e. physically separated from the mother's body (not prior to or after conception), then it will follow that they will be able to withdraw from their parental responsibilities only once they become parents.[1593] On the one hand, for the natural father it should be more difficult to withdraw from parental responsibilities or only with the mother's consent.[1594] On the other hand, for the donor, it should be mandatory to follow the obligations undertaken with the prior consent to withdraw from parental responsibilities.[1595] Inevitably, parental links exist through genetics and this fact should not be hidden. Alongside this, parenthood is a legal concept that develops over time between persons who have the intention of sharing life together. Even if a known donor who has withdrawn from parental responsibilities establishes family links with his child with the cooperation and consent of the mother, he could recognise the child as his later on and thus establish legal family links.

Parenthood is initially a genetic and only afterwards a social relationship between parent and child. If these facts are integrated in the concept of parenthood in practice, parental responsibilities should start from childbirth. The same should also apply in cases of medically assisted conceptions.

Firstly, donors should be informed of the birth of their genetically related children.

Secondly, they should be asked to withdraw from their parental responsibilities (according to the previously expressed intention). Only afterwards should the transfer of the parental responsibilities be made possible (to another father). While the White Paper acknowledges that nowadays the only legal form of change of parentage is adoption, it also recognises the potential for the development of

---

Quebec considered that a "parental project" can also exist even if conception occurs via sexual intercourse. Nevertheless, the Court found that there was no sufficient interest from the donor to prove that he intended to be more than that in the first year after the birth of the child.

1593 *Keegan v. Ireland*, European Court of Human Rights, No. 16969/90, judgment of 26.05.1994, para. 44, holding that the relationship between parents and their children constitutes family lifestarting from the moment of birth and by the very fact of it, it is irrelevant whether the child was born in or out of wedlock.

1594 For more on the mother's consent, see footnote 1336.

1595 A case making a distinction when parental responsibilities of the father can or cannot be withdrawn was judged by the New Jersey Superior Court in 2011 (*E.E. v. O.M.G.R.*, 420 N.J. Super. 283, 285–86 (N.J. Super. Ct. Ch. Div. 2011)). The Court drew a difference between sperm donation by a friend of a single woman executed at home and a sperm donation in a licensed clinic. After not allowing the man to relinquish his parental rights and responsibilities and as such him being proclaimed the child's parent against the initial will of both mother and father, the Superior Court reaffirmed the decision starting from the premise that "a child has the right to the security of two parents at the time of birth" (p. 286). This followed the rationale that parties cannot contract to terminate parental rights. For a critique of this decision, see Garcia M.A., "In with New Families, Out with Bad Law: Determining the Rights of Known Sperm Donors Through Intent-Based Written Agreements", *Duke Journal of Gender Law & Policy*, Vol. 21, 2014, pp. 207, 208 and 209.

new forms of change of parentage, taking account of the inventiveness of the legal profession with regard to the new social, medical and legal changes when it comes to the establishment of parenthood.[1596] If parental responsibilities start for both women and men at the time of birth, and the idea is to make "natural" and "artificial" conceptions equal as far as possible, then they should also start at the same moment for sperm donors. If they are just *sperm donors*, then they will have to withdraw or resign from being *parents*, and firmly acknowledge their status after childbirth. In these terms, donors' parental responsibilities will be terminated and available to be transmitted to the commissioning parents. This is how donors will be notified that their progeny are born, and from there on they can explicitly reject paternity, leaving no vacuum or place for further contestations or paternal conflicts. This is also how donations will legally come closer not only to adoptions, but also to surrogacies (in countries that regulate them), making the legal system more harmonised as a whole. In this way, the approach to donations will be taken with a decent dose of procreational responsibility, making donors aware that they do not give an object as a gift to somebody else, but procreate a child who may wish to know their identity in the future. Therefore there should be another way to terminate parental responsibilities, with explicit reference to sperm donors.[1597]

Parental proceedings should be available for every parent and child under equal conditions. Once the case is considered admissible, the merits of the claim should be evaluated based on the interaction between three facts: (1) biology/genes, (2) social and factual family life, and (3) intention of the parties, as additionally perceived through the prism of the best interests of the child in each particular case.

Children should enjoy two aspects of private and family life.

Firstly, they should enjoy the informational aspect envisaged in the right to know their family origins.

Secondly, they should enjoy the legal and functional aspect of having parental care as established on grounds of intention (expressed prior to the conception as a presumption in the cases of "natural" conceptions *via* coitus or explicitly expressed in written consent in cases of gamete donations). These intentions should

1596 White Paper, p. 23. For this purpose, Principle 17 was drafted, stipulating: "any new form of change of parentage shall take place under the control of the competent authority in procedures which have due regard to the best interests of the child. Any such form should be subjected to the same safeguards as adoption". From the explanation of the principle, it can be concluded that it was drafted with the primary reason to cover surrogacies (along these lines, the identification with adoption would mean that still, the principle *mater semper certaest* is obeyed, as it is, for instance, in the UK). Nevertheless, other possible forms of change of parentage are not excluded.

1597 For instance, Principle 3:30 of the *Principles of European Family Law Regarding Parental Responsibilities* regulates the termination of parental responsibilities in cases when the child: (1) reaches majority, (2) enters into marriage or registered partnership, (3) is adopted, or (4) is dying. Next to these, the case of withdrawal of the parental responsibilities of the sperm donor has to be explicitly added.

be additionally confirmed or rebutted after birth (if they do not match "natural" conceptions, and are transferred to other parents, it should be considered that the legal parental responsibilities are established via adoption).

If these facts are accepted and integrated into the legal system, there will be no reason to ban parental proceedings for a group of misfortunate children born after gamete donation without their choice. Additionally, the national legal systems will not compromise the accessibility of justice and the internationally accepted conventions, and thus will be more coherent.

The conclusions resulting from the research conducted do not deal with the technical aspects of the provisions in the national legal systems. On the contrary, the impact of the results is on a level of shifting concepts upon which the Macedonian legal system (and many others in Europe and worldwide) traditionally rest to concepts that correspond with the newly developed realities (*correspondence theory of truth*).[1598] The technical aspects of it should be part of some future project if the ideas are accepted.

The application of the assisted reproductive technologies remains controversial in changing family laws and affiliations. The suggested solution for equalising the positions of families irrespective of the relationship between parents or modus of conception of children is just one aspect of it. Future research will have to elaborate profoundly the experiences of families created in one way or the other. In the context of the Republic of Macedonia, the new amendments regulating surrogacies have already opened up new terrain for elaborating the further possible fragmentations of parenthood, and the technical aspects of performing it in practice. Nevertheless, the suggested concepts in this work strive for universal application. Moreover, once the ramifications of parenthood become even more apparent than they already are, the necessity for strengthening legal certainty and protection of the interests of the most vulnerable ones – children – should be of paramount importance.

[1598] See footnote 16.

REFERENCES

BOOKS

Andersen, M.L., Taylor H.F., *Sociology: Understanding a Diverse Society*, Thomson Wadsworth, 2008.

Anthias F., Yuval-Davis N., *Women-Nation-State*, St. Martin's Press, 1989.

Antokolskaia M., *Harmonisation of Family Law in Europe: A Historical Perspective, A Tale of Two Millennia*, Intersentia, 2006.

Aries P., *Centuries of Childhood. A Social History of Family Life*, Baldick R. (trans.), A Vintage Giant, 1962.

Aristotle, *Nicomachean Ethics*, Irwin T. (trans.) (2nd edition), Hackett, 1999.

Avineri S., De-Shalit A. (eds.), *Communitarianism and Individualism*, Oxford University Press, 1992.

Bainham A., *Children: The Modern Law* (3rd edition), Jordan Publishing, 2005.

Balen A.H., Jacobs H.S., *Infertility in Practice* (2nd edition), Informa Healthcare, 2003.

Baran A., Pannor R., *Lethal Secrecies: the Psychology of Donor Insemination, Problem and Solution*, Amistead Press, 1993.

Barett M., Macintosh M., *The Anti-Social Family*, Verso, 1985.

Beauchamp T.L., Childress F.J., *Principles of Biomedical Ethics* (5th edition), Oxford University Press, 2001.

Beck U., Beck-Gernsheim, E., *The Normal Chaos of Love*, Polity Press, 1995.

Beck-Gernheim E., *Reinventing the Family. In Search of New Lifestyles*, Polity Press, 2002.

Blankenhorn D., *Fatherless America. Confronting Our most Urgent Social Problem*, Basic Books, 1995.

Blauwhoff J.R., *Foundational Facts, Relative Truths. A Comparative Law Study on Children's Right to Know their Genetic Origins*, Intersentia, 2009.

Boele-Woelki K. (ed.), *Perspectives for the Unification and Harmonisation of Family Law in Europe*, Intersentia, 2003.

Boele-Woelki K. *et al.*, *Principles of European Family Law Regarding Parental Responsibilities*, Intersentia, 2007.

Bok S., *Secrets*, Vintage, 1984.

Borland M., O'Hara G., Triseliotis J., *Adoption & Fostering: The Outcome of Permanent Family Placements in 2 Scottish Local Authorities*, Scottish Office, 1991.

Bowlby J., *The Making and Breaking of Affectional Bonds*, Tavistock, 1979.

Burke E., *Reflections on the Revolution in France, and on the Proceedings in Certain Societies in London Relative to that Event. In a Letter Intended to have been sent to a Gentleman in Paris*, Dodsley, 1790.

Callahan S., Monagle E.J., Thomasma C.D. (eds.), *Medical Ethics: A Guide for Health Care Professionals*, Aspen Publishers, 1987.

Chadwick F.R. (ed.), *Ethics, Reproduction and Genetic Control*, Routledge, 1992.

Clayton R., Tomlinson H., *The Law of Human Rights*, Oxford University Press, 2000.

Clayton, R., Tomlinson T., *The Law of Human Rights* (2nd edition), Oxford University Press, 2009.

Cohen S., Taub N. (eds.), *Reproductive Laws for the 1990s, Contemporary Issues in Biomedicine, Ethics, and Society*, Humana Press, 1989.

Coleman J.C., Hendry L., *The Nature of Adolescence* (3rd edition), Routledge, 1999.

Coleman L., Glenn F., *When Couples Part. Understanding the Consequences for Adults and Children*, One Plus One, 2009.

Croli E., Davin D., Kane P. (eds.), *China's One-Child Policy*, St. Martin's Press, 1985.

De Beauvoir S., *The Second Sex*, Parshley H.M. (trans.), Vintage Books, 1989 (the original title: *Le deuxième Sexe*, Vols. 1 and 2, Gallimard, 1949).

Detrick S., *A Commentary on the United Nations Convention on the Rights of the Child*, Kluwer Law International, 1999.

Devlin P., *The Enforcement of Morals*, Oxford University Press, 1965.

Donovan C., *Genetics, Fathers and Families. Exploring the Implications of Changing the Law in Favour of Identifying Sperm Donors*, Sage, 2006.

Dostal J., *Ethical and Legal Aspects of Assisted Reproduction. Situation in the Member States that Joined the European Union in 2004* (1st edition), Olomouc Palacky University, 2007.

Dworkin R., *Law's Empire*, Harvard University Press, 1986.

Eckhard B., *Toegangsregte tot buite-egtelike kinders – behoort die wetgewer in te gryp?*, TSAR, 1992.

Edwards J., *Born and Bred. Idioms of Kinship and New Reproductive Technologies in England*, Oxford University Press, 2000.

Eisenstein H., *Contemporary Feminist Thought*, Allen & Unwin, 1984.

Ezzy D., *Qualitative Analysis: Practice and Innovation*, Allen & Unwin, 2002.

Fairclough N., *Analysing Discourse*, Routledge, 2003.

Feinberg J., *Harm to Others. The Moral Limits of the Criminal Law*, Oxford University Press, 1984.

Fenwick H., *Civil Liberties and Human Rights*, Cavendish Publishing, 2005.

Field M.J., *The Comparative Politics of Birth Control. Determinants of Policy Variation and Change in the Developed Nations*, Praeger, 1983.

Finegold W.J., Charles C.T., *Artificial Insemination*, Charles C. Thomas, 1964.

Fineman M., *The Sexual Family. Family and Queer Legal Theory. Intimate Encounters, Uncomfortable Conversations*, Ashgate, 2009.

Firestone S., *The Dialectic of Sex. The Case for Feminist Revolution*, Bantam Books, 1970.

Foucault M., *The History of Sexuality, Vol. 1, An Introduction*, Hurley R. (trans.), Vintage Books, 1990.

Foucault M., *The Order of Things. An Archaeology of the Human Sciences*, Vintage Books, 1994.

Frankfurt, G.H., *The Importance of What we Care* About, Cambridge University Press, 1988.

Franklin S., *Embodied Progress: A Cultural Account of Assisted Conception*, Routledge, 1997.

Fratter J., Rowe J., Sapsford D., Thoburn J., *Permanent Family Placements: A Decade of Experience*, BAAF, 1991.

Freeman M. (ed.), *Children's Rights. A Comparative Perspective*, Dartmouth Publishing, 1996.

Freeman M., *The Moral Status of Children, Essays on the Rights of the Child*, Martinus Nijhoff, 1997.

French M., *Beyond Power: Woman, Man and Morals*, Cape, 1985.

Freud, S., *Die Sexualität in der Ätiologie der Neurosen*, Psychanalyse.lu, 1898.

Gal S., Kligman G., *The Politics of Gender after Socialism*, Princeton University Press, 2000.

Gerson K., *No Man's Land. Man's Changing Commitments to Family and Work*, Basic Books, 1993.

Giddens A., Eichler M., *Family Shifts. Families, Policies, and Gender Equality*, Oxford University Press, 1997.

Giddens A., *The Transformation of Intimacy. Sexuality, Love and Eroticism in Modern Societies*, Polity Press, 1993.

Gilby T., *The Political Thought of Thomas Aquinas*, University of Chicago Press, 1958.

Glandon M.A., *Rights Talk. The Impoverishment of Political Discourse*, Free Press, 1991.

Goldberg V., *The Right of Access of a Father of an Extramarital Child: Visited Again*, SALJ, 1993.

Gomien D., Harris D.J., Zwaak L., *Law and Practice of the European Convention on Human Rights and the European Social Charter*, 1996.

Greer S., *The Margin of Appreciation: Interpretation and Discretion under the European Convention on Human Rights*, Council of Europe, 2000.

Guggenheim M., *What's Wrong with Children's Rights?*, Harvard University Press, 2005.

Hart H.L.A., *Law, Liberty and Morality*, Oxford University Press, 1963.

Henn M., Weinstein M., Foard N., *A Short Introduction to Social Research*, Sage, 2006.

Hertz R., *Single by Chance, Mothers by Choice. How Women are Choosing Parenthood without Marriage and Creating the new American Family*, Oxford University Press, 2006.

Herzfeld M., *The Social Production of Indifference. Exploring the Symbolic Roots of Western Bureaucracy*, Berg, 1992.

Heyd D., *Genetics: Moral Issues in the Creation of People*, University of California Press, 1992.

Hodgkin R., Newell P., *Implementation Handbook for the Convention on the Rights of the Child*, UNICEF, 2007.

Ignovska, E., *Bio- reproduktivna etika i pravo. Novite reproduktivni tehnologii i roditelskoto pravo*, Biggos, 2010.

Jagger G., Wright C. (eds.), *Changing Family Values*, Routledge, 1999.

Jasanhoff S. (ed.), *States of Knowledge: The Co-Production of Science and Social Order*, Routledge, 2004.

Jones H.W., Cohen J., Cooke I., Kempers R. (eds.), *IFFS Surveillance 07*, 2007.

Jones P., *Rights, Issues in Political Theory*, Palgrave Macmillan, 1994.

Jonsen A.R., *The Birth of Bioethics. An Historical Memoir of the Origins and Evolution of Bioethics in the United States, 1947–1987*, Oxford University Press, 1998.

Kaplan J.L., Tong R., *Controlling Our Reproductive Destiny. A Technological and Philosophical Perspective*, MIT Press, 1994.

Keller H., Sweet A.S., *The Impact of the ECHR on National Legal Systems*, Oxford University Press, 2008.

Kingston H.M., *ABC of Clinical Genetics* (3rd edition), BMJ Books, 2002.

Kleijkamp G.A., *Family Life and Family Interests, A Comparative Study on the Influence of the European Convention of Human Rights on Dutch Family Law and the Influence of the United States Constitution on American Family Law*, Kluwer Law International, 1999.

Kruger J.M., *Die toegangsbevoegdhede van die ongetroude vader – Is die finale wordgespreek? B. v S., 1995 3 SA 571 (A)*, THRHR, 1996.

Levinas E., *Otherwise than Being, or Beyond Essence*, Martinus Nijhoff, 1981.

Lowe N.V., Douglas G. (eds.), *Bromley's Family Law* (10th edition), Oxford University Press, 2007.

Luker K., *Abortion and the Politics of Motherhood*, University of California Press, 1984.

MacKinnon C.A., *Toward a Feminist Theory of the State*, Harvard University Press, 1989.

Malinowski, B., *The Family Among the Australian Aboriginies: a Sociological Study*, University of London Press, 1913.

Malthus T., *An Essay on the Principle of Population*, London, 1798.

Martin A., *The Lesbian and Gay Parenting Handbook*, Harper Perennial, 1993.

McLanahan S., Sandefur G., *Growing up with a Single Parent. What Hurts, What Helps*, Harvard University Press, 1994.

Melo-Martin I., *Making Babies. Biomedical Technologies, Reproductive Ethics, and Public Policy*, Kluwer Academic Publishers, 1998.

Minow M., *Making All the Difference. Inclusion, Exclusion and American Law*, Cornell University Press, 1990.

Mitchell A., *Children in the Middle London*, Tavistok, 1985.

Morgan L.H., *Ancient Society*, Macmillan, 1877.

Mosikatsana T.L., *Is Papa a Rolling Stone? The Unwed Father and his Child in South African Law – a Comment on Fraser v. Naude*, CILSA, 1996.

Mount F., *The Subversive Family: an Alternative History of Love and Marriage*, Counterpoint, 1983.

Narayan U., Bartkowiak J.J. (eds.), *Having and Raising Children: Unconvetional Families, Hard Choices and the Social Good*, Pennsylvania State University Press, 1999.

O'Brien M., *The Politics of Reproduction*, Routledge & Kegan Paul, 1981.

Ory S.J., Devroey P. *et al.* (eds.), *IFFS Surveillance*, 2013.

Overall C., *Ethics and Human Reproduction: A Feminist Analysis*, Allen & Unwin, 1987.

Pateman C., *The Sexual Contract*, Polity Press, 1988.
Philips A., *Endangering Democracy*, Polity Press, 1991.
Pintens, W., Vanwinckelen K., *Casebook European Family Law*, Leuven University Press, 2001.
Plato, *The Laws*, Saunders T.J. (trans.), Penguin, 1970.
Popenoe D., *Life Without Father. Compelling New Evidence that Fatherhood and Marriage are Indispensable for the Good of Children and Society*, Free Press, 1996.
Purdy L.M., *Reproducing Persons. Issues in Feminist Bioethics*, Cornell University Press, 1996.
Putnam H., *Pragmatism: An Open Question*, Blackwell, 1996.
Rasmussen D. (ed.), *Universalism v. Communitarianism. Contemporary Debates in Ethics*, MIT Press, 1990.
Rawls J., *Political Liberalism*, Columbia University Press, 1993, 1996, 2005.
Rawls J., *Theory of Justice* (revised edition), The Belknap Press of Harvard University Press, 1971, 1999.
Richards, A.I., *Hunger and Work in a Savage Tribe: A Functional Study of Nutrition Among the Southern Bantu*. G. Routledge and Sons, 1932.
Rifkin J., Perlas N., *Algeny*, Viking Press, 1983.
Robertson J.A., *Children of Choice: Freedom and the New Reproductive Technologies*, Princeton University Press, 1994.
Rothstein M.A., Murray T.H., Kachnick G.E., Majumder M.A. (eds.), *Genetic Ties and the Family, Baltimore*, Johns Hopkins University Press, 2005.
Saffron L., *Challenging Conceptions: Pregnancy and Parenting Beyond the Traditional Family*, Cassell, 1994.
Sandal J.M., *The Case Against Perfection*, Harvard University Press, 2009.
Sandel M., *Liberalism and its Critics*, New York University Press, 1984.
Sandel M., *Liberalism and the Limits of Justice*, Cambridge University Press, 1982.
Schneider D., *A Critique of the Study of Kinship*, University of Michigan Press, 1984.
Schweitzer P.P., *Dividends of Kinship: Meanings and Uses of Social Relatedness*, Routledge, 2000.
Scott J., Treas J., Richards M. (eds.), *The Blackwell Companion to the Sociologies of Families*, Blackwells Publishing, 2004.
Shanlev C., *Birth Power: The Case for Surrogacy*, Yale University Press, 1989.
Shanley M.L., *Making Babies, Making Families, What Matters Most in an Age of Reproductive Technologies, Surrogacy, Adoption, and Same-Sex and Unwed Parents*, Beacon Press, 2001.
Silva E.B., Smart C. (eds.) *The New Family?*, Sage, 1999.
Singer P., Wells D., *The Reproduction Revolution. New Ways of Making Babies*, Oxford University Press, 1984.
Smart C., Neale B., *Family Fragments?*, Polity Press, 1999.
Smith R.K.M., *The Essentials of Human Rights*, Oxford University Press, 2005.
Soiseth A., *Choosing You. Deciding to have a Baby on my Own*, Seal Press, 2008.
Spaas L., (ed.), *Paternity and Fatherhood: Myths and Realities*, Macmillan, 1998.

Stacey J., *Brave New Families. Stories of Domestic Upheaval in the Late Twentieth Century*, Basic Books, 1990.

Steiner, H., *An Essay on Rights*, Blackwell, 1994.

Stafford C.L., *Separation and Reunion in Modern China*, Cambridge University Press, 2000.

Strathern M., *Reproducing the Future: Anthropology, Kinship and the New Reproductive Technologies*, Routledge, 1992.

Van Bueren G., *Child Rights in Europe*, Council of Europe, Strasbourg, 2007.

Van Dijk, Van Hoof, *Theory and Practice of the European Convention on Human Rights*, Kluwer, 1998.

Van Onselen D., *TUFF – the Unmarried Fathers' Fight*, De Rebus, 1991.

Vonk, M., *Children and their Parents, A Comparative Study of the Legal Position of Children with Regard to their Intentional and Biological Parents in English and Dutch Law*, Intersentia, 2007.

Wallerstein J.S., Kelly K.B., *Surviving the Breakup*, Grant Mcintyre, 1980.

Warnock M., *A Question of Life. The Warnock Report on Human Fertilization and Embryology*, Blackwell, 1985.

Wedge P., Mantle G., *Sibling Groups and Social Work*, Gower, 1991.

Weeks J., Heaphy B., Donovan C., *Same Sex Intimacies: Families of Choice and Other Life Experiments*, Routledge, 2001.

Weismantel, M., *Food, Gender and Poverty in the Ecuadorian Andes*, University of Pennsylvania Press, 1988.

Westermark, E., *The History of Human Marriage*, Macmillan, 1891.

Ziemele I., *A Commentary on the United Nations Convention on the Rights of the Child. Article 7 – The Right to Birth Registration, Name and Nationality, and the right to Know and Be Cared for by Parents*, Martinus Nijhoff, 2007.

ARTICLES IN BOOKS

Asch A., "Licensing Parents, Regulating Assisted Reproduction", in Cutas D., Chan S. (eds.), *Families Beyond the Nuclear Ideal*, Bloomsbury Academic, 2012.

Asch A., "The Lessons of Oncofertility for Assisted Reproduction", in Woodruff T.K., Zoloth L., Campo-Engelstein L. *et al.* (eds.), *Oncofertility. Reflections from the Humanities and the Social Sciences*, Springer, 2010.

Bainham A., "Birthrights? The Rights and Obligations Associated with the Birth of a Child", in Spencer A.R., Du Bois-Pedain A. (eds.), *Freedom and Responsibility in Reproductive Choice*, Hart Publishing, 2006.

Berg, F.B., "Listening to the Voices of the Infertile", in Callahan J.C. (ed.), *Reproduction, Ethics and the Law. Feminist Perspectives*, Indiana University Press, 1995.

Bennett B., "Gamete Donation, Reproductive Technology and the Law", in Petersen K. (ed.), *Intersections: Women on Law, Medicine and Technology*, Ashgate, 1997.

Bentham J., "Critique of the Doctrine of Inalienable Natural Rights", *Anarchical Fallacies*, Vol. 2 of Bowring (ed.), Works, 1843.

Berkman J., "Virtuous Parenting and Orphaned Embryos, Human Embryo Adoption, Bioetechnology, Marriage, and the Right to Life", in Berg T.V., Furton E.J. (eds.), *Human Embryo Adoption: Biotechnology, Marriage, and the Right to Life*, The National Bioethics Center and the Westchester Institute for Ethics and the Human Person, 2006.

Boele-Woelki K., "European Challenges in Contemporary Family Law: Some Final Observation", in Boele-Woelki K., Sverdrup T. (eds.), *European Challenges in Contemporary Family Law*, Intersentia, 2008.

Callahan J.C., "Introduction", in Callahan J.C. (ed.), *Reproduction, Ethics and Law. Feminist Perspectives*, Indiana University Press, 1995.

Campbell J., Moyers B., "The Power of Myth", in Flowers B.S. (ed.), *The Power of Myth*, Doubleday, 1988.

Carsten J., Hugh-Jones S., "Introduction", in Carsten J., Hugh-Jones S. (eds.), *About the House: Levi-Strauss and Beyond*, Cambridge University Press, 1995.

Carsten J., "Substantivism, Antisubstantivism, and Anti-antisubstantivism", in Franklin S., McKinnon S. (eds.), *Relative Values: Reconfiguring Kinship Studies*, Duke University Press, 2001.

Chadwick R.F., "Having Children: Introduction", in Chadwick R.F. (ed.), *Ethics, Reproduction and Genetic Control*, Routledge, 1990.

Cohen J., "Respect for Private and Family Life", in MacDonald R.S.J., Matscher F., Petzold H. (eds.), *The European System for the Protection of Human Rights*, Martinus Nijhoff, 1993.

Collier R., "Men, Heterosexuality and the Changing Family. (Re)constructing Fatherhood in Law and Social Policy", in Jagger G., Wright C. (eds.), *Changing Family Values*, Routledge.

Daniels K., "The Semen Providers", in Daniels K., Haimes E. (eds.), *Donor Insemination. International Social Science Perspectives*, Cambridge University Press, 1998.

Deanoska-Trendafilova A., Cadikovski V., "Legal and Medical Issues Concerning the Transplantation of Human Body Parts for Treatment in the Republic of Macedonia", in Jansen B.C.S., Ignovska E. (eds.), *Law, Public Health Care System and Society. Macedonia – Social Policy, Legislation, Biomedicine and Ethics of Organ Transplantation, Fertilization and ART*, Academische Verlagsgemeinschaft, 2012.

Dewar J., "Fathers in Law", in Lee R., Morgan D. (eds.), *Birthrights, Law and Ethics at the Beginning of Life*, Routledge, 1989.

Dobozi V., "The Right to Know One's Biological Identity", *The International Conference Challenges of the Knowledge Society* (7th edition), Bucharest, 17–18 May 2013.

Dobinson I., Johns F., "Qualitative Legal Research", in McConville M., Hong Chui W. (eds.), *Research Methods for Law*, Edinburgh University Press, 2007.

Doek J.E., "The Nuclear Family: Who are the Parents?", in Eekelaar J., Nhlapo T. (eds.), *The Changing Family: International Perspectives on the Family and Family Law*, 1998.

Dostal J., "Specific Ethical and Legal Aspects of ART Practice in Eastern European Countries", in Schenker J.G. (ed.), *Ethical Dilemmas in Assisted Reproductive Technologies*, Walter de Gruyter, 2011.

Eriksson A., Saldeen A, "Parenthood and Science-Establising and Contesting Parentage", in Eekelaar J., Sarcevic P. (eds.), *Parenthood in Modern Society: Legal and Social Issues for the Twenty-First Century*, Martinus Nijhoff, 1993.

Floyd S.L., Pomerantz D., "Is there a Natural Right to Have Children?", in Arthur J. (ed.), *Morality and Moral Controversies*, Prentice-Hall, 1981.

Fortes M., "Introduction", in Goody J. (ed.) *The Developmental Cycle in Domestic Groups*, Published for the Department of Archaeology and Anthropology by Cambridge University Press, 1959.

Gong Z., Zheng Li., "Sperm Donation and Sperm-Bank Management", in Schenker J.G. (ed.), *Ethical Dilemmas in Assisted Reproductive Technologies*, Walter de Gruyter, 2011.

Gracia D., "History of Medical Ethics", in ten Have H.A.M.J., Gordijn B. (eds.), *Bioethics in a European Perspective*, Kluwer Academic Publishers, 2001.

Graham S., "Choosing Single Motherhood? Single Women Negotiating the Nuclear Family Ideal", in Cutas D., Chan S. (eds.), *Families – Beyond the Nuclear Ideal*, Bloomsbury Academic, 2012.

Green Y., "Informed Consent for Treatment of Fertility", in Schenker J.G. (ed.), *Ethical Dilemmas in Assisted Reproductive Technologies*, Walter de Gruyter, 2011.

Haimes E., "Gamete Donation and the Social Management of Genetic Origins", in Stacey M. (ed.), *Changing Human Reproduction*, Sage, 1992.

Hare R.M., "In Vitro Fertilization and the Warnock Report", in Chadwick R.F. (ed.), *Ethics, Reproduction and Genetic Control*, Routledge, 1990.

Harris J., "The Right to Found a Family", in Scarre G. (ed.), *Children, Parents and Politics*, Cambridge University Press, 1989.

Hetherington E.M., Stanley-Hagan, M.M., "Parenting in Divorced and Remarried Families", in Bornstein M.H. (ed.), *Handbook of Parenting*, Vol. 3, Lawrence Eribaum Associates, 2002.

Hirsch E., "Negotiated Limits. Interviews in South-East England", in Edwards J. *et al.* (eds.), *Technologies of Procreation. Kinship in the Age of Assisted Conception*, Manchester University Press, 1993.

Hong Chui W., "Quantitative Legal Research", in McConville M., Hong Chui W. (eds.), *Research Methods for Law*, Edinburgh University Press, 2007.

Ieven A., "Privacy Rights in Conflict: In Search of the Theoretical Framework Behind the European Court of Human Rights' Balancing of Private Life against Other Rights", in Brems E. (ed.), *Conflicts Between Fundamental Rights*, Intersentia, 2008.

Ignovska E., "The Impact of Assisted Reproduction on Affiliation within the Family Law of the Republic of Macedonia", in Jansen B.C.S., Ignovska E. (eds.), *Law, Public Health Care System and Society. Macedonia – Social Policy, Legislation, Biomedicine and Ethics of Organ Transplantation, Fertilization and ART*, Academische Verlagsgemeinschaft, 2012.

Ignovska E., "The Value of Life of the Embryo, the Argument of Potentiality to Develop, and the Context in which is Embedded", in Hongladarom S. (ed.), *Genomics and Bioethics: Interdisciplinary Perspectives, Technologies and Advancements*, 2011.

Jänterä-Jareborg M., "Parenthood for Same-Sex Couples – Scandinavian Developments", in Boele-Woelki K., Fuchs A. (eds.), *Legal Recognition of Same-Sex Relationships in Europe* (2nd revised edition), Intersentia, 2012.

Kant I., "Grounding for the Metaphysics of Morals", in Cahn, S.M. (ed.) *Classics of Western Philosophy*, Hackett, 1995.

Killerby M., "The Council of Europe's Contribution to Family Law (Past, Present and Future)", in Lowe N., Douglas G. (eds.), *Families Across Frontiers*, Martinus Nijhoff, 1996.

Kingdom E., "Birthrights. Equal or Special?", in Lee R., Morgan D. (eds.), *Birthrights, Law and Ethics at the Beginning of Life*, Routledge, 1989.

Kittay E.F., "Womb Envy. An Explanatory Concept", in Treblicott J. (ed.), *Mothering. Essays in Feminist Theory*, Rowman & Allanheld, 1984.

Klink B., Taekema S. "On the Border. Limits and Possibilities of Interdisciplinary Research", in Klink B., Taekema S. (eds.), *Law and Method, Interdisciplinary Research Into Law*, Mohr Siebeck, 2011.

La Cour Mosegaard M., "Stories of Fatherhood. Kinship in the Making", in Inhorn M. C., Tjørnhøj-Thomsen T., Goldberg H., la Cour Mosegaard M. (eds.), *Reconceiving the Second Sex. Men, Masculinity and Reproduction*, Berghahn Books, 2009.

Lamb M.E., "How do Fathers Influence Children's Development? Let me Count the Ways", in Lamb M.E. (ed.), *The Role of the Father in Child Development*, John Wiley & Sons, 2010.

Laqueur T., "The Facts of Fatherhood", in Hirisch M., Keller F.E. (eds.), *Conflicts in Feminism*, Routledge, 1990.

Locke J., *Second Treatise of Government*, 1689, McPherson C.B. (ed.), *John Locke Second Treatise of Government*, Hackett, 1980.

Maclean S., "The Right to Reproduce", in Campbell *et al.* (eds.), *Human Rights: from Rhetoric to Reality*, Blackwell, 1986.

Malinowski B., "Parenthood – the Basis of Social Structure", in Calverton V., Schmalhausen S.D. (eds.), *The New Generation*, Macaulay, 1930.

Marauhn T., Ruppel N., "Balancing Conflicting Human Rights: Konrad Hesse's Notion of "Praktische Konkordanz" and the German Federal Constitutional Court", in Brems E. (ed.), *Conflicts Between Fundamental Rights*, Intersentia, 2008.

Marina S., Marina F., Marina D., "Access to Fertility Treatment by Lesbian Couples", in Schenker J.G. (ed.), *Ethical Dilemmas in Assisted Reproductive Technologies*, Walter de Gruyter, 2011.

Masson J., "Parenting by Being. Parenting by Doing – in Search of Principles for Founding Families", in Spencer J.R., Bois-Pedain A. (eds.), *Freedom and Responsibility in Reproductive Choice*, Hart Publishing, 2006.

McLeod C., "Morally Justifying Oncofertility Research", in Woodruff T.K., Zoloth L., Campo-Engelstein L. *et al.* (eds.), *Oncofertility. Reflections from the Humanities and Social Sciences,* Springer, 2010.

Meyer D.D., "Partners, Care Givers, and the Constitutional Substance of Parenthood", in Wilson R.F. (ed.), *Reconceiving the Family: Critique on the American Law Institute's Principles of the Law of Family Dissolution*, 2006.

Mickovik D., Ristov A., "Bio-medically Assisted Fertilization in Republic of Macedonia", in Jansen B.C.S., Ignovska E. (eds.), *Law, Public Health Care System and Society. Macedonia – Social Policy, Legislation, Biomedicine and Ethics of Organ Transplantation, Fertilization and ART*, Academische Verlagsgemeinschaft, 2012.

Mill J.S., "On Liberty", in Warnock M. (ed.), *Utilitarianism,* Fontana, 1972.

Millar J., "State, Family and Personal Responsibility. The Changing Balance for Lone Mothers in the United Kingdom", in Allen G. (ed.), *The Sociology of the Family. A Reader*, Blackwell, 1999.

Morton M., Irving M.A., "Common Questions that Arise in Adoption", in Turnpenny P. (ed.), *Secrets in the Genes: Adoption, Inheritance and Genetic Disease*, British Agencies for Adoption and Fostering, 1995.

Mottier V., "Reproductive Rights", in Waylen G., Celis K., Kantola J., Weldon S.L. (eds.), *The Oxford Handbook of Gender and Politics*, Oxford University Press, 2013.

Nordgren A., "Personal Genomics. Consumer Genomics Companies and their Rhetoric", in Tupasela A. (ed.), *Consumer Medicine*, TemaNord, Nordic Council of Ministers, 2010.

O'Donovan K., "What Shall We Tell the Children? Reflections on Children's Perspectives and the Reproduction Revolution", in Lee M., Morgan D. (eds.), *Birthrights, Law and Ethics at the Beginning of Life*, Routledge, 1989.

Prodanov, V., "Cultural Pro-Attitudes, Reproductive Ethics and Embryo Protection", in Evans D. (ed.), *Conceiving the Embryo, Ethics, Law and Practice in Human Embryology*, Martinus Nijhoff, 1996.

Richards B., "What is Identity?", in Gaber I., Aldridge J. (eds.), *The Best Interests of the Child, Culture, Identity, and Transracial Adoption*, Free Association Books, 1994.

Richards M., "Genes, Genealogies and Paternity: Making Babies in the Twenty-first Century", in Spencer J.R., Bois-Pedain A. (eds.), *Freedom and Responsibility in Reproductive Choice,* Hart Publishing, 2006.

Ruddick W., "When Does Childhood Begin", in Scarre G. (ed.), *Children, Parents and Politics*, Cambridge University Press, 1989.

Senaeve P., "The Reform of Affiliation Law in France and in Benelux Countries", in Eckelaar J., Sarcevic P. (eds.), *Legal and Social Issues for the Twenty-First Century*, Dordrecht, Martinus Nijhoff, 1993.

Shanley M.L., "Father's Rights, Mother's Wrongs? Reflections on Unwed Fathers' Rights, Patriarchy, and Sex Equality", in Callahan J.C. (ed.), *Reproduction, Ethics and the Law, Feminist Perspectives*, Indiana University Press, 1995.

Shaw A., "The Contingency of the Genetic Link in Constructions of Kinship and Inheritance – An Anthropological Perspective", in Spencer J.R., Bois-Pedain A. (eds.), *Freedom and Responsibility in Reproductive Choices*, Hart Publishing, 2006.

Sheldon S., "Reproductive Choice. Man's Freedom and Women's Responsibility", in Spencer J.R. and Bois-Pedain A. (eds.), *Freedom and Responsibility in Reproductive Choice*, Hart Publishing, 2006.

Shenfield F., Surreau C., "The Welfare of the Child. Whose Responsibility?", in Shenfield F., Surreau C. (eds.), *Contemporary Ethical Dilemmas in Assisted Reproduction*, Abingdon, 2006.

Sinclair J.D., "Family Rights", in Van Wyk D. *et al.* (eds.), *Rights and Constitutionalism: The New South African Legal Order*, Juta, 1994.

Sinclair J.D., "Legal Personality", in Van Heerden B. *et al.* (eds.), *Boberg's Law of Persons and the Family* (2nd edition), Juta, 1999.

Smith, P., "The Metamorphosis of Motherhood", in Callahan C.J. (ed.), *Reproduction, Ethics and the Law. Feminist Perspectives*, Indiana University Press, 1995.

Stafford C.L., "Chinese Patriliny and the Cycles of *Yang* and *Laiwang*", in Carsten J. (ed.), *Cultures of Relatedness: New Approaches to the Study of Kinship*, Cambridge University Press, 2000.

Steinberg A., "The Foundations and Application of Medical Ethics", in Schenker J.G. (ed.), *Ethical Dilemmas in Assisted Reproductive Technologies*, Walter de Gruyter, 2011.

Steinbock B., "Defining Parenthood", in Spencer J.R., Bois-Pedain A. (eds.), *Freedom and Responsibility in Reproductive Choices*, Hart Publishing, 2006.

Stoddard J.C., Fox J., "Egg Donation Consent Forms", in Seibel M.M., Crockin S.L. (eds.), *Family Building through Egg and Sperm Donation. Medical, Legal, and Ethical Issues*, Jones and Bartlett Publishers, 1996.

Stoljar S.J., "Persons and Family", in Rheinstein M., Stoljar S.J. (eds.), *International Enciclopedia of Comparative Law*, Vol. 4, Mouton, 1973.

Thompson C., "Strategic Naturalizing. Kinship in an Infertility Clinic", in Franklin S., McKinnon (eds.), *Relative Values. Reconfiguring Kinship Studies*, Duke University Press, 2001.

Trieseliotis J., "Identity and Genealopgy", in Bruce N., Mitchell A., Priestley K. (eds.), *Truth and the Child. A Contribution to the Debate on the Warnock Report*, Family Care, 1988.

Triseliotis J., "Obtaining Birth Certificates", in Bean P. (ed.), *Adoption: Essays in Social Policy, Law, and Sociology*, Tavistock, 1984.

Van Balen F., Inhorn M.C., "Introduction: Interpreting Infertility. A View from the Social Sciences", in Inhorn M.C., Van Balen F. (eds.), *Infertility Around the Globe*, University of California Press, 2002.

Van der Burg W., "Law and Ethics. The Twin Disciplines", in Klink B., Taekema S. (eds.), *Law and Method, Interdisciplinary Research Into Law*, Mohr Siebeck, 2011.

Vonk M., 'Towards a New Concept of Parenthood: Procreational Responsibility", in Boele-Woelki K., Sverdrup T. (eds.), *European Challenge in Contemporary Family Law*, Intersentia, 2008.

Weiss R.S., "The Attachment Bond in Childhood and Adulthood", in Paros M.C., Stevenson-Hinde J., Marris P. (eds.), *The Attachment Across the Lifecycle*, Routledge, 1991.

Weston K., "Parenting in the Era of AIDS", in Stein A. (ed.), *Sisters, Sexperts and Queers Beyond the Lesbian Nation*, Plume, 1993.

Williams B., "Classification Systems Revisited. Kinship, Caste, Race, and Nationality as the Flow of Blood and the Spread of Rights", in Yanagisako S., Delaney C. (eds.), *Naturalizing Power: Essays in Feminist Cultural Analysis*, Routledge, 1995.

Yanagisako J., Junko S., Collier J.F., "Towards a Unified Analysis, Gender and Kinship", in Collier J.F., Yanagisako J. (eds.), *Gender and Kinship: Essays Toward a Unified Analysis*, Stanford University Press, 1987.

Zucca L., "Conflicts of Fundamental Rights as Constitutional Dilemmas", in Brems E. (ed.), *Conflicts Between Fundamental Rights*, Intersentia, 2008.

Мицковиќ Д., "Вонбрачната заедница во земјите на Европската унија", *Centre for Regional Research and Cooperation Studiorum*, 25 December 2013.

Мицковиќ Д., Ристов А., "Реформите во наследното и семејното право и ингеренциите на нотарите", Нотариус, бр. 19, available online: www.nkrm.org.mk/dokumenti/notarius/84_426597554.pdf.

JOURNAL ARTICLES

Adrian W., "The Infancy of the History of Childhood. An Appraisal of Philipp. Aries", *History and Theory*, Vol. 19, No. 2, 1982.

Allen G., Hawker S., Crow G., "Family Diversity and Change in Britain and Western Europe", *Journal of Family Issues*, Vol. 22, No. 7, 2001.

Amato P., "Children's Adjustments to Divorce: Theories, Hypothesis and Empirical Support", *Journal of Marriage and Family*, Vol. 55, No. 1, 1993.

Amato P., "The Impact of Family Formation on the Cognitive, Social and Emotional Well-Being of the Next Generation", *Future of Children*, Vol. 15, No. 1, 2005.

Antokolskaia M., "Legal Embedding Planned Lesbian Parentage. Pouring New Wine into Old Wineskins", *Familie & Recht*, February 2014.

Antokolskaia M., Boele-Woelki K., "Dutch Family Law in the 21st Century: Trend-Setting and Straggling Behind at the Same Time", *Nederlande Vereniging Voor Rechtsvergelijking (Netherlands Comparative Law Association)*, Vol. 6, No. 4, December 2002.

Asada H., Sueoka K., Hashiba T. *et al.*, "The Effect of Age and Abnormal Sperm Count on the Nondisjunction of Spermatozoa", *Journal of Assisted Reproduction and Genetics*, Vol. 17, No. 1, 2000.

Barnes J.A., "African Models in the New Guinea Highlands", *Man*, Vol. 62, 1962.

Barnes J.A., "Physical and Social Kinship", *Philosophy of Science*, Vol. 28, No. 3, 1961.

Bartholomew G.W., "The Development and Use of Artificial Insemination", *Eugenics Review*, Vol. 49, No. 4, 1958.

Becker G., Nachtigall R.D., "Eager for Medicalisation. The Social Production of Infertility as a Disease", *Sociology of Health & Illnesses*, Vol. 14, No. 4, 1994.

Benagiano G., Gianaroli L., "The New Italian IVF Legislation", *Reproductive BioMedicine Online*, Vol. 9, No. 2, 2004.

Bernstein G., "Regulating Reproductive Technologies. Timing, Uncertainty and Donor Anonymity", *Boston University Law Review*, Vol. 90, 2010.

Berry M., "Risks and Benefits of Open Adoption", *The Future of Children, Adoption*, Vol. 3, No. 1, Spring 1993.

Biblarz T., Stacey J., "How does the Gender of Parents Matter?", *Journal of Marriage and Family*, Vol. 72, No. 1, 2010.

Blauwhoff J.R., "Tracing down the Historical Development of the Legal Concept of the Right to Know One's Origins. Has 'To Know or Not to Know' ever been the Legal Question?", *Utrecht Law Review*, Vol. 4, No. 2, 2008.

Blyth E., "Gamete Donation – Where is the Evidence that there are Benefits in Removing Anonymity of Donors? A Patient's Viewpoint", *Reproductive Biomedicine Online*, Vol. 7, No. 6, 2003.

Blyth E., Frith L., Jones C., Speirs J.M., "The Role of Birth Certificates in Relation to Access to Biographical and Genetic History in Donor Conception", *International Journal of Children's Rights*, Vol. 17, 2009.

Bock J.D., "Doing the Right Thing? Single Mother by Choice and the Struggle for Legitimacy", *Gender and Society*, Vol. 14, No. 1, 2000.

Boggio, A., "Italy Enacts New Law on Medically Assisted Reproduction", *Human Reproduction*, Vol. 20, No. 5, 2005.

Bohlen C., "Anything Goes in Italian Birth Science", *The Edmonton*, C6, 1995.

Boivin J., Pennings G., "Parenthood Should be Regarded as a Right", *Archives of Disease in Childhood*, Vol. 90, No. 8, 2005.

Bossema E.R., Janssens P.M.W., Landwehr F., Treucker R.G.L., Kor Van Duinen, Nap A.W., Geenen R., "A Taxonomy of Possible Reasons For and Against Sperm Donation", *Acta Obstetricia et Gynaecologica Scandinavica*, 2012.

Bouchard, T.J., "Genetic Influence on Human Psychological Traits. A Survey", *Current Directions in Psychological Science*, Vol. 13, No. 4, 2004.

Brawaeys A., de Bruyn J., Louwe L., Helmerhorst F., "Anonymous or Identity-Registered Sperm Donors? A Study of Dutch Recipients' Choices", *Human Reproduction*, Vol. 20, No. 3, 2005.

Brewaeys A., Golombok S., Naaktgeboren N., "Donor Insemination: Dutch Parents' Opinions About Confidentiality and Donor Anonymity and the Emotional Adjustment of their Children", *Human Reproduction*, Vol. 12, No. 7, 1997.

Brewaeys A., Ponjaert I., Van Hall EV, Golombok S., "Donor Insemination. Child Development and Family Functioning in Lesbian Mother Families", *Human Reproduction*, Vol. 12, No. 6, 1997.

Brindle D., White M., "Thatcher Rounds on Absent Fathers", *Guardian*, 18.01.1990.

Brunet L., Kunstmann J.-M., "Gamete Donation in France: the Future of the Anonymity Doctrine", *Medicine, Health Care and Philosophy*, No. 16, 2013.

Burr J.A., Reynolds P., "Thinking Ethically about Genetic Inheritance. Liberal Rights, Communitarianism and the Right to Privacy for Parents of Donor Insemination Children", *Journal of Medical Ethics*, Vol. 34, No. 4, 2008.

Cahn N., "Necessary Subjects. The Need for a Mandatory National Donor Gamete Databank", *DePaul Journal of Health Care*, Vol. 12, No. 1, 2008.

Cannold L., "DNA tests, Paternity 'Fraud' and Moral Panic about Single Women and Lesbians forming Families with Donor Sperm", *Journal of Professional and Applied Ethics*, Vol. 4, No. 2, 2003.

Carbone J., Gottheim P., "Markets, Subsidies, Regulation, and Trust. Building Ethical Understandings into the Market for Fertility Services", *Journal of Gender, Race, and Justice*, Vol. 9, No. 3, 2006.

Carsten J., "The Substance of Kinship and the Heat of the Hearth: Feeding, Personhood, and Relatedness among Malays in Pulau Langkawi", *American Ethnologist*, Vol. 22, No. 2, 1995.

Chan R., Raboy B., Patterson C., "Psychological Adjustment Among Children Conceived via Donor Insemination by Lesbian and Heterosexual Mothers", *Child Development*, Vol. 69, No. 2, 1998.

Chan, S., Quibly M., "Frozen Embryos, Genetic Information and Reproductive Rights", *Bioethics*, Vol. 21, No. 8, 2007.

Chandra A., Martinez G., Mosher W., Abma J., Jones J., "Fertility, Family Planning, and Reproductive Health of U.S. Women. Data from the 2002 National Survey of Family Growth", *Vital and Health Statistics*, Vol. 25, 2005.

Charo R.A., "And Baby Makes Three – or Four, or Five, or Six: Redefining the Family After the Reprotech Revolution", *Wisconsin's Women's Law Journal*, Vol. 7, No. 1, 1992.

Chestney E.S., "The Right to Know One's Genetic Origin. Can, Should, or Must a State that Extends the Right to Adoptees Extend an Analogous Right to Children Conceived with Donor Gametes?", *Texas Law Review*, Vol. 80, No. 2, 2001.

Cho C., "Defining Parenthood: Assisted Reproduction in France", *Yale Journal of Medicine & Law, (special edition) International Health Care*, Vol. 7, No. 2, 2011.

Churchman D. "The Debate Over Open Adoption", *Public Welfare*, Vol. 44, No. 11, 1986.

Clapshaw D., "Legal Aspects of Artificial Human Reproduction: Can the Law Afford to Play Ostrich?", *Auckland University Law Review*, Vol. 4, No. 3, 1982.

Cohen G., "Response. Rethinking Sperm-Donor Anonymity. Of Changed Selves, Non-Identity, and One-Night Stands", *Georgetown Law Journal*, Vol. 100, No. 2, 2013.

Cohen S.R., "The Invisible Man. Artificial Insemination by Donor and the Legislation on Donor Anonymity: A Review", *Journal of Family Planning and Reproductive Health Care*, Vol. 30, No. 4, 2004.

Conelly A.M., "Problems of Interpretation of Article 8 of the ECHR", *International and Comparative Law Quarterly*, Vol. 35, No. 3, 1986.

Cook R., Golombok S., "A Survey of Semen Donation: Phase II – The View of the Donors", *Human Reproduction*, Vol. 10, No. 4, 1995.

Cook R., Golombok S., Bish A. *et al.*, "Disclosure of Donor Insemination Parental Attitudes", *American Journal of Orthopsychiatry*, Vol. 65, No. 4, 1995.

Cooper T.G., Noonan E., von Eckardstein S, *et al.*, "World Health Organization Reference Values for Human Semen Characteristics", *Human Reproduction Update*, Vol. 16, No. 3, 2010.

Correia H., Broderick P., "Access to Reproductive Technologies by Single Women and Lesbians. Social Representations and Public Debate", *Journal of Community & Applied Social Psychology*, Vol. 19, No. 4, 2009.

Crawshaw M., "Prospective Parents' Intentions Regarding Disclosure Following the Removal of Donor Anonymity", *Human Fertility*, Vol. 11, No. 2, 2008.

Cummings E.M., Davies P.T., "Maternal Depression and Child Development", *Journal of Child Psychology and Psychiatry*, Vol. 35, No. 1, 1994.

Cutas D., "The Right to Reproduce. Sex is Over-rated. On the Right to Reproduce", *Human Fertility*, Vol. 12, No. 1, 2009.

Daniels K., "Donor Gametes. Anonymous or Identified?", *Best Practice & Research Clinical Obstetrics and Gynecology*, Vol. 21, No. 1, 2007.

Daniels K., Blyth E., Crawshaw M., Curson R., "Short Communication. Previous Semen Donors and their Views Regarding the Sharing of Information with the Offspring", *Human Reproduction*, Vol. 20, No. 6, 2005.

Daniels K., Gillett W., Grace V., "Parental Information Sharing with Donor Conceived Offspring. A Follow-up Study", *Human Reproduction*, Vol. 24, No. 5, 2009.

Daniels K., Lalos O., "The Swedish Insemination Act and the Availability of Donors", *Human Reproduction*, Vol. 10, No. 7, 1995.

Daniels K., Lewis G., Carson R., "Information Sharing in Semen Donation. The Views of Donors", *Social Science and Medicine*, Vol. 44, No. 5, 1995.

Daniels K.R., "Semen Donors in New Zealand: Their Characteristics and Attitudes", *Clinical Reproduction and Fertility*, Vol. 5, No. 4, 1987.

Daniels K.R., "Semen Donors: Their Motivation and Attitudes to their Offspring", *Journal of Reproductive and Infant Psychology*, Vol. 7, No. 2, 2007.

Daniels K.R., Grace V.M., Gillett W.R., "Factors Associated with Parents' Decisions to Tell Their Adult Offspring about the Offspring's Donor' Conception", *Human Reproduction*, Vo. 26, No. 10, 2011.

Daniels K.R., Hall D.J., "Semen Donor Recruitment Strategies – A Non Payment Based Approach", *Human Reproduction*, Vol. 112, No. 110, 1997.

Dargan F., "New IVF Rules to Include Lesbians", *The Herald Sun*, Vol. 12, No. 2, 2001.

De Groot, G.R., "Op Weg naar een Europees Personen – en familie recht?", *Ars Acqui*, No. 44, 1995.

De Melo-Martin, I., "On Cloning Human Beings", *Bioethics*, Vol. 16, No. 3, 2002.

DePaulo B.M., Morris W.L., "Singles in Society and in Science", *Psychological Inquiry*, Vol. 16, No. 2, 2005.

DePaulo B.M., Morris W.L., "The Unrecognized Stereotyping and Discrimination Against Singles", *Current Directions in Psychological Science*, Vol. 15, No. 5, 2006.

Cooper T.G., Noonan E., von Eckardstein S. *et al.*, "World Health Organization Reference Values for Human Semen Characteristics", *Human Reproduction Update,* Vol. 16, No. 3, 2010.

Dempsey D., "Donor, Father or Parent? Conceiving Paternity in the Australian Family Court", *International Journal of Law, Policy and Family*, No. 18, 2004.

Denier, Y. "Need or Desire? A Conception and Moral Phenomenology of the Child Wish", *International Journal of Applied Philosophy*, Vol. 20, No. 1, 2006.

DiFonzo J.H., "Toward a Unified Field Theory of the Family: The American Law Institute's Principles of the Law of Family Dissolution", *Brigham Young University Law Review*, 2001.

Dillen A., "Foundations of Responsibility for Children", *International Journal of Children's Spirituality*, Vol. 13, No. 1, 2008.

Donovan C., "Who Needs a Father? Negotiating Biological Fatherhood in British Lesbian Families Using Self-Insemination", *Sexualities*, Vol. 3, No. 2, 2013.

Dunn J., Deater-Deckard, Pickering K., O'Connor T.G., Golding J., ALSPAC Study Team, "Children's Adjustment and Prosocial Behavior in Step-, Single-Parent, and Non-Stepfamily Settings. Findings from a Community Study", *Journal of Child Psychology and Psychiatry*, Vol. 39, No. 8, 1998.

Dunne G.A., "Opting into Motherhood: Lesbians Blurring the Boundaries and Transforming the Meaning of Parenthood and Kinship", *Gender and Society*, Vol. 14, No. 1, 200.

Dzehtsiarou K., "European Consensus and the Evolutive Interpretation of the European Convention of Human Rights", *German Law Journal*, Vol. 12, No. 10, 2011.

Dziak E., Janzen B.L. Muhajarine N., "Inequalities in the Psychological Well-Being of Employed, Single and Partnered Mothers. The Role of Psychological Work Quality and Work-family Conflict", *International Journal for Equity in Health*, Vol. 9, No. 6, 2010.

Epstein L., King G., "Empirical Research and the Goals of Legal Scholarship: The Rules of Inference", *University of Chicago Law Review*, Vol. 1, No. 69, 2002.

Eran S., Dalit S., "Incest Avoidance, the Incest Taboo, and Social Cohesion: Revisiting Westermarck and the Case of the Israeli Kibbutzim", *American Journal of Sociology*, Vol. 114, No. 6, 2009.

Ernst E., Ingerslev H.J., Schou O., Stoltenberg M., "Attitudes Among Sperm Donors in 1992 and 2002. A Danish Questionnaire Survey", *Acta Obstetrica et Gynecologica Scandinavica*, Vol. 86, No. 3, 2007.

Ethics Committee of the American Society for Reproductive Medicine, "Interests, Obligations and Rights of the Donor in Gamete Donation", *Fertility and Sterility*, Vol. 91, No. 1, 2009.

Ethics Committee of the American Society for Reproductive Medicine, "Access to Fertility by Gays, Lesbians and Unmarried Persons", *Fertility and Sterility*, Vol. 92, No. 4, 2009.

Fisher S.N., Markovic K., Radat J. Ogresta, "'Za' i 'O' Jednoroditeljskim Obiteljima", Zagreb, *Udruga za Unapredgenje Kvaliteta Zivljena, LET*, 2006.

Fitzgerald W.A., "Maturity, Difference, and Mystery.Children's Perspectives and the Law", *Arizona Law Review*, Vol. 36, No. 11, 1994.

Flaks D. *et al.*, "Lesbians Choosing Motherhood. A Comparative Study of Lesbian and Heterosexual Parents and their Children", *Developmental Psychology*, Vol. 31, No. 1, 1995.

Fokkema T., Liefbroer A.C., "Trends in Living Arrangements in Europe. Convergence or Divergence?", *Demographic Research*, Vol. 19, 2008.

Fortescue E., "Gamete Donation – Where is the Evidence that there are Benefits in Removing Anonymity of Donors? A Patient's Viewpoint", *Reproductive Biomedicine Online*, Vol. 7, No. 2, 2003.

Frank R., "Compulsory Physical Examinations for Establishing Parentage", *International Journal of Law and the Family*, Vol. 10, No. 2, 1996.

Frankfurt G.H., "Necessity and Desire", *Philosophy and Phenomenological Research*, Vol. 45, No. 1, 1984.

Franz M, Lensche H. "Psychosocial Distress and Symptoms of Single Mothers and their Children in a Large Community Sample", *Z Psychosomatic Medicine and Psychotherapy*, Vol. 49, No. 2, 2003.

Freeman T., Jadva V., Kramer W., Golombok S., "Gamete Donation: Parent's Experiences of Searching for Their Child's Donor Siblings and Donor", *Human Reproduction*, Vol. 24, No. 3, 2009.

Frith L., "Beneath the Rhetoric. The Role of Rights in the Practice of Non-anonymous Gamete Donations", *Bioethics*, Vol. 15, No.15/16, 2001.

Frith L., "Gamete Donation and Anonymity. The Ethical and Legal Debate", *Human Reproduction*, Vol. 16, No. 5, 2001.

Frith L., Blyth E., Farrand A., "UK Gamete Donors' Reflection on the Removal of Anonymity Implications for Recruitment", *Human Reproduction*, Vol. 22, No. 6, 2007.

Frost C., "Feminism and Infertility", *Resolve Inc. Newsletter*, 1980.

Garcia M.A., "In with New Families, Out with Bad Law: Determining the Rights of Known Sperm Donors Through Intent-Based Written Agreements", *Duke Journal of Gender Law & Policy*, Vol. 21, 2014.

Garcia S.A., "Sociocultural and Legal Implications of Creating and Sustaining Life through Biomedical Technology", *Journal of Legal Medicine*, Vol. 17, No. 4, 1996.

Garrison M., "Law Making for Baby Making: An Interpretative Approach to the Determination of Legal Parentage", *Harvard Law Review*, Vol. 113, No. 4, 2000.

Cahn N., Singer J., "Adoption, Identity, and the Constitution: The Case for Opening Closed Records", *Journal of Constitutional Law*, Vol. 2, No. 1.

Gavella N., Stvarno Pravo, Svezak 2, Narodne Novine, 2007.

Glezerman M., "Two Hundred and Seventy Cases of Donor Insemination. Management and Results", *Fertility and Sterility*, Vol. 35, 1981.

Godman K.M., Sanders K., Rosenberg M., Burton P., "Potential Sperm Donors' and their Partners' Opinions Towards the Release of Identifying Information", *Human Reproduction*, Vol. 21, No. 11, 2006.

Goldeberg A.E., "Lesbian and Gay Parents and their Children", *Washington, DC. American Psychological Association*, 2010.

Golombok S., Tasker F., Murray C., "Children Raised in Fatherless Families from Infancy. Family Relationships and the Socio-emotional Development of Children of Lesbian, Single and Heterosexual Mothers", *Journal of Child Psychology and Psychiatry*, Vol. 38, 1997.

Golombok S., "New Families, Old Values. Considerations Regarding the Welfare of the Child", *Human Reproduction*, Vol. 13, No. 9, 1998.

Golombok S., Badger S., "Children Raised in Mother-Headed Families from Infancy. A Follow up of Children of Lesbian and Single Heterosexual Mothers at Early Adulthood", *Human Reproduction*, Vol. 25, 2010.

Golombok S., MacCallum F., "Children Raised in Fatherless Families from Infancy. A Follow up of Children of Lesbian and Single Heterosexual Mothers at Early Adolescence", *Journal of Child Psychology and Psychiatry*, Vol. 45, 2004.

Golombok S., Spencer A., Rutter M., "Children in Lesbian and Single-Parent Households. Psychosexual and Psychiatric Appraisal", *Journal of Child Psychology and Psychiatry*, Vol. 24, No. 4, 1983.

Goodwin M., "A View from the Cradle. Tort Law and the Private Regulation of Assisted Reproduction", *Emory Law Journal*, Vol. 59, 2010.

Goodwin M., "Assisted Reproductive Technology and the Double Bind: The Illusory Choice of Motherhood", *Journal of Gender, Race and Justice*, Vol. 9, No. 1, 2005.

Gordon, K., van Houten, N., "IFFS Surveillance 07", *Fertility & Sterility*, Vol. 87, No. 4, 2007.

Gottlieb C., Lalos O., Lindblad F., "Disclosure of Donor Insemination to the Child. The Impact of Swedish Legislation on Couples' Attitudes", *Human Reproduction*, Vol. 15, 2000.

Grace V.M., Daniels K.R., Gillett W., "The Donor, the Father, and the Imaginary Constitution of the Family. Parents' Construction in the Case of Donor Insemination", *Social Science & Medicine*, Vol. 66, 2008.

Green N.S., "Risks of Birth Defects and Other Adverse Outcomes Associated with Assisted Reproductive Technology", *Pediatrics*, Vol. 114, No. 1, 2004.

Green R., Mandel J.B., Hotvedt M.E., Gray J., Smith L., "Lesbian Mothers and their Children. A Comparison with Solo Parent Heterosexual Mothers and their Children", *Archives of Sexual Behavior*, Vol. 15, No. 2, 1986.

Gunning J., "Oocyte Donation. The Legislative Framework in Western Europe", *Human Reproduction*, Vol. 13, No. 2, 1998.

Haimes E., Weiner K., "'Everybody's Got a Dad ...' Issues for Lesbian Families in the Management of Donor Insemination", *Sociology of Health and Illness*, Vol. 22, No. 4.

Hanson F., "Donor Insemination. Eugenic and Feminist Implications", *Medical Anthropology Quarterly*, Vol. 15, No. 3, 2001.

Hawkins D., Amato P., King V., "Parent-Adolescent Involvement. The Relative Influence of Parent Gender and Residence", *Journal of Marriage and Family*, Vol. 68, No. 1, 2006.

Hedrih A., Hedrih V., "Attitudes and Motives of Potential Sperm Donors in Serbia", *Vojnosanitetski Pregled*, Vol. 69, 2012.

Hendrick H., "Children and Childhood", *Refresh*, Vol. 15, Autumn 1992.

Held V., "No-Contractual Society: A Feminist View", *Canadian Journal of Philosophy*, Vol. 17, Suppl. 1, Special issue: Suppl. Vol. 13, *Science, Morality & Feminist Theory*, 1987.

Helfer L.R., Consensus, "Coherence and the European Convention on Human Rights", *Cornell International Law Journal*, Vol. 26, No. 133, 1993.

Hertz R., Ferguson I.T.F., "Kinship Strategies and Self-Sufficiency Among Single Mothers by Choice. Post Modern Family Ties", *Qualitative Sociology*, Vol. 20, No. 2, 1997.

Hodgson D., "The International Legal Protection of the Child's Right to a Legal Identity and the Problem of Statelessness", *International Journal of Law, Policy and the Family*, Vol. 7, No. 2, 1993.

Ignovska E., Verschelden, G., "De rechterlijke toetsing van het belang van het kind bij het onderzoek naar het vaderschap", case-note by the Constitutional Court nr. 30/2013, 7 March 2013, *Tijdschrift voor Jeugd en Kinderrechten*, Vol. 2. 2013.

Inhorn M.C, "Defining Women's Health. A Dozen Messages from More than Ethnographies", *Medical Anthropology Quarterly*, Vol. 20, No. 3, 2006.

Inhorn M.C., Patrizio P., "Rethinking Reproductive 'Tourism' as Reproductive 'Exile'", *Fertility and Sterility*, Vol. 92, No. 3, 2009.

Jadva V., Badger S., Morrissette M., Golombok S., "'Mom by Choice, Single by Life's Circumstance ...' Findings from a Large-scale Survey of the Experiences of Single Mothers by Choice", *Human Fertility*, Vol. 12, No. 4, 2009.

Jadva V., Freeman T., Kramer W., Golombok S., "Experiences of Offspring Searching for and Contacting their Donor Siblings and Donor", *Reproductive BioMedicine Online*, Vol. 20, No. 4, 2010.

Jadva V., Freeman T., Kramer W., Golombok S., "Sperm and Oocyte Donors' Experiences of Anonymous Donations and Subsequent Contact with Their Donor Offspring", *Human Reproduction*, Vol. 26, No. 3, 2011.

Jadva V., Freeman T., Kramer W., Golombok S., "The Experiences of Adolescents and Adults Conceived by Sperm Donation. Comparison by Age of Disclosure and Family Type", *Human Reproduction*, Vol. 24, No. 8, 2009.

Janssens P.M.W., Simons A.H.M., Van Kooij R.J., Blokzijl E., Dunselman A.A.J., "A New Dutch Law Regulating Provision of Identifying Information of Donors to Offspring: Background, Content and Impact", *Human Reproduction*, Vol. 21, No. 4, 2006.

Johnston J., "Mum's the Word: Donor Anonymity in Assisted Reproduction", *Health Law Review*, Vol. 11, No. 1, 2002.

Jones H.W., Cohen J., Cooke I., Kempers R. (eds.), "IFFS Surveillance 07", *Fertility and Sterility*, Vol. 87, Sup. 1, 2007.

Jordana-Pröpper O., "An Anthropological Approach to Voluntarily Single Motherhood in Barcelona", *Journal of Comparative Research in Anthropology and Sociology*, Vol. 4, No. 1, 2013.

Joskow P.L., "Commercial Impossibility, the Uranium Market and the Westinghouse Case", *Journal of Legal Studies*, Vol. 6, No. 1, 1977.

Kass L., "Babies by Means of In Vitro Fertilization. Unethical Experiments on the Unborn?", *New England Journal of Medicine*, Vol. 285, No. 21, 1971.

Keiser C.R., Kashy D.A., "The Contextual Nature and Function of Singlism", *Psychological Inquiry*, Vol. 16, No. 2, 2005.

Kelly F., "(Re)forming Parenthood: The Assignment of Legal Parentage Within Planned Lesbian Families", *Ottawa Law Review*, Vol. 40, 2008.

Kelly F., "Equal Parents, Equal Children: Reforming Canada's Parentage Laws to Recognize the Completeness of Women-led Families", *University of New Brunswick Law Journal*, Vol. 64, 2013.

Kirkman M., "Saviours and Satyrs. Ambivalence in Narrative Meanings of Sperm Provision", *Culture, Health & Sexuality*, Vol. 6, No. 4, 2004.

Kirkpatrick M., "Clinical Implications of Lesbian Mother Studies", *Journal of Homosexuality*, Vol. 14, No. 1–2, 1987.

Kirkpatrick M., Smith C., Roy R., "Lesbian Mothers and their Children. A Comparative Survey", *American Journal of Orthopsychiatry*, Vol. 51, No. 3, 1981.

Kopac J., "Otrok, Zenin Dar Ocetu i Narodu (A Child, Wife's Gift to the Father and to the Nation)", *Sobotna Priloga Dela*, 2000.

Korac A., "Draft of the Croatian Act on Medically Assisted Procreation – Balancing Procreative Rights", *Drustvena Istrazivanja*. Zagreb, god. 9, br. 2–3, 1999.

Koropatrick, S. *et al.*, "Infertility: A Non-event Transition", *Fertility and Sterility*, Vol. 59, No. 1, 1993.

Kovaček-Stanić G., "Porodicni Zakon Srbije iz 2005 godine u kontekstu planiranja porodice", Zbornik Matice srpske za drustvene nauke, br. 121, 2006.

Kovaček-Stanić G., "Porodično pravni aspect biomedicinski potpomognutog oplođenja u pravu Srbije I Evropskim pravima", Zbornik Matice srpske za društvene nauke, br. 131, 2010.

Ladau R., Weissenberg R., "Disclosure of Donor Conception in Single-Mother Families: Views and Concerns", *Human Reproduction*, Vol. 25, No. 4, 2010.

Laftman S.B., "Family Structure and Children's Living Conditions. A Comparative Study of 24 Countries", *Child Indicators Research*, Vol. 3, 2010.

Lalos A., Daniels K., Gottlieb C., Lalos O., "Recruitment and Motivation of Semen Providers in Sweden", *Human Reproduction*, Vol. 18, No. 1, 2003.

Lalos A., Gottlieb C., Lalos O., "Legislated Right for Donor-Insemination Children to Know their Genetic Origin: A Study of Parental Thinking", *Human Reproduction*, Vol. 22, No. 6, 2007.

Landau R., "The Management of Genetic Origins: Secrecy and Openness in Donor Assisted Conception in Israel and Elsewhere", *Human Reproduction*, Vol. 13, 1988.

Landau R., and Weissenberg R., "Disclosure of Donor Conception in Single-mother Families: Views and Concerns", *Human Reproduction*, Vol. 25, No. 4, 2010.

Lansac J., "French Law Concerning Medically-assisted Reproduction", *Human Reproduction*, Vol. 11, No. 9, 1996.

Lavender N., "The Problem of the Margin of the Appreciation", *European Human Rights Law Review*, No. 4, 1997.

Leckey R., "'Where the Parents Are of the Same Sex': Quebec Reforms to Filiation", *International Journal for Law, Policy and the Family*, Vol. 23, 2009.

Lester L., Herne Q.C., "Universality *v.* Subsidiarity: A Reply", *European Human Rights Law Journal*, Vol. 3, No. 1, 1998.

London S., "Risk of Pregnancy-Related Death is Sharply Elevated for Women 35 and Older", *Perspectives on Sexual and Reproductive Health*, Vol. 36, No. 2, 2004.

Louw A., "The Constitutionality of a Biological Father's Recognition as a Parent", *Potchefstroom Electronic Law Journal*, Vol. 13, No. 3, 2010.

Lui S.C., Weaver S.M., Robinson F., Debono M., Nieland M., Killich S.R., Hay D.I.M., "A Survey of Semen Donor Attitudes", *Human Reproduction*, Vol. 10, No. 1, 1995.

Lycett E., Daniels K., Curson R., Golombok S., "Offspring Created as a Result of Donor Insemination: A Study of Family Relationships, Child Adjustment, and Disclosure", *Fertility and Sterility*, Vol. 82, No. 1, 2004.

Machado H., "Biologising Paternity, Moralizing Maternity. The Construction of Parenthood in the Determination of Paternity through the Courts in Portugal", *Feminist Legal Studies*, Vol. 16, No. 2, 2008.

Mahlstedt P.P., Probasco K.A., "Sperm Donors, Their Attitudes Towards Providing Medical and Psychosocial Information for Recipient Couples and Donor Offspring", *Fertility and Sterility*, Vol. 56, No. 4, 1991.

Manderson D., Mohr R., "From Oxymoron to Intersection: An Epidemiology of Legal Research", *Law/Text/Culture*, Vol. 6, 2002.

Mannis V.S., "Single Mothers by Choice", *Family Relations*, Vol. 48, No. 2, 1999.

Mattoras R., "Reproductive Exile *versus* Reproductive Tourism", *Human Reproduction*, Vol. 20, No. 12, 2001.

McConachie H., "Psychological Correlates of Depressive Symptoms among 12–14 year old Norwegian Adolescents", *Child: Care, Health and Development*, Vol. 30, No. 2, 2004.

McGee G., Brakman S.V., Gurmankin A.D., "Gamete Donation and Anonymity. Disclosure to Children with Donor Gametes should not be Optional", *Human Reproduction*, Vol. 16, No. 10, 2001.

McWhinnie A., "Ethical Dilemmas in the Use of Donor Gametes", *Medicine and Law*, Vol. 17, No. 3, 1998.

McWhinnie A., "Gamete Donation and Anonymity. Should Offspring from Donated Gametes Continue to be Denied Knowledge of their Origins and Antecedents?", *Human Reproduction*, Vol. 16, No. 5, 2001.

Mickovikj, D., "Dilemi vo vrska so Zakonot za Bio-medicinsko potpomognato oploduvanje", *Pravnik*, 2008.

Morgan L.H., "Systems of Consanguity and Affinity of the Human Family", *Smithsonian Contributions to Knowledge*, Vol. 17, Washington Smithsonian Institution, 1870.

Motluk A., "Canadian Court Bans Anonymous Sperm and Egg Donation", *Nature News*, 27.05.2001.

Moulton R., "Who's Your Daddy?: The Inherent Unfairness of the Marital Presumption for Children of Unmarried Parents", *Family Court Review*, Vol. 47, No. 4, 2009.

Mucklow B.M., Phelan G.K., "Lesbian and Traditional Mothers' Responses to Child Behavior and Self-Concept", *Psychological Reports*, Vol. 44, No. 3, 1979.

Murray C., Golombok G., "Going it Alone. Solo Mothers and their Infants Conceived by Donor Insemination", *American Journal of Orthopsychiatry*, Vol. 75, No. 2, 2005.

Nachtigall R.D., "Secrecy. An Unresolved Issue in the Practice of Donor Insemination", *American Journal of Obstetrics and Gynecology*, Vol. 168, No. 6, 1993.

Novakov M., "Jednoroditeljske Porodice", *Socioloski Pregled*, Vol. XLVI, No. 3, 2012.

Ostrovski A.A., "How the Margin of Appreciation Doctrine Preserves Core Human Rights within Cultural Diversity and Legitimizes International Human Rights Tribunals", *Hanse Law Review*, Vol. 1, No. 1, 2005.

Parolin L.L., Metzler I., Schuster A., "(Not) Making 'Heternologous' Fertilization. The Italian ART Law and its Paradoxes", *Tecnoscienza, Italian Journal of Science & Technology Studies*, Vol. 4, No. 1, 2013.

Patterson C., "Children of Lesbian and Gay Parents. Psychology, Law and Policy", *American Psychologist*, Vol. 64, No. 8, 2009.

Pedersen B., Nielsen A., Lauritsen G.J., "Psychosocial Aspects of Donor Insemination", *Acta Obstetricia et Gynecologica Scandinavica*, Vol. 72, No. 9, 1994.

Pennings G., "Ethical Issues of Infertility Treatment in Developing Countries", *Oxford Journals, ESHRE Monographs*, Vol. 2008, No. 1, 2008.

Pennings G., "The 'Double Track' Policy for Donor Anonymity", *Human Reproduction*, Vol. 12, No. 12, 1997.

Pennings G., "The Right to Choose your Donor. A Step Towards Commercialization or a Step Towards Empowering the Patient?", *Human Reproduction*, Vol. 15, No. 3, 2000.

Pennings G., Mertes H., "Ethical Issues in Infertility Treatment", *Best Practice & Research Clinical Obstetrics & Gynecology*, Vol. 26, No. 6, 2012.

Peterson S.V., "Sexing Political Identities. Nationalism as Heterosexism", *International Feminist Journal of Politics*, Vol. 1, No. 1.

Pluym L., "Het recht van het kind om zijn ouders te kennen (art. 7.1 IVRK) na heterologe medisch begeleide voortplanting, adoptie en draagmoederschap in België", *Tijdschrift voor Jeugd en Kinderrechten*, March 2012.

Potter V.R., "Evolving Ethical Concepts", *Bioscience*, Vol. 27, No. 4, 1977.

Provencal L.V., "The Family in Aristotle", *Animus*, Vol. 6, 2001.

Przeska T., "Things that May be Object of Contractual Pledge in the Legal System of Republic of Macedonia", *Iustinianus Primus Law Review*, Vol. 1, No. 1, 2010.

Radin M.J., "Market-Inalienability", *Harvard Law Review*, Vol. 100, 1987.

Ramsey P., "Shall we 'Reproduce'? II Rejoinders and Future Forecast", *Journal of the American Medical Association*, Vol. 220, No. 11, 1972.

Ravelingien A., Pennings G., "The Right to Know your Genetic Parents. From Open Identity Gamete Donation to Routine Paternity Testing", *American Journal of Bioethics*, Vol. 13, No. 5, 2013.

Resetar B., Emery R.E., "Children's Rights in European Legal Proceedings: Why are Family Practices so Different from Legal Theories?", *Family Court Review*, Vol. 46, No. 1, 2008.

Richards J.L., "Redefining Parenthood. Parental Rights Versus Child Rights", *Wayne Law Review*, Vol. 40, 1993–1994.

Riggs D.W., Russell L., "Characteristics of Men Willing to Act as Sperm Donors in the Context of Identity-Release Legislation", *Human Reproduction*, Vol. 26, No. 1, 2010.

Riley J., "Utilitarian Ethics and Democratic Government", *Ethics*, Vol. 100, No. 2, 1990.

Robertson J.A., "Noncoital Reproduction and Procreative Liberty", *Embryos, Families, and Procreative Liberty. The Legal Structure of the New Reproduction*, Southern California Law Review, Vol. 59, No. 5, 1986.

Robertson J.A., "Reproductive Technology in Germany and the United States. An Essay in Comparative Law and Bioethics", *Columbia Journal of Transnational Law*, Vol. 43, No. 1, 2004.

Rochon M., "Sterility and Infertility: Two Concepts", *Cahiers Quebecois de Demographie*, Vol. 15, No. 1, 1986.

Roos E., Burstrom B., Saastamoinen P., Lahelma E., "A Comparative Study of the Patterning of Women's Heal by Family Status and Employment Status in Finland and Sweden", *Social Science & Medicine*, Vol. 60, No. 11, 2005.

Russo N.F., "The Motherhood Mandate", *Journal of Social Issues*, Vol. 32, No. 2, 1976.

Ryburn M., "Contact After Contested Adoptions", *Adoption and Fostering*, Vol. 18, 1994.

Sants H., "Genealogical Bewilderment in Children with Substitute Parents", *The British Journal of Medical Psychology*, Vol. 37, No. 2, 1964.

Scheib J., Riordan M., Schaver P., "Choosing between Anonymous and Identity-release Sperm Donors. Recipient and Donor Characteristics", *Reproductive Technologies*, Vol. 10, 2000.

Schelb J., Riordan M., Rubin S., "Choosing Identity-Release Sperm Donors: The Parents' Perspective 13–18 Years Later", *Human Reproduction*, Vol. 18, No. 5, 2003.

Schrauwers, A., "Negotiating Parentage: the Political Economy of 'Kinship' in Central Sulawesi, Indonesia", *American Ethnologist*, Vol. 26, No. 2, 1999.

Schenner, J.G., "Assisted Reproduction Practice in Europe: Legal and Ethical Aspects", *Human Reproduction Update*, Vol. 3, No. 2, 1997.

Schokkenbroek J., "The Basis, Nature and Application of the Margin of Appreciation Doctrine in the Case-Law of the European Court of Human Rights", *Human Rights Law Journal*, Vol. 19, No. 30–31, 1998.

Schover L.R., Rothman S.T., Collins R.L., "The Personality and Motivation of Semen Donors. A Comparison with Oocyte Donors", *Human Reproduction*, Vol. 7, No. 4, 1992.

Schwenzer I., "Tensions Between Legal, Biological and Social Conceptions of Parentage", *Electronic Journal of Comparative Law*, Vol. 11, No. 3, 2007.

De Melo-Martin, I., "On Cloning Human Beings", *Bioethics*, Vol. 16, No. 3, 2002.

Shalev C., "Rights to Sexual and Reproductive Health. The ICPD and the Convention for the Elimination of All Forms of Discrimination against Women", *Health and Human Rights*, Vol. 4, No. 2, 2000.

Shanley M.L., "'Surrogate Mothering' and Women's Freedom: A Critique of Contracts for Human Reproduction", *Signs*, Vol. 18, No. 3, 1993.

Sharon R.C., "The Invisible Man. Artificial Insemination by Donor and the Legislation on Donor Anonymity: A Review", *Journal of Family Planning and Reproductive Health Care*, Vol. 30, No. 4, 2004.

Shehab D., Duff J., Pasch L.A., MacDougall K., Scheib J.E., Nachtigall R.D., "How Parents Whose Children have been Conceived with Donor Gametes make their Disclosure Decision. Contexts, Influences, and Couple Dynamics", *Fertility and Sterility*, Vol. 89, No. 1, 2008.

Sheldon S., "Reproductive Technologies and the Legal Determination of Fatherhood", *Feminist Legal Studies*, Vol. 13, No. 3, 2005 (a).

Sheldon S., "Fragmenting Fatherhood: The Regulation of Reproductive Technologies", *Modern Law Review*, Vol. 68, No. 4, 2005 (b).

Shenfield F., Pennings G., De Mouzon J., Ferraretti A.P., Goossens V., on behalf of the ESHRE Task Force Cross Border Reproductive Care (CBRC), "ESHRE's Good Practice Guide for Cross-Border Reproductive Care for Centers and Practitioners", *Human Reproduction*, Vol. 26, No. 7, 2001.

Shenfield F., Steele S., "What are the Effects of Anonymity and Secrecy on the Welfare of the Child in Gamete Donation?", *Human Reproduction*, Vol. 12, No. 2, 1997.

Shentfield F., "Filiation in Assisted Reproduction. Potential Conflicts and Legal Implications", *Human Reproduction*, Vol. 9, No. 7, 1994.

Shukla U., Deval B., Jansa M.P., Hamoda H., Savvas M., Narvekar N., "Sperm Donor Recruitment, Attitudes and Provider Practices – 5 Years After the Removal of Donor Anonymity", *Human Reproduction*, Vol. 28, No.3, 2013.

Schultz M.M., "Reproductive Technology and Intent-Based Parenthood. An Opportunity for Gender Neutrality", *Wisconsin Law Review*, Vol. 297, 1990.

Ramsey P., "Shall we Reproduce? II Rejoinders and Future Forecast", *Journal of the American Medical Association*, Vol. 220, No. 11, 1972.

Stein P., "Singlehood. An Alternative to Marriage", *The Family Coordinator*, Vol. 24, No. 4, 1975.

Storrie R., Equivalence, "Personhood and Relationality: Processes of Relatedness Among the Hoti of Venezuelan Guiana", *Journal of the Royal Anthropological Institute*, Vol. 9, No. 3, 2003.

Storrow R., "The Pluralism Problem in Cross-Border Reproductive Care", *Human Reproduction*, Vol. 25, No. 12, 2010.

Storrow, R.F., "The Bioethics of Prospective Parenthood. In Pursuit of the Proper Standard for Gatekeeping in Infertility Clinics", *Cardozo Law Review*, Vol. 28, No. 5, 2007.

Suh M.M., "Surrogate Motherhood. An Argument for Denial of Specific Performance", *Columbia Journal of Law and Social Problems*, Vol. 22, 1989.

Suppon J.M.F., "Life after Death: the Need to Address the Legal Status of Posthumously Conceived Children", *Family Court Review*, Vol. 48, No. 1, 2010.

Sutton D.E., "Local Names, Foreign Claims: Family Inheritance and National Heritage on a Greek Island", *American Ethnologist*, Vol. 24, No. 2, 1997.

Svanberg A.S., Sydsjo G., Selling K.E., Lampic C., "Attitudes towards Gamete Donation among Swedish Gynaecologists and Obstetricians", *Human Reproduction*, Vol. 23, No. 4, 2008.

Sykes M.R., "Adoption with Contact: A Study of Adoptive Parents and the Impact of Continuing Contact with Families of Origin", *Journal of Family Therapy*, Vol. 23, No. 3, 2001.

Thorn P., Katzorke T., Daniels K., "Semen Donors in Germany: A Study Exploring Motivations and Attitudes", *Human Reproduction*, Vol. 23, No. 11, 2008.

Turner A. J., Coyle A., "What Does it Mean to be a Donor Offspring? The Identity Experiences of Adults Conceived by Donor Insemination and the Implications for Counseling and Therapy", *Human Reproduction*, Vol. 15, No. 9, 2000.

Turney L., Wood P., "'Paternity Fraud' and the Invisible Child", *Australian Journal of Emerging Technologies and Society*, Vol. 5, No. 2, 2007.

Ulrich M., Weatherall A., "Motherhood and Infertility: Viewing Motherhood through the Lens of Infertility", *Feminism & Psychology*, Vol. 10, No. 30, 2000.

Shenfield F, De Mouzon J., Pennings G. *et al.*, "ESHRE Task Force on Cross-Border Reproductive Care. Cross-Border Reproductive Care in Six European Countries", *Human Reproduction*, Vol. 25, No. 6, 2010.

Van Crombrugge H., "'Ik zal er zijn voor jou'. Van Huwelijksgezin naar contractueel gezin: het instituut van het opvoedingscontract en de cultuur van de belofte" ("'I will be there for you'. From marital family to contractual family: the institute of the educational contract and the culture of promise"), *Rondom Gezin* 25, 2005.

Van den Broeck U., Vandermeeren M., Vanderschueren D., Enzlin P., Demyttenaere K., D'Hooghe T., "A Systematic Review of Sperm Donors. Demographic Characteristics, Attitudes, Motives and Experiences of the Process of Sperm Donation", *Human Reproduction Update*, Vol. 19, No. 1, 2012.

Van Hoof W., Pennings G., "The Consequences of S.H. and Others v. Austia for Legislation on Gamete Donation in Europe. An Ethical Analysis of the European Court of Human Rights Judgments", *Reproductive BioMedicine Online*, Vol. 25, No. 7, 2012.

Van Hoof, Pennings G., "Extraterritorial Laws for Cross-Border Reproductive Care. The Issue of Legal Diversity", *European Journal of Health Law*, Vol. 19, No. 2, 2012.

Vanfraussen K., Ponjaert-Kristoffersen I., Brewaeys A., "An Attempt to Reconstruct Children's Donor Concept. A Comparison Between Children's and Lesbian Parents' Attitudes Towards Donor Anonymity", *Human Reproduction*, Vol. 16, No. 9, 2001.

Velleman D., "Family History", *Philosophical Papers*, Vol. 34, No. 3, 2005.

Vilaca, A., "Making Kin out of Others in Amazonia", *Journal of the Royal Anthropological Institute*, Vol. 8, No. 2, 2002.

Walker K., "1950s Family Values v. Human Rights: In Vitro Fertilization, Donor Insemination, and Sexuality in Victoria", *Public Law Review*, Vol. 11, No. 4.

Warner J., "Mommy Madness. What Happened When the Girls Who Had it All Became Mothers? A New Book Explores Why This Generation Feels so Insane", *Newsweek*, 21.05.2005.

Warner M., "Introduction. Fear of Queer Planet", *Social Text*, No. 29, 1991.

Warnock M., "The Good of the Child", *Bioethics*, Vol. 2, 1987.
Weber W., "Dutch Sperm Donors will Remain Anonymous for Another Two Years", *The Lancet*, Vol. 355, No. 9211.
Weinberg R., "The Moral Complexity of Sperm Donation", *Bioethics*, Vol. 22, No. 3, 2008.
Weissenberg R., "Are Two A Family? Older Single Mothers Assisted by Sperm Donation and their Children Revisited", *American Journal of Orthopsychiatry*, Vol. 82, No. 4, 2012.
Weissenberg R., Landau R., Madgar I., "Older Single Mothers Assisted by Sperm Donation and their Children", *Human Reproduction*, Vol. 22, No. 10, 2007.
Weitoft G.R., Hjern A., Haglund B., Rosen M., "Mortality, Severe Morbidity, and Injury in Children Living with Single Parents in Sweden. A Population Based Study", *The Lancet*, Vol. 361, 2003.
Whitehead M., Burstroom B., Didericksen F., "Social Policies and the Pathways to Inequalities in Health. A Comparative Analysis of Lone Mothers in Britain and Sweden", *Social Science & Medicine*, Vol. 50, No. 2, 2000.
Woodhouse B.B., "Child Custody in the Age of Children's Rights: The Search for a Just and Workable Standard", *Family Law Quarterly*, Vol. 33, No. 3, 1999.
Yeung W.J., Sandberg J.F., Davis-Kean P.E., Hofferth S.L., "Children's Time with Fathers in Intact Families", *Journal of Marriage and Family*, Vol. 63, No. 1, 2001.
Zerjav T., "The Politicization of Singlehood", *CEU eTD Collection*, 2012.

INTERNET SOURCES

"Family on Your Own Terms", *Al Jazeera*, 24.02.2014 (http://stream.aljazeera.com/story/201402242305-0023501).
"Груевски: наталитетот е особено загрижувачки", *Глас на ВМРО-ДПМНЕ*, 23.11.2013 (http://glas.mk/2012/10/gruevski-natalitetot-e-osobeno-zagrizuvacki/).
"No Child Support if Dad is Anonymous Sperm Donor", *The Local* (Germany's News in English), 17.05.2013 (www.thelocal.de/20130517/49763).
"Meet the 40-something Childless Singles Turning to Co-parent partnerships where Raising a Family Doesn't Include Romance", *MailOnline*, 11.02.2013 (www.dailymail.co.uk/femail/article-2277027/Meet-40-childless-singles-turning-parent-partnerships--raising-family-doesnt-include-romance.html).
"Article 8: The Right to Respect for Private and Family Life, Home and Correspondence", *Human Rights Review*, 2012 (www.equalityhumanrights.com/uploaded_files/humanrights/hrr_article_8.pdf).
"Nurse Hopes to have World's First Baby from a Transplant Womb Donated by her own Mother", *MailOnline*, 18.10.2011 (www.dailymail.co.uk/health/article-2050401/Married-nurse-hopes-worlds-baby-womb-transplant-donated-MOTHER.html).
"Call to End Sperm Donor Anonymity", *BBC News Online*, 14.05.2002 (http://news.bbc.co.uk/2/hi/health/1986683.stm).

Almeida S., "The Right to Respect for (Private and) Family Life in the Case-Law of the ECtHR; the Protection of New Forms of Family", *academia.edu* (https://www.academia.edu/2269426/The_right_to_respect_for_private_and_family_life_in_the_caselaw_of_the_European_Court_of_Human_rights_the_protection_of_new_forms_of_family).

Blackburn-Starza A., "Australian Known Sperm Donor Granted Parenthood", *bionews.org.uk*, 24.06.2013 (www.bionews.org.uk/page_315706.asp).

Blyth E., Crawshaw M., Van den Akker O., "What are the Best Interests of the Child in International Surrogacy?", *bionews.org.uk*, 17.02.2014 (www.bionews.org.uk/page_397263.asp).

Brennan S., "How Many Parents Can a Child Have? Philosophical Reflections on the Three Parent Case", *Western University*, 2013 (http://papers.ssrn.com/sol3/papers.cfm?abstract_id=1451926).

Carpenter L., "Meet the Co-parents", *The Guardian*, 15.12.2013 (www.theguardian.com/lifeandstyle/2013/dec/15/meet-the-co-parents-modern-families).

Cassidly P., "Canada: Three Parents Listed on Baby's Birth Certificate", *bionews.org.uk*, 17.02.2014 (www.bionews.org.uk/page_396795.asp).

Collins N., "Three Parents Babies "Incompatible" with Human Dignity", *The Telegraph*, 04.10.2013(www.telegraph.co.uk/science/science-news/10356387/Three-parent-babies-incompatible-with-human-dignity.html).

Ellin A., "Making a Child Without the Couple", *New York Times*, 08.02.2013 (www.nytimes.com/2013/02/10/fashion/seeking-to-reproduce-without-a-romantic-partnership.html?pagewanted=all&_r=0).

Engels, F., *The Origin of the Family, Private Property and the State,* 1884, Introduction by Brewer P., Resistance, 2004 (http://readingfromtheleft.com/PDF/EngelsOrigin.pdf).

European Court of Human Rights: The ECHR in 50 Questions, July 2012 (www.echr.coe.int/Documents/50Questions_ENG.pdf).

Friedman M., "N.J. Legislator Proposes Bill Requiring Genetic Testing for all Newborns, Parents to Verify Paternity", *N.J. com*, 01.03.2012 (www.nj.com/news/index.ssf/2012/03/nj_legislator_proposes_measure.html).

Gibbs N., "A Man's Right to Choose", *Time US*, 15.03.2006 (www.time.com/time/nation/article/0,8599,1173414,00.html).

Gill C., "Why I'm Happy to Tell my Child I Don't Know who Her Father Is", *MailOnline*, 14.03.2011 (www.dailymail.co.uk/femail/article-1365913/sperm-donors-why-im-happy-tell-child-I-dont-know-father-.html).

Grimez K., "Ethics around Womb Transplanttaion", *bionews.org.uk*, 10.03.2014 (www.bionews.org.uk/page_404116.asp?dinfo=0esSyGvLnIgvoXEHYEU8ANqO&PPID=404298).

Henley P., "Business Booms for Danish Sperm", *BBC News*, Copenhagen, 19.05.2011 (www.bbc.co.uk/news/world-europe-13460455).

Hobbes T., *The Leviathan*, 1651, Project Gutenberg (www.gutenberg.org/ebooks/3207).

Holland M.P., "Social Bonding and Nurture Kinship: Compatibility Between Cultural and Biological Approaches", 2004 (http://ssrn.com/abstract=1791365 or http://dx.doi.org/10.2139/ssrn.1791365).

Hsu C., "Denmark Tightens Sperm Donation Law After "Donor 7042" Passes Rare Genetic Disease to 5 Babies", *Medical Daily*, 25.10.2012 (www.medicaldaily.com/denmark-tightens-sperm-donation-law-after-donor-7042-passes-rare-genetic-disease-5-babies-242737).

Hyder H., "Craigslist Sperm Donor is Legal Father, US Court Rules", *bionews.org.uk*, 27.01.2014 (www.bionews.org.uk/page_390812.asp).

ICCS (www.dialogueuroafricainmd.net/web/uploads/activity/civil_registry/more_documents/Supporting-Documents-ICCS.pdf).

John Harris interview for BBC, 11.09.2002 (http://news.bbc.co.uk/2/hi/health/2249442.stm).

Krista A., "Genetic Sexual Attraction", *The Guardian*, 17.05.2003 (www.theguardian.com/theguardian/2003/may/17/weekend7.weekend2).

Leleu Y.H., "The Great Shift in Belgian Law", *Reflexions*, Université de Liège (http://reflexions.ulg.ac.be/cms/c_11968/the-great-shift-in-belgian-law).

Maine H.J.S., *Ancient Law*, London, J.M. Dent and Sons Limited, 1917, 1861 (Project Gutenberg, www.gutenberg.org/files/22910/22910-h/22910-h.htm).

Marusic S.J., "No Extra Tax for Macedonia's Bachelors", *Balkan Insight*, 05.11.2012 (www.balkaninsight.com/en/article/no-extra-tax-for-macedonia-s-bachelors).

Merriam-Webster online dictionary, defining "artificial" (www.merriam-webster.com/dictionary/artificial).

Moore S., "Does a Man have the Right to Decide on Abortion?", *MailOnline*, 17.08.2013 (www.dailymail.co.uk/news/article-33265/Does-man-right-decide-abortion.html).

Natzis N.A., "The Regulation of Surrogate Motherhood in Greece", *Social Science Research Network*, 2010 (http://papers.ssrn.com/sol3/papers.cfm?abstract_id=1689774).

New Indian Express, "Croatia's Government Proposes Law on Gay Partnership", 12.12.2013 (www.newindianexpress.com/world/Croatias-government-proposes-law-on-gay-partnership/2013/12/12/article1942238.ece#.UvuTYxA1CiU).

Notes of the Parliamentary debate over the proposal for changes in the Constitution of the Republic of Macedonia: *Стенографски белешки од 72-та седница на Собранието на Република Македонија*, одржана на 23 септември, 2013 (www.sobranie.mk/default.asp?pSearch=%D0%B1%D1%80%D0%B0%D0%BA+&x=0&y=0).

Official State's statistics website: *Државен завод за статистика, население* (www.stat.gov.mk/OblastOpsto.aspx?id=2).

Openness about using DI (http://humrep.oxfordjournals.org/content/18/5/1115.long).

Programme of Action of the International Conference on Population and Development (www.unfpa.org/public/home/sitemap/icpd/International-Conference-on-Population-and-Development/ICPD-Programme#ch7).

Rai N., "Revolutionary 'Womb Transplant' Performed in Turkey – World's First", 11.08.2011 (www.allvoices.com/contributed-news/9926041-revolutionary-womb-transplant-performed-in-turkey-worlds-first).

Sarfraz M., "Come Inside: The World's Biggest Sperm Bank", *The Guardian*, 02.11.2012 (www.theguardian.com/society/2012/nov/02/worlds-biggest-sperm-bank-denmark).

Sperm Donation and Possible Inbreeding – Oops! "One Sperm Donor, 150 Offspring", *Human Biological Diversity*, 09.07.2011 (http://hbdchick.wordpress.com/2011/09/07/sperm-donation-and-possible-inbreeding-oops/).

The Margin of Appreciation, Council of Europe (www.coe.int/t/dghl/cooperation/lisbonnetwork/themis/echr/paper2_en.asp).

VS Pages Comparing Difference between Things. Insemination vs. Fertilization (http://vspages.com/insemination-vs-fertilization-25363/).

WHO website (www.who.int/genomics/gender/en/index6.html).

Wijlaars L., "Gay Man Who Donated Sperm to Lesbian Ex-Wife Seeks Parental Access", *bionews.org.uk*, 13.02.2012 (www.bionews.org.uk/page_124417.asp)

Влада на Република Македонија, *Предлог за донесување на Закон за биомедицинско потпомогнато оплодување со предлог на закон*, Скопје, јануари, 2008 (www.sobranie.mk/default.asp?pSearch=%D0%B1%D1%80%D0%B0%D0%BA+&x=0&y=0).

Хера Уставниот суд да го запре законот за абортус (http://plusinfo.mk/vest/107490/HERA-Ustavniot-sud-da-go-zapre-zakonot-za-abortus).

REPORTS, SURVEYS AND HANDBOOKS

New Zealand Law Commission's Report, No. 88 on New Isssues in Legal Parenthood, 2005 (www.lawcom.govt.nz/sites/default/files/publications/2005/04/Publication_91_315_R88.pdf).

Artificial Human Insemination. Report of a Commission Appointed by His Grace the Archbishop of Canterbury, London, SPCK, 1948.

Artificial Human Insemination. Report of a Commission Appointed by His Grace the Archbishop of Canterbury, London, SPCK, 1952.

Burell R., *Assisted Reproduction in the Nordic Countries: A Comparative Study of Policies and Regulation*, Nordic Committee of Bioethics, 2005.

Committee on the Rights of the Child, *Report on the Forty-Third Session*, September 2006, Day of General Discussion, Recommendations, Preamble (www.ohchr.org/english/bodies/crc/discussion.htm).

Communication from the Commission – *Towards an EU strategy on the rights of the child* {SEC (2006) 888} {SEC (2006) 889} COM/2006/0367 final (http://eur-lex.europa.eu/legal-content/en/ALL/;jsessionid=8vlVTxjKjthhvD40pbF21N3wV7lCt8chyGGsc3cxC0dvzRcYRFpD!-639655971?uri=CELEX:52006DC0367).

Communication from the Commission to the European Parliament, the Council, the European Economic and Social Committee and the Committee of the Regions. An EU Agenda for the Rights of the Child, COM/2011/0060 final.

Comparative Analysis of Medically Assisted Reproduction in the EU: Regulation and Technologies, Final Report, SANCO/2008/C6/051.

Medically Assisted Procreation and the Protection of the Human Embryo. Comparative Study on the Situation in 39 States, Council of Europe, 1998.

Council Report on the Need to Approximate Member States' Legislation in Civil Matters of 16 November 2011, 13017/01 justciv 129.

Currie I., De Waal J., Erasmus G., *The Bill of Rights Handbook* (5th edition), Juta, 2001.

Daniels K.R., "Gamete Donation and Its Impact on Relationships", *Western Australia Reproductive Technology Council Annual Report*, 1996.

European Commission, Directorate General XII, Office for Official Publications of the European Communities, Luxembourg, *Science, Research, and Development, Studies on the Socio-Economic Impact of Biotechnology: Genetic Fingerprints, Scientific Truth and Affiliation Law*, OOPEC, 1997.

European Observatory on National Family Policies, *A Synthesis of National Family Policies*, 1994.

European Observatory on National Family Policies, *Policy and the Employment of Lone Parents in 20 Countries, the University of York*, 1996.

European Parliament, Directorate General for Internal Policies, Policy Department, Citizens' Rights and Constitutional Affairs, Legal Affairs, *Recognition of Parental Responsibility: Biological Parenthood v. Legal Parenthood, i.e. Mutual Recognition of Surrogacy Agreements: What is the Current Situation in the MS? Need for EU Action?*, 2010.

Explanatory Report of the Convention on Contact concerning Children (www.conventions.coe.int/treaty/EN/Reports/HTML/192.htm).

Explanatory Report on the European Convention on the Exercise of Children's Rights (http://conventions.coe.int/Treaty/en/Reports/Html/160.htm).

Gallup, Inc., *Global Study of Family Values*, 1997 (www.gallup.com/poll/9871/1997-global-study-family-values.aspx).

Glover J., *Fertility and the Family. The Glover Report on Reproductive Technologies to the European Commission*, Fourth Estate, London, 1989.

Hodgkin R., Newell P., *Implementation Handbook for the Convention on the Rights of the Child*, UNICEF, 2007.

Howard W.J. *et al.*, International Society of Fertilities Sciences, *IFFS Surveillance*, 2010.

International Federation of Fertility Societies Surveillance 2010, American Society for Reproductive Medicine, Elsevier Inc. 2010.

International Surrogacy and Donor Conceived Persons 'Preserving the Best Interest of Children' Call for Action by the International Social Service Network, July 2013 (http://iss-ssi.org/2009/assets/files/maternite-substitution/ISS%20call%20for%20action%20-%20Surrogacy%20-ENG.pdf).

A Preliminary Report on the Issues Arising from International Surrogacy Arrangements, Hague Conference on Private International Law, March 2012 (www.hcch.net/upload/wop/gap2012pd10en.pdf).

Jänterä-Jareborg M., Singer A., Sorgjerd C., *National Report: Parental Responsibility, Sweden*.

Law Commission Preliminary Paper 54, New Issues in Legal Parenthood. A Discussion Paper, Wellington, New Zealand, 2004.

Lowe N., "An Evaluation of the Council of Europe's Legal Instruments in the Field of Family Law, A Report for the Attention of the Committee of Experts of Family Law (CJ-FA)", *Cardiff Law School Research Papers*, No. 2, Presented to the 36th Plenary Meeting of the CF-FA, Strasbourg, 15–17 November, 2006.

Lowe N., *A Study into the Rights and Legal Status of Children being Brought Up in Various Forms of Marital or Non-Marital Partnerships and Cohabitation*, A Report for the Attention of the Committee of Experts on Family Law, September 2009.

Reply by the Member States to the Questionnaire on Access to Medically Assisted Procreation (MAP) and on the Right to Know about their Origin for Children born after MAP, Steering Committee of Bioethics, Strasbourg, 9 February 2012.

Report of the Committee of Inquiry into Human Fertilisation and Embryology, Department of Health & Social Security (Warnock Report), London, Cmnd. 9314, Her Majesty's Stationery Office, July 1984.

Report of the Interdepartmental Committee on Human Artificial Insemination, Feversham Committee, 1958.

Report of the International Conference on Population and Development, United Nations, Cairo, 1994.

Report on Human Artificial Protection, Principles Set Out in the Report of the Ad Hoc Committee of Experts on Progress in the Biomedical Sciences (CAHBI), 1989.

Report on Principles Concerning the Establishment and Legal Consequences of Parentage – White Paper, Committee of Experts on Family Law, 2006.

Research Report, Bioethics and the Case-law of the Court, Council of Europe, European Court of Human Rights, 2012.

Second Report from the Commission to the European Parliament, the Council, the European Economic and Social Committee and the Committee of the Regions on Voluntary and Unpaid Donation of Tissues and Cells, 17.06.2011 (COM(2011)0352).

United Nations, CRC, *General Guidelines for Periodic Reports*, 11/20/1996, CRC/C/58.

Van Bueren G., "Child Rights in Europe", Council of Europe, Strasbourg, 2007.

Working Party on the New Legal Instrument(s) on the Rights and Legal Status of Children and Parental Responsibilities, Committee of Experts on Family Law, CJ-FA-GT3, 2010.

World Health Organization's Guiding Principles on Human Cell, Tissue and Organ Transplantation. Guiding Principle 5 (www.who.int/transplantation/Guiding_PrinciplesTransplantation_WHA63.22en.pdf).

Yannakoudakis M., *Report on Voluntary and Unpaid Donation of Tissues and Cells*, 2011/2193 (INI), European Parliament, Committee on the Environment, Public Health and Food Safety, 29 June 2012 (www.europarl.europa.eu/sides/getDoc.do?type=REPORT&reference=A7-2012-0223&language=EN).

INTERNATIONAL DOCUMENTS

Additional Protocol to the Convention on Human Rights and Biomedicine concerning Transplantation of Organs and Tissues of Human Origin, Council of Europe, 2002.

Brussels II bis Regulation (EC) No 2201/2003 (http://eur-lex.europa.eu/LexUriServ/LexUriServ.do?uri=CELEX:32003R2201:EN:HTML).

Constitution of the World Health Organization, World Health Organization.

European Convention on the Exercise of Children's Rights, Council of Europe, Strasbourg, 25.05.1996.

Convention on Contact Concerning Children, Council of Europe, 15.05.2003.

Convention on Recognition and Enforcement of Decisions concerning Custody, Council of Europe, 20.05.1980.

Convention on the Elimination of All Forms of Discrimination against Women, United Nations General Assembly, 18.10.1979.

Convention on the Rights of the Child, United Nations, General Assembly, 20.11.1989.

Convention for the Protection on Human Rights and Dignity of the Human Beings with regard to the Application of Biology and Medicine: Convention on Human Rights and Biomedicine, Council of Europe, Oviedo, 04.04.1997.

Human Rights and Rule of Law, Family, Council of Europe (www.coe.int/t/dghl/standardsetting/family/Introduction_en.asp).

Council Regulation (EC) No. 2201/2003 of 27 November 2003 concerning Jurisdiction and the Recognition and Enforcement of Judgments in Matrimonial Matters and the Matters of Parental Responsibility repealing Regulation (EC) No. 1347/2000.

Directive 2004/23/EC of 31 March 2004 of the European Parliament and European Council on Setting Standards of Quality and Safety for the Donation, Procurement, Testing, Processing, Preservation, Storage and Distribution of Human Tissues and Cells (OJ L 102, 07.04.2004).

Directive 2010/53/EU of 7 July 2010 of the European Parliament and European Council on Standards of Quality and Safety of Human Organs Intended for Transplantation (OJ L 207, 06.08.2010).

Draft Recommendation on the Rights and Legal Status of Children and Parental Responsibilities, Committee of Experts on Family Law (CJ-FA), Explanatory Memorandum, Revised version proposed by Nigel Lowe after the 4th Meeting held in Strasbourg from 16 to 18 March, 2011; Preamble of the Draft Recommendation on the Rights and Legal Status of Children and Parental Responsibilities, Committee of Experts on Family Law Tasked to Draft One or More Legal Instruments on the Rights and Legal Status of Children and Parental Responsibilities (CJ-FA), Strasbourg, 13 July 2011; Appendix IV, Draft Recommendation on the Rights and Legal Status of Children and Parental Responsibilities, Explanatory Memorandum, CJ-FA, 2011 RAP 5 prov.

Recommendation No. R (84) 4 on Parental Responsibilities, Council of Europe, 28.02.1984

Draft Treaty for a European Constitution, CONV 820/03, Brussels, 20.07.2003.

Charter of the Fundamental Rights of the European Union, Official Journal of the European Communities, 364/01, 18.12.2000.
European Commission Directive 2004/23/EC, 2006/17/EC.
European Commission Directive 2006/86/EC.
Convention for the Protection of Human Rights and Fundamental Freedoms (European Convention of Human Rights), Council of Europe, Rome, 04.11.1950.
European Convention of the Legal Status of Children Born Out of Wedlock, European Council, Strasbourg, 15.10.1975.
European Convention on the Adoption of Children (revised), Council of Europe, Strasbourg, 27.11.2008.
Convention on the Civil Aspects of International Child Abduction (Hague Child Abduction Convention), Hague Conference on Private International Law, 25.10.1980.
Hague Convention on Jurisdiction, Applicable Law, Recognition, Enforcement and Cooperation in Respect of Parental Responsibility and Measures for the Protection of Children, Hague Conference on Private International Law, 19.10.1996.
Proclamation of Teheran, International Conference on Human Rights, 1968.
Universal Convention of Human Rights, United Nations, General Assembly, 10.12.1948.
Universal Convention on Bioethics and Human Rights, UNESCO, 2005.
Universal Declaration on the Human Genome and Human Rights, UNESCO, 1997.

NATIONAL LAWS/ACTS

CROATIA

Act for Exercising the Right to Free Decision of Giving Birth to Children, *Official Gazette of the Republic of Croatia,* 18/1978.
Constitution of the Socialist Republic of Croatia, *Official Gazette of the Republic of Croatia,* 8/1974.
Constitution of the Republic of Croatia, *Official Gazette of the Republic of Croatia,* 56/90 and 135/97.
Medical Fertilization Act, *Official Gazette of the Republic of Croatia*, 88/2009.
Obiteljski Zakon, Broj: 01-081-03-2596/2, Zagreb, 16. Srpnja 2003.
Predlog Zakona o Medicinski Potpomognutoj Oplodnji, Vlada Republike Hrvatske, Zagreb, 2012.

FRANCE

Code de la Santepublique, amendment Loi n 2011-814 du juillet 2011.
Bioethics Bill, No. 2911, French National Assembly, 20 October 2010.
Civil Code, France. English Version (Légifrance), Rouchette G., Berton A. (trans.) www.legifrance.gouv.fr/content/download/1950/13681/.../Code_22.pdf).

Les Lois de Bioéthique. Cinq ans après, Étude Adoptee par l'Assemblée générale du Conseil d'État le 25 novembre 1999, La Documentation Française, Paris, 1999.

Loi n° 2011-814 du 7 juillet 2011 relative à la bioéthique, *Journal Officiel*, 8 July 2011.

ITALY

Guidelines on Medically Assisted Reproduction, *Official Gazette*, No. 191, 12 August 2004.

Il Codice Civile Italiano, *Official Gazette*, No. 79 del 4 aprile, 1942, Libro Primo – Delle Persone e della Famiglia.

Italian Constitution, *Official Gazette*, No. 298, 27 December 1948.

Rules on Medically Assisted Procreation, *Official Gazette*, No. 45, 24 February 2004 (www.ieb-eib.org/en/pdf/loi-pma-italie-english.pdf).

MACEDONIA

Constitution of the Republic of Macedonia (Устав на Република Македонија), *Official Gazette of the Republic of Macedonia*, No. 52, 22.11.1992.

Criminal Code (Кривичен законик) *Official Gazette of the Republic of Macedonia*, No. 37/96, 80/99, 4/2002, 43/03, 19/04.

Decree of the Supreme Court (Решение на Врховниот суд на Република Македонија), No. 38/98, 16.12.1999.

Family Law, *Official Gazette of Republic of Macedonia*, No. 80/92, 22.12.1992 (unofficial translation: http://minoritycentre.org/sites/default/files/law_on_family_mac.pdf).

Law on Extracting and Transplanting Human Body Parts for Medical Treatment, (Закон за земање и пресадување на делови од човечкото тело заради лекување), *Official Gazette of the Republic of Macedonia*, No. 47, 08.04.2011.

Law on Inheritance (Закон за наследувањето), *Official Gazette of the Republic of Macedonia*, No. 08/95, 15.02.1995.

Law on Obligations (Закон за облигационите односи), *Official Gazette of the Republic of Macedonia*, No. 18, 05.03.2001.

Law on Ownership and Other Real Rights, (Закон за сопственост и други стварни права), *Official Gazette of the Republic of Macedonia*, No. 18, 05.03.2001.

Law on Prevention and Protection from Discrimination (Закон за спречување и заштита од дискриминација), *Official Gazette of the Republic of Macedonia*, No. 50, 13.04.2010.

Law on Registers of Birth (Закон за матичната евиденција), *Official Gazette of the Republic of Macedonia*, No. 08/95, 15.02.1995.

Law on Bio-medically Assisted Fertilization (Закон за био-медицинско потпомогнато оплодување), *Official Gazette of Republic of Macedonia*, No. 37, 19.03.2008 (for an English version see the appendix at the end).

Law on Termination of Pregnancy (Закон за прекинување на бременоста), *Official Gazette of the Republic of Macedonia*, No. 87, 17.06.2013.
Law on Litigation (Закон за парнична постапка), *Official Gazette of the Republic of Macedonia*, No.79/05, 21.09.2005.
Law on Termination of the Pregnancy (Закон за прекинување на бременоста), *Official Gazette of the Republic of Macedonia*, No. 87/2013, 17.06.2013.

THE NETHERLANDS

Wet van 25 april 2002, houdende regels voor de bewaring, het beheer en de verstrekking van gegevens van donoren bij kunstmatige donorbevruchting (Wet donorgegevens kunstmatige bevruchting), *Stbl.* 2002.

SERBIA

Law on Infertility Treatment through a Procedure of Bio-medically Assisted Fertilization, Republic of Serbia (Закон о лечењу неплодности поступцима биомедицински потпомогнутог оплогења), *Official Gazette of the Republic of Serbia*, 72/2009.
Породични закон Србије, *Службен гласник Републике Србије,* 18/05, 2005.

UNITED KINGDOM

Family Law Reform Act, 1987 c. 42, Part II Rights and Duties of Parents (www.legislation.gov.uk/ukpga/1987/42/part/II/crossheading/parental-rights-and-duties-general).
Human Fertilisation and Embryology Act, 1990.
Human Fertilisation and Embryology Authority, Disclosure of Donor Information, Regulations, 2004.
Human Fertilisation and Embryology Authority, Human Fertilisation and Embryology Act, 2008.
Human Tissue Act, 2004 (legislation.gov.uk: www.legislation.gov.uk/ukpga/2004/30/section/45).

EUROPEAN COURT OF HUMAN RIGHTS CASE LAW

Ahrens v. Germany, European Court of Human Rights, No. 450071/09, judgment of 22.03.2012.
Anayo v. Germany, European Court of Human Rights, No. 20578/07, judgment of 21.12.2010.
Bellet v. France, European Court of Human Rights, No. 23805/94, judgment of 04.12.1995.

Berrehab v. the Netherlands, European Court of Human Rights, No. 10730/84, judgment of 21.06.1988.
Bianchi v. Switzerland, European Court of Human Rights, No. 7548/04, judgment of 22.06.2006.
Boyle v. United Kingdom, European Court of Human Rights, No. 15680/90, judgment of 28.02.1999.
Brayer v. Germany, European Court of Human Rights, No. 3545/04, judgment of 28.05.2009.
Burghartz v. Switzerland, European Court of Human Rights, No. 16213/90, judgment of 22.02.1994
Camp and Bourimi v. the Netherlands, European Court of Human Rights, No. 28369/95, judgment of 03.10.2000.
Chavdarov v. Bulgaria, European Court of Human Rights, No. 3465/03, judgment of 21.11. 2010.
Di Lazzaro v. Italy, European Commission of Human Rights, No. 31924/96, judgment of 10.07.1997.
Dickson v. United Kingdom, European Court of Human Rights, No. 44362/04, judgment of 04.12.2007.
Emonet and Others v. Switzerland, European Court of Human Rights, No. 39051/03, judgment of 13.12.2007.
Evans vs. the United Kingdom, European Court of Human Rights, No. 6339/05, judgment of 10.04.2007.
Fretté v. France, European Court of Human Rights, No. 36515/97, judgment of 26.02.2002.
Gaskin v. the United Kingdom, European Court of Human Rights, No. 10454/83, judgment of 07.07.1989.
Godelli v. Italy, European Court of Human Rights, No. 33783/09, judgment of 25.09.2012.
Golder v. United Kingdom, European Court of Human Rights, No. 4451/70, judgment of 21.02.1975.
Harroudj v. France, European Court of Human Rights, No. 43631/09, judgment of 04.10.2012.
Hokkanen v. Finland, European Court of Human Rights, No. 19823/92, judgment of 22.10.1994.
Ignaccolo-Zemide v. Romania, European Court of Human Rights, No. 31679/96, judgment of 25.01.2000.
Inze v. Austria, European Court of Human Rights, No. 8695/79, judgment of 28.10.1987.
J.R.M. v. the Netherlands, European Commission of Human Rights, No. 16944/90, decision of 08.02.1993
Jaggi v. Switzerland, European Court of Human Rights, No. 58757/00, judgment of 13.07.2006.
Johnston and Others v. Ireland, European Court of Human Rights, No. 9697/82, judgment of 18.12.1986.
K. and T. v. Finland, European Court of Human Rights, No. 25702/94, judgment of 12.06.2001.

Kalacheva v. Russia, European Court of Human Rights, No. 3451/05, judgment of 07.06.2009.

Karadzic v. Croatia, European Court of Human Rights, No. 71099/01, judgment of 05.04.2005.

Kautzor v. Germany, European Court of Human Rights, No. 23338/09, judgment of 22.03.2012.

Kearns v. France, European Court of Human Rights, No. 35991/04, judgment of 10.01.2008.

Keegan v. Ireland, European Court of Human Rights, No. 16969/90, judgment from 26.05.1994.

Kroon and Others v. the Netherlands, European Court of Human Rights, No. 18535/91, judgment of 27.10.1994.

Lebbik v. the Netherlands, European Court of Human Rights, No. 45582/99, judgment of 01.06.2004.

Loizidov v. Turkey, European Court of Human Rights, No. 15318/89, judgment of 18.09.1996.

M.B. v. the United Kingdom, European Commission on Human Rights, No. 22920/93, judgment of 06.04.1994.

Maire v. Portugal, European Court of Human Rights, No. 48206/99, judgment of 26.06.2003.

Marckx v. Beelgium, European Court of Human Rights, No. 6833/74, judgment of 13.06.1979.

Maumousseau and Washington v. France, European Court of Human Rights, No. 39388/05, judgment of 06.12.2007.

Mazurek v. France, European Court of Human Rights, No. 34406/97, judgment of 01.02.2000.

Merger and Cros v. France, European Court of Human Rights, No. 68864/01, judgment of 22.12.2004.

Mikulic v. Croatia, European Court of Human Rights, No. 53176/99, judgment of 07.02.2002.

Mizzi v. Malta, European Court of Human Rights, No. 26111/02, judgment of 12.01.2006.

Monory v. Romania and Hungary, European Court of Human Rights, No. 71099/01, judgment of 05.04.2005.

Morfis v. France, European Court of Human Rights, No. 10978/04, judgment of 12.04.2007.

Neulinger and Shuruk v. Switzerland, European Court of Human Rights, No. 41615/07, judgment of 06.07.2010.

Nylund v. Finland, European Court of Human Rights, No. 27110/95, judgment of 29.06.1999.

Odièvre v. France, European Court of Human Rights, No. 42326/98, judgment of 13.02.2003.

Paulik v. Slovakia, European Court of Human Rights, No. 10699/05, judgment of 10.09.2006.

Pini and Others v. Romania, European Court of Human Rights, No. 78028/01 and 78030/01, judgment of 22.09.2004.

Rasmussen v. Denmark, European Court of Human Rights, No. 8777/79, judgment of 28.11.1984.
Relating to Certain Aspects of the Laws on the Use of Languages in Education in Belgium v. Belgium, European Court of Human Rights, No. 2126/64, judgment of 23.06.1968.
Roman v. Finland, European Court of Human Rights, No. 13072/05, judgment of 29.03.2013.
Różański v. Poland, European Court of Human Rights, No. 55339/00, judgment of 18.05.2006.
Runke and White v. United Kingdom, European Court of Human Rights, No. 42949/98, judgment of 10.05.2007.
S.H. and Others v. Austria, European Court of Human Rights, No. 57813/00, judgment of 03.11.2011.
Schneider v. Germany, European Court of Human Rights, No. 17080/07, judgment of 15.09.2011.
Scozzari and Giunta v. Italy, European Court of Human Rights, No. 39221/98, 41963/98, judgment of 13.07.2000.
Shofman v. Russia, European Court of Human Rights, No. 74826/01, judgment of 24.11.2005.
Söderbäck v. Sweden, European Court of Human Rights, No. 24484/97, judgment of 28.10.1998.
Tavli v. Turkey, European Court of Human Rights, No. 11449/02, judgment of 09.11.2006.
Wagner and J.M.W.L. v. Luxembourg, European Court of Human Rights, No. 76240/01, judgment of 28.06.2007.
X v. Latvia, European Court of Human Rights, No. 27853/09, judgment of 13.12.2011.
X. v. Belgium and the Netherlands, European Commission of Human Rights, No. 6482/74, judgment of 10.07.1975.
Yousef v. the Netherlands, European Court of Human Rights, No. 33711/96, judgment of 05.11.2002.
Z and Others v. United Kingdom, European Court of Human Rights, No. 29392/95, judgment of 10.05.2001.
Znamenskaya v. Russia, European Court of Human Rights, No. 77785/01, judgment of 02.06.2005.

www.ingramcontent.com/pod-product-compliance
Ingram Content Group UK Ltd.
Pitfield, Milton Keynes, MK11 3LW, UK
UKHW051919100926
8556IPUK00021B/1266

9 781780 683362